Ex Líbris

Out of the Storm

Out of the Storm

THE END OF THE CIVIL WAR,
April–June 1865

NOAH ANDRE TRUDEAU

LITTLE, BROWN AND COMPANY

BOSTON   NEW YORK   TORONTO   LONDON

Library of Congress Cataloging-in-Publication Data

Trudeau, Noah Andre.
    Out of the storm : the end of the Civil War, April–June 1865 /
Noah Andre Trudeau. — 1st ed.
        p.   cm.
    Includes bibliographical references (p.   ) and index.
    ISBN 0-316-85328-3
    1. United States — History — Civil War, 1861–1865.   2. United
States — History — Civil War, 1861–1865 — Peace.   I. Title
E477.6.T78   1994
973.7 — dc20   93-34683

10 9 8 7 6 5 4 3 2

MV-NY

Published simultaneously in Canada
by Little, Brown & Company (Canada) Limited

Printed in the United States of America

To Burke Davis,
author of *To Appomattox, Sherman's March, The Long Surrender,*

the father of us all

Contents

———◄○►———

List of Maps

Preface

———◄○►———

OUT OF THE STORM completes a saga I unknowingly began in 1989 with my first book, *Bloody Roads South,* and continued two years later with *The Last Citadel*. I say "unknowingly" because only now do I realize that one presaged the next with an inevitability that seems, in hindsight, quite obvious.

Each of these books sought to answer a question. For *Bloody Roads South* the starting point was Cold Harbor — how could such a terrible and particularly senseless bloodletting ever have happened? To answer that I began a journey that took me to the Wilderness, Spotsylvania Court House, and the North Anna River. After that book was finished, I started to wonder what had happened to those men in the long period between Cold Harbor and Appomattox Court House. That led me into the maze of events that constituted the Petersburg siege. Finally, having spent so much time with the leaders and common soldiers of both sides through their letters, diaries, and memoirs, and having become immersed in the passions and ideals that drove them forward, I was curious to know how it had all ended. This time I found I could not limit my investigations to the eastern theater of the war but needed to cast my net as wide as possible.

In April 1865, the United States was a nation totally at war with itself.

It had more men under arms (approximately 1.3 million), and was spending more to keep them under arms (more than $2.5 million a day), than any other nation in the world. On the first day of April, a Confederate government in Richmond still claimed suzerainty over a nation that stretched from Texas to Virginia and was defended by standing armies in Virginia, North Carolina, Alabama, and the Trans-Mississippi. In three months it would all be gone — the nation, the armies, and, most important, the will to fight on. Within those same three months would occur the assassination of a U.S. President, the worst maritime tragedy in our history, and one of the major municipal disasters of the nineteenth century. This period would be followed by another traumatic time as hundreds of thousands of veteran soldiers returned to the folds of civilian life. Added to this were profound fissures of change that would crack the very foundations of American society: emancipation, industrialization, and a transformation of the national identity as the North came to terms with its victory, and the South with its defeat.

Confederate general Robert E. Lee's surrender at Appomattox Court House, on April 9, 1865, did not end the Civil War. There remained intact and active forces of significance in North Carolina, Alabama, and the Trans-Mississippi, all of which would have to be subdued. C.S. President Jefferson Davis, his Cabinet, and key departments of the Confederate government were still functioning, albeit no longer with a permanent capital, and Abraham Lincoln was girding himself for the greatest political fight of his life, even though he had been having disturbing premonitions that the end of that life was near. Against this backdrop of large events unfolding, there were also the countless personal tales of individuals caught up in the final scudding squalls of the terrible storm that had swept across the land. There were men and women alive on April 9 who would not live to see the day when the last gun was fired.

It was during the period of April–June 1865 that the shooting finally stopped. These months, and the six or so following, marked a time between times, a period during which, to choose lines from the poet Walt Whitman, the American nation stopped marching to the "terrible drums" and looked ahead to a horizon where there were "vistas again to peace restored." For four awful years Americans north and south had stood at the edge of the abyss and endured what Herman Melville termed the "tempest bursting from the waste of Time." Sectional and racial hatreds had burned with a blinding flame of slaughter and desolation. Now, within a remarkably short interval, the great national trauma was spent. The passions and fears that had driven the machines of war were no longer the ruling sentiments of the nation. The dark, incomprehensible force that had reigned over the country during those four years of madness dissipated with amazing swiftness.

It is a forgotten time in American history. Scholars are anxious to move quickly into the political and social aspects of later Reconstruction, while general readers are so taken with the simple drama of Appomattox that many continue to believe that the Civil War ended with that incident. How the people across the land came to terms with the great bloodletting (360,222 Union and 258,000 Confederate lives lost), how they stopped fearing the latest news and began to dream about the future, how they adapted (or failed to adapt) to the tremendous social changes the war had wrought — all this is subtext to the great saga of Americans' groping toward a new equilibrium.

This is the story of the final months of the Civil War.

Author's Note

—◁○▷—

IN MY PREVIOUS BOOKS it was possible for me to include a detailed table of organization for the forces engaged so that the interested reader might orient himself or herself to the units and leaders described in the text. This book, however, treats four major campaigns in four different theaters of the war (along with several other, lesser actions), making such a table prohibitively large. In lieu of such a listing, I can direct those who want to follow along to consult the appropriate volumes of the *Official Records:* volume 46, part I, for the Appomattox campaign (Union forces on pages 564–580, Confederate forces on pages 1267–1276); volume 47 for North Carolina operations (Union forces in part I, pages 46–60, and Confederate forces in part III, pages 732–736); volume 49, part I, for the Mobile campaign (Union forces on pages 105–109, Confederate forces on pages 1046–1048); volume 49, part II, for Wilson's campaign (Union forces on pages 542–543, no table for Confederate forces).

For the most part, the military forces of each side were organized along the hierarchy of corps, divisions, brigades, regiments, and companies. I prefer to refer to the units above regimental level by the names of their commanders (e.g., Gordon's corps, Long's division, and Cockrell's brigade), though the Union predilection for simply numbering these units will be followed when appropriate (e.g., Fifth Corps, Six-teenth Corps, Third Division). References to regiments are always by number and state — so, for example, 8th Iowa and 16th Mississippi.

The essential battle tactic of this era was to maneuver the long, usu-ally four-abreast marching columns into two (or often three, with the third serving as a reserve) lines of battle, with as many rifles as possible facing the enemy. Regimental and national flags were generally placed in the center of a regimental front, with either end of this extended line being the flank. Geographic directions are always given from the point of view of the side under discussion.

Finally, I have again applied a variable rule on spelling in order to eliminate the qualifier *sic* from the text. Where I feel a particular spelling conveys a vivid sense of character, I have preserved the original; other-wise I have exercised some judicious editorial cleaning-up of manuscript passages. Where a place-name exists in several variants, I have explained my choice in a footnote at the first occurrence of the place.

Part One

WORLD ON THE EDGE

With its cloud of skirmishers in advance,
With now the sound of a single shot snapping like a whip,
    and now an irregular volley,
The swarming ranks press on and on,
    the dense brigades press on,
Glittering dimly, toiling under the sun — the dust-cover'd men,
In column rise and fall to the undulations of the ground,
With artillery interspers'd — the wheels rumble, the horses
    sweat,
As the army corps advances.

       Walt Whitman, "An Army Corps on the March"

Chapter One

"We may expect weighty news any minute"

---◄○►---

THE DYING WINDS of winter blew fitfully across the somber landscape of a nation still at war. They struggled to breathe life into the Confederate flags that flew defiantly over the five state capitals as yet untouched by the enemy: Richmond, Raleigh, Montgomery, Tallahassee, and Austin. They whirled in and out of the encampments of the armed forces that wearily confronted each other in Virginia, Tennessee, North Carolina, Alabama, South Carolina, Texas, and elsewhere. They brought the promise of spring, of renewal, but also the inevitability of the end. The last winter of the Civil War was drawing to a close.

Dawn had yet to touch this final March day of 1865 as a small party of resolute men made its way through the thickets of Johnson County in eastern Tennessee. The armed group, numbering thirty or so, were all local Unionists under the command of Daniel Ellis, a hardened veteran of the state's four-year guerrilla war. Ellis had led his band into this portion of the county in hopes of ambushing one of the supply trains that still shuttled goods into Confederate western Virginia. The wagons had proved elusive, but an informant had reported that a detachment of Rebels was resting on a farm a few miles away.

Ellis brought his command to within a short distance of the enemy camp and settled down to wait for daylight. It was just before dawn when he roused his men and moved them forward. "We found that the rebels were in a log barn, which, of course, gave them the advantage of us in regard to position," Ellis observed, "and, besides, we had no means of ascertaining the number of the rebels, about which there was a great contrariety of opinion, some saying that there were sixty or seventy of them, and others said there were at least a hundred."

Ellis advanced his men in a tight column of fours until they were about sixty yards from the barn, where they spread out into a single line abreast. Suddenly a warning cry sounded from the enemy encampment. They had been discovered! Ellis shouted to his men to open fire and charge. The shock of this unexpected assault bursting out of the cold morning gloom unnerved the Rebels, most of whom fled. Several ran through a nearby sheep pen, driving ahead of them the lone animal kept there. "It was hard to determine which would win the race," Ellis later wrote, "the pet sheep or its rebel companions."

Some of the enemy party attempted to hide in the log barn, but a volley from Ellis's men soon flushed them into the open, where they were taken prisoner. Fifteen of the Rebels were killed in the dawn attack, at a cost of one Unionist mortally wounded. Ellis's men helped themselves to thirty-six horses as well as some equipment and food. The captured men were paroled and turned loose, and Daniel Ellis led his company off to search for more Rebels. Tennessee's private Civil War had entered another day.

The citizens of Mobile, Alabama, awoke this morning to their second day under a state of siege. The condition had been declared by the district military commander, Major General Dabney H. Maury, and fully supported by Lieutenant General Richard Taylor, commanding the Confederate Department of Alabama, Mississippi, and East Louisiana. Maury's declaration allowed the military authorities to arrest suspicious persons and to close all drinking establishments. It also called for the burning of all cotton stored in the city. Fearing that this action might spread a conflagration throughout Mobile, Major William H. Ketchum had municipal workers hauling the material to an open field where it might be safely destroyed. No private cache was immune. A Mobile resident never forgot the scene: "Going home one day, I was surprised to see bales of cotton tumbling from the attic windows of some of the best mansions in the city. . . . Almost everyone had secreted a little of that commodity in their homes to serve their wants when the Confederate money should collapse."

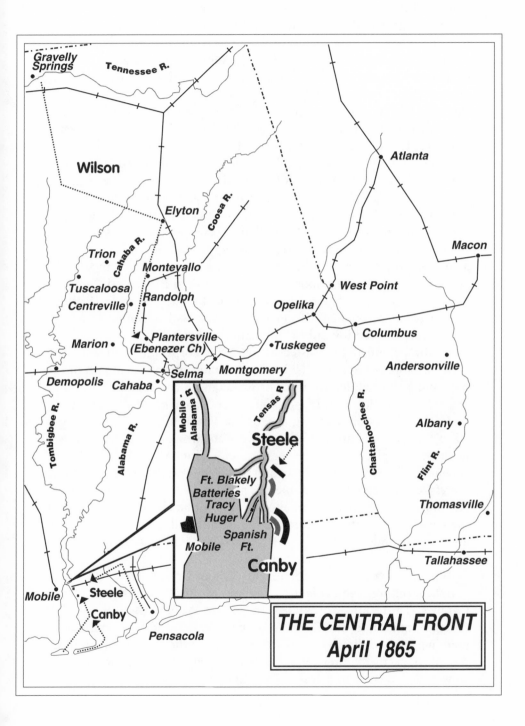

THE CENTRAL FRONT
April 1865

The cause of these desperate measures was the long-awaited Union offensive against Mobile, which had begun in earnest on March 17. It was the oft-postponed sequel to Admiral David Farragut's celebrated forcing of the mouth of Mobile Bay on August 5, 1864. While that engagement had ended Mobile's operation as a viable Confederate port and provided the United States West Gulf Blockading Squadron with a sheltered harbor, it had left untouched the city itself, which was situated thirty miles up the bay and protected by a deadly seeding of underwater mines (called torpedoes) and a network of forts and earthworks.

Responsibility for sealing Mobile's fate rested with the commander of the Federal Military Division of West Mississippi, Major General Edward R. S. Canby. Canby had already angered U.S. military chief Ulysses S. Grant by his failure to reorganize his forces after Farragut's victory in time to support Major General William Tecumseh Sherman's march to the sea. Now, by targeting Mobile for capture, Canby was once again acting against Grant's wishes. Grant believed that Selma and Montgomery were far more important military targets; he wanted Canby to bypass the blockaded port unless it could be taken with little effort. Canby, worried about advancing into Alabama with a Confederate force in his rear, decided instead to eliminate the threat.

Canby's command consisted of two army corps, the Thirteenth and Sixteenth, operating out of Union bases established at the mouth of the bay, and an expeditionary force of white and black soldiers encamped around Pensacola, Florida — about 45,000 men in all. According to C. C. Andrews, commanding one of the Thirteenth Corps's divisions, "The fortifications around Mobile were so strong that a direct movement on the place, from the western shore [of the bay], would have encountered unequal resistance, and involved a protracted siege. It was therefore determined to flank them. The base could be fixed on the eastern shore; and the main army moving up on that shore with the aid of the navy, would carry the forts on the islands and main land, and then approach Mobile by the Tensas River or one of the channels coming in above."

While the expeditionary force, under Major General Frederick Steele, marched out of Pensacola to close on Mobile from the northeast, Canby's Thirteenth Corps, led by Brevet Major General Gordon Granger, and Sixteenth Corps (Major General Andrew J. Smith commanding) moved directly along the east side of the bay. What Andrews described as the "unreliable and swampy character of the ground" slowed the advance to a crawl. Two Confederate bastions guarded this route to Mobile: Fort Blakely,* ten miles northeast of the city, and three miles south of Blakely, Spanish Fort. Granger's column made the first serious contact with the enemy and on March 27 began to close in on Spanish Fort.

The patterns of the siege were quickly established. Yankee soldiers dug approach trenches at night, then defended and strengthened them during the day. "We are now 'in the field,' sure," a Federal officer from Wisconsin wrote home on the last day of March. "The fall of this fort & Blakely will be a good start toward the reduction of Mobile." In addition to the deadly litany of artillery and rifle fire, the Union troops digging toward Spanish Fort also faced a relatively new battlefield terror: land mines, called torpedoes like their nautical counterparts. These infernal devices were often simply buried artillery shells that had been set to explode when touched. Even those that had been excavated and defused could still kill, as a New York artilleryman explained in a letter written this day: "One of Company A's boys was mortally wounded by a torpedo that someone was fooling with and threw it down in front of him and it exploded and tore one of his arms nearly off and one of his legs. That is what boys get by fooling with these things. So goes soldiering."

"The siege of Spanish Fort," reported Mobile commander Maury, "was prosecuted with great industry and caution. The defense was active, bold and defiant." Just how defiant was demonstrated this very evening, when a party of fifteen enlisted men and one officer overran an advanced Union picket line and captured twenty-two Federals. Confederate artillery was also quick to anger. A Chicago newspaperman gamely penned one dispatch from the front lines today while subjected to the "hissing, shrieking 64-pounder shells which, burying themselves in the ground, tear and root like an earthquake."

But the C.S. defenders nonetheless had to pay a price for their boldness and defiance. Shortly after noon, Colonel William E. Burnett, Chief of Artillery, was shot and killed by a sniper while attempting to do a little sharpshooting of his own from Spanish Fort.

The Union commander, Canby, was still in the process of bringing up all of his big guns and placing them around Spanish Fort. An Illinois soldier named Alphonse Wolfe was among those who prepared positions for the heavy artillery. "Today we are all engaged in a new and novel employment," he wrote to his family. "Our whole Division turned out to

---

* Spelled Blakely in accounts contemporary with the war. Some years afterward, the name was changed to its modern spelling, Blakeley. The earlier version will be used here.

make baskets to be used as gabions, on our new fortifications. It looked funny to see several thousand men scattered through the woods making baskets, and you will hardly be surprised if I tell you that many an odd-shaped concern was brought into camp to pass for a basket. These baskets are used for port-holes, where our cannon are planted, to prevent the breastworks from caving in. . . . Our siege pieces are mounted as fast as possible. . . . I expect to hear some awful cannonading in a short time."

Throughout the North and South, noncombatants of both sides looked to the coming days with a mixture of apprehension and anticipation.

In New York, a patrician observer of the world scene named George Templeton Strong catalogued in his diary entry for this day the reports from Mobile and other fronts, concluding, "We may expect weighty news any minute." A glance at his own storm-streaked window prompted an additional note: "I hope this rain may not have spoiled the party." A friend who had recently returned from a visit to Sherman's army in North Carolina met Strong today and ventured the comforting opinion that the "Southern 'masses' [are] an effete people, unable to take care of themselves now that their slaveholding lords and magnates are gone."

One of those "masses," a Georgia woman named Minerva Mc-Clatchey, faced the future with dogged hope. "We are succeeding beyond all expectation in making a garden and preparing for a small crop," she wrote in her journal for this month. "It seems cheerful to hear the loom and wheel again, and see domestic matters moving on." Yet thoughts of the conflict were never far away as she closed her March entry: "We are waiting with intense anxiety to hear the result of matters at the front, where greek meets greek to face."

The meeting was anything but Greek facing Greek in a large field outside Goldsboro, North Carolina, where stone-faced members of Sherman's army were drawn up in a hollow square to witness a fellow soldier be executed for the crime of rape. Despite recent inaction and boredom on this front, many were reluctant to have to watch such extreme punishment. "Nobody wished to see so sad a sight," wrote a drummer boy in the 2nd Minnesota. "Some of the men begged to be excused from attending, and others could not be found when their drums beat 'assembly'; for none could well endure, as they said, 'to see a man shot down like a dog.'"

An open grave lay in the center of the three-sided square. While the troops shifted nervously, the sound of the "Dead March" grew more distinct as the condemned man and his escort drew near. An Ohio veteran recalled what happened next. "He was conducted to the grave, and the two chaplains who accompanied him knelt, and one of them offered a prayer, after which the prisoner's hands were tied behind him and his eyes bandaged. Then he knelt beside his coffin, and twelve of the guard fired at him at a distance of twelve paces. He fell forward on his face, dead. I do not desire to witness another scene like this."

"An odd feature of the execution," remembered a Massachusetts man in the crowd, "was that hundreds of the Confederate soldiers witnessed the execution from across a stream about three hundred yards away. No shots, however, were fired by either side."

This grim part of the army routine was not even noted at command headquarters in Goldsboro, where William Tecumseh Sherman had just returned from a high-level conference with Abraham Lincoln and U. S. Grant.

Following the celebrated march from Atlanta to the sea, and their devastating movement through South and North Carolina, Sherman's men had been engaged in just one serious battle (at Bentonville, North Carolina, on March 19–20) before settling into watchful inaction around Goldsboro while their chief traveled up to U.S. Army headquarters near Petersburg, Virginia, for the final strategic conference of the war.

When Sherman and Grant finally saw each other on March 27 (their last face-to-face meeting had been in early 1864), it was, remembered one of Grant's aides, "like two schoolboys coming together after a vacation." The pair were joined by President Lincoln and other military leaders, all hoping to hammer out a policy to guide the military men in the coming critical days. Few specific actions were dictated by Lincoln, but he did take pains to convey a general course of conduct — or at least Sherman so believed. "I know, when I left him," Sherman wrote, "that I was more than ever impressed by his kindly nature, his deep and earnest sympathy with the affliction of the whole people, resulting from the war, and by the march of hostile armies through the south, and that his earnest desire seemed to be to end the war speedily, without more bloodshed or devastation, and to restore all the men of both sections to their homes."

The military plans decided at City Point had more specificity. Grant would move at once to force C.S. General Robert E. Lee to abandon Petersburg and Richmond. On April 10 Sherman's forces would begin their advance against the small Confederate army under General Joseph

E. Johnston, now drawn up between Goldsboro and Raleigh. Today Sherman acted to complete his preparations for the operation. To Secretary of War Edwin Stanton he wrote, "All things are working well and I have troops enough to accomplish the part assigned me, and only await the loading [of] our wagons, [and the] patching up and mending made necessary by the wear and tear of the past work." To U. S. Grant, Sherman vowed, "I shall keep things moving and be all ready by the date fixed, April 10."

A mood of hot anger swept through the headquarters of Sherman's opponent Joseph E. Johnston, but it had nothing to do with the Federal troops arrayed against the general. "General Hood's report of operations from the time of taking command at Atlanta until his succession by Johnston, has just been received," an officer at Confederate headquarters wrote today. "He abuses a great many for tardiness and dereliction of duty, and, I think, some unjustly." That was putting it mildly: the report of Lieutenant General John B. Hood — who had replaced Johnston as commander of the Army of Tennessee in July 1864 and then led it into a series of crushing defeats culminating in the disastrous Battle of Nashville in December — was less an account of events than an indictment of Johnston's stewardship before Hood took over. This was the kind of blow that the proud and highly sensitive Johnston could not ignore, and the coming days would see a bitter exchange of messages between the two, with Johnston vainly seeking an investigation and court-martial.

Matters pertaining to the military problem facing him were also on Johnston's mind this last day of March. Hard campaigning, battle losses, and persistent desertions had whittled his army to around 20,000 men. One element not lacking in this reduced command was officers; in fact, Johnston had too many. In a dispatch sent today to the Confederate secretary of war, he asked that no more be sent to him for assignments. "I can give none," Johnston explained, "having now only a small body of troops with officers enough for a very large one."

In Danville, Virginia, some 130 miles northwest of where Joe Johnston sat, C.S. Senator Williamson S. Oldham waited phlegmatically for the next train connection on his journey home to Texas. The hardworking, conscientious Oldham had left Richmond on the evening of March 30, following the close of the Confederate Congress five days earlier. "At the time of adjournment, members of Congress, executive officers of the government, and citizens were filled with painful forebodings of evil," he recollected, "but none entertained the thought that the crisis was so near at hand."

While Oldham did not harbor any false hopes for the security of the Confederate capital ("All intelligent men were satisfied that the defense of Richmond could not be sustained much longer," he admitted), he nevertheless believed that the heart of the Confederacy remained strong. The previous December, en route from Texas to Richmond, it had taken him nearly forty-eight hours to cover the stretch from Greensboro to Danville. Today, Oldham found solace and faint hope for the future in the fact that he expected to make the return journey between those points in less than twelve.

Battlefield miracles were virtually standard procedure for Confederate Lieutenant General Nathan B. Forrest. The hard-driving, occasionally brilliant, and always unorthodox Tennessee officer had been in the war from the beginning, entering the service as a private on June 16, 1861. In four years of fighting, Forrest had acquired a top army rank, three wounds, and the kind of reputation that gave his adversaries nightmares. His apparently easy victories over the often numerically superior Union forces sent against him by William T. Sherman in the summer and fall of 1864 drove that exasperated officer to proclaim, "That devil Forrest must be hunted down and killed if it costs ten thousand lives and bankrupts the Federal Treasury." In the end, Sherman just marched away from the problem.

Following the Confederate defeat at Nashville in December, as the focus of attention moved with Sherman to the sea, hard-pressed C.S. military authorities were forced to shift most of their troops out of the Deep South to meet the Union threat. This left Forrest to defend the region with only his battered cavalry, which was scattered throughout Mississippi, Alabama, and Tennessee. But if his command was spread thin, Forrest's name still possessed all its fierce magic. As one Alabama newspaper proclaimed to its readers in February, "He will bring rejoicing to every true Southern beating heart, as he is now getting ready . . . , and when he does move he will make the sound of his roaring heard among the Negroes and Yankees in the West."

Forrest was in fact frantically reorganizing his widely dispersed commands, hoping to consolidate them before the winter-muddied roads hardened enough to allow the Yankees positioned north and south of him to begin active operations. He went so far as to have the trees along several key concentration routes marked with an X so there would be no error on the part of his subordinates. His attempts were frustrated, however, by Federal diversionary forays that required his department commander, Lieutenant General Richard Taylor, to redirect units in response. Forrest was still struggling to pull the pieces together when, on March 22, the onslaught began. A huge Union cavalry army moved from its camps in northwest Alabama on a purposeful march south, toward the still-functioning industrial centers at Elyton (modern Birmingham) and Selma.

Elyton fell on March 29, with Forrest's troops still too scattered to mount a defense. Two days later the Yankee column pushed Forrest's advance out of the important railroad junction town of Montevallo. The Federals met their first serious resistance just south of that town, with clashes ranging for miles across the surrounding fields and dirt roads.

Forrest himself rode into the heart of the confused fighting, joined in some briefly violent combat, and then continued south to establish his headquarters sixteen miles from Montevallo. Couriers went racing off to his various subordinates with instructions for them to join him to stop the enemy juggernaut. It was all a question of time. Given enough of it, Forrest was confident he could turn back the enemy expedition. His own sense of purpose was crystal-clear: he was, as he declared at this time, "honor bound to fight to the bitter end, unless authorities should direct otherwise."

The commander of the Federal forces opposing Forrest was equally determined to allow his adversary no respite from the constant, unrelenting pressure. The entire expedition was the brainchild of Brevet Major General James H. Wilson, a protégé of U. S. Grant and an outspoken advocate of massed cavalry tactics. The twenty-seven-year-old "boy general" had been pushing for a large-scale mounted raid into central Alabama since January, but not until late February had he been told to proceed. Wilson had immediately begun the time-consuming task of organizing the men and material for the expedition, which was then further delayed by the worst late-winter rainstorms in memory. His 13,500-man cavalry army finally broke camp on March 22. The next eight days saw Wilson's column make steady progress, even as Confederate units began to converge on his line of march. On March 30 Wilson detached a brigade under Brigadier General John T. Croxton, with orders to raid to the west to further confuse enemy defensive schemes.

Wilson rode into Montevallo at 1:00 P.M. on March 31. Learning from his scouts that enemy troops were making a stand south of the town, he at once ordered his lead elements to engage them. "In less time than it takes to tell it," he boasted afterward, "the rattle of cannon and carbine began." An officer in one of the units under fire this day wrote in his journal, "Rebels in line. The 5th Iowa makes a gallant charge and it's a four mile chase. Then the enemy get a strong position and we have a sharp engagement. Our Spencers and enthusiasm too much for them, and we see their backs again in retreat. . . . General Forrest commanded the rebs today, but his name has lost its terror, however, we expect hot work tomorrow."

The stage was set for what everyone believed would be the closing operations of the war. Yet even as Sherman confronted Johnston, Canby dug toward Mobile, and Wilson stood poised to burst into central Alabama, events in the Virginia theater of operations were about to come to a sudden and decisive climax.

Chapter Two

Breakthrough in the East

Friday, March 31

Petersburg–Richmond

ALONG THE MILES of trenches that wriggled from Richmond to Petersburg, soldiers of both sides were waiting. Sometime this day, the officer in charge of the Union lines across the neck of Bermuda Hundred called to his counterpart north of the James, "Nothing new along my line. Have you any news?" Back came the reply: "Nothing new here."

For ten grueling months Lieutenant General Ulysses S. Grant had personally directed Union operations in and around the strategically important transportation and manufacturing town of Petersburg, Virginia. An attempt to seize the city in June 1864 had turned into a tedious siege that stretched through to spring. Approximately 42,000 Yankee boys had been lost — killed, wounded, or missing — in fighting for what were little more than points of temporary advantage, such as Peebles Farm, Hatcher's Run, and the Jerusalem Plank Road.

Throughout it all, Grant had held his lines with a tenacious grip, forcing his opponent to do the same. The coming of spring meant that the muddy southside roads would become firm enough to support a rapid movement of troops. Now Grant worried that Robert E. Lee would somehow find a way to slip his forces out of the ring that was tightening around Petersburg and escape south to link up with Joseph E. Johnston's army, near Raleigh. If that happened, declared Grant's mili-

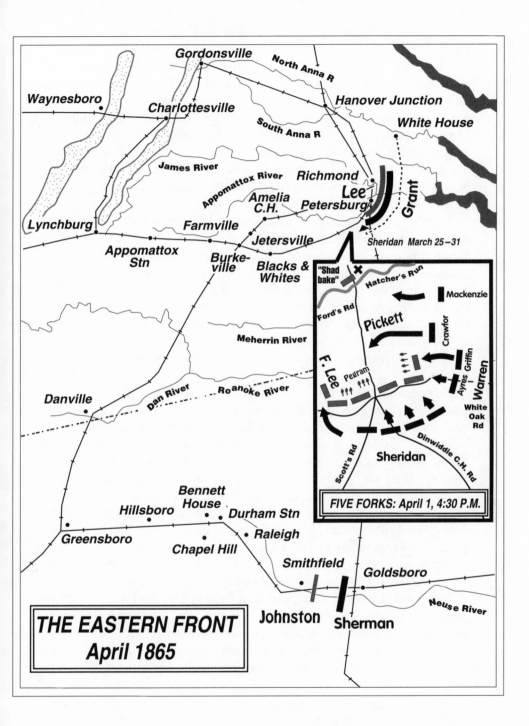

Waynesboro

Gordonsville

North Anna R

Hanover Junction

White House

Charlottesville

South Anna R

James River

Appomattox River

Richmond

Lee

Grant

Amelia
C.H.

Petersburg

Lynchburg

Farmville

Jetersville

Sheridan March 25–31

Appomattox
Stn

Burke-
ville

Blacks &
Whites

"Shad
bake"

Hatcher's Run

Mackenzie

Ford's Rd

Pickett

Crawfor

Meherrin River

F. Lee

Pegram

Ayres Griffin
Warren

Danville

Dan River

Roanoke River

White
Oak
Rd

Scott's Rd

Sheridan

Dinwiddie C.H. Rd

Bennett
House

Hillsboro

Durham Stn

FIVE FORKS: April 1, 4:30 P.M.

Greensboro

Raleigh

Chapel Hill

Smithfield

Goldsboro

**THE EASTERN FRONT
April 1865**

Johnston

Sherman

Neuse River

tary secretary, Adam Badeau, "a long and tedious and expensive campaign, consuming most of the summer, might be inevitable."

The situation this day was more active along the southern stretch of the Petersburg lines, where the deadly routine of siege war continued without pause. Portions of the Twenty-fourth Corps had recently arrived here from north of the James to free up Army of the Potomac units. As some of these fresh troops moved into the trenches today, they were taught a quick lesson about survival. "At 9:30 A.M. firing commenced in our front," a Maine soldier wrote in his diary. "We remained behind our new works as a reserve while the shells go screaming over us. Some are killed and others wounded."

Nearby, four regiments from the Second Corps, led by Brevet Brigadier General Robert McAllister, tested the enemy positions. "They went forward under a terrific fire of musketry, canister and shell," McAllister proudly reported. Once up close to the Rebel positions, the Yankee boys found it impossible to advance further and hopeless to retreat now that the defenders were fully alert. "On some parts of the line one man at a time ran the gauntlet and made good his escape," McAllister noted. "Others were cut down in their attempts to get back, and quite a number were taken prisoner." At this cost, a small bit of battlefield intelligence was gained.

From his just-established headquarters south of the city at Dabney's Mill,* U. S. Grant continued to monitor a critical operation that he had ordered Major General Philip Sheridan to lead against the Confederate right flank. As Adam Badeau later recorded, "From daylight till daylight again, Grant was sending messages to Lincoln and Sheridan and Meade [commanding the Army of the Potomac] and Ord [commanding the Army of the James], directing first a division and then a corps of infantry, and afterwards another division of cavalry, to the support of his beleaguered subordinate; planning a battle on a field he had never seen, persisting in his effort to break through the right of Lee."

The siege of Petersburg had been a death sentence for Robert E. Lee's once vaunted army, which had suffered about 28,000 casualties thus far. A brutal fall season of steady combat, followed by a winter marked by periods of near starvation and mass desertion, had left the forces defending Petersburg and Richmond dangerously weakened, with morale at an ebb point. For Lee, making a tactical move at any one point of his overstretched lines meant risking disaster at another. For three days now he

---

* Noted in Grant's dispatches as Dabney's *Mills*. Only a large pile of sawdust remained to mark the site of the steam-powered sawmill that had operated there before the war.

had been anxiously watching the buildup of enemy strength against his vulnerable right flank. He rode today to the threatened point, at the intersection of the White Oak Road and Claiborne Road, and personally directed a local counterattack against a Federal probe. Despite routing the first units they faced, Lee's fighters were soon pressed back to their original positions by the presence of strong Union supports. It was near the end of this little engagement that Lee spotted one of his officers, Brigadier General Eppa Hunton, sporting several fresh bullet holes in his uniform coat.

"I wish you would sew those places up," Lee chided the officer. "I don't like to see them."

Hunton thought a moment, then brightened. "General Lee," he said, "allow me to go back home and see my wife and I will have them sewed up."

"The idea," Lee replied with mock sternness, "of talking about going to see wives; it is perfectly ridiculous, sir."

Shortly before setting out on his ride to the right, Lee had penned a brief note to his daughter Agnes, who had been hoping to visit him. After apologizing for being absent when she called at his headquarters, Lee closed with innocent words full of darker meaning: "I . . . do not know when I shall have the pleasure of seeing you."

City Point, Virginia

Abraham Lincoln spent much of this day in a bad mood. According to his personal bodyguard, William H. Crook, the "President (then at City Point, Virginia)* knew that Grant was to make a general attack upon Petersburg, and grew depressed. The fact that his own son [Robert Todd Lincoln] was with Grant was one source of anxiety. But the knowledge of the loss of life that must follow hung about him until he could think of nothing else."

Lincoln spent part of this Friday talking with Admiral David Porter and chatted for half an hour with Brigadier General Marsena Patrick, provost marshal general of the U.S. armies operating against Richmond. The President had come down to City Point from Washington on March 25, partly because he wished to escape the intrigues of the capital for a while and partly out of a desire to be near the front when the end came.

---

* Located near the confluence of the James and Appomattox rivers, City Point was the central supply depot and administrative headquarters for all the military forces operating against Petersburg and Richmond.

Events here had been building to a climax ever since then. Early on the morning of Lincoln's arrival, Confederate troops had launched a well-planned assault on the Federal siege lines east of Petersburg. Despite an initial success that included the capture of Union Fort Stedman, the Rebels had been driven back with great loss, and their bloody effort had not stayed in the slightest Grant's plans for an all-out offensive.

This new operation had opened on March 29, when Grant began to shift the weight of his forces against the Confederate right flank. The last progress report Lincoln received this day from Grant arrived shortly after dark. "Sheridan has had hard fighting to-day," Grant wrote, "I am very anxious to hear the result; will let you know when I do hear."

Although Lincoln was in no way managing the military campaign from City Point, his being here was important. How much so was affirmed by Secretary of War Stanton, who wired Lincoln today, "I have strong faith that your presence will have great influence in inducing exertions that will bring [down] Richmond; compared to that no other duty can weigh a feather."

Richmond

In the Rebel capital this night, Jefferson Davis, President of the Confederate States of America, bade a sad farewell to his wife and family. He had made the decision to send his loved ones away despite Varina Davis's urgent protests that she should remain. The family holdings were packed, and whatever could not be easily transported was sold at auction. This painful scenario was made even more ominous when Davis insisted that his wife carry a pistol with her at all times. "You can at least, if reduced to the last extremity, force your assailants to kill you," he told her.

Their parting was filled with tears. "Mr. Davis almost gave way," Varina recalled, "when our little Jeff begged to remain with him, and Maggie clung to him convulsively, for it was evident he thought he was looking his last upon us."

Davis had asked his personal secretary, Burton Harrison, to accompany the family to its destination in Charlotte, North Carolina. Before the train left the station, Davis took Harrison aside to give him his final instructions: "My latest information from General Lee is, that Sheridan has been ordered to move with his cavalry to our right flank and to tear up the railroad; he is to remain there, destroying as much of the railroad as he can, until driven off. . . . After establishing Mrs. Davis in Charlotte, you will return to Richmond as soon as you can."

It was nearly ten o'clock at night when the two-car special chugged wearily out of the city. Remembered Harrison, "After proceeding twelve or fifteen miles, our locomotive proved unable to take us over a slight up-grade. We came to a dead halt, and remained there all night." Added Mrs. Davis, "There were no arrangements possible for sleeping."

Southside Virginia, near Petersburg

Sleep was also elusive for the weary Yankee troopers spread in soggy bivouacs near Dinwiddie Court House, Virginia, fifteen miles southwest of Petersburg. There had been a battle here this day, a clangorous, fluid combat of cavalry against cavalry and cavalry against infantry. The gun-fire had sputtered out soon after dark, and the exhausted men tried to catch what rest they could. An Ohio trooper named Roger Hannaford remembered that the "night was cold, with slight frost, & we suffered bitterly. . . . We could not move around briskly, it made too much noise, and if we laid down, it was dreadful cold on the wet ground and no cover."

There were some difficult decisions to be made in the next few hours by the man running the show. Philip H. Sheridan's mission had been to swing his cavalry force around the Confederate defenses in order to sever the South Side Railroad, Petersburg's last functioning rail connection to distant supply depots. Stymied by the horrendous weather, Sheridan's men had made slow progress on March 29 and 30.

Robert E. Lee had promptly dispatched a strong infantry and cavalry force to challenge Sheridan's advance. The result was a sharp engagement throughout March 31 near Dinwiddie Court House. Sheridan's communications to Grant reflected his changing situation at the close of the engagement. His first message, sent by courier at dark, announced his intention "to stay at Dinwiddie" but also sketched the retreat route he would follow if the enemy attacked in the morning. A short time later, after Sheridan had time to better assess the condition of his troops, his outlook improved. A second courier conveyed to Grant Sheridan's promise to "hold on at Dinwiddie till forced to go." By the time one of Grant's aides rode down the muddy roads to Sheridan's headquarters, the bantam officer was breathing fire. "This force [of the enemy's] is in more danger than I am," he declared. "If I am cut off from the Army of the Potomac, it is cut off from Lee's army and not a man in it should ever be allowed to get back to Lee."

Sheridan's optimism was further buoyed by Grant's promise to send him help to do the job — more cavalry, and a full infantry corps. The only drawback was that Grant was sending Sheridan the Fifth Corps instead of the Sixth, the corps that had successfully served under him in the Shenandoah Valley. Sheridan had had some run-ins with the Fifth Corps's touchy commander, Major General Gouverneur K. Warren, and he sensed a cloud of doubt about the man that suggested he might be wanting in a pinch. Whatever his misgivings, however, Sheridan realized that these reinforcements would allow him to resume the offensive in the morning. Grant's message indicated that the lead elements of the Fifth Corps should be on hand by around midnight.

Five miles northeast of Sheridan's busy headquarters, Lieutenant Colonel Theodore Lyman of Massachusetts mourned the loss of a friend. Major Charles J. Mills had been a convivial, capable, and much-liked aide to Major General Andrew A. Humphreys, who commanded the Union Second Corps. The corps had come into action this morning in support of the Fifth, which was pressing the enemy lines along the White Oak Road near the Boydton Plank Road. Mills had been mounted, in sight of Lyman, when he was struck and killed by an artillery shell. Despite his pressing duties as an aide to Army of the Potomac commander Major General George G. Meade, Lyman spent time this evening contemplating Mills's body. The sight brought back memories of another young comrade killed almost a year earlier, in the Wilderness. "It is the same thing over and over again," Lyman reflected. "And strange too, this seeing a young man in full flush of robust health, and the next moment nothing that we can make out but the broken machine that the soul once put in motion."

Not far from where Lyman was holding his private vigil, Major General Warren was trying to make some sense out of the conflicting orders he had received this evening. Warren's troops had already fought a sizable battle this day when fresh instructions came at 4:30 P.M. for him to go on the defensive and to send a small force west along the White Oak Road to Five Forks to assist Sheridan. Warren suspected that this was *not* Sheridan's real location, but he sent one brigade off in that direction in any case. A new directive arrived at 6:30 P.M. telling him to divert that brigade from its westward trek and to send it along the Boydton Plank Road to Dinwiddie Court House. Not wanting to waste the time it would take to turn around the unit already in transit, Warren ordered a closer one to proceed to Sheridan.

At eight o'clock that night, Warren received word from Meade of Sheridan's embattled condition at Dinwiddie, with the commanding general's recommendation that the brigade on its way there should not be allowed to march too far away, lest the rear of the Fifth Corps be left open to attack. Warren, however, saw an opportunity here. He suggested to Meade that the Fifth Corps might be able to attack the rear of the force that was threatening Sheridan at Dinwiddie. Then, at 10:50 P.M., a fresh dispatch directed Warren to send Brevet Major General Charles Griffin's division down to Sheridan.* Headquarters could not have made a worse selection, as Griffin's men held Warren's right flank and would have to pass behind two other divisions to get to Sheridan. Overriding the directive, Warren selected the division closest to Sheridan, Brigadier General Romeyn Ayres's, and, at eleven o'clock, ordered it to proceed at once. It took Ayres some time to draw in his outposts, regroup units scattered by the day's fighting, and then get them onto the muddy roads — all with only a quarter moon to light the way. As if all that weren't bad enough, Ayres's lead elements marched only a short distance down the Boydton Plank Road before they found the Gravelly Run bridge out and the usually fordable stream swollen by the recent rains. More time was lost while Federal engineers labored in the darkness to get a crossing span erected. It was not until two o'clock the next morning that Warren's men were able to renew their march; they were still several hours from the linkup that an increasingly impatient Sheridan had been told to expect at midnight.

There were fateful decisions being made on the Confederate side as well this night. The mixed infantry-cavalry command that had so punished Sheridan's riders at Dinwiddie Court House was led by Major General George E. Pickett, a sad-eyed romantic whose division had found tragic immortality at Gettysburg. His men had done well in the fighting around Dinwiddie Court House this day, despite having to maneuver over swollen streams, inundated floodplains, and muddy fields. "The enemy were severely punished," Pickett later reported, "half an hour more of daylight and we would have gotten to . . . [Dinwiddie] Court House."

Pickett's men shared their commander's glow of victory. "In this engagement . . . ," wrote one of them, "the famous cavalry officer, General Phil Sheridan, with all his brag, was scared out of his boots." Crowed another, "The enemy had fled. We were masters of the field." A Virginia cavalryman named Rufus Peck was not celebrating this night. Try as he might, he could not erase from his mind the image of a comrade killed in the fighting. Peck had come across the corpse, "a splendid looking fellow, who didn't look to be more than fifteen years old, lying across a

---

* The message was written at nine o'clock but not received by Warren until the time noted.

clump of rock lilies." Reflecting years later on this image, Peck wrote, "I never see the beautiful waxy bloom of the rock lily, that I don't think of the fate of that fine looking boy, almost a child. I laid him flat on the ground, but could do no more."

Darkness brought George Pickett little opportunity to further enjoy his success. He worried about his dwindling ammunition supplies, and he was anxious about his relative isolation from the rest of Lee's army around Petersburg. Sometime after nine o'clock he received a report that one of his cavalry outposts on the Crump Road, near Gravelly Run, had picked up some prisoners from the enemy Fifth Corps.* This likely meant that Yankee foot soldiers were coming down to reinforce Sheridan. A glance at the map made it clear that they were positioned in such a way as to easily break Pickett's already tenuous connection to Lee's main body and trap him in a deadly pocket.

As Pickett viewed the matter, his mission had been to turn back Sheridan's flanking move and to protect the approaches to the South Side Railroad. He had accomplished the first and could carry out the second without needlessly exposing his command.

Shortly after midnight, Pickett made his decision. Couriers and aides splashed off through the mud and puddles to coordinate the movement. George Pickett had decided to pull his entire force back across Hatcher's Run.

The situation at Petersburg had come down to a balance point. Whether the stalemate would continue or be broken would be decided by the men in blue and gray in the next twenty-four hours.

Saturday, April 1

Union

A light, misty fog lay across the fields north of Dinwiddie Court House. Ohio cavalryman Roger Hannaford was one among many who peered into the thinning haze and wondered if the new day would bring battle, pursuit, or retreat. "Every minute added to the light and we soon saw that the rebels were indeed gone," he noted with relief. The sun was just rising as the first squadron of Yankee riders trotted out to see how far back the enemy had pulled.

It was 4:50 A.M. when Gouverneur Warren received a dispatch writ-

---

* The Union POWs were from the small force that Warren had sent out to the west in accordance with the orders he received at 4:30 P.M.

ten nearly two hours earlier by Phil Sheridan, which put a whole different spin on affairs. In it Sheridan directed Warren's men to cooperate with him in a pincer movement against the enemy force near Dinwiddie Court House. Ironically, it was similar to the plan Warren had proposed during the night to Meade and Grant, which they had ignored in their rush to reinforce Sheridan. Warren immediately left his headquarters to personally order out Griffin's and Crawford's divisions, taking pains to avoid waking most of his staff. "I expected a hard day's work before us," he recalled, "and I ordered them to get some sleep if they could."

Confederate

George Pickett's intention had been to take up a line along Hatcher's Run, a mile or so north of Five Forks. Hardly had he begun his retrograde movement from Dinwiddie Court House, however, when a dispatch arrived from Robert E. Lee that changed everything.

> Hold Five Forks at all hazards. Protect road to Ford's Depot and prevent Union forces from striking the Southside Railroad. Regret exceedingly your forced withdrawal, and your inability to hold the advantage you had gained.

It was still dark when the first of Pickett's men began taking positions at Five Forks, the infantry filing slowly into a line that ran parallel to the White Oak Road. "We went to work immediately throwing up intrenchments," recalled the officer in charge of one of the brigades. "We made a very respectable breastwork with what we had to work with, in about an hour and a half or two hours." A watching artilleryman marveled at the men's industry. "They were working like beavers then," he later declared.

The cannon with Pickett's infantry were under the command of Colonel William Ransom Pegram, a bespectacled twenty-three-year-old who was one of the most highly regarded artillerists in the Army of Northern Virginia. Personally fearless, Pegram could be counted upon to find his way into the thickest combat.

With his aide and close friend Captain W. Gordon McCabe, Pegram now waited in the damp dawn for the infantry line to be set so he could place his cannon. The constant movement during the night had separated the gunners from their support wagons, and there was little food on hand, so the pair munched on some parched corn they had taken from their horses' feed bags.

Union

General Warren's infantry column made contact with Sheridan's cavalry outposts shortly after dawn. The leading files had been moving along the Boydton Plank Road, directly toward Dinwiddie Court House, when they were redirected by one of Sheridan's aides onto a turnoff that would bring them to the Dinwiddie Court House Road north of the village.

Colonel Richard Bowerman accompanied the skirmishers who spearheaded the column. He remembered hearing perhaps as many as six guns fired in the distance, then a faintly audible band playing "John Brown's Body." His men passed some still-smoldering picket fires before going to ground when several warning shots were fired ahead of them. It proved to be a Union cavalry vidette. "Being on the line," Bowerman recollected, "the first officer I encountered was Genl. Sheridan himself, who inquired for the commanding officer of the Division. I told him Genl. Ayres, who at that instant himself came up."

Sheridan believed that a matchless opportunity to smash Pickett's force had been frittered away by Warren's lackadaisical management of his night march. "That we had accomplished nothing but to oblige our foe to retreat was to me bitterly disappointing," he later wrote. For the moment Sheridan had no plans for the infantry, so Ayres was instructed to hold his men in readiness near the J. Boisseau residence, "about two miles and a half north of Dinwiddie Court House."

Sheridan believed that an officer's merit was directly related to his proximity to the front, so his estimation of Warren continued to sink as more and more of the Fifth Corps arrived with no sign of the general commanding. When a fresh gaggle of mounted men appeared at 7:00 A.M., Sheridan rode up to the group, only to discover that it was led by Brigadier General Joshua Chamberlain, commanding a brigade in Brevet Major General Charles Griffin's division. "General Sheridan asked me where General Warren was," Chamberlain later recalled. "I told him I understood him to be at the rear of the column with the rear guard."

"That is where I should expect him to be," Sheridan snapped.

For his part, General Warren was exactly where he believed he *should* be. Withdrawing as large a body of men as a corps from close contact with the enemy was an operation fraught with danger. A sudden enemy advance might catch the corps strung out on the roads and unable to defend itself. Accordingly, as he later reported, Warren "remained with General Crawford's division, [the last to be withdrawn,] which we formed to retire in line of battle to meet the enemy should he pursue us from his breast-works, as I confidently expected he would as soon as he discovered our movements. I also deployed my escort to retire toward the plank road to take back any men or supplies which might be coming to the point through ignorance of the change [in orders] that had been made in the night."

It was not until 9:00 A.M. that Warren received instructions placing his corps directly under Sheridan's command. Even then, Warren felt no urgency to meet with the cavalry officer. Two of his division commanders had already made personal contact, and Sheridan had not expressed to either the need to see him. And as things appeared quiet, Warren decided to improve the moment by sitting down to eat breakfast.

At his headquarters near Dabney's Mill, Lieutenant General U. S. Grant was anxiously keeping track of Sheridan's operation. Shortly before 9:00 A.M. he called in his trusted aide Lieutenant Colonel Horace Porter. "I wish you would spend the day with Sheridan's command," he instructed, "and send me a bulletin every half-hour or so, advising me fully as to the progress of his movements. . . . Tell him the contemplated movement is left entirely in his hands, and he must be responsible for its execution." Porter set out promptly to find Sheridan, accompanied by "half a dozen mounted orderlies to act as couriers in transmitting field bulletins."

While Grant had absolute confidence in Sheridan's ability to carry out his part in the operation, he had almost none in Warren. Because of the proximity of Warren's men to Sheridan, Grant had had no choice but to hand the support assignment to the Fifth Corps, even though he had profound doubts, as he later stated, with "General Warren in this critical position, which I then expected to make the last battle of the war, [and I worried] that he would probably fail [Sheridan]."

The final straw for Grant occurred at about ten o'clock in the morning, when an aide just back from a ride to Sheridan's headquarters erroneously reported that the Fifth Corps was still stalled at Gravelly Run. Grant's anxiety now turned into anger. In the presence of this aide and other staff officers, he declared that he had wanted to relieve Warren of his command back in May at Spotsylvania Court House, "but that at General Meade's solicitation he did not do it, and that he was sorry now that he had not done it — had not relieved him."

Grant called in another of his inner circle, Lieutenant Colonel Orville E. Babcock, and gave him a personal message for Sheridan's ears only. "Tell General Sheridan that if, in his judgment, the Fifth Corps would do better under one of the division commanders, he is authorized to relieve General Warren and order him to report to me."

Confederate

The cavalry attached to George Pickett's command, which had covered his withdrawal, began to arrive at Five Forks between ten and eleven o'clock this morning. There had been little fighting during the operation, with the Federals merely following up the rear guard. Most of the troopers were posted on the right of the White Oak Road line. Brigadier General R. M. T. Beale recollected that his men immediately "cut pines and made a pretty heavy breast-work through those woods. I suppose they did it in an hour. I think it was a pretty heavy work for cavalry, it was nothing like what the infantry threw up." Beale's immediate superior, Major General W. H. F. Lee, arrived with the last of the screening force at 11:00 A.M. Approximately 9,200 men — infantry, cavalry, and artillery — now occupied the position.

Willie Pegram began to distribute his six guns along the line shortly after 10:00 A.M.. Three cannon were placed at the intersection to cover approaches by either Scott's Road or the Dinwiddie Court House Road. The other three were unlimbered further to the west to sweep a broad open field owned by a family named Gilliam. There was an orchard upwind of these guns, and as the sweating artillerymen wrestled their pieces into place and prepared them for action, they did so amidst that "delicious haze so common in lowland Virginia." On Pickett's left, four guns of the horse artillery, commanded by Major William M. McGregor, took station.

The Confederate line now extended for about a mile and three-quarters along the White Oak Road. Additionally, the left, or east, flank was refused (that is, bent back) to provide some protection. This return extended about 150 yards north of the line.

Robert E. Lee spent part of this morning on the right flank of his main line, near Burgess' Mill, hoping to uncover something of his enemy's intentions. He learned that the Yankee infantry he had fought here yesterday had moved off to the west, in Pickett's direction. The Confederate commander even rode a short distance outside his entrenchments to confer with officers in Roberts's brigade, his only link to Five Forks. An aide on Roberts's staff, worried that fighting was likely to break out at any moment, was "rather pleased" when Lee at last rode "slowly away in the direction of Burgess' Mill."

In the absence of any indication from Pickett that he was in trouble, Lee decided not to further weaken his Petersburg defenses by sending reinforcements to Five Forks.

Union

Grant's aide Horace Porter found Sheridan "about 10 A.M., on the Five Forks [i.e., Dinwiddie Court House] road not far from J. Boisseau's house." Sheridan reviewed the morning's events and grumbled that he had "had his patience sorely tried by the delays that had occurred in getting the infantry to him," but he vowed "to make every effort to strike a heavy blow with all the infantry and cavalry as soon as he could get them into position."

Porter was still talking to Sheridan when Gouverneur K. Warren arrived. Warren later described that meeting: "As I approached the place, I think he had been lying down on a blanket, and he rose up. I spoke to him, half reclining or maybe sitting upon the blanket. I know there was a log between me and him, and I sat down upon it, and we had some conversation there together." Although he was inwardly fuming over what he perceived as Warren's lack of urgency, Sheridan said nothing about the matter. "I directed General Warren to hold fast at J. Boisseau's house, refresh his men, and be ready to move to the front when required," Sheridan later reported.

The politeness did not last long, however. Hoping to make the point that his men had already fought a sharp engagement within the past twenty-four hours, Warren remarked that his corps "had had rather a field day of it since yesterday morning."

Sheridan's reply was icy: "Do you call that a field day?"

Remembered Warren, "I saw by the tone of his remark that he was not very well pleased with what I had said, so I, in a measure, apologized for it by saying that it was perhaps a little ironical, and I referred to the fact that we had been directed to cease operations and have a quiet time of it, but the dispositions General Lee had made had given us about as lively a time as I had in my experience."

That ended their conversation. According to an officer present, "Sheridan left Warren there, mounted his horse, and . . . said he was going right to the front and see what they were doing there."

Some two miles up the road, Sheridan's troopers were at last coming upon the entrenched Confederate position at Five Forks. Colonel Alexander C. M. Pennington, commanding a brigade in Brigadier General George A. Custer's division, was riding toward a sudden outburst of firing when he met one of his regimental officers. "He told me he had just encountered the enemy and had quite a little fight with them. While I was talking with him I heard artillery firing, and an aide-de-camp came and told me we had found the enemy."

Even as that conversation was taking place, Grant's aide Babcock located Sheridan "in rear of his line . . . passing from the left to the right giving instructions to his command." Babcock delivered Grant's verbal authorization for Sheridan to replace Warren if he believed "the Fifth Corps would do better under one of the division commanders."

Sheridan accepted the message with no sign of emotion. "I did not wish to do it," he later stated, "particularly on the eve of battle." For the moment, Sheridan decided to say "nothing at all about the message brought me." He and Babcock rode along the cavalry position, and the aide listened while Sheridan explained to each of his division commanders that "the attack would be made upon the left with cavalry, and at the same time he intended to throw infantry on to the right."

The reports that his officers were sending him painted a distorted picture of the enemy's defenses. Custer, for instance, described them as "extending for miles" and consisting of "heavy lines of earthworks. . . . Every point seemed to be strongly manned with infantry and artillery." Fearing that too much scouting of the enemy position might reveal his intentions, Sheridan satisfied himself with these long-distance observations. He based his plan on an understanding of the White Oak Road line that placed its refused flank nearly seven-tenths of a mile further to the east than it actually lay.

It was almost 1:00 P.M. when Sheridan sent word to Warren to move the Fifth Corps into a relatively open staging area near Gravelly Run Church. An aide waiting near Warren watched as a cavalry officer delivered the message. He recalled, "General Warren immediately turned to me and told me to go back and bring up the corps at once."

Confederate

As morning passed into afternoon with no sign of a serious enemy attack at Five Forks, Pickett's men began to relax. "No fight today, boys; only an April fool!" one artilleryman called out merrily to his comrades.

Union

Upon receiving Sheridan's orders to advance his infantry to the jump-off point, Gouverneur K. Warren rode on to reconnoiter so that no time would be lost once his men reached the area. The Fifth Corps commander again sought out Sheridan, who "explained to me the state of affairs and what his plan was for me to do." To help screen the advance,

Warren ordered his escort to patrol ahead as far north as the White Oak Road.

Brigadier General Samuel W. Crawford's 4,100-man division was the first to come up from the J. Boisseau house to the marshaling point near Gravelly Run Church. "The roads were heavy with mud, and the men worn down by four nights of marching and battle," one of Crawford's men later wrote.

Next to move was Brevet Major General Charles Griffin's 5,800-man division. Brigadier General Joshua Chamberlain, commanding one of Griffin's three brigades, remembered that the "road had been much cut up by repeated scurries of both the contending parties and was even yet obstructed by cavalry led horses, and other obstacles. . . . We . . . were brought to frequent standstill. This was vexatious — our men being hurried to their feet in heavy marching order, carrying on their backs perhaps three days' [rations and ammunition] . . . , and now compelled every few minutes to come to a huddled halt in the muddy road."

The 2,600-man division of Brigadier General Romeyn B. Ayres was the last to come up. "The column advanced along the road," recalled a Pennsylvanian in the ranks, "with frequent halts, which indicated that we were nearing the foe. Ere-long we could hear skirmishing, and an occasional discharge of cannon."

Those battle sounds signaled that Sheridan's cavalrymen were testing the Rebel lines. There was no pattern to these actions; rather, each unit acted in its own way to realize Sheridan's directive to press the enemy. On the Union left, troopers from Pennington's brigade scrapped with Southern parties posted near the Gilliam family home. The fight ended with the Confederate riders' pulling back to the White Oak Road line and the Federals' digging in.

On the right of the long cavalry line, men from Brigadier General Thomas C. Devin's division closed on Pickett's infantry. A Rhode Island trooper later recollected moving "through woods and fields, over fences and ditches [to take position] . . . in a cleared field at the edge of woods, slightly protected by an elevation, while the shells were coming thick and fast, knocking off limbs and felling small trees." One of Sheridan's many rides along the line today was noted by a New York officer, who never forgot him "in his earnest, energetic manner shaking his fingers in the direction of the enemy. I remarked, 'Boys, that means business, there's lively work before us.'"

As the afternoon unfolded with no dramatic action on the Federal right, where the Fifth Corps was coming into line, the cavalrymen grew increasingly impatient. A soldier under Devin's command spoke for all of them when he reflected, "For the anxious cavalrymen who were forced to lie inactive before a vigilant and formidable enemy, watching the lengthening shadows which marked the fast waning day, the three hours seemed an eternity, and the delay unaccountable."

Phil Sheridan mirrored his men's mood. "Here began his dissatisfaction with General Warren in connection with this battle," one of Sheridan's aides later wrote. "It was a time for personal effort and example." The aide long remembered Sheridan this afternoon, "walking up and down in an impatient way . . . constantly asking staff officers what time it was, and being rather strenuous in such remarks that he did make."

For all his anxiety and irritation, Sheridan never lost sight of the larger tactical problem facing him. As long as the enemy at Five Forks maintained a connection with the rest of Lee's army along the White Oak Road, that route could be used either to send reinforcements or to mount a counterstroke. Sheridan now decided to break that link, using the cavalry reinforcements that Grant had sent him when he dispatched the Fifth Corps. These troopers, Brigadier General Ranald S. Mackenzie's small-sized division from the Army of the James, moved at around 1:00 P.M. from Dinwiddie Court House to J. Boisseau's, where they turned northeast, up the Crump Road. As they approached the White Oak Road, the blue-coated riders ran into a strong enemy force posted in a line of rifle pits. Mackenzie himself led a charge that pounded into the left flank of the position and routed the enemy troopers, who proved to be North Carolinians of Brigadier General William P. Roberts's brigade, detached from W. H. F. Lee's division. The Tar Heel cavalrymen scattered, some fading eastward to the main army, others turning west to take word of their disaster to Five Forks.

Confederate

An aide to Brigadier General Matthew W. Ransom, whose five North Carolina infantry regiments held the extreme left of Pickett's line, noted that the "men were tired and were feeling confident and simply resting in their places." There had been some small action among the pickets when Sheridan's riders scouted their position, but then, remembered one of Ransom's soldiers, "as if by mutual consent, both sides ceased firing and lay behind the trees watching each other."

This lack of concern was shared by the senior officers present. According to Fitzhugh Lee, in overall command of the cavalry, "When we moved towards Five Forks, hearing nothing more of the infantry's [i.e., the Union Fifth Corps's] move which we had heard of the night before, I thought that the movements just there, for the time being, were suspended, and we were not expecting any attack that afternoon." Also contributing to this relaxed attitude was the officer's assumption that Robert E. Lee would send help if he detected any significant movement of enemy troops toward them.

Any information that ran counter to this rosy assessment was discounted. "Heavy columns of infantry . . . were observed moving on our left, and moving around our flank," recalled one of Ransom's pickets. "Frequent reports were made of this . . . , but apparently no steps were taken to oppose or prevent this movement." At one point Colonel Thomas T. Munford, whose cavalry was posted directly north of the Fifth Corps's assembly area, asked Ransom for some of McGregor's guns, but Ransom refused to release them.

George Pickett now received a request from Major General Thomas Rosser, commanding the reserve, to join him north of Hatcher's Run for a little feast. Before linking up with Pickett's force, Rosser's men had been stationed along a section of the Nottoway River, where Rosser had caught a good number of shad. Since nothing seemed to be happening, Rosser decided to have a shad-bake. Both Pickett and Fitzhugh Lee accepted Rosser's invitation with pleasure.

It was sometime after 2:00 P.M., likely very close to 3:00, when Pickett left the front for the two-mile ride to Rosser's headquarters. Just before Fitzhugh Lee departed, Colonel Munford handed him a dispatch written by the officer handling liaison with Roberts's brigade. The message indicated that Roberts's brigade, holding the connection between Five Forks and Petersburg, had been scattered by an overwhelming force of the enemy.

Lee was skeptical. "Well, Munford," he said after reading the note, "I wish you would go over in person at once and see what this means and, if necessary, order up your Division and let me hear from you." He then rode off to catch up with Pickett. Through either an oversight or overconfidence, the next individuals in the chain of command were not informed that the two senior officers at Five Forks were no longer on the field. As Munford later observed, "The Generals left on the line were *left* like *tin soldiers,* to hold their position without orders for any emergency."

Union

Phil Sheridan's impatience at the slow pace of the Fifth Corps was growing. A watchful Horace Porter observed, "He made every possible appeal for promptness, he dismounted from his horse, paced up and down, struck the clinched fist of one hand into the palm of the other, and fretted like a caged tiger. He said at one time: 'This battle must be fought and won before the sun goes down. All the conditions may be changed in the morning; we have but a few hours of daylight left us. My cavalry are rapidly exhausting their ammunition, and if the attack is delayed much longer they may have none left.' "

Sheridan complained directly to Warren, who was supervising the arrival and placement of his corps near Gravelly Run Church. The infantry commander was making a conscious effort to keep his own anxieties concealed. He later allowed that Sheridan's "impatience was no greater apparently than I felt myself, and which I strove to repress and prevent any exhibition of, as it would tend to impair confidence in the proposed operations." In response to Sheridan's anxious inquiries, Warren promptly offered to lead into action such troops as were then on hand, but the cavalryman wanted all the infantry to go in together. Warren was also determined that his senior officers should fully understand the plan. A sketch map based on Sheridan's scouting reports was drawn up and given to each division commander, with instructions "as far as time would admit, to explain it to the brigade commanders."

Sheridan at one point corralled several of Warren's brigade commanders for an impromptu briefing. As one later recalled, "General Sheridan called us around him in the road — his plan was very short: he drew his saber in the dust and says: 'There is the White Oak road; the enemy are intrenched behind that, they have refused their left; somewhere near an old church; whether it is within their lines or not I do not know.' He said: 'I will attack their entire front; I will deploy my cavalry, dismounted[,] and engage their entire front, and with the strong arm I will strike this salient and wheel on to their left and rear.' " Another officer present thought that the plan was "perfectly clear, and struck us all as a splendid piece of tactics, cyclone- and Sheridan-like, promising that our success was to be quick and certain."

The last of Warren's three divisions, Ayres's, was just coming into position when Brevet Brigadier General Frederick Winthrop, in charge of its leading brigade, found his friend Joshua Chamberlain of Griffin's division. "Have you managed to bring anything to eat?" Winthrop asked. "We moved so suddenly I had to leave everything." Chamberlain sent off an orderly, who returned with what little he could find. Remembered Chamberlain, "We sat there on a log, close behind the lines, and acted host and guest, while he opened his heart to me as men sometimes will quite differently from their custom, under the shadow of a forecasting presence." They had not yet completed their modest meal when it became apparent that the assault was imminent. The two parted, each for his own command.

A member of the 190th Pennsylvania, in Ayres's division, sketched the troops as they waited for the order to advance. "Most of them are young men. A few days ago they were so neat and tidy in dress and appearance, you might almost mistake that they were college students playing soldier. Now they are dirty, smeared with mud, half wet still from the rain. . . . Some are seated, leaning against the trees, taking it easy, conversing as pleasantly as if these were the ordinary occurrences of life. . . .

"But our waiting is over at last; and, at the word of command, every soldier is in his place. These men were *not* stolid, ignorant, nor inexperienced. Their thinned ranks show how well they know what battle means. You can see some pale faces, and lips compressed, as 'FORWARD' passes down the line."

Ayres's division made up the left of Warren's formation, and Crawford's the right, with Griffin following Crawford as the reserve. In his final instructions to his divisional officers, Warren stressed the need "to keep closed to the left and to preserve their direction in the woods, by keeping the sun, then shining brightly, in the same position over their left shoulders."

It was close to 4:30 P.M. when Warren's infantry went into motion. Sheridan was sitting with Warren as Ayres passed at the head of his men, and he called out to the infantry commander, "I will ride with you." Warren remained behind to coordinate the complicated movement. An aide who was present remembered that "General Warren gave orders to one or two staff officers who were there, and sent them to different parts of the command."

Ayres's battle lines moved out of the wooded bottomland and onto a broad, open field near the center of which stood the Bass House. "Here we caught sight of the White Oak Road, some two hundred yards before us, and a little party of the enemy's cavalry moving restlessly about in the edge of the woods in our front," recalled an aide with Sheridan.

Suddenly a cavalry officer galloped in from the right. It was Ranald Mackenzie, coming to report that his small division, in obedience to orders received from Sheridan after it cleared the enemy roadblock, was approaching from the east along the White Oak Road. Sheridan quickly instructed Mackenzie to hook up on the right of Crawford's division to protect that flank, and to guide on it so as to "move west and get possession of the Ford road in the enemy's rear."

Ayres, meanwhile, advanced with two brigades forming his front line — Bowerman's all-Maryland brigade on the left and Brevet Brigadier General James Gwyn's mixed Delaware-Pennsylvania brigade on the right — and one, Winthrop's, following as the reserve. Ayres later recalled that as "we came through the woods into [the Bass field], . . . a staff officer says, 'It looks as if the enemy might be at our left.' . . . Says I, 'Yes, ride back immediately to General Winthrop, and give him my order to observe carefully to our left.' "

By now Warren's leading divisions — Ayres's and Crawford's — were crossing the White Oak Road. A Pennsylvania soldier never forgot the sight: "This was the grandeur, the sublimity of war. The corps was coming in order of battle, line after line sweeping on with steady step[,] . . . guns at a right shoulder, glittering in the sunlight like silver, battle-flags fluttering in the air."

Continued Ayres, "Just after [the warning was sent to Winthrop] . . . there came a little fire from the woods in front. . . . Coming along a little more there came a volley from a little piece of woods in my front, a small fire that struck the right of my right brigade. . . . The commander of that brigade gave the command 'double quick' to his troops — my right brigade — contrary to directions he had received, and his brigade struck a double quick and had the appearance of being in disorder." Added one of Sheridan's aides, "Fortunately General Sheridan happened to be at hand, and together with his staff rode into the ranks of the faltering troops, which were soon reassured."

But Ayres was now facing a much bigger problem than a somewhat disorganized brigade. He recalled that as his troops forged ahead and entered the woods, "I got a sharp, full volley from the left, out of the dense woods [in that direction], raking my left flank." The officer realized that the sketch map had placed the enemy entrenchments too far to the east. Instead of striking them head-on, his troops were passing them on their left.

Ayres at once ordered a radical shift in his formation. His reserve brigade, Winthrop's, which had yet to cross the White Oak Road, was told to wheel 70 degrees to its left. He then took personal charge of the Maryland brigade (its commander having already been wounded) and turned it to form on Winthrop's right, while his third brigade guided on the Marylanders and turned with them. Thus Ayres's two-brigade front line, which had been facing north, became a three-brigade line of battle facing west. This reorientation, Ayres later estimated, took "not more than 15 minutes I guess."

Sheridan's plan called for the two leading divisions to wheel against the enemy line in concert, but Ayres's sudden redirection had severed his connection to Crawford's division. Untouched by, and unaware of, the flanking fire that had so startled Ayres, Crawford kept his men on their original course, slowly forcing back stubborn groups of Confederate cavalrymen in their front. His foremost elements had moved perhaps two hundred yards north of the White Oak Road when a frantic aide informed Crawford that "there was no connection with General Ayres." Crawford, who was better suited to following orders than improvising them, sent an officer to find Warren for new instructions. Meanwhile, his standing directive was to advance, and this his division did, widening the gap between it and Ayres's command.

Riding in the rear of Ayres's original front line, Warren perceived the sudden change in the picture at the same instant Ayres did. Turning to one of his aides, he ordered the man off to the right, saying, "Go over and see if you cannot get Crawford in." Warren now realized, as he later stated it, "that the fight for the angle of the works was going to come on Ayres instead of Crawford, as we had planned it, [so] I sent an officer to Griffin to come in that direction as quickly as he could to sustain Ayres."

Griffin's orders were to follow in Crawford's wake to provide support where it was needed. Recalled one of the soldiers in his advance, the "ground was rough and cut up with numerous ravines." Another felt that the briefing had not completely prepared the men for what they encountered. He recollected that when they came upon the White Oak Road, "it looked smaller than we thought it was going to be, and we came upon it sooner than we thought, and there was a discussion as to whether it was the White Oak Road; we thought it was a by-road."

This confusion, coupled with the rugged terrain, opened up the distance between Crawford and Griffin, so that when the reserve force did cross the White Oak Road, Crawford's men were nowhere in sight. A staff officer later remembered that they had proceeded about half a mile beyond the White Oak Road when Griffin began to suspect that things were not as they were supposed to be. According to this aide, Griffin "remarked that we were getting away from the firing and that Ayres had got hotly engaged." Griffin then ordered the left brigade in his two-brigade first line (Bartlett's; Chamberlain's was on the right) to halt while he figured out what was happening. A short ride brought Griffin to Ayres's position, where he asked his fellow division commander what was up. "Nothing much," Ayres replied with a touch of battlefield humor, "nothing new. The same old story; Crawford has gone off and left me to fight alone."

Griffin rode off to make his own plans. Ayres, meanwhile, advanced his men in a westerly direction, where his course brought him directly against the short bend back, or return, in the enemy's White Oak Road line. According to a Maryland man in the fray, "A charge being ordered the boys rushed gallantly forward, going over fields, through woods, and apparently not heeding any obstacles at all. By some means, regiments in our right hand brigade became separated, and confusion was likely to result, but at this moment Genl. Sheridan and staff rode through open space[,] ordered the troops to close up, and spoke the words 'follow me' which with many cheers was done." A member of Sheridan's staff recalled, "As we went along the line, and as he was urging the line forward to go into the timber, the expression he made use of several times was, 'Go in there! There is nothing in there.' "

By this time the Confederates occupying the return were putting up all the firepower they could manage. "Bullets were humming like a swarm of bees," wrote Horace Porter. A Maryland soldier in this charge observed that "bullets and shells rapidly fell among us putting many poor fellows out of the way."

Ayres's assault brought Winthrop's and most of the Maryland brigade directly against the fortified return. However, some of the Marylanders, as well as Gwyn's brigade on the extreme right, overlapped the enemy's position. One of Gwyn's skirmishers came dashing back to the main line with the news. "We've got them! we've got them!" he shouted. "We're right in their rear. We'll take them all!"

It was around 5:00 P.M. when the left and center of Ayres's line struck the eastern flank of Pickett's White Oak Road line.

Confederate

W. A. Day of Ransom's brigade was one of the soldiers manning the return. The enemy, he recalled, "rushed over the low breast-works like an avalanche, and ordered us to surrender." He added that "our old flag was shot to pieces, nothing but a bunch of rags tied to a stick, but we stood by it like a wall of iron. . . . We poured the hot Minies into them as long as we had time to load our guns, but we could not stop them." In the 56th North Carolina, "Lieutenant Palmer had his men to load for him, and he stood on the parapet, and fired as fast as the guns could be handed to him, until he was surrounded." "The Yankees simply run over us and crowded us so that it became impossible to shoot," an officer in the 49th North Carolina remembered. "They literally swarmed on all sides of us, and by and by, as I looked toward the center of the regiment, I saw our old tattered banner slowly sinking out of sight."

The Federal assault also engulfed Wallace's brigade, posted on Ransom's right. A member of the 26th South Carolina later described the action: "The fighting was fierce and bloody until we were completely overlapped by superior numbers and stood as it were between the blades of scissors, the enemy being within twenty steps of our front and rear." One of Ransom's aides galloped toward the South Carolinians. Like many in Lee's army, he wore captured clothes, in this case a Yankee overcoat. Seeing this rider suddenly appear out of the fog of gunsmoke, someone cried out, "Shoot the Federal spy!" "Instantly," a horrified onlooker recalled, "a half dozen bullets pierced his body, and he fell from his horse dead."

Confederate defense here simply ceased to exist. Many of Ransom's men were captured, while others fled to the west, hoping either to reform their ranks or to escape.

Union

Phil Sheridan was in his glory. As an admiring Horace Porter watched, "Sheridan spurred [his horse] 'Rienzi' up to the angle, and with a bound the horse carried his rider over the earth-works, and landed in the midst of a line of prisoners who had thrown down their arms and were crouching close under their breastworks. Some of them called out, 'Whar do you want us-all to go to?' Then Sheridan's rage turned to humor, and he had a running talk with the 'Johnnies' as they filed past. 'Go right over there,' he said to them, pointing to the rear. 'Get right along, now. Drop your guns; you'll never need them any more. You'll be safe over there. Are there any more of you? We want every one of you fellows.' "

Gouverneur Warren finally decided to find Crawford's division himself. He blundered through the wooded terrain and at last came upon the left brigade in Crawford's two-brigade front line — Colonel John A. Kellogg's. Warren instructed Kellogg "to change direction at right angles and remain halted until the other brigade came on the line." Then the Fifth Corps commander continued to search for his errant division officer.

Hardly had Warren ridden out of sight when a light gunfire erupted from nearby woods, probably from some of Munford's troopers. "I ordered my men to lie down to protect them from this fire temporarily," Kellogg recalled. "Just then Colonel [George A.] Forsyth [of Sheridan's staff] appeared in front of the Seventh Wisconsin Regiment, which was my left regiment, . . . and . . . gave them some order. . . . I immediately rode out to Colonel Forsyth and . . . told him . . . if he had any orders, to give them to me, and he says: 'Your orders are to move into action,' . . . and he gave it as coming from General Sheridan. I asked him if General Sheridan was aware [that the rest of Crawford's division was] to guide upon my right. We had some italicized conversation about that time." Forsyth rode off, leaving Kellogg with a difficult decision: whether to follow Warren's instructions to wait or obey Sheridan's to move. After four minutes' reflection, Kellogg ordered his brigade to advance toward the west.

Some distance to the rear of Crawford's men, Charles Griffin was scouting the route he planned to follow with his division. Joshua Chamberlain, who today led the right brigade in Griffin's two-brigade front line, had a terrible feeling "that something was 'all wrong.' " He spotted Griffin's headquarters flag dutifully following as the general galloped toward the firing. If Griffin was heading in that direction, Chamberlain reasoned, so should he be. The young officer pivoted his brigade to the left and, after telling the other two brigadiers what he was doing, moved his men after Griffin. Hardly had the maneuver been completed when Griffin himself rode up. "He gave the look I wanted," Chamberlain wrote, "and without coming near enough for words waved me to . . . attack."

Griffin now met Joseph Bartlett, whose brigade had begun the advance on the left of his front line. Together, they sent these regiments in on Chamberlain's right. This force, soon joined by the reserve brigade, crossed the Sydnor field to come into the fight on Ayres's right. Griffin's men struck a battle line made up of the left flank of Steuart's brigade and the remnants of Ransom's and Wallace's brigades, which, in an effort to halt the blue wave coming from the east, had been reinforced by a Virginia regiment hurriedly detached from Mayo's command.

Along the White Oak Road, Ayres's assault on the return became the signal for Sheridan's cavalry to press its attacks against the front. Wherever the enemy line was well manned, the troopers made little headway. "Useless, worse than useless," complained one of Pennington's men, "to expect that a thin line of dismounted men, not indeed much thicker than a skirmish line, could unaided carry such breastworks." Only along the section nearest to the captured return did the troopers enjoy any success. As Sheridan remarked, "After we had captured the works thrown to the rear, I directed a halt [of Ayres's men] for a few moments because the cavalry were coming over the works on the White Oak road, and I was afraid Ayres's men would kill the cavalry." Sheridan believed that victory had been achieved. "The battle was won, in my opinion," he later declared, "when the angle was taken."

Confederate

The commanding officers left on the line in the absence of Pickett and Fitzhugh Lee tried in vain to stop the overwhelming enemy assault. Colonel Joseph Mayo, whose brigade held a position immediately west of the intersection, was summoned by Brigadier General George H. Steuart, commanding the men just on the east side of the fork. "Colonel, I have just received an important message from Ransom to bring my brigade to his support," Steuart said. "I will send him two regiments, if you will send him one." According to Mayo, "I told him I did not like to take that responsibility, and asked him where General Pickett was. He said he did not know, he had not seen him." Already enemy rifle fire was hitting Steuart's men from the rear. Mayo raced back to his command and sent the 11th Virginia off to support Ransom.

The regiment arrived just as the survivors of Ransom's and Wallace's brigades, along with some of Steuart's men, managed to form into line of battle a short distance northwest of the lost return. A Tar Heel in the 49th Regiment watched as the Virginians "moved down to where our Regiment was stationed, then left-faced and moved in line of battle to the rear. . . . In a short time the Virginians came rushing back with the enemy close behind them. . . . The Virginia Colonel rode up the line at full speed to make his escape, leaving his men to take care of themselves."

"There was no throwing down of guns at this point," wrote one of those in the 49th. "The men fought until the Federals literally ran over them. The only time during the war that I saw guns clubbed and blows struck with them was at this time and place." "A regular stampede now commenced," wrote another member of the 49th North Carolina. "The enemy were pressing on all sides; the men confused and various commands mixed with each other. . . . The cowardly ran, the timid were dumbfounded, the brave, alone, could not withstand the vastly superior force of the enemy."

Colonel Pegram and Captain McCabe were asleep when the firing broke out to the east. By the time they mounted and reached their three guns at Five Forks, the firing near the return was, McCabe remembered, "terrific beyond anything I have ever seen." Pegram's gunners were smoothly serving their cannon against the Yankee cavalrymen in their front as the young artillery commander rode into the battery. He reeled suddenly and fell heavily to the ground. McCabe rushed to his side and saw a reddening stain spread along his left side and arm. "Oh, Gordon," Pegram cried, "I'm mortally wounded, take me off the field." McCabe yelled for some stretcher bearers, waited until his friend had been lifted off the ground, and then returned to give the gunners Pegram's last order: "Fire your canister low." McCabe hurried to catch up with the stretcher bearers, determined to remain with his friend to the end.

Union

Still unable to locate General Crawford, Gouverneur Warren returned to where he had left Kellogg's brigade, only to find it gone. Fearing that by racing around the battlefield he had compromised his ability to control the corps, Warren decided to stay put for a while so that his staff might locate him. "I . . . continued to send officers to General Crawford and General Griffin until, I think, I had none left," he later recalled. At one point Sheridan rode up. "We flanked them gloriously," he declared, then complained that Crawford's and Griffin's failure to follow the plan might still ruin everything. Warren tried to assure the cavalry commander that these were good officers who knew their duty, but Sheridan was not mollified.

Stung by Sheridan's criticism, and despite his instinctive feeling that a commander should stay in one place, Warren rode off again — alone this time — in search of Crawford and Griffin. He came across Griffin and his men moving across the Sydnor field to attack the remnants of Ransom's and Wallace's brigades. After confirming Griffin's reorientation of his division, Warren rode back toward the return, saw that everything there was well in hand, and again sought Crawford. "I had a first-rate horse and I went on as fast as anybody could through those woods," he later insisted.

Confederate

From a social perspective, Tom Rosser's shad-bake was a great success. As he remembered, "Some time was spent over the lunch, during which no firing was heard. And we concluded that the enemy was not in much of a hurry to find us at Five Forks." Tragically for Pickett's future reputation, the combination of soggy woods and heavy atmosphere so blanketed the sounds of gunfire just two miles away that no one in the shad-bake party could hear them. "Some time after we had finished lunch," continued Rosser," . . . Pickett asked for a courier to take a message to Five Forks . . . and I gave him two of my couriers with the usual instruction to follow (in sight) each other, but not together. The foremost courier while passing through a clearing on the other side of Hatcher's Run and in full view of us, was fired on and captured and at the same time we saw a line of blue coats across the road."

The realization came to Pickett like an electric shock. He scrambled for his horse and galloped south across Hatcher's Run. He had gone only a short distance when he came upon a group of Munford's cavalrymen who were slowly retreating before the determined Federal advance. Already some enemy detachments were close to cutting off the road to Five Forks. Catching sight of Tom Munford, Pickett asked to what command these troopers belonged. Told that they were part of Fitzhugh Lee's division, Pickett asked if some could not be used to keep the enemy off the road long enough for him to get by. A young captain in the 2nd Virginia Cavalry heard Pickett's appeal and led a charge that momentarily stopped the Yankee advance. Pickett threw himself forward on his horse and, using the animal's head and neck to shield himself, raced safely past the choke point under a hail of gunfire. The gap closed behind him, and over the body of the youthful officer who had bought Pickett time with his life. Fitzhugh Lee, equally anxious to reach his men, followed after Pickett but could not break through the blue cordon. The cavalry commander returned to the north side of Hatcher's Run to organize the forces there.

Once George Pickett reached Five Forks, he immediately began to assemble a force to block the Federals who would soon be moving down Ford's Road in his rear. An aide was dispatched to Colonel Mayo with orders for him to pull most of his brigade out of the line and then bring it up. Mayo rode ahead of his men and met Pickett near the southern edge of the Young-Boisseau field.

"Colonel," Pickett called out, "the enemy are in our rear, and if we do not drive them out we are gone up."

Mayo later recalled his answer: "I said that was perfectly apparent to everybody."

Pickett missed, or ignored, the sarcasm. "File off to the left, and, with your right resting on the road, advance until you strike them," he ordered.

Union

By following a trail of wounded soldiers, Gouverneur Warren was at last able to locate Samuel Crawford. Alerted to the true situation by one of the aides dispatched by Warren, Crawford not only had made a turn to the west but had advanced his men to Ford's Road. Crawford's battle lines now ran parallel to the road. As Warren later related, "I immediately rode to him and told him to change his direction at once to the southward and move down upon those guns that were firing south of us. . . . General Crawford immediately executed that movement with a great deal of promptitude."

Crawford's men completed their maneuver, then descended on the scratch force that Pickett had organized. "The fire of the enemy now became severe," recalled a Pennsylvania soldier, ". . . [and] shouts and cheering, rising above the din of clashing arms, were heard from every part of the field." Another Pennsylvanian remembered how a "Confederate officer on horseback galloped along their front waving his sword above his head . . . when the order rang out loud and clear, 'Fix bayonets.' Instantly the clanging of steel rose above the din of battle supplanting for the moment the incessant discharge of guns."

"McGregor's four gun battery, which had escaped at the return, was also here in position," a New Yorker noted. "Crawford's division made a spirited attack upon the enemy's line and the defense was sharp and determined, but it was brief; when Mayo returned in the direction of [Brigadier General Montgomery D.] Corse and the Five Forks, leaving his four guns in our possession."*

Crawford's men, joined on their left by some of Griffin's, completed their sweep down to the intersection. One Massachusetts man ran up to the rear of the enemy earthworks, where he saw a young Rebel firing on bluecoats approaching from the east. Said the Union soldier, "Jamming on my bayonet I jumped to the works and ordered him to come out; he looked up and had the impudence, with a smile on his face, to say, 'I wish you would let me fire these five cartridges.' I think I swore some and told him I'd put the bayonet right through him unless he came out at once, and he came."

A jubilant Warren turned to his chief of staff, Lieutenant Colonel Frederick T. Locke, and told him to ride to Sheridan with the joyous news that the Fifth Corps had "gained the enemy's rear and had taken over 1,500 prisoners, and that he was pushing in a division as rapidly as he could."

Confederate

Mayo's attempt to stem the Union tide had failed. "It was sheer recklessness to stay a moment longer in that place," the C.S. officer recalled,

---

* Some accounts of this action insist that only three of McGregor's guns were captured.

"and telling us to get out the best way we could, General Pickett rode slowly to the rear."

All those manning the White Oak Road line who were not already dead, wounded, captured, or running rallied on the western end, where Corse's infantry brigade and two of W. H. F. Lee's cavalry brigades remained in good order. "I was rallying the refugees, part of my own brigade and the men from the other commands," General Corse recalled. "We stood there until it was nearly dark. . . . I could see the flashes of the guns. . . . I know that some of my officers came to me and said: 'Why, general, there is no use standing here any longer, they will gather us all up.' I said: 'No, I suppose not.' There was a little cessation, and I broke off to the left through the woods." One of the cavalrymen caught a glimpse of the whole embattled line and later swore that he "saw more Yankees then than in all the four years [of] war put together." A foot soldier in Corse's brigade looked up from the fighting in time to see "General Pickett[,] his long hair streaming behind him[,] as he rode from the ill-fated field."

The brigades of Barringer and Beale skillfully blunted several strong attempts by the Federal cavalry to cut off all retreat. A Rebel trooper afterward vowed that he would never forget the "blare of the Yankee bugles blowing the charge, and the deep voice of . . . [Major Roger] Moore [of Barringer's brigade], 'Form a line, men, form a line.' " "We then charged the enemy & counter charged & by so doing saved a good many of our infantry & wagons, ambulances & artillery belonging to our Division," recounted one of Beale's riders.

Union

The final organized action of the day took place as pieces of the Fifth Corps (mostly from Crawford's and Griffin's divisions) joined with elements of Custer's division to attack the enemy infantry and cavalry still holding the west side of the White Oak Road line. The weary Federal battle lines soon faltered in the face of this last-ditch Confederate resistance, and the hesitation continued, remembered one soldier, "till Warren [took] the Fifth Corps flag and [rode] forward with it, his troops follow[ing] him to the charge. His horse was shot under him in crossing the [Gilliam] field." Another soldier heard Warren calling out, "Now, boys[,] follow me, this will be the last fight of the war." Lieutenant Colonel Hollon Richardson of the 7th Wisconsin was severely wounded when he purposely rode between Warren and the enemy riflemen in order to shield the Fifth Corps commander.

This makeshift Union battle line hurried the Confederate rear guard off the field, then pushed along the White Oak Road until, as Warren later described it, "there was no longer any enemy in sight." Seeing that there was nothing more to be done, Warren sent another of his aides "for orders to General Sheridan, to learn what he wished."

In the meantime, the aide whom Warren had sent earlier to find Sheridan, Frederick Locke, had located the general near Five Forks and delivered Warren's message that he had "gained the enemy's rear, and had taken over 1,500 prisoners, and that he was pushing in a division as rapidly as he could."

Sheridan turned his horse around, gestured with his hand, and exclaimed, "Tell General Warren, by God! I say he was not at the front. That is all I have got to say to him."

This devastating reply stunned the young aide. "Must I tell General Warren that, sir?" he asked at last.

"Tell him that, sir!" Sheridan thundered.

Sheridan watched Warren's man depart and then looked around. His gaze rested on Charles Griffin's brigadier Joseph Bartlett, who was sitting within earshot on horseback. "You are in command of Griffin's division," he told Bartlett. "Griffin is in command of the corps."

Everything Sheridan had seen, or failed to see, on the field today had confirmed his belief that Warren was not a combat commander who could lead and inspire his men. The unsteadiness of Ayres's division during its advance and the wandering of Crawford's and Griffin's divisions were both blamed by Sheridan on Warren's command failings. Today's achievement could be lost tomorrow if vigorous and aggressive pressure was not maintained. "I felt that though my troops were victorious, they were isolated from the Army of the Potomac," Sheridan later explained, " . . . [and] I surmised that [the enemy] . . . might march down the White Oak Road that night or early next morning and take my command in rear. It was therefore necessary for me to make new dispositions to meet this new emergency."

Even as Sheridan began issuing new orders, Warren rode up, his face a mask of concern. Not only had Frederick Locke conveyed Sheridan's cutting comment to him, but Warren had also met one of the cavalryman's aides, who had delivered the written orders formally removing him from command. "General, I trust you will reconsider your determination," he said, in a manner that one of Sheridan's aides later termed "very insubordinate." Sheridan had no time for this. "Reconsider?" he said. "Hell! I don't reconsider my determination." "I will not rest under it," Warren retorted. "Go on, General," Sheridan said, ending the interview.

"It was a good fight," a soldier in the 20th Maine noted in his diary. "4 bullet holes in my pants." "It is impossible to overrate the exhilaration of the men in and after this action," remembered a Massachusetts man in the 32nd Regiment. Said a member of the 88th Pennsylvania of the bivouac this night, "There wasn't a man in that jubilant camp but felt he had grown a foot taller since sunrise." "Gave them a complete whipping and captured a great many prisoners," wrote a Pennsylvania cavalryman. Added a New York trooper, "One of the peculiar circumstances of the surrender of prisoners was that, almost without exception, they at once appealed to their captors for something to eat. . . . The way they ate was astonishing. It seemed as if their voraciousness would never be satisfied."

Not all the scenes this night were celebratory ones, however. "A little white country church was utilized as a hospital, where the wounded of both sides were carried on stretchers dripping with blood," one of Sheridan's men remarked. A temporarily paralyzed cavalryman was brought to this hospital, where "the dead and the dying are all about, and the saw and the knife are constantly at work." A reporter named George Townsend looked for and found the body of Frederick Winthrop, who had been mortally wounded in the charge of Ayres's division, just minutes after his final meal with Joshua Chamberlain. "He was pale and beautiful, marble rather than corpse, and the uniform cut away from his bosom showed how white and fresh was the body, so pulseless now."

Winthrop was one of 103 Federals killed in the fighting at Five Forks this day. With the 670 wounded and 57 missing added in, the final count of Union infantry and cavalry casualties for Five Forks was 830, most of which (633) came from the Fifth Corps.

Confederate

Although Federal sources claimed between 3,200 and 4,500 Rebels taken captive this day, a more careful modern accounting puts that figure at about 2,400, and the number of killed and wounded at 605, for total casualties of approximately 3,000 out of perhaps 9,200 engaged. Even more devastating was the psychological blow this had on the Southern troops. A Virginia cavalryman assigned to round up stragglers encountered two foot soldiers who seemed unfrightened by the course of events. As the trooper recalled, "They said they were going home; they had been in as many hard-fought battles as I had, and maybe more. They said there was no use to fight any more. . . . They stopped, though, and I sent them with all I had gathered back to their commands." Reflected another cavalryman, "I wonder when it will end & how."

Although Robert E. Lee would not learn the full details of the Five Forks debacle until the next day, there were enough danger signs from that quarter that he decided to send help. At 5:45 P.M. Major General Bushrod Johnson was directed by Lieutenant General Richard H. Anderson to pull his three brigades out of the trenches near the place where the Claiborne Road crossed Hatcher's Run and to march them up to the Church Road crossing. Johnson's men left at 6:30 P.M., took a northerly course to the South Side Railroad, and then followed the tracks west. It was a slow night march, and most would not reach their destination until morning.

Meanwhile, the troops remaining in the trenches abandoned by Johnson had to spread out to cover the gap. Fully recognizing the danger this posed to his defenses, Lee also decided to pull troops down from Richmond, where things were relatively quiet, to Petersburg, where further enemy attacks seemed imminent. He then returned to his headquarters at the Turnbull House, just west of Petersburg, and tried to get some sleep.

The ambulance carrying Captain McCabe and his dying friend William Pegram somehow managed to elude the Federal columns and cross safely to the north side of Hatcher's Run. "While in the ambulance," McCabe wrote shortly afterward, "I held him in my arms & prayed for him & kissed him over & over again." Several times Pegram said, "If it is God's will to take me, I am perfectly resigned." At one point McCabe, moved beyond discretion by his helplessness, cried out, "My God, my God, why hast thou forsaken me." "Don't say that, Gordon," Pegram chided him, "it isn't right." "Willie," McCabe said through his tears, "I never knew how much I loved you until now." Pegram pressed his hand. "But I did," he said.

They traveled to Ford's Station on the South Side Railroad, arriving there at about ten o'clock at night. Early the next morning the young artillery commander fell into a coma. "At 8 A.M., Sunday morning, he died without a struggle," McCabe noted.

Union

Horace Porter was in a gleeful mood as he brought word of Sheridan's victory at Five Forks to Grant's headquarters. Grant listened attentively, saying little as his exuberant aide spilled out the details. The instant

Porter finished his report, Grant walked to his tent and hurriedly scribbled out a series of dispatches. Rejoining his staff, Grant said (as "coolly as if remarking upon the state of the weather"), "I have ordered a general assault along the lines." Porter put the time at 9:00 P.M.

Among the hangers-on at Grant's headquarters was Sylvanus Cadwallader, chief of the *New York Herald*'s operations at Petersburg. In three years of association with Grant, the newspaperman had successfully ingratiated himself into a favorable position. Now the absence of any available aides or orderlies prompted Grant to ask Cadwallader if he would carry the news of Sheridan's victory back to City Point, along with some captured Confederate regimental battle flags.

Cadwallader set out at once. "The roads were execrable," he recalled, "filled with moving troops and trains, and the ride a distressing one to myself and horse." He reached City Point well after the President had retired for the night, but an interview was immediately arranged on Lincoln's steamboat, the *River Queen*. Lincoln was waiting expectantly as the reporter came aboard, and he took up the captured flags in his hands and slowly unfolded them one by one. "Here is something material — something I can see, feel, and understand," he said. "This means victory. This *is* victory."

By the time Cadwallader left, the distant rumble of artillery could be heard all along the Petersburg front. Lincoln knew that the sounds presaged Grant's all-out assault on the Confederate citadel, an action that was likely to result in more terrible casualty lists. "Mr. Lincoln would not go to his room," recalled his bodyguard, William Crook. "Almost all night he walked up and down the deck, pausing now and then to listen or to look out into the darkness to see if he could see anything. I have never seen such suffering in the face of any man as was in his that night."

Richmond

"The air is full of strange rumors, events are thickening around us," wrote a resident of the Confederate capital this day. Even a government clerk had no better luck trying to pierce the veil of misinformation that hung over everything: "We have vague and incoherent accounts from excited couriers of fighting without result in Dinwiddie County, near the South Side Railroad," he scribbled in his diary. "It is rumored that a battle will probably occur in that vicinity to-day." Jefferson Davis put his finger on the crux of the matter in a letter he wrote this day to Robert E. Lee. "The question is often asked, 'will we hold Richmond,' to which my only answer is, if we can; it is purely a question of military power."

A distinguished visitor from England made calls on several of the Confederacy's military leaders today. Mr. Thomas Conolly, a member of the British Parliament and a wholehearted supporter of the South, had made his way through the blockade in late February, partly to watch over his investment in a smuggling ship and partly because he was curious to see the nation he so admired. Conolly had arrived in Richmond on March 31 and was now enjoying his first full day of socializing. He spent part of the morning with Lee's veteran corps commander James Longstreet. The lieutenant general unrolled a large-scale map to explain the military situation to his visitor, and while they were talking, an aide arrived with a captured enemy seven-shot Spencer rifle. The staff officer had a low opinion of this fast-firing weapon, Conolly noted: "[He] thinks it would make men unsteady[,] thinks one shot sufficient, men are too much inclined to throw away their fire."

Conolly would end this day at a party, watching with droll amusement as seemingly happy couples danced "curious quadrilles unlike anything I ever saw [—] a sort of country dance!"

Just a few miles to the east, Union troops besieging Richmond waited for something to break the monotony of the past three months. A soldier in the 98th New York recalled this Saturday as a fine one, "with rather high wind. . . . Rumor flies through the air with a hundred eyes, a hundred tongues. . . . All is quiet in camp and front; our works simply hold themselves.

"In the evening our bands exhausted their list of tunes: Sacred Music, National Airs, waltzes, reels and hornpipes. The men encored, danced and sang responsive."

Chapter Three

CAPTURED!!

---◁○▷---

Sunday, April 2

Petersburg — Bermuda Hundred — Richmond

Union

THE BOMBARDMENT of the Confederate lines at Petersburg, which had begun at 10:00 P.M. on April 1, rumbled unceasingly for five hours. The Union veterans crouching in the trenches had seen their fair share of artillery exchanges during the course of the siege, but this one was different. "Storms of fire were pouring steadily into the rebel works," marveled one Rhode Island soldier. "Exploding shells illumined their ramparts as rebounding, they flashed in midair, while coruscating bombs penciled the heavens with curves unmatched e'en by Aurora's fairy touches."

Not everyone had a grandstand view. A Maine soldier further down the line complained that it was a "bright moonlight night and the shells did not show very plainly except when they burst."

Confederate

Only the Union batteries opposite Petersburg took part in the cannonade. Those along the lines to the north — stretched across Bermuda Hundred and along the eastern face of Richmond's defenses — were silent. A Maryland captain, McHenry Howard, "asleep in the tent on the lines a little north of Chaffin's Bluff on the north side of [the] James

River," was awakened by a "low muttering like distant thunder." Opening his eyes, he noticed that the tent canvas was bathed in an eerie red glare. A little closer to Petersburg, a Virginia gunner named Creed T. Davis was more directly affected. The "very earth trembled," he declared. "The heavens were illumined by the flash of the guns. I thought the world would fall to pieces."

The commotion finally tempted Captain Howard to dress and step outside his tent. He and some friends stood on their works, listening for half an hour to the distant cannon fire. Satisfied that whatever it meant, it did not involve them, Howard and his friends went back to sleep, determined to "make the most of this present exemption."

Union

Try as he might, Abraham Lincoln just could not sleep as long as the cannon were booming around Petersburg. Then, when the gunfire did subside, at about two in the morning, he fell into a fitful sleep and had a disturbing dream. In it he was back in the White House, and, as he later related, "There seemed to be a death-like stillness about me. Then I heard subdued sobs, as if a number of people were weeping. . . . I left my bed and wandered downstairs. . . . I went from room to room, no living person was in sight, but the same mournful sounds of distress met me as I passed along. . . . I was puzzled and alarmed. What could be the meaning of all this? Determined to find the cause . . . I kept on until I arrived at the East Room, which I entered. There I met with a sickening surprise. Before me was a catafalque, on which rested a corpse wrapped in funeral vestments. Around it were stationed soldiers who were acting as guards. . . . 'Who is dead in the White House?' I demanded of one of the soldiers. 'The President,' was his answer, 'he was killed by an assassin!' Then came a loud burst of grief from the crowd, which awoke me from my dream."

There would be no more sleep for Lincoln this night. He got dressed and walked outside and onto the deck of the *River Queen*. To the east the sun was rising on what would be the decisive day in the siege of Petersburg.

Thousands of blue-coated soldiers were moving this morning in response to Grant's instructions for an all-out assault on the Confederate citadel. The Union lines began at the Appomattox River east of Petersburg, swung south for about three miles, and then turned west along the city's southern perimeter for eight miles before turning again — this time southwest — to parallel the Boydton Plank Road for five miles, with a last westward jog across the road itself. Four Federal army corps pressed this line — the Ninth Corps from the east, the Sixth along the southern boundary, and the Second and Twenty-fourth along the Boydton Plank Road extension.

It had become axiomatic by 1865 that no attack against a well-defended entrenched line could succeed. Yet two Federal corps commanders were preparing to launch just such an attack. Their planning had gone forward under the belief that Lee had so thinned his defenses to meet emergencies elsewhere that a breakthrough was now possible. To further improve their chances, both generals had scheduled their assaults to take place at first light.

Along the lower eastern edge of the Union line, at the point where the Jerusalem Plank Road passed through the Federal position and into the Rebel defenses,* Ninth Corps commander Major General John G. Parke intended to send in nearly two full divisions, between 9,000 and 10,000 men. "The Confederates had several forts, redans and batteries, near the Jerusalem Plank Road," remembered one of Parke's men, which "swept the approaches in every direction. Back of these were other forts and works which could fire over the front ones or into them, as the occasion might demand. . . . Here were the siege guns, light batteries, rifles, howitzers, and mortars, all trained to repel assault."

Parke's two divisions began to move into assault formation immediately behind their picket line at around one o'clock in the morning. At first some of the troops moving toward the front thought they were needed to repel an attack, but, recalled one, "when [we] . . . could see the men in columns of four clambering over the works, [we] . . . then knew it meant an assault on the strongest part of the rebel works."

First light would not come until 4:30 A.M., so the men waited in the darkness. It was, recalled a Maine man, an "anxious period of suspense, . . . mingled with fear that we might not get started before we ourselves were attacked at a disadvantage." At 4:00 A.M., a noisy diversion was staged by Union troops near the Appomattox River. Then, thirty minutes later, the order to advance was passed along the waiting columns of troops.

"We at once started . . . with a yell (too early)," noted a New Yorker in one of the first waves. "We passed their pickets' earthworks quickly,

---

* On the Federal side, the point where the Jerusalem Plank Road crossed the line was the site of Fort Sedgwick.

then on toward a high fortification with a wide, deep ditch to get over under a terrible fire from those works. Our men swayed right and left to find a more convenient place to cross the ditch." Preceded by squads of axmen who cut paths through the wooded entanglements, three of Parke's brigades clawed their way into several enemy batteries placed in the forward line.

Confederate

"When the first streaks of gray was appearing in the east Yanks made a heavy charge on our works in front of our brigade and carried the works with apparent ease," recollected an Alabama soldier in the trenches facing Fort Sedgwick. "The men were posted at the distance of ten paces apart in the works and could offer but feeble resistance to the dense columns of Yanks that was opposing us."

The initial enemy success in this sector, defended by Major General John B. Gordon's corps, was deceptive. Once the massed Federals had overrun the forward Confederate positions, they were forced by fire from the still-intact inner line to go to ground and spread into a mazelike trench system that acted to dissipate the force of their charge. The combat abruptly shifted to small groups battling other small groups amid the deadly twists and turns of the entrenchments. Every two hundred feet or so along the trenches there was an extra earthwork, or traverse, running at right angles to the first, designed to provide a rallying place in the event that the enemy penetrated into the ditch system. "All day long the men of this division fought between these traverses," said a North Carolina soldier, "slowly yielding one after another when compelled to do so by overwhelming forces."

The Confederate defensive positions on the flanks and rear of the breach were fully alert by the time the Yankee attackers reached them, and here the defenders were able to hold. When a worried staff aide asked the artilleryman in charge of C.S. Battery No. 30 if he would be able to maintain his position, he was told in no uncertain terms, "Don't you see I am giving them double charges of canister? They'll never get up that ravine, sir."

The struggle within the captured trench system now seesawed back and forth as reinforcements from one side tipped the balance, only to give way again when a fresh group of troops from the other side regained much of the lost ground. "The fight was from traverse to traverse as we slowly drove them back," a Confederate officer recalled. "The Yankees would get on top of them and shoot down at our men, and when we would retake them our men did the same thing."

Some of the bitterest fighting was over a detached battery known as Fort Mahone. Blue and Gray soldiers grappled over its mud-slicked ramparts, but neither side was able to gain the final advantage before darkness fell. Losses on both sides were heavy, with a C.S. officer later declaring that the "open space inside of Fort Mahone was literally covered with blue-coated corpses." One defender, his face black from his tearing open countless cartridges with his teeth, turned to an equally painted comrade and asked how many rounds he thought he had fired. The other soldier replied, "I know from the number of times I have replenished my supply of cartridges that I have fired more than two hundred rounds."

Darkness ended the fighting here with no breakthrough achieved or allowed. Weary Federals held on to fragments of their initial gains, while equally weary Confederates managed to recapture some, though not all, of their lost trenches. John Parke's casualties exceeded 1,700 killed, wounded, or missing; Confederate losses were unreported, though Parke claimed to have taken 800 prisoners.

Union

Major General Horatio Wright's Sixth Corps held the lines to the south and southwest of Petersburg. Wright's men had overrun the Confederate picket posts in their front eight days earlier, and in so doing had secured an excellent jump-off area for an assault. Soon after the cannonade ended at 2:00 A.M., soldiers from all three of Wright's divisions — perhaps fourteen thousand men in all — began to file out between Union Forts Fisher and Welch and into the staging area. It was a high-risk move on Wright's part, for once his men were outside the main fortifications, they would be without protection. Should the enemy defenders become aware of the move and open up with all their guns, they would turn the marshaling place into a charnel house.

"While the troops were thus silently stealing into position," recalled a staff officer in Wright's Second Division, "the pickets commenced firing on both sides and many brave Union officers and men were killed or wounded. . . . This harassing picket firing at length died away. The night was pitchy dark. . . . The troops lay benumbed and shivering on the damp ground, anxiously awaiting the signal. . . . How long it seemed waiting in the darkness and cold! Would the signal gun never sound!" One New York soldier turned to a friend lying beside him on the chill earth and said, "I would rather charge than lie here in this suspense and misery."

Wright decided to wait for the fog to lift before he gave the order, with the result that it was closer to 4:40 A.M. when the signal gun was fired. Because of the noise of the Ninth Corps's assaults further to the east, not everyone heard it, so the order to advance had to be delivered by hand in some cases. Then the battle lines began to rush forward, crossing over the new enemy picket positions and moving directly on the powerful line of earthworks. The men advanced under what Wright later reported as a "heavy fire of artillery and a more deadly though less noisy fire of musketry from the parapets." "The shooting was very poor, though," a reporter declared, "and scarcely discommoded our men, who soon discovered that everything was passing harmlessly over their heads." A Pennsylvanian in that charge remarked that the "ground was somewhat broken as we rapidly neared their line, and many a soldier who fell into an old [rifle] pit or trench wondered whether he was hit or had stumbled."

Then, incredibly, the waves of blue-coated figures surged up and over the main enemy line. A New York soldier never forgot how he and his comrades "carried the works with a yell that would have alarmed the 'seven sleepers.' The rebels fled, pell-mell, over the country, with our good boys charging after them, capturing them, or killing them if they would not halt or surrender." Another New Yorker, in a letter to his parents, explained, "We got in the rear of the forts and mowed the Johnies down like grass. The Johns was panic stricken and run like sheep."

The Confederate lines defending Petersburg, which had withstood nine months of siege, were now decisively breached.

Confederate

Robert E. Lee had slept little during the night. It was not yet dawn when his Third Corps commander, Lieutenant General A. P. Hill, entered Lee's headquarters at the Turnbull House. Hill, whose overextended command had responsibility for the lines that ran southwest out of Petersburg, was worried about his men's condition and had come to speak with Lee about it. The two fell into an easy conversation that was still in progress when Lieutenant General James Longstreet, Lee's First Corps commander, arrived at about 4:00 A.M. Longstreet was riding in advance of the division of his corps that Lee had ordered down to Petersburg from the Richmond defenses. The three men bent thoughtfully over a map as Lee indicated the route he wanted Longstreet's men to take to bolster the right flank, near Hatcher's Run.

Colonel Charles Venable of Lee's staff suddenly rushed into the room with the dramatic news that wagons and panic-stricken teamsters were racing down the Cox Road toward Petersburg. According to a staff officer whom Venable had spoken to, there were Yankees well behind the main line. The three generals hurried out onto the front porch of the Turnbull House to try to see the situation for themselves. There was a skirmish line coming up slowly from the southwest, but was it Union or Confederate? Telling Venable to investigate, Lee turned as if to give Hill some orders, but the Third Corps's commander was already running toward his horse. The trouble was in his sector and was his responsibility. There were no last words between the two as Hill galloped off, accompanied only by a pair of couriers. Lee redirected Venable after Hill, with a caution for the general to be careful.

Lee went inside and put on the rest of his clothes, then came back out and rode down the driveway to the road to get a better view of the countryside. He had been sitting still for a few moments, contemplating the fresh problems facing him, when several officers came up in the company of one of Hill's couriers, who was leading the general's dapple-gray horse. A staff officer began to say something about Hill but then broke down in sobs, leaving the courier to tell his story. A. P. Hill was dead, killed by a pair of Yankee soldiers who had confronted the general as he and the courier* tried to reach the broken lines. Lee turned away to hide his own tears. "He is now at rest, and we who are left are the ones to suffer," he said at last, adding words of concern that the general's widow be properly notified.

Lee's situation was now only too apparent. As one of his staff officers later stated, "Our line was so thin that it had been penetrated with little opposition and so little excitement that the fact was not made known to either General Lee or General Hill." He continued, "It was apparent that our position [at Petersburg] could be no longer maintained."

Couriers dashed off with orders to hurry along troops and to stiffen Petersburg's interior defenses for the enemy assault that was certain to come. Lee found time in the midst of this activity, at around nine-thirty in the morning, to dictate a dispatch to the Confederate War Department in Richmond.

While his aide Walter Taylor scribbled frantically, Lee bluntly

---

* Venable and the other courier had been dispatched by Hill on separate errands.

sketched his present circumstances. "I see no prospect of doing more than holding our position here till night," he declared. "I am not certain that I can do that." The enemy breakthrough had isolated Lee's troops west of Petersburg, and there was no way they would be able to rejoin him as long as they remained south of the Appomattox River. He would try to buy as much time here as he could in order to facilitate a general withdrawal to the north side of the river, where his army might concentrate at Amelia Court House. "I advise that all preparations be made for leaving Richmond to-night," Lee finished. Colonel Taylor stuffed his notes into his pocket and galloped off to find a telegrapher.

Wright's breakthrough was achieved at a cost to the Union of 123 killed and 958 wounded or missing, for a total of 1,081. Confederate losses were never reported, but just one of Wright's three divisions claimed to have taken more than 2,100 prisoners.

City Point, Virginia

Soon after it was light, Abraham Lincoln, accompanied by Admiral David Porter, took a stroll through the sizable village that had sprung up at City Point during the siege, reflecting its role as a major supply depot. The pair stopped near one of the post's forts, where a member of the headquarters provost guard was sitting. The foot soldier watched as Porter pointed out some of the defensive positions and talked generally about the hardships of the siege operation. "President Lincoln was greatly moved, and his feelings were apparent in his rough-hewn features," the infantryman observed. As the two men turned to retrace their steps, the President was heard to say, "The country can never repay these men for what they have suffered and endured."

Back at the telegraph office, Lincoln reviewed the day's actions thus far. An 8:25 A.M. note from Grant indicated that "Wright has gone through the enemy's line, and now has a regiment tearing up the track on the South Side [Rail]road west of Petersburg. . . . I do not see how the portion of the rebel army south where Wright broke through . . . are to escape." A follow-up message, sent at 10:45 A.M., declared, "We are now closing around the works of the city immediately enveloping Petersburg. All looks remarkably well."

Richmond

Robert Garlick Hill Kean, head of the Bureau of War, arrived at his office at eight in the morning to find quite a crowd of notables present.

Colonel F. R. Lubbock of Jefferson Davis's staff was there, as were Post-master General John H. Reagan and Secretary of War John C. Breckinridge. As the minutes passed, this group was joined by Secretary of State Judah P. Benjamin and Judge John A. Campbell. At around nine-thirty,* as Kean recalled, "the messenger from the telegraph office brought in a telegram from General Lee that his lines were broken in three places and he doubted his ability to re-establish them; that prepara-tions should be made to evacuate Richmond at once." The communica-tion promised that further details would be forthcoming.

Kean saw to it that copies were made and properly distributed, while Reagan and Lubbock went off to tell Davis. They found him on his way to Sunday services at Saint Paul's and quickly briefed him on Lee's message. Since the note indicated that more details would follow, Davis decided not to change his plans.

A young naval officer who was at Saint Paul's this morning later re-membered that the church "was crowded with the beauty, elite, and fashion of the capital." Stephen Mallory, Davis's secretary of the Navy, was already in his pew when the President entered. Mallory stared hard at Davis's face for some sign but found none. As Mallory recalled, "The cold, calm eyes, the sunken cheek, the compressed lip, were all as impen-etrable as an iron mask."

According to a Richmond lady who was also present, the "services were progressing as usual, no agitation nor disturbance withdrew the thoughts from holy contemplation, when a messenger was observed to make his way up the aisle, and to place in the hands of the President a sealed package." Another of Richmond's ladies, soon to be Mrs. Burton Harrison, was sitting directly behind Davis and remembered that sealed package as a "scrap of paper." She never forgot the "sort of gray pallor that came upon his face" as he read it.

> Petersburg
> April 2, 1865
>
> His Excellency President Davis, Richmond, Va.:
>
> I think it is absolutely necessary that we should abandon our posi-tion to-night. I have given all the necessary orders on the subject to the troops; and the operation, though difficult, I hope will be performed successfully. I have directed [Brigadier] General [W. H.] Stevens to

---

* Although Lee's message is published in the *Official Records* with the notation "Re-ceived 10.40 o'clock," Kean's diary notes the time of receipt as 9:30 A.M.

send an officer to your Excellency to explain the routes to you by which the troops will be moved to Amelia Court-House, and furnish you with a guide and any assistance that you may require for yourself.

R. E. Lee

The future Mrs. Harrison kept her eyes on Davis. "With stern set lips and his usual quick military tread, he left the church, a number of other people rising in their seats and hastening after him, [while] those who were left [were] swept by a universal tremor of alarm." "I felt that something was going wrong with our cause when I saw the President withdraw," noted another of those present. Also at Saint Paul's was Captain Howard, the officer whose sleep had been but briefly interrupted by the night bombardment of Petersburg. He recalled, "Many persons somewhat tumultuously got up and left the church and for a while there was a good deal of confusion among those who remained, but order was presently restored, and, being Communion Sunday, the services were conducted to the conclusion without further interruption and with unusual solemnity." One of the communicants prayed as she went up to the sacred table, "God grant that it may be blessed to us this sad, last communion perhaps in our free city!"

Southside Virginia, near Five Forks

The Union victors at Five Forks spent part of this morning cleaning up the battlefield. There were, recalled a Pennsylvania soldier, "between three and four thousand stand of arms and several caissons and wagons [that] were destroyed, there being no means available for their transportation."

Among the prisoners taken in the fighting was a member of the 25th North Carolina named J. C. L. Gudger. He awoke this morning following the best sleep he had had in a long time. "It was the first night," he later reflected, ". . . that I had been out of danger of death, the first night in nine months that I was free from the dread of being killed before the sun should rise again."

The captured men were marched to City Point during the day, an experience that came as a revelation to Gudger. "I knew much about our army, its size, equipment, and strength, but I was simply amazed at the evidences that met my gaze on every hand, of the size, equipment and strength of the army that opposed us, and I wondered, and we all wondered, how our little army had so long held at bay so mighty a force."

* * *

Most of the Confederate soldiers who had not been captured at Five Forks found their way to the South Side Railroad and eventually gathered around Crowder's Crossing, just about midway between Ford's Station and Sutherland Station. They were joined there by the three brigades under Bushrod Johnson that Robert E. Lee had ordered sent up from Hatcher's Run.

During the morning, George Pickett received orders to move his men east in order to rejoin Richard Anderson at Sutherland Station. Hardly had he begun to comply with that instruction when, as he later reported, "I found the road strewn with stragglers without arms, from [Major General Cadmus] Wilcox's and [Major General Henry] Heth's divisions, who informed me [that] the lines in front of Petersburg had been forced."

Pickett now turned his battered columns north, hoping to find a crossing to the north side of the Appomattox River. Remembered one of his foot soldiers, "We pushed on that day, learning en route that General A. P. Hill had been killed before Petersburg. We went into camp near Deep Creek, hungry and conscious of loss, both in the breaking of the lines at Petersburg and in the death of the sturdy, gallant Hill — and still there was no murmuring."

The victorious infantry and cavalry under Sheridan did not press Pickett heavily during the day. Sheridan's first impulse was to establish a connection back to the main army, so he ordered the Fifth Corps, now commanded by Charles Griffin,* to move east along the White Oak Road. Griffin's men had barely begun their march when they encountered elements of the Second Corps moving west along the road to reinforce them. Matters were quickly straightened out, with the Second Corps retracing its steps while the Fifth headed north.

By the time the infantrymen, who had now been joined by Sheridan's cavalry, reached Crowder's Crossing, the Rebels were nowhere to be seen. One of Sheridan's officers observed that the "earth was yet damp on their breastworks as we rode through, and some grinning darkey, hard by informed us that the rebels had 'done took out' about two hours before."

Some of Sheridan's riders pushed on from the railroad and came into contact with Pickett's rear guard at about sunset. There was a brief firefight that ended when the Federals fell back. According to Phil Sheridan,

---

* On the morning of April 2, Gouverneur K. Warren had been put in command of rear-echelon positions at City Point.

"The darkness prevented our doing more than to pick up some stragglers."

New York City — Halifax, North Carolina

The military events of this day rippled outward like waves from a stone dropped in a pond. New York diarist George Templeton Strong smelled victory. "There is reason to hope this day may be long remembered," he noted. Its being Sunday, Strong and his family attended church, after which they shared a carriage with a military notable, General Robert Anderson of Fort Sumter fame. They halted at the *New York Tribune* office to check the latest news. "There was an extra with a dispatch from Lincoln at City Point to Stanton — brief but weighty. Read it to the general, and his Thank God was fervently uttered and good to hear."

The image that lingered with Catherine Edmondston today was that of the first swallow of the season. Mrs. Edmondston and her family lived near Halifax, North Carolina, just below the Virginia border and nearly sixty-five miles directly south of Petersburg. She always thought of the swallow as a harbinger of peace, but seeing the bird today, she wrote in her diary, "made me heartsick with hope deferred." A letter she received from her brother, who was serving with Joe Johnston, only reinforced her depression. "Sherman can go anywhere for Johnston is too weak to oppose him," he wrote. Another army acquaintance passed along the intelligence that "Richmond will be evacuated this spring." "I hope he will be mistaken," Edmondston added after this entry.

She also wrote of a neighbor with remarkable hearing who told her that he had listened to "heavy and continuous firing all the morning." Once before this man had told of hearing such sounds, and that was on the same days in March that the battle of Bentonville had been fought more than eighty miles away. "This cannonade is, however," Edmondston noted, "in a Northerly direction some where on Lee's lines."

Petersburg

Confederate

Following the Sixth Corps's breakthrough of his lines west of Petersburg, Robert E. Lee received the surprise gift of a lull in the fighting near the city. The Federals had not halted operations but were instead busy rolling up the Confederate line from the breakthrough point as far south as Hatcher's Run. Lee used the opportunity to gather intelligence and begin implementing his withdrawal plans and organizing the defenses along Petersburg's western interior lines.

It was likely during this period of relative calm that he learned for the first time of the full extent of Pickett's disaster at Five Forks. A little later, Lee heard from John Gordon, whose troops on Petersburg's eastern front had blunted the worst of the attacks by the enemy Ninth Corps, and who was even then preparing a counterattack to regain the lost ground. Lee signaled Gordon to abandon those plans and to concentrate instead on holding what he had in preparation for a nighttime pullout.

It was not certain whether Lee's army would be able to get out of Petersburg in an organized fashion. Only a few hundred soldiers manned the western inner line, and many of those were disorganized remnants of Hill's corps. Unless fresh troops arrived soon from Richmond, a strong Yankee attack against the city's western perimeter would spell catastrophe. Lee was mulling over these sour possibilities when he was interrupted by a civilian named Nottingham, who lived with his family just across the road from the Turnbull House, Lee's headquarters.

"General, do you think the reinforcements will be here from Richmond in time to restore the lines?" the citizen asked.

"No, sir," Lee answered with uncharacteristic pessimism.

"Then you will have to give us up?"

"Yes, sir," Lee said, adding, "Give my kind regards to Mrs. N. and the little girls."

By the time his aide Colonel Taylor returned from sending dispatches to Richmond, Lee had regained his normal confidence. Taylor thought Lee "self-centered and serene[. He] ... acted as one who was conscious of having accomplished all that was possible in the line of duty, and who was undisturbed by the adverse conditions in which he found himself."

Lee's only hope to retard the returning Federal battle lines lay in a pair of small three-sided redoubts named after the farms on which they were built — Forts Gregg and Whitworth. "These two works were constructed to meet the very emergency that had now risen," one of Lee's officers observed, "i.e., to protect the rear of the lines in the immediate front of Petersburg in the event our lines further to the right were forced by the enemy." Lee first ordered Brigadier General James Lane, whose sector this was, to round up as many of his men as he could and put them into the forts to hold them. But Lane's men were too disorganized to form the cohesive command necessary to defend the position, so when

Brigadier General Nathaniel Harris arrived, leading the first of Longstreet's reinforcements, his brigade got the assignment.

Harris placed two of his Mississippi regiments — the 19th and 48th — in Fort Whitworth, while two others — the 12th and 16th — filed into Fort Gregg. He took personal charge of the Whitworth defenses and sent Lieutenant Colonel James H. Duncan to direct the men in Gregg.

"Stand like iron, my brave boys!" Harris called to the Gregg garrison as he checked it one last time.

Inside Gregg, the soldiers were busy gathering as many discarded rifles as they could handle. It was a trick they had learned in the bloody campaign of 1864: by placing two to four loaded guns next to each soldier, the defenders practically had the advantage of repeating rifles.

It was shortly after midday when the Yankees finally began to move against Petersburg's western defenses. These were not the same troops that had broken the line, but rather fresh columns that came out from the old Federal position "with the same precision as though on parade," as one of the watching Confederates observed. "No obstacles were in their path," he continued, "the ground being level and clear. The Mississippians were crouched low on one knee, waiting the living flood which came in their direction and threatened all with destruction."

There were some final exhortations from various officers, and then all outsiders were gone, leaving the two garrisons to fend for themselves. At 12:30 P.M. Union cannoneers posted south and west of the two bastions began a bombardment that lasted about thirty minutes. Recalled one of Gregg's defenders, "When the artillery fire ceased the infantry hastily approached for the assault."

Union

The battle lines closing on Forts Gregg and Whitworth came from the Twenty-fourth Corps, part of the Army of the James. These soldiers had been moved south of the James River only a few days earlier to fill in the gaps that were created as Union strength was massed on the extreme left. The troops had originally been slated to assault the works in their front at dawn, but following the Sixth Corps's success, the Twenty-fourth had been moved up to exploit the breach.

It was about one o'clock in the afternoon when the first blue-coated wave approached Fort Gregg. An untutored Pennsylvanian in those ranks later wrote, "Whe knew if whe take that fort that Rich and Petersburg would fall. So our Curnel he wanted the praise of takin that fort for it was the key of Petersburg and Richmd so he gave us the orders to advance and he determined to have that fort." The initial assault ran right into a murderous sheet of flame as the battle-wise Southerners used their multiple guns to full advantage. This fire, one Illinois veteran remarked, "mowed down our men most unmercifully." An Ohio skirmisher close to the blazing ramparts looked back in horror as Rebel cannon shot tore gaps in the advancing lines, but then proudly observed that as "soon as the men passed those cut down they came together like drops of water."

Nevertheless, the first Union wave was blasted back. Soon a second rolled forward, and this one surged into the broad moat that fronted Fort Gregg. One Ohio soldier recalled standing waist-deep in the muck, "with shot and shell flying in a terrible hurricane from all parts of the compass. . . . The ditch was so full of water at one end that the men had to swim across."

There were not enough Federals here yet to climb over the parapets, but there were too many to be forced back. A few ran around to the rear of Fort Gregg, only to find its open fourth side completely blocked by a loopholed palisade behind which Rebel riflemen were posted. Then, under protest but with orders to do so, General Harris pulled out of Fort Whitworth and retreated with his men to Lee's main line. This exposed Gregg's northern side to a strong Federal column that descended on it from that quarter and decisively swung the balance to the offense. A surgeon in one of the West Virginia regiments engaged described what happened next: "When they reached the parapet of the fort it was found so difficult to ascend that a temporary halt was made for the men to breathe. . . . A few moments and they began the difficult and perilous task of climbing the parapet, and in this was displayed the true heroism of brave men, a hand to hand conflict ensued."

Confederate

A North Carolina captain watching the battle from the main line chronicled Gregg's last moments: "The Federals have reached the ditch. They climb up the sides of the works, and, as the foremost reach the top, we can see them reel and fall headlong on their comrades below. . . . [At last] we can see the Federals as with impunity they mount the works and begin a rapid fire on the defenders within. Their ammunition is exhausted, and, unwilling to surrender, they are using their bayonets and clubbing their guns in an unequal struggle."

Another Tar Heel officer had a much closer view. Lieutenant A. B.

Howard was among a handful of North Carolina soldiers who fought alongside the Mississippians in Gregg. " 'Tis true," he later wrote of the Yankees, "that when they rushed into the fort upon us, they were yelling, cursing and shooting with all the frenzy and rage of a horde of merciless barbarians."

Union

"When we rushed over the top the sight was truly terrific," a Federal officer recalled. "Dead men and the dying lay strewn all about, and it was [only] with the greatest difficulty that we could prevent our infuriated soldiers from shooting down and braining all who survived of the stubborn foe."

Major General John Gibbon, commanding the Twenty-fourth Corps, remembered the struggle for Fort Gregg as "one of the most desperate ever witnessed. . . . We now confronted the last line of entrenchments between us and our long sought prize, Petersburg."

But there would be no final assault this day. The Twenty-fourth Corps had spent itself taking Gregg and Whitworth, and the triumphant Sixth Corps was equally exhausted from its sweep along the enemy's lines. The Ninth Corps was bogged down in the trench fighting east of Petersburg, the Fifth Corps was with Sheridan, and the Second Corps had been drawn off to the west at Sutherland Station, where several C.S. brigades that had been cut off from the city were making a stand.

Robert E. Lee would have the time he needed to withdraw his army from the defenses of Petersburg and Richmond.

Fifty-six of the men who defended Fort Gregg were killed, and approximately 200 were wounded and captured, along with the few who were not injured. The Federal losses in taking the fort were 122 killed and 592 wounded, for a total of 714.

City Point, Virginia

Throughout the day Abraham Lincoln was able to track the progress of the Union assaults on Petersburg, thanks to reports he received from U. S. Grant. At 4:40 P.M. Grant indicated that his men had at last closed the ring around the city and now held a line stretching "from the Appomattox, below Petersburg, to the river above." In that same dispatch, Grant invited Lincoln to pay him a visit the following morning.

Lincoln replied:

Allow me to tender to you and all with you the nation's grateful thanks for this additional and magnificent success. At your kind suggestion I think I will meet you to-morrow.

Grant's last message of the day came in at 8:40 P.M., reporting the final actions at Sutherland Station.

Lincoln stepped outside the telegraph office to listen for a while to the military bands that had assembled there to play for him. He then left shore to go aboard Admiral Porter's flagship, the *Malvern*, since the presidential vessel was in Norfolk for two days. He and the admiral sat on the upper deck and listened for a while to the distant sounds of combat around Petersburg.

"Can't the Navy do something at this particular moment to make history?" Lincoln at last asked Porter.

The admiral explained that the best thing for the Navy to do was to keep the enemy ironclads bottled up along the James River.

"But can't you make a noise?" Lincoln persisted.

"Yes," Porter replied, "and if you desire it I will commence."

Lincoln nodded, and Porter gave orders to be telegraphed upstream to where the James River squadron was anchored. Minutes passed before the slow rumble of naval artillery fire could be heard. It continued in a steady rhythm until about 11:30 P.M., when it was punctuated by a boom that rattled the admiral's boat.

"I hope to Heaven one of our vessels has not blown up!" Lincoln exclaimed in alarm.

Porter guessed that it was more likely the enemy destroying their own craft to keep them from falling into Union hands. He predicted that there would be more such explosions, and they eventually counted four in all. Porter believed that those sounds accounted for the enemy's entire ironclad fleet.

"That's all of them," he assured the President. "No doubt the forts are evacuated and to-morrow we can go up to Richmond."

Richmond

Immediately after leaving Saint Paul's, Jefferson Davis called the members of his Cabinet to his office for an emergency meeting. Also present were several city and state representatives, including Richmond's mayor, Joseph Mayo. Navy Secretary Stephen Mallory recalled the meeting's brief agenda: "In few words, calmly, solemnly, the President expressed to his Cabinet and other high officials, gathered around him at his office, his views of the situation and of the measures which it demanded, and each at once entered upon his allotted duty."

Many outside the President's office who heard the evacuation rumors were simply not prepared to believe them. One young Richmond socialite left Saint Paul's at the end of the service determined to enjoy her usual Sunday afternoon promenade. "I . . . was surprised to meet people in considerable numbers . . . hastening in the opposite direction," she remembered. "Some called out: 'Have you heard that Richmond is to be evacuated?' I remember how I laughed and how I replied that I . . . knew all about panics." "From lip to lip, from men, women, children and servants, the news was bandied, but many received it at first, as a 'Sunday sensation rumor,' " recalled another of the capital's ladies.

Yet few could deny that the government's activity this Sabbath day was anything but normal. From the city military command came orders for the Home Guard to assemble at 3:00 P.M. By that hour the rumors had become official statements, and the city's population was suddenly divided into two camps: those who were to leave and those who were to stay. A member of the quartermaster's department who came into town at around three o'clock that afternoon described what he saw: "The streets crowded with throngs of human beings — men, women and children — vehicles hurrying to and fro, officers on horse dashing rapidly hither and thither — cinders of burning official papers falling everywhere. . . . Boxes of paper and archives hurried forth and packed into the huge wagons of the Express Co. for transportation to Danville — Horses saddled up and awaiting their riders at the Govt. stables. Ladies seated on their doorsteps bareheaded to get a last look at brothers and friends &c. All pictures of distress & woe."

Individuals now moved to play their part in the drama that was unfolding. Peter Helms Mayo, a private in the governor's mounted guard and at twenty-nine already a veteran railroad man, was instructed "to have prepared at once a special train to move over the Richmond and Danville Railroad to carry the President, his Cabinet, their effects and horses." Secretary of State Judah Benjamin was busy packing when the French consul, Alfred Paul, paid a call. "We are going to Danville," Benjamin explained. "It is simply a measure of prudence. I hope that we will return in a few weeks."

The admiral of the James River Fleet, Raphael Semmes, was sitting quietly in the cabin of his flagship when a dispatch boat came down from Richmond. Semmes was handed fresh orders that entailed the destruction of his squadron and the provisioning of his sailors for land duty as infantry. After remarking that "this was rather short notice," Semmes began issuing the necessary commands. Another navy man, Captain William H. Parker, was told to destroy his vessel, the training ship *Patrick Henry,* and then muster his cadet crew "to take charge of the Confederate [Treasury] . . . and convey it to Danville."

The visiting M.P., Thomas Conolly, could only watch in sadness as the once proud Confederacy unraveled before his eyes. He noted in his journal that "painful rumours follow thick on one another . . . and as the day goes on the confirmation of all! The Govt officials all leave for Danville by train. Streets filled with departures, a regular stampede has begun." Toward the end of the afternoon, Conolly spotted an officer of his acquaintance on Longstreet's staff and invited him to dinner. "I had to beg off," the harried aide recalled. "I could not have accepted the invitation of His Royal Highness then."

The departure of James Longstreet for Petersburg left Lieutenant General Richard S. Ewell in charge of all the troops north of the James. Ewell had been near the front at Chaffin's Bluff this morning when he received an urgent summons to return to the capital. Following a quick briefing on the situation, Ewell began issuing orders to pull out all the troops posted in the trenches east of Richmond and move them to the rendezvous point he had selected, the village of Manchester. He was also determined to carry out a Confederate law that designated cotton and tobacco contraband of war, subject to destruction. Before he left Richmond, Ewell intended to order that all stocks of those materials be burned.

The troops manning Richmond's eastern defenses began retreating as soon as it was dark. Some crossed the James on the pontoon bridge near Chaffin's Bluff, while others were routed through town. A young courier who passed along the evacuation route this night recollected, "I found the main road filled with wagons, artillery, and small bodies of troops. The latter . . . seemed to be in a very good humor. . . . My old horse, whose gait was rather unsteady, and whose bony frame could be plainly discerned, even in the moonlight, was a special source of comment.

" 'Say, Mister!' exclaimed one, 'let's see you rattle them bones between them spurs.'

" 'I wonder how he keeps that animal in such good order?' said another.

" 'He feeds him on shavings,' replied a third. 'And saw-dust,' added another in a gruff voice.

"It seemed to me that every man noticed the leanness of my poor Sally," the courier reflected.

The growing number of people in the streets worried General Ewell. With the troops rapidly pulling out, the task of maintaining order was left to the undermanned city constabulary and the few Home Guard units that had bothered to respond to his summons. Ewell decided that the mob needed something to distract it while the business of evacuation continued. A short conference with Mayor Mayo yielded a plan to throw open the doors to the government food depots. The army had taken all it could carry, and if Richmond's citizens were kept busy grabbing free food, they might well be too distracted for other mischief. Accordingly, at about seven o'clock in the evening, the locks were removed from the commissary, government bakery, and quartermaster store.

Ewell's plan seemed to be working. "Delicate women tottered under the weight of hams, bags of coffee, flour and sugar," wrote one observer. "Invalided officers carried away articles of unaccustomed luxury for sick wives and children at home. Every vehicle was in requisition, commanding fabulous remuneration, and gold or silver the only currency accepted." Said another, "You could see old men, women, and children snatching for something, whether it was useful or not. I made many trips back and forth to carry my pick-ups home, and there were any number who were doing as I did."

The next phase of Ewell's plan went into operation about ninety minutes later, when soldiers set fire to the tobacco and cotton stores in the Shockoe Warehouse and three other large storage areas. The buildings were soon in flames, but the carefully planned conflagration did not spread beyond the structures that had been targeted.

It was about eleven o'clock when the special train carrying Jefferson Davis and members of his staff and Cabinet left the Danville Depot. Davis had spent much of the afternoon and evening packing away his belongings at the executive mansion and preparing his own modest travel kit. He had arrived at the station at the appointed hour — eight o'clock — but it had taken his Cabinet another three hours to trickle in. During that time Davis discussed plans and contingencies with Secretary of War Breckinridge, who was going to remain behind and retreat with the troops. The train finally got under way, pulled out of the station, and was quickly swallowed up by the darkness.

A government clerk who chose to remain behind wrote in his diary at about this time, "All is yet quiet. No explosion, no conflagration, no riots, etc. How long will this continue?"

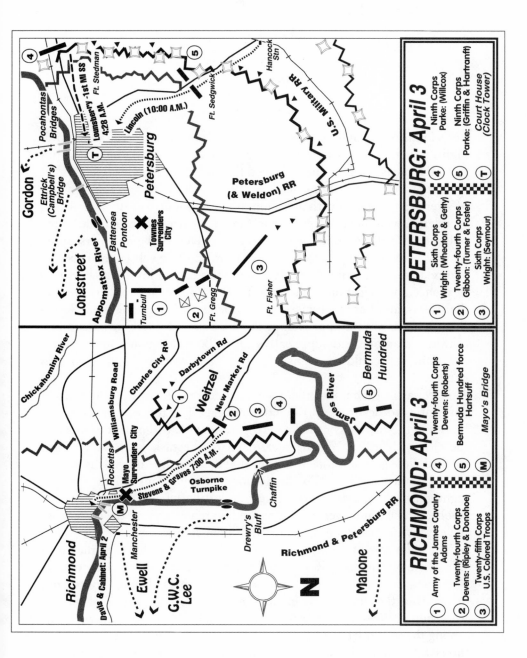

PETERSBURG: April 3

(1) Sixth Corps
Wright: (Wheaton & Getty)

(2) Twenty-fourth Corps
Gibbon: (Turner & Foster)

(3) Sixth Corps
Wright: (Seymour)

(4) Ninth Corps
Parke: (Willcox)

(5) Ninth Corps
Parke: (Griffin & Hartranft)

(T) Court House
(Clock Tower)

RICHMOND: April 3

(1) Army of the James Cavalry
Adams

(2) Twenty-fourth Corps
Devens: (Ripley & Donohoe)

(3) Twenty-fifth Corps
U.S. Colored Troops

(4) Twenty-fourth Corps
Devens: (Roberts)

(5) Bermuda Hundred force
Hartsuff

(M) Mayo's Bridge

Monday, April 3

Petersburg

Confederate

Lee's infantry began to quietly abandon their fortifications at about midnight. "Silently and gloomily the army in long columns marched out from the breast-works, and marched through the desolate streets of Petersburg," remembered one veteran. "We had little to say, the intuition of every man told him that Richmond was about to fall, and we all wondered, what next." A gunner in Martin's Battery recalled that as the pullout was getting under way, "leave was given to the members of the battery who could be spared from duty to say farewell to their friends and relatives in the city." "The Confederates passed through Petersburg in silence and dejection," said an officer. "No one but soldiers were in the streets, and but few houses gave evidence of being inhabited. Sometimes females would approach at the windows of different houses and ask, in a plaintive and supplicative tone, 'Boys, are you going to leave us?' And you could see signs of sorrow and distress in their countenances."

Here, as in Richmond, there was a concerted effort by C.S. military authorities to destroy contraband supplies. "The tobacco in the warehouses in the city was burned where it stood and at some risk of burning the city with it," an engineer assigned to the task later wrote. Also torched were ammunition stockpiles that could not be moved, as well as other military surplus. "To the despondent reflections which the midnight retreat suggested," remarked an artilleryman, "the flame and smoke, which hung over the depots and warehouses, and the glare from the exploding magazine, gave an additional somber tint."

The main part of the army passed through town and over to the north side of the Appomattox River well before dawn. Among the last to leave were the pickets, whose job it had been to keep the Union scouts from discovering the movement. In the confusion, a few groups of pickets were not notified that it was time to withdraw. I. G. Bradwell was among these. "In front of me, and only a hundred yards or more, were thousands of enemies who had nothing to do but come over and take me," he reminisced, "but they remained silent and did not make any movement until the hour appointed for our relief had arrived and I had become restless." Marshaling his comrades, Bradwell led them out of the trenches, into town, and across a bridge to the north bank.

As these last men passed over, the job of burning the bridges began. Major Giles B. Cooke was in charge of the railroad span. "As soon as it was dark enough," he wrote, "I put my large force of bridge burners with tar, axes, etc., to work, who saturated the immense structure with tar and set fire to the bridge; all the obstructions were cut away and what remained of the bridge fell into the river about daylight." Engineer John E. Roller was responsible for destroying another of the structures. "After waiting until all the men who desired to leave Petersburg had crossed the river, we set fire to the bridge at Ettrick and waited until its destruction was assured," he reported. The Pocahontas Bridge, used for vehicular traffic, came under a heavy shelling while the burners were at work. A young North Carolina soldier named Cummings Mebane volunteered to start the blaze and ran to the center of the bridge to ignite it. He was hit by a piece of shell before he could strike the flame. According to one observer, "He walked back to the bank, but expired in a few moments." It was afterward claimed that Mebane was the last soldier killed at Petersburg. Someone else finally set the bridge on fire, but advancing Union troops were able to save it.

Robert E. Lee, who had left town with the first of his columns, stationed himself at a key intersection to see that the troops were properly directed. A staff officer who took part in the retreat never forgot the image of Lee, "standing with the bridle of his horse in his hand [as he] . . . gave his orders. His bearing still remained entirely composed, and his voice had lost none of its grave strength of intonation. When the rear was well closed up, Lee mounted his horse, rode on slowly with his men; and, in the midst of the glare and thunder of the exploding magazines at Petersburg, the small remnant of the Army of Northern Virginia . . . went on its way through the darkness."

Union

Soon after midnight, the Yankee pickets outside Petersburg began to grow suspicious. Up to that time the firing from the Confederate side had been steady and spiteful, but suddenly, recalled one of the advanced parties, "the firing ceases."

Pennsylvanian J. L. Pounds was standing watch near the site where the terrible battle of the Crater had taken place in July. Three deserters came into his post after the firing died down and, under careful questioning, declared that "their pickets [had] withdrawn and their army [was] falling back."

Word now raced up the chain of command all along the Union siege lines as post after post reported evidence that Lee's men, as one Federal private put it, had "skinned out."

The silence along the enemy positions lasted for perhaps an hour. Then distant detonations began, accompanied by what a Michigan man remembered as the "glare of suddenly rising flames from various places in Petersburg [that] told of a effort to destroy what could not be carried away, the flames being punctuated by repeated explosions."

Along the Union positions directly east of the city, Colonel Ralph Ely had his men all mustered and ready to advance well before daylight. He was determined that his command would be the first to enter the city and had even detailed two regiments with specific orders to race into town the moment the way seemed clear. Ely moved the bulk of his command into the enemy's forward lines shortly after 3:10 A.M., occupying them without a shot. Now the two chosen regiments — the 1st Michigan Sharpshooters and the 2nd Michigan — moved quickly along the City Point Road into Petersburg. A flying squad from the Sharpshooters out-distanced the 2nd Michigan and, at 4:28 A.M., hung the United States flag from the tall courthouse clock tower.

The longest siege of an American city was at an end.

Federal troops were now filtering into Petersburg from three points of the compass. The first Yankees to approach from the west encountered a trio of officials empowered to surrender the city. This group, headed by Petersburg's mayor, W. W. Townes, was one of several sent out by the civilian government to avoid needless bloodshed. The officer in charge of the Union skirmishers, Colonel Oliver Edwards, later claimed that he had "received the surrender of Petersburg."

The document that Mayor Townes handed to Edwards was succinct:

> The city of Petersburg having been evacuated by the Confederate troops, we, a committee authorized by the Common Council, do hereby surrender the city to U.S. forces, with a request for the protection of the persons and property of its inhabitants.

Another trio, this one on the city's southern outskirts, approached the first mounted figure that came into view. This proved to be Sylvanus Cadwallader, the reporter who had brought word of Five Forks to Abraham Lincoln. Cadwallader curtly dismissed the group's painfully self-conscious attempts to capitulate with the comment that he "should have been glad to have met them on that errand at any time for many months last past; but it was now too late."

According to U. S. Grant's military secretary, Adam Badeau, "At nine o'clock, the general-in-chief rode into Petersburg to obtain what information he could in regard to the movements of Lee. The streets were nearly vacant, but here and there groups of women and children gazed curiously at the conqueror. . . . Grant rode through the narrow streets, attended only by his staff, and alighted at the home of a citizen, where he sat in the porch, receiving intelligence and examining prisoners."

"As the Federal troops entered the city," a Massachusetts man recalled, "they found that most of the citizens of the better class had left. . . . The women kept themselves behind closed doors and curtained windows, though many faces were seen cautiously peering out with an angry look of despair in their eyes." Despite the fires that had been set to destroy the city's tobacco stores, enough of the leaf still lay about that the Yankee boys had no trouble helping themselves. According to a Vermont chaplain, "The men gathered all they cared to for smoking and chewing, and some companies festooned themselves with the withered weed, in imitation of Malcolm's soldiers moving from Birnam wood to Dunsinene."

A Wisconsin man tried to take some measure of the damage done to Petersburg in the long campaign. "The lower part of the city bore severe traces of the siege, hardly a home being unmarked by either shot or shell. . . . The clock on the Town Hall had also been perforated by a three inch shell, though strange to say, the missile had not damaged the works in the least. . . . A fine strong bridge . . . had been loaded with two new locomotives and all the cars that could be placed on it, and then set fire to, cars and locomotives being thus precipitated into the river."

Abraham Lincoln left City Point for Petersburg at about midmorning. He and a small party rode the U.S. Military Railroad train as far as Hancock Station, where they met Lincoln's son Robert, then serving as an aide on Grant's staff, and changed to horseback. They rode into town along the Jerusalem Plank Road, stopping along the way to view the Confederate Fort Mahone, still dotted with bodies left unburied after the previous day's fighting.

The group continued into the downtown area, passing columns of happy Union soldiers. Remembered one of these, "With hat in hand [Lincoln] graciously acknowledged the greetings of the soldiers, who enthusiastically swung their caps high in the air, and made the city ring with their loud hurrahs." Said another, "President Lincoln passed us on horseback, and as he went by our boys cheered him, as the rebs used to say, 'right smart.' "

Lincoln met with Grant at the house he was using, and the two talked for ninety minutes about the current situation and Grant's plans. They had hoped to receive word of Richmond's capture, but none had yet arrived by the time they parted company — Lincoln to return to City Point, Grant to take charge of the final operation of this campaign.

Grant was determined not to merely pursue Lee. His goals were to block the Confederate general from turning south to link up with Joe Johnston's army, and, in the process, to force Lee and his men to surrender. As Grant later put it, "I hoped to capture them soon."

Very little of the Union army was to remain behind in Petersburg; most of it was, in fact, already moving along roads leading west. Morale among the men was high. A Second Corps soldier later wrote, "We marched twenty miles during the day, and the soldiers seemed to think that they were for once in a fair way to tie up that famous 'Bag,' which the army of the Potomac had so long been preparing for the reception of Lee's army."

The only fight of any significance today took place at midday along the leading edge of the Federal pursuit, when Sheridan's cavalry caught up with the rear guard protecting George Pickett's and Richard Anderson's men. The engagement occurred about ten miles northwest of Sutherland Station, near a local meeting place named Namozine Church. At first the North Carolina cavalry under Brigadier General Rufus Barringer was able to blunt the Yankee advance, but blue-coated reinforcements were readily on hand and quickly flanked Barringer's line. The Rebels withdrew, losing about 350 men as prisoners. Federal casualties were 4 killed and 15 wounded.

In his campaign report, U. S. Grant summarized the Union movements this day: "General Sheridan pushed for the Danville road, keeping near the Appomattox, followed by General Meade with the Second and Sixth Corps, while General Ord moved for Burkeville along the South Side [Rail]road; the Ninth Corps stretched along that road behind him."

Richmond

Confederate

The past twenty-four hours had seen a surfeit of dramatic incidents in this theater of the war, but perhaps none quite so personally dramatic as that which befell young Walter Taylor, one of the most trusted members of Robert E. Lee's staff. Taylor began this day in Petersburg, at Lee's side. Immediately after the evacuation orders were written up and distributed, Taylor asked Lee's permission to go to Richmond, promising to return by early the next morning. In response to Lee's surprised look, Taylor added that he planned to marry. Even with Lee's approval, Taylor almost didn't make it. He missed the final passenger train to Richmond, had to commandeer the last available engine at Dunlop Station, and only just overtook the passenger train before the engine had to return.

Shortly after midnight, Taylor stood proudly alongside his bride, Miss Elizabeth Selden Saunders, and spoke the words making them husband and wife. "As will be readily understood," he later explained, "the occasion was not one of great hilarity, though I was very happy; my eyes were the only dry ones in the company."

Even as that ceremony was concluding, the train carrying the Confederate Treasury was at last pulling out of town. Right behind it was another, on which rode Brigadier General Josiah Gorgas, C.S. chief of ordnance. "All was still and orderly on the streets," he wrote in his diary, ". . . and everything promised an orderly evacuation. I had given directions that nothing in my control should be burned lest fires might be general and the innocent inhabitants suffer."

Gorgas's sanguine outlook was not shared by Captain Parker, commanding the Treasury escort of naval cadets. Everything he saw pointed to trouble. "The whiskey, which had been 'started' by the Provost guard, was running in the gutters, and men were getting drunk upon it. As is the case under such circumstances . . . , large numbers of ruffians suddenly sprang into existence. . . . These were the men who were now breaking into stores and searching for liquor."

Not long after one o'clock in the morning, the sporadic incidents of burglary and theft began to gain strength and cohesion. The dark night was suddenly dotted with bright embers of flame as buildings well clear of those that had been torched by Ewell's order were set afire.

"After night-fall Richmond was ruled by the mob," one resident later declared. "In the principal business section of the city they surged in one black mass from store to store, breaking them open, robbing them, and in some instances (it is said) applying the torch to them."

The troops moving in retreat through Richmond's streets passed in and out of these chaotic pockets. The young courier whose bony horse had been the object of derision just hours earlier now found himself caught up in the rampage. "I had just stepped out upon the pavement," he recalled, "when I saw a crowd of about a dozen men walking rapidly upon the opposite side of the street. All of them seemed to be soldiers, but only two or three carried muskets. They seemed to be much excited, and filled the air with their cries.

" 'Show us a shoe store!' — 'a hat store!' 'Let's make a raid on the speculators!' "

The group settled on a hat store and soon broke into one of Richmond's largest. Caught in the grip of a compulsion he could not shake, the young courier followed the little squad, which by now had been joined by a great many others, into the store. "Men were busily engaged in ransacking drawers, overturning boxes, and stripping shelves — all in search of the handsomest articles." The youth gathered three hats into his arms and fought his way back outside, but by the time he made it through the door, the clutching mob had torn and crushed his trophies. "With an exclamation rather profane than the opposite, I kicked my plunder into the middle of the street and turned away in disgust," he remembered. He watched an adult emerge from the same building with an armful of intact hats and caps. "It is every man for himself, and the devil for us all, tonight," the man said as his eyes met the boy's. The courier asked for a hat and, to his surprise, was handed two. "Placing one upon my head and the other under my arm, with many thanks, I left the spot," he recalled.

General Ewell did his best to regain control of the situation. As he later reported, "I . . . ordered all my staff and couriers who could be spared to scour the streets, so as to intimidate the mob by a show of force, and sent word to [Major] General [Joseph B.] Kershaw, who was coming up from the lines, to hurry his leading regiment into town." Kershaw's men began arriving at about three in the morning. One of his soldiers noted that "everything was in confusion and uproar — the city was on fire in more than one place. Soldiers on horse and on foot were going in every direction — old men and women and children were on the streets weeping."

An artillery officer who passed through the town recollected, "As I rode by the principal jewelry store, I saw an old woman come crawling backward out of a window. One of the mounted men [with me] rode up and whacked her with the flat of his sword. She tumbled out with a yell, and her lapful of plunder from the showcases of Mitchell and Tyler, the leading jewelers of Richmond, poured over the sidewalk."

A cleric moving in the crowd's wake was deeply affected by the sight of those who had lost everything. "And among all of those people no one spoke," he wrote, "everywhere there was grim silence, drawn faces and a sense of hopelessness and horror. Except for an occasional exclamation from a child or from a negro who had salvaged something from the flames, no human voice was heard."

Sometime around two o'clock the fires reached the arsenal stockpiles, setting off a series of powerful explosions. A bedridden C.S. soldier never forgot the instant when "a flash of light came into my room, brighter than the brightest lightning. It was accompanied immediately by a loud report that rumbled and shook the house, and by a crash that sounded as if the front had fallen!"

An even greater display of explosive destruction lay in store, courtesy of Admiral Semmes, who was doing remarkably well on short notice. Shortly after three o'clock his sailors set fire to the four small ironclads that constituted the metal heart of the James River fleet. One by one the ships disintegrated as the flames touched the ammunition that had been packed into their holds — the *Virginia,* the *Richmond,* and the *Fredericksburg.* Most memorable was the end of Semmes's flagship, the *Virginia No. 2.* "The spectacle was grand beyond description," Semmes recorded. "Her shell-rooms had been full of loaded shells. The explosion of the magazine threw all those shells, with their fuses lighted[,] into the air. The fuses were of different lengths, and as the shells exploded by the dozen, the pyrotechnic effect was very fine." A pious artilleryman crossing over the pontoon bridge downriver declared, "I distinctly remember feeling that after this I could never more be startled — no, not by the catastrophes of the last great day."

It was nearing first light when Ewell found Captain Clement Sulivane, a cavalry staff officer on detached service, and put him in charge of the detail guarding Mayo's Bridge over the James. All the other crossing spans either had been dismantled or destroyed or would soon be gone. Ewell told Sulivane he was to hold this final escape route open until the last possible moment, then burn it to prevent the enemy from crossing. Sulivane hurried to his post, organized the detail there, and turned his gaze on the doomed city. "Every now and then, as a magazine exploded, a column of white smoke rose up as high as the eye could reach, instantaneously followed by a deafening sound. The earth seemed to rock and tremble as with the shock of an earthquake, and immediately afterwards hundreds of shells would explode in air and send their iron spray down far below the bridge."

The last soldiers and officials now passed out of Richmond. Secretary of War Breckinridge arrived clad in a "suit of plain black, with a short cape or talma thrown over his shoulders," recollected an engineer who saw him. "But notwithstanding his unassuming garb, many soldiers recognized the familiar face of 'Old Breck,' and acknowledged his presence by hearty cheers, which the Secretary returned by touching his cap." At about this same time, the newlywed staff officer, Walter Taylor, crossed the bridge. The way, he later wrote, was well lighted by the "lurid glare of the fire."

Among the officers waiting anxiously at the bridge for their commands to appear was Brigadier General E. Porter Alexander, Longstreet's chief of artillery. He later remembered a tense moment: "Soon after daylight I noticed canal boats on fire in the canal [that ran beneath the bridge], & at least one of them . . . got directly under the bridge. One of my batteries was still behind, but presently, when flames began to rise through all the cracks in the floor, with my staff we sped across lest we should be cut off." A squad of Georgia soldiers, marching along at the time, had to "run with all of our might and shimmy from side to side of the bridge to keep from being burned to death," one declared. "Some soldiers, however, in the nick of time, managed to push the burning boat out, & presently my last battery came along & then we all crossed," Alexander added.

Captain Sulivane saw the first Yankee scouts in Richmond's streets at about the same time that the last of the Confederate rear guard came hurrying toward him. Supply wagons led the way, instantly attracting the attention of a mob that was blocking the approach to the bridge. Sulivane led a charge that cleared a lane for the wagons to escape. As his small command fell back, the mob closed behind it like quicksand. Then the veteran cavalry of Brigadier General Martin W. Gary's command appeared. "The mob scattered right and left before the armed horsemen," Sulivane noted with satisfaction. The troopers clattered over the bridge quickly, save for a lone squad that waited until the last possible moment, then galloped wildly across. "My rear-guard," General Gary explained to Captain Sulivane. Gary touched his hat to the young officer and said, "All over, goodbye; blow her to hell."

Sulivane and his men applied their torches, and in a few minutes, as the captain remembered, "Mayo's bridge [was] wrapped in flame and smoke."

Union

Philadelphia Press correspondent Thomas Morris Chester, the only black reporter for a major daily covering the Richmond campaign, sketched this scene in the hours after midnight: "The soldiers along the line gathered upon the breastworks to witness the scene [of the burning city] and exchange congratulations. While thus silently gazing upon the columns of fire one of the monster rams was exploded, which made the very earth tremble. If there was any doubt about the evacuation of Richmond that report banished them all."

A trickle of Rebel deserters helped spread the news. Along the front held by Colonel Edward Ripley's brigade, a Virginia soldier brought in at 3:30 A.M. revealed that the "Confederates were leaving their line in front" and further explained that the "Confederacy was 'busted up,' and that he did not wish to fight any longer." In front of Colonel Michael T. Donahoe's brigade there appeared what a Vermont officer later called "an intelligent young fellow [who] . . . told us that the picket line in our front had been withdrawn and ordered back to camp, and that he believed it meant an abandonment of Virginia."

With Major General Ord away at Petersburg, the Army of the James north of that river was commanded by Major General Godfrey Weitzel. A career military man for whom caution was a watchword, Weitzel was not prepared to do anything rash. Even though he would later claim that as early as 3:00 A.M. "it was evident that the enemy was abandoning my immediate front," Weitzel decided to wait until dawn before acting. According to one of his subordinates, "Much apprehension and fear in regard to torpedoes was created in the command by the warning instructions of Genl. Ord, and no attempt was made to advance until after daylight."

This did not, however, prevent the more adventurous among Ord's men from setting out on their own. Colonel George A. Bruce commanded the pickets in front of Brigadier General Charles Devens's division, of which Ripley's and Donohoe's brigades were a part. Bruce's experiences this night encompassed the full course of incidents, beginning with the eerie silence soon after midnight, followed by the sight of large fires in the distance, and culminating in the powerful explosions that marked the end of the enemy's James River fleet. "Then," recalled Bruce, ". . . I ordered the pickets to advance to the first line held by the Confederates." As his soldiers cautiously poked forward, they picked up a Rebel deserter who obligingly showed them a clear path through the obstructions and mines. In another instant Bruce's men were into the enemy works that had so long defied them. Bruce deployed his skirmishers to hold his uncontested gains, then rode back to announce his success. On the way he met a courier from General Devens, carrying instructions not to advance the pickets for fear that a serious accident might occur in the dark. Bruce hurried on, found Devens in front of the divisional headquarters, and reported that the message had come too late, "as I had already taken possession of [the enemy's] Fort Gilmer and the whole Confederate line." Devens held his hand out to the young officer and said in mock courtliness, "Hail to thee, Count of Gilmer."

The troops that Bruce had left behind in the enemy works were not about to wait for his return. Captain Warren M. Kelley of the 10th New

Hampshire organized a force of about two hundred skirmishers, and as he later claimed, "I advanced my line, and finding no opposition I kept on until I entered the city before it was fairly light." Kelley and his men made it as far as the lower portion of the city, known as Rocketts, where most of Richmond's deep-water docks were located.

At about 5:30 A.M. Godfrey Weitzel selected two staff officers, Major Atherton H. Stevens and Major Eugene E. Graves, and sent them with an escort from two companies of the 4th Massachusetts Cavalry "to receive the surrender of the city, and to direct the authorities and citizens to cause all liquor to be destroyed and to preserve order until my troops arrived."

A member of the advance party later left this reminiscence of the ride into the enemy capital:

> We proceeded at once through our fortified line and approaching the Confederate line found that the troops were gone. . . . We continued "on to Richmond," and soon were inside the inner works. . . . As we entered those works we saw a man approaching with a flag of truce.
>
> In the distance were mounted men and carriages. We halted and Stevens and his officers went forward and conferred with the party, who proved to be the Mayor of Richmond, Judge [John] Meredith and others. The city was formally surrendered to Stevens, and we then went forward at a rapid pace. At the Rocketts we came in full view of Richmond.
>
> . . . We gave three cheers and were on, and were soon in the streets of Richmond. We passed Libby Prison and clattering up the street on the gallop were soon in the space in front of the Capitol building.
>
> Major Stevens, with some of the officers, rushed into the building, and soon the guidons of Companies E and H were fluttering from the top of the building. We were formed around the equestrian statue of Washington, and cheered. Richmond was ours.

Even as this group was entering the town, General Weitzel organized a general advance. The rest of Devens's division moved along the New Market Road, the black infantry under Brevet Major General August V. Kautz advanced up the Osborne Road, and the cavalry, commanded by Colonel Charles F. Adams, rode out the Darbytown and Charles City roads. As Devens's white troops approached the intersection with the Osborne Road, they noticed the black troops closing from their left. Suddenly it became a contest to see which organized unit would be the first to enter the enemy's inner works. "For more than a mile we raced it," recalled a Vermont officer. "I became so heated that I tore off my sword-belt and threw it with scabbard and revolver behind me, saying that if there were any that could not keep up they might, if they pleased, bring them along. My dress coat and vest soon followed, collar and necktie followed suit and my panting breast was bared to the breeze. Soon our colored braves gave up the race and we entered the inner line of defense."

According to the commander of the black troops, his men had the clear lead before they were halted by an order from General Devens. "The delay was a great annoyance to the negroes who seemed to feel that whoever could get in front should be allowed to do so," he later protested.

Union soldiers now flooded into Richmond. "Everything was in confusion," a Connecticut man recalled. Fires still raged, creating a terrible, stormlike condition. Wrote Colonel Bruce, "The wind, increasing with the conflagration, was blowing like a hurricane, hurling cinders and pieces of burning wood with long trails of flame over the houses to distant quarters of the city. The heated air, dim with smoke and filled with the innumerable particles that float from the surface of so general a fire, rendered it almost impossible to breathe."

Godfrey Weitzel and his staff reached Richmond's Capitol Square at about 8:15 A.M. "A sad sight met us," Weitzel later wrote. "[The square] was covered with women and children who had fled here to escape the fire. . . . It was a sight that would have melted a heart of stone. I first ordered my aide, Captain Horace B. Fitch . . . to write a dispatch to General Grant, announcing my entrance into Richmond. . . . Then I sent an order to Devens to march his division into the city and endeavor to extinguish the flames. . . . I directed Kautz to occupy the detached forts nearest the city, and Manchester and [Colonel Charles F.] Adams to picket the roads."

Union flags now fluttered from the roofs of public buildings and other well-known sites. The 81st New York laid claim to raising the first U.S. colors over the notorious Libby Prison. "Details were made to pick up all men that wore the gray uniform and bring them into the prison, which was soon pretty well filled," a member of the regiment recollected. When Lieutenant Johnston Livingston de Peyster rode into town as a member of Weitzel's staff, he carried in front of his pommel a United States flag that had flown over occupied New Orleans. The young officer galloped directly to the Capitol building, where he and a fellow officer rushed to the roof. "Together we hoisted the first large flag over Richmond and on the peak of the roof drank to its success," he wrote home today.

Reporter Thomas Morris Chester made his way to the building that housed the Confederate Congress, determined to fulfill a personal promise. He went inside to the desk of the Speaker of the House and began to write: "Seated in the Speaker's chair, so long dedicated to treason, but in the future to be consecrated to loyalty, I hasten to give a rapid sketch of the incidents which have occurred." Chester's labor was interrupted by a paroled Confederate officer who rushed into the chamber and shouted at him to leave. When the black reporter pointedly ignored the request, the officer tried to throw him out. Chester rose and delivered a punch that sent the C.S. soldier sprawling. Glancing about and spotting a Union officer nearby, the Rebel demanded to use the Yankee's sword. The amused Federal refused but offered to clear a space for a fair fight. At this the frustrated Confederate officer fled, leaving Chester to comment, "I thought I would exercise my rights as a belligerent."

April 3, 1865

Lieutenant-General Grant:

We took Richmond at 8:15 this morning. I captured many guns. The enemy left in great haste. The city is on fire in two places. [I] am making every effort to put it out. The people received us with enthusiastic expressions of joy.

G. Weitzel
Major-General*

New York City and Elsewhere

In four years of war, George Templeton Strong had seen enough good news suddenly turn sour that he girded himself carefully against anything approaching premature jubilation. The reports of Union victories in the April 2 fighting at Petersburg were encouraging, but when Strong headed downtown at midday he expected "only to learn . . . more positively that the South Side Railroad was cut; that Lee had returned to his entrenchments badly punished, and that it was confidently expected that he would have to evacuate them at some future period."

Passing the offices of the *Commercial Advertiser,* however, Strong noticed a war bulletin announcing that "Petersburg is taken." Stepping inside for more particulars, he saw a clerk slowly lettering a large sign: "Richmond is ——"

---

* Although this message was received at City Point before 11:00 A.M., it did not catch up with U. S. Grant until nearly 2:00 P.M.

"What's that about Richmond?" Strong asked. The clerk ignored the interruption and continued at his task: C-A-P-T-U-R-E-D. Strong felt a rush of joy. CAPTURED!!

He raced up to Trinity Church, convinced the sexton to have the chimes rung, then hurried down to Wall Street, where a large crowd had gathered to listen to speeches. "Never before did I hear cheering that came straight from the heart," Strong reflected. "They sang 'Old Hundred,' the Doxology, 'John Brown,' and 'The Star-Spangled Banner,' repeating the last two lines of Key's song over and over, with a massive roar from the crowd and a unanimous wave of hats at the end of each repetition. I think I shall never lose the impression made by this rude, many-voiced chorale. It seems a revelation of profound national feeling."

Word of Richmond's fall spread all along the telegraph network, touching other communities as well. In Wilmington, Delaware, stores closed, an outdoor thanksgiving service was held, and a victory procession filled the streets well into the night. In occupied Norfolk, Virginia, flags appeared everywhere. "Bands in wagons played to the echo in every street, bells were rung and cannon fired till 'further orders.' Till nightfall the carnival continued," recalled the officer commanding the garrison.

In Washington, the word that the enemy capital had been taken was received at the War Department by a sixteen-year-old telegrapher named W. E. Kettles. Hardly able to contain himself, the boy jumped up, threw open a window, and shouted happily to people in the street: "Richmond has surrendered!" An artilleryman riding past the War Department soon afterward "saw a great commotion and excitement of some kind going on, . . . my first impression was that the building was on fire, but when I saw one old grey haired man throw his hat up in the air and yell Hurrah! . . . I went into the enclosure . . . and was told that Richmond and Petersburg were evacuated." Here, too, the celebrations continued far into the night.

Richmond

For many of Richmond's residents, the hours immediately preceding the Yankee occupation were a time of great anxiety. "Into every house terror penetrated," wrote one of the city's ladies. Daylight brought the hated enemy. "Before long," wrote an observer, "eager watchers from Chimborazo Heights saw bluecoats rise dim over the distant crest. Then came the clatter of cavalry, sabers drawn and at a trot; still cautiously feeling their way into the long-coveted stronghold."

The single symbolic act most remembered by Richmond's faithful was Lieutenant de Peyster's raising of the United States flag over the Capitol. "The Yanks came in . . . and first of all placed the horrible stars and stripes (which seemed to me to be so many bloody ashes) over our beloved capitol. O, the horrible wretches!" cried a thirteen-year-old girl. "The saddest moment of my life was when I saw that Southern Cross dragged down and the Stars and Stripes run up above the Capitol," said another witness. "We covered our faces and cried aloud." One seventeen-year-old woman watched helplessly as celebrating Yankee soldiers trampled over a Confederate flag. "I felt as if I would have given anything to have gone and picked it up," she confessed to her diary.

Throughout this momentous day, the citizens took the measure of their conquerors. For those too young to understand all that was happening, these new people were something of a game. "Almost every minute Flory and I run out to the gate to see if the Yankees are coming," a little girl recollected, "and if we see them we run in as fast as our feet can carry us." Among the many kind gestures made this day by the occupation troops was the small guard detail sent to watch over the house, wife, and family of Robert E. Lee. Older residents stared with great curiosity as the first African-American soldiers marched in. "They certainly were the blackest creatures I ever saw," one declared. The Federal troops, both black and white, soon brought order to the town and by nightfall had extinguished the worst of the fires.

More than twenty square blocks — the heart of Richmond's commercial district — had been consumed in the terrible flames. Gone was the huge Gallego Flour Mill, the sprawling arsenal, and a host of warehouses and banks, as well as all of the city's newspaper offices, save one. From this time forward the blackened area between Capitol Square and the James River would be known as the Burnt District.

Despite the ruin around them, the Federals would not be denied their celebrations. "An inspiring feature of the first evening of our occupation of the city was the music of the military bands," noted one of the Yankees present, "discoursing such patriotic airs as 'Yankee Doodle,' 'Hail, Columbia,' 'The Star Spangled Banner,' etc. — airs that must have fallen rather oddly on the ears of the citizens, after having listened four years to the music of treason." "For us," wrote one Richmond lady of this serenade, "it was a requiem for buried hopes."

City Point, Virginia

Abraham Lincoln completed his tour of Petersburg and returned to the main Union supply base shortly before five o'clock in the afternoon.

Waiting for him there was a copy of General Weitzel's 8:15 A.M. dispatch announcing Richmond's capture, along with a 10:30 A.M. telegram from Edwin Stanton in which the secretary of state worried that it might be too dangerous for Lincoln to visit Petersburg. "Thanks for your caution," Lincoln answered, "but I have already been to Petersburg. . . . It is certain now that Richmond is in our hands, and I think I will go there to-morrow."

Before joining Admiral Porter aboard the *Malvern* for dinner, Lincoln stopped at another vessel, the *Mary Martin,* where he called on Mrs. Grant to assure her that her husband was well and hopeful of success. Upon boarding the *Malvern,* Lincoln turned his attention to a nearby transport loaded with Confederate POWs. "They were in a pitiable condition, ragged and thin," remarked Lincoln's bodyguard. "They looked half starved."

Lincoln stared at these fruits of Union victory and then said at last, "Poor fellows. It's a hard lot. Poor fellows —."

Something in Lincoln's voice caused the bodyguard to take a close look at his charge. "His face was pitying and sorrowful," the man remembered. "All the happiness had gone."

Part Two

AN END TO VALOR

"Tell brave deeds of war."

Then they recounted tales:
"There were stern stands
And bitter runs for glory."

Ah, I think there were braver deeds.

Stephen Crane,
"Tell Brave Deeds of War"

Chapter Four

The Death of an Army

———◆———

Monday, April 3

Confederate Retreat

THE MOOD among many of the soldiers along the roads leading
out of Petersburg and Richmond was expressed by one cannoneer, who
insisted that the "men experienced a sense of relief — that of getting rid
of some hideous dream in leaving behind the trenches, and once more
moving in column on the road." A staff officer recalled Lee's remarking
today, "I have got my army safe out of its breastworks, and in order to
follow me, the enemy must abandon his lines, and can derive no further
benefit from his railroads or James River."

The various components of Lee's force were moving on courses that
would bring them together at Amelia Court House, a point some forty
miles west of Richmond and Petersburg. Here Lee expected to find supply trains for his army. After replenishing his food and military stocks,
Lee intended to follow the railroad south toward Danville, 104 miles
away.

How many Confederate soldiers were involved in the retreat has long
been a matter of contention. Southern sources, which tend to emphasize
the disparity between the two sides, suggest that between 25,000 and
30,000 soldiers left the Richmond-Petersburg theater on the night of
April 2. Modern researchers, working backward from the known figures
of those captured, killed, or surrendered in the course of the campaign,

have established a likely figure of about 58,000. If a similar measure is applied to the Union troops actually engaged in the pursuit, the result is a total Federal force of more than 76,000 men.

The first natural obstacle in the way of Lee's men was the Appomattox River. Longstreet's and Gordon's columns (which included the troops belonging to A. P. Hill) were to cross at Bevill's Bridge, the troops from Bermuda Hundred under Major General William Mahone would use Goode's Bridge, and another column of Ewell's and G. W. C. Lee's soldiers was to move over at Genito Bridge.

But plans were one thing, and reality was another. Scouts and couriers came in to report that the bridge Longstreet and Gordon were hoping to use was flooded and impassable, which meant that they would have to shift their line of march northward and cross at Goode's Bridge, along with Mahone's men. There would be delays, but there was no other option. Then Lee learned that the temporary bridgework that should have been on hand at Genito's crossing was not there, so he sent instructions to Ewell to come south to Goode's Bridge if he could not otherwise ford the Appomattox. In the end, Ewell's troops were able to utilize the railroad bridge at Mattoax for their purposes, though they did not all get safely across until nightfall on April 4.

The day was not all problems, however. Lee was able to enjoy a short midday respite when he received a dinner invitation from Judge James H. Cox of Clover Hill. It was gladly accepted by Lee, his staff, and other general officers. Presiding over the whole affair was Miss Kate Cox, Judge Cox's daughter.

"General Lee," she said at one point, "we shall still gain our cause; you will join General Johnston and together you will be victorious."

"Whatever happens," Lee replied, "know this — that no men ever fought better than those that have stood by me."

Tuesday, April 4

Confederate Retreat: Amelia Court House

"Just before dawn, April 4, a drizzling rain began to fall and the morning broke dismally enough," recalled Captain McHenry Howard with Ewell's column. When Robert E. Lee rode across Goode's Bridge shortly after 7:30 A.M., he did not know the location or condition of the troops that had come out of Richmond. The courier he had sent to Ewell to apprise that officer that the Genito Bridge was down had not found the command. Leaving orders for William Mahone to keep Goode's Bridge open until it was known that Ewell was over the Appomattox, Lee rode with Longstreet's men on the road to Amelia Court House.

With his crossing of the Appomattox, Lee had overcome one obstacle, but he now faced a new problem. Up to this point the Federal pursuit had been more expectation than fact, with the Appomattox providing an effective screen for Lee's left. But by moving over the river, Lee had opened that quarter to pressure from the Union columns that were pacing him to the south. Reflecting on this day's march, James Longstreet made careful note of the "enemy's cavalry constantly threatening our left flank."

The rebound in morale that had followed the abandonment of the trenches was proving to be of short duration. "The troops were silent and seemed depressed, except the Second Corps [i.e., Gordon's], who cheered vigorously as General Lee rode along the moving columns," recollected one soldier. "Had an awful hard march," a diarist in Longstreet's corps added. During this day the troops under Richard Anderson and George Pickett, which had been isolated from the army after Five Forks, made contact again. "To rejoin our main army, after having been cut off for three days, was indeed like getting home from a distant voyage," a Tar Heel soldier noted, "and I don't think I ever saw men more rejoiced at anything than we were at being again with our comrades."

There should have been rations for Lee's men waiting at Amelia Court House, but upon his arrival there Lee was shocked to discover that the railroad cars sent from Richmond just before its fall were loaded with munitions, not foodstuffs. Although many motives — from greed to incompetence to outright sabotage — were later advanced to explain this circumstance, the facts suggest that confusion among Lee's overworked staff during the chaotic period of April 1–2 in Petersburg, coupled with the disruption that occurred in the management of the Commissary Department during its hasty evacuation of Richmond, led to Lee's requests' arriving too late for proper action.

Lee faced a fateful decision. Should he continue the retreat and maintain his thin lead over the pursuing enemy at the risk of serious starvation among his troops, or should he stop long enough to regroup and resupply as best he could, trusting that the enemy would not block his way south? "No one who looked upon him then," an artillery officer later recorded, "as he stood there in the full view of the disastrous end, can ever forget the intense agony written upon his features." A staff officer was even more explicit, claiming that "no face wore a heavier shadow than that of General Lee. The failure of the supply of rations completely paralyzed him."

At last the orders went out: the army would camp around Amelia Court House while supply wagons spread out into the countryside to forage for food. The quartermasters traveling with these wagons carried a personal appeal from Lee "To the Citizens of Amelia County, Va.," in which he asked them in their "generosity and charity to supply as far as each one is able the wants of the brave soldiers who have battled for your liberty for four years."

Other instructions were issued that drastically reduced the number of artillery pieces and wagons accompanying the army. Those remaining were to move out ahead of Lee's columns in order to place the Southern infantry between them and the pursuing Federals.

The various units of Lee's army began to gather at Amelia Court House by early afternoon. A cannoneer later recalled that "about that time . . . food was not to be had, and we began to eat parched corn. A panicky feeling has begun to seize the army." Exhaustion was also taking its toll. Hardly had the Richmond Howitzers gone into camp when a call went out for a guard detail; "four men answered to their names, but declared they would not keep awake if placed on guard. . . . They were marched off to picket a road leading to camp, and when they were relieved, said they had slept soundly on their posts. No one blamed them."

By nightfall Lee at last received some good news. Ewell's column, out of Richmond, was safely across the Appomattox and making for Amelia Court House. Lee's army, such as it was, was together again, and that meant anything was possible.

Union Pursuit: Roads West

Sheridan was the key today. The aggressive cavalry commander's troopers were in direct contact with the retreating enemy, and how effectively they handled the pursuit might well determine the success or failure of this campaign. Sheridan, for his part, had a simple plan of action, as described by his chief of staff: "It was to pursue and attack the left flank of the retreating army at any possible point with the cavalry division that first reached it, and, if possible, compel it to turn and defend its wagon trains and artillery, then to send another division beyond and attack the Confederate army again at any possible point, and to follow up this method of attack until at some point the whole [enemy] army would be obliged to turn and deliver battle."

Federal riders now spread along a broad front as they pushed north to develop the extent and direction of the enemy's movement. "This was the most exciting race we ever had," a Rhode Island trooper remembered, "chasing the invincible rebels . . . through mud and water, up hill and down, across meadows and brooks, through plantations and villages." There were countless small, sharp encounters as Sheridan's probing riders struck the left flank of the Confederate columns marching west from Goode's Bridge.

During one of these clashes, some Michigan cavalrymen overran a small house and plantation. The Federal officer in charge was told by one of his men that the owner and his wife and children and slaves were hiding in the cellar. This news was followed by a visit from the owner himself, who insisted that a guard be placed over his property to protect the provisions stored there. The Union officer curtly informed the Virginia planter that his men were here to do battle, not to perform guard duty.

"Then you will not grant me protection?" the planter asked.

"I am here to fight Rebels," the exasperated officer replied, "not protect them, and am in favor of fighting them until the last one surrenders or finds that last ditch, & so long as food is in the country my men shall not want."

The Yankee foot soldiers following behind the cavalry saw unmistakable signs that the enemy forces were unraveling. An officer in the Sixth Corps observed that the "road is filled with broken wagons and the things thrown away in the flight of the Rebels." "Great numbers of prisoners, cannon, caissons, and quantities of all sorts of equipments were taken through the day," a Pennsylvanian in the Second Corps reported. In the Fifth Corps the men began to ignore the groups of Rebel stragglers they passed. "Some one would remark, 'See the squad of Johnnies, we ought to pick them up!' Some one else would reply, 'Let them alone, they are going home, the war has ended for them!' and they would be allowed to go." All of this capped a difficult day of marching. A Maine officer in the Second Corps stated that some of the roads were "almost impassable, but we corduroyed, patched, mended, and pushed on."

Throughout the day reports came to Sheridan suggesting that, as he later stated, "the enemy was at Amelia Court-House, and everything indicated that they were collecting at that point." He ordered one of his divisions to strike for the railroad — Lee's direct link to Danville — and cut it.

Sheridan realized that if he could control the road system near the village of Jetersville, eight miles southwest of Amelia Court House, he would block Lee from making a turn to the south. After issuing orders to the Fifth Corps and all available cavalry to join him there, Sheridan rode ahead with his personal escort of two hundred men from the 1st United States Cavalry.

A member of the escort recalled arriving near Jetersville in the afternoon: "Here we took possession of the station and telegraph office, and, throwing out pickets, prepared to dispute the further advance of the Confederate army, feeling confident that, with the General's assistance, we should be able to do so with success." The Yankee troopers also captured a courier who was carrying dispatches from Lee's commissary general requesting that rations be sent from Danville to Burkeville. Sheridan turned these messages over to his resourceful chief of scouts, Major Harry Young.

Although it was one of the smaller commands engaged in the Appomattox Campaign (Sheridan later acknowledged its strength as "thirty or forty men"), Major Young's band had an influence far out of proportion to its size. Operating singly or in small groups, these scouts — disguised either in official Confederate uniforms or in otherwise nondescript clothing — infiltrated Lee's retreating columns to gather information or to sabotage their movement whenever possible.

Now Major Young decided to have his men continue the captured messages on their way; with Federal troops astride the Danville line, he reasoned, any supplies sent along it would be sure to fall into their hands. As a further refinement, Young sent out two pairs of his scouts in different directions, each bearing a copy of the original orders. One duo proceeded south along the rail line in hopes of reaching a station still in telegraphic connection with Danville, while the other struck west, intending to get the same message through to the C.S. supply depot at Lynchburg. In this particular instance the operation was without result, but in summing up the activities of Major Young's unit, Sheridan wrote that the "information gained through him was invaluable."

There were some tense hours as Sheridan's small command waited for reinforcements to arrive. It was late afternoon before the first elements of the infantry came on the scene, but the veteran foot soldiers knew exactly what to do. Remembered one, "The Fifth Corps immediately occupied the cavalry works, and in a short time with pick and shovel had them thick and high." "As the enemy was within striking distance no fires were lighted, and the corps was kept in readiness for battle," noted another. "We seem to have cut the rebels off," a Maine infantryman penned in his diary. This observation echoed one that Sheridan had made earlier in the day in a message to U. S. Grant: "If we press on we will no doubt get the whole army."

Richmond & Danville Railroad: South of Burkeville

Even as the two armies settled down for the night, a young Confederate officer was undertaking the adventure of his life. John S. Wise had been on duty at Clover Station when he learned that a volunteer was needed to try to establish contact between the Confederate government in Danville and Lee's army. Wise, whose father commanded a brigade in the Army of Northern Virginia, at once stepped forward. An engine with a tender and a baggage car was sent up from Danville at about eight o'clock at night, and Wise received some last-minute instructions. He was to try to get as far north as Burkeville, and if he made it there, he was to switch over to the South Side Railroad and run westward until he made contact. If it was not possible for him to reach Burkeville, Wise was to pull the train back to Meherrin Station, obtain a horse, and attempt to intercept Lee overland.

The train set out on its desperate mission with Wise riding alone in the baggage car. "The night was chilly, still, and overcast," he remembered. "The stations were deserted. We had to put on our own wood and water. . . . The solitude of the car became unbearable." Wise went up front to converse with the train engineer, and the two decided to detach the baggage car. With its headlight masked and all its running lights extinguished, the Confederate probe moved cautiously forward into the night.

Wednesday, April 5

Richmond & Danville Railroad: South of Burkeville

The engine and tender carrying John Wise pulled into Meherrin Station at two o'clock in the morning. Wise got out of the train and pounded on the door of a nearby house until the owner appeared.

"Have you heard anything from Lee's army?" Wise inquired.

"Naw, nothin' at all," the civilian replied. "I heerd he was at Amelia Court House yesterday."

Wise asked a few more questions, all of which were met with equal unhelpfulness. "Where is Grant's army?" he finally asked.

"Gord knows. It 'pears to me like it's everywhere."

Wise reboarded the engine and continued on his journey into the early-morning gloom. As they drew closer to Burkeville, Wise and the engineer were able to make out a faint glow on the horizon, as if many fires were being reflected by the low cloud cover. The engineer was all for turning back, but Wise, none too gently, insisted that they go on. They eased around one final curve and beheld an incredible sight. Remembered Wise, "Lines of men were heaving at the rails by the light of fires built for working." The realization came to him like a dash of cold water: the Yankees were not wrecking the line, they were changing the track gauge to fit the width of their supply trains! If the Union rear echelon was south of Burkeville, the front must be somewhere above that point, so Lee must be either north or west. So intent were the Federals on their work that several minutes passed before anyone noticed the interlopers. Then men began to run toward the locomotive, shouting and waving weapons.

"Reverse the engine!" Wise yelled to the engineer. When he hesitated, Wise took out his revolver. "Reverse or you're a dead man!" he shouted menacingly. The engineer obeyed, and with agonizing slowness, the engine pulled away, soon outdistancing its pursuers.

Once back at Meherrin Station, Wise gave the engineer a report for Jefferson Davis and got off the engine to continue his mission. A walk of three or four miles into the country brought him to a house, in front of which was tied "a pretty mare . . . saddled and bridled, as if waiting for me." Wise knocked on the door and learned that the animal belonged to a Virginia trooper who had soon to return to his command. When Wise told the man that he wanted to borrow his horse, the soldier laughed and refused, but when he was shown the order from Jefferson Davis, "he yielded, very reluctantly."

It was too late in the day to start this leg of the journey, so John Wise determined to set out first thing in the morning.

Confederate Retreat: Amelia Court House, Virginia

The burden of command was something that usually sat easily on the shoulders of Robert E. Lee, but this morning it was a great, bulky weight that bore down on him unmercifully. He had gambled by halting, gambled that he could concentrate his army and gather supplies quickly enough to be able to move south again before the pursuing Federals could cut him off. Not only were the rations he had expected to find here not on hand, but in order to scour the countryside for foodstuffs, he had been forced to press most of his men into immediate service, negating whatever rest they might otherwise have obtained. And when the quartermaster wagons returned today, they were for the most part empty. As Lee later reported, his "troops, wearied by continued fighting and marching for several days and nights, obtained neither rest nor refreshment."

Lee decided that he could tarry no longer. As soon as his command could be prepared to move, it would continue south along the railroad line toward Danville and hope to meet supplies along the way. Before that, however, there was much to do. As one of his artillery officers put it, "We stopped at Amelia all morning reorganizing commands, & waiting for the rear to close up."

Among the troops closing up were those under Richard Ewell that had come from Richmond. It was a patchwork command, consisting of some veteran infantry and green garrison troops along with local defense forces (including a detachment of black C.S. troops only recently organized as an experiment) and a smattering of naval personnel under Commodore John Randolph Tucker. This last outfit turned more than one head with its strange uniforms and hybrid commands, such as "To starboard, march!"

The process of consolidating commands and reducing the size of the horse-drawn trains was a discouraging one. Recalled a man in Lee's ranks, "Just as I was passing up a hill beyond Amelia Court-house, I saw a party of cannoneers digging a trench. I thought at first they were . . . burying some of the slain, but was surprised to find out that they were burying their GUNS." Added a Tar Heel officer in John Gordon's corps, "The horses, of our artillery, ordnance train, wagons, and ambulances, like ourselves had been on short rations all the winter, were poor and weak, and with scarcely time to eat what little was given them on the march, could scarcely drag themselves along, many falling in harness had to be cut loose and dragged out of the way." "Today we abandoned several thousand rounds of artillery ammunition with the caissons," a Virginia soldier in the same corps noted. "While the caissons were being burned . . . a terrific explosion occurred. Thousands of shells exploded at once, and filled the air with their fragments. Many men were wounded, and a few killed."

Sometime before noon, the reduced wagon train creaked out of the camps, heading west around the right flank of the army, beyond which it would then swing south. At 1:00 P.M. the infantry column, preceded by a cavalry screen, began its tramp south along the rail line — the same one Jefferson Davis had used only a few days earlier. James Longstreet's corps led the way. "Our purpose," he recalled, "had been to march through Burkeville to join our forces to those of General J. E. Johnston in North Carolina, but at Jetersville . . . we found the enemy square across the route in force and intrenching."

E. P. Alexander, the artillery officer, remembered riding with Lee "& his staff & Gen. Longstreet, & we were not long in coming to where our skirmish line was already engaged. I never saw Gen. Lee seem so anxious to bring on a battle in my life as he seemed this afternoon; but a conference with Gen. W. H. F. Lee in command of the cavalry in our front seemed to disappoint him greatly. [W. H. F.] Lee reported that Sheridan . . . was more than we could venture to attack."

The Confederate army commander now decided to shift the line of march from south to west, in order to strike for a still-usable stretch of the South Side Railroad linking Farmville with the supply depot at Lynchburg. No local guides could be found to direct the army, so Lee had to rely on his maps. A soldier in Longstreet's ranks saw Lee at this time and described his countenance as "very serious."

More bad news awaited Lee as his columns took up roads leading west, toward Amelia Springs and Deatonville. Ewell had brought with him from Richmond a small supply train that had moved toward Amelia Court House on a more roundabout route than the one used by the foot soldiers. Just a few miles from their destination, the wagons had been ambushed. As one of Lee's horsemen remarked, "The enemy's cavalry had swooped down, captured and fired our wagon train." Not only had hundreds of vehicles been lost, including some carrying desperately needed rations, but the wreckage was creating a monumental tie-up for the men, animals, and wagons now seeking to follow that route. A Virginia soldier recalled, "We marched, or tried to march, all night, but only progressed a short distance, frequently we would move a few yards and then halt for an hour or two." "A good many fell out and lay down and were captured by the enemy or gave themselves up," a soldier in Richard Anderson's ranks wrote in his diary of this march, adding, "the straggling is terrible."

A small measure of revenge was extracted by Lee's cavalry, which caught up with the Yankee raiders before they had completed their destruction. "As we approached they began to retreat," remembered a C.S. Maryland trooper, "when a running fight commenced. We pursued them for several miles[, and the] . . . road was strewn with guns, sabers, and knapsacks, which they threw away in their flight." When South Carolina troopers came on the scene, the first thing they saw was a pretty woman "standing in the mud by the roadside with a soldier in a 'grey jacket.' " She shouted her story as the cavalrymen galloped past. She was from Mississippi and had left Richmond in an ambulance with some artillerymen friends. Her transportation had been taken by the Yankees, and she had been left to fend for herself. One of the Carolina riders recalled that "she stood there in the mud . . . and gesticulated as she told her story, making up a picture striking and peculiar."

Portions of the slow night march became a nightmare for the troops, whose nerves were already stretched thin by fatigue. Maryland Captain

McHenry Howard was moving with his column when a brief spatter of gunfire broke out somewhere ahead. "Most of the men became panic-stricken," he wrote, and "broke and sought cover behind trees or fences, while not a few skulked disgracefully to the rear. They began to discharge their pieces at random, in many instances shooting their own comrades, and bullets were flying from and to every direction." It took a considerable while for officers to restore order. Captain Howard never learned whether the spark that had set off the panic was caused by enemy scouts or Confederate carelessness.

Lee paused on the road to Amelia Springs at a residence known as Selma, where he was invited to supper. A houseguest, a young woman named Eliza Willson, took station on the front porch and refused to allow anyone to see General Lee until he had finished his meal. She proved impervious to all entreaties until one of Lee's staff, Lieutenant Colonel Charles Marshall, presented himself before her and wrapped a Confederate flag around her waist. The stalwart young lady let Marshall pass.

There would be little sleep for Lee this night. An engineer officer called forward to help repair a small country bridge that had buckled under the unusually heavy traffic was surprised to see Lee waiting at the site for the work to commence. Recalled that officer, "He explained his anxiety by saying that [his men] . . . had captured a dispatch from General Grant [at Jetersville] to General Ord . . . ordering an attack early the next morning, and [he] did not leave until he was assured that material for a new bridge was close at hand."

Union Pursuit: Jetersville

Two Union corps, Humphreys's Second and Wright's Sixth, were pushing hard to join Sheridan near Jetersville. "Had to march very rapidly in the afternoon and a great many fell out," one of Wright's men wrote in his diary today, adding proudly, "but I made out to keep up with the regiment though it was pretty hard work."

Ironically, the pace of the Federal pursuit put the most advanced units in much the same predicament as their Confederate counterparts. Noted the chaplain of a New Jersey regiment, "Men straggled and grumbled. Gen. Meade & staff passed. 'Hard tack! Hard tack!' they shouted." But unlike the C.S. soldiers, the Federal troops had adequate rations, and throughout the day units halted long enough to grab supplies before being hustled back onto the roads. Even when food was not readily at hand, the Yankee boys improvised. "We passed a molasses factory and arrived at a large mansion inhabited by an old gentleman," recalled a New Yorker in Humphreys's corps. "We halted, stacked arms and immediately charged a row of bee-hives, securing the honey, and utterly demoralizing the bees."

Time and again the files of marching foot soldiers were brought to a halt when cavalry units rushing to Sheridan's support took possession of the road, with the result that, as Humphreys later wrote, "it was half-past two in the afternoon . . . when the Second Corps began to arrive at Jetersville, followed by the Sixth Corps. Both went into position, the Second Corps on the left, the Sixth on the right of the Fifth Corps."

Even before these fresh troops came up, Phil Sheridan was busy looking for an opening. He sent out a brigade that morning "on a reconnaissance to Paine's crossroads"* to find out if Lee was marching by that flank. These troopers, noted one of them, soon "discovered the enemy's artillery and wagon trains were moving westward."† "The escort was dispersed and the dingy vehicles consigned to the flames," crowed a New York trooper. An exuberant staff officer long remembered the cascade of images of men "dashing up and down the road, now shooting the drivers, now charging the guards, now unceremoniously overhauling the contents of a heavily laden wagon, or attempting to drive off mules, drivers, wagons, and all." "After sending the plunder on the road to Jetersville, the boys were reminded that there was some of the Confederacy still alive, as a vigorous attack was made on their rear," recalled one of the New York riders. It took the timely arrival of two more blue-coated brigades to enable the raiders to pull back toward Jetersville with most of their trophies — five guns, eleven flags, over six hundred prisoners, and more than four hundred bony animals.

Finding C.S. wagons this far north on a westerly heading convinced Sheridan that "Lee would attempt to escape as soon as his trains were out of the way." This opinion was not shared by the commander of the Army of the Potomac, Major General George G. Meade, who, though ill, was now in charge of operations at Jetersville. After studying the situation, Meade concluded that Lee was making a stand at Amelia Court House, so he planned to fight a set piece battle by moving against the Rebels from the east once all of the Second and Sixth Corps were up — a process that would not be completed until after dark. Meade and his staff fully expected that a major battle would be fought at Amelia Court House on April 6.

* Also known as Paineville.
† This was the supply train that had traveled with Ewell from Richmond.

At Five Forks Sheridan had possessed the authority to override the hesitancy of the infantry commander, but the only way he could change Meade's plan was to go right to the top. As Sheridan later wrote, "I sent dispatches to General Grant . . . telling him that . . . I wished he himself was present. I assured him of my confidence in our capturing Lee if we properly exerted ourselves."

Sheridan gave the message to one of his "irregulars," who rolled it into a tight ball that he then placed in a tin-foil pellet in his tobacco pouch. If captured, he would take a chaw and hide the message in his mouth. The scout managed to locate Grant's headquarters along the South Side Railroad, about halfway between Nottoway Court House and Burkeville. Grant's aide Horace Porter was present when the messenger arrived. "The general said he would go at once to Sheridan. . . . It . . . was thought that it would be prudent to take some cavalry with us, but there was none near at hand, and the general said he would risk it with our mounted escort of fourteen men. . . . I . . . found that we would have to follow some cross-roads through a wooded country and travel nearly twenty miles. It was now dark, but there was enough moonlight to enable us to see the way without difficulty." Sylvanus Cadwallader, the reporter who had told Lincoln about Five Forks, scented a story and tagged along. "The ride was lonely, somewhat hazardous, and made at a slow pace part of the way," he wrote. "Occasionally our gait was quickened on a good stretch of road; but farm houses, possible places of ambush, junctions and crossing of roads, were approached with caution." Continued Porter, "About half-past ten o'clock we struck Sheridan's pickets. . . . Sheridan was awaiting us, feeling sure that the general would come after getting his dispatch."

Grant met first with Sheridan, whose headquarters were located in a small log cabin in the middle of a small tobacco field, and then the two went over to talk with Meade. Remembered Grant, "I explained . . . that we did not want to follow the enemy; we wanted to get ahead of him, and that . . . I had no doubt that Lee was moving right then. Meade changed his orders at once." Now the advance in the morning would be directly toward Amelia Court House, with the cavalry sweeping out to the west.

Thursday, April 6

Union Pursuit: Morning

Dawn found the Union Second, Fifth, and Sixth Corps (under overall command of George Meade), as well as much of Sheridan's cavalry, concentrated at Jetersville, ready to advance on Amelia Court House. The infantry moved out early, but at 8:30 A.M., after the Union troops had covered about four miles, an enemy column was seen heading off to the west. More information came in to confirm that Lee's army had indeed abandoned Amelia Court House and taken up roads leading toward Farmville. George Meade promptly shifted his three corps to pursue along that axis, with the Sixth taking up the left of the three parallel columns, the Second the center, and the Fifth the right. By the time this repositioning was accomplished, Sheridan's riders were already racing west along the country roads, striking at whatever enemy units they encountered.

This morning also found a portion of the Twenty-fourth Corps, under Major General Ord, firmly established at Burkeville. Ord was operating on information that was already several hours old, indicating that Lee was still at Amelia Court House. Along with that report, the Union officer received orders to cut the bridges that Lee would have to use if he moved west. The biggest of these was a real colossus, fully 2,500 feet long and 126 feet high, built on 21 brick piers — no wonder it was called High Bridge. The span was located about twelve miles northwest of Burkeville — too far to send a large force, but just close enough to be reached by a fast-marching raiding party. Ord made up a strike force consisting of two infantry regiments (the 54th Pennsylvania and 123rd Ohio) and added to it the only cavalry he had on hand, his personal escort of eighty members of the 4th Massachusetts Cavalry — about nine hundred men in all. Colonel Francis Washburn of the 4th Massachusetts was put in overall charge, with "orders to push as rapidly as the exhausted condition of men and horses would permit, for the bridge . . . and, if not too well guarded, to burn it." The raiding party was gone before daylight.

Confederate Retreat: Morning

It had been a grueling night tramp for Robert E. Lee and his men. "The soldiers were worn out, almost starved, and thoroughly discouraged," recollected a Maryland soldier. "The march now assumed every appearance of a rout," wrote a Virginia artilleryman. "Soldiers, from every command, were straggling all over the country, and our once grand army was rapidly melting away." Lee's tactical situation was also serious. His columns were moving along parallel roads, but once past Deatonville, they would all have to use the same road, making one long, vulnerable procession of men and wagons. There was no alternative,

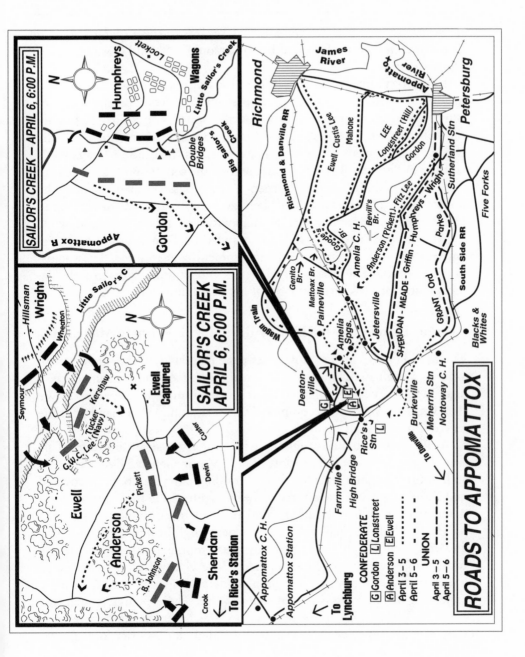

SAILOR'S CREEK – APRIL 6, 6:00 P.M.

Humphreys

Lockett

Wagons

Little Sailor's Creek

Double Bridges

Big Sailor's Creek

Gordon

Appomattox R

N

SAILOR'S CREEK
APRIL 6, 6:00 P.M.

Hillsman

Wright

Wheaton

Seymour

Little Sailor's C

Ewell Captured

Kershaw

Tucker (Navy)

G.W.C. Lee

Custer

Devin

Pickett

Ewell

Anderson

Sheridan

B. Johnson

Crook

To Rice's Station

N

James
River

Richmond

Richmond & Danville RR

Ewell - Custis Lee

Mahone

LEE

Longstreet (Hill)

Gordon

Appomattox
River

Petersburg

Bevill's
Br.

Anderson (Pickett) - Fitz Lee

Humphreys - Wright

Griffin

Sutherland Stn

Parke

Five Forks

Amelia C. H.

Goode's
Br.

Genito
Br.

Mattoax Br.

Paineville

Jetersville

SHERIDAN - MEADE - GRANT - Ord

South Side RR

Blacks &
Whites

Wagon Train

Deaton-
ville

Amelia
Spgs.

Burkeville

Meherrin Stn

Nottoway C. H.

Rice's
Stn

to Danville

G

A
E

L

Farmville

High Bridge

Appomattox C. H.

Appomattox Station

To
Lynchburg

CONFEDERATE
G Gordon   L Longstreet
A Anderson E Ewell
April 3–5
April 5–6

UNION
April 3–5
April 5–6

ROADS TO APPOMATTOX

103

however, so instructions were issued regarding the order of march: Longstreet in the van, followed by Anderson, Ewell, and Gordon guarding the rear.

Longstreet's men crossed Little Sailor's Creek* in the morning and headed toward Rice's Station to prevent Yankees operating out of Burkeville from seizing that depot on the South Side Railroad. Just up the rail line from Rice's Station was Farmville, where 80,000 badly needed rations were waiting for Lee's men. As the head of Longstreet's column pulled into Rice's Station, some of the scouts spotted the rear of Colonel Washburn's bridge burners as they passed out of sight to the north. Longstreet guessed their likely destination and was just trying to figure out how he could intercept them with only infantry on hand when a division of cavalry appeared, commanded by Tom Rosser. Longstreet wasted few words in turning the assignment over to him: "He was ordered to follow after the bridge-burners and capture or destroy the detachment, if it took the last man of his command to do it."

Union Expedition to High Bridge: Morning–Early Afternoon

The raiding party moved slowly, its pace regulated by the infantrymen, who had been marching without much rest since the pursuit of Lee's army began. They were halted shortly after sunrise for breakfast. "We then learned what troops comprised this forlorn hope," a member of the 123rd Ohio recalled.

A rider in Union blue caught up with the party a short time later. This was Brigadier General Theodore Read, Major General Ord's chief of staff, who brought a warning that the raiding party had been discovered and should look out for a force of Lee's cavalry.[†] He took overall command from Colonel Washburn and decided to continue the mission.

The head of the small column drew near High Bridge around midday and was immediately fired upon "by a few mounted rebels," as the 4th Massachusetts adjutant later reported. The eighty Union riders raced ahead to the span, which had been rendered impassible by the simple expedient of removing some of the flooring. These planks, which had been stacked nearby, were replaced by the Massachusetts men, who were also able to drive away the small Confederate security force guard-

---

* Noted in many period accounts as *Sayler's* Creek. It is now generally referred to as Sailor's Creek, and will be so designated in this text.

† A second staff officer was sent after Read with instructions for the party to return by way of Prince Edward Court House, but he was unable to break the cordon created by Longstreet's advancing corps and Rosser's pursuing force.

ing the bridge. A sergeant in the Union ranks later recalled, "At the same time quite a brisk firing was heard in our rear, and we surmised that our infantry had been attacked, which proved to be true. Our cavalry at once fell back, and arriving at a ridge, saw upon the partly wooded plain just below, and directly in our front, our forces in a brisk engagement with the enemy."

This was the cavalry sent by James Longstreet to intercept the raiders. The Rebels had dismounted to fight on foot, a tactic that Colonel Washburn believed gave his small mounted force an advantage. Recalled Lieutenant J. H. Lathrop of the cavalry command, "Immediately on our arrival Colonel Washburn held a consultation with General Read, and at once determined to charge the enemy. Forming the squadron on the brow of the hill we moved forward in column of fours, at a trot, until beyond the right flank of our infantry, and then, wheeling to the left, by fours we charged. . . . This charge was eminently successful, the enemy scattering in every direction, and we captured a number of them."

The Federal squadron re-formed in time to see a large mounted force of the enemy approaching from the rear. Hoping to cut a path back to the infantry, Washburn led his men charging into what proved to be three lines of Rebel cavalry. Reported Lieutenant Lathrop, "The men fought desperately hand to hand, but the conflict lasted a few minutes, for, overpowered by numbers and all the officers being disabled or captured, many of our men surrendered." Among the crumpled bodies on the ground was that of Colonel Washburn, who had been shot in the mouth and slashed across the head.

High Bridge: Afternoon

The Confederate interception force of about 1,200 men (made up of portions of Rosser's and Fitzhugh Lee's divisions) came upon the Yankee force at around 1:00 P.M. The Federal infantry was drawn up in a strong defensive position along the edge of a woods, behind a high fence. Munford's Brigade of Lee's division dismounted and tackled the infantry head-on, while two of Rosser's brigades — Brigadier General James Dearing's and Brigadier General John McClausland's — moved to flank the line. It was Munford's men who were hit by the charge of the 4th Massachusetts, and Dearing's riders who closed in behind the impetuous Yankees. "We were soon on them pell-mell in the woods and a desperate hand to hand fight ensues," recalled a Virginia cavalryman.

The melee quickly broke up into small groups and individual combats. Major James Breathed, commanding a horse battery, was cornered by a pair of saber-wielding Federals. Breathed slashed one from his horse but was knocked to the ground by the other, who bent over the fallen C.S. officer to finish the job. At that moment, a nearby Confederate sent the Yankee crashing to the ground with a well-aimed pistol shot. Then, recalled an onlooker, "Breathed sprang up with his saber still in his hand, [and] exclaiming 'Oh! damn you! I've got you now,' . . . killed him."

With its small screening force destroyed, the Union infantry fell back to the hillcrest near the bridge for a last stand. In a final dismounted charge, the 6th Virginia Cavalry overran this position and took most of the Yankees prisoner.

Aftermath

The Union bridge-burning force was wiped out. More than 800 were taken prisoner, with 42 reported killed or wounded. Among the dead was General Read; the mortally wounded Washburn would succumb to his injuries on April 22. Confederate losses were uncounted but included a high proportion of officers, most notably the twenty-five-year-old Brigadier General James Dearing, who died of his wounds on April 23. Several other popular regimental commanders were killed in the fighting this day: Major John Locher Knott (commanding the 12th Virginia Cavalry), Major James W. Thomson (of Stuart's Horse Artillery), and Colonel Reuben B. Boston (5th Virginia Cavalry). When someone remarked to a Virginia officer that the victory here had been complete, his reply was, "Yes, complete, but dearly bought."

High Bridge had been preserved as an escape route for Lee's army.

Confederate Retreat: Morning–Afternoon

Robert E. Lee's desperate attempt to funnel his forces along the single road from Deatonville to Rice's Station began to come apart soon after daylight. Except for the safe arrival of Longstreet's corps at the railroad depot, little went right. "Gen. Lee was with us very early," Longstreet's artillery chief wrote, "& I remember his getting very impatient & worried because the troops we were expecting to come up & pass us did not appear."

Longstreet's forced march to Rice's Station had opened the gap between his corps and the next in line, Richard Anderson's. Anderson was further slowed by what he later reported as "wagon trains which still blocked up the road" as well as almost constant skirmishing with de-

tachments of Sheridan's cavalry. Richard Ewell's corps, following Anderson's, held a defensive position at Amelia Springs for three hours to
let the lumbering vehicles move past. Not until 2:00 P.M. was he able to
move onto the road, pass the wagons, and fall in behind Anderson. John
Gordon's corps, protecting the rear, had the hardest time. "On and
on, hour after hour, from hilltop to hilltop, the lines were alternately
forming, fighting, and retreating, making one almost continuous shifting
battle," Gordon recalled.

There was a sharp little fight at an intersection a few miles west of
Deatonville known as Hott's Corner.* Here the road split, with one lane
leading directly to Rice's Station after crossing Little Sailor's Creek, and
the other making a roundabout loop to the north before likewise running down to the railroad depot. Anderson took a defensive position
around the crossroads and soon had to fend off an aggressive probing
attack by the Yankee cavalry. When Ewell's men trudged into sight, Anderson moved off along the direct route, leaving Ewell in charge of the
roadblock. When he rode forward to reconnoiter, Ewell met up with the
cavalry commander, Fitzhugh Lee, who told him that "a large force of
cavalry held the road just in front of General Anderson, and was so
strongly posted that he had halted a short distance ahead."

Ewell decided to clear the wagons off the infantry route by sending
them up the northern loop road, and at the same time to move his command up to support Anderson. Even as the creaking procession was
turning in this new direction, Ewell rode ahead to confer with his fellow
corps commander and found himself facing a crisis.

Union Pursuit: Morning–Afternoon

The pressure on the Confederate rear guard was coming largely from
Andrew Humphreys's Second Corps, which made contact with Gordon's corps at about 9:00 A.M. and kept up a constant running fight
from then on. "We have got the enemy now on the run, and go for them
on the double-quick," a Michigan soldier wrote. Closely supporting the
Second Corps was Horatio Wright's Sixth. A Pennsylvania soldier in
those ranks never forgot the moment when the men "received orders to
double-quick; for three miles we went on at a run over hills, across
swamps and through brambles. Many poor fellows fell by the wayside,
unable to keep up."

---

* Though referred to by residents as Hott's Corner, it was actually named after a local
farmer, John Holt, and was also known as Holt's Corner.

Confederate Retreat: Sailor's Creek

It was a nightmare come true: the Yankee cavalry had gotten in front in sufficient strength to block the way to Rice's Station, while the infantry was pressing hard from behind. Ewell and Anderson were trapped.

Ewell hurried back to his command, where he learned that the wagons had been successfully shunted to the northern route and that Gordon's men had "turned off after the trains." The closely pursuing Yankee corps had turned north to follow Gordon, but there would be no respite for Ewell's men because yet another Union corps had quickly filled the roads and begun pushing Ewell's skirmishers back toward Little Sailor's Creek.

Even as Anderson's men spread out to confront the cavalry forces that threatened them from the south, Ewell's troops were moved into a defensive alignment along the ridge west of Little Sailor's Creek, facing east and northeast. Joseph Kershaw's division was posted on the right of Ewell's line, with G. W. C. Lee's Richmond defensive forces on the left and the out-of-the-water Naval Battalion in the middle. There was no artillery on hand, so the soldiers had to face the enemy without the comforting presence of friendly cannon. "The odds against us were fearful," recalled one of Ewell's men.

Union Pursuit: Sailor's Creek

There was a brief firefight at Hott's Corner as the tail of John Gordon's corps held off the approaching Federals, but Gordon's men were soon pushed away from the intersection by Humphreys's troops and a few units from the Sixth that remained attached to the Second Corps for this phase of the combat. "The running contest with Gordon's Corps continued for three miles further," Humphreys recounted, with "the road for many miles strewn with tents, camp equipage, baggage, battery-forges, limbers, and wagons."

Three Sixth Corps regiments turned onto the direct route to Rice's Station. In the report of their brigade commander, Brevet Brigadier General J. Warren Keifer, "The rear guard of the enemy [i.e., Ewell's rear guard] was soon overtaken and attacked, it was vigorously pressed for about one mile, to and across [Little] Sailor's Creek."

Portions of two Sixth Corps divisions now hurried forward to take up a line of battle that stretched perpendicular to the road along a ridge on the east side of Little Sailor's Creek. Near the center of the line was a house owned by a family named Hillsman. Troops from two brigades of

Brigadier General Truman Seymour's division took station on the right side of the dirt lane, while a pair of brigades from Brevet Major General Frank Wheaton's command moved into line on the left side. A New York soldier in Wheaton's ranks remembered the sight as the men deployed: "Beyond on the opposite hillside we could see across the valley about a mile away, the enemy's line of battle formed and awaiting our attack. We instantly realized the work we had to do, and a tough job it looked to be." Phil Sheridan had ridden over to confer with Wright as the infantrymen spread out. A soldier watching from nearby recalled that "by the few words I caught and by the motions Gen. Sheridan made, I took it for granted that the object was to surround the enemy and close in on them on all sides."

Just behind the forming Union ranks, Brevet Major Andrew Cowan was lining his cannon along the ridge. At about 5:15 P.M. his guns opened fire and began pounding the enemy positions.

Confederate Lines: Sailor's Creek

Once he found his route to Rice's Station blocked by Yankee cavalry, Richard Anderson spread his corps along the main road with his battle line facing south. His position was almost a mile south of the ridge along which Richard Ewell's men were waiting for the Federals to attack.

After fending off some sharp cavalry rushes soon after their arrival, Anderson's men were told to dig in and wait, an order that satisfied few of the infantrymen. "Along our front and fully five hundred yards away we could see passing to our right heavy bodies of the enemy, evidently bent upon getting ahead of us," observed a Virginia soldier. "That somebody blundered, there is no doubt, as any enlisted man in the ranks could clearly see. We should have moved on."

Anderson held another hurried conference with Ewell. According to Ewell, he "suggested two methods of escape — either to unite our forces and break through, or to move to the right through the woods and try to strike a road which led toward Farmville." Ewell favored moving off, but the deep rumble of the Union artillery pummeling his men signaled that it was too late to disengage.

Along Ewell's line, a soldier recollected, "the enemy began the attack by shelling us from the woods, while with our hands and bayonets we threw up what fortification we could, and awaited the charge. In a little while a large body of infantry emerged from the woods and came right toward us at double quick."

Two miles further north, John Gordon's men were also facing an imminent attack. The road they had followed had taken them north from Hott's Corner, then west into a marshy valley, through which flowed the northern neck of Sailor's Creek, which emptied into the Appomattox River. At the southern end of the valley, Sailor's Creek split into two branches, one angling to the southwest (Big Sailor's Creek), and the other to the southeast (Little Sailor's Creek). The roadway crossed these two streams on a pair of wooden spans known as the Double Bridges, which had been built to handle light farm traffic, not a long procession of heavy military wagons and ordnance. Recalled one of Gordon's men, "The bridge across Sailor's Creek had broken down and hundreds of our wagons were detained. The enemy were pressing us hotly." Gordon attempted a stand on the east side of the valley, but "the enemy came upon our rear in great force," another soldier wrote, "and a 'sauve qui-peut' [every man for himself] engagement ensued." "The scene among the wagons was one of pell-mell confusion," noted an officer with the ordnance train. "They were driving in lines, eight or ten abreast, across the field towards the stream. . . . Its high banks interposed an effectual barrier, and there the teamsters, unhitching a horse or mule from the wagons, attempted to ford the stream, in which many of them failed." "I fear that a portion of the train will be lost as my force is quite reduced and insufficient for its protection," Gordon informed Lee.

Union Lines: Sailor's Creek

A New Jersey soldier in Humphreys's command remembered John Gordon's attempt to hold the east side of the valley: "The enemy made a spirited resistance, but were soon driven from this position." "Their line was swept away in an instant," a Maine soldier insisted. "Several hundred prisoners, thirteen flags, three guns, and a large share of Lee's wagon train were among the fruits of this victory," a Pennsylvanian recalled. "Gordon attempted to form [again] on the high ground on the opposite [i.e., west] side of the creek," Humphreys later stated, "but fell back quickly from it as our troops crossed. Night put a stop to the pursuit."

Three miles to the south, where Sheridan's cavalry confronted Anderson's infantry, the sound of fighting on Ewell's front had unleashed a series of mounted charges against the Confederate line. The Rebels, a Pennsylvania trooper later wrote, "fought savagely." A New Yorker noted that the "Confederates fought heroically, but were out-matched by the determined Federals, who saw victory and home but a short distance ahead."

The blow that finally shattered Anderson's defense was delivered by Colonel Henry Capehart's brigade of George Custer's division. A West Virginia trooper who was present later described the action: "The bugles sounded the charge, and forward up the face of that ridge swiftly swept that grand cavalry command with an irresistible force. . . . The rebels rose and fired a terrific volley . . . but they fired too quickly and too high, and before they could reload the most of our brigade had leaped the works and were among them. . . . The scene at this time was fierce and wild, but the saber, revolver and Spencer carbine of the cavalry were too much for the bayonet, and the musket that could not be quickly loaded." Other Federal units joined in all along the line, and Anderson's position collapsed. "As [the line] broke, [the C.S. infantry] lost all formation and went across the country," a trooper in the 10th New York Cavalry remembered, "scattering like children just out from school, our boys chasing up and gathering them in."

Along Horatio Wright's front, facing Ewell's position, the Federal cannonade lifted after about thirty minutes to let the battle lines advance. The time was just past 6:00 P.M.

The Union formation managed to keep its shape until it reached the streambed. As Frank Wheaton later reported, "Instead of finding it like most of the streams we had passed that day, it was discovered to be a swamp, varying in width from forty to a hundred yards, and traversed by several streams, the water in many places above the shoulders of the troops." "Many were shot down in the water and on both sides of the creek," a Vermont man in Truman Seymour's ranks wrote. "They went over with arms at a shoulder and in numerous instances cartridge boxes were also swung over the shoulder." One skirmisher, who managed to cross over dry-shod by jumping from grass clump to grass clump, looked back and enjoyed the scene. "It was laughable to see the boys floundering through the mud and water," he afterward reflected.

"Remained a short time under the crest of the hill to reform, the creek being quite deep and the crossing difficult," one of Wheaton's officers later recorded. When the advance resumed, the center of the line moved up a fairly open slope, while the two wings had to struggle through heavier undergrowth; as a result, the center of the line progressed more rapidly and was exposed to a more concentrated musketry of the enemy. "A scathing and murderous fire was opened," recalled a Rhode Island soldier in the center of the Sixth Corps's line. A staff officer watching from the nearby Hillsman house was startled when "suddenly the [center of the] brave Union line breaks into scattered fragments, which flow tumultuously down the hill before an unbroken gray line which charges furiously upon and after them. . . . The rebel yell rises exultant from their swift pursuing line. There is nothing between it and the artillery but the fugitives. . . . Thirty guns reopen and shatter the yelling gray line."*

The slower-moving wings of the Union advance were relatively unaffected by the momentary collapse of the center; they not only continued forward but began to envelope the Confederate line. Now it was the turn of the counterattacking Rebels to scramble back to their original lines. A captured Pennsylvania skirmisher had just been herded into a small gully when the Federal artillery pieces again ranged the open hillside. "We were scarcely down when the rebels came tumbling in and filled the ditch, nearly smothering me," he recalled. As soon as the cannonade ceased, heavy musketry erupted on the flanks as the attacking wings closed in. The POW was hustled out of the ravine. "Then saw a sight I will never forget," he continued. "Men were lying in every direction, heads shot off and arms and legs scattered and bleeding."

The fighting became hand-to-hand as the closing jaws encountered pockets of defenders. "The lines of Blue and Gray, half hidden in the veil of smoke, seemed to mingle in one mass as they swayed back and forth," said a Massachusetts soldier. "Thus almost simultaneously both flanks of the Sixth Corps broke the enemy's line, [while the Federal] . . . center was repulsed and driven back," observed a staff officer. "The enemy was soon routed at all points, and many general officers and many thousands of prisoners threw down their arms and surrendered," reported Brevet Brigadier General Keifer.

Among the last of the surrounded Confederate units to capitulate was the drydocked Naval Battalion. "They fought better and longer than any other troops upon the field," wrote Keifer to his wife afterward. The Union officer, believing that the sailors were ready to give up the fight, rode into their ranks to accept their surrender. The naval men began to follow his instructions, not recognizing him as a Yankee officer. When they understood what he was attempting to do, several leveled their muskets at the intruder. Said Keifer, "Commander Tucker, who commanded the Brigade, knocked up the muzzles of the guns nearest to me and saved my life. I succeeded in escaping to my lines unhurt. I at once bore down upon them and in a few moments captured the Brigade entire." Quipped one of Keifer's men, "Although sailors themselves, yet Sailor's creek had no charms for them."

---

* "Thirty guns" represents a touch of poetic license. The actual count was twenty cannon, in five batteries of four guns apiece.

Confederate Lines: Sailor's Creek

Richard Anderson believed that Sheridan's attacks had virtually wiped out his small corps. As he later reported, "After a feeble effort to advance[, my men] ... gave way in confusion and with the exception of one hundred and fifty or two hundred men the whole of General Ewell's and my command was captured."* One wounded officer hastily assembled all that remained of his regiment. "Men, I will dismiss you right here, in the hope you may succeed in escaping and joining the army under Lee," he told them. "Break ranks, march!" As the officer later recalled, "The men looked at me a moment, then the line wavered, broke, and melted into the brush and I was left alone."

John Gordon's report of his action against Humphreys's infantry concluded with the statement that his "greatly inferior numbers ... could not protect their flanks, and about 6 o'clock P.M. the enemy again renewed his attack in front and on both flanks and drove these commands from the field in considerable confusion." "That night our army marched the entire night," one of Gordon's men remembered, "and efforts were made to reorganize our shattered divisions, but the men being worn-out and weakened for want of rest and food, many of them threw their guns away, while others were with the wagon trains and embarrassed their progress materially."

Richard Ewell's report of his action against Wright's infantry made note of a last-minute attempt to organize a breakout using Anderson's men, which failed. "On riding past my left I came suddenly upon a strong line of the enemy's skirmishers advancing upon my left rear. This closed the only avenue of escape, as ... my right was completely enveloped. I surrendered myself and staff to a cavalry officer."† Ewell was not witness to the final moments of his command, which included some of the most vicious close-in combat of the campaign. "I saw numbers of men kill each other with bayonets and the butts of muskets, and even bite each others' throats and ears and noses, rolling on the ground like wild beasts," wrote an officer. Another Confederate soldier watched the blue lines envelope the Naval Battalion. "They clubbed their muskets, fired pistols into each other's faces, and used the bayonets savagely," he recalled. Then suddenly it was over. "Our men then threw down their arms, and we were prisoners of war," a Virginia officer recollected. "I

---

* Anderson's figures are reflective more of his demoralized state of mind than of reality. Included on the Appomattox surrender rolls are the names of 2,277 men from his corps and 294 from Ewell's.

† Actually Sergeant Angus Cameron, of the 5th Wisconsin.

remember that in the hot blood of youth, I broke my sword over a sapling rather than surrender it."

Aftermath: Confederate

"When the infantry which we had so recently repulsed came up to us again," a Confederate soldier at Little Sailor's Creek remembered, "it was with smiling faces. They commenced opening their haversacks, offering to share their 'hard tack' with us, which in our famished condition we most eagerly and gratefully accepted."

Robert E. Lee had spent the afternoon reconnoitering the roads around Rice's Station while he waited for word that the rear of his long troop column had closed up. Vague reports were received of fighting involving Gordon, but there was nothing definitive, and no word from either Anderson or Ewell. Lee had stopped to talk with one of his officers, William Mahone, when Charles Marshall of his staff rode up and announced that a large number of wagons were reported captured. Lee was skeptical and asked Mahone to lead his men back to investigate. Lee himself tagged along.

When they reached a ridge that overlooked much of the terrain to the east, Lee saw a disturbing sight. As Mahone later described it, there were "hurrying teamsters with their teams and dangling traces (no wagons), retreating infantry without guns, many without hats, a harmless mob, with the massive columns of the enemy moving on."

"My God!" Lee exclaimed, as if talking to himself, "Has the army dissolved?"

Mahone's men remained firm, and the distant Federal columns came no closer. It was a worn, weary Confederate commander who returned that evening to his headquarters outside Rice's Station. There, at least, things were quiet. More reports began to arrive sketching the magnitude of the disaster that had struck Confederate arms at Sailor's Creek. Lee put aside whatever feelings he may have had on the matter and concentrated on planning the next stage of his retreat. Longstreet would move through Farmville in the direction of Lynchburg, with the cavalry covering his rear, while Mahone's men, and all that was left of Gordon's corps, would use High Bridge, being sure to burn it once they were across.

Even as these orders were being transcribed for transmission to the various commands, a young officer appeared out of the darkness and stepped up to the Confederate commander.

"General Lee?" he asked, touching his hat. It was John Wise, the courier sent by Jefferson Davis. Wise had spent a nerve-racking day dodging Yankee cavalry patrols as he made his way toward Rice's Station. Now he produced Davis's written order, which satisfied Lee.

"You may say to Mr. Davis that, as he knows, my original purpose was to adhere to the line of the Danville Road. I have been unable to do so and am now endeavoring to . . . retire in the direction of Lynchburg."

Wise ventured to ask the great commander if he foresaw making a stand at any particular place. "No," Lee said sadly. "No; I shall have to be governed by each day's developments." There was a moody moment of silence before he added, with a touch of bitterness, "A few more Sailor's Creeks and it will be over — ended — just as I have expected it would end from the first."

Wise was astonished at Lee's frankness. Their conversation ended with Lee solicitously suggesting that the young man get some sleep before setting out on his dangerous trip back to Danville. Wise began to leave, stopped, and asked Lee if he had any news of his father, Brigadier General Henry Wise.

"No, no," Lee said, after a moment of thought. "At nightfall his command was fighting obstinately at Sailor's Creek, surrounded by the enemy. . . . I fear they were captured, or — or — worse."

Feeling older than his tender years, John Wise walked away from Lee's flickering campfire. He reclaimed his horse, rode toward Farmville until he struck the rear of one of Longstreet's divisions, and lay down to sleep in a pile of leaves.

Aftermath: Union

"This was a glorious day for the Army of the Potomac," one of Sheridan's cavalrymen crowed. "The result has been a complete success," Horatio Wright reported to headquarters at 9:10 P.M. Ewell had lost 3,400 men out of slightly more than 3,600 engaged, while Anderson had suffered 2,600 casualties out of 6,300 on the field. In its fight against the Second Corps, Gordon's corps counted 300 killed and more than 1,700 captured, making the total Confederate loss in all three sectors of the Sailor's Creek fighting approximately 8,000 men. Included among the captured were six Confederate generals taken in the fighting against Wright — Ewell, G. W. C. Lee, Kershaw, Brigadier General Seth Barton (serving under Lee), and Brigadier Generals James P. Simms and Dudley Du Bose (both with Kershaw) — and two brigadiers — Montgomery D. Corse and Eppa Hunton, serving under George Pickett — snared in the cavalry battle with Sheridan. Both Pickett and Anderson had managed to escape.

The Union loss was 1,180 killed and wounded. In a brief report of the action sent this night to U. S. Grant, Phil Sheridan concluded, "If the thing is pressed I think Lee will surrender."

Chapter Five

"After four years of arduous service"

---◆---

Friday, April 7

Confederate Retreat: Farmville

THE SOUNDS of the tail end of Longstreet's column breaking camp woke John Wise well before daylight. The young soldier mounted his horse and headed toward Farmville, where he expected to receive any last-minute messages from Lee for Jefferson Davis.

Wise had ridden only a short distance when he spotted a military unit camped in a grove of trees, the "troops . . . lying there more like dead men than live ones." Something prompted him to investigate further, and in an instant he recognized it as part of his father's command. Wise searched anxiously among the sleeping figures for his father. When he at last found him, the two hugged, happy to find each other alive. After catching up on recent events, the elder Wise insisted on joining his son to meet with General Lee. As a former governor of Virginia, Henry Wise was used to getting what he wanted.

John Wise found the ride to Farmville terribly dispiriting. "Demoralization, panic, abandonment of all hope, appeared on every hand," he reflected. When they came to Lee's headquarters, Wise's father stepped forward to confront the Confederate commander.

"General Lee," he exclaimed, "my poor, brave men are lying on yonder hill more dead than alive. . . . [By] God, sir, they shall not move another step until *somebody* gives them something to eat!"

"They deserve something to eat, and shall have it," Lee said soothingly.

The three men moved into the house Lee was using. Once inside, Lee asked the politician-turned-general for his opinion of the current situation. "Situation?" the elder Wise exploded. "There is no situation! . . . I say to you, sir, emphatically, that to prolong the struggle is murder, and the blood of every man who is killed from this time forth is on your head, General Lee."

"Oh, general, do not talk so wildly," Lee answered wearily. "My burdens are heavy enough. What would the country think of me, if I did what you suggest?"

Wise snorted and replied that Lee himself was all the country the men of the Army of Northern Virginia either knew or cared about. Those soldiers would die obeying his orders to fight, Wise continued, but if Lee chose the course of surrender, "no men or government or people will gainsay your decision."

Lee went to the window to watch his ragged columns trudge past. He turned back to the young Wise and wrote a brief note confirming that he had given the courier a verbal report. John Wise hugged his father good-bye and then rode off to complete his mission. Wise remembered feeling that he was "in the midst of the wreck of that immortal army which, until now, I had believed to be invincible."

James Longstreet's men had begun arriving in town at about nine in the morning and immediately set to devouring the rations handed to them from the Commissary Department supply trains. "Up to this time they had lived chiefly on parched corn, with a few bags of flour and a little meat which the sergeants picked up in the country," an artillery officer recalled. "At Farmville the Confederates feasted," a cavalryman declared. "It was the first occasion since leaving Richmond that rations were issued; previous to this the men had subsisted on parched corn." One of Longstreet's infantrymen later described how, "without orders, the men charged that [corn]meal, with which they filled their pockets and any other available receptacles. The meat was seized upon and slashed into pieces as they ran. Several of the men stuck their bayonets into middlings, and bore them proudly aloft."

There was little time to enjoy the food, however, as the Union forces were still pressing hard. Longstreet's men grabbed what they could, moved through town, and crossed to the north side of the Appomattox River. Lee soon followed them, seeking information on the troops under Mahone and Gordon that were crossing the river at High Bridge. He met up with Secretary of War John C. Breckinridge, who had ridden most of the way from Richmond with Ewell's wagon train. The trip had been far from uneventful, with Breckinridge, a veteran general in the Confederate service, successfully directing the train's defense against hit-and-run Yankee raiders. The two briefly reviewed Lee's plans, then Breckinridge continued on his journey to reach the Confederate government in Danville.

Lee had hoped that by moving his entire army to the north side of the Appomattox and burning the spans at High Bridge and Farmville, he might isolate himself for a while from Federal pursuit. Now word arrived that someone had failed to carry out his orders to destroy both High Bridge crossings,* and that the fast-advancing Federals had captured one of them intact. Union infantry was even now on the north bank of the river in strength. Lee flared with uncharacteristic anger; as one aide later tactfully phrased it, "He spoke of the blunder with a warmth and impatience which seemed to show how great a repression he ordinarily exercised over his feelings."

The best he could hope for now was to keep the Federals who were approaching Farmville from uniting with those coming from High Bridge. He called on Longstreet's artillery chief, E. P. Alexander, and gave him the job of burning the wagon and railroad bridges at Farmville after the last of the Confederate rear guard had crossed. He also wanted Alexander to position some guns at the point where he expected the Federals moving from High Bridge to intercept his line of march. To better explain his purpose, Lee took out a small map of the region and pointed out the situation to the young artillery officer. Alexander's own examination of the map left him puzzled and disturbed. It was clear to him that the route Lee intended to follow — heading north over the river, then skirting west along it before crossing south to rejoin the South Side Railroad at Appomattox Station — was longer than the path the Federals could follow by simply assuming a parallel course along the south side of the river. "Well there is time enough to think about that," was Lee's response when Alexander put the question to him. "Go now and attend to these matters here."

---

* In addition to the towering railroad bridge, there was a small wagon bridge that crossed the river along the valley floor.

Union Pursuit: High Bridge

The Federal advances this day were targeted at Farmville, Lee's likely point of concentration. Ord's Army of the James (which included elements of the white Twenty-fourth Corps and the black Twenty-fifth Corps), followed by Griffin's Fifth Corps, moved from Rice's Station (which Ord had reached late the previous evening) toward Farmville, while Wright's Sixth Corps marched from the Sailor's Creek battlefield to that same point. The bulk of Sheridan's cavalry hurried to keep ahead of Lee by striking for Prince Edward Court House, seven miles southwest of Farmville, while one division was left behind to screen the infantry advance into Farmville itself. Humphreys's command, meanwhile, moved directly from the area near the Double Bridges toward High Bridge. If the latter crossing point could be captured intact, Lee would be squeezed from two sides.

Brevet Major General Francis Barlow's division got the High Bridge assignment, and Barlow sent the 19th Maine racing ahead to secure the span. Lieutenant Colonel Joseph W. Spaulding, the regiment's second-in-command, never forgot the sight that met his eyes as his men topped the last crest: "[The bridge] had twenty-one spans of a hundred feet each, . . . and three of the spans at the further end were on fire and one or more had already fallen. A few rods below the railroad bridge was a low wooden bridge, for the dirt road, and that too was on fire with a few of the enemy still encouraging the fire."

The Maine soldiers tumbled down the valley slope toward the wagon bridge. "We were ordered to put out the fire on [it] . . . so as to be able to cross which was done," a laconic soldier in the ranks wrote in his diary. Spaulding was somewhat more forthcoming in his reminiscence, describing how his men extinguished the flames "by reaching down from the low bridge with dippers, canteens, hats — anything that could hold water — and throwing the water upon the blazing bridge."

The Confederate rear guard attempted to push the Maine soldiers back, but the rest of Barlow's division came up in time to solidify their hold. Meanwhile, Federal engineers contained the fire on the railroad bridge, saving most of its arching spans and ensuring that it could be quickly repaired.

Andrew Humphreys had all his men on the north side of the Appomattox River by 9:15 A.M.

Confederate Retreat: Farmville

The enemy appeared in force at Farmville starting at around midday. The cavalry came first, steadily pushing back the rear guard, whose job it was to keep the bridges open for as long as possible. From his position overlooking the vital railroad span, E. P. Alexander anxiously watched the combat unfold, waiting to give the necessary orders to the men standing at the ready below to burn the crossings. To Alexander's disgust, the Confederate cavalry, which was supposed to fall back across the bridge, instead broke off to the east, leaving him without any protection. "By the time I realized this," Alexander later remembered, "the enemy's skirmishers were very close to the bridge. I gave the signal . . . & the bridge was soon in flames from one end to the other. But there was little margin & had the enemy rushed a force up at double quick, they might have saved it." The nearby wagon bridge was also torched in time.

Well before the first Federal riders entered the town, Lee's commissary general sent the railroad cars containing provisions off to the west, in the expectation that Lee would be able to march around and meet them.

The troops under Mahone and Gordon, who had crossed the Appomattox at High Bridge, coiled up into a strong defensive position along a ridgeline north of Farmville, on which was located Cumberland Church. Although Longstreet's men and the Confederate cavalry soon reinforced the position, it was struck throughout the afternoon by elements of the Federal Second Corps that had followed Gordon and Mahone over High Bridge, and by Union cavalry units that had managed to ford the river just west of town.

There was nothing tentative about the combat that swirled around the Cumberland Church ridge all afternoon and into the early evening. It was, a South Carolina soldier later wrote, "a good stiff fight." E. P. Alexander remarked that it seemed as if the Confederates "had gotten into a certain habit of fighting, which they could not change, although they were now beginning to foresee the inevitable end."

At nightfall, Lee's lines remained unbroken. The Confederate commander came to a cottage close to the church to rest and confer with some of his generals. It was around 9:30 P.M. when a courier arrived with a message for Lee from U. S. Grant.

Federal Pursuit: Farmville

Andrew Humphreys later reckoned that the engagements around Cumberland Church cost his corps "five hundred and seventy-one officers and men killed, wounded, and missing." Among the mortally wounded was Brigadier General Thomas A. Smyth, who would linger until April 9 and thus become the last Union general killed in the war. Included among those captured was a cavalry brigade commander, Brevet Brigadier General J. Irvin Gregg.

Ulysses Grant rode into Farmville this afternoon. He set up his headquarters at the Prince Edward Hotel, listened to the fighting at Cumberland Church, and watched as Wright's Sixth Corps moved through town. By evening Federal engineers had constructed a pontoon bridge across the Appomattox so that Wright's men could get over to reinforce Humphreys. When Grant came onto the hotel porch to see the troops pass by, the event was instantly transformed into an impromptu review. Grant's aide Horace Porter later described the scene: "Bonfires were lighted on the sides of the street, the men seized straw and pine-knots, and improvised torches; cheers arose from their throats, already hoarse with shouts of victory; bands played, banners waved, and muskets were swung in the air."

A note had arrived from Sheridan reporting his safe arrival at Prince Edward Court House and passing along the intelligence that supplies sent to Lee from Lynchburg had reached Appomattox Station. Sheridan vowed to send a column out at once to capture or destroy that cache.

Enjoying the unofficial review with Grant were Generals Ord and Gibbon, the latter commanding the Twenty-fourth Corps. John Gibbon sensed something historical about the mood of the moment. "It was very evident that, having been cut off from all prospect of a junction with Johnston and his whole army forced to the north side of the Appomattox River with the loss of much of his artillery and transportation, Lee's only hope now was to reach Lynchburg with his much reduced force and half-famished men and his chances for that against our largely superior force and active cavalry were very slim."

Gibbon was not surprised when Grant turned to him and remarked, in a quiet way, "I have a great mind to summon Lee to surrender." It was but a short time afterward, as Gibbon recalled it, that Grant's adjutant general Seth Williams was on his way across the river bearing Grant's note.*

---

* Williams was shot at by nervous enemy pickets and the orderly riding with him killed before the former could establish his identity and deliver Grant's note to a Rebel officer.

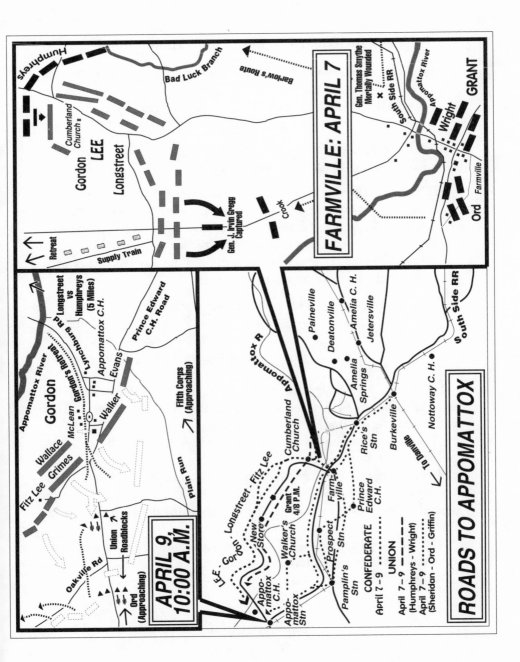

FARMVILLE: APRIL 7

Bad Luck Branch

Barlow's Route

Gen. Thomas Smythe Mortally Wounded

South Side RR

Appomattox River

GRANT

Humphreys

Cumberland Church

LEE

Gordon

Longstreet

Wright

Retreat

Supply Train

Gen. J. Irvin Gregg Captured

Crook

Farmville

Ord

APRIL 9, 10:00 A.M.

Appomattox River

Lynchburg Stage Rd

Gordon's Retreat

Longstreet vs Humphreys (5 Miles)

Appomattox C.H.

Prince Edward C.H. Road

Evans

McLean

Walker

Gordon

Wallace

Grimes

Fitz Lee

Union Roadblocks

Oakville Rd

Plain Run

Fifth Corps (Approaching)

Ord (Approaching)

ROADS TO APPOMATTOX

Appomattox R

Paineville

Deatonville

Amelia C. H.

Jetersville

Amelia Springs

Cumberland Church

Rice's Stn

Burkeville

Nottoway C. H.

South Side RR

New Store

Walker's Church

Grant 4/8 P.M.

Farm- ville

Prospect Stn

Prince Edward C.H.

to Danville

Appo- mattox C.H.

Appo- mattox Stn

Pamplin's Stn

LEE - Gordon - Longstreet - Fitz Lee

CONFEDERATE
April 7 - 9

UNION
April 7 - 9
(Humphreys - Wright)
April 7 - 9
(Sheridan - Ord - Griffin)

Lee's Headquarters, near Cumberland Church

Robert E. Lee took Grant's note from the courier and read it to himself.

HEAD-QUARTERS ARMIES OF THE UNITED STATES
5 P.M., April 7, 1865

General R. E. Lee,
    Commanding Confederate States Army:

GENERAL: The results of the last week must convince you of the
hopelessness of further resistance on the part of the Army of Northern
Virginia in this struggle. I feel that it is so, and regard it as my duty to
shift from myself the responsibility of any further effusion of blood by
asking of you the surrender of that portion of the Confederate army
known as the Army of Northern Virginia.

Very respectfully, your obedient servant,
U. S. Grant
Lieutenant-General,
Commanding Armies of the United States

Lee passed the message over to his aide Charles Venable, waited until
the staff officer had finished reading it, and then asked him, "How
would you answer that?"

"I would answer no such letter," Venable replied.

"Ah, but it must be answered," Lee said.

Several other officers looked at the note and made comments. There
was, recalled Charles Marshall, "some difference of opinion among the
general officers as to the nature of the reply to be made to Grant's letter."

The last word came from James Longstreet, who spent a silent moment reading it and then returned it to Lee.

"Not yet," Longstreet said.

---◄○►---

Saturday, April 8

Union Pursuit: Farmville

It was well after midnight when Grant received Robert E. Lee's reply.*

---

* Having already been the target of one set of pickets, Seth Williams had no desire to
repeat the experience, so he took the long way back to Farmville, via High Bridge.

He was asleep when the note arrived but quickly came downstairs from the bedroom to read it.

7th Apl '65

Genl

I have rec'd your note of this date. Though not entertaining the opinion you express of the hopelessness of further resistance on the part of the Army of N. Va. — I reciprocate your desire to avoid useless effusion of blood, & therefore before considering your proposition, ask the terms you will offer on condition of its surrender.

Very respy your obt. Servt
R. E. Lee
Genl

"This was not satisfactory," Grant thought, "but . . . it [was] deserving [of] another letter."

April 8, 1865

General R. E. Lee,
Commanding C.S.A.

Your note of last evening in reply of mine of same date, asking the condition on which I will accept the surrender of the Army of Northern Virginia is just received. In reply I would say that, peace being my great desire, there is but one condition I would insist upon, namely: that the men and officers surrendered shall be disqualified for taking up arms again against the Government of the United States until properly exchanged. I will meet you, or will designate officers to meet any officers you may name for the same purpose, at any point agreeable to you, for the purpose of arranging definitely the terms upon which the surrender of the Army of Northern Virginia will be received.

U. S. Grant,
Lieut.-General

Grant sent the message off and went back to bed. When he got up a few hours later, he was feeling ill — he called it a "sick headache." Nevertheless, he was determined to keep pace with the Union pursuit.

Lee's men had left Cumberland Church during the night and moved off to the west. Humphreys's Second and Wright's Sixth corps picked up the trail, and south of the Appomattox River the cavalrymen once again led the way, galloping west toward Appomattox Station from camps surrounding Prospect Station. Behind them marched Army of the James troops under Ord, followed by Griffin's Fifth Corps. Ord set the tone for the day as he restlessly moved along his dusty, footsore columns with encouragements such as "Legs will win this battle, men," "They can't escape, if you keep up to it," and "I promise you, boys, that this will be the last day's march you will have to endure."

On his way out of the hotel to join in this pursuit, Grant met the proprietor, who identified himself as a colonel in Lee's army. Remembered Grant, "He said that when he came along past home, he found that he was the only man of the regiment remaining with Lee's army, so he just dropped out, and now wanted to surrender himself. I told him to stay there and he would not be molested. That was one regiment which had been eliminated from Lee's army."

Confederate Retreat: Roads West

Shortly after Lee finished writing his response to Grant's April 7 message, his men began pulling out of their positions around Cumberland Church. The plan was for them to move west in two parallel columns, with Longstreet (commanding all that remained of the old First and Third corps) taking the northernmost route and Gordon (commanding everything else) using the southern one. Once the columns reached New Store, however, they would have to use the same road, so it was decided that Gordon would then take the lead, while Longstreet assumed rearguard responsibilities.

The ragged files were moving into a region of Virginia that had not seen much military action. More than one soldier later recalled enjoying the view of what one of them described as "a picturesque country." Yet signs of the Confederacy's perilous condition were never far away: an Alabama soldier noted the carefully tended farm he passed, but the sight he never forgot was that of some nearby artillerymen "burying two twelve pound brass Napoleon guns."

Union Pursuit: Roads West

One of Sheridan's divisions, moving along the south bank of the Appomattox River, entered Pamplin's Station on the South Side Railroad around midday. A Pennsylvania officer recorded in his diary that the Yankees there "captured 3 Engines and some rolling stock." These were the cars containing rations that Lee's commissary general had sent away from Farmville for safekeeping on April 7.

Sheridan's other two divisions kept their course for Appomattox Station. The Federal officer had targeted the place on the intelligence that a large stock of Rebel supplies was waiting there for Lee's army. This morning, thanks to a little covert action by one of the cavalryman's scouts, operating behind enemy lines in a Confederate uniform, the presence of supplies at Appomattox Station was more than speculation. Several trains had been sent down from Lynchburg but had skittishly hung back from approaching the depot for fear of the Yankee horsemen. Sheridan's scout, disguised as a C.S. courier, convinced the trainmen of Lee's desperate need for the supplies they were carrying, so they patriotically pressed on to the station. The scout at once galloped to Sheridan with his story, and the cavalry commander became more determined than ever to see that his men got there before Lee's did. Orders went out to all his commands to converge on Appomattox Station.

Confederate Retreat: New Store–Appomattox Station

The Union infantry was not following very closely, and most of the Yankee cavalry was south of the Appomattox, so Lee's retreat was relatively unimpeded. "We marched undisturbed all day," one of Gordon's brigadiers reported. As each section of the column reached New Store, where the parallel lines singled up, there was even an opportunity for a brief rest.

It was at New Store that Robert E. Lee found time to take care of a few administrative matters. Three generals — Richard H. Anderson, Bushrod Johnson, and George E. Pickett — were relieved of command, ostensibly because their forces had been too depleted by combat loss and attrition to continue as independent organizations, though the generals' lackluster performances during the retreat were certainly also a factor. The existing units were shifted to other commands, and the three officers told to report home for further orders, though only Anderson appears to have been formally notified.*

While Lee was sitting by the roadside, his artillery chief, Brigadier General William N. Pendleton, asked to speak with him. Pendleton had been appointed to represent a group of officers who had met the pre-

---

* Both Pickett and Johnson remained with the army through Appomattox Court House and were among those paroled.

vious evening to discuss a hitherto unmentionable possibility: surrender. The time had come, these officers agreed, to open negotiations with the enemy.

"I trust it has not come to that!" Lee replied with some surprise. "We certainly have too many brave men to think of laying down our arms. They still fight with great spirit, whereas the enemy does not. And, besides, if I were to intimate to General Grant that I would listen to terms, he would at once regard it as such an evidence of weakness that he would demand unconditional surrender — and sooner than that I am resolved to die. Indeed, we must all determine to die at our posts."

Pendleton's reply was that "every man would no doubt cheerfully meet death with him in discharge of duty, and that we were perfectly willing that he should decide the question."

Lee's determination may have been unshaken, but the slow decay of his army continued unabated. A Virginia cavalryman with the rear guard never forgot the sight this day of muskets "thrown away by the dozen, showing that the men had left the ranks in groups." A veteran line officer thought it strange that his superiors did so little to stop the straggling: "They seemed to shut their eyes on the hourly reduction of their commands, and rode in advance of their brigades in dogged indifference," he observed.

Moving well ahead of the long column of infantry and cavalry was Lee's surplus artillery, which had been taken on a northern route from Amelia Court House on April 5, not rejoining the line of march until April 7 at Cumberland Church, where it had once again been sent out ahead of the main body. Brigadier General R. Lindsay Walker was in command. His gunners reached Appomattox Station in the afternoon and went into bivouac on high ground not far from the railroad depot. Closer to the station, C.S. engineer troops were going into camp as well. Nearby were the engines and cars containing the rations sent down the line from Lynchburg.

Several of the military engineers were startled when the locomotives suddenly jerked into motion, whistles screaming. An engine and its cars chugged past the soldiers, who looked down the track to see a man running toward them, "yelling like all fury."

"The Yankees are coming," he cried. "The Yankees are coming."

Union Pursuit: Roads West–Appomattox Station

Grant had hoped to keep pace with Humphreys's men today, but that was not to be. According to his military secretary, Adam Badeau,

"Worn out with the mental anxiety and physical fatigue, loss of sleep and the weight of responsibility, he became very unwell, and was obliged to halt at a farm-house on the road, where he spent most of the day."

North of the Appomattox River, Union infantry reached the vicinity of New Store at about four o'clock in the afternoon. "Stragglers are found scattered all along the line of march, and as the troops pass they come in and surrender themselves, expressing their determination to fight no longer, as they consider the rebellion as good as over," a Yankee noted. Humphreys's Second Corps reached New Store first, rested for two hours, and then pushed on for seven more miles before stopping for the night. Behind the Second Corps came the Sixth, which camped around New Store at 9:00 P.M.

South of the Appomattox, the Army of the James and the Fifth Corps plodded through the day without incident. Ord's men would rest this night within three miles of Appomattox Station, while Griffin's men halted just five miles further away.

It was a little after 4:00 P.M. when the first of George A. Custer's three brigades arrived at Appomattox Station. There the Yankee riders found a small squad of Confederate cavalry guarding trains loaded with supplies for Lee's army. As his lead regiment scrambled into a battle line, Custer galloped up to the unit commander. "Go in, old fellow, don't let anything stop you, now is the chance for your stars," he said. "Whoop 'em up. I'll be after you."

The brigade formed into a charge that raced into the depot, scattered the small guard unit, and captured several trains. A few cavalrymen with railroad experience managed to get three of them moving and headed down the tracks toward the approaching Federal columns.

From their bivouac near the depot, Walker's Rebel artillerymen guessed what was happening and unlimbered their guns for action. For the next several hours the fighting was largely artillery against cavalry, as numerous blue-coated battalions lunged repeatedly at the flaming semi-circle of cannon, only to be stopped cold by what one trooper described as "a blaze of canister and musketry."[*] Not until nearly 9:00 P.M. would Custer be able to mobilize his scattered brigades into an all-out attack that swamped one flank of Walker's line. It was not an easy fight for the cavalrymen, many of whom had to advance on foot through prickly undergrowth. "The men lost their caps, tore their clothes, and scratched their faces," one grumbled. Most of the Rebel gunners were able to hitch

---

[*] A few dismounted Confederate cavalry units also joined in the defense.

up and escape, but more than twenty-five pieces were taken by Custer's men.

A small squad of New York troopers brashly pursued the retreating gunners down the road and through to the east side of the village of Appomattox Court House, where they abruptly came up against the steady skirmishers of John Gordon's corps. A volley emptied saddles, and the survivors melted away, leaving behind several dead and wounded, including a sergeant who was found by one of the villagers. The civilian never forgot the Yankee, "whose vitals had been shot away, and who begged [me] . . . to take the carbine by his side and shoot him through the head; so great was his agony. In five minutes the soldier was dead."

Back at Appomattox Station, more of Sheridan's troopers had arrived, including the cavalry leader himself, who, at 9:20 P.M., wrote Grant, "If General Gibbon [i.e., the Twenty-fourth Corps] and the Fifth Corps can get up tonight we will perhaps finish the job in the morning. I do not think Lee means to surrender until compelled to do so."

Confederate Retreat: Near Appomattox Court House

It was late afternoon by the time a courier found Lee and handed him the note that U. S. Grant had penned that morning in Farmville. Its terms were surprising: rather than calling for unconditional surrender, Grant had indicated a willingness to let the men disarm and return home until exchanged. This time Lee did not discuss his response with anyone. He sat down by the roadside and wrote:

8th Apl '65

Genl

I rec'd at a late hour your note of today. In mine of yesterday I did not intend to propose the surrender of the Army of N. Va. — but to ask the terms of your proposition. To be frank, I do not think the emergency has arisen to call for the surrender of this Army, but as the restoration of peace should be the sole object of all, I desired to know whether your proposals would lead to that and I cannot therefore meet you with a view to surrender the Army of N. Va. — but as far as your proposal may affect the C.S. forces under my command & tend to the restoration of peace, I shall be pleased to meet you at 10 A.M.

tomorrow on the old stage road to Richmond between the picket lines
of the two armies.

Very respy your Obt Sevt

R. E. Lee

Genl.

Lee gave the note to Charles Marshall to be copied and then delivered. He rode on, reaching a point about two miles from Appomattox
Court House when the sound of Custer's 9:00 P.M. attack on Walker's
artillery position made it painfully clear that the enemy had once again
cut across his path. Lee sent orders to Fitzhugh Lee, whose cavalrymen
had been covering the rear of the retreating column, to pass Longstreet's
and Gordon's men and take over the van. It was nearing midnight when
Robert E. Lee's senior officers began to gather for a conference that
history would call his last council of war.

Longstreet was there, as were Gordon and Fitzhugh Lee. Robert E.
Lee was certain that only the Federal cavalry barred his route, and that
once it was pushed aside, the retreat could continue. Gordon, with no
evidence other than his intuition, believed that there was Federal infantry near at hand, a supposition that Fitzhugh Lee supported. Lee disagreed and overruled the two, but he assured them that if it was
discovered that there were Union foot soldiers behind the cavalry, and
that a breakthrough was not possible, he would "accede to the only
alternative left us."

The battle plan was straightforward enough. First thing in the morning
Fitzhugh Lee's men would charge the enemy cavalry, scatter it, and take
control of the Lynchburg Stage Road. Gordon's infantry would back up
Fitzhugh Lee's move and quickly clear out any enemy strongpoints. Once
the route had been opened, the infantry and cavalry would push south
toward Danville, while the supply wagons would veer off to the west and
make for Lynchburg. Fitzhugh Lee spoke up. "I only stipulated that if I
saw a surrender was inevitable," he recalled, "I should get the cavalry out
of it, if possible, for I feared their horses would be taken from them — a
serious loss to troops where each owned the animal he rode."

Years later, John Gordon reflected that "no tongue or pen will ever be
able to describe the unutterable anguish of Lee's commanders as they
looked into the clouded face of their beloved leader and sought to draw
from it some ray of hope."

There was nothing left to say. The conference came to an end as the
officers made off to their commands. John Gordon was well on his way

back to his headquarters when he realized that he had not bothered to ask how far he should press his attack in the morning. He sent off a courier to ask Lee. The aide returned with a reply that signaled that the Confederate commander might be down but was certainly not out: "Tell General Gordon that I should be glad for him to halt just beyond the Tennessee line."

One way or another, it would all be decided tomorrow, April 9.

---◁◦▷---

Sunday, April 9

---◁◦▷---

Southside Virginia, near Appomattox Court House

Confederate

The infantrymen assigned to the breakout attempt were roused from their camps at around two o'clock in the morning and moved toward the village of Appomattox Court House. "The night was dark," one of them recalled, "but our men seemed to be in good spirits and ready for any duty." Another recollected, "We moved at 3 A.M. into the principal street of the town and lay there shivering until daylight." Fitzhugh Lee's cavalry had preceded them, though one of the arriving foot soldiers remembered that most of the troopers he observed were "apparently asleep mounted."

During the night, Major General Bryan Grimes's division had taken up a defensive line west of the village. When his skirmishers reported that the enemy was blocking the escape road, Grimes went looking for instructions. The sun had not yet risen when he found his corps commander, John Gordon, arguing with the cavalry commander, Fitzhugh Lee. According to Grimes, "General Gordon was of the opinion that the troops in our front were cavalry, and that General Fitzhugh Lee should attack. Fitzhugh Lee thought they were infantry and that General Gordon should attack." Grimes was astonished at the behavior of these two senior officers, and he interrupted them with the comment that "it was somebody's duty to attack." He then offered to do the job himself.

"Well, drive them off," Gordon snapped.

"I cannot do it with my division alone, but require assistance," Grimes replied.

"You can take the two other divisions of the corps," Gordon said.

Grimes rode off to organize his advance. "By this time it was becoming sufficiently light to make the surrounding localities visible," he later wrote.

Union

A soldier serving in Ord's Army of the James, which had bivouacked approximately three miles from Appomattox Station, recalled that it was "between three and four o'clock in the morning of the 9th of April [when] we were on the march again. Shortly after daybreak we reached a large field in which Sheridan's headquarters tents were pitched."

Ord and John Gibbon met with the cavalryman to work out their attack plan. A surgeon who watched this exchange later remarked that the " 'battlelight' is not a myth nor a figure of speech; on that morning it fairly transfigured Sheridan."

Twenty-five miles to the northeast, above the Appomattox River and in the rear of Humphreys's Second Corps, U. S. Grant finished breakfast and made plans to cross the river to join Sheridan. He had received Lee's note proposing a ten o'clock conference for "the restoration of peace," but at the insistence of his chief of staff, he had decided that such a broad-ranging political agenda exceeded his military authority. Grant never explained why he rode this morning away from Humphreys's front — where Lee had proposed they meet — and toward Sheridan, a trip that put him out of contact for several fateful hours.

Before leaving, Grant sent Lee his reply:

Headquarters Armies of the United States
April 9, 1865

General R. E. Lee,
Commanding C.S. Armies:

General: Your note of yesterday is received. As I have no authority to treat on the subject of peace the meeting proposed for 10 A.M. today could lead to no good. I will state, however, General, that I am equally anxious for peace with yourself, and the whole North entertain the same feeling. The terms upon which peace can be had are well understood. By the South laying down their arms they will hasten the most desirable event, save thousands of human lives, and hundreds of millions of property not yet destroyed. Sincerely hoping that all our difficulties may be settled without the loss of another life, I subscribe myself,

Very respectfully, your obedient servant,
U. S. Grant
Lieutenant-General U.S. Army

Confederate

Robert E. Lee established himself on a hilltop about a mile and a half northeast of Appomattox Court House, roughly midway between Gordon's and Fitzhugh Lee's men west of the village and Longstreet's corps a few miles further north. He was in full dress uniform. When one of his officers asked him why he had dressed that way, Lee answered, "I have probably to be General Grant's prisoner, and thought I must make my best appearance." Lee's aide Lieutenant Colonel Charles Venable returned from Gordon's front with distressing news. Already lukewarm about the breakout operation, Gordon had had no optimistic words for Lee's emissary; according to Venable, he had said, "Tell General Lee I have fought my corps to a frazzle, and I fear I can do nothing unless I am heavily supported by Longstreet's Corps."

In the distance Lee could hear the crackle of small arms and the occasional boom of cannon. Whatever his misgivings, Gordon was attacking. The sun had come up by this time; when Lee spotted Longstreet's artillery chief, E. P. Alexander, he waved to the young man to come over.

"Well, here we are at Appomattox, & there seems to be a considerable force in front of us. Now, what shall we have to do today?" Lee asked him.

Alexander was for fighting through the blue cordon, but Lee said he thought that would be impossible. The gunner then responded that but two courses of action remained: either surrender the army or let the troops scatter to make their way to Johnston.

Lee listened impassively as Alexander marshaled his arguments for sparing the army the indignity of surrender. He then countered each point, dwelling on the chaos that an unorganized mass of armed men was sure to bring upon the Virginia countryside. "We must consider only the effect which our actions will have upon the country at large," Lee declared.

West of the village, the Confederate battle lines now stretched at a right angle to the Richmond-Lynchburg Road, with Fitzhugh Lee's cavalry constituting the extreme right flank. It was these riders who drew first blood. Two North Carolina regiments charged eight hundred yards across an open field and overran a Union battery section that had been shelling them since first light. Fortunately for them, the Yankee cannoneers did not stick to their weapons: "Some went into the woods, some took shelter under the gun carriages, and all quit firing," a Tar Heel trooper recalled. Other Rebel horsemen pushed ahead across the

Oakville Road, where they met and scattered a second Federal strong-point, taking another gun in the process.

Gordon's infantry lines swung out from Appomattox Court House like a door hinged to the southern edge of the village. They crossed over the Richmond-Lynchburg Road in a formation parallel to it so as to clear the route for the rest of the army. In the wake of these advancing files lay the bodies of those who had fallen in the brief actions, clothed in blue and gray.

Gordon's and Fitzhugh Lee's men had carried out their assignment and broken the enemy roadblocks. The way seemed open for Lee's army to continue its retreat. The time was about 8:30 A.M.

Union

Following the brief conference at Appomattox Station, John Gibbon moved his Twenty-fourth Corps in the direction of Appomattox Court House. He later wrote that "it soon became evident that the cavalry was heavily engaged." Brigadier General Robert S. Foster's division was the first of Gibbon's units to deploy across the Richmond-Lynchburg Road and move toward the enemy. Foster's leading brigade pushed too far out in front of the rest of the division and was repulsed when it struck the right flank guard of John Gordon's battle line. This brigade fell back with the rest of the division as the Union line was stabilized by the arrival of Brevet Major General John W. Turner's division of Gibbon's command and two brigades of black troops from the Twenty-fifth Corps — the latter troops deployed but not engaged in any fighting.

A solid line of Union infantry now blocked the Richmond-Lynchburg Road. Lee's escape route, so briefly open, was once more firmly closed.

Confederate

Robert E. Lee knew it was over. The persistent sounds of battle off to the west made it clear that the enemy still blocked his way. James Longstreet arrived in response to Lee's summons and stood impassively as the senior officer explained that "the advanced columns stood against a very formidable force, which he could not break through." Longstreet asked whether sacrificing the Army of Northern Virginia might possibly benefit some other quadrant of the Confederacy. Lee indicated that it would not.

"Your situation speaks for itself," Longstreet said.

Lee turned to General Mahone, who agreed with Longstreet's assessment. Lee then called for Colonel Taylor, the newlywed.

"I have had a conference with these gentlemen around me, and they agree that the time has come for capitulation," Lee told him.

Taylor tried to argue the point, but Lee cut him off. "I have arranged to meet General Grant with a view to surrender, and wish you to accompany me."

Taylor found Colonel Marshall, and the two made up Lee's escort. Lee rode with this small party toward Longstreet's lines, where he assumed he would find Grant. They entered the no-man's land between the Confederate and Union positions, but instead of meeting one of Grant's emissaries, they encountered an aide to the Union Second Corps commander, Andrew Humphreys, who carried Grant's letter of this morning rejecting the idea of a meeting to discuss a general peace. Lee read the note, then turned to Colonel Marshall and said, "Well, write a letter to General Grant and ask him to meet me to deal with the question of the surrender of my army."

Marshall penned a short message to that effect and passed it over to the Federal officer, who sent it to the rear to be delivered to Grant. The time was about 9:00 A.M.

Lee had hoped that his request for a surrender conference would automatically suspend the fighting, but the Federal officers on the scene claimed to lack the authority to order a ceasefire. An enemy skirmish line even began to advance toward Lee, forcing him to retreat a short distance. At last a note arrived from Army of the Potomac commander George Meade, granting a one-hour truce.

While Lee was waiting for the matter to be resolved, a courier arrived from James Longstreet, bearing a message from Fitzhugh Lee claiming that an unblocked escape route had been located for the army. Robert E. Lee doubted that his cavalry commander could be right, but he instructed Longstreet to use his own judgment. Lee's skepticism, as it turned out, was justified: not long after, another courier appeared to report that Fitzhugh Lee had been wrong. This served to remind Lee that he had neglected to authorize John Gordon to seek a ceasefire on his front, so the courier returned with those instructions.

From General Meade came the suggestion that Lee send a second note to Grant — this one on a more direct route, through Sheridan's front. Lee agreed and wrote:

Headquarters, Army of Northern Virginia
April 9, 1865

Lieut. Gen. U. S. Grant
  Commanding U.S. Armies:

General:

I sent a communication to you to-day from the picket-line, whither I had gone in hopes of meeting you in pursuance of the request contained in my letter of yesterday. Major-General Meade informs me that it would probably expedite matters to send a duplicate through some other part of your lines. I therefore request an interview, at such time and place as you may designate, to discuss the terms of the surrender of this army in accordance with your offer to have such an interview, contained in your letter of yesterday.

Very respectfully, your obedient servant,
R. E. Lee
General

This letter was sent on its way at around ten o'clock in the morning.

Union–Confederate

The last killings of the Appomattox Campaign took place between nine-thirty and ten-thirty this morning.

One was accounted for by a small company of Confederate engineers who had been given muskets and orders to support a battery on the southwest side of the village. The artillerymen were pulling back according to instructions as the engineers arrived, so the soldiers pushed on and soon spotted a cavalry fight in front of them. As the men fell into a long forward-facing line of battle, a lone horseman appeared, "gesticulating wildly with his sword and shouting something which I did not catch," an engineering officer remembered. He yelled at the rider to get out of the line of fire, but then some of the men in the ranks cried, "Lieutenant, it's a Yankee." Someone else called out, "Kill him!" and before the officer could intervene, a volley flashed along the line. "Man and horse went crashing to earth," the officer recalled, "both dead before they touched the ground."

Not far away, Lieutenant Colonel Joseph B. Pattee's brigade of the Fifth Corps was among the last Federal units to engage the enemy. The all-Pennsylvania outfit was advancing on the right of Gibbon's corps and had reached the outskirts of Appomattox Court House when a flag of truce passed through its lines. A few enemy sharpshooters kept firing from the cover of the village houses, however, and some of Pattee's command began shooting back. As the brigade commander rushed forward to order his men to stop, a sharpshooter's bullet passed close by him and struck a mounted cavalryman who had come up to observe the fracas. According to a soldier who was present, the rider "bowed forward on the pommel of his saddle, but seemed unable to dismount or help himself in any way. A couple of the boys lifted him to the ground, but he died within a few minutes. He did not utter a word."

A bit further to the right of this occurrence, skirmishers from Joshua Chamberlain's brigade were moving toward the village when an artillery shell landed in their midst, mortally wounding Lieutenant Hiram Clark of the 185th New York. "A group of sad-eyed officers gathered around the body," wrote one observer, "and it seemed, under the circumstances, a particularly hard fate."

Union

The firing west of Appomattox Court House began to die down soon after 10:00 A.M. By now the leading elements of Griffin's Fifth Corps had linked up on Gibbon's right, further closing the circle. Then, at various points along the contending lines, flags of truce began to appear.

One of the more dramatic incidents in this phase of the action took place when one of those flags was raised in the position held by George Custer's division, inspiring the impetuous officer to ride into the enemy lines and demand an unconditional surrender. He confronted James Longstreet, who listened with barely suppressed irritation as the young Federal threatened to renew the action and vowed that Longstreet would be held responsible for any further bloodshed. Longstreet curtly dismissed Custer and, according to one bystander, told him to "go ahead and have all the bloodshed he wanted." By the time Custer returned to his lines, a ceasefire had been ordered to allow Grant to meet with Lee.

Confederate

The moment John Gordon learned from Lee that "there was a flag of truce between General Grant and himself," he ordered that a corresponding message be sent to the Union troops on his front. At the same time, he began to pull his troops back to the east, through Appomattox Court House, leaving only a skirmish line to mark the former Confederate position west of the village. True to his vow, Fitzhugh Lee sent two of his brigade-sized divisions off toward Lynchburg, while a third fell back with

Gordon's foot soldiers. Some of the escaping Rebel cavalry units got caught in a firefight with Union troopers prowling the flank, but the combat was soon broken off and the Southern horsemen allowed to withdraw.

Once he had sent his men on their way, Fitzhugh Lee turned to his staff and said, "I don't wish to be included in the surrender. Come, let us go. General Lee no longer requires my poor services." Bullets were still buzzing about the command group, and before Fitzhugh Lee could leave the field, one of his aides tumbled from his horse with a shriek of pain. The general hurried to his side. It was Lieutenant Charles Minnigerode, his favorite aide-de-camp. The wound was a bad one, and the young officer could not be moved. "Take your pistol and kill me," he cried to his commander in agony. Believing the boy to be dying, Fitzhugh Lee told the surgeon to pin a note to his jacket, identifying the body and requesting that his father, the Reverend Charles Minnigerode of Richmond, be notified of his son's death. Lee and the rest of his staff rode off toward Lynchburg.

Somehow the badly wounded officer managed to pen a few last lines to his mother. "I am dying — but I have fallen where I expected to fall," he wrote. "Our cause is defeated but I do not live to see the end of it."

Robert E. Lee, meanwhile, had ridden toward Appomattox Court House before deciding to wait under an apple tree in Sweeney's Orchard for some definite word from Grant. While waiting, he had a number of conversations with various officers, among them a colonel of engineers who remembered his saying that "he felt it to be his duty to meet General Grant for the purpose of negotiating terms of surrender, and stopping further sacrifice of life." Lee also spoke for a while with James Longstreet, who had known Grant before the war. Lee worried that his failed attempt to transform Grant's surrender request into a larger peace discussion might now cause the Federal to impose harsher terms. Longstreet tried to assure Lee that Grant was as good as his word, but Lee seemed unconvinced. At last Longstreet declared that "in that event he should break off the interview and tell General Grant to do his worst." Recalled Longstreet, "The thought of another round seemed to brace him, and he rode with Colonel Marshall, of his staff, to meet the Union commander."

Union

Grant and his party had reached a point approximately four miles west of Walker's Church when Meade's courier found them and delivered the note that Lee had dictated to Colonel Marshall. John Rawlins, Grant's chief of staff, read it first and then handed it to Grant, who scanned it without expression before returning it to Rawlins with the comment, "You had better read it aloud, General." According to reporter Sylvanus Cadwallader, who was also present, "Rawlins drew a long breath, and in his deep sepulchral voice, a little tremulous by this time, read the following dispatch from Lee":

April 9, 1865

Lieut. Gen. U. S. Grant,
    Commanding U.S. Armies.

General:
    I received your note of this morning on the picket-line, whither I had come to meet you and ascertain definitely what terms were embraced in your proposal of yesterday with reference to the surrender of this army. I now request an interview in accordance with the offer contained in your letter of yesterday for that purpose.
                    Very respectfully, your obedient servant,
                                R. E. Lee,
                                    General

There was a halfhearted attempt to raise three cheers, but everyone was simply too choked up over the news. Grant at last turned to Rawlins, whose voice had been the loudest in counseling him to reject Lee's previous request for broad peace talks.

"How will that do, Rawlins?" Grant asked.

"I think *that* will do," Rawlins replied.

Grant later recalled that his headache was cured the instant he read Lee's message. He turned to Lieutenant Colonel Ely S. Parker of his staff and dictated a reply:

Headquarters Armies of the U.S.
April 9, 1865

General R. E. Lee
    Commanding C.S. Army:

Your note of this date is but of this moment (11:50 A.M.) received. In consequence of my having passed from the Richmond and Lynchburg road to the Farmville and Lynchburg road I am at this writing about four miles west of Walker's church, and will push forward to the front for the purpose of meeting you. Notice sent on this road where you wish the interview to take place will meet me.

> Very respectfully, your obedient servant,
> U. S. Grant,
> Lieutenant-General

The note was given to another member of Grant's staff, Lieutenant Colonel Orville E. Babcock, who spurred ahead to deliver it while the rest of the party followed behind.*

Officers from both sides now began to congregate near Appomattox Court House. General Sheridan and his staff and escort, a hundred or so riders in all, were passing through the Union lines toward the Confederate outposts when a group of Rebel skirmishers fired a volley at them. Recollected a New York cavalryman, "They were about 500 yards away, and no one was hurt. Sheridan stopped his horse and stood up in his stirrups and the language he used was rather emphatic. The firing ceased and he rode forward to the Court House."

A small group of Federal and Confederate officers gathered near the old courthouse building "and talked over old times," as one recalled. Most tried to keep the conversation on the light side, but not Sheridan. "He is for unconditional surrender and thinks we should have banged right on and settled all questions without asking them," a participant later remembered. A reporter standing well outside this circle of officers noted that this "time of remaining together was spent waiting the arrival of Lieutenant-General Grant and an interview between the latter and General Lee."

Other Union soldiers wandered across the recently contested fields. One Yankee found young Charles Minnigerode, Fitzhugh Lee's badly wounded aide. Still in terrible pain, Minnigerode again asked to be put out of his misery. "No I won't Johnny Reb, you might get well," the Federal said.

Four days later, from a Union hospital bed in Farmville, Minnigerode wrote his father, "I suffer intensely, but my hopes of recovery are good." He would live.

---

* En route to meet Lee, Grant encountered another courier, this one carrying the duplicate note that Lee had written at Meade's suggestion. As it contained no new information, it was received without comment.

Confederate

Grant's emissary Babcock found Lee before 1:00 P.M., waiting under the apple tree. He handed Grant's note to the Confederate general, who fastidiously noted the time of receipt on the envelope. After reading it, Lee asked Babcock if he would send a message in Grant's name to Meade, requesting an extension of the ceasefire until Grant could send his own directive. Babcock agreed and sent off the message.

Lee then asked Charles Marshall to find a place in the village where he and Grant might meet. Marshall had been gone only a short while when his orderly returned to lead the party to the place the staff officer had chosen — the residence of Wilmer McLean.*

Lee had wanted Colonel Walter Taylor to be with him at this time, but the young aide could not face the prospect of surrender and had begged off. Accompanied by an orderly, Joshua B. Johns, Lee rode to the McLean House with Babcock and his orderly, Captain William Mckee Dunn. While Johns and Dunn waited outside, Lee and Babcock went into the front room, where Marshall was waiting. As the Confederate staff officer later recalled, "General Lee, Babcock and myself sat down in McLean's parlour and talked in the most friendly and affable way," killing time until Grant arrived.

The Surrender

Grant and his party arrived at the McLean House at about 1:30 P.M. Grant led the group inside so that the Union officers could be introduced to Lee, and then the two commanders spent a few moments in private conversation. According to Charles Marshall, "They engaged for a short time about their former acquaintance during the Mexican War."

The normally phlegmatic Grant was struggling in the grip of conflicting emotions. He had achieved a great military triumph but could find no elation in his victory. "I felt anything rather than rejoicing at the downfall of a foe who had fought so long and valiantly, and had suffered so much for a cause," he later wrote.

It was Lee who finally put matters back on track when, as Marshall recalled, he reminded Grant "that he had come to discuss the terms of

---

* Ironically, McLean had moved his family to Appomattox Court House in 1863 from Bull Run, the site of major engagements in 1861 and 1862. McLean had promised his family that they would live in a place "where the sound of battle would never reach them."

surrender of his army . . . and he suggested to General Grant to reduce his proposal to writing."

Grant asked Colonel Parker for his order book and bent thoughtfully over the blank paper. "I did not know the first word that I should make use of in writing the terms," he reflected. "I only knew what was in my mind, and I wished to express it clearly, so that there could be no mistaking it." Grant wrote quickly and reviewed the result with Parker, who made a few changes and then passed it over to Lee.

The terms were generous: soldiers and officers to be paroled and allowed to return to their homes, officers to retain their side arms and other personal property. Lee noticed a word omission and, with Grant's permission, corrected it. Remembering Fitzhugh Lee's concern about his men's horses, Lee explained to Grant that soldiers in the C.S. cavalry and artillery personally supplied their mounts, and he asked if they would be able to retain them. Grant replied that while it was not part of the terms as he had written them, he would see to it that orders were issued to allow the men to keep their animals.

Lee thanked him. "This will have the best possible effect upon the men," he said, "it will be very gratifying and will do much toward conciliating our people."

Ely Parker now made a clean copy of the surrender terms. While he was doing so, some of the officers present took the opportunity to say a few words to General Lee. When Parker was finished, Lee asked Marshall to draft an acceptance. The officer's first draft was too formal for Lee's taste.

"Don't say, 'I have the honor to acknowledge the receipt of your letter of such a date,'" he chided Marshall. "He is here, just say, 'I accept those terms.'" Marshall redrafted the letter, and Lee approved the revision. While Marshall was finishing the clean draft, there was further negotiation among those in the room, with Lee agreeing to return the thousand or so Union prisoners he was holding, and Grant promising to provide 25,000 rations for the hungry Confederate soldiers.

Headquarters, Army of Northern Virginia
April 9, 1865

Lieut-Gen. U. S. Grant,
    Commanding Armies of the United States

General: I have received your letter of this date containing the terms of surrender of the Army of Northern Virginia as proposed by you. As they are substantially the same as those expressed in your letter of the 8th instant, they are accepted. I will proceed to designate the proper officers to carry the stipulations into effect.

> Very respectfully, your obedient servant,
> R. E. Lee
> General

Then it was over. The time was just before 3:00 P.M.

After a little more talk, Lee and Marshall left. Grant and his party filed out the door to see them off, Grant stepping down off the porch and saluting his adversary by raising his hat. Then the Union commander went back into the house to supervise the drafting of a series of orders necessitated by the new circumstances. So engrossed was he in making certain that all the necessary instructions were issued that it was not until he had left the McLean House and was riding back toward his headquarters that he realized he had never officially notified Washington. Grant dismounted at once, sat down on a large stone alongside the road, and wrote the following message to be sent to the secretary of war:

> General Lee surrendered the army of Northern Virginia this afternoon on terms proposed by myself. The accompanying additional correspondence will show the conditions fully.

Union

Word of Lee's surrender quickly spread along the Union positions on both fronts. The message was brought to the 39th Illinois, in Ord's command, by a mounted officer who appeared out of nowhere, shouting "Lee's surrendered!" over and over. Recalled a soldier, "When the astounding news was fairly comprehended that Gen. Lee had surrendered — that the war was over — these weary, war-worn veterans began to yell at the top of their voices — some rolling on the ground and yelling, others shouting and singing; others, again, flinging to the air their hats and blankets shouting!"

A New Jersey infantryman in Humphreys's corps never forgot the moment when George Meade passed along the line calling out, "Boys, it's all right." "Then a glad shout went up, which was echoed, and re-echoed all along our line, like magic the glad tidings spread. Men were shouting, batteries firing, hats were in the air, and after the excitement had subsided, we realized that the war was over and our occupations gone, and now for home, sweet home."

A staff officer with Meade felt a brief rush of pity for the man they had defeated. "Poor old Robert Lee! His punishment is too heavy — to hear those cheers, and to remember what he once was!"

Confederate

"It was some time before we knew the crushing truth," a North Carolina officer later wrote. "Oh! but it is a bitter, bitter humiliation." "When the news came," recalled an Arkansas officer, "notwithstanding I had been partially prepared, to me it was a mental shock that I am unable to describe, just as if the world had suddenly come to an end." "Men expressed in various ways the agonizing emotions that shook their souls and broke their hearts," one gunner noted.

A few learned of the surrender from Lee himself. Captain Frederick M. Colston was with a group that gathered around Lee as he returned from the McLean House. Colston later described the scene: "He stopped his horse, and looking around, said: 'Men, we have fought the war together and I have done the best I could for you. You will all be paroled and go to your homes until exchanged.' I was close to him and climbed upon a wagon-hub to see and hear distinctly. . . . I looked around and the tears were in my eyes and on many cheeks where they had never been brought by fear. . . . The rest of the day was given to sad reflection and gloomy forebodings."

Monday, April 10–Thursday, April 13

The thunderclap of Lee's surrender echoed throughout the North louder than any other event of the war, save perhaps the firing on Fort Sumter. "Everybody *here* is half crazy," exclaimed a Delaware woman. "The men have holiday, and all the bells, including the Church bell, have never ceased ringing! It is a great day!" In Keokuk, Iowa, the sister of a soldier serving with Sherman likewise noted that all the bells of that town, "fire, school, and church bells, merrily jangled together. The fire companies displayed their skill by throwing a stream of water over the Estes Hospital. Every horse nearly, had a flag attached to his head and I never saw Main Street look as gay as it did with the flags today."

The importance of the event was underscored in countless different ways. The philosopher Ralph Waldo Emerson wrote that it was "a joyful day . . . & proud to Allegheny ranges, Northern Lakes, Mississippi rivers & all kinds & men between the two Oceans, between morning & evening stars." In New York, diarist George Templeton Strong celebrated the end of "the rebel army of the Peninsula, Antietam, Fredericksburg, Chancellorsville, The Wilderness, Spotsylvania Court House, and other battles. . . . It can bother and perplex none but historians henceforth forever. . . . God be praised!"

The novelist Herman Melville, testing the paths of poetry, sought to elevate the event to a higher plane with verse that read, in part:

> *The warring eagles fold the wing,*
> *But not in Caesar's sway;*
> *Not Rome o'ercome by Roman arms we sing,*
> *As on Pharsalia's day,*
> *But Treason thrown through a giant grown,*
> *And Freedom's larger play.*
> *All human tribes glad token see*
> *In the close of the wars of Grant and Lee.*

Other poetic lines, aimed at a broader audience, were penned by a Virginia woman for a song titled "General Lee's Surrender":

> *I can never forget the day Lee*
> *And his soldiers had to part,*
> *There was many a tear to wipe away,*
> *And many a sad and weary heart.*
>
> *'Twas vain! for an unnumbered host*
> *Closed round our small heroic band,*
> *The General saw that hope was lost*
> *And sadly gave up his command.*

The pleasant weather began to change during the night of April 9, and by dawn on April 10 the encampments around Appomattox Court House were hunched under what one diarist called a "drizzling rain." The mood of most of the Southern soldiers was one of relief. "The Blue and Gray mix very freely together, many of the Blue dividing rations with our boys," a South Carolinian wrote. "All are glad that the war is over." For one Tar Heel, the "universal sentiment was that the question in dispute had been fought to a finish and that was the end of it." "So good-natured have we become that we would probably even consent to being rolled in the mud," a Maine volunteer noted in his journal. At least one Yankee officer believed that the "last hope of the Rebellion is extinguished. They are and feel themselves to be a whipped people."

Soldiers of both sides began a lively trade in selling pieces of the apple tree under which, it was said, Lee had surrendered. "Why they were paying $5.00 and $10.00 for chips," a Pennsylvania soldier exclaimed. No one was ever sure how many trees disappeared to satisfy this suddenly lucrative market for mementos. A Maine cavalryman recalled it as being a "large whitewood tree," adding that soon after he first saw it, "you couldn't find a piece of it as big as a two-cent piece. It has literally been dug up by the roots. Even the old dead leaves on the ground had been gathered as souvenirs."

A similar wave of trophy hunting engulfed the Wilmer McLean residence. One observer noted that "curious officers of every grade inundated the house. Everything that would do for a relic, however unwieldy, was confiscated or bought, and Mr. McLean seemed likely to pay a high price for the glory of going down to history on the arm of a great event." Horace Porter, who wrote that McLean seemed near a nervous breakdown at that time, also recorded that no item was too small or inappropriate for the souvenir hunters. "A child's doll was found in the room, which the younger officers tossed from one to the other, and called the 'Silent Witness.' This toy was taken possession of by Colonel Moore of Sheridan's staff." After reading Porter's comment concerning McLean's state of mind, the latter's son-in-law wondered why Porter should have expressed surprise at his condition. "Any man would be so when his house was being robbed before his eyes," he declared.

Six high-ranking officers — three Union, three Confederate — met at the McLean House to draw up the formal terms of surrender. They spent much of the day working through the fine print and at last emerged with a five-point document that specified the protocol of the surrender ceremony; called for all public horses and seized private property to be confiscated; promised that officers' baggage would be shipped by the U.S. Quartermaster Department; allowed artillerymen and cavalrymen to keep their personal animals; and set a twenty-mile zone around Appomattox Court House, beyond which any units operating on April 8 were excluded from the capitulation.

At about nine o'clock in the morning, U. S. Grant left his headquarters for an unscheduled meeting with Robert E. Lee. Grant halted at the Confederate picket line while word of his arrival was carried to the Rebel chief. Lee promptly rode out, and the two met at about ten o'clock on a small knoll east of the village, just off the Richmond-Lynchburg Stage Road. They sat on horseback and had what Grant later described as "a very pleasant conversation of over half an hour." He had hoped to convince Lee to use his prestige to urge all other Confederate military forces to lay down their arms, but this Lee would not do "without consulting the President [i.e., Davis] first." Grant decided not to press the issue: "I knew there was no use to urge him to do anything against his ideas of what was right," he reflected.

At Lee's headquarters, the lone staff officer who had been present at the surrender, Colonel Marshall, struggled with the most difficult task he had ever been given.

"Fred," Marshall said to his friend Captain Frederick Colston, "General Lee has told me to write a farewell address. What can I say to those people?"

Colston's only help was to leave Marshall alone, but there were enough other interruptions that when Lee returned from his meeting with Grant, Marshall had to confess "that the order had not been prepared." Lee had Marshall put into the headquarters ambulance to ensure the necessary solitude, and posted an orderly outside to guarantee his privacy.

Charles Marshall finally produced the document, which Lee then reviewed. He crossed out one paragraph that he thought would "tend to keep alive the feeling existing between the North and South," and made several other small changes. Marshall took the marked-up copy to Norman Bell, a young headquarters clerk, who made copies to be distributed to all commands.

GENERAL ORDER, NO. 9
Headquarters, Army of Northern Virginia
April 10, 1865

After four years of arduous service, marked by unsurpassed courage and fortitude, the Army of Northern Virginia has been compelled to yield to overwhelming numbers and resources.

I need not tell the brave survivors of so many hard fought battles, who have remained steadfast to the last, that I have consented to the result from no distrust of them.

But feeling that valor and devotion could accomplish nothing that would compensate for the loss that must have attended the continuance of the contest, I determined to avoid the useless sacrifice of those whose past services have endeared them to their countrymen.

By the terms of the agreement officers and men can return to their homes and remain until exchanged. You will take with you the satis-

faction that proceeds from the consciousness of duty faithfully performed, and I earnestly pray that a Merciful God will extend to you
His blessing and protection.

With an increasing admiration of your constancy and devotion to
your country, and a grateful remembrance of your kind and generous
considerations for myself, I bid you all an affectionate farewell.

R. E. Lee
Genl

The formal surrender ceremony for the infantry at Appomattox
Court House began early on the morning of April 12. The honor of
receiving the surrender had been given to Brigadier General Joshua
Chamberlain, who was instructed that the whole affair should be carried
out as simply as possible, "and that nothing should be done to humiliate
the manhood of the southern soldiers." A temporary promotion came
with the honor, and so, for the occasion, Chamberlain commanded the
First Division of the Fifth Corps. It would be these troops from Maine,
Massachusetts, Michigan, New York, and Pennsylvania who would take
part in the ceremony. "It was a chill gray morning, depressing to the
senses," Chamberlain recalled. "But our hearts made warmth."

The gray Confederate columns began unwinding from their camps
northeast of the village shortly after 9:00 A.M. "A thrill of excitement
ran along the line," a Maine veteran later wrote, "and exclamations like
the following: 'There they are,' 'The Johnnies are coming,' 'The Confederacy had found its last ditch,' were whispered among the men."

"While we felt humiliated, we were proud of our army record," a
Confederate soldier declared. Riding at the head of their procession was
John Gordon, whom Chamberlain thought looked "downhearted and
dejected ... almost beyond description." The Union officer had given
orders that the passing Confederates be rendered the dignity of a military
salute, and this gesture brought life back to Gordon. He smoothly returned the salutation with his sword and sent back word to his men to
return the compliment. It was, Chamberlain later recalled, "honor an-
swering honor."

Then, as the Rebel units reached an assigned point before the waiting
Federal regiments, there came the sad sequence of commands: "Halt!"
"Close up!" "Front face!" "Stack arms!" "Unsling cartridge boxes!"
"Hang on stacks!" One Federal remembered that a few of the Johnny
Rebs said "very witty things" as they gave up their arms. "If you kill as
many Rebels as you have killed Yanks, you will do very well," remarked

one to his weapon. Said another, "Good-bye gun; I am darned glad to get rid of you. I have been trying to for two years." A Maine soldier noted that it was "quite an affecting scene to see some of the various color guards, as they were about to leave the old flags they had carried so long and defended so bravely, turn and tear small pieces from the old banner, and hastily put them in their pockets as if fearing our officers would forbid their doing it." "We did not surrender our old flag but tore it to pieces," a South Carolina veteran recollected. "We surrendered an old headquarters flag instead." A Tar Heel reminisced, "While we were stacking our arms in the street I saw a young lady standing on a veranda in front of us crying. I wanted to go to her, take her in my arms and kiss her, but could not break ranks just then — too many Yankees between us."

It was not until nearly four o'clock in the afternoon that the last Confederate troops finished stacking their arms and folding their regimental flags. Remembered one teary-eyed Union man, "The Army of Northern Virginia, the pride of the Confederacy, the invincible, upon which their hopes and faith had been reposed, had disappeared forever, existing thenceforth in memory only." Before the end of the ceremony, Robert E. Lee, with a small personal escort, left for Richmond. Some of his veterans who saw him ride off ran down to the roadside, where they waved their hats and shouted, "Goodbye General, goodbye."

Most of Lee's soldiers received their paroles by April 13. Then, recalled a Tar Heel, "We were turned out into the world most of us without any money, with one weather-beaten suit of clothes, and nothing to eat, entirely on the mercy of strangers." General Chamberlain never forgot the sight that morning of these men, "singly or in squads, making their way into the distance, in whichever direction was nearest home, and by nightfall we were left there at Appomattox Court House lonesome and alone."

Aftermath

The various C.S. units that managed to elude the Federal net at Appomattox only postponed the inevitable. Many made their way to Lynchburg, where they either disbanded under orders or simply melted away without instructions. Fitzhugh Lee, who had led the last breakout from Appomattox Court House, soon gave up the "fond, though forlorn, hope that future operations were still in store for the cavalry," ordered his men to go home, and "accepted for myself the terms offered the officers of the Army of Northern Virginia." A group of diehards, numbering (one artilleryman guessed) between 1,200 and 1,500 men, "banded together, and ... ran the blockade to reach Joe Johnston's army."

On April 12, Union cavalry led by Ranald Mackenzie arrived at Lynchburg. In accepting the town's surrender, the Federal officer told the city fathers, "We come to do you no harm; let us be friends."

It was raining on April 15, the day Robert E. Lee returned to Richmond. A Baptist minister saw the general as he rode through Manchester on his way into town. "Even in the fleeting moment of his passing by my gate, I was awed by his incomparable dignity," the cleric remarked. "His majestic composure, his rectitude and his sorrow, were so wrought and blended into his visage and so beautiful and impressive to my eyes that I fell into violent weeping." A Richmond resident who observed Lee immediately after he crossed the James on one of the Yankee pontoon bridges recalled that he "looked neither to the right nor to the left, but straight ahead. The streets were filled with debris from the fire, and it was difficult to make your way through, even in the middle of the roadway."

Word quickly spread that Lee was in town, and by the time he approached his house on Franklin Street, quite a crowd had gathered to welcome him. A staff officer who knew Lee later wrote, "He seemed desirous, however, of avoiding this ovation, and, returning the greeting by simply raising his hat, rode on and reached his house ..., where, respecting his desire for privacy under circumstances so painful, his admirers did not intrude upon him."

The surrender and parole of Lee's army at Appomattox Court House did not mean that the hatreds of four years could be instantly set aside. A Massachusetts man, pulling guard duty, wrote in his diary on April 17, "A Reb, after taking the oath [of allegiance], was caught tearing up our RR tracks. The guard shot him dead where he stood." A Pennsylvania surgeon, in a letter finished on April 18, reported a similar incident: "Yesterday some rebels were hung in the vicinity.... They were caught tearing up the Railroad.... They violated their parole and were justly and summarily dealt with. There is no truth or honor in a Rebel."

A New York cavalryman on a patrol south of Petersburg saw a different aspect when his unit came upon many hundreds of ex-Confederate soldiers on their way home: "Most of them avoided our column, emerging from the woods and spreading over the fields in all directions, battle-worn veterans in dingy gray and butternut, silent and cast down. Our men respected their feelings as they passed on in scattered groups, and were as silent as they."

A hundred or so miles north of Appomattox Court House, another, smaller, and far less well known — though no less feared — Confederate force ceased to exist on April 21. Colonel John S. Mosby's 43rd Battalion of Virginia Cavalry, a unit of fewer than two hundred men, sat in sad silence as Mosby's final orders were read to them on a rainy day in Salem, Virginia. A Rebel to the last, Mosby — whose raiders had for two years kept a 1,600-square-mile region immediately west of Washington in such turmoil that an exasperated U. S. Grant had ordered that they be summarily executed when caught — had chosen to scatter his men back to their home communities rather than have them surrender to Federal authorities. Once his orders to this effect had been read, Mosby stood alongside the road to shake hands with each of his soldiers. Remembered one, "It was the most trying ordeal through which we have ever passed."

On April 27 the Union Sixth Corps, following the route Lee had once intended to take, completed a five-day march from Burkeville to Danville, Virginia. "The people looked at us with disgust in their faces as we marched through the streets with drums beating and colors flying," remembered a Rhode Island officer. "I did not see a smiling face except among the slaves, who of course were glad to see us. 'We have been waiting for you!' was shouted to us many times."

While the bulk of the corps entered campsites located south of Danville proper, a provost force was established to maintain order and dispense justice in the city itself. It was not always an easy task. One ex-slave, who had been a foreman for a nearby planter, presented himself to the provost marshall and asked for his share of the plantation so that he could put in a crop to feed his family. When the Federal officer in charge explained that he had no authority to dispense land, the black man seemed puzzled. "If you had the right to take Master's niggers you had the right to take Master's land too," he said. "And what good will freedom do the niggers if they get no land to work to make their bread?"

Chapter Six

"For God's sake, cease firing! We have the fort!"

———◁◦▷———

Even as Lee's army wound its way toward Appomattox Court House, military operations in the heartland of the Confederacy continued apace. In central Alabama, James Wilson and his cavalry army pressed toward Selma, while along the eastern side of Mobile Bay, Union forces under E. R. S. Canby closed the ring around the two bastions that defended Mobile. The war would not be over until every Confederate force had laid down its arms.

———◁◦▷———

Saturday, April 1

South Alabama, near Mobile

The siege of Spanish Fort entered its sixth day to the boom of artillery fire and the stray cracks of sharpshooters' rifles. Morale on the Federal side was high. An Illinois boy writing home today reported that "our heavy artillery & mortars . . . are now pounding away at the Johnnies. They do not seem to reply with their artillery as much as I should think they would. . . . I scarcely ever see the boys in better spirits than now, in every camp the boys play ball & other games." Yet the likelihood that they would soon be ordered to charge the enemy's works somewhat muted the lighthearted mood. "Jokes for 1st of April have been scarce," an Iowa soldier observed.

Nobody on the Federal side was expecting Spanish Fort to be a walkover. "Those who came here under the impression that we had an easy job have had that idea dispelled several days since," an officer in the 122nd Illinois explained in a letter. The commander of the nearby 117th Illinois concurred: "If the Rebels [are] determined to hold Mobile to the last, we shall have to fight our way inch by inch," he wrote his wife.

North of Spanish Fort, the Fort Blakely warning posts were put on alert after scouts reported the approach of Major General Frederick Steele's expeditionary column out of Pensacola. W. P. Chambers stood with a detail of a hundred men from the 46th Mississippi, watching over one of the main roads leading in from that direction. A Yankee probing force appeared in the afternoon but was turned back so easily that the men felt a surge of cockiness. When their worried commander sent orders for them to withdraw from their exposed position, the captain in charge begged to remain.

Then the enemy suddenly reappeared, this time in great strength. "Judged by the number of flags in sight, there were three or four regiments bearing down on our little handful of men," Chambers recalled.

A fighting retreat was attempted, but blue-coated cavalry cut in behind the small Mississippi detail and then charged from the rear. "In a moment more they were among us," remembered Chambers, "slashing with their sabers and with oaths and opprobrious epithets . . . calling on us to 'halt' and to 'surrender.' " The little command dissolved, with some men finding their way to safety, others to death or captivity.

Central Alabama: On the Road to Selma

Union

James Wilson's cavalrymen were on the move early this morning. It was, recalled one of Wilson's aides, "in the glow of a generous Springtime" that the Union troopers left their camps outside Montevallo and took up the roads leading south. "The first two miles were without incident," continued the aide, "and then began again the keen crack of the spencer and the frequent clang from the 'draw saber.' This continued for several miles, with few and short interruptions, to the indifferent hamlet of Randolph."

It was here that Wilson's luck took a decided turn for the better. One of his patrols reported in at 9:00 A.M. with an important prisoner, a courier carrying three messages from Nathan B. Forrest to his subordinates. The young Federal general felt a rush of elation as he examined the dispatches, which not only pinpointed the locations of one of Forrest's largest units (Brigadier General William H. Jackson's division) and many of his smaller ones but also detailed the enemy leader's plan to concentrate his forces in front of and behind Wilson. Jackson was to come in from the northwest and assail the Union rear while Forrest himself blocked the front. Crowed Wilson, "I now knew exactly where every division and brigade of Forrest's corps was, that they were widely scattered and that if I could force the marching and the fighting with sufficient rapidity and vigor, I should have the game entirely in my hands."

The key to checkmating Jackson lay in Centreville, fifteen miles west of Randolph, where a single bridge spanned the rain-swollen Cahaba River. Wilson dispatched a brigade to block that crossing and, if possible, to link up with Croxton's brigade, which he had detached in that direction two days earlier. At the same time, he ordered Brigadier General Eli Long and Brevet Major General Emory Upton to move their divisions south along parallel roads to break up any concentration of forces that Forrest might attempt.

Once more the powerful mounted columns pushed along the dirt roads, and once more the thin crackle of carbine fire marked the points where the Federal advance met the Rebel rear guards. A trooper in Long's division remembered it as "one of the finest countries for skirmishing I ever saw."

Confederate

Nathan B. Forrest was furious. Try as he might, he just could not get his subordinate commanders to move as quickly as the situation demanded. The small force under his immediate command — perhaps two thousand men altogether, members of Colonel Edward Crossland's Kentucky brigade, Brigadier General Philip D. Roddey's division, and a scattering of other cavalry and state militia units — was doing its best to delay Wilson's advance, but Forrest was desperately counting on Brigadier General James R. Chalmers to bring more troops up from the south to meet him near Plantersville. Word now arrived that these reinforcements were not south of him but off to the west, where they were bogged down in miry terrain. Forrest fired off an angry message to his errant commanders and then made a characteristically bold decision to turn and fight the advancing Federals.

Brigadier General Frank C. Armstrong, commanding his militia, reported finding a good defensive site six miles north of Plantersville. Forrest promptly ordered his troops to occupy it. The position his men took stretched across the convergence of the Selma and Old Maplesville roads, with the right flank anchored on Mulberry Creek and the left lying across a low ridgeline to a point just above Bolger Creek. The state militia covered the right, while Roddey's division blocked the Selma Road and Crossland's Kentuckians took position on the far left flank. Four guns swept the Selma Road, with two more posted on the right.

Union

The Federal column moving down the Selma Road engaged Forrest's outposts at about four o'clock in the afternoon.

Eli Long's division struck Forrest's picket line first. Four companies of the 72nd Indiana made the contact: "We encountered the enemy in force . . . ," an Indiana soldier reported, "in a good position with . . . artillery planted." The rest of the regiment was deployed on the west side of the road and closed on the enemy's fence-rail barricades. As the opposing lines swayed together, the order to charge rang out in the Union rear, and four saber-wielding companies of the 17th Indiana dashed through Forrest's front line.

Upton's division had by this time come on the scene by way of the Old Maplesville Road. Upton and his staff stared at what one of them later described as a "line of earthworks hurriedly constructed upon the brow of a gently sloping hillside, manned by a presentable body of dismounted cavalry, supporting a battery of ten-pound iron guns." Brevet Brigadier General Andrew J. Alexander, commanding Upton's leading brigade, promptly ordered one Iowa and two Ohio regiments into a battle line.

Confederate

The four Indiana saber companies from Long's division punched through Forrest's Selma Road line and slashed their way into the four-gun battery. Forrest, who had ordered his personal escort to support the cannon, watched coolly as the blue-coated riders pounded through the gun positions. One Federal rider lost control of his horse, which crashed against a gun wheel, dismounting the weapon and throwing the terrified Yankee to the ground, where he was killed by an artilleryman swinging a rammer staff.

Forrest's supports charged into the Federal column, breaking it just behind the lead squadron. The main body was deflected into some woods and managed to cut its way back to friendly lines. The isolated lead group of sixteen men, under Captain James D. Taylor, spotted Forrest's headquarters flag and hacked a path toward it. "Fortunately for the escort," recalled one of Forrest's bodyguards, "the Federals were using the saber while we had our six-shooters." Remembered another, "Every one of us, the general, staff, and escort, were surrounded by Federals, and it . . . was . . . every man for himself." "It seemed as if those fellows were bent on killing the general," a staff officer noted, "whom they recognized at once as an officer of high rank. I saw five or six slashing away at him with their sabers at one time. He was very hard pressed by these men."

A lieutenant in the escort company watched in horror as one of the enemy troopers knocked the pistol out of Forrest's hand. "Private Phil Dodd was fortunately near and spurred his horse to the general's rescue, and shot the Federal soldier," the lieutenant recalled. Taylor, the Yankee captain, then closed with Forrest, who desperately fended off the cutting saber blows with his arm. Another member of the escort, Lieutenant John Eaton, asked Forrest if he wanted his assailant shot. As a friend of the young officer later related, "The General said yes, and Eaton dropped him out of the saddle."

Union

Hardly had the Indiana attack been beaten back when Upton's men charged forward along the Old Maplesville Road. One of Upton's aides recollected, "There is a fast rush and a stubborn fight against odds, but we literally ride over their rail barricades capturing many prisoners and two guns."

Even as Forrest was trying to withdraw his men to a secondary position on the south side of Bolger Creek, a fresh enemy battle line pressed down the Selma Road. Caught between the two fires, Forrest's hope for a controlled retreat dissolved. "The road was strewn with guns, belts, cartridge boxes, coats and hats," an Iowa cavalryman exulted. " 'Too fast for their *goods!*' the boys would say."

Reviewing this action long afterward, one of Upton's officers mused on its name. "The proportions of this affair graded it up, in the nomenclature of war, to the name and dignity of a battle. In this remote region, so barren of designations, it seemed difficult to find a suitable appellation. But a little meeting-house, hitherto unnoticed, cropped out from the midst of the timber. Its people had christened it Ebenezer, and, as the fight was nearest this as any known place, the triumph went down among the annals as 'The Battle of Ebenezer Church.' " "This is certainly 'April Fools' day," an officer with Long wrote at the end of his memorandum of this action.

Confederate

"It was impossible to concentrate our troops," a Confederate soldier bitterly observed. The Southern newspapers were unforgiving. "The disaster is not attributed to a want of men," editorialized one of them. "There has been a want of co-operation. Some of Forrest's men did not come to time, and some of his men disgraced themselves. This is the secret of our failure."

Union

Wilson's men captured three hundred prisoners and three artillery pieces, at a cost of twelve dead and forty wounded. Forrest had no choice but to shepherd his units toward the waiting entrenchments at Selma. Word again went out to his scattered commands to join him there for what was shaping up to be his last stand.

James Wilson had scarcely finished celebrating his little victory when Fortune not only smiled on but positively grinned at him. Emory Upton personally delivered a prisoner whom his men had picked up, "an English civil engineer named Millington, who had been employed on the fortifications at Selma." Well before daybreak, Wilson had a full sketch of the Selma defenses in his hands. He now held the key to the main object of the campaign.

Sunday, April 2

South Alabama, near Mobile

To hear Alabama artilleryman Robert Tarleton tell it, the Federal investment of Mobile was a bust. "Our city is not at all changed in appearance," he wrote to his bride-to-be today. "The band plays in the square as usual and to judge from the display on such festive occasions, you would never suppose it is in a state of siege, although Gen'l. Maury says so." An officer at headquarters concurred. "We are confident of holding our own," he noted in a dispatch. "The men in fine spirits." Continued Tarleton, "I think we are going to win this little game."

Tarleton would have found limited agreement among the soldiers in blue on the east side of the bay. "This work of taking Mobile is a job of more magnitude than I at first imagined," an Iowa soldier in the Sixteenth Corps wrote in his diary, "but it must come at last."

The Federals undertook their assigned tasks knowing full well that death awaited the unwary and the unlucky. Lieutenant Colonel Jonathan Merriam was on a voluntary detail, riding as an aide with a small party sent to establish communication between the troops besieging Spanish Fort and those investing Fort Blakely, when the horse directly behind his stepped on a torpedo. "Blinded by the smoke and sand and stunned by the terrific explosion we staggered like drunken men," Merriam recounted. "I realized in a moment that I was not killed[,] but for some moments could not comprehend what had happened. . . . That we were not all killed is certainly a wonder and that none were seriously hurt is more than strange. . . . As I sat upon my horse for a few minutes afterward and reflected upon what had occurred I could but thank God for preserving me."

While the siege of Spanish Fort was entering its seventh day, that of Fort Blakely was just beginning. Black soldiers serving with Major General Frederick Steele made first contact this morning as they closed on the fort's northern perimeter. More of Steele's men marched up throughout the day and gradually extended the Union line southward. A lieutenant in the 97th Illinois described the enemy's setup: "There was no town here[,] but there was a strong fort with breastworks and rifle pits stretching out for a mile or more. In front of these works was a wide and deep ditch. A wire was stretched about one foot from the ground so as to catch our feet when we tried to jump over the ditch. Between our line and the Rebels was a quarter of a mile of ground all planted full of torpedoes over which we had to pass to get to them."

By nightfall Steele's men had cut off all land access to Fort Blakely.

Central Alabama: Selma

Confederate

After spending part of the night rounding up troops scattered in the fighting near Ebenezer Church, Lieutenant General Nathan B. Forrest rode south to Selma, arriving there at about ten o'clock in the morning. According to a member of his escort, "He found the place in wild confusion. . . . Long trains of cars loaded with stores and prisoners were being dispatched toward Demopolis. Steamers at the landing were being loaded with other stores of all description to be sent up the river to Montgomery. The streets were thronged with wagons and drays laden with boxes, barrels, and parts of machinery and being driven in confusion in all directions."

Selma was a significant military prize. The city's relatively safe location in the heart of Alabama, coupled with its easy access to river and rail transportation, had prompted Confederate authorities to transfer a great deal of war manufacturing there. Selma, in 1865, housed a large arsenal, a naval foundry, a munitions plant, and a variety of other factories producing clothing and accoutrements for the war effort. In 1863 C.S. officials had used slave labor to construct a defensive ring that by 1865 had reached formidable proportions. The only flaw in this impressive scheme was that it required a very large force to hold the works, and military manpower was in sore supply at the moment.

Once in town, Forrest rode to the Gee House, headquarters for his Military Department commander, Lieutenant General Richard Taylor. As Taylor recalled, Forrest "appeared, horse and rider covered with blood, and announced the enemy at his heels, and that I must move at once to escape capture." The two conferred briefly, then separated, Taylor to finish his evacuation and Forrest to organize Selma's defenses.

Forrest mobilized the citizens of Selma using a simple rule of thumb: every male citizen had two choices — to "go into the works or into the river." As one resident later recollected, "Everybody who could walk was called upon to go into the breastworks with whatever arms could be procured. Squads of armed men were traversing the streets and examining the various buildings for soldiers to go to the breastworks, sparing nothing that wore pantaloons."

Forrest stationed his best troops in the likeliest trouble spots. According to one of those veterans, "The escort took position in the trenches on the extreme left, the weakest point, and Roddey's troops were placed on our right. Then the home guards and mixed multitude were strung out in a thin line along the remainder of the works, and instructed to hold the trenches at all hazards and never leave until they should receive orders to retire."

Even with all these bodies in position, Forrest's men still offered only a facade of defense. "The place was well fortified, but we didn't have men enough to man the trenches," one Mississippi cavalryman complained. "They were from five to ten steps apart in the ditches." Yet the old hands were far from disheartened: "I really wanted to go in the fight, as it appeared we were going to have good breastworks, and in all the fighting we had ever done, we had to fight them in the open or in their own works," declared one.

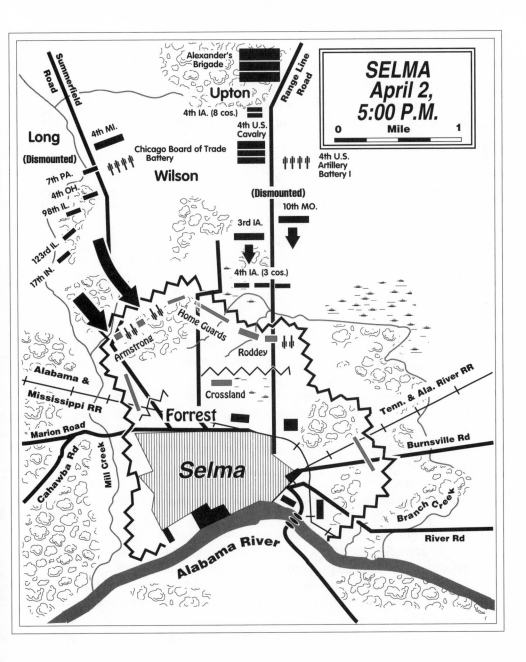

SELMA
April 2,
5:00 P.M.

0   Mile   1

Summerfield Road

Alexander's Brigade

Upton

4th IA. (8 cos.)

4th U.S. Cavalry

Range Line Road

4th MI.

Long

(Dismounted)

Chicago Board of Trade Battery

Wilson

4th U.S. Artillery Battery I

7th PA.

4th OH.

98th IL.

(Dismounted)

10th MO.

123rd IL.

3rd IA.

17th IN.

4th IA. (3 cos.)

Home Guards

Armstrong

Roddey

Alabama &

Crossland

Mississippi RR

Tenn. & Ala. River RR

Forrest

Marion Road

Burnsville Rd

Cahawba Rd

Mill Creek

Selma

Branch Creek

River Rd

Alabama River

161

Shortly before two o'clock in the afternoon, Richard Taylor left Selma on a yard locomotive bound for Demopolis. Soon after, when Forrest was in the telegraph office sending out urgent appeals for reinforcements, a black youngster came racing down the street screaming, "The Yankees is cum." Forrest bounded out of the office and sprang into the saddle. The battle for Selma was under way.

Union

Brevet Major General James H. Wilson had his men up before daybreak and on the road before sunrise. "Mile after mile through a thickly settled country, dotted with houses and enclosures, and broken by corn and cotton fields, was crossed without firing a single shot," he remembered. Wilson fully expected Forrest to defend Selma with everything he had, and he worried that if his own men failed to take the city, it "would be defeat for us and would bring the entire rebel force of that region together on our back."

Wilson's column moved south along the Selma Road, also known as Range Line Road. Eli Long's division had the lead, with Emory Upton's following. Wilson planned to press Selma from the north (Upton) and northwest (Long), with the major thrust coming from the north. While his troops deployed according to this plan and his artillery began a desultory shelling of the enemy's line, Wilson, as he later recalled, "made a reconnaissance [of Selma's defenses] with my staff to verify the English engineer's plan and, much to my gratification, found it to be surprisingly accurate."

A Missouri officer under Upton recollected that in the course of an hour, "the cannon spoke plainly all along the whole line of works & the rattling of small arms became quite lively, but I knew that all this was nothing but play, & that before we could reach the city the very earth would tremble. We laid quietly on the ground, the most of the men asleep — awaiting the order for the attack." Trooper Edward Smith was riding in front of his company's lieutenant along Eli Long's battle line when a Rebel shell screamed over his head. "I looked back to see it explode," he recounted. "The Lieutenant seemed to be the object for which the shell was making and it burst under him, but he rode right on as though nothing had happened."

Wilson's careful plans were all thrown into a cocked hat at about 4:30 P.M., when Eli Long learned that a "force of rebel cavalry, estimated from 500 to 1,000 men," was attacking the troops he had left to protect the supply trains in his rear. The Confederates likely came from

Chalmers's long-absent division, with the attack itself representing a halfhearted attempt by that officer to comply with Forrest's orders. Even though the Yankee rear guard was capable of handling the slight threat posed by this force, Long feared there might be more of the enemy nearby — enough to threaten the entire operation if he hesitated. Accordingly, and without consulting Wilson, Long ordered his men to attack.

Confederate

An officer in the 1st Mississippi Cavalry reckoned that Forrest spent the last minutes before the enemy attack "either cursing Chalmers for not coming up, or praying that he might come in at night. While we were all looking — the sun was nearly down — a long, dark line of men appeared on the brow of the ridge, they moved slowly forward for a while, and then broke into a cheer and charged. . . . I hastened to my place in line, and was barely in time to caution the men not to fire till I gave the word, as they were as yet too far away for our fire to be effectual."

Union

At "General Long's 'forward' the entire line started up with a bound, yelling, shooting, and all pushing forward under a most terrific cannonade and through a perfect shower of bullets," an Illinois officer reported. The Federal line struggled across a deep ravine in front of the enemy works and then picked its way through the wooden entanglements fronting the fortifications. "Our troops charged nobly," observed a Pennsylvania trooper on the skirmish line, and "went right over the works."

Confederate

The Confederates defending alongside the Summerfield Road gave as good as they got for a few minutes. But then the Yankees came crowding right up to the foot of the earthworks. A Mississippi captain stood on the edge of the parapet and fired his revolver "five times into the struggling mass, and had commenced to reload when I heard wild cheering to the right." Remembered another Mississippian, "We thought we were getting the advantage when a shell exploded amongst the horses and they stampeded, thus a break was made through the militia." At this point, continued the captain on the ramparts, "I knew all was lost."

Union

Corporal John H. Booth of the 4th Ohio Cavalry was later reported to have been the first man on the works. According to another soldier in the regiment, Booth was "killed literally at the cannon's mouth, as a portion of his body was blown away, just as he was entering the embrasure." Another Ohio man in the charge described his close call in a letter written this evening: "When within a few yards of the fortification a bullet passed through my clothes, slightly grazing my right shoulder, then passed on, I wishing it God-speed." Not so lucky was General Long. He was within 150 yards of the main line when he was severely wounded.

"Upton," recorded James Wilson, "hearing the noise of battle to his right, punctuated as it was by the rattle and roar of the opposing artillery, waited for neither signal nor orders, but made his way through the brush, across the swamp, carrying the works in his front with a rush and but trifling loss."

The Missouri men got the word when some officers rode up to where they were lying and yelled, "Go in boys, give them hell, we have the city, we are all right, give them hell." The men scrambled to their feet and coalesced into a wild charge toward the frowning earthworks. "Every second I expected a deadly volley," remembered one officer, "but to our greatest astonishment our skirmishers bounded ahead, scaled the works, and waved their hats in triumph. The rebels were seen skedaddling in all directions."

Wilson arrived at the works carried by Long's men only moments after they had been taken. He saw that some of the fleeing Rebels were attempting to make a stand along an interior line, and hoping to scatter this concentration before it could gel, he ordered his escort detachment, the 4th United States Cavalry, to charge.

The Yankee riders quickly discovered that they were not facing a panicked foe. A noncom in the attack noted that "all at once the whole top of the embankment was one sheet of fire, flame and smoke and the bullets fairly piped and screamed through the air, . . . the fort had all of a sudden become choked full of gray uniforms and bristling with muzzles of guns and bayonets."

Deciding that it was time for some personal leadership, Wilson rode with the attacking escort detachment. He was tumbled to the ground when his horse took a bullet in its chest, but the animal regained its feet in an instant and Wilson rode it for the rest of the engagement.

A second charge was organized, this one employing the 3rd Ohio and

17th Indiana. The regrouped 4th U.S. joined in as well, and this time the enemy position was swamped by blue.

Confederate

One survivor of this last stand later recalled that the fighting was hand-to-hand at times. Only Forrest's veterans were left. The militia, one Georgia soldier wryly recollected, "threw away everything they could shed without checking speed." "The last to leave their position were the 1st Mississippi Cavalry," a member of that regiment proudly recalled. "The Confederates, beaten from their breastworks, rushed to their horses, while the streets were choked with soldiers and citizens hurrying wildly to and fro."

For all his battlefield fury, Nathan B. Forrest could also recognize when a little judicious discretion was needed. Yelling to all those who could hear him that the time had come to escape, Forrest led his escort and other survivors out of the city on the Burnsville Road.

Union

Wilson's men poured into Selma from the north and northwest. Suddenly, remembered a trooper in the 3rd Ohio, "we found ourselves in the midst of . . . blazing buildings, . . . terror-stricken citizens, [and] . . . disorganized squads and companies of Confederates." An Iowa man never forgot the Union soldiers' "yelling vengeance, for some of our men were shot from their saddles after entering the city, citizens scared, women and children screaming, excitement high everywhere."

Scattered fighting continued well into night. The combination of darkness, unfamiliar surroundings, and the disorganization that always follows a major action made it almost impossible for Federal officers to control their men, many of whom took advantage of the confusion to roam the now helpless city.

One of Wilson's aides believed that the "confusion of sounds" this night could only be "equalled . . . by Babel." "The night that followed beggars description," a member of the headquarters escort later declared. "Houses and stores were broken into and plundered. Fires broke out and threatened the city with destruction. . . . The frightened citizens could not be made to take charge of their [fire] engines, but our provost-guards managed to check the fires by morning." "A number of large buildings are on fire, making a hideous glare," another staff officer noted. "Battle and excitement join together a distracted mob on the streets, and whiskey does its part. Officers ride through the swaying crowd in search of their men, but order is not restored until the hours are small."

Taking Selma had cost Wilson 46 dead, almost 300 wounded, and 13 missing. According to his report, the "immediate fruits of our victory were 31 field guns and one 30-pounder Parrott which had been used against us, 2,700 prisoners, including 150 officers, a number of colors, and immense quantities of stores of every kind."

James Wilson's triumph was complete. "I regard the capture of Selma [as] the most remarkable achievement in the history of modern cavalry," he afterward reported. "The capture of Selma having put us in possession of the enemy's greatest depot in the Southwest was a vital blow to their cause."

Monday, April 3

Central Alabama: Selma

"Selma was a sad-looking city," wrote one of James Wilson's men as daylight revealed the extent of the damage caused by yesterday's fighting and the Confederate evacuation. "Several squares were burning," an Iowa cavalryman observed this morning, "and soldiers running with the [fire] engines, more for amusement than to put out the fire, splashing the fire and unlucky citizens." "The business part of the city was burnt," added an Illinois artilleryman, who also noted that "plenty of silver and gold coin was found and all kinds of goods."

James Wilson was awake early, with lots to do. As he wrote, "It was necessary to make our position secure and the first measure to that end was to draw in our detachments and trains and send out scouts to ascertain the enemy's position and movements." Among their other actions this day, Wilson's men rounded up all the loose horses and mules they could find. After they had replaced all they needed, there were still some five hundred excess horses and many extra mules on hand. "Fearing that these might fall into the enemy's hands when we left," Wilson later recorded, "I ordered them shot and thrown into the Alabama River, which was done."

Nathan B. Forrest, his escort, and some other Selma survivors had circled around to the north side of the city after escaping and now headed directly for Plantersville. During this late-night ride, Forrest's escort overwhelmed a lone Union outpost, killing or wounding most of the troopers from the 4th United States Cavalry who manned it.

After resting his men at Plantersville for a while, Forrest resumed his retreat toward Marion, Alabama, which lay west of Plantersville, across the Cahaba River. He skirmished briefly with the brigade Wilson had sent to Centreville on April 1, which was just now rejoining the main body. The scrap ended as quickly as it had begun, however, and Forrest continued on his way. He did not yet know it, but he had fought his last engagement.

South Alabama, near Mobile

As the siege of Spanish Fort entered its eighth day, the tempo of artillery fire picked up somewhat. Chortled one Yankee, "Parrotts, Napoleons, siege, Howitzers &c. Fun! How we did warm the Johnnies! A caisson with a reb on top of it blown up — an awful sight."

Three miles north of Spanish Fort, where the siege of Fort Blakely was in its second day, General Steele pushed his earthworks ever closer to the Confederate fortifications. On the Union right, African-American troops labored under a direct shelling from the fort as well as an enfilade fire from Rebel gunboats in the river. "Our colored boys fight well, better than the white troops," wrote an admiring Connecticut artilleryman, adding, "I pity the poor Johnnies if they ever get a chance at them."

When the guns stopped firing, the men dug. "It was by no means smooth work," a Federal officer declared, "for in some places the ground was rocky, in others it was filled with stumps and roots, and covered with large logs." In a communication sent today to General Maury in Mobile, the officer commanding Spanish Fort exclaimed, "I never saw such digging as the enemy does — he is like a mole. . . . I wish I had more men and guns. . . . It is digging all night and fighting all day."

Tuesday, April 4

Central Alabama: Selma

James Wilson continued to wait for the arrival of his detached units before making any moves away from Selma. Should he want to cross to the south side of the Alabama River, it would be necessary to rebuild the pontoon bridge that had been destroyed in the Confederate evacuation, so orders were issued today to one of his brigadiers to impound all the material needed and to press into service "all the carpenters that can be found" to do the job.

At the same time, Wilson pressed on with his grim plan to completely destroy all of Selma's "immense shops, arsenal, and foundries." His cold resolve was matched by that of his troopers, one of whom declared, "The arsenal and foundry at Selma are next to those at Richmond in extent, and their destruction will help end the war." Later in this day, this same soldier would note in his journal, "Foundry is now burning[,] shells exploding."

South Alabama, near Mobile

"Inch by inch we are moving on the Gibraltar that protects Mobile," a *Chicago Tribune* reporter wrote of this ninth day of the siege of Spanish Fort. Work on the Union entrenchments began in earnest when the sun went down and continued nearly until daylight. "We shoveled hard," remembered a Wisconsin soldier. "It was sandy enough so it was easy shoveling, but the Rebs could see the bright shovels glisten in the moonlight, and they would fire a volley at us. Then we would hug the ground, or if in the ditch would hug the bottom of that." An Ohio soldier assigned to work in the advance lines recalled how this morning his detail "went to work for dear life, every unlucky stroke against a root bringing a swift messenger from the enemy as much as to say, 'I do not know what is going on in the darkness, but there must be something going on.'"

"During the day," reported an officer, "the [Spanish Fort] garrison were quite annoying with their coehorn mortars, and troubled the infantry in their advanced pits exceedingly."* "These shells could easily be seen in their flight and were generally successfully dodged," maintained an Illinois officer, "but it kept the men very busy running backward and forward and around corners the day long."

The Union boys in the trenches found ways to hit back. An Iowa soldier facing Fort Blakely in this third day of the operations against it wrote home about one of these improvisations: "Our boys showed a little 'Yankee' ingenuity to the 'Rebs' which they never dreamed of, we made wooden mortars out of live oak, and banded them with iron to strengthen them, took them into our advanced rifle pits. By taking a small charge of powder we could throw twelve-pound shell just over the entrenchments into the very midst of the enemy, scattering death and destruction wherever they burst."

By evening Canby's men had placed seventy-five cannon of both

---

* Coehorns were light-caliber field mortars, portable enough to be used in the trenches.

heavy and light caliber around Spanish Fort. At 5:00 P.M. these guns opened a two-hour bombardment. As soon as the firing commenced, a Connecticut gunner in the artillery reserve noted, "our boys gave a cheer along the whole line. [The guns are] . . . firing as often as every second, sometimes it resembles the rolling thunder." "It was pretty noisy on our side," remarked an Illinois man in the trenches, "and looked from here as if it were pretty hot & dusty in their lines." "The earth seemed to shake like an aspen leaf," a correspondent wrote. "It seemed as if heaven had opened its artillery, and was avenging itself for the previous sins of man."

Yet such was the art of the Confederate engineers who had designed the Spanish Fort complex that, as one pointedly wrote in his diary entry for this day, there were "but few casualties on our side, not exceeding six or eight all told."

Wednesday, April 5

South Alabama, near Mobile

The siege of Spanish Fort, now in its tenth day, was taking its toll on the overextended defenders. "Enemy sweeps my flanks with heavy batteries, and presses on at all points," the post commander complained today to General Maury. "My men are worked all the time [and are] . . . wider apart than they ever were under Generals Johnston and Hood. . . . Can't you send a force of negroes, with axes[?] I can make good soldiers of the negroes." Things were somewhat better for the garrison at Fort Blakely, which was in only its fourth full day under fire. Although the Yankee lines were still outside normal rifle range, this did not prevent some Federal marksmen from making a serious nuisance of themselves, prompting Blakely's commandant to request a special squad of Confederate sharpshooters to help him deal with the problem.

An Illinois soldier busily engaged in burrowing toward Spanish Fort found time today for a tongue-in-cheek diary update: "Making fine progress with new line, a long stride towards a more intimate acquaintance with our friends on the other side. They do not seem to appreciate our advances. They will feel better in a few days when we take them by the hand, which we shall."

News of the fall of Richmond and that of Selma became official today, and was commemorated with orders for a hundred-gun salute to be fired on April 6.

Central Alabama: Selma

James Wilson continued to fret over his missing brigades — Croxton's, which he had sent on a diversionary raid on March 30, and Colonel Oscar H. LaGrange's, dispatched toward Centreville on April 1. Upton's division, which had been searching for the two since April 3, had not yet reported back, so Wilson had no information to assuage his anxiety.

In a move designed to gather information from the enemy and at the same time relieve him of the more than 2,000 prisoners taken at Selma, Wilson wrote to the Confederate commander, Richard Taylor, to propose a parole arrangement. The message was carried by his aide Captain Lewis M. Hosea, who took with him a captured Rebel officer as proof of his good faith. The two crossed the Alabama River and rode south until they were opposite the small town of Cahaba, which lay on the west bank of the north-south-running Cahaba River. In attempting to convey his intentions by shouting to a civilian party on the other side of the river, Captain Hosea was pleasantly embarrassed to be told by the group that it was empowered to surrender the city to him. Hosea brought forward the Rebel officer, who explained their particular mission. The Yankee captain and his prisoner-aide were promptly rowed over to the far bank and entertained by one of the town's finer families. Hosea never forgot how he "found in this society the most delightful gratification of being with persons of education and culture."

Thursday, April 6

Central Alabama: Selma

The division that James Wilson had sent out to locate his two wayward brigades returned today with a mixed report. Of Croxton's brigade, detached more than a week ago on a diversionary mission, there was still no news, but the other brigade, LaGrange's, returned with the search force, relieving at least some of their commander's worries. Wilson's aide Captain Hosea also came in to report that he had made contact with a member of General Forrest's staff, and that a face-to-face meeting between the Confederate officer and Wilson was scheduled for the next day.

In town, the sober work of wrecking the arsenal of the Confederacy continued. "Large conflagrations everywhere," a Yankee artilleryman noted. "Shells exploding and gunpowder blowing up. The beautiful city is in ruins."

South Alabama, near Mobile

The fifth day of the Fort Blakely siege was announced violently at 3:00 A.M. by a sortie from the garrison "with much noise and shouting, for the purpose, as it appeared, of dislodging the [Federal] . . . skirmishers." At one point the raiding force threatened to overrun a line of rifle pits held by about a dozen Yankees, who fortunately included among their number a sergeant with some imagination. As the Rebels pressed close to the position, he called out to the empty trenches behind him, "First and Second Brigade supports, forward!" Fearing a counterattack, the enemy troops fell back.

At Spanish Fort, now in its eleventh day of siege, there was little deviation from the standard program of steady spadework and deadly nuisance fire. A Wisconsin man wrote home today that the "men dig, dig, dig, day & night. . . . The rebels dig too, and we have to be cautious not to expose ourselves too far, or whiz goes a bullet, much too close to one's head to be pleasant for a timid man." "When a cannonball comes close over the reserve post, the way the boys hunt their holes is a caution," an Illinois soldier observed. "Sometimes when in a hurry, they go in head foremost, like a frog into the water."

Underlying all the grim jocularity, however, was the common assumption that, as a reporter on the scene put it, if the forts did not "capitulate ere long, . . . the works will be assaulted, and thus the affair will be short but bloody."

Friday, April 7

South Alabama, near Mobile

The Confederate defenders of Fort Blakely raided the Union trenches again this morning, inaugurating the sixth day of the siege. "They came out apparently in strong force, delivering repeated volleys and charging with cheers up to the pits of the federals," a Union officer wrote. The artillery on both sides joined in, so that, as the same officer recalled, "the tumult . . . was startling." "The Johnnies seem determined to disturb our slumbers as much as possible," the commander of an Illinois regiment wrote to his wife today. "I am becoming so accustomed to it that it doesn't disturb me much. In fact, I begin to feel fidgety when there is a lull in the discharge of artillery & musketry." The raiders were once more beaten back, with a loss to the Federal side of one man killed and two wounded.

Things were relatively quiet at Spanish Fort, where the sniping and the trench excavations continued on this twelfth day of siege. "It would be certain death to get in front of the breastworks in daylight," a soldier in the 44th Missouri confided to his wife. "Yesterday, one of the 49th [Missouri] just on our left had his gun in the port hole ready to shoot and looked over the top of the work to see something to shoot at, when a bullet struck him in the mouth, killing him instantly."

Central Alabama: Selma

Still feeling anxious about his lost brigade, James Wilson rode out to meet with Nathan B. Forrest, wondering how he might trick the wily Rebel leader into revealing what he knew about the matter. But the face-to-face session would not take place today, as the rain-swollen Cahaba River was too flooded to cross. Remembered Wilson, "I reluctantly gave up the trip and returned to the city for the night." At his orders, the 4th Kentucky Cavalry was detailed to ride out to learn the "whereabouts of General Croxton, join him, and direct him to move with his command as fast as circumstances will permit to this place."

All the while, work on the next stage of Selma's destruction proceeded. Gangs of black laborers swarmed over the arsenal grounds, "piling timber [and] tar and pouring oil over the wood work in the arsenal and yards, tearing down the out buildings so as to prevent the spread of fire to dwellings near[by,] . . . for all shall be burned some night."

Wilson was already thinking ahead to the next phase of his operation and had targeted the capital of Alabama, Montgomery, as his likely destination. In order to get there, though, his men would have to cross the flooded Alabama River with their wagons and ordnance. Fortunately, a detachment of 211 pontoniers had just arrived in Selma and was put to that task. "The bridge was over 800 feet long," one of the military engineers later wrote. "The bottom of the stream was soapstone and almost impossible to get anchors to hold."

While the pontoniers struggled against the river current, driftwood, and the slick river bottom, James Wilson planned his next move and continued to worry about his missing brigade.

Saturday, April 8

Central Alabama: Selma Area

The meeting arranged by Captain Hosea between James H. Wilson and Nathan B. Forrest took place at 1:00 P.M. this day in Cahaba, Alabama.

Forrest, recalled the young captain, "had ridden far, and was in common fatigue uniform, much soiled." Wilson thought the enemy commander "neither as large, dignified, nor striking as I expected." For his part, Forrest, whose injured arm was still in a sling, wrote no reminiscence of the meeting.

After the usual preliminaries, the two commanders left the company of their aides to speak alone for a while.

"Well, General," Forrest said, "you have beaten me badly, and for the first time I am compelled to make such an acknowledgement."

"Our victory was not without cost," Wilson returned. "You put up a stout fight, but we were too many and too fast for you."

The two went on to discuss their competing strategies at Selma, and then came the part of the conversation during which Wilson hoped to learn something about Croxton's brigade. The Federal officer suggested that they consider an exchange of prisoners, but Forrest begged off, saying that he lacked the authority for such an action. He did offer, however, to tell Wilson how many POWs he was holding and proceeded to enumerate the various Union commands represented in his prison pens. Wilson's ears pricked up when the Rebel leader mentioned having a few of Croxton's men, who had been taken around Trion and Tuscaloosa, Alabama. Noting Wilson's interest, Forrest obligingly added that the bulk of Croxton's command seemed to be going pretty much wherever it wanted to go. Wilson had heard enough. "I brought the conference to a close with the remark that it was getting late and I must return to Selma," he recalled.

As he rose to leave, Wilson inquired about Forrest's wounded arm. The Confederate explained that he had been injured at Ebenezer Church by a Yankee captain who had engaged him in personal combat and slashed him with saber strokes. "While warding these off with my arm I feared that he would give me the point of his saber instead of its edge, and, had he known enough to do that, I should not have been here to tell you about it," Forrest said.

James Wilson rode back to Selma, satisfied that Croxton was safe and that the larger operation could continue, "first against Montgomery, and afterward onward to Columbus, West Point, and central Georgia." Work on the pontoon bridge across the Alabama River was nearly completed, and Wilson could see nothing to prevent his men from getting off as scheduled, tomorrow, April 9.

South Alabama, near Mobile

Confederate

Major General Dabney H. Maury, in overall command of Mobile's defenses, visited Spanish Fort today to determine "how much longer it would be safe to keep the garrison in the place." Maury did not believe that a Federal attack was imminent and left instructions for the defenders to prepare to withdraw on April 11.

The garrison commander, Brigadier General Randall L. Gibson, did not agree with his superior's assessment. He decided to develop the extent of the enemy's preparations by opening a bombardment and skirmish-line fire. Everything was set to go at 5:30 P.M.

Union

Brevet Brigadier General Cyrus Comstock was frustrated and angry. A trusted member of U. S. Grant's inner circle, he had arrived on this front in March with the avowed purpose of urging General Canby to act quickly and decisively. Since his arrival Comstock had watched the siege unfold as a succession of opportunities lost. By April 5 he was demanding that Spanish Fort be taken ("Think we might & should do it, at once," he wrote) and, further, that eight thousand men be sent immediately to assist Wilson in Alabama's interior.

Comstock believed that the end of this tedious siege was in sight. "At last the general decided to assault in about 36 hours. A little bombardment [scheduled] in pm. beginning at 5½ pm.," he noted in his diary.

Confederate

General Gibson's artillery barrage got off just before Canby's, but his gunners were quickly smothered by the weight of the nearly simultaneous Union bombardment. A dazed Louisiana cannoneer recalled that the "din was so great it distracted our senses. . . . The cracking of musketry, the unbroken roaring of artillery, the yelling and shrieking of the shells, the bellowing boom of the mortars, the dense shroud of sulphurous smoke thickening around us — it was thought the mouth of the pit had yawned and the uproar of the damned was about us."

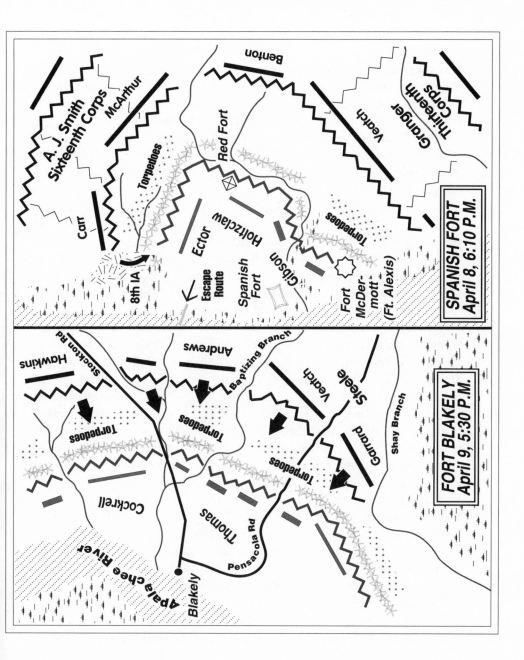

SPANISH FORT
April 8, 6:10 P.M.

A. J. Smith
Sixteenth Corps

McArthur

Carr

Torpedoes

8th IA

Ector

Holtzclaw

Gibson

Escape
Route

Spanish
Fort

Red Fort

Benton

Veatch

Granger
Thirteenth
Corps

Torpedoes

Fort
McDermott
(Ft. Alexis)

FORT BLAKELY
April 9, 5:30 P.M.

Hawkins

Stockton Rd

Andrews

Baptizing Branch

Veatch

Steele

Garrard

Shay Branch

Torpedoes

Torpedoes

Torpedoes

Cockrell

Thomas

Pensacola Rd

Blakely

Apalachee River

175

Union

Federal siege engineers had managed to plant fifty-three heavy guns and thirty-seven field pieces around Spanish Fort. When these instantly answered the blast of guns from the Confederate lines, "the effect was terrific," an Illinois soldier remembered. "This firing . . . made it seem impossible for any in the fort to survive," added an Iowa man. Another Iowa bluecoat referred to it as "one terrible storm of fire," while a *New York Times* reporter who was present felt that the effect "can be better imagined than described."

Brigadier General Eugene A. Carr, whose division held the extreme northern end of the semicircular siege lines embracing Spanish Fort, met with Colonel James L. Geddes, commanding his third brigade. Geddes, though feeling ill (Carr recalled that he was "shaking with a chill" as they talked), listened intently as Carr outlined his mission "to press with skirmishers on his right against the rebel left, feel their strength, ascertain the nature of the ground, and take as much as he could hold."

Geddes hurried back to the front, where he detailed two companies from the 8th Iowa for the assignment. The regiment's commander noted the time as precisely 6:10 P.M. when Companies A and G set out, with Company H in close support. The boggy nature of the ground on this flank was such that trenches could not be dug, so the line was established by means of gabions, aptly defined by one soldier as "grapevines made into hoops and filled with dirt." The Iowa men filed out from behind the gabion wall and plunged into what a member of the regiment later described as a "swamp thickly covered by fallen trees cut waist high and left hanging to the stumps and lying criss-cross in all shapes."

The three companies pressed ahead in the face of heavy fire from the widely spaced defenders. Then, with a last quick rush, the Iowa soldiers overran the rifle pits representing the extreme left of the Spanish Fort defenses. A member of the regiment who watched this advance from the main Union line recalled the soldiers' "frantically calling to us, 'Come on! Come on!' " The regimental commander sent a courier running back to Colonel Geddes to request permission to put the rest of the regiment in to support the three companies. The reply was slow in coming, so the Iowa colonel, believing that further hesitation would imperil the men already engaged, ordered his men forward on his own initiative. "The movement was executed with as much regularity as could be expected considering the nature of the ground," he reported. "As soon as the regiment gained the crest of the hill where our skirmishers were[,] the fight commenced in full force."

Confederate

The small Yankee party had overrun the rifle pits held by Texas troops belonging to Colonel Julius A. Andrews's brigade. A few Texans rallied around Captain James A. Howze and counterattacked. "He gave the word to charge," remembered one of them, "and the boys gave the Rebel yell and charged. Here I saw our brave young flag bearer, Billy Powers, go down. This checked us. Some one gathered up the colors and we retreated."

Union

The 8th Iowa now began the grim task of clearing out the enemy line. The Iowans were helped in this instance by the design of the works, which consisted of a series of large rifle pits unconnected by trenches. "This enabled us to attack them in detail," reported the regimental commander. "We here witnessed the spectacle of dying in the last ditch, as quite a number of rebels refused to surrender and were shot in their ditches, and on the other hand quite a number of them who were taken prisoner ought, in justice to our men, to have been killed, as they would first fire at our men after being ordered to surrender, then throw up both hands and surrender."

Colonel Geddes now ordered the rest of his brigade to advance. These additional regiments joined with the 8th Iowa and began to dig a new line of trenches at right angles to the enemy's pits.

Confederate

Following the failure of the Texans to dislodge the enemy intruders, a second attack was launched by the provost guard, which also failed. General Gibson now viewed the Spanish Fort position as irrevocably lost. The enemy had overwhelmed his weak left flank and was entrenching to secure its gains. The lodgement also commanded the garrison's only line of retreat, but thanks to the confusion and darkness the enemy seemed not yet to realize the extent of its success. Gibson's standing orders from General Maury were not to risk the loss of the garrison, so, as he later reported, "I determined . . . to withdraw my troops.

"The retreat was along a narrow treadway, about eighteen inches wide, which ran from a small peninsula, from the left flank, across the river, and over a broad marsh to a deep channel opposite Battery

Huger." Huger was one of two powerful artillery positions situated on marshy islands in the river channel.

A Louisiana gunner recalled that it was about ten o'clock at night when he and his batterymates were ordered to spike their guns and march down a steep, narrow gully to the river. "At the word, all shoes and boots were off and we stood in our stocking or naked feet in a single line upon that narrow treadway. And then, after orders to keep our guns on the off-side from the enemy, to prevent their glistening being noticed, . . . and after orders not to whisper a word on pain of being shot, we went forth." "The night was rather dark and the movement could not be hurried," Gibson explained.

Most of the troops successfully evacuated the Spanish Fort lines by midnight. Noted one officer, "The whole garrison after a terrible march through mud & water and a dense thicket of marsh canes exceeding four miles in length reached Blakeley by daylight on the next day." Most were then carried by steamer to Mobile. In his after-action report, Gibson praised the "steady valor and cheerful endurance" of his men.

Union

All along the Spanish Fort siege lines, impromptu advances were ventured as outposts reported that the enemy positions had fallen silent. Most of Carr's division now crowded into the left half of the enemy trenches, while other groups of Federals pushed into the three forts and crept toward the river. "The moon had now risen, and the reflection on the bright barrels of our infantry as they marched to take position, the signal officers with torches signaling the gunboats that we had possession, the rebel transports in the distance steaming up the bay, made it a scene long to be remembered," an Illinois soldier wrote. Although most of the garrison had fled, another Illinois man recalled that "many skulked away to be taken prisoner and all seem glad to be taken. . . . Our companies soon moved inside [the forts, and then] . . . you ought to see the boys go for the clothing and everything else they found. Well, the women of Mobile sent them out the good things."

So unexpected was this success that supporting units to the south and in the river did not at first realize that the enemy troops were gone. Federal gunboats, anchored offshore for their usual night bombardment, threw several shells into the forts before frantic signalmen could tell them to cease fire. Troops belonging to the Thirteenth Corps, holding the lines on the left of the Sixteenth, also fired at the distant targets. "For God's sake, cease firing," an Iowa officer bellowed at them. "We have the fort!"

Captain Charles J. Allen, acting chief engineer of the Sixteenth Corps, undertook a personal reconnaissance of the newly captured positions. "As I walked along," he recalled, "the moonlight appeared to grow brighter, and the sand hillocks looked like snow drifts." He had not got far when he saw the body of a well-built Rebel soldier. "I stopped, for a few seconds, and looked at him with a feeling something like wonder at the thought that a small projectile of lead could lay low such a sample of human vigor." There was another body a few steps beyond, that of a young man whose open but lifeless eyes seemed to recognize Allen. The pensive officer reflected, "I thought that, possibly, probably, the boy's parents . . . in their home, perhaps far distant, were at that moment . . . praying to the Good God to preserve their boy."

Allen continued on his journey but had gone only a few yards when a voice challenged him. "Who goes there?"

"An officer of the Union Army," Allen replied. He stepped forward to find a wounded Confederate officer who identified himself as Captain Clark. He said he had been leading a charge of the provost guard, trying to stop the Federal advance, when he was wounded. Clark was very thirsty, so Allen went off to look for some water. He found three Union soldiers, like him wandering along the abandoned works, who agreed to carry the injured Southerner back to a field hospital. Allen watched as they improvised a litter and bore him off. "It was a pleasure to me to think that I had, at least, been able to rescue him from the battlefield and get him to a place where he could be comfortable, and kindly treated."

In his final report of this action, General Canby stated, "The immediate fruits of this success were the capture of these strong forts, two miles of intrenchments with all the armament, material, and supplies, 4 flags, and more than 600 prisoners."* Federal losses for the Spanish Fort operation were 52 killed, 575 wounded, and 30 missing, for a total of 657.

Work now hurried forward on plans to assault Fort Blakely on April 9.

—◦—

Sunday, April 9

Central Alabama: Selma

James Wilson began moving his men over the pontoon bridge across the Alabama River today. "The passage was characterized by several exciting incidents," Wilson wrote, referring to the drifting trees carried against the span by the swift current. "The work of protecting the bridge

---

* The forts mentioned by Canby were strongpoints along the Spanish Fort defenses — Red Fort and Fort McDermott, sometimes called Fort Alexis.

was difficult in the extreme, but by use of skiffs the floating trees were guided either to the shore above and fastened there or through the openings of the bridge." In the course of the day's operation, one high-ranking officer, Brigadier General Andrew J. Alexander, was pitched into the swirling waters and nearly crushed by a log, but he was finally fished out without serious injury.

Behind the departing troopers, smoke curled into the cloudy sky as the remaining military stores and properties in the city were put to the torch. "The picture I beheld beggars all description," noted a Missouri cavalryman. "It was one of the grandest imaginable. In front was the dark river, with the bridge crowded. To our right were the burning buildings. To the left were the woods & in the rear were the remains of the arsenal. . . . Here were a crowd of negroes of both sexes, of all colors & of all ages, there a squad of Confederate prisoners with their guards . . . & everything illuminated by the burning buildings. I cannot describe it, but it was beautiful."

Reflected one of Wilson's staff officers, "What a wreck of a place we have left."

South Alabama, near Mobile

At Spanish Fort the unpleasant task this day was cleaning up after the battle. "The whole interior is in a perfect smash," wrote Benjamin C. Truman of the *New York Times*. "All the debris of a battlefield met our gaze. The enemy had managed to remove his wounded, but his dead he had left, right where the poor fellows lie."

In Mobile itself, rumors that Spanish Fort had been lost were confirmed when the survivors arrived and marched through the town. "I had to believe the evidence of my own eyes," remembered one civilian, "for our soldiers were passing by in squads, from an early hour, dirty, wet and completely worn out."

All attention was now on Fort Blakely. The Federal commander, Canby, had wasted little time celebrating the fall of Spanish Fort. Hardly had the victory cheers died away when whole divisions were on the move to support the Fort Blakely besiegers. Canby knew that it would not be easy to take this second fort: "The enemy's line had a development of two miles and a half," he reported. "It consisted of nine strong redoubts connected by rifle-pits and palisades, and was covered in front by slashings and abatis, and in some places by outworks of telegraph wire and by torpedoes or subterra shells."

Blakely's defenders were on full alert. Gunners in some of the C.S.

river batteries noted Canby's buildup and notified the garrison's commander, Brigadier General St. John Liddell, who placed all units "in readiness for an assault at any moment." Approximately 3,500 infantrymen and artillerists manned the redoubts and earthworks; they included everything from veterans who had fought at Vicksburg to the teenage Alabama Reserves, called up late in the war as the Confederates scraped the bottom of the manpower barrel.

Throughout the morning and well into the afternoon, the front-line fire at Fort Blakely was, if anything, lighter than usual. That, plus reports of steamers' carrying soldiers (actually Spanish Fort survivors) from the fort to Mobile, led most Union observers to conclude that the Rebels were pulling out. "The talk had been all day that the enemy were evacuating and that in a short time we would be inside their works," an Ohio infantryman affirmed.

Things were especially quiet on the Federal right, which was held by black troops belonging to Brigadier General John P. Hawkins's division. A number of line officers began to fear, as one put it, "that the prize was slipping through our fingers," so several squads were moved out into the no-man's land to find out if Blakely was being abandoned. They ran into a torrent of fire that answered that question. Supports rushed up to help the stranded parties, and for a while it seemed as if a full-scale assault were under way. Some of the enemy's rifle pits and advance trenches were taken, but attempts to pierce the main line were blasted back. "We slaughtered them fast," a C.S. veteran later bragged. The fighting here began to die down shortly before 5:00 P.M.

These actions did not impede Federal plans for an all-out attack. Each of the four divisions confronting Fort Blakely was to advance a strong skirmish line, closely backed up by heavier lines of battle. The widely spaced skirmish formations would be able to move more easily through the obstructions and get close enough to the main enemy lines to pin the defenders down long enough for the denser lines of battle to press the attack. Everything was set to go at 5:30 P.M.

All along the Union lines, the forward trenches began to fill as the skirmishers filed into their jump-off positions. An Illinois soldier assigned to one of these groups recalled, "We marched through the zig-zag ... to our advanced rifle-pits, which were within forty yards of the rebel sharpshooters' pits, and about five hundred yards from the line of forts." Behind them, more men marched into the reserve trenches in response to the order that, according to one of them, "all anticipated, and yet the boldest shrunk from hearing."

"The waiting and suspense was a severe test of courage," wrote an

Iowa soldier. "Some tried to conceal their anxiety by an effort to appear reckless, careless and brave, and whispered jokes and puns, pretending they enjoyed it immensely." "As I looked over the space between us and the fort, covered with fallen timbers, brush and everything that could hinder our progress, and thought of the torpedoes thickly planted in the ground, I will own that I never wanted to go home so badly in all my life," declared an Illinois veteran.

Then it was time.

The skirmishers began to scramble forward all along the two-and-a-half-mile front. In the portion of the line held by Brigadier General Christopher C. Andrews's division, the leading regiments were the 83rd Ohio and 97th Illinois. A man in the Ohio ranks vividly recollected "scrambling in the brush, jumping over logs, now stumbling over sharpened stakes, at another time tripping up with the telegraph wires that were laced through here and there — knee high." One of the Illinois soldiers remembered, "As we got out of the rifle pits the Captain of Company D struck a torpedo and it blew his leg off below the knee and sent it up in the air about fifty feet, and my Captain who stood next to me on my right was shot through the left shoulder."

Along Brigadier General James C. Veatch's line, bluecoats from the 8th Illinois led the way. "To reach the enemy's works it was necessary to cross three distinct lines of abatis," the regiment's commander reported. "At the second line . . . there were a number of . . . trenches filled with the enemy's skirmishers. These pits were carried and the skirmishers killed or captured."

Advancing on the Union left were troops from Illinois, Wisconsin, New York, Kansas, and Iowa, belonging to Brigadier General Kenner Garrard's division. "As a cloud we raised from the rifle-pits and with a shout and cheer onward we went," said an officer. "The enemy swept the ground with shell, grape, canister and musketry," wrote an Iowa man in the ranks. "Many brave men fell, but still we pressed forward as fast as we could run, and without firing a shot."

Behind this screen of skirmishers came the main battle formations. "It was the greatest sight I ever saw," declared a Connecticut cannoneer. "It was a glorious sight," seconded a batterymate, "a line of 15,000 men marching steadily into the jaws of death." "Had about six hundred yards to go before the works were reached," observed an officer in the reserve, "which the men did in most gallant style, on the full run, in the face of a heavy fire, falling at every jump." Added an Illinois onlooker, "Soon after a loud cheer arose from the center — another from the left and then on the right, indicating the successive points at which the works had been successfully stormed."

In some cases the skirmishers themselves actually overran the main enemy positions, while in others the impetus came from the heavier lines of battle. At all points the combat was briefly violent. "The wild scene which followed cannot be depicted," an Illinois soldier in Garrard's division maintained. "The Rebel infantry left the works or surrendered as soon as we got to them, but the artillerymen fought to the last, some of them choosing to be shot down sooner than stop shooting their pieces." Some of Garrard's Federals came up against the teenage Alabama Reserves. "Young as they were, they fought like devils," an Indiana veteran attested. In just one incident of the hand-to-hand fighting that raged all along the line, Lieutenant Angus R. McDonald, of the 11th Wisconsin, waded into the enemy trenches armed only with his sword. "He . . . succeeded in felling several of his foes, when he was shot in the thigh and bayonetted twice in the shoulder," it was reported.

The action was much the same along Veatch's and Andrews's lines. "We went over the ditch, over their breastworks and jumped down in the rifle pits right on top of them, too close to shoot them, too close to stick them with our bayonets, but we could still use the butts of our guns," recalled an Illinois soldier.

On the Union right, once it became clear that a general advance was taking place, the black troops dropped their entrenching tools, picked up their muskets, and launched an impromptu charge. "The command moved with a yell through the abatis and over torpedoes, several [of] which exploded, driving the rebels from their works and guns," recounted one officer. Another noted that many Confederates "threw down their arms and ran toward their right to the white troops to avoid capture by the colored soldiers, fearing violence after surrender." A Confederate artilleryman later testified that black troops had rushed into his battery after it raised a white flag, "brandishing their guns in great rage, accusing us of having fired upon them after we had surrendered, shooting down Captain Lanier, . . . and clubbing 'Long' Smith of Tarrent's Battery. It looked as though we were to be butchered in cold blood." Federal officers soon brought their men under control, and one later insisted that "not a rebel soldier was shot by the darkies after they had surrendered."

Most of the garrison were rounded up near the lines they had defended, but several hundred ran to the river and tried to swim to Confederate vessels anchored nearby. "By this time the Federals were on the bluffs of the river, about two hundred yards off, and were firing at every object in the river," wrote one of those would-be escapees. The majority of those in the water, about two hundred men, made it to safety; the rest were either killed or turned back to shore and captured.

Fort Blakely was now in Union hands. "General Steele reached the works soon after their capture," recalled an Iowa man, "and in his squeaky voice exclaimed: 'I knew you'd do it, I knew you'd do it.'" Some 3,700 Confederates were taken prisoner in the assault, including Generals Cockrell, Thomas, and Liddell. Federal losses totaled 571, of which 105 were killed in action. In an emergency conference held this night, General Maury decided that the loss of his two bastions on the eastern shore made any further defense impossible. Mobile would have to be evacuated.

The battle for Fort Blakely was over, but the wounding and dying would continue for a few more hours. As General Andrews remembered, "All the fore part of the night, there were occasional explosions of torpedoes, and a few men were killed by them while searching for the dead and wounded. It was a discordant and melancholy sound to hear."

———◦———

Monday, April 10–Friday, April 14

For two days, April 10 and 11, Major General Dabney H. Maury organized the evacuation of Mobile, Alabama, and the destruction of the military stores that his men could not carry away with them. "Most of the army gone," a resident wrote on April 11. "I saw them march past with resolute step. Perhaps I shall never look upon a gray coat again." The artillerists manning the forts that protected the city proper were kept especially busy in these two days. "Rolled all the shot and shell into the bay, destroyed all the powder by emptying all the cartridge bags into the bay," recalled a gunner. "On account of the nearness of the enemy, the evacuation had to be conducted as quietly as possible."

Food- and clothing-supply depots were thrown open to the public. "Commissary stores having been left by our military authorities, and being turned over to the poor, each of that class . . . endeavoring to carry off as much as possible [created] . . . much scuffling and rioting," a resident scribbled in her journal.

The greater part of the town's garrison boarded steamers that took them up the Tombigbee River. Maury left early on April 12, leaving one battery and a Mississippi cavalry regiment behind to cover the rear. After setting fire to the bales of cotton piled around the city's outskirts, these troops, too, withdrew. Hardly had they moved out of sight, however, when citizens appeared to knock down the fires and recover as many of the cotton bales as possible.

All this did not go unnoticed by the Union forces across the bay, and on the morning of April 12 — while at Appomattox General Chamberlain's soldiers were waiting to receive the formal surrender of Lee's men — General Canby sent two divisions under General Granger to take possession of Mobile. An Iowa soldier described some of the events in his diary: "Crossed over to Catfish Landing, a Man-of-War came up close & lifted a shell over which called no reply, but caused a display of white flags at every house along the landing." "Sent a boat ashore and learned the city was evacuated," explained an officer. "Immediately the landing began. Water was so shallow we could not get in very readily, but were soon got off and we secured to land. A deputation from the city, consisting of the Mayor[, R.H. Slough,] and some of the Common Council, met us and surrendered the city. Everything was joy and hilarity."

A soldier from the 8th Illinois received permission to ride ahead to place the U.S. flag on the prominent Battle House Hotel. "When I got into the city I had to go slowly, as the streets were full of men, women and children, and they crowded the thoroughfares," he remarked. "They treated me kindly and helped me to a hammer and nails and showed me the way to the top of the five-story building, where I nailed Old Glory."

Behind the young herald, the blue columns formed up and marched into Mobile. "The bands played most beautifully, and the boys cheered most loudly," an officer recalled. An Ohio soldier saw "many ragged women and children. A great many colored people were watching us with happy faces." A few conversations were struck up. "I don't see any horns on your head," one resident said to a Yankee boy. "No," the Federal replied, "I got mine knocked off at Blakely."

A more formal flag raising occurred later in the afternoon. A Mobile teenager named Willie Fulton watched sourly as the "flag of the dis-United States" was hauled up the pole. Then the city's mayor appeared and made a speech, "telling the citizens to go to their homes and behave as quietly as possible." The Yankees, another resident reluctantly admitted, "have only conducted themselves according to the rules of civilized warfare, but they are so seldom accustomed to act with such moderation that some of our people seem to be carried away by such unexpected treatment." "My feeling this afternoon and tonight, has been anything but pleasant," a young woman penned in her journal. "I believe I was never so gloomy — but there will be a bright day for us yet."

The abandonment of the city by Confederate forces allowed the

Federal naval units to undertake the deadly task of clearing enemy explosives from Mobile Bay. "The channel is lined with torpedoes of the
most explosive and dangerous character," a sailor had complained earlier in the siege. The Unionists had learned from experience to be wary of
the underwater mines: in the few weeks immediately preceding Mobile's
capitulation, the sailors had lost two monitors and two gunboats to the
infernal devices. "Some of those," a Wisconsin boy explained in a letter
to his mother, ". . . were common kegs filled with powder & covered
with resin to the depth of about two inches." The end of hostilities in the
region did not mean that these weapons were rendered harmless. On
April 14, a launch from the gunboat U.S.S. *Cincinnati* was dragging up a
torpedo near Fort Blakely when the weight anchoring it in place snapped
and threw it against the stern of the small craft. The ensuing explosion
sank the launch and killed three of those aboard.

Back on land, General Canby spent April 13 refitting his forces. On
April 14 he ordered the Sixteenth Corps to set out on roads leading to
Montgomery.

James Wilson had already rendered Canby's march superfluous. His men
had made good time in their eastward march from Selma, slowed only
by having to corduroy swampy stretches of ground and engage in brief
firefights with isolated Confederate detachments. They camped on the
night of April 11 within striking distance of the city that had been the
first capital of the Rebel nation and the cradle of the Confederacy —
Montgomery.

A small Southern force under the overall command of a one-eyed
brigadier general named Daniel W. Adams had gathered there ahead of
Wilson to fulfill Adams's promise of "a full defense of the city." Hardly
had the C.S. officer begun to make his plans, however, when new instructions arrived from Lieutenant General Richard Taylor, ordering
him to "attempt no defense at Montgomery." Adams and his men were
to follow the officials of the Alabama government and join the exodus to
Columbus, Georgia. In a last act of defiance before leaving, Adams had
his men torch more than 85,000 bales of cotton and freely distribute the
commissary stores. The large cotton-bale barricades that had been set up
alongside many residences to block the streets were likewise slated for
burning. A Montgomery newsman described the scene: "Dense columns
of smoke piled above the city and almost shut out the light of the sun.
Women with affrighted countenances were seen running hither and
thither, crying and wringing their hands, and hundreds of excited persons were endeavoring to secure their furniture from the adjacent

houses." One intrepid group of women saved their homes by perching on the bale barricades and daring the soldiers to set them alight. Other portions of the town were saved by the heroic exertions of firefighters, including an all-black company. As the newsman reported, the "night [of April 11] was passed in dreadful suspense."

Early on the morning of April 12 — the day Mobile fell — a deputation of Montgomery city officials rode out, met Wilson, and turned over the city to him. The Federal officer promptly exchanged his assault plans for a public entry full of pomp and circumstance. "With perfect order in column of platoons, every man in his place, division and brigade flags unfurled, guidons flying, sabers and spurs jingling, bands playing patriotic airs, and the bugles now and then sounding the calls, the war-begrimed Union troops, batteries, ambulances, and wagons passed proudly through the city," he wrote afterward. "It was a grand sight, our triumphal entry into Montgomery," a Wisconsin cavalryman recalled. "It was truly a fine display," added an Illinois man.

Wilson and his men remained in Montgomery for two days, and then they were again on the move, this time headed for Columbus, Georgia. Wilson had learned of Lee's fate, and he suspected that a death blow had been struck, but he was nevertheless determined to keep on " 'breaking things' along the main line of Confederate communications."

Chapter Seven

Heads of State

————◦►————

As THE MILITARY issue was being decided on battlefields in Virginia and Alabama, the chief political leaders of both sides were experiencing profound personal odysseys. For Abraham Lincoln that meant a somber journey of victory; for Jefferson Davis, a race against the approaching specter of defeat.

————◦►————

Monday, April 3
Danville, Virginia

The train carrying President Davis, his Cabinet, and other members of the refugee Confederate government, which had left Richmond shortly before midnight on April 2, pulled into the Danville station around three o'clock this afternoon. "A large number of the people of the town were assembled at the depot as the train entered it," Navy Secretary Mallory observed, "and the President was cordially greeted, but there was that in the cheers which told as much of sorrow as of joy." Davis did not share Mallory's pessimistic view of affairs. "Nothing could have exceeded the kindness and hospitality of the patriotic citizens," he declared. "They cordially gave us an 'Old Virginia welcome,' and with one heart contributed in every practicable manner to cheer and aid us in the work in which we were engaged."

Danville now became the temporary capital of the Confederacy. One factor in the choice was its location, midway between Lee's army in Virginia and Johnston's in North Carolina, along with its access to both river and rail transportation. A less practical but perhaps more significant explanation for its selection lay in Davis's reluctance to take the government out of Virginia and, in so doing, abandon the state to its enemies.

The crowds that had thronged to the railroad station were now rewarded with a procession of notables representing a virtual who's who of the Confederate government. There was Secretary of State Judah P. Benjamin, Navy Secretary Mallory, Treasury Secretary George A. Trenholm, Attorney General George Davis,* Postmaster General John H. Reagan, and a host of lesser lights.

Their journey along the 140 miles of track from Richmond to Danville had been enough to try everyone's patience. Such was the sorry condition of the roadbed that the engine could manage only ten to fifteen miles per hour, with frequent stops as trains in front of theirs experienced breakdowns and other problems. One of the grisliest of these latter occurred about thirty miles from Danville, when the floor of a troop train ahead of theirs collapsed, throwing a half dozen screaming soldiers under the moving wheels. During some of the delays, citizens approached the presidential car to gawk at the Chief Executive or to shake his hand.

Carriages now conveyed Davis and his entourage to their respective quarters in Danville. Davis, along with his staff, Trenholm, and Mallory, was taken to a large home on the southwestern outskirts of town, owned by Major William T. Sutherlin. The remaining Cabinet members found places in other residences, while various officials and clerks filled the town's two public houses.

Davis made inquiries about Lee's army but could learn nothing of its condition. He sent a telegram off to his wife in Charlotte, North Carolina, telling her of his safe arrival. A few C.S. departments even managed to do a little business before night fell. Treasury officials placed some of their funds in local banks and exchanged paper money for hard currency — the going rate was 70 to 1 — while War Department clerks began to review the correspondence that had been loaded aboard the train in Richmond, and John Reagan established the Post Office Department in Danville's Masonic Hall.

Davis's next moves would depend upon those made by Robert E. Lee.

* No relation to Jefferson Davis.

Davis believed that once the Confederate general abandoned Petersburg, he was planning to move his army toward Danville, where it could take up a strong defensive position behind the Dan and Roanoke rivers. Lee would then unite with Johnston's army, "make a combined attack upon Sherman," and, after defeating him, turn on Grant, who by then would have been lured far from his base of supply and would be "in the midst of a hostile population." Should the scenario play out that far, Davis was confident that Lee would at last be able to drive Grant "from the soil of Virginia and restore to the people a government deriving its authority from their consent."

----◄○►----

Tuesday, April 4

Richmond

A civilian diarist set the tone in the fallen capital when she wrote, "All is very quiet today. The Yankees are behaving very well considering it is them." Many of the blue-coated victors spent the day sightseeing. A Connecticut man picked his way through the rubble-filled streets of the Burnt District and reflected that " 'poetic justice' was here represented." Another soldier took stock of the U.S. banners that now flapped in the breeze throughout the city. "As I gazed upon the Stars and Stripes floating gaily over Libby Prison in Richmond, I felt that the day of our deliverance was indeed at hand," he declared. "The Rebels is gone," a New York officer wrote home today, "the devil knows where, for I don't."

Abraham Lincoln today fulfilled his vow to visit the captured capital, coming ashore off the James River from a small barge that landed him a hundred yards or so below Libby Prison. When the President set out this morning from City Point, his party consisted of four ships. One fell behind, and another was unable to squeeze past the obstructions below Chaffin's Bluff, while the remaining two found themselves similarly blocked at Drewry's Bluff. There Lincoln transferred to a barge, which was towed by a tug until the presidential party could see the spires of the enemy city. The tug itself then went aground, leaving it to the sailors in the barge to row the President to shore. Most of Lincoln's escort was stuck on the tug, so when he stepped onto dry land at around 2:30 P.M., there were only twelve armed sailors forming the escort for him, his son Tad, Admiral Porter, two staff officers, a signal officer, and William Crook, the bodyguard.

A black dockworker recognized the tall, lanky figure and ran toward him, crying, "Bress de Lord, dere is de great Messiah!" The man fell on his knees and kissed the President's feet.

"Don't kneel to me," Lincoln admonished him gently. "That is not right."

Reported correspondent Thomas Morris Chester, "Some of the negroes, feeling themselves free to act like men, shouted that the President had arrived. This name having always been applied to [C.S. President] Jeff [Davis], the inhabitants, coupling it with the prevailing rumor that he had been captured, reported that the arch-traitor was being brought into the city. As the people pressed near they cried 'Hang him!' 'Hang him!' 'Show him no quarter' and other similar expressions, which indicated their sentiments as to what should be his fate. But when they learned that it was President Lincoln their joy knew no bounds." "I thought we all stood a chance of being crushed to death," Admiral Porter later admitted. He quietly ordered his men to fix bayonets and form a protective circle around the President.

It finally took a direct plea from Lincoln to open a path. Walking slowly along the hot and still-smoky streets toward the center of town, his guards pushed wearily against the crowds, which only grew in size as word spread. At last help arrived from the Federal provost guard, and the group was able to make its way to Jefferson Davis's former residence, now Godfrey Weitzel's headquarters. Lincoln went into the room Davis had used for his office. Remembered one of Weitzel's staff officers, "As he seated himself he remarked, 'This must have been President Davis's chair,' and, crossing his legs, he looked far off with a serious, dreamy expression."

Several prominent Confederate leaders heard that Lincoln was in town and met with him late this afternoon. Among these was Judge John A. Campbell, who had been part of the negotiating team during the futile Hampton Roads Peace Conference in February. Campbell asked the U.S. President not to rule with an iron hand, and Lincoln invited him to return tomorrow for further discussions. Then the President and his party were driven to see the Virginia state capitol. "There is no describing the scene along the route," observed reporter Chester, ". . . when the President passed through the Capitol yard it was filled with people. Washington's monument and the Capitol steps were one mass of humanity to catch a glimpse of him." When General Weitzel asked Lincoln's advice regarding the treatment of the conquered people of Richmond, Lincoln declined to provide any directives, but he did offer a suggestion: "If I were in your place I'd let 'em up easy," he said. "Let 'em up easy."

It was getting late, so Admiral Porter guided the group back to the river and suggested that Lincoln spend the night aboard the *Malvern*, which had just completed its journey up from City Point. It would prove to be a tense vigil for Porter, with two attempts made by shadowy figures to come aboard the vessel. This night he would insist that Lincoln allow an armed guard to be posted outside his cabin door.

Danville, Virginia

There was a steady drizzle outside this morning when Jefferson Davis met with his Cabinet at the Sutherlin House. All the Cabinet officers save Secretary of War Breckinridge were present. Much of their discussion revolved around the problems of reestablishing governmental operations in the new location. It was also decided that the populace should hear something about the current situation from their President, so immediately following the meeting, Davis set to work writing a proclamation.

Addressing it "to the People of the Confederate States of America," he began by acknowledging that Richmond had indeed been lost to the enemy, but he quickly argued that this fact was not such a bad thing. "We have now entered upon a new phase of the struggle," he declared. "Relieved from the necessity of guarding particular points, our army will be free to move from point to point, to strike the enemy in detail far from his base. Let us but will it, and we are free." Davis went on to vow that he would never "consent to abandon to the enemy one foot of the soil of any of the States of the Confederacy," and he exhorted those who read these words to "meet the foe with fresh defiance and with unconquered and unconquerable hearts."

He gave the draft to Secretary of State Judah P. Benjamin, who went off to have it printed and distributed. Throughout the rest of this day Davis sent several telegrams to a military detachment at Clover Station, twenty-five miles further north along the railroad line, seeking fresh information about Robert E. Lee's army. The only news the officer in charge was able to send back consisted of a chilling litany of stations along the line that had suddenly gone silent. The wire through to Amelia Court House ceased operating in the morning, followed a few hours later by the telegraphic connection to Jetersville.*

---

* As part of his quest for information, Davis authorized a scout to be sent toward Burkeville, an assignment given to John S. Wise, whose story is told in Chapter 3.

---◄◦►---

Wednesday, April 5

Danville, Virginia

Jefferson Davis spent much of this day in frustrated ignorance of larger happenings. "I have in vain sought to get into communication with Genl. Lee," he wrote to his wife in Charlotte, adding, "I do not wish to leave Virginia, but cannot decide on my movements until those of the army are better developed."

A diversion was provided by the arrival this day of the indefatigable Admiral Semmes and his naval unit, currently serving on dry land. Semmes reported to Navy Secretary Mallory, who, he wryly observed, "could scarcely be said now to have a portfolio." Mallory checked with Davis, and it was arranged that Semmes's men "should be organized as a brigade of artillery and assigned to the defenses around Danville." The question of Semmes's adjusted rank was raised; on water he was a rear admiral, but in Danville he agreed to serve as a brigadier general. Semmes felt that he was entitled to the higher rank of major general but agreed to waive his claim in the interests of the common good. "That is the right spirit," Jefferson Davis said.

The proclamation Davis wrote yesterday was printed today in the *Danville Register* and sent out along the existing telegraphic network.

Richmond–City Point, Virginia

Abraham Lincoln kept up a busy schedule of meetings this morning aboard the *Malvern*, anchored in the James off Richmond. Soon after breakfast, a Vermont colonel, Edward H. Ripley, arrived with a prisoner in tow and a disturbing story to relate. The Rebel claimed to have been a member of the Confederate Secret Service and said he knew of a plot to assassinate the head of the Yankee government. Ripley wanted Lincoln to speak with the man personally and then to take more stringent measures to ensure his own security. Lincoln rejected both suggestions. "I deeply appreciate the feeling which has led you to urge them on me," he explained to Ripley as he ended the interview, "but I must go on as I have begun in the course marked out for me, for I cannot bring myself to believe that any human being lives who would do me any harm."

Next to visit was the city military commander, General Weitzel, in the company of Judge Campbell and Gustavus A. Myers, a citizen of some standing in the Richmond community. The talk was of the political future of the states that had tried to secede from the Union. Lincoln reminded the pair of Southerners of the three nonnegotiable points he had presented during the failed Hampton Roads Peace Conference in February: restoration of the Union; acceptance of all laws passed by the U.S. Congress regarding slavery; and an end to all hostilities. On the matter of pardons, Lincoln indicated that a blanket amnesty was out of the question, but that he would be generous in the matter and was fully prepared to "save any repentant sinner from hanging." The one exception was Jefferson Davis, who would have to stand trial for his crimes.

Lincoln revealed that he was considering allowing the Virginia legislature, which had been elected under the Confederate regime, to reconvene for the purpose of petitioning to reenter the Union. Campbell favored such a plan as providing the quickest return to normal state operations. The President turned to Weitzel and said, as Myers recalled, "that he would send to him privately points on the subject in a day or two." Myers also remembered Lincoln's stating that he "professed himself really desirous to see an end of the struggle, and said he hoped in the Providence of God that there never would be another."

The final visitor this morning was an old acquaintance from Kentucky, an irascible incorrigible named Duff Green. If Lincoln was hoping for a friendly chat, he did not get his wish. Green berated Lincoln as a tyrant come to gloat over his victims. Green's purpose in coming was to request a pass to leave the city, and Lincoln ended the interview by giving him one.

Lincoln had no further desire to visit the captured capital, which was already becoming something of a tourist attraction. Recalled one resident, "Crowds of curious strangers thronged the pavements, while squads of mounted male pleasure seekers scoured the streets. Gayly-dressed women began to pour in also, with looped-up skirts, very large feet, and a great preponderance of spectacles."

The presidential party now returned by water to City Point. Lincoln's spirits, which had been soured by Green's visit, were considerably improved when they sailed past a transport filled with well-treated Confederate POWs, who not only recognized the Chief Executive but gave him three cheers. Back on land, Lincoln reviewed the communications that had piled up during his absence and spoke with several officers, including Brigadier General Charles H. T. Collis, in charge of City Point. Collis mentioned that a captured Confederate general who was waiting to be transported to a Northern prison had expressed an interest in seeing the

U.S. President. "Do you know," Lincoln said with a faint smile, "I have never seen a live rebel general in full uniform."

Collis brought in the prisoner, Rufus Barringer, who had been picked up by Yankee scouts on April 3, only a few hours after directing the Rebel side of the battle at Namozine Church. The two men chatted for a while; it seemed that Barringer's brother had served in Congress when Lincoln was part of the Illinois delegation. Lincoln ended their talk by asking if there was anything he might do for the captured officer. Now it was Barringer's turn to smile. "If anybody can be of service to a poor devil in my situation, I presume you are the man," he said. Unbidden, Lincoln wrote out a note to War Secretary Stanton, requesting that Barringer's detention in Washington be "as comfortable as possible."*

Barringer read the note and left without further comment, with Collis leading the way. The Federal officer had walked only a few yards when he realized that the captured Rebel was no longer behind him. He went back and found Barringer standing alone, "audibly sobbing and terribly overcome."

Thursday, April 6

Danville, Virginia

This was another day of no news for the refugee Confederate government in Danville, Virginia. Most of its departments were up and running, though more for show than anything else. As the head of the Bureau of War later explained, "I deemed it of great importance that the country should see that a government was in operation though Richmond was evacuated." In a letter to his wife, Jefferson Davis reflected the mix of determination and ambivalence that was affecting everyone. "We are now fixing an executive office where the current business may be transacted here," he told her, adding, however, that he did not "propose at this time definitely to fix upon a point for a seat of Govt. in the future."

The train carrying the Confederate Treasury left Danville today for Greensboro, North Carolina, carrying an estimated $327,000 in coin and bullion. Still guarding it was the cadre of naval cadets commanded by Captain Parker, who was more than a little annoyed at the Treasury Department for failing to assign any senior official to accompany the

---

* Ironically, Lincoln's gesture ended up having the opposite effect. In the hysteria following the President's assassination, the note made Barringer a suspect. He was interrogated repeatedly and kept imprisoned until July 1865.

funds. Parker had nothing against the low-level clerks who rode with him, but he felt strongly that "it was a time when every man should be made to do his duty. It was not a time to be falling sick by the wayside, as some high officials were beginning to do."

It was during this period that Jefferson Davis had a number of conversations with his hosts, the Sutherlins. "I think under all circumstances we have done the best we could," he told Major Sutherlin, who was completely convinced of Davis's devotion to the cause. Wrote Sutherlin, "I believe he would have cheerfully laid down his life at any time if it would have saved [the Confederacy] from defeat."

City Point, Virginia

Abraham Lincoln's sojourn at City Point had provided him with something of a sanctuary from the political intrigues and distractions that so nattered at him in Washington. That sanctuary was violated twice today, much to his annoyance. Around midday, a vessel carrying his wife and some of her friends dropped anchor off City Point. Lincoln received them aboard the *River Queen,* where he explained the current military situation and then made arrangements for them to visit Richmond — without him. After they left, he went ashore to wait in the telegraph office for the latest reports from the front. He was sitting there in quiet contemplation, idly playing with some kittens kept by the telegraphers, when an aide appeared to announce that a second vessel had arrived, carrying the Vice President and a friend. Lincoln's mood abruptly changed.

"Don't let those men come into my presence," he told the messenger. "They have no business here, any way; no right to come down here without my permission."

Admiral Porter, who was never far away, stepped in and promised that the gentlemen would be looked after. He gave orders that they were to be properly entertained and kept at a distance.

During this day, Lincoln sent Richmond's military commander, Godfrey Weitzel, a note authorizing him to allow the Virginia legislature to convene, as long as it was willing to accept his conditions and take the state out of the war. If at any time the representatives attempted any move "hostile to the United States," Weitzel was to disperse the meeting at once and arrest anyone who refused to leave.

Lincoln then sent off another note to inform U. S. Grant of this decision, observing with a touch of humor that Grant himself seemed to be "effectively withdrawing the Virginia troops from opposition to the government."

————◆————

Friday, April 7

Danville, Virginia

It was as if Danville lay in the calm eye of the great final storms that were sweeping the land. To the west a Yankee raiding force under General Stoneman was on the loose, and to the north Lee's army was in retreat, while to the south Johnston's thinning ranks awaited Sherman's on-slaught. But in Danville, the temporary capital of the Confederacy, life assumed a languid routine for the small host of government officials left with no nation to govern.

Navy Secretary Stephen Mallory could only remark the slow diminu-tion of the once vital energies of his department's workers. "At any hour of the day after nine o'clock A.M., these officers ... might be seen perched around the [naval] store upon the beef and bread barrels, some abstractedly shaping strands of cord or marline into fancy forms.... Others were overhauling their trunks and bags.... Others were writing letters.... They were generally grave and silent[;] ... with all Confeder-ate ports, bays, and waters in the hands of the enemy, their occupation as naval men was gone."

Jefferson Davis still had not heard from Robert E. Lee, and all that came in on the telegraph lines today was rumors. One declared that Lee's army of "60,000 men" (which was regrouping at Farmville today, fol-lowing the disaster at Sailor's Creek) was in fine shape; another an-nounced that the Virginian had whipped the enemy. "Yankee cavalry is not in their way in retreating," the second message ended, "as they keep a good distance from General Lee's troops."

City Point, Virginia

When Abraham Lincoln went ashore this morning from the *River Queen,* he found a small pile of telegraphic reports waiting for him, including Phil Sheridan's summary of the Sailor's Creek victory. Lincoln wrote Grant a reply: "Gen. Sheridan says: 'If the thing is pressed I think Lee will surrender.' Let the *thing* be pressed."

Lincoln had another, this time more welcome, visitor — his assistant secretary of war, Charles Dana, who had served as the President's eyes at the front since the spring campaign of 1864. Lincoln told Dana about his decision to allow the Virginia Legislature to reconvene, then, with a smiling reference to Sheridan's report, added that the cavalryman "seemed to be getting rebel soldiers out of the war faster than the Legislature could think."

Lincoln's wife and her party returned from Richmond later in the morning and cajoled the President into accompanying them to Petersburg. While in the siege-damaged city, Lincoln spoke with the city military commander, Major General George L. Hartsuff. During the train ride back to City Point, the President shared with his guests that officer's views, concluding, "There still remains much for us to do, but every day brings new reason for confidence in the future."

Saturday, April 8
Danville, Virginia

The information blackout surrounding the fate of Lee's army was pierced twice today. After leaving Lee just outside Farmville, War Secretary Breckinridge had found a point on the Richmond and Danville Railroad that was still in telegraphic communication with the temporary Confederate capital. From that station he sent the President a three-hundred-word summary of current operations.

Lee's reverses at Sailor's Creek and High Bridge were described, along with the movements being made by ancillary units to counter Stoneman's raiders, now in western Virginia. Regarding Lee's intentions, Breckinridge was definite: "He will still try to move around toward North Carolina." Regarding Lee's chances, however, the secretary could offer little reassurance: "The straggling has been great, and the situation is not favorable," he admitted.

Davis met with his Cabinet this evening over dinner to discuss the implications of Breckinridge's report. While they were talking, an aide entered with word that someone had arrived with important news. It was John Wise, bone-weary but uninjured after another harrowing ride across countryside swarming with Yankee patrols. The young man felt suddenly very self-conscious in the presence of so many notables, but Jefferson Davis quickly put him at ease and listened attentively as Wise told his story. The floor was then opened to questions.

"Do you think that General Lee will be able to reach a point of safety with his army?" someone asked.

Wise thought back to the scenes he had witnessed on the Farmville road, especially the condition of his father's men, and took a deep breath. "I regret to say no. From what I saw and heard, I am satisfied that General Lee must surrender." (As he spoke, Wise watched the faces of his audience. He never forgot the men's collective shudder.) "In my opinion, Mr. President, it is only a question of a few days at furthest. . . . I believe the result is inevitable, and postponing the day means only the useless effusion of noble, gallant blood." ("It was not a popular speech to make," Wise afterward reflected.)

The young man was asked to wait outside, where a sympathetic Mr. Sutherlin got him something to eat. Inside the dining room, the discussion of the future of the Confederate government continued. After the Cabinet members had either left the house or gone to their rooms, Davis beckoned Wise to join him.

"Do you feel equal to another trip?" he asked.

Wise nodded and was told to report back for instructions at nine o'clock the next morning, April 9.

City Point, Virginia

This would be Abraham Lincoln's final day at City Point. There were pressing matters in Washington that required his presence,* so plans were made for him to depart this evening. Before he left, however, he was determined to spend some time visiting wounded soldiers. When he arrived at the Depot Field Hospital,† he discovered that officials were prepared only to give him a brief tour of the facilities. He set them straight at once.

"Gentlemen," Lincoln said, "you know better than I *how to conduct* [these] hospitals, but I came here to take by the hand the men who have achieved our glorious victories."

He proceeded to visit each of the corps hospitals. A Vermont soldier detailed as a guard at the Sixth Corps Hospital described Lincoln's visit: "When the President came all the men that were able arranged themselves by common consent into line, on the edge of the walk that runs along by the door of the stockades, and Mr. Lincoln passed along in front, paying personal respect to each man. 'Are you well, sir?' 'How do you do to-day?' 'How are you, sir?' looking each man in the face, and giving him a word and a shake of his hand as he passed. He went into each of the stockades and tents, to see those who were not able to be out."

In another ward, Lincoln stopped beside a cot and extended his hand to the man lying there.

* Not the least of these was the incapacity of his secretary of state, William Seward, who had been badly injured in a carriage accident.
† The Depot Field Hospital was essentially the administrative and supply center for the five separate corps hospitals located nearby.

"Mr. President," the patient said, "do you know to whom you offer your hand?"

"I do not," Lincoln replied.

"Well, you offer your hand to a Confederate colonel who has fought you as hard as he could for four years."

"Well, I hope a Confederate colonel will not refuse me his hand."

"No, sir," the wounded Rebel answered, and he returned the President's gesture. Reflecting years afterward on this moment, the officer said, "He had me whipped from the time he first opened his mouth."

By the end of the afternoon Lincoln had grasped the hands of more than five thousand wounded and sick military personnel.

His sojourn at City Point ended with an evening soiree aboard the *River Queen*. The party broke up at ten o'clock, and after the guests departed, the vessel got up steam and started for Washington. One of Mrs. Lincoln's friends looked on as Lincoln stood on the deck, silently watching the lights of City Point recede into the distance. "Mr. Lincoln's mind seemed absorbed in the many thoughts suggested by this scene, and we saw him still pursue his meditation long after the quickened speed of the steamer had removed it forever from him," the observer noted.

Lincoln expected to return to Washington by early evening on April 9.

<hr/>

Sunday, April 9

Danville, Virginia

Jefferson Davis met briefly this morning with his intrepid young courier John Wise. "I received my return dispatches, and I set forth to rejoin General Lee," the officer recalled.* After Wise left, Davis dictated a telegraph message to be sent to Lee by another route. "You will realize the reluctance to leave the soil of Virginia and appreciate my anxiety to win success north of the Roanoke," Davis wrote. "I hope soon to hear from you at this point, where offices have been opened to keep up the current business, until more definite knowledge would enable us to form more definite plans. May God sustain and guide you."

Davis then left the Sutherlin residence to attend a prayer service. On his way he passed groups of weary stragglers from Lee's army who had drifted into town. It was not the best of omens.

---

* The dispatches were never delivered. On April 10 Wise learned conclusively of Lee's surrender, and when he returned to Danville he found the C.S. government no longer there. Wise joined up with Johnston's army and surrendered with it.

Washington

The *River Queen,* bearing Lincoln, his wife, and her guests, steamed up the Potomac throughout the morning and afternoon. "That whole day the conversation turned to literary subjects," remembered a member of Mary Lincoln's party. "Mr. Lincoln read aloud to us for several hours. Most of the passages he selected were from Shakespeare, especially *Mac-Beth.* The lines after the murder of Duncan, when the new king falls a prey to moral torment, were dramatically dwelt on."

The presidential vessel arrived at the Capitol around sundown. During the carriage ride back to the White House, Mrs. Lincoln stared fearfully out the window and said, "That city is full of enemies." "Enemies," Lincoln said with impatience. "Never again must we repeat the word."

Shortly after 9:00 P.M., Edwin Stanton hurried over from the War Department bearing Grant's dispatch announcing Lee's surrender. Lincoln and his secretary of war hugged each other out of joy.

William Crook, the President's bodyguard, went for a walk with Lincoln's son Tad just before Stanton arrived with the news. The two could see that something was happening. "The streets were alive with people, all very much excited. There were bonfires everywhere," Crook recalled. Tad was so curious to learn the cause that Crook stopped a stranger to ask what all the excitement was about.

"Why, where have you been?" the man exclaimed. "Lee has surrendered."*

Monday, April 10–Friday, April 14

Danville, Virginia–Greensboro, North Carolina

The C.S. government officials manning the departments of the temporary capital in Danville began to move with a purpose on April 10. Reliable news of Lee's surrender had changed everything. "Well, sir," Jefferson Davis told the governor of Virginia, who had only just arrived in town, "though unofficial, I have no doubt of the fact. You see my people are packing up and I shall be off as soon as I can get ready."

There was an ominous reluctance on the part of several key Cabinet members as the chief officials of the Confederate government boarded a

---

* Crook's narrative places this incident immediately upon Lincoln's arrival in Washington. However, word of Lee's surrender did not reach the War Department until about 9:00 P.M., so Crook's memory appears faulty in this regard. I have placed the incident where it seems to me most likely to have occurred.

twelve-car train that finally puffed off into the rainy gloom at eleven o'clock at night. Not everyone was so eager this time to join the exodus, and a number of government workers decided to go home instead.

It was late afternoon on April 11 before Davis and his party arrived at their destination: Greensboro, North Carolina. The distance between Danville and Greensboro might be only fifty miles, but the differences in attitude could hardly have been greater. No welcoming committees were on hand here to greet the arriving officials, nor were the doors of the best homes thrown open. Davis's secretary, Burton Harrison (who had re-joined the President after seeing Mrs. Davis safely to Charlotte), observed that it was "rarely that anybody asked one of us to his home; and but few of them had the grace even to explain their fear that, if they entertained us, their houses would be burned by the enemy when his cavalry got there."

Lending credence to these fears was the report that a Yankee raiding force detached from Stoneman's expedition — which was on the return swing of a diversionary movement into western Virginia — had burned the railroad bridge at Jamestown, little more than ten miles *south* of Greensboro. Another group of vandals, also part of Stoneman's command, destroyed the Reedy Fork Bridge — less than ten miles *north* of Greensboro — not an hour after the President's train passed over it. When informed of this near catastrophe, Davis tried to make light of it, saying that "a miss is as good as a mile."

With Lee now out of the picture, Davis had no choice but to try to work with Joe Johnston. It was an unfortunate pairing, as the two had had serious disagreements over war strategy, and Davis's decision to replace him with John B. Hood at the height of the Atlanta Campaign still rankled Johnston. Nevertheless, on the night of April 11, Davis sent his general a message suggesting a conference. Johnston arrived the next day.

Tracking close behind Jefferson Davis were dark signs of things to come. Mere hours after he and his Cabinet left the gentle embraces of Danville, that city was caught up in a wave of great unrest as crowds of civilians and unattached soldiers descended upon it, seeking caches of C.S. Government foodstuffs and clothing. The small provost detail left in charge was no match for the mob, especially when a leader emerged and began shouting, "The Confederacy is gone up! Let us help ourselves!"

"The drunken disorder was disgusting and alarming," declared a soldier who was passing through on furlough. At the height of the riot, either as an act of vandalism or as an attempt on the part of the provost guard to deny weapons to the crowd, the Confederate Arsenal was set on fire. A paroled soldier on his way home remembered "a tremendous explosion that shook the entire town, and pieces of shell began to drop about us and everywhere in the city." At least fourteen people were killed by the explosions that followed. It took martial law, finally imposed on the morning of April 13 by an Army of Northern Virginia veteran, to restore order. One resident wrote of the experience, "Unreasoning terror and disarray had taken full possession of the community and discipline had given place to utter and aimless confusion."

Even as Davis and his Cabinet were gathering in Greensboro, detachments of Stoneman's cavalry were proceeding almost unopposed into Salisbury, fifty miles to the south. A civilian there never forgot the "Yankees riding into the public square with drawn swords in their hands and oaths in their mouths." "The army stores captured in Salisbury were immense," an Ohio cavalryman bragged. "Artillery, ammunition, wheat, army cloth, and millions of Confederate money."

The raiders remained in town for less than twenty-four hours, pulling out on April 13 when it became apparent that Confederate defense forces were approaching from Greensboro. Before leaving, however, the cavalrymen heaped great stocks of captured goods in the streets and torched them. As the flames threw dense, dark clouds into the air, residents watched in horror as a mob of poor whites and ex-slaves clambered over the goods, "carrying and dragging away as much of the pillage as they could by hand, chanting weird alleluias."

On the afternoon of April 12, Jefferson Davis met in Greensboro with members of his Cabinet and Generals Beauregard and Johnston. Neither of the officers was in a good mood, especially Johnston, who had been steadily giving ground before Sherman's advance since it began, on April 10. Both generals thought they had been asked here to brief officials on the military situation, but instead they had to endure a Davis pep talk. The President believed that the spirit of the South was unbroken. "Neither soldiers nor civilians have shown a disposition to surrender," he insisted, and he went on to describe a plan to fill the armies' depleted ranks with men who had left in difficult times but would be animated by a spirit of patriotism to return to arms. Beauregard and Johnston were, to put it mildly, skeptical. Further discussion was postponed until the next day, when it was anticipated that Secretary of War Breckinridge would be present.

The former C.S. general arrived in Greensboro late on April 12, briefed Davis on Lee's surrender, and conferred with Beauregard and

Johnston. When Davis reconvened the group at 10:00 A.M. on April 13, he expected to consider offensive options. "Though I was fully sensible of the gravity," he observed afterward, "I did not think we should despair."

Beauregard and Johnston were of quite another opinion. "My views are, sir, that our people are tired of war, feel themselves whipped, and will not fight," the latter declared. Beauregard agreed. When Davis turned to his Cabinet for support, he found that all but Judah Benjamin agreed with the generals.

Under heavy pressure from the doves, Davis at last dictated a letter to be given to Sherman, requesting a general ceasefire to allow "the civil authorities to enter into the needful arrangements to terminate the existing war." The two generals departed with vague promises to continue their efforts to preserve what remained of a Rebel fighting force in the east. "I . . . never expected a Confederate army to surrender while it was able either to fight or to retreat," Davis later said.

As if to add to the crushing weight of misfortune already on his shoulders, Davis that evening was handed Robert E. Lee's official report of his surrender. The Confederate President at last lost his composure and, in the presence of a few intimates, began to weep uncontrollably. "He seemed quite broken by this tangible evidence of the loss of his army and the misfortune of its general," one of those present recalled.

Interlude

Oldham's Odyssey (Part One)

———◦▸———

ON SUNDAY, *April 2, while Grant's troops were assaulting Petersburg and Wilson's were attacking Selma, and the Confederate government was preparing to abandon Richmond, Texas Senator Williamson Old-ham covered the distance between Greensboro and Charlotte in about twelve hours as he proceeded on his journey home. The day was full of events that the Confederate official thought worthy of noting. Just south of Greensboro, Oldham's train passed another that was stopped at a siding for repairs. Glancing at the passengers milling outside the halted train, Oldham recognized the slim figure of Burton Harrison, Jefferson Davis's private secretary. Speaking with the presidential aide as his own train slowly eased past, Oldham learned that Mrs. Davis and her children and servants were waiting on board, anxious to continue their trip south.*

Oldham's end of the conversation was carried out under the baleful glare of several Union POWs who were riding in his car on their way to Salisbury, where there was a prison compound. "They were a hard look-ing set," Oldham remembered. "Many of them were insolent and insult-ing in their remarks, and, like all Yankees, seemed to be insensible to the fact that their language was offensive."

It was evening when Oldham's train pulled into Charlotte, where he spent the night. The next day, April 3, he made it as far as Chester, South Carolina, where he would have to wait for space on a wagon to carry him overland to his next stop, Newberry. From that point the route would be by rail to Abbeville, and then by dirt road to Washington, Georgia.

On April 5, copies of Jefferson Davis's proclamation to the people of the Confederate States arrived in Chester. Oldham believed that Davis's appeal failed in its attempt to rouse popular support. "Hope seemed immediately to flee, and the gloom of despair appeared to settle upon the people," he reflected. "From that day no cheering word was ever spoken for the Confederate States. The cause was lost."

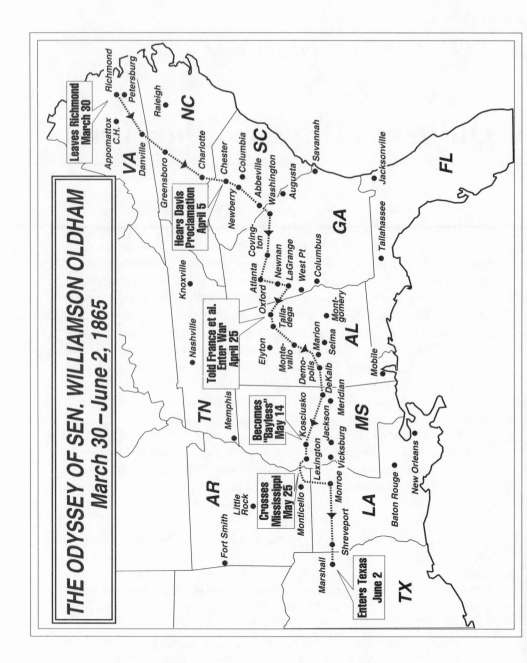

THE ODYSSEY OF SEN. WILLIAMSON OLDHAM
March 30 – June 2, 1865

Leaves Richmond
March 30

Hear's Davis
Proclamation
April 5

Told France et al.
Enter War
April 25

Becomes
"Bayless"
May 14

Crosses
Mississippi
May 25

Enter's Texas
June 2

Richmond
Petersburg
Appomattox C.H.
Raleigh
NC
VA
Danville
Greensboro
Charlotte
Chester
Columbia
Abbeville
Washington
SC
Newberry
Augusta
Savannah
Jacksonville
FL
Knoxville
Atlanta
Coving-ton
Newnan
LaGrange
West Pt
Columbus
GA
Oxford
Talla-dega
Mont-gomery
AL
Nashville
Elyton
Monte-vallo
Marion
Selma
Mobile
Demo-polis
DeKalb
Meridian
TN
Memphis
Kosciusko
Jackson
MS
Lexington
Vicksburg
Monroe
LA
Baton Rouge
New Orleans
AR
Little Rock
Monticello
Fort Smith
Shreveport
Marshall
TX
Tallahassee

Senator Oldham's slow journey back to Texas was revealing a side of the Southern homefront that appalled him. For the next two nights in a row, he and his companions, traveling by wagon to reconnect with the rail service at Newberry, stopped at large, well-appointed residences to seek food and a place to sleep. On both occasions they were grudgingly allowed a little floor space and nothing else. "It is a fact not to be denied that individual selfishness was a character of many Southern planters," Oldham later noted. "Possessing within themselves all, both of the comforts and luxuries of life, they drew themselves all, back into their shells, and refused all hospitality to strangers, and to those engaged in the defense of the country."

By April 10, the day the Confederate government quit Danville, Oldham had got as far as Washington, Georgia, where he was able to catch a train that took him toward Atlanta. The rail line, which had been extensively wrecked by Sherman's men the previous year, had been rebuilt to within a few miles of the capital. After a night's rest on a cot placed in the hallway of the only hotel in the town of Covington, Oldham hitched a wagon ride into the city. The damage wrought by Sherman's vandals nearly a year earlier was still shocking. "Nothing was to be seen but crumbled ruins, and naked, blackened standing walls," the senator recalled.

While waiting in Atlanta for his next connection west, Oldham learned of the capture of Mobile and Selma, seemingly blocking his way. But from another source he gleaned the comforting (albeit wrong) intelligence that the Yankees who had taken Selma had turned south after their conquest, and that a route through to Texas was possible. On April 13 Oldham caught the West Point train for Montgomery, "fondly dreaming that all my difficulties were over."

Chapter Eight

Slow Dance in North Carolina

—◄◦►—

THE GOAL of the Army of Northern Virginia after it left Petersburg, and the point of sanctuary for Jefferson Davis and the rest of the Confederate government after they fled Richmond, was Joseph E. Johnston's army in North Carolina. There Johnston faced an old enemy from the Georgia Campaign of 1864, William T. Sherman. Johnston, outmanned, outsupplied, and outgunned, could only watch and wait while events elsewhere took center stage.

Near Smithfield, N.C.
April 1, 1865

General R. E. Lee:

Do you think that [a] conference between us would be advantageous? If so, I'll go to your headquarters.

J. E. Johnston

—◄◦►—

Headquarters
April 1, 1865

General J. E. Johnston

I think what you propose advisable if you can come on. I am informed that Sherman has returned to N.C.

R. E. Lee

"All fools' Day was noisily observed in camp," an Illinois soldier in Sherman's Fifteenth Corps remembered. "Every man who did not stay close in quarters and hold his peace became sooner or later the victim of some ridiculous joke." "Considerable fun is enjoyed by the regiment getting off April fool sells etc.," a comrade in the nearby Seventeenth Corps observed.

The sheer size and power of Sherman's army brought confidence to everyone who saw it. "It was a magnificent sight, and there is scarcely a likelihood that a similar scene will ever again be witnessed in this country," a New Jersey soldier bragged. A member of the 85th Illinois agreed: "It was, perhaps, as nearly perfect in instruction, equipment, and general efficiency as volunteer troops can be made while in the field."

Confederate General Joseph E. Johnston spent much of April 2 not dealing with the large enemy army confronting him, but instead concentrating on a raiding force operating behind him. The first was military. In late March a Yankee raiding column of four to five thousand cavalry, commanded by Major General George Stoneman, had moved out of east Tennessee and into western North Carolina. There was little organized resistance in that region, so Stoneman's veterans had no trouble scattering the few Home Guard units that they did encounter. On March 28 the Union riders passed through Boone, North Carolina, where they burned the jail along with all the county records, and then proceeded in an easterly direction, seemingly intent on capturing Salisbury, an important supply depot and the site of a Confederate POW camp.

The task of coordinating the region's defenses had been handed by Johnston to one of the Confederacy's senior generals, P. G. T. Beauregard. The appointment was less an indication of the importance Johnston attached to the raid than a sad reminder that there were more high-ranking officers available than there were appropriate command assignments for them to fill.

From his field headquarters in Greensboro, seventy-five miles west of Raleigh, Beauregard issued a stream of dispatches ordering all his commands to concentrate at Salisbury. From his own HQ at Smithfield, Johnston monitored the progress of the enemy raiding party and moved what troops he could toward them.

A few miles east of Johnston's headquarters, William T. Sherman spent another busy day preparing his armies for their April 10 offensive. "There is not much stir here, except the stir that naturally arises from getting ready for another campaign," a Wisconsin soldier wrote to his wife from the Seventeenth Corps camp near Goldsboro. "All is in [a] bustle in that way." Even though the newspapers the soldiers received were four days old by the time they got them, the stories in them still boosted morale. Wrote a Kentucky Unionist in the Twenty-third Corps, "From our unparalleled chain of success I am more than ever firm in the belief that the boasted Southern Chivalry will be forced to succumb to Yankee prowess." In one of the few communications he sent today, Sherman echoed this confidence: "All well here and everything works well," he wrote.

The slow passage of the current campaign in North Carolina began to blur the dates together for many of Sherman's soldiers, remarkably few of whom left any written record of April 3.

"Cold and cloudy," complained a young Minnesota diarist, while an Ohio man noted, "Did nothing but drill a little." They lined up to draw supplies in the 20th Illinois, where one member of the regiment griped that the "price of clothing has been increased to nearly fifty per cent the July 1st 64 schedule and hence it costs one far more than his allowance to clothe himself properly." In the 27th Ohio the troops were mustered to see an Illinois man drummed out of camp with his head shaved. "His offense was an assault upon a woman living near the picket line," wrote one diarist.

Yet the business of war was never entirely forgotten. A Michigan man in the Twenty-third Corps observed that the "Rebel cavalry are scouting around the country in our front. To be sure in case of an attack by a superior force we are putting up light works."

Sherman heard from Grant late in the day regarding the enemy's abandonment of Petersburg and Richmond. "The mass of Lee's army was whipped badly south of Petersburg, and to save the remnant he was forced to evacuate Richmond," Grant wrote. The lieutenant general worried that Lee might outdistance his pursuers long enough to turn south for a linkup with Johnston. "If Lee goes beyond Danville you will have to take care of him with the force you have for a while," Grant commented.

Sherman was lavish in his response. "Lee has lost in one day the repu-

tation of three years," he told Grant, "and you have established a reputation for perseverance and pluck that will make Wellington jump out of
his coffin."

From his headquarters near Smithfield, Joe Johnston continued to
keep tabs on the progress of Stoneman's raiding party in western North
Carolina. General Beauregard reported from Greensboro that he had no
reliable information about Stoneman's whereabouts and complained
that he did not have "sufficient force to guard well at the same time this
place, Salisbury, and Danville."

The matter of not having sufficient force on hand was driven home to
Johnston today as he received the tallies of effective strength turned in by
his various corps commanders. Lieutenant General William J. Hardee's
corps, made up of divisions drawn largely from the East Coast, numbered slightly more than 8,700 fit for action. This presented a vivid contrast with the three battered corps that constituted the once proud Army
of Tennessee, the force that Hood had taken from Johnston and then
driven bloodily into the ground. Its three corps commanders counted
fewer than 7,000 effectives among them, and some of those were without arms. Adding artillery and cavalry, Johnston showed a paper
strength of approximately 22,000 men. Against this, Sherman's armies
would field nearly 90,000 soldiers.

Joe Johnston was using the breathing space created by Sherman's unexpected inactivity to reorganize his small forces. The units were consoli-
dated into three infantry corps, commanded by Lieutenant Generals
William J. Hardee, Alexander P. Stewart, and Stephen D. Lee,* and a
cavalry corps under Lieutenant General Wade Hampton.

A series of military reviews were held on April 3 and 4 to mark the
completion of this consolidation. The sight of the ragged veterans of the
Army of Tennessee (now Stewart's and Lee's corps) was too much
for one of Johnston's officers, who later pronounced it "the saddest
spectacle of my life. . . . The march of the remnant was so slow — colors
tattered and torn with bullets — that it looked like a funeral procession."

The passing in review of Hardee's corps was far more successful. An
officer present remarked that with this body, "once more we began to
look like soldiers." The morale in the North Carolina Junior Reserves,
made up of seventeen- and eighteen-year-olds, was high. "There was not
in the grand parade of that day — the last grand review of the Confederate Army — a more soldierly body of troops than the Junior Reserves,"

* No relation to Robert E. Lee.

one proudly declared. "Gov. Vance and many ladies from Raleigh came down to the review of Hardee's corps," recorded an observer. "The ladies cheered Gen. Hoke's division of North Carolinians."

A soldier commented of Johnston during the ceremony that "he seemed from that piercing look to give each soldier as he passed a most scrutinizing look." A Georgia man returning to the army today from leave wrote in his diary, "Gen'l Johnston passed me on the road. I lift my hat [in] salute — he was never known to pass unnoticed."

Only a few miles to the east of Johnston's reviewing stand, Sherman's men continued to prepare themselves for the upcoming campaign. "The hundreds of huge boxes that daily disappear from our store-houses here," a correspondent wrote from Goldsboro, "will prove to any one that the herculean task of refitting these armies for field-work is being speedily accomplished."

The heaviest blow that fell on Joe Johnston on April 5 came in the form of a press dispatch announcing the evacuation of Richmond three days earlier. It was the first he knew of it. "The shades of sorrow are gathering upon us," a staff officer lamented. "Heavens, the gloom and how terrible our feelings!" Lacking any information to the contrary, Johnston believed that Lee would move toward him so they could combine their forces. Until that happened, it would be up to him to preserve his army, a task that was becoming increasingly difficult: desertions had become so epidemic that, in one division, the men were lined up for roll call as many as five times a day in order to deny the runaways much of a head start.

For his part, General Sherman today issued his operational instructions for the April 10 advance. Sherman's plan, which also assumed that Lee was coming this way, called for his armies to march north, cross the Roanoke River, then pivot to face west so they could join with the Army of the Potomac to meet the Lee-Johnston combination. Remembered one of Sherman's army commanders after reading these orders, "We went to bed that happy night in the belief that we were soon to be in front of Richmond [and] . . . have the honor of taking part in the capture of Lee's army."

The reports coming into Joe Johnston's headquarters on April 6 brought both gloom and faint hope. Noted one staff officer, "It never rains but it pours, and still the bad news comes — Selma, Alabama, we hear officially, has been given up to a raiding party." Closer to home, General Beauregard in Greensboro confirmed that Stoneman and his cavalry had turned north, so the threat to Salisbury was, at least for the moment, past. Johnston was quick to take advantage of what little opportunity beckoned. "If there is no longer danger from Stoneman please send on our troops rapidly," he wrote Beauregard. "It is important to consolidate."

Johnston realized that it was only a matter of time before the Sherman juggernaut would begin rolling. To General Braxton Bragg in Raleigh, Johnston sent a request for every available wheeled vehicle. "Please let us have all you can possibly spare, no matter how small the number," he pleaded. He still had no definite information about Lee's situation in Virginia. Johnston was operating in a vacuum, with hearsay his only guide. "Rumors say General Lee is between Richmond and Danville," one of his aides recorded today, "but we have no information on the subject."

The reports coming into Sherman's headquarters had quite the opposite affect. "Drills — cheers throughout the camp — shouts of Peace! Peace! Grant has taken Richmond! Thanks to Almighty God!" observed an Illinois soldier in the Seventeenth Corps. "At brigade headquarters . . . the expert fife-player . . . says he's getting scared; the war will soon be over, and he'll be out of a job!"

The army brass was not quite so sanguine. Brevet Major General Alpheus S. Williams, commanding a division in the Twentieth Corps, admitted in a letter today that he could not join in the celebrations. "I think if Lee had held a little longer it would be better for us, as we should have made a junction with Grant. Now the whole Rebel army I fear, will get between us," he wrote. The news from the north also caused Sherman to reconsider the directives he had issued only yesterday. "This will alter our plans," he told his cavalry commander. "We must move on Raleigh. Be all ready. I think Johnston is still near Smithfield. We must hit him hard."

William T. Sherman chose April 7 to make his change of operations official by sending fresh instructions to his corps commanders. The new plan was a classic Sherman ploy — heavy pressure up the middle accompanied by strong encircling moves on both flanks. Major General Henry W. Slocum's Army of Georgia would drive directly on Smithfield and Raleigh, with support on its left from Major General John M. Schofield's Army of the Ohio and on its right from Major General Oliver O. Howard's Army of the Tennessee.* To his cavalry commander, Major General Judson Kilpatrick, Sherman suggested, "You

---

* Not to be confused with the Army of Tennessee under Joe Johnston. Union armies tended to be named after rivers, while Confederate forces were most often named for the territory they had been created to defend.

may act boldly and even rashly now, for this is the time to strike quick and strong." All preparations continued toward the April 10 jump-off.

In Joe Johnston's camp, the only official word arriving today was that contained in Jefferson Davis's April 5 proclamation. A staff officer summarized it: "President Davis issues an address to the people of the Confederacy imploring them to stand by him in reverses and to be not disheartened, for he'll steer us safely through." Davis's message struck home for one dedicated Georgia cavalryman, who remarked, "It is a strong address — full of fire, patriotic and shows a degree of fortitude truly remarkable."

Reports from U. S. Grant outlining the situation in Virginia as of April 6 reached Sherman the evening of April 8. "He is pressing Lee hard and expects to scatter his whole army," Sherman informed a subordinate. Sherman's biggest concern now was how to coordinate his planned moves with Grant's, so that their operations might be mutually supporting. "Get a message to General Grant, at any cost," he directed the officer commanding at Morehead City, "that I will push Joe Johnston to the death."

Still lacking any official word regarding Lee's army, Johnston continued to rely on hearsay for information. Today he received a telegram from a friend who passed along what he had heard about Lee's men. "All private accounts cheering and represent the army in good condition and spirits," the note insisted. By the time this tidbit trickled down to the staff level, it had been polished up a bit. "Lee has had another fight at Amelia Court House since the evacuation of Richmond, in which he was successful," wrote one officer in his journal today. The intelligence gathering nearer home was much closer to the mark. Wrote this same officer, "Prisoners taken state that Sherman will commence his movement upon us Monday."

Some fifty miles from where Johnston wondered about Lee, a quiet scholar and ex–North Carolina governor sat down on the morning of April 8 to write a letter that he hoped would remove North Carolina from the war. David Lowry Swain, president of the University at Chapel Hill, addressing his note to W. A. Graham, another former governor of the state, proposed that the two meet with the current governor, Zebulon Vance, to discuss the steps that might be taken to "arrest the downward tendency of public affairs."

Graham replied this very day, concurring with Swain's sentiments and declaring that now was the time for the state government "to move for the purpose of effecting an adjustment of the quarrel with the United States."

The two agreed to discuss their plan the next day.

On April 9 Swain and Graham met at Graham's house at the agreed-upon time to hammer out a course of action. Together they drew up a four-point agenda for Governor Vance, advising him to (1) summon the General Assembly into emergency session; (2) have the assembly pass a resolution calling for peace; (3) appoint a commission to treat with the United States on the subject; and, (4) if Sherman's advance began before the legislators could convene, negotiate an immediate ceasefire to last until the General Assembly could be gathered.

Swain took the document away with him, promising to give it to Vance when he met with him in Raleigh on April 10.

At his headquarters near Smithfield, General Johnston was still in the dark about Lee's situation. He was clearer about Sherman's intentions.

Near Smithfield, N.C. April 9, 1865

General S[amuel] Cooper[, C.S. Inspector General, Danville]:

General: Prisoners and citizens from Goldsborough say that it is understood in the Federal army that it is to advance on Raleigh to-morrow. It is of great importance that General Lee should know this, in order to combine the movements of his army and these troops. I earnestly suggest, therefore, that you communicate with him as soon as possible, by the most trusty messengers, who may bring back his orders, as well as explanations of his intentions. It is necessary for me to know them before being pressed back beyond Raleigh.

Most respectfully, your obedient servant,
J. E. Johnston,
General

"There seems to be a great stir in the camp about moving," an Indiana soldier wrote from the Union camps around Goldsboro today. "On the 9th, the whole army was eager to move," recalled another. "They seemed to long for the excitement of battle and of the march." "Whether we will have much hard fighting or not, God only knows," wrote an Illinois infantryman to his wife. "There cannot be many more battles."

* * *

215

William T. Sherman's three armies of infantry, with accompanying cavalry and artillery, uncoiled from their camps around Goldsboro as scheduled on April 10. "The occasion was quite like a gala-day performance," observed a Wisconsin soldier. "All the bands of the great army were filling the air with lively music, and the men sang songs and shouted." "We have started and had a little skirmish this afternoon," noted an Indiana officer. "The Johnnys soon ran away."

The pace of Sherman's advance was determined less by enemy resistance than by natural obstacles. "The day we started quite a heavy rain set in, and in a short time the roads were awful," remembered a Wisconsin man. "It was generally a low and wet sandy country that we had to go through," added an Iowa bluecoat, "and it was hard for the trains to get along."

The Confederate forces falling back before the Yankee columns paused to make brief stands wherever the terrain allowed it or stubbornness dictated the mood. "Sherman is moving toward Raleigh," Joseph Johnston informed the Confederate government at 10:00 A.M. on April 10, "and we [are] falling back."

On April 11, the various prongs of Sherman's three-column advance touched and in some places even crossed the Neuse River, the first significant water barrier between Goldsboro and Raleigh. "Near the village of Smithfield, however," wrote a New Jerseyman, "a small body of cavalry was met, who held our force in check long enough to enable them to destroy the bridge across the Neuse river. . . . The town was entered and occupied by our forces." An Indiana veteran recalled that it "soon became evident that [Johnston] was not disposed to fight, and the prospect seemed to indicate a chase of our old antagonist, who had so often exhibited his skill in retreating before Sherman's forces, in Mississippi, Georgia and the Carolinas."

Early on the morning of April 11, Joe Johnston received another blow in the form of a message from Jefferson Davis. "A scout reports that General Lee surrendered the remnant of his army near to Appomattox Court House," it read. "No official intelligence of the event, but there is little room for doubt as to result." Whatever hope Johnston may have harbored of keeping this shattering intelligence from the rank and file was dashed instantly by the unofficial grapevine. Hours before Johnston read the cipher-encoded telegram, a South Carolina officer heard from a passing artilleryman that "General Lee had met with a disaster; a few hours later the army was filled with vague rumors upon the subject." "On the 10th of April we hear that General Lee has surrendered, which has a very demoralizing effect on the army," seconded a Texas officer.

The news of Lee's surrender meant a reprieve for one C.S. soldier sentenced to be shot for desertion. Johnston had been firm in his decision to carry out the court-martial verdict despite the pressures of a major military operation, but he suspended the execution after receiving Davis's telegram. The staff officer who carried the commutation order reasoned that as long as there was a chance that the fight would continue, Johnston had been determined to do what was required to maintain discipline, but once that chance disappeared, he was unwilling to needlessly sacrifice a life. "Then I knew, was positively certain, that the war was over," the officer declared.

Sherman did not learn of the events at Appomattox Court House until nearly twenty-four hours after Johnston. "I hardly know how to express my feelings, but you can imagine them," he wired Grant. Word of mouth was as spontaneous in Sherman's force as it had been in Johnston's. "The whole army was electrified," an Illinois soldier exclaimed. "Cheer after cheer swept up and down the long line of the great moving columns," said an Iowa man. An Ohio diarist noted that there "was a wild hullabaloo as the boys began shooting off their ammunition in celebration, saying they would have no further use of it in battles." When an orderly on horseback shouting the glad tidings pounded along a line of marching men, one of them called out from the ranks, "Be dad! You're the man we've been looking for for the last four years."

When Johnston's retreating units reached Raleigh, on April 11, the Confederate general was handed a communication from Jefferson Davis summoning him to an urgent conference. Johnston departed on the morning of April 12, leaving the army under the command of Lieutenant General William J. Hardee.

Even as Johnston's train was rolling west out of the North Carolina capital, another engine, carrying the peacemakers David Swain and W. A. Graham, was getting up steam for a trip in the opposite direction. As promised, Swain had laid the matter of a ceasefire before Governor Vance on April 10, whereupon Vance had promptly asked that Graham join them for a fuller discussion. The end result was that Vance approved the plan and authorized the pair to carry it out. Armed with a pass from General Hardee, the two commissioners headed toward Sherman's advancing troops, carrying with them a letter proposing a ceasefire.

The train was allowed to pass through the Confederate lines, but it had hardly gone two miles when Major General Wade Hampton rode up, stopped it, and, under fresh orders from Raleigh headquarters, revoked its safe passage. The only problem was that Hampton did not control that area, and as the train backed up, it was overtaken and captured by Yankee cavalry. The more mobile Hampton was able to escape, but the commissioners were roughly herded out of their car and had some of their possessions plundered by their captors. By the time they explained their mission and were conducted to meet Sherman, the two North Carolina statesmen were, Sherman observed, "dreadfully excited" by events.

Swain and Graham were given a note by Sherman that expressed sympathy for their plight but promised nothing. Allowed to reboard their train on April 13, they returned to Raleigh to find it nearly empty. Governor Vance had left soon after midnight with the last organized units of Johnston's army; Raleigh was now an open city. Whatever hope the two ex-governors had had for a negotiated peace settlement had disappeared with Vance. Graham decided to try to make it back to his home in Hillsboro, while Swain waited for the Yankees to arrive.

April 12, Raleigh's last day under Confederate rule, was filled with incidents of pride and shame. Johnston's men continued to pass through until after dark. "How sad did Raleigh look that day," a Tar Heel soldier reflected. Another had happier memories. "How the servants stood at the fence with supplies of water for us to drink! How the fair girls trooped down to see us pass!" The Confederate rear guard, under Major General Joseph Wheeler, was a different matter. Wheeler's men, one Raleigh resident wrote, "were a wild set." Another remembered the night of April 12, with Wheeler's men in the streets, as "one of extreme anxiety."

It was shortly after dawn on April 13 when mounted troopers belonging to Colonel Michael Kerwin's brigade of Kilpatrick's command came in sight of the city. "We rode forward, with carbines held ready," remembered Sergeant J. A. Gilberg of the 5th Ohio Cavalry. "As we came near a movement was seen in a street on the outskirts of the capital. For a few moments we thought it was the advance of the Johnnies. Upon getting nearer we saw vehicles approaching with a white flag in the foremost buggy." It turned out to be a procession of Raleigh citizens led by Mayor William H. Harrison, coming to surrender the city. They were taken to General Kilpatrick, who accepted the capitulation.

"We then entered the city and took possession," Sergeant Gilberg continued. "There was no haste or rush — the column moved at a walk." On Kilpatrick's orders, Adjutant Lew McMakin placed guards in front of private homes. When McMakin tried to pacify one especially anxious Southern matron by assuring her that the Federal army would guard Raleigh as well as it had protected Richmond, she flew into a rage at the mere suggestion that the Confederate capital had fallen. "That is a nasty Yankee lie," she snapped, and then she fled indoors.

Not everything went so smoothly for McMakin. After setting the property guards, he and the brigade staff hurried toward the capital building to raise the U.S. flag. "It appeared that there were about half a dozen [Confederate] stragglers . . . who were looting a store just opposite the Capitol. These fellows, hearing us, rush[ed] out, fired at Kerwin and I and galloped down the street." Another diehard spotted Judson Kilpatrick making his triumphal entry and fired five shots at him, all of which missed. Members of Kilpatrick's escort swarmed after the foolhardy Confederate, caught him, and, with their chief's grim approval, strung him up as an example to others.

Leaving behind one regiment of cavalry to wait for the infantry, Kilpatrick pushed on and was soon engaged in what one bluecoat described as a "nice running fight" with the main body of the Confederate rear guard. General Sherman, riding with the Fourteenth Corps, arrived in the capital at about 7:30 A.M. Raleigh got mixed reviews from some of those in the ranks. An Illinois man thought it the "handsomest city in all famous Dixie," while an Indiana soldier dismissed it as the "poorest excuse for a State capital we ever saw." A Minnesota veteran long remembered how the Federal troops marched into the city "with colors flying, bands playing and everybody, including apparently most of the resident people, in fine spirits." Only two of the capitals of the eleven seceding states — Austin and Tallahassee — now remained in Confederate hands.

William Sherman used the next day, April 14, to allow his army to regroup and resupply following its advance to Raleigh. "A beautiful spring morning," one of his officers noted in his diary. "Nature is putting on her green clothes." Sherman was himself paying some social calls in the city's outskirts when a courier arrived from Kilpatrick to inform him that a note had come in from Johnston under a flag of truce. Sherman returned to town to read the message. It was the text Davis had dictated at the April 12 Cabinet meeting, sent over Johnston's signature, requesting a general ceasefire. Sherman quickly replied, promising to limit his advances for the moment and to suspend the operations of collateral forces over which he had jurisdiction (such as Stoneman's). He further offered "the same terms and conditions as were made by Generals Grant and Lee at Appomattox Court House." The reply went back that same evening.

In a communication sent to Kilpatrick at this time, Sherman declared that Johnston's letter was "the beginning of the end."

Chapter Nine

"My God — the President's shot!"

—◦—

Friday, April 14

FOR FOUR YEARS Assistant Adjutant General Edward D. Townsend of the War Department had been an offstage player in that great drama known as the Civil War. Orders issued over his name had removed certain officers from command and elevated others to positions of prominence; directives from his pen had redrawn military boundaries, given the stamp of approval to national war policies, and otherwise filled in the minutiae of a massive military administration. Such was War Secretary Edwin Stanton's trust in Townsend's abilities that he handed him full responsibility for what promised to be *the* symbolic event marking the end of the war — the restoration of the U.S. flag over Fort Sumter.

A flag had been fluttering over the fort since its recapture in February, but Stanton's plan was to restore, in a very public ceremony, the same standard that had been hauled down in defeat by Major Robert Anderson in April 1861. That relic of national calamity had been kept safely stored in New York's Bank of Commerce ever since, waiting for the right moment. Stanton judged that April 14, 1865, would be that moment, and in March he began the wheels turning to organize the event. The job was given to Townsend, who was to accompany a delegation of dignitaries to the site and make certain that "no embarrassment should grow out of any speech making, &c."

The rough plans were shown to Lincoln during his sojourn at City Point. His only objection was that the proposed date was wrong. "I feel quite confident that Sumter fell on the 13th and not on the 14th of April, as you have it," he wired the secretary. "Look up the old almanac and other data and see if I am not right." Stanton agreed that the President's memory was correct, but he cited Major Anderson's report stating that he had "marched out of the fort on Sunday afternoon, the 14th instant, . . . saluting my flag with fifty guns." That settled the matter.

To ensure that the ceremony would not get out of hand, Townsend decided to draw up a simple game plan and stick to it. "Anderson [now a brevet major general] wanted it all to be a religious service; but I did not see why it should be, & I proposed singing the Star Spangled Banner to let off the enthusiasm a little, to atone for the prohibition on speeches." The one exception to the latter injunction was to be the keynote address, which that great public speaker Henry Ward Beecher agreed to deliver. "There is a profound feeling about [the] Charleston celebration," Beecher exclaimed. "It is a grand national event."

Whether in testament to Townsend's organizational abilities or just out of plain luck, the Fort Sumter ceremony came off without any serious hitch. The weather cooperated, more than four thousand citizens flocked from the North to be present, and the program — two prayers, four psalm readings, a recitation (by Townsend) of Anderson's April 18, 1861, dispatch announcing the fort's fall, the singing of the "Star-Spangled Banner" and the "Doxology," Beecher's speech, and the actual flag raising — unfolded strictly according to plan. ("But for that," Townsend boasted more than a month later, "I suppose we should now be listening to some burst of eloquence in the ruins of Sumter.") Only the fortress itself was not dressed up for the occasion, having been pounded into near rubble by two years of steady bombardment.

But no plan, however well crafted, could have predicted the tidal wave of emotion that swept over all those present as Anderson stepped forward, grasped the halyards, and slowly pulled the flag up the staff. "I thank God that I have lived to see this day, and to be here, to perform this perhaps the last act of my life, of duty to my country," he said. According to one account, "The whole audience sprang to their feet. Bands began to pay their most inspired music. Men swung their hats and grasped each other by the hand; women and children waved their handkerchiefs, and many wept for joy."

Beecher's speech followed. He was unsparing in his condemnation of the Southern elite who had led their region into war, but conciliatory toward the great masses who, he believed, had simply marched to the tune. "For the people misled . . . ," he said, "let not a trace of animosity remain." The celebration continued well into the evening with a dinner at the Charleston Hotel, accompanied by what Townsend remembered as "some very fine speeches."

Three days later, following a return voyage by sea to New York, Anderson filed his report of the event with Edwin Stanton:

> The duty assigned me by you has been performed. The flag lowered at Fort Sumter April 14, 1861, was by God's blessing restored to its standard April 14, 1865. Would to God you could have been present to have witnessed the ceremony. Great God! what saddening, crushing news meets us.

The battle for a conciliatory postwar Southern policy was joined as soon as Lincoln returned to Washington from City Point. In the midst of the joyous street celebrations that filled the city on April 10, Lincoln still managed to find small ways to express his own views. When a happy crowd gathered at the White House and called for him to give a speech, the President put them off, saying that he already had one planned for the next day and did not want to spoil it. He spotted several bands with the crowd and asked if the musicians might play a tune for him. "I have always thought 'Dixie' one of the best tunes I ever heard," Lincoln said. "Our adversaries over the way attempted to appropriate it, but I insisted yesterday that we fairly captured it. I presented the question to the Attorney General and he gave it as his legal opinion that it is now our lawful prize. I now request the band to favor me with its performance."

Lincoln's promised speech was delivered on April 11 to a large crowd packed onto the White House lawn. "There was something terrible in the enthusiasm with which the beloved Chief Magistrate was received," an observer noted. "Cheers upon cheers, wave after wave of applause, rolled up, the President patiently standing quiet until it was over."

"The evacuation of Petersburg and Richmond, and the surrender of the principal insurgent army, give hope of a righteous and speedy peace whose joyous expression cannot be restrained," Lincoln told the audience. It soon became apparent, however, that his subject was not celebration but rather the obstacles to a just reconstruction of the nation. "We simply must begin with, and mold from, disorganized and discordant elements," Lincoln warned. He recognized that the South was not a monolith but a confederation of very different components, so much so that "no exclusive and inflexible plan can safely be prescribed." It was not the kind of happy-slap-on-the-back speech that the crowd was expecting.

On April 12 Lincoln acted quickly to correct a misstep in his slowly evolving Reconstruction policy on the matter of the Virginia legislature. Members of his Cabinet, led by Edwin Stanton, had been aghast that Lincoln would even consider allowing a representative body elected under Confederate auspices to convene under Union control; for his part, Lincoln, always the pragmatist, had seen his olive branch allowing Judge Campbell to explore the possibilities of such a convention as an experiment. Now it became clear that the experiment was getting out of hand. Judge Campbell was moving, or being pushed, too far too fast, and an agenda was being set up for this legislative body that far exceeded anything Lincoln had wanted or suggested. In a message sent at 6:00 P.M. today to Richmond's military commander, Godfrey Weitzel, Lincoln noted that Campbell "assumes . . . that I have called the insurgent legislature of Virginia together, as the rightful legislature of the state, to settle all differences with the United States. I have done no such thing." Putting his best legal fine point on it, Lincoln further stated that he had viewed the former Virginia state legislature simply as a group of gentlemen who might help convince other Virginians still in armed rebellion to put down their guns. "I meant this and nothing more. . . . Do not allow them to assemble," he instructed Weitzel.

The subject of reconstruction came up again the next day, during a discussion between the President and his Navy secretary, Gideon Welles. According to Welles, Lincoln insisted that "civil government must be reestablished . . . as soon as possible; there must be courts, and law, and order, or society would be broken up, the disbanded armies would turn into robber bands and guerrillas, which we must strive to prevent."

There was another Cabinet meeting the following day, Good Friday, April 14. Lieutenant General Grant was present and afterward approached the President to apologetically decline an invitation to join the Lincolns at the theater that evening. Mrs. Grant was exceedingly anxious to visit family in New England, he explained, and they had tickets on an afternoon train. (A more likely reason was that Mrs. Grant, who had been with her husband at City Point, did not get along at all well with Mrs. Lincoln and had no desire to spend the evening with her.)

Lincoln accepted Grant's regrets and turned to other matters, among them the signing of a number of military pardons. "Well, I think this boy can do more good above ground than under ground," he said after commuting one death sentence. A little while later Charles Dana, the assistant secretary of war, came in with an order from Stanton for the arrest of a minor Confederate official who was reliably reported to be entering Maine from Canada on his way to England.

"He says arrest him," Dana told Lincoln, "but that I should refer the question to you."

"Well," Lincoln replied, "no, I rather think not. When you have got an elephant by the hind leg, and he's trying to run away, it's best to let him run."

Late in the afternoon, Lincoln made a quick visit over to the War Department, accompanied by his bodyguard, William Crook.

"Crook," Lincoln said suddenly, "do you know I believe there are men who want to take my life?" He paused thoughtfully. "And I have no doubt they will do it."

"I hope you are mistaken, Mr. President," was all Crook could manage in response.

A few blocks from where Lincoln and Crook were talking, a darkly handsome, deeply troubled young actor was putting the final touches on a plot of transcendent infamy. Twenty-six-year-old John Wilkes Booth came from a stage family. His father was a British-born Shakespearean player of eccentric and ultimately self-destructive tendencies, while his older brothers Edwin and Junius were already widely recognized for their stage appearances and, as such, a source of passionate envy for John Wilkes. More than one acquaintance later commented on the youngest Booth's often-expressed "desire to do some deed or accomplish some act that had never been done by any other man, so that his name might live in history."

Booth, who had little respect for black Americans (he once declared that slavery was "one of the greatest blessings . . . that God had ever bestowed upon a favored nation"), was in full sympathy with the Confederate cause. He had chosen not to enlist in the Rebel military proper, preferring instead to become involved, by the end of 1863, in the shadowy world of clandestine operations. At first he used his ability to pass between North and South to smuggle medical supplies into the Confederacy, but soon he found he had a flair for conspiracy, and by mid-1864 he had been recruited by the Confederate Secret Service to help organize an ambitious plot to kidnap Abraham Lincoln.

Booth became a man with a purpose. Over the course of the next few months he put together a network of operatives, many of whom would later suffer for their association with him. Well-placed Confederate agents assisted him in his planning and recruitment. Lincoln's kidnapping would be no wild-eyed act of desperation but rather a carefully choreographed operation with full logistical support. The abduction was to take place in mid-March 1865, in Washington, but a combination of missed chances, poor intelligence, and bad luck resulted in the complete failure of the plan. Then Lincoln was gone, off to Petersburg, where he would remain until after Richmond had been captured.

The clandestine apparatus designed to support the kidnap plot fell apart, but Booth had come too far down this personally tortuous road to turn back. Moved by a turbulent mix of passions and self-perceptions, he remained resolved to commit a decisive act. Booth now turned to the pool of operatives he had contacted, and selected a handful to assist him in a new plan — his own plan — to assassinate Abraham Lincoln.

It was an easy matter for Booth to learn of Lincoln's intention to attend the theater this evening. He ordered his group into action, its goal to strike the heads of the United States government in one night of slaughter. To George Atzerodt went the assignment of killing Vice President Andrew Johnson, while coconspirator Lewis Paine* was to murder the injured and bedridden secretary of state, William Seward. Booth had saved the greatest prize for himself. His plan called for the fatal blows to be struck simultaneously, at 10:00 P.M.

Lincoln and his wife left the White House for Ford's Theater at around eight o'clock. On the way there they picked up the guests Mrs. Lincoln had chosen to replace the absent Grants — Major Henry R. Rathbone and his fiancée, Miss Clara Harris. William Crook had gone off duty, and his replacement† remained downstairs when the party arrived at the theater at about eight-thirty and went up to their seats in the presidential box on the south side of the building, dress-circle level. Lincoln tried to enter without any fuss, but the audience spotted him and applauded, stopping the actors, until he acknowledged their reception with a solemn bow.

A military man who was present recalled that the "people now gave their undivided attention to the play, happy to share its humor, wit and gaiety, with one who had earned that right, if ever relief, followed by relaxation, was due to one who had led the nation through the sea of trouble to a triumphant ending." Then, at approximately ten-fifteen, a shot rang out. "My first thought was that a boy in the gallery had fired off one of these large firecrackers which we have been hearing for the

---

* "Paine" was an alias; his real name was Lewis Powell.
† The substitute bodyguard is usually identified as John F. Parker, but recent investigation has determined that Parker was not present at Ford's Theater this night. The bodyguard on duty was likely Charles Forbes, a White House messenger.

last week," a doctor in the house later told a friend. "I . . . thought [it] to be part of the performances," said a New Jersey officer seated in the orchestra section. A nearby businessman watched as a "man of about 5 ft. 9 inches dressed in a black suit of clothes leaped onto the stage apparently from the President's box. . . . He did not strike the stage *fairly* on his feet, but appeared to stumble slightly. Quickly recovering himself he ran with lightning speed across the stage & disappeared. . . . The whole occurrence, the shot, the leap, the escape — was done while you could count eight." A restaurateur named James P. Ferguson shouted, "My God — the President's shot!" "Everyone was struck with astonishment until he had disappeared behind the scenes, when it was announced that the President was shot," said the New Jersey officer.

"Such a scene I never saw before," another patron recalled. Cries that Lincoln had been assassinated mingled with appeals for a doctor. The performance of *Our American Cousin* was forgotten as the now milling crowd made its way outside. "Groups gathered at the corners of the streets, speaking in hushed breath of the awful thing that had happened," one member of the audience remembered.

Saturday, April 15 – Wednesday, April 26

Abraham Lincoln, sixteenth President of the United States, died at 7:22 A.M. on April 15, in the Petersen House, across the street from Ford's Theater, where he had been carried after being shot. Secretary of War Stanton, just one of the approximately sixty-five people who spent some time in the small (9½-by-17½-foot) room, was there at the end. "Now he belongs to the ages," Stanton sobbed.

A cleric living in the city caught the mood and mind of the moment in his diary:

> *We have the saddest tidings* this morning *that ever shocked our Country.* It almost chills my heart's blood to record it. *President Lincoln was murdered at Ford's Theater last night!!!* The dwelling house of Mr. Seward, Secretary of State, was also entered about the same time, and an attempt made to assassinate him, from which it would appear that these sad occurrences are the result of *a foul conspiracy* against *the Government* represented by these distinguished men. . . . The murderer of Mr. Lincoln is reported to have exclaimed, after he shot him, "Sic Semper Tyrannus! The South is avenged. I have done it." Was he an agent for the Rebel authorities? Was it the same man that entered Mr. Seward's home? What will be done with him, and any

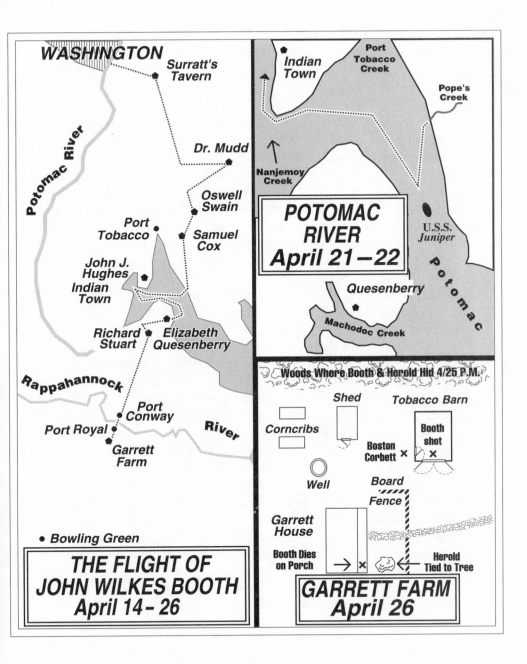

WASHINGTON

Surratt's
Tavern

Potomac River

Dr. Mudd

Oswell
Swain

Port
Tobacco

Samuel
Cox

John J.
Hughes

Indian
Town

Richard
Stuart

Elizabeth
Quesenberry

Rappahannock

Port
Conway

Port Royal

River

Garrett
Farm

• Bowling Green

THE FLIGHT OF JOHN WILKES BOOTH
April 14 - 26

Indian
Town

Port
Tobacco
Creek

Pope's
Creek

Nanjemoy
Creek

U.S.S.
Juniper

POTOMAC RIVER
April 21–22

Potomac

Quesenberry

Machodoc Creek

Woods Where Booth & Herold Hid 4/25 P.M.

Shed

Tobacco Barn

Corncribs

Booth
shot

Boston
Corbett ×

×

Well

Board
Fence

Garrett
House

Booth Dies
on Porch

→ ×

Herold
Tied to Tree

GARRETT FARM
April 26

227

that may have been accomplices to these foul deeds, if caught by our authorities? What will be the effect of these awful transactions on the affairs of our Country for the future? These and many such questions are now being asked.*

For a few tense hours on the morning of Lincoln's death it seemed as if mob madness would rule Washington's streets. "The excitement then was intense, words fail to describe it," one of the officers assigned to keep order recalled. Some in the crowd that gathered near the Petersen House called for the burning of Ford's Theater, while others congregated into a group about two thousand strong and advanced on the Old Capitol Prison, where a number of Confederate POWs were being held. Only a strong showing by armed troops turned the angry mass away.

In contrast, the actual transition of authority was carried out with subdued but calm deliberation. Between ten and eleven o'clock in the morning, Chief Justice Salmon P. Chase administered the oath of office to Andrew Johnson of Tennessee. "You are President," Chase said once the ceremony had been completed. "May God support, guide, and bless you in your arduous duties."

The morning papers all confirmed the identity of Lincoln's assassin. Washington's *Morning Chronicle* declared, "Developments have rendered it certain that the hand which deprived our President of life was that of *John Wilkes Booth,* an actor." City, military, and government investigators scrambled to determine the full extent of the plot and to identify those involved. Booth himself was more than twenty miles south of the city this morning, having talked his way across the Navy Yard Bridge shortly before eleven o'clock the night before and then crossed unchallenged through the line of fortifications that ringed the Capitol. Although some writers would later point to the ease of his escape as evidence of a conspiracy in high places, it was more likely the result of confusion and poor communication in the hours immediately following the fatal gunshot.

Booth had now been joined by another conspirator, David E. Herold, who had guided Lewis Paine to Seward's house and whose knowledge of the area made him invaluable. The two arrived at the residence

---

* Paine's knife attack on Seward left the secretary of state badly slashed but alive. Atzerodt lost his nerve and never got closer to Andrew Johnson than the bar of his hotel.

of Dr. Samuel Mudd at four o'clock in the morning. Here his broken leg* was set and he was allowed to rest throughout the day while Mudd tried to scare up a carriage for his use. Mudd's defenders would later press their claim that the doctor was only acting the part of the Good Samaritan, but Mudd had been part of a Confederate intelligence network throughout the war and had, in fact, met with Booth on at least three previous occasions. Booth told Mudd nothing of what he had done.

Booth and Herold left Mudd's place at about four in the afternoon and continued south to the home of a black tobacco farmer, Oswell Swann,† whom they paid twelve dollars to lead them to the house of Colonel Samuel Cox, a Southern sympathizer. Not far from Cox's was an area of pine thickets where people moving in and out of the Confederacy often hid. Here Booth and Herold would spend the next five days.

It was likely at this time that Booth made the first of two entries in what would afterward be referred to as his "diary."

April 13th   14 Friday the Ides

Until to day nothing was ever *thought* of sacrificing to our country's wrongs. For six months we had worked to capture.‡ But our cause being almost lost, something decisive & great must be done. But its failure was owing to others, who did not strike for their country with a heart. I struck boldly and not as the papers say. I walked with a firm step through a thousand of his friends, was stopped, but pushed on. A Col-§ was at his side. I shouted Sic semper *before* I fired. In jumping broke my leg. I passed all his pickets, rode sixty miles that night, with the bone of my leg tearing the flesh at every jump. I can never repent it, though we hated to kill. Our country owed all her troubles to him, and God simply made me the instrument of his punishment. The country is not what it *was*. This forced union is not what I *have* loved. I care not what becomes of me. I have no desire to outlive my country. This night (before the deed), I wrote a long article

---

* Although it is accepted as fact that Booth broke his leg in his leap from the presidential box to the stage at Ford's Theater, some who have studied the matter believe it was broken in a fall from his horse *after* he left Washington.
† Referred to in some accounts as Oswald Swann.
‡ A reference to the plot to kidnap Lincoln in early 1865.
§ Reference to Major Rathbone.

and left it for one of the Editors of the National Inteligencer, in which
I fully set forth our reasons for our proceedings.* He or the Govmt†

Telegraph wires crackled across the country with the awful story. A
New York officer serving in the Army of the Potomac was awakened at
two o'clock in the morning and handed a telegram by an orderly who
could only repeat over and over again, "My God! can it be, can it be!"
"A few moments later I walked out in the open air trying to convince
myself that it was all a dream," the officer recalled. "Everything about
the camp was quiet, and the shelter tents of my men had an unusually
uniform appearance; but they were all empty, and the men with heavy
hearts and speechless tongues, were gathered in groups about the smol-
dering campfires. They all seemed stupefied by the terrible news." "For
the second time in my army experience, the first was after the reception
of the news of the battle of Bull Run, I saw men, even unemotional
Americans, shed tears over a public misfortune," a nearby cavalryman
remembered. "Every soldier felt that he had lost a dear friend in the
lamented chief magistrate, whose heart always beat with joy at their
successes in the field, and sorrowed with the truest sorrow over their
reverses and misfortunes." A Confederate soldier imprisoned at Fort
Delaware wrote in his diary, "Lincoln was assassinated last night. When
we awoke this morning the flags were at half mast. What a pity. What a
pity."

The terrible cloud of guilt by association soon spread over the Booth
family. Government investigators averred, with no evidence other than
hearsay, that John Wilkes's brother Joseph had known of the plot beforehand. A confiscated letter from the assassin to another brother, Junius, contained a reference to the "oil business," which some authorities
thought might be a code for something more sinister. The unfortunate
Junius was held in the Old Capitol Prison until it was determined that
the reference was indeed to an innocent oil speculation. John Wilkes's
sister Asia lamented, "The tongue of every man and woman was free to
revile and insult us . . . , if we had friends they condoled with us in secret;
none ventured near."

On April 20 Edwin Booth, the senior brother of the family, released
an open letter "To the people of the United States," which read, in part:

---

* The editor who received this note burned it, fearing he would be incriminated in the
plot.
† The entry ended in midsentence at this point.

It has pleased God to lay at the door of my afflicted family the life-blood of our great, good and martyred President. Prostrated to the very earth by this dreadful event, I am yet but too sensible that other mourners fill the land. To them, to you, one and all go forth our deep, unutterable sympathy; our abhorrence and detestation of this most foul and atrocious of crimes.

In the immediate aftermath of the assassination, Federal authorities moved with great energy but little coordination to round up the conspirators. Cavalry patrols crisscrossed Booth's escape route, finding bits of a cold trail but no real leads regarding his whereabouts; the clandestine Confederate network in that region was functioning well enough to preserve the secret of Booth's hiding place. Other members of the plot were less fortunate. Lewis Paine was picked up on April 17 when he foolishly returned to Mary Surratt's boardinghouse, a known hangout for the group. Three days later George Atzerodt was arrested after a tip led investigators to the farm near Germantown, Maryland, where he was hiding.

While all of this was taking place, John Wilkes Booth and David Herold lay low in the pine thickets not far from the Cox House, where they were kept supplied with food and information by Thomas A. Jones, a C.S. agent to whom they had been passed by Samuel Cox. Not until late on Thursday, April 21,* did Jones feel it was safe to move Booth and Herold across the Potomac River. He led the two to a small boat cached up a creek tributary of the river and gave them a course for Machodoc Creek, on the Virginia side, where they were to make their next contact. Booth and Herold rowed into the Potomac at about ten o'clock at night, at a point where the river was approximately two miles wide.

A strong river current pushed the pair forward of their destination, where they unexpectedly came upon an anchored Union warship, the U.S.S. *Juniper*, and only just managed to pull back without being detected. Now thoroughly confused, Booth and Herold attempted to retrace their route, but a strong wind had come up, causing them to overshoot in the other direction. Dawn of April 22 found them at the mouth of Nanjemoy Creek — several miles *north* of their starting point, and still on the Maryland side of the Potomac. Herold knew this region

* There is some uncertainty about this date. Jones gave it as April 21, but Booth's diary clearly indicates that he believed it was April 20. The log of the U.S.S. *Juniper*, however, shows that the only night the vessel was anchored along Booth's route to Machodoc Creek was April 21.

well enough so that the two were able to find sanctuary on a farm named Indian Town, then the residence of John J. Hughes. Here they would remain until sundown.

It was while they were at Indian Town that Booth made the second, and final, entry in his "diary."

Friday 21 —

After being hunted like a dog through swamps, woods, and last night being chased by gun boats till I was forced to return wet cold and starving, with every mans hand against me, I am here in despair. And why; For doing what Brutus was honored for, what made Tell a Hero. And yet I for striking down a greater tyrant than they ever knew am looked upon as a common cutthroat. My action was purer than either of theirs. One, hoped to be great himself. The other had not only his countrys but his own wrongs to avenge. I hoped for no gain. I knew no private wrong. I struck for my country and that alone. A country groaned beneath this tyranny and prayed for this end. Yet now behold the cold hand they extend to me. God *cannot* pardon me if I have done wrong. Yet I cannot see any wrong except in serving a degenerate people. The little, the very little I left behind to clear up my name, the Govmt will not allow to be printed. So ends all. For my country I have given up all that makes life sweet and Holy, brought misery upon my family, and am sure there is no pardon in the Heaven for me since man condemns me so. I have only *heard* of what has been done (except what I did myself) and it fills me with horror. God try and forgive me, and bless my mother. To night I will once more try the river with the intent to cross, though I have a greater desire and almost a mind to return to Washington and in a measure clear my name which I feel I can do. I do not repent the blow I struck. I may before my God but not to man.

I think I have done well, though I am abandoned, with the curse of Cain upon me. When if the world knew my heart, *that one* blow would have made me great, though I did desire no greatness.

To night I try to escape these blood hounds once more. Who who can read his fate. God's will be done.

I have too great a soul to die like a criminal. Oh may he, may he spare me that and let me die bravely.

I bless the entire world. Have never hated or wronged anyone. This last was not a wrong, unless God deems it so. And its with him, to damn or bless me. And for this brave boy with me who often prays (yes before and since) with a true and sincere heart, was it crime in him, if so why can he pray the same[.] I do not wish to shed a drop of blood, but "I must fight the course[.]" Tis all thats left me.*

From April 18 to April 21, Washington paid its final respects to the martyred President. "Everywhere lie insignia of sorrow," a visitor noted. A resident named Helen McCalla was among those who came to the White House on Tuesday, April 18. "There was a dense crowd (mostly blacks) extending from the gate down to the avenue, and through that we were obliged to force our way," she remembered. "Ladies fainted near us and children screamed, and a violent shower rained [upon] the scene. . . . Upon entering, we marched in a slow silent procession through the Reception Room, into the East Room, where the remains were lying in state, but we were not permitted to wait a moment near the corpse, so that it was impossible to obtain a satisfactory view. The effect was imposing, the coffin being placed upon a high platform, covered with black cloth, surmounted by a canopy of the same material."

On April 19, following a morning funeral service at the White House, the body was borne to the Capitol, where it would remain until April 21. "All felt the solemnity and sorrowed as if they had lost one of their own household," Navy Secretary Welles wrote of Wednesday's events. "By voluntary action business was everywhere suspended, and the people crowded the streets."

April 19 was Patriot's Day in Massachusetts, where the town of Concord marked the occasion with a few words from its great sage Ralph Waldo Emerson. He gave a eulogy on Lincoln's assassination. "Old as history is," Emerson told those gathered, "and manifold as are its tragedies, I doubt if any death has caused so much pain to mankind as this has caused."

Few of America's intellectuals had embraced the war as wholeheartedly as Emerson. To Nathaniel Hawthorne he seemed as "merciless as a steel bayonet." Emerson saw this terrible bloodletting as a way of purging the body politic of its great evils; he considered Southerners to be the "enemies of mankind" and the North's cause a veritable "battle for Humanity." The cost, however high, was worth it, for Emerson believed

> *That one broad, long midsummer day*
> *Shall to the planet overpay*
> *The ravage of a year of war.*

* Some modern writers believe that the last two paragraphs of the diary were written as late as April 25.

In Lincoln Emerson found the heroic symbol that brought closure to the conflict. The President, Emerson declared, served "his country even more by his death than by his life."

Even as Emerson's words filled the columns of newspapers everywhere, a harsh wind of vengeance was beginning to blow across the land. The mood started at the very top. A member of the new President's beefed-up security force never forgot Andrew Johnson's pacing the floor of his room and exclaiming, "They shall suffer for this, they shall suffer for this." The slightest suggestion of someone's implication in the assassination plot was reason enough for his or her arrest, imprisonment, and often brutal interrogation.

There were other deaths connected with the events of April 14 that reflected the grim mood of the North. A Michigan soldier on garrison duty in Nashville wrote to his wife on April 18 that the "excitement was immense. The solders were almost ungovernable. One man died in the City — said that it was good enough for Lincoln ought to have died before. A soldier shot him dead." After telling his mother of another such incident, a man named William Daggett assured her, "My seven shooter is in my pocket and I shall not fail to use it should I hear any such remark."

John Wilkes Booth and David Herold left Nanjemoy Creek at sundown on April 22, and this time successfully landed on the Virginia shore. They were given food at the home of Elizabeth Quesenberry, where they also obtained horses and a local guide through the assistance of a Confederate agent named Thomas Harbin. The guide led them to the house of Dr. Richard Stuart, who reluctantly provided some food but offered no other hospitality. Stuart directed the local man to take the pair to a nearby cabin owned by a free black man named William Lucas, where they might hire a wagon to convey them further south, to Port Conway.

For Booth, who had a low opinion of black people, having to spend the night in the cabin of such a family was a deep personal insult. His mood grew so surly that Lucas, with his wife and children, moved outdoors for the night. The next day, April 24, Lucas's son drove Booth and Herold ten miles to the Rappahannock River ferry at Port Conway. They arrived at the crossing at about eleven o'clock in the morning and, after failing to convince a local resident to row them across, sat down to wait until they could catch a ride on the ferry. There they were joined by three former Confederate cavalrymen. While Booth remained tight-lipped about his identity, Herold let the cat out of the bag, admitting to the soldiers, "We are the assassinators of the President!"

The troopers agreed to help the pair, and after crossing on the ferry, they took them (riding double, five men on three horses) to a farm owned by a loyal Confederate sympathizer, Richard Garrett. Told that Booth was a wounded C.S. soldier named James W. Boyd,* Garrett agreed to provide him with temporary room and board while the three ex-cavalrymen and Herold continued on to Bowling Green. That night after supper, recalled Garrett's son Richard, "Our guest seemed much refreshed after his rest and joined freely in the conversation, which became quite lively as my [older] brothers told of some of the stirring scenes they had witnessed during the war."†

Early the next morning, April 25, young Richard Garrett happened to view their guest, "Boyd," as he slept. "I was but a boy, but the thoughts came to me then that he was different from all the soldiers I had seen[,] for they were rough and tanned from exposure." At lunch the family received confirmation of a rumor they had heard: Lincoln had been assassinated, and a reward of $100,000 was being offered for his killer. "I wish he would come this way, and I could capture him," exclaimed Richard's brother William. The man known as Boyd never even flinched. "Would you do such a thing?" he asked. "Betray him?"

Later in the day, David Herold returned from Bowling Green with two of the troopers who had crossed with them on the ferry the day before. The third trooper, William S. Jett, had remained in the village with a girl he knew.

After dropping Herold off, the two riders set out for Port Royal, but they had been gone for only a few minutes when they returned at a gallop with news that a Yankee cavalry detachment had already crossed from Port Conway and was coming their way. "You must take care of yourselves the best way you can," one called to Booth as they spurred their horses on.

Booth and Herold hurried into a stand of pines behind the Garrett tobacco barn and listened anxiously as the sound of hoofbeats grew louder and louder, then faded away. The cavalrymen had ridden past the farm, intent only on getting to Bowling Green as quickly as possible.

The Garretts now suspected that the strangers were not who they claimed to be, and when "Boyd" asked for transportation west to Guinea Station, he was put off until morning. Garrett's son John further insisted that the two sleep in the tobacco barn instead of the house. To ensure that their "guests" did not make off with some of their horses, John and his brother William settled down for the night in a nearby shed.

* An alias likely chosen to explain the initials J.W.B., tattooed on the back of Booth's hand.
† Both John and William Garrett had served in the Confederate military.

It was approximately two o'clock on the morning of April 26 when the shadowy figures of the Union detachment began to filter into positions surrounding the Garrett Farm. The Federals had located William Jett in Bowling Green and identified him as one of the soldiers who had crossed on the ferry on April 24. Pressed hard by his interrogators, Jett had admitted that Booth had been with his group, and that he was now hiding on the Garrett Farm. The dismounted Yankee cavalrymen woke up the Garretts' dog, which in turn roused the household. When the elder Garrett professed having no knowledge of the two strangers, one of the Federals threatened to hang him on the spot and burn his house.

The noise brought John Garrett on the run from the shed. He was grabbed and pushed over to the circle of angry men surrounding his father. "The men you seek are over there," young Garrett volunteered, indicating the tobacco barn. The soldiers quickly encircled the structure and sent John inside with a message for the men to give themselves up. "Damn you!" Booth cursed. "You have betrayed me!" John Garrett fled back outside.

A few tense minutes passed, and then Booth called out, "There is a man here who wishes to surrender very much." The barn door opened, and David Herold stumbled out; he was hustled away to be tied to a tree.

When the Federal officer in charge demanded that Booth now surrender, the actor asked for some time to think. After about fifteen minutes he requested that he be allowed to die a hero, by charging alone into the drawn-up ranks of the cavalrymen. The Federal officer refused. "Well, my brave boys," Booth cried, "prepare a stretcher for me."

In short order, the barn was set ablaze. Booth was soon fully illuminated by the flames; as he began to hobble toward the door, he was shot in the back of the head by Sergeant Boston Corbett, who was positioned by a side window. Several of the Federals dragged the mortally wounded assassin out of the burning barn and onto the front porch of the Garrett House.

Booth lingered for three and a half hours. The officers who leaned over him remembered some of the statements he made. "Tell Mother that I died for my country," he said to one. "I thought I did for the best," another recalled hearing him say.

The bullet had damaged Booth's spinal cord and paralyzed him. Just as it became light enough to see, he asked that his hands be raised so he could look at them.

"Useless," he muttered. "Useless." Then John Wilkes Booth was dead.

Chapter Ten

The Bennett Farmhouse

———◁○▷———

In NORTH CAROLINA, April 14 was a day of important —
albeit far less dramatic — developments in the winding-down of the war.
Union general William T. Sherman received a note from his Confederate
opposite number, Joseph E. Johnston, requesting a ceasefire. He replied
at once in the affirmative and handed his response to Judson Kilpatrick,
the Union cavalry commander, for delivery. Kilpatrick, however, suspected a Rebel trick and delayed passing the note on to the Confederate
side until sundown of April 15; as a result, it did not reach Johnston until
early the next day. Johnston at once trained from Hillsboro to Greensboro to consult with Jefferson Davis, only to discover that the C.S. President had "quitted the town" and was heading toward Charlotte. This
left Johnston on his own. He returned to Hillsboro and sent a message to
Sherman through his own cavalry chief, Wade Hampton, asking for a
face-to-face meeting at a point midway between the two picket lines.

Kilpatrick, who had been dressed down by Sherman for his earlier
dilatoriness, forwarded the note at once. Sherman made plans to travel
by train from Raleigh to Durham Station, where he and his staff would
switch to horses for the ride to meet Johnston.

"No news," a soldier under Sherman's command wrote on April 16.
"This suspense is oppressive. We want to know what is going on." "All

kinds of rumors afloat," an Ohio diarist recorded. "All seem pretty confident that this great war is played out."

The development these soldiers were hoping for was set in motion the very next morning, when William T. Sherman and his staff boarded a special train in Raleigh, bound for the front. "Just as we were entering the car," Sherman recalled, "the telegraph-operator, whose office was up-stairs in the depot building, ran down to me and said that he was at that instant of time receiving a most important dispatch in cipher from Morehead City, which I ought to see. I held the train for nearly half an hour. . . . It was from Mr. Stanton, announcing the assassination of Mr. Lincoln. . . . Dreading the effect of such a message at that critical instant of time, I asked the operator . . . not to reveal the contents by word or look till I came back."

A clerk in Sherman's entourage later wrote of the events once the train arrived at Durham Station. "At General Kilpatrick's headquarters horses were furnished us and we rode through our lines with a flag of truce at the head of the column. General Johnston was met about four miles out . . . riding along the road with a portion of his staff, and also flying a flag of truce. The two Generals shook hands with each other and rode back to the house of a Mr. [James] Bennett, where they went into a room by themselves and talked for an hour."

Sherman showed Johnston the message about Lincoln's death. "The perspiration came out in large drops on his forehead," Sherman observed, "and he did not attempt to conceal his distress." Johnston said that the assassination was the "greatest possible calamity" that could befall the South. Then the two got down to the business at hand. Sherman began by offering Johnston the same terms that Grant had offered Lee, but Johnston stopped him by pointing out that the purpose of this meeting was not to discuss the surrender of his army but rather to explore the possibility of a larger ceasefire, one that would allow the civilian authorities time to seek a peace settlement.* He also remarked that unlike Lee, who had been surrounded, he still had options, especially as his army was several days' march from Sherman's.

Johnston now took the plunge: he suggested that they "make one job of it" and "arrange the terms of a permanent peace." When Sherman asked if he had that kind of authority, Johnston offered to produce Secretary of War Breckinridge to speak for the Confederacy. This was a problem for Sherman, who was forbidden to hold any discussions with members of the civilian government, but Johnston neatly flanked that

---

* This was the same approach Lee had tried with Grant on April 8.

obstacle by reminding him that Breckinridge was also a major general in the Confederate service and could meet with him as such. Sherman gave his approval, and the two agreed to reconvene in twenty-four hours.

Sherman quickly returned to Raleigh, where he prepared the general order announcing Lincoln's death. Before releasing it, he was careful to increase the provost patrols in the city, instructing them to stop any trouble before it got out of control.*

"Boys, there is sad news, terrible news," a Wisconsin officer told his company. "President Lincoln has been shot, and is dead!" "A grape-shot through the heart would not have struck me more dumb," an Illinois soldier declared. "People generally were perfectly stunned by the news," seconded another. "It brought great sorrow to the soldiers for Lincoln was particularly endeared to them," an Ohio man noted. "They stood in groups and talked seriously of the murder." "Awful was the excitement," wrote an Indiana soldier. "The boys are raving about it. Revenge is uttered from most every lip." "The army is crazy for vengeance. . . . We hope Johnston will not surrender. God pity this country if he retreats or fights us," was the grim promise of an Illinois bluecoat.

Sherman met with Johnston again at the Bennett House on April 18, shortly after midday. Johnston was anxious to clarify a few points regarding the future political rights of the surrendered soldiers, and he asked if Breckinridge might join them. Sherman agreed. A Federal clerk waiting outside watched as a C.S. staff officer left and returned with the secretary of war. "His clothes looked rather seedy, but he was haughty and his manner was proud," the clerk remembered.

Inside the Bennett House, the three officers got down to the business at hand. Their conversation had already touched upon several sore points when a courier arrived bearing a memorandum that had just been drafted for this meeting by the C.S. postmaster general, John Reagan. Sherman read through Reagan's recommendations, which included, among other things, the preservation of the existing state governments in the South, the protection of all property rights of former Confederates, and a general ceasefire. After indicating that Reagan's terms were unacceptable, Sherman took up his pen to write his own version. He drew upon his recollections of Lincoln's ideas, as the President had expressed them just a few weeks earlier at City Point, "and wrote off the terms, which I thought concisely expressed his views and wishes, and explained

---

* Sherman's precautions paid off. With a few minor exceptions, Raleigh was quiet this night.

that I was willing to submit these terms to the new President, Mr. Johnson, provided that both armies should remain *in statu quo* until the truce therein declared should expire."

While Sherman led the two C.S. officers outside to introduce them to his staff, clerk Arthur O. Granger sat inside the Bennett House and made clean copies of Sherman's terms. There were seven points in all. The first established the truce, which could be terminated by either party with forty-eight hours' notice. The second allowed for the disbanding of all "Confederate armies now in existence." The third recognized existing state governments, while the fourth reestablished the Federal courts in those states. The fifth protected property rights, the sixth guaranteed surrendered Confederates relief from prosecution, and the seventh declared "the war to cease; a general amnesty." It was understood that this agreement would not be binding until it was approved by the civil authorities on both sides.

Johnston and Breckinridge returned to their lines, with the latter entrusted with carrying the terms to Jefferson Davis and the rest of the C.S. government, by now probably established in Charlotte. Sherman dispatched his copy to Washington by means of a staff aide. Recalled Sherman, "I reckoned that it would take him four or five days to go to Washington and back."

Sherman's peace terms arrived in Washington on April 21, at a time when the nation's leaders were still reeling from Lincoln's assassination and caught in the grip of paranoia as fears of treachery and conspiracy continued to spread across the land. Grant read the documents and immediately contacted Stanton to suggest that an emergency Cabinet meeting be convened to discuss the matter. Stanton took one look at the material and quite lost control of himself with rage and indignation. He had barely cooled to room temperature by the time President Johnson and the Cabinet gathered at 8:00 P.M. Stanton had Grant read the dispatches received and then the terms offered by Sherman, which, it was apparent to everyone, went well beyond the purely military considerations established by Grant at Appomattox Court House. As Navy Secretary Welles wrote in his diary, "Among the Cabinet and all present there was but one mind on this subject. The plan was rejected, and Sherman's arrangement disapproved. Stanton and [Attorney General James] Speed were emphatic in their condemnation. . . . General Grant . . . while disapproving . . . was tender to sensitiveness of his brother officer and abstained from censure. . . . It was decided that General Grant should immediately inform General Sherman that his course was disapproved, and

Richmond, April 1865: A view of the Burnt District.

Sailor's Creek, April 6, 1865: The last of Ewell's corps. The artist wrote, "This was quite an effective incident in its way the soldiers silhoutted against the western sky — with their muskets thrown butt upwards in token of surrender, as our troops closed in."

Appomattox Court House, April 9, 1865: General Robert E. Lee and Colonel Charles Marshall leaving the McLean House.

Appomattox Court House, April 10, 1865: Union souvenir hunters chopping up the apple tree under which Lee waited for word from Grant.

Appomattox Court House, April 12, 1865: The formal surrender of the Army of Northern Virginia.

Fort Sumter, South Carolina, April 14, 1865: Major General Robert Anderson raises the same U.S. flag he had taken down in surrender four years earlier.

Selma, Alabama, April 1865: Ruins of the Confederate States Naval Foundry, destroyed by Wilson's troopers.

The Bennett Farmhouse, North Carolina: Here General Joseph E. Johnston surrendered his forces to Major General William T. Sherman.

The Lonesome Train, 1865: One of several engines used to pull the Lincoln funeral train on its journey from Washington, D.C., to Springfield, Illinois.

Abraham Lincoln: Crowds in Cleveland, Ohio, wait to view Lincoln's body, which lay in state there on April 28, 1865.

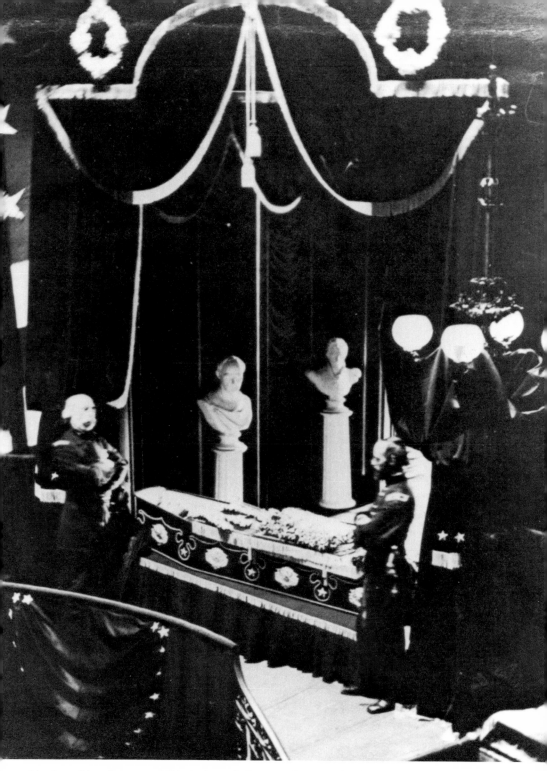

Abraham Lincoln at rest: This is the only known photograph of Lincoln in death. Rear Admiral Charles Davis (*left*) and Adjutant General Edward D. Townsend (*right*) stand guard. When he learned of this photograph, Secretary of War Edwin Stanton ordered the negative and all prints destroyed, but one survived.

The *Sultana*, April 26, 1865: The doomed vessel, overloaded with recently released Union prisoners of war, is seen here during a brief stopover at Helena, Arkansas. The next day she sank, killing perhaps as many as 1,800 of her passengers.

(Library of Congress)

(Alfred Waud, Library of Congress)

Jefferson Davis: The captured C.S. President in his cell at Fortress Monroe, Virginia.

(Frank Leslie's Illustrated Newspaper)

Mobile, Alabama, May 25, 1865: Soldiers and citizens searching the ruins for survivors following the explosion of the munitions warehouse.

Mobile, Alabama, 1865: The site of the munitions warehouse that exploded on May 25, 1865. (United

The Grand Review, May 23, 1865: Major General Andrew Humphreys and his staff, followed by the Second Corps of the Army of the Potomac, pass in review down Pennsylvania Avenue.

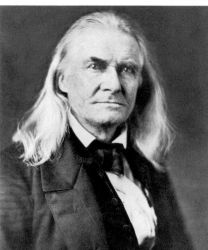

Edmund Ruffin: The archtypical fire-eating secessionist killed himself on June 17, 1865, rather than outlive his beloved Confederacy.

The windup: Former officers of the Confederate States of America arrive in Richmond to take the Oath of Allegiance.

C.S.S. *Shenandoah*: The last warship of the Confederacy, she finally hauled down the Confederate flag on November 6, 1865.

Bull Run, Virginia, June 10, 1865: Soldiers gather for the dedication of a monument commemorating the battles fought here.

that generals in the field must not take upon themselves to decide on political and civil questions."

William T. Sherman, in Raleigh, grew increasingly anxious as he waited to hear if his broad peace terms would be ratified in Washington. On April 23 he sent a bundle of newspapers containing the latest news on the assassination to General Johnston, along with a personal note. "The feeling North on this subject is more intense than anything that ever occurred before," he said. Sherman was also savvy enough to sense the changing mood in the land, which, he took pains to warn Johnston, "may thwart our purpose of recognizing 'existing local governments.'" In the evening of that same day Sherman learned that the aide he had sent to Washington with his terms had reached Morehead City and would be in Raleigh early on April 24. In a dispatch sent at 8:00 P.M., Sherman informed Johnston, "Please be in readiness to resume negotiations when the contents of dispatches [from Washington] are known."

The train carrying Sherman's aide arrived at 6:00 A.M. the following morning, with more than just dispatches aboard. It also carried U. S. Grant, who had come from the capital "as quietly as possible, hoping to see [Sherman] ... without even his army learning of my presence," Grant wrote. Said Sherman, "Of course, I was both surprised and pleased to see the general, and soon learned my terms with Johnston had been disapproved." Added Grant, "I told him that ... he was authorized to offer [Johnston] the same terms I had given General Lee." Sherman promptly sent off two messages to Johnston. The first officially notified him that the ceasefire would be terminated in forty-eight hours; the second offered "the same terms as were given to General Lee at Appomattox, April 9th instant, purely and simply."

Even though he had been sent from Washington with instructions to "take charge of matters there myself," Grant was determined that his friend should be allowed to handle them on his own. "As soon as possible I started to get away," Grant later wrote, "to leave Sherman quite free and untrammelled."

At noon on April 26 Johnston met once again with Sherman at the Bennett House. Johnston's very presence here was an act of insubordination, for on April 25 he had been instructed by Jefferson Davis to scatter his army, with orders for it to reassemble at a different location. Also, all mounted troops were to be sent directly to Davis to join his escort. "We have to save the people, spare the blood of the army, and save the high civil functionaries," Johnston had replied to the C.S. President. "Your plan, I think, can only do the last."

At first it seemed as if the two sides would be unable to reach a settlement, as Sherman and Johnston emerged from their long negotiation still deadlocked over the issue of providing provisions and transportation for the paroled soldiers. Since this was not specifically included in Grant's April 9 terms, Sherman felt he could not add it in this case. Major General John M. Schofield, commanding Sherman's Army of the Ohio, had a suggestion. Since he, as senior officer, would be responsible for overseeing the disbanding of Johnston's army, he promised to fully address its commander's concerns. Schofield's word was good enough for Johnston. Schofield drew up the military convention of surrender and signed it with the Confederate general.

In a proclamation that he prepared soon afterward, Johnston declared, "I made this convention to spare the blood of the gallant little army committed to me, to prevent further suffering of our people by the devastation and ruin inevitable from the marches of invading armies, and to avoid the crime of waging hopeless war."

The surrender ceremony for Lee's army at Appomattox Court House would have no complement for the men of Joe Johnston's army. Anxious to begin healing what he called the "wounds made by the past war," Sherman dispensed with any formal act of capitulation. "According to immemorial custom," an Illinois soldier explained, "Sherman's victorious legions should have been drawn up in line with sounding trumpet and waving plume, while the captives should in that imposing presence furl their flags and ground their arms. But instead of this triumphant pageant, the rebel army was permitted to furl its ill-starred banners and lay down its arms in the seclusion of its own camp, and there was neither blare of band nor peal of cannon heard in the quarters of the Federal army." "The Rebel men began to wept and lament like small children," a Yankee cavalryman observed. "They were hert stricken that theer cawse had failed."

"Remained quietly in camp all day," a South Carolina officer noted on April 27. "Rumors rife as usual, at length culminating in the sad and solemn truth of surrender." "All is confusion and unrest, and the stern realization that we are subdued, and ruined, is upon us," added another officer. "We had a dreadful night," a Texas soldier remarked that next morning, "all hands up and talking over the situation. They go over the war again, count up the killed and wounded, then the results obtained — It is too bad! If crying would have done any good, we could have cried all night." "There is no use commenting upon it," a Georgian wrote in his diary.

"I never witnessed such a scene as that which presented itself, when it became fully known that we were to lay down our arms," a Tennessee man said. "All phases of human feeling were exhibited. Some raved and swore that they would never submit to it. Some paced back and forth like caged lions. Some seated themselves on logs and buried their faces in their hands." "Everything we had fought for and believed in had come down to nothing," declared a Louisiana cavalryman. There were gestures of defiance; in one such instance the officer commanding a regiment of North Carolina Junior Reserves called his boys together and announced, "My advice to you is to surrender, but, if you will not, we will cross the Mississippi River, join Gen. Kirby Smith, and fight it out to the bitter end." Others salvaged what measure of pride they could manage. "The battle flag of the 54th Alabama regiment was never surrendered," a soldier proudly recollected years afterward. "It was literally honeycombed with bullet holes, and was finally torn into small pieces and divided up among the boys, each getting a piece."

Private Sam Watkins found himself remembering the faces of the many men who had passed through the ranks of the 1st Tennessee in its nearly four years of service. "The day that we surrendered our regiment it was a pitiful sight to behold," he recalled. "A mere squad of noble and brave men, gathered around the tattered flag that they had followed in every battle through that long war. It was so bullet-riddled and torn that it was but a few blue and red shreds that hung drooping while it, too, was stacked with our guns forever."

While no official celebrations were authorized in Sherman's armies, little could be done to prevent unofficial ones from breaking out all over. An Iowa soldier remembered that "flags and banners were all unfurled; the drum corps were called out; guns were fired; bonfires were kindled; we paraded the camp; gathered at the various headquarters of the commanding Generals and were entertained with thrilling and eloquent speeches." "The war is over or virtually so," an Ohio man exulted. "Happy day! Happy hour!" "No words could tell our gladness at the final accomplishment of this great work," said another Ohio veteran, "nor our deep sense of relief when we fully realized that we had fought our last battle."

William T. Sherman returned to his headquarters in Raleigh to discover that he had ended one campaign only to begin another. The recent newspapers awaiting him there fired salvo after salvo in a personal attack against him for his discredited peace offering — many of these inspired by the innuendos of misconduct contained in official War Department bulletins signed by Edwin Stanton. "General Sherman could not have surprised his country more if he had surrendered his army to Johnston," one editor exclaimed. Another columnist lamented the "few unlucky strokes of [Sherman's] pen" that had "blurred all the triumphs of his sword."

The news reports, one of Sherman's men admitted, "astonished us all." "I lament it exceedingly for I do think he had done more than any other one General to crush the rebellion and I shall always give him credit for that, whatever he does now," said a Connecticut soldier. Sherman's response was, at first, unprintable. An officer recalled his pacing the floor "like a caged lion, talking to the whole room with a furious invective which made us all stare. He lashed Stanton as a mean, scheming, vindictive politician who made it his business to rob military men of their credit earned by exposing their lives. . . . He berated the people, who blamed him for what he had done, as a mass of fools, not worth fighting for. . . . He railed at the press which had become the engine of vilification."

When Sherman left Raleigh on April 29 for a brief tour of his other commands, which were spread south along the coast, he was still fuming. Stanton's behavior, he later declared, "was an outrage on me."

Chapter Eleven

Potter's Raid

———◄○►———

FEDERAL MILITARY OPERATIONS against the remaining forces and resources of the Confederacy were carried out on both large and small scales. At 7:30 A.M. on April 5 (the day Lee found his route south blocked at Jetersville), a force numbering 2,700 men left the Atlantic coast port of Georgetown, South Carolina, and headed inland to destroy the "locomotives and rolling-stock collected on the railroad between Sumterville and Camden, South Carolina." The expedition, under the command of Union Brigadier General Edward E. Potter, consisted of two provisional brigades — one composed of white troops, the other of black — with an accompanying artillery battery, a small cavalry contingent, and a detachment of engineers.

Among the white officers in the 54th Massachusetts — the first black regiment in the North to have been recruited into Federal service* — was a Harvard man from Brighton, Massachusetts, named Edward L. Stevens. Lieutenant Stevens kept a journal of this operation, titling it "Notes on Potter's Raid." His account began with the column's stepping onto the sandy South Carolina road, where it was joined by what Stevens described as a "large train of contrabands [who] came with us for the purpose of getting their families which they had left in 'Rebbdum.' "

---

* Several other black military units were raised before the 54th, but they all began under state jurisdiction and were organized in either the South or Midwest.

He continued, "The country we passed through is the most desolate imaginable. We passed through but two or three houses all day and those of the meanest kind."

The column covered about seventeen miles on this first day of the operation and went into camp on the road to Kingstree. As young Stevens completed his journal entry that night, he remained blissfully unaware that he had only thirteen days left to live.

The raiding column of white and black U.S. troops covered some fifteen miles on April 6 as it drew near Kingstree. There was nothing out of the ordinary to report in the movement, save an incident recorded by Lieutenant Stevens in his journal: "About a mile out we came to a house, said to be occupied by a union man. Our boys rushed in & began to slay chickens & take horses so one woman pulled out her handkerchief & waved it as a signal of neutrality, but as it seemed to do no good, she uttered an exclamation & rushed frantically into the house & snatched a table cloth from the Breakfast table & waved it aloft & screamed, 'Mr. Officer, see those big men coming in here[!]' " A white officer in another black regiment complained that the "colored troops of the 2nd Brigade have been conducting themselves awfully today in straggling and pillaging on all sides."

The main column of Potter's raiding force marched fifteen more miles on April 7 without seeing anything of the enemy. Less lucky were two detachments sent off from the main line of march to destroy a pair of bridges: both parties were fired upon, and four men were wounded.

Lieutenant Stevens accompanied the group sent to burn the Kingstree bridge across the Black River. "Here was the meanest place I ever saw, black water and black mud," he wrote in his journal. The plain approaching the bridge was flooded, so the lieutenant and his men had to wade through two and a half miles of knee-deep water before getting close enough to their goal to see that the Rebels had already torched it. An enemy rear guard on the far side of the river opened fire, wounding an officer with Stevens's party and several enlisted men. By the time they returned to the main column, Stevens figured that his men had marched nearly twenty-one miles. "I was well wet through and got to bed late," he scribbled.

The Federal soldiers in the column, both black and white, continued to pillage the countryside. They did so not only with the tacit approval of their superiors but with their calculated encouragement. In a communication sent today regarding Potter's expedition, the matter of providing food to his troops was discussed. "You will keep General Potter supplied with rations, seeing that he uses them very frugally and lives as far as

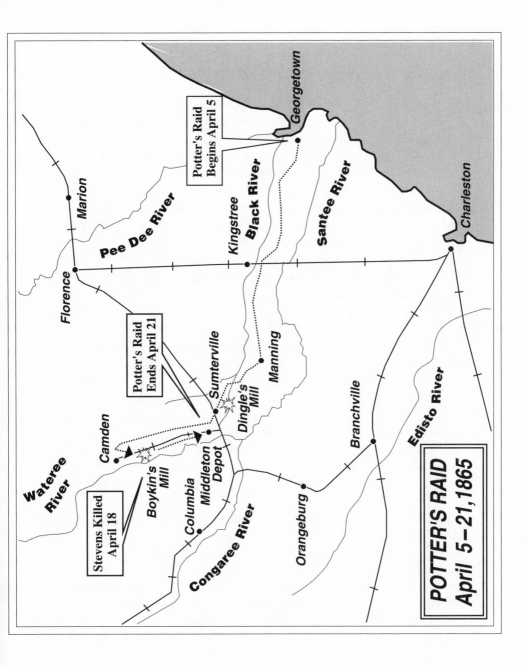

Georgetown

Potter's Raid
Begins April 5

Marion

Pee Dee River

Kingstree

Black River

Santee River

Charleston

Florence

Potter's Raid
Ends April 21

Sumterville

Manning

Dingle's
Mill

Camden

Branchville

Edisto River

Wateree
River

Boykin's
Mill

Columbia

Middleton
Depot

Orangeburg

Stevens Killed
April 18

Congaree River

POTTER'S RAID
April 5–21, 1865

possible off the country," the orders read. This policy did not sit well with all of the officers on the raid, one of whom noted in his diary, "All kinds of plunder is beginning to come in and to an extent that is positively sickening."

Potter's raiders entered the small town of Manning at dusk on April 8, after a march of more than eighteen miles. For Lieutenant Stevens, the highlight of the day came when he caught sight of a large procession of ex-slaves, some seven to eight hundred strong, trudging along next to the soldiers. "Such a sight for an artist it is to see these poor people just liberated, going on happy, under such burdens as they bear, keeping up with veteran soldiers in the long wearisome marching. It is Sad & yet encouraging to see the hope in their countenances & their perfect trust in us. What is to become of this Race of uneducated, hopeful, anxious people[?] What a change has the war bro't about!"

There was talk in the Union camps this night that the armed Rebels in the region were gathering up the road at Sumterville.* Everyone anticipated that the next day, April 9, would bring a fight.

Sunday, April 9, was a day of decision throughout the embattled South. In Virginia, Lee faced the inevitability of surrender at Appomattox Court House; at Mobile, Canby's troops prepared to assault the last bastion defending the city; and in South Carolina, Confederate defenders pooled their meager resources in an all-out attempt to turn back Potter's raiders. If the Yankees were to be repulsed, then Dingle's Mill — three miles south of Sumterville — was the place. As a Southern woman living in the area recalled, it was "the only position in the line of march from Manning which could be defended with any possibility of success."

Nearly five hundred militia — old men and boys — augmented by a small force of Kentuckians and some furloughed veterans, marched along the sandy road to the mill, dragging three cannon along. The point where the Sumterville Road crossed Turkey Creek had been dammed to form a broad millpond that was too large and too marshy to ford. The only way to traverse it was by means of a two-hundred-foot causeway flanked by heavy undergrowth. Two of the small guns hauled from Sumterville were placed in hurriedly erected earthworks on the right side of the road, ready to sweep the causeway. The third gun was found to be useless because the right primers had not been brought along; nevertheless, it too was placed in position, on the left side of the road.

Midday came and went with no sign of the enemy. The ladies of

* Modern Sumter.

Sumterville thought to send a basket dinner to one of the gunners, a convalescing Louisiana lieutenant named Pamperya, who shared it around. One of the boys in the militia watched as his uncle wolfed down a portion. "Help yourself, son," the man told him. "If we must die, die with a full stomach."

As the boy wandered back to his position, he passed another of the furloughed officers, Lieutenant W. A. McQueen, who was commanding one of the guns. The lieutenant was a picture of lightheartedness, twirling his glasses and joking with other members of the battery.

It was a little past two in the afternoon when the Yankees came into view.

General Potter was expecting trouble at Dingle's Mill, so he had detached his black brigade to flank the enemy's left by means of a roundabout plantation road that a guide had offered to show them. The white troops pressed on, coming under fire the moment they caught sight of the millpond. A first rush by Ohio troops was repulsed by the disciplined fire of the Kentucky veterans, but even as the Ohio men were falling back, two guns of Battery F, 3rd New York Light Artillery, went into action along the road. One of the fifty-five rounds fired by the battery struck the smiling Lieutenant McQueen, killing him and silencing his gun.

Potter learned from a contraband that there was a path through the swamp on the enemy's right. A detachment of New York soldiers followed this guide, gained the enemy's rear, and fired a volley that sent most of them running back toward Sumterville. Among the dead and dying left behind was Lieutenant Pamperya, killed by a rifle shot to the head.

The black brigade appeared on the scene just as the fighting was coming to a close. Their guide had lost his way, leaving the officer in charge no choice but to retrace his steps back to the main road. Lieutenant Stevens arrived in time to see the captured mill defenders. "Some of the prisoners we got were old men, some little boys, the cradle & grave," he wrote. "One of our men said as we went along, there's a soldier almost old enough to vote, referring to a 75 yr. older."

The Yankee column pushed on and by evening entered Sumterville itself. One resident recalled that the "troops came in . . . devastating everything on the way." Lieutenant Stevens, for his part, saw only the military targets: "There was fine, costly machinery here, which it will be hard for the Rebels to get replaced," he wrote in his journal. "We burned lots of cotton. . . . We went through the city singing 'Year of Jubilee['] & 'John Brown[,'] etc."

With the occupation of Sumterville, South Carolina, Potter's raiders had achieved one of the objectives of their operation. The city itself was of decent size, boasting "some good dwellings, two female seminaries and the usual public buildings," as the historian of the 54th Massachusetts later recorded. More important, it was located near the intersection of the Manchester and Wilmington Railroad with the trunk line that ran to Camden — a collecting place for Rebel rolling stock forced up from Columbia or down from Wilmington. Small columns were sent out from Sumterville to locate some of this transportation, and by the time they reported back, on April 14, they had destroyed eleven locomotives and more than seventy-four cars.

Although Lieutenant Stevens, of the 54th Massachusetts, continued to disparage the pillaging he witnessed, he had few qualms when he was offered a chance to share in some of the plunder: "I found several books which I wanted," he wrote after a stroll through looted Sumterville. Rations were again late in arriving, so when the march was resumed toward Camden on April 12 and 13, Stevens's men once more foraged off the land. "We are living splendidly with no expense to us," the lieutenant wrote in his journal. "Poultry, Honey, Potatoes, Corn Bread[,] Molasses, &c."

On the morning of April 14 Stevens ruminated about an event that was on the minds of many across the nation this historic day. He wrote, "Four years ago today the Stars & Stripes were lowered at Fort Sumter & Maj. Anderson marched out as Prisoner of War — as my man Jones says; What has happened to the country & especially to the South since then 'sets a man thinking many a way.' "

The last three days of Lieutenant Edward L. Stevens's life were filled with steady boredom and occasional action as Potter's expedition pushed north toward Camden, South Carolina. April 15 was passed in almost constant marching, to the staccato accompaniment of skirmishers up ahead firing at enemy detachments. On April 16 a fresh wave of former slaves flocked to the blue-coated columns. Wrote Stevens, "It is a joyful sight to see families and squads strolling across the fields to join their Liberators." On the same day that Johnston and Sherman first met at the Bennett House, Potter's weary raiders at last entered Camden. There it was discovered, as the general later reported, "that the locomotives and trains had been removed to Boykin's Mill, eight miles below."

On April 18 Potter ordered his men toward where the trains were said to be. Enemy troops were also on hand at Boykin's Mill, on Swift Creek, in a position reminiscent of the one the militia had taken up nine days earlier at Dingle's Mill. Here too the road bridge was blocked, there were swamps on either flank, and the usually fordable creek was flooded by water released from the millpond dam. Repeating his maneuver at Dingle's Mill, Potter swung troops around both flanks while the main body kept the enemy busy in the center. As an advance party from the 54th Massachusetts under Lieutenant Stevens pushed down to the water's edge on the enemy's left, the young officer formed them to deliver a volley. According to the regiment's historian, "As if acting under the same impulse, at the very moment this order was executed, the enemy also fired a volley, one shot striking Lieutenant Stevens in the head, killing him instantly. He fell partially into the stream. It was a dangerous duty to remove him, but two men were selected from volunteers, who, crawling forward, brought back his body."

Another regiment found a way across the marsh, and the enemy was soon flanked and sent running. Stevens was one of two Union fatalities in this action, and perhaps the last Union officer to die in combat. The other fatality was James P. Johnson, a black corporal.

Potter's men fought a similar engagement on each of the next two days (with no reported losses) as they closed inexorably on Middleton Depot, where they found and destroyed fifteen locomotives and many boxcars. On April 21 a courier arrived with news of the Sherman-Johnston armistice and instructions to cease active operations. "The war was over," an Ohio officer in the expedition declared. Lieutenant Edward L. Stevens had missed the end by three days.*

---

* Stevens was buried on the battlefield at Boykin's Mill. In 1885 his body was transferred to the National Cemetery at Florence, South Carolina.

Chapter Twelve

"The whole country seemed to be alive with demons"

———◆◇◆———

I T WAS ALL a question of bridges. The major obstacle in the way of James Wilson's cavalry sweep into the heart of Georgia was the rain-swollen Chattahoochee River, which delineated the Alabama–Georgia border. If Wilson could seize an intact span, he would not have to call upon his pontoniers, who would have to haul their campaign-battered equipment a long, time-consuming distance to do the job. There were bridges to be found at two places along his line of march — West Point, Georgia, and, thirty-five miles below that, Columbus. Wilson decided to try for both crossings by detaching one brigade to capture the West Point bridge while the rest of his command moved against the other.

West Point, Georgia

The Rebel defenses at West Point consisted of a single thirty-five-yard-square redoubt on the Alabama side of the river, garrisoned by a scratch force of Georgia militia and Louisiana and South Carolina artillerymen, with a sprinkling of furloughed soldiers stuck here by circumstances elsewhere. Commanding this forlorn hope was Brigadier General Robert C. Tyler, an invalided survivor of Shiloh and Missionary Ridge.

Tyler had no choice but to concentrate his defenses in the three-gun redoubt (equipped with a thirty-two-pounder siege gun and two twelve-pounders), which the locals had taken to calling Fort Tyler in his honor. An officer who inspected the position with him exclaimed, "Why, General, this is a slaughter pen!" "I know it," Tyler replied, "but we must man and try to hold it." The time was about eight o'clock on the morning of April 16 when a horseman galloped into town with the dreaded news that the Yankees were coming.

Colonel Oscar H. LaGrange's brigade of Indiana, Kentucky, and Wisconsin riders had drawn the West Point assignment. They broke camp at 2:00 A.M. and arrived near the town about eight hours later. While skirmishers from the 2nd Indiana Cavalry pushed Tyler's pickets back into their defenses, gunners from the 18th Indiana Artillery swung into action to begin a slow bombardment that continued until almost one-thirty in the afternoon. One of the fort's young defenders recalled that it was not long before the enemy cannoneers found the range, and thereafter "every ball hit the mark, that is, every few minutes while squatting against the parapet when loading my gun, I could feel the jar." When a shell fragment severed the flagpole halyards, a Georgia sergeant squirreled up the staff and tacked the standard back in place.

LaGrange had come here to secure a crossing, so his first move was aimed at accomplishing that goal. A dismounted battle line from the 2nd Indiana, 7th Kentucky Cavalry, and 1st Wisconsin Cavalry moved up to engage the bastion's defenders while the 4th Indiana Cavalry went all out for the river. "Our regiment was then directed to get up as close to the fort as possible — behind buildings, fences, posts, and anything affording the slightest cover, and act as sharpshooters to silence the fire of the fort," a Kentucky rider recollected. Shortly after midday, the Indiana horsemen charged. "Surprised the garrison and took possession of the bridge across Chattahoochie," a Hoosier wrote in his journal.

Now it was Fort Tyler's turn. By this time the Federals had noted the broad and deep ditch surrounding the redoubt, so while skirmishers banged away at any defender who showed his head, other Yankees began ripping up neighboring houses to obtain enough planking to bridge the gap. It was sometime during this phase of the scrap that General Tyler was killed by a sharpshooter hidden in a nearby group of houses, which Tyler himself had spared from demolition out of consideration for the hardship it would cause the owners.

The Federal assault finally got under way near sundown. A Wisconsin officer with the reserve watched the events unfold: "Our boys are rapidly approaching the works. There they go into the ditch; now up on the embankment! There they lie within 10 feet of the enemy, waiting for the rest of the brigade to get up close as they are. While in the ditch lighted fuse shells are thrown over among our boys, but they prove boomerangs in every instance, for our boys pitch them back into the fort, where they explode. . . . Then they threw over great rocks, and some of our boys are badly bruised by them. . . . The Bugler is sounding the charge. Up they spring to the top of the embankment like a swarm of bees. Up goes the white flag, they have surrendered!" A Wisconsin sergeant made it official by chopping down the flagpole holding the garrison's nailed-up standard.

Fort Tyler and, more importantly, the West Point bridge were now firmly under Union control, at a cost of 36 killed or wounded. Among the 120 or so Confederates who held the fort, along with others who defended the bridge, Colonel LaGrange reported 18 dead, 28 wounded, and 218 captured. Most of the Confederate killed were in the fort, which one artilleryman described as having "a awful look."

Columbus, Georgia

While darkness marked an end to the fight at West Point, it only signaled the commencement of Wilson's attack on Columbus. His lead brigade hauled within sight of the river early in the afternoon. Wilson's target was actually two towns — Columbus, Georgia, on the east bank of the Chattahoochee, and Girard, Alabama,* on the west. It was on the Girard side that the Confederate authorities had decided to concentrate their defenses, with the heaviest earthworks protecting the upper wagon bridge, while the lower crossing was less well guarded. Nevertheless, the mixed force of civilians and soldiers was able to turn back the initial U.S. rushes against the south side. A young soldier manning the line never forgot the moment of first contact: "I heard the minie ball hiss near my ears. And the clanking of the swords of the Federal cavalry in front of me. The whole battle lines of the Confederates popped like firecrackers." What the Yankee scouts had not realized was that the lower bridge had been rendered impassible by the removal of much of the floor planking. The first Union troopers on the scene discovered the stratagem rather quickly when they rushed and gained entrance to the lower bridge, only to have to pull back when they saw the large gap in the floor. At this point a C.S. engineer on the Columbus side ordered the lower bridge to be set afire, and it was soon fully engulfed.

* Modern Phenix City.

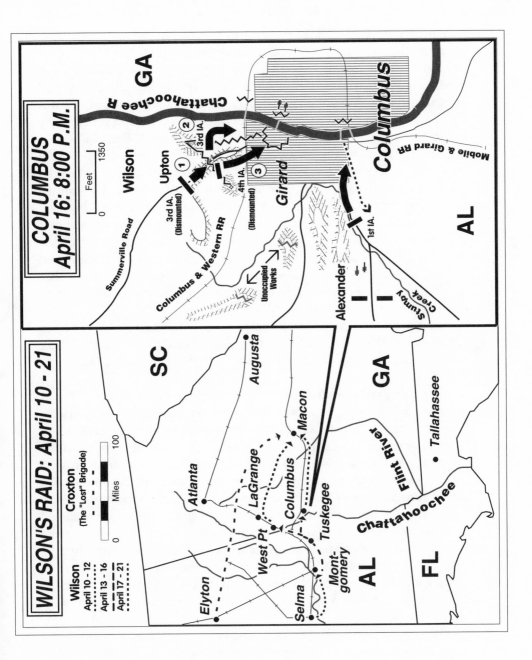

COLUMBUS
April 16: 8:00 P.M.

GA

Chattahoochee R

Wilson

Upton

3rd IA.

Feet
0   1350

Summerville Road

3rd IA.
(Dismounted)

4th IA.
(Dismounted)

Girard

Columbus & Western RR

Unoccupied
Works

Columbus

Mobile & Girard RR

Alexander

1st IA.

Stinoy Creek

AL

WILSON'S RAID: April 10 - 21

SC

Augusta

Atlanta

LaGrange

Macon

Elyton

West Pt

Columbus

Tuskegee

Mont-
gomery

Selma

GA

Chattahoochee

Flint River

Tallahassee

AL

FL

Wilson
April 10 - 12
April 13 - 16
April 17 - 21

Croxton
(The "Lost" Brigade)

Miles
0   100

255

Wilson promptly shifted his forces to take on the defenses protecting the upper bridge. He had hoped to make his attack before dark, but a communications mixup resulted in the key brigade's not coming into position until after sundown. "As we had already become pretty well accustomed to night fighting and its advantages," Wilson said afterward, "it occurred to me that an attack after dark would be accompanied by less loss and greater success than one in full daylight." The troops who would have to make the attack were all under the command of Emory Upton, an officer who reveled in devising new combat tactics and implementing difficult tactical exercises. When told of Wilson's decision, he responded, "By jingo, I'll do it; and I'll sweep everything before me."

Federal scouts had identified what they considered to be the enemy's main line of defense running at right angles across the Summerville Road. The plan called for Upton to crack this line with a dismounted charge, which would be followed immediately by a mounted force that would race through the breach to seize the upper bridge before it could be burned.

Phase one — the dismounted charge — was launched at 8:30 P.M. Six companies of the 3rd Iowa Cavalry "went forward at once with a cheer under the heavy fire and cleared the works," the regiment's commander reported.

Then came the mounted phase. Two companies of the 10th Missouri Cavalry rode through the captured lines to take possession of the bridge. The only problem was that the Union scouts had badly misread the Confederate defenses: the earthworks stormed by the 3rd Iowa were not the enemy's main line but only a forward outpost. A heavily manned row of works ran along the river parallel to the road, with an additional small belt of fortifications protecting the western approach to the bridge itself. At first everything went according to plan, as the Confederates assumed that the troopers (indistinguishable as Yankees in the darkness) were their own and let them pass along the works without a challenge. But the Federal riders were found out before they reached their goal, and "all of a sudden there was a shot, another, and in a second 10,000 more," a Missouri officer remembered. "The whole country seemed to be alive with demons."

The two mounted companies reeled back. "We tried to retrace our steps, but were so mixed up that we took a road leading direct to the fort of the enemy," the officer wrote. After taking fire from this strongpoint, the scattered soldiers finally scrambled up the road and back into the Union lines.

The Confederate reaction to the rush of the Missouri troops also served to outline their position in pinpoints of flame. A young girl watching with her family from high ground on the Columbus side of the river vividly recollected how the "flashes from the guns looked like streaks of lightning darting from the lower bridge up the river as far as we could see." The six companies of the 3rd Iowa now pivoted to their left to take on this new objective. "The ground over which this evolution had to be performed was very much broken, but the officers and men went forward with a cheer, passing in the profound darkness over fences, ditches, and sloughs, with no other guide than the light and the roar of the rebels' fire," noted the regimental commander. The Iowa boys stormed a battery located just east of the road, then swung to their right and began rolling up the enemy lines. Veteran Confederate troops now realized, as one artillerist put it, that the time had come "to take care of ourselves."

The 4th Iowa Cavalry, which had been waiting in reserve, advanced in a charge. "Boys, go for the bridge," the brigade commander shouted as the troops moved forward. "And we did go, as fast as horses' legs could carry us," a member of the regiment recalled. This mounted rush carried the Yankees onto the bridge itself, which was crowded with panicked defenders. "It was a covered wooden bridge, with two carriageways, and the whole space was now filled with the flying rebels and the advancing Iowans," remembered one of the soldiers. "The air was full of the odor of turpentine. The angles of the woodworks had been stuffed with cotton saturated with that fluid, so that the whole could be burned instantly in case of defeat in the works; but the persons charged with the duty of setting the fire could not determine the moment of action, perhaps because enemies appeared before their friends were all through."

Another Iowa horseman recollected, "On the Columbus side of the river two cannon were mounted in the road, loaded with canister, to sweep the bridge. . . . We and the enemy were all mixed up together on the bridge, so the Johnnies could not fire the cannons. When we got across the bridge we had a struggle for the two cannons. The officer in command of the cannons was killed, and we had one man killed. Then we fought the rebels by their own gas lights in the streets of Columbus, Ga."

Civilians caught in the confused terror of a night fight fled the city in panic. A participant in the mad rush observed that "at one place the women and children were running through the streets like people deranged, and men, with mules and wagons, driving in every direction."

The combat was over by eleven o'clock. Girard, Columbus, and the vital bridge were all in Union hands, at a cost of twenty-four Federals killed or wounded. "The capture of Columbus settled the fate of

Georgia," wrote an Ohio trooper, ". . . and convinced Gen. Wilson that he was master of the situation, and could march his command in any way his mood dictated."

Behind all the congratulations was the somber reality of a Civil War battlefield. It was viewed immediately after the fighting had ceased by an officer on Upton's staff who recorded the scene: "The ground is strewn with blankets, guns, haversacks and camp debris, while at intervals stood silent abandoned cannon. There are but few dead and wounded left on the field, but here and there is a marble face, or a wounded man who has raised himself up to hail the chance passers, or begging for water. It is all impressive, even weird, and rendered more so by the added light of some nearby burning buildings. As I turn back, the ambulance corps, with lights and stretchers, comes out to pick up the unfortunates."

The flames from burning war matériel were still crackling around Columbus when James Wilson acted to ensure the success of the next phase of his raid. A two-regiment strike force was sent out late on April 17 to seize intact the bridges across the Flint River. This was accomplished after a brief fight on the morning of April 18. Wilson and the rest of his command were not far behind, averaging about thirty miles per day, making this, he later bragged, "one of the most rapid and important campaigns made by either side."

Wilson's next target was Macon, whose defense had been entrusted to Major General Howell Cobb, a former Speaker of the U.S. House of Representatives. Cobb's defense force consisted mostly of raw militia levies and inspired no one. "The demoralization is complete," a woman refugee in town wrote in her journal. "We are whipped, there is no doubt about it. Everybody feels it, and there is no use for the men to try to fight any longer." On April 20 Cobb received a message from General Beauregard announcing the Sherman-Johnston truce. He wasted no time dismantling his defenses and sent messengers off to meet Wilson with the news.

When Cobb's representatives encountered Wilson's van, under Colonel Robert H. Minty, they tried to convince the Federals that the terms of the ceasefire required them to halt their advance. Minty would have none of it. He told the truce party that it had five minutes to get back to Macon and then ordered his lead elements to continue. Despite the Georgians' head start, the first details quickly caught up again with Cobb's emissaries, who seemed to be purposely moving slowly in order to stall the Federal column. Minty ordered a charge, which cleared the road and took the bluecoats into the outskirts of Macon. Faced with this action, General Cobb grudgingly surrendered the city.

Word that Macon had been taken, and that there was a general truce, made its way quickly along Wilson's weary columns. The news was at first greeted with astonishment by the men of the 4th Michigan Cavalry, but once it became clear that these were not idle rumors, "a terrific shout went up, a regular old cavalry charging yell soon taken up by the other regiments in line, repeated and enlarged as the wave of news struck the column that had been gradually massing in column of brigades in our rear, and it was a long time to be remembered."

At six o'clock on the evening of April 21, Wilson, in Macon, received a cipher message from Sherman sent via Johnston, ordering him to "desist from further acts of war and devastation until you hear that hostilities are renewed."

The greatest cavalry raid of the Civil War had come to an end.

The column of Union infantry dispatched from Mobile to assist Wilson's cavalry arrived at Montgomery and Selma long after the Federal riders had passed through those places. Elements of the Sixteenth Corps reached the outskirts of the Alabama capital on April 25 and paraded through town two days later. "The streets were full of negroes and a few citizens," an Iowa soldier recollected. "The citizens did not seem very glad to see us." Units from the Thirteenth Corps arrived at Selma on April 27. "Selma, you know, a short time ago was visited by Wilson's cavalry and a perfect wreck they made of the business part of the city," an Ohio foot soldier wrote to his sweetheart a few days after getting there. "Large arsenals and extensive foundries lie in ruins — cannon of the largest caliber and in every state of construction lie about in heaps. . . . Nearly everyone expresses a longing desire for the war to end and, I fancy, the desire to come under the wing of the old government is daily increasing."

The writing on the wall was becoming painfully evident to the Confederate charged with the defense of the Department of Alabama, Mississippi, and East Louisiana. The patrician officer, Lieutenant General Richard Taylor, worried as much about the excesses of his own troops as he did about the actions of the enemy. "One great trouble the citizens of your section will have to contend with," he warned an Alabama planter in late April, "is the outrages of our own stragglers and deserters." When word of Lee's surrender and news of the (first) Sherman-Johnston armistice reached him, Taylor asked for a conference with his opposite number, Major General E. R. S. Canby.

The two met on April 29, at a point "ten miles north of Mobile, near the railway." Canby made quite a production of the whole affair, arriving with a large escort, a military band, and ample culinary service. Taylor's entrance was equally dramatic, albeit indicative of the low fortunes of the Confederacy. "With one officer, Colonel William Levy ..., I made my appearance on a hand-car, the motive power of which was two negroes," Taylor later wrote.

Following what Taylor remembered as a "bountiful luncheon," and a concert at which Canby asked for "Dixie" and Taylor requested "Hail Columbia," the two agreed to a ceasefire with the by now standard provision for termination upon forty-eight hours' notice. Hardly had Taylor issued orders to that effect, however, when word came from Canby that Sherman's terms had been rejected and that hostilities would resume in two days' time.

Taylor briefly considered and then firmly rejected the notion that his forces might scatter into guerrilla bands to continue the struggle. Should any of his men attempt that, he warned a subordinate, "they will be hunted down like beasts of prey, their families will be persecuted, and ruin thus entailed not only upon the soldiers themselves, but also upon thousands of defenseless Southern women and children." The time had come for action. "There was no room for hesitancy," Taylor later declared. "Folly and madness combined would not have justified an attempt to prolong a hopeless contest."

Taylor met with Canby again on May 4, at Citronelle, Alabama, and surrendered all the troops under his command. As he recalled the moment, "I delivered the epilogue of the great drama in which I had played a humble part." In a parallel action, the Confederate naval vessels in his department also hauled down their flags, and a number of former C.S. transports were pressed into service returning Union troops to Mobile from the Alabama interior. A Yankee sailor thought it "a splendid sight to witness those prize steamers coming down in line together. They were quite forlorn-looking — emblematic of the so-called confederacy. The leading one ... had a calliope, which played the tune, whilst passing us, 'Ain't I glad I'm out of the wilderness?' which seemed to speak its sentiments, as it looked rather the worse for wear."

One by one, like candles guttering in a gusty wind, the newspapers of the Confederacy were going out. That there had ever been any at all was a proud tribute to the indomitable will of publishers who persevered in the face of shortages of paper, ink, type, and news services. The communication network throughout the South had been fragile at the best of times, and the blunt blows of the final weeks of the war completely disrupted telegraphic and rail connections between most Southern cities.

Wilson's capture of Columbus ended the saga of what was perhaps the Confederacy's most peripatetic newspaper, the *Memphis Appeal*. From 1862 to 1865 it became so good at changing its base in time to keep one jump ahead of the enemy that admiring competitors referred to it as the "Moving Appeal." Its luck finally ran out at Columbus, where Wilson singled out its presses for destruction. Three years earlier the paper's editors had prophetically declared, "Our fate is indissolubly connected with that of the Confederacy."

One of the last grasps for hope came from the May 2 issue of the *Jackson* (Mississippi) *Free Trader*. Lacking any hard information on events in faraway Virginia, the paper reported the comments of a Doctor H. J. Holmes, who had arrived in Jackson with an armful of Columbus papers dated April 15. "No mention is made in them of LEE's surrender," the *Free Trader*'s writer crowed. "It is officially reported that Gen. LEE and JOHNSTON whipped Gen. Grant in two successive engagements. Grant has lost 100,000. A truce was thus agreed upon to try and arrange difficulties." Turning to another Southern paper, this one dated April 25, the *Free Trader* quoted, "What becomes of that address of Gen. Lee to his troops upon capitulating, and which so many so greedily swallowed? Our readers will notice that it bears the stamp of forgery upon its face. It is 'Headquarters Army of Virginia.' Gen. Lee is too exact a man to make such a mistake, and it should be 'Headquarters Armies of the Confederate States.' But enough. The tale is told."

On May 3 Nathan Bedford Forrest sat in on a conference of Southern leaders and listened incredulously as one of them outlined a plan to retreat across the Mississippi River to join Kirby Smith's Trans-Mississippi Department. "Men, you may all do as you damn please," he said as he abruptly rose to leave the room, "but I'm a-going home." When someone reminded Forrest that he still commanded troops in the field, the legendary Confederate fighter responded, "Any man who is in favor of a further prosecution of this war is a fit subject for a lunatic asylum, and ought to be sent there immediately."

Six days later Forrest formally surrendered his command. In his farewell address, he told his men, "Civil war, such as you have just passed through, naturally engenders feelings of animosity, hatred, and revenge. It is our duty to divest ourselves of all such feelings, and, so far as it is in our power to do so, to cultivate feelings toward those with whom we have so long contested, and heretofore so widely but honestly differed. . . . Whatever your responsibilities may be to government, to society, or to individuals, meet them like men."

On May 16 James Wilson enjoyed the satisfaction of placing under arrest a man who had recently sought his protection. Nine days earlier, the figure who would soon be known throughout the North as "the demon of Andersonville" had written to Wilson:

> I am a native of Switzerland, and was before the war a citizen of Louisiana, by profession a physician. Like hundreds and thousands of others I was carried away by the maelstrom of excitement and joined the Southern Army. . . . [In] February, 1864 . . . I was ordered to report to the commandant of military prisoners at Andersonville, Ga., who assigned me to the command of the interior of the prison. The duties I had to perform were arduous and unpleasant and I am satisfied that no one can or will justly blame me for things that happened here and which were beyond my power to control. . . . Still I now bear the odium, and men who were prisoners here seem disposed to wreak their vengeance upon me. . . . My life is in danger, and I most respectfully ask of you help and relief. . . . My intention is to return with my family to Europe as soon as I can make the arrangements.

The letter was signed *Hy. Wirz, Captain, C.S. Army.*

The day after Wilson received this plea, he ordered his aide Henry E. Noyes "to go to Andersonville and arrest Wirz." A week later Wilson reported to Washington, "I have arrested Capt. H. Wirz, C.S. Army, notorious as commandant of the Andersonville prison. . . . I respectfully request that this miscreant be brought before a general court-martial."

Troops under Wilson's command removed another Confederate state capital from the map with a flag-raising ceremony in Tallahassee on May 20. The Federals had entered the town unopposed nine days earlier, in what one resident remembered as "a long line of blue." The official flag ceremony, accompanied by a cannon salute for every state in the Union, met with a mixed reaction from the crowd. "The soldiers and Negroes were in ecstasy; the citizens were not so enthusiastic, but some of them removed their hats in token," wrote a Yankee sympathizer.

Chapter Thirteen

"My husband and baby are gone!"

————◦————

THE SURRENDER of the Confederacy's two largest standing armies, and the ability of Union forces to penetrate at will into hitherto secure areas, posed a vexing problem for C.S. military authorities: What to do with the Union prisoners of war who were scattered in camps throughout the South? The answer to the question varied. In some cases the exchange system was speeded up; in others, scarce transportation resources and military assets were employed to keep the POWs out of Federal hands.

In early April several thousand inmates of the notorious prison camp at Andersonville were brought down to Albany, Georgia. From there they were marched sixty miles to Thomasville, only to find that the rail line to Darien had been destroyed and they would have to retrace their steps. The prisoners remained in Andersonville until April 17, when they were suddenly moved to Macon, then to Albany again, and then on to Thomasville. Finally, when it was apparent that the Confederate commissary was no longer capable of supplying them, they were allowed to pass into the Union lines in Florida. According to a reporter who witnessed their arrival, "Their clothing was in tatters; their faces were begrimed with dirt and black smoke from pine wood; they nearly were all without shoes; many were without hats. Large numbers were affected with scurvy."

Thousands of other prisoners clogged the exchange pipeline when the C.S. military administration began to unravel. Prisoner exchange had been the accepted practice until 1863, when the system had fallen apart due to mutual distrust and a hardline Union policy that recognized that the North, with its larger population base, was better able to replace the men lost as prisoners than was the South. Exchanges on a man-for-man basis were resumed in 1865, when a combination of humanitarian concerns and political pressures caused the Federals to end their boycott. By the war's end more than four hundred thousand men would have spent time in prison camps (both North and South), where the generally squalid conditions, malnourishment, lack of adequate sanitary and medical facilities, and occasionally brutal supervision would claim over fifty-six thousand lives.

Once the exchange system was again in operation, officials began to move the prisoners to designated sites where rolls could be prepared for use in later accountings. In early April Robert Ould, a Confederate exchange commissioner, selected Vicksburg, Mississippi, as one of those sites (though it had already been functioning in that capacity for several weeks). Thousands of Union prisoners were shipped to Jackson, Mississippi, where, if they were lucky, they caught a train or hitched a wagon ride to Vicksburg; if not, they had to walk the thirty miles. Once at Vicksburg, they were placed in a parole camp (managed by Federal authorities) known as Camp Fisk, located four miles east of the river city. More than 5,500 men passed through Camp Fisk in March and April 1865, most of them coming from either Andersonville or the prison compound at Cahaba, Alabama. An agent for the Sanitary Commission who was charged with helping these men described many of them as being "in very feeble and distressing condition."

The collapse of the Confederacy's infrastructure made it virtually impossible for the government to manage the exchange mechanism, so Confederate authorities agreed to ignore the time-consuming protocols of the system and allow Union POWs to be moved to northern camps, where they could be better treated. This created, in its turn, both a financial windfall for contractors who could provide steamboats capable of handling the traffic, and the potential for great corruption among the officers charged with oversight.

The exchange post of Vicksburg had, in April 1865, more than its share of officers who had come there under a cloud of suspicion. Captain George A. Williams, commissary of musters, had been brought up on

charges of "excessive cruelty . . . and gross neglect of duty" while running a military prison and hospital in Memphis in 1864. Only his friendship with U. S. Grant had saved him from a dishonorable discharge.
Lieutenant Colonel Reuben B. Hatch, chief quartermaster, had already
faced down indictments of fraud and accepting kickbacks when he took
the lucrative Vicksburg assignment.

The situation at Vicksburg seemed designed for abuse. Vessels carrying POWs from there to camps in the North were paid by the head (the
going rate was $5.00 per enlisted man and $10.00 per officer); it was all
extra profit, and the more soldiers aboard, the better the black ink. It
was left to the officers on the scene to decide how many men a particular
ship would be allowed to take, and which ships would be assigned this
human cargo. Boat selection was made by either Lieutenant Colonel
Hatch or his assistant, Captain W. F. Kerns, while responsibility for actually selecting and shipping the parolees rested with Captain Williams
and his assistant, Captain Frederic Speed. As Williams was absent from
his post in early April on a mission to Mobile, Captain Speed was in
charge of shipment.

At first everything seemed to function smoothly. Some 1,300 men
were sent north on the steamboat *Henry Ames* on April 21, followed two
days later by 700 more on the *Olive Branch*. Hardly had the latter
cleared port, however, when trouble began on shore. Captain Speed met
with Major General Napoleon J. T. Dana, commander of the Department of the Mississippi, to report a breach of orders and rumors of
corruption. The arrival of all boats at Vicksburg was to be promptly
reported to Captain Speed's office, so that he might then assign paroled
soldiers to them. This had not been done in the case of the *Olive Branch*.
When Speed informed Lieutenant Colonel Hatch of this omission, he
was told that Hatch suspected his assistant, Kerns, of taking bribes to
ensure that only certain boats would be loaded with prisoners. General
Dana listened to Speed's unsubstantiated allegations and promised to
investigate.

That same evening, April 23, the steamboat *Sultana* limped into
Vicksburg on its journey upriver from New Orleans. Some ten hours
earlier the ship's chief engineer, Nathan Wintringer, had discovered a
crack in one of the four boilers that provided steam for the engines.
Fearing an explosion, Wintringer had immediately reduced the steam
pressure, and thus the boat's power. Once the steamer was tied up at
Vicksburg, a local boilermaker was summoned. He at first insisted that
only a major overhaul would restore the boiler to safe operating condition, but Wintringer eventually convinced him that a temporary patch

would be enough to get the *Sultana* to St. Louis, where a proper repair job could be done.*

The master of the *Sultana,* Captain J. Cass Mason (who, as part owner, shared in all profits), was anxious to get under way again as soon as possible. He had been promised a full load of returning prisoners and worried that too long a stopover would see that cash cargo shipped in other hulls. Throughout the day of April 24, while the reluctant boiler-maker performed the makeshift repairs, Captain Mason pulled every string he could to assure himself of rich pickings. At first Speed informed the captain that no men could be shipped on his steamer, but then he changed his mind and told Mason to expect no more than five hundred or so, since the rolls for only that many had been prepared. Mason com-plained to Captain Williams (who had returned to Vicksburg on April 23 but had not yet formally assumed his duties), and after trying and failing to change Speed's mind, Williams brought Speed over to speak with Lieutenant Colonel Hatch. The two persuaded him that it was not necessary to work up the rolls *before* the men boarded; rather, it would be sufficient to check in the soldiers as they went on the boat, so more than the five hundred then on the rolls could be sent. Speed finally agreed to their "suggestion."

The transfer of prisoners from Camp Fisk to the *Sultana* began on April 24, even as the boiler repairs continued. Lacking an accurate count of the soldiers then in camp, Speed supervised the Fisk side of the opera-tion believing their number to be only 1,300 or so. There were actually nearly 2,400.

As the men began to arrive from Camp Fisk and go on board the *Sultana,* Captain Kerns, standing near the loading ramps, grew increas-ingly worried that the steamer was becoming dangerously crowded. There was another vessel already at the dock, with a second soon to follow, and Kerns wondered if some of the men might not be placed on them instead. He sent a note off to Speed at Camp Fisk, who, still un-aware of the numbers involved, rejected the request. Lieutenant Colonel Hatch and Captain Williams observed the overloading of the *Sultana* without comment, while General Dana chose to remain oblivious to what was happening just a short distance from his headquarters. At one point Williams even thought that Speed was purposely delaying the sol-diers at Camp Fisk, and told General Dana he suspected collusion to keep them there for another ship. Kerns tried once again to get Hatch or

---

* The boilermaker, R. G. Taylor, later admitted to having had serious misgivings about the repair, but the fix was approved by Wintringer.

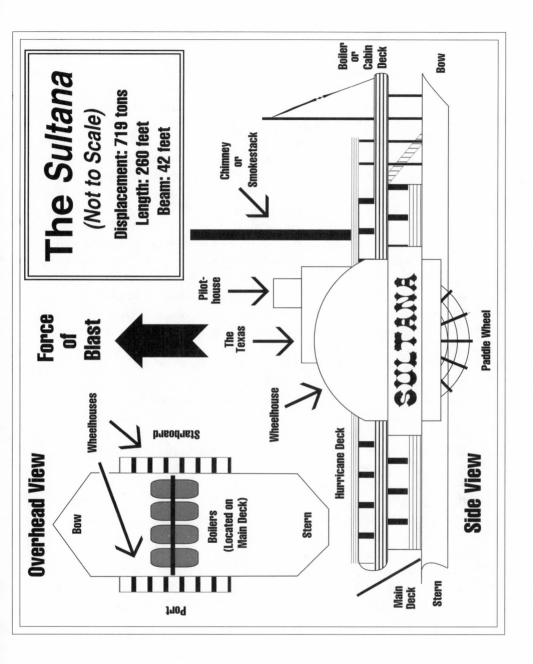

The Sultana
(Not to Scale)

Displacement: 719 tons
Length: 260 feet
Beam: 42 feet

Overhead View

Force of Blast

Wheelhouses

Starboard

Bow

Boilers (Located on Main Deck)

Stern

Port

Side View

Chimney or Smokestack

Boiler or Cabin Deck

Bow

Pilot-house

The Texas

Wheelhouse

SULTANA

Paddle Wheel

Hurricane Deck

Main Deck

Stern

the post commander, Brigadier General Morgan L. Smith, to do something, but neither would interfere. Someone, it would seem, wanted as many prisoners as possible put on the *Sultana*.

For the most part, the soldiers were just happy to be going home. "Everybody *was* ready," a Michigan soldier declared. Yet few were pleased with the situation they found on the *Sultana*. "Our condition on this boat was more like a lot of hogs than men," an Ohio veteran complained. The ex-prisoners came from the camp in three trainloads spread throughout the day.* As each wave made its way up the gangplank, the new arrivals had to squeeze into a vessel that was already filled with those who had arrived ahead of them as well as a cargo consisting of approximately a hundred mules and horses, 150 tons of sugar, and ninety cases of wine. When the few officers present† tried to object, they were told that there was no problem. An assistant quartermaster stationed at Vicksburg began to ask questions and was sharply reminded that "officers sometimes get dismissed from the service for meddling with that which is none of their business." To add to the misery of those aboard the *Sultana,* no provision had been made for their medical care or treatment during the voyage home.

Captain Speed arrived at the ship about dark with the third and final trainload of men. When Captain Kerns complained to him about the overloading, Speed took up the matter with Captain Williams, who assured him that "there is plenty of room and they can all go comfortably." Speed, at the end of what must have been a long and frustrating day, simply gave up caring and became anxious to see his problem (and miscalculation) go away.

By nine o'clock at night, everything was ready. The leaking boiler had been patched,‡ and extra supports had been hammered into place to buttress the upper decks, which were sagging under the weight of so many men. With a final blast of its whistle, the *Sultana* backed away from the wharf, then turned its blunt nose into the surging river. The Mississippi was running wide and fast because of recent rains, and the side wheels labored to move the heavily laden craft forward into the current. "It was quite late in the evening," noted Sergeant Nicholas Karns of the

---

* Both Williams and Speed later testified that they believed just two trainloads of POWs had been sent.

† Officers were usually separated from enlisted men at the time of capture and kept apart from them. Very few officers were sent to either Andersonville or Cahaba.

‡ Lacking the proper materials, the boilermaker had placed a ¼-inch thick patch on the boiler skin, which had an actual thickness of $^{17}/_{48}$ inch.

18th Ohio, "and as she pulled out from her moorings we cheered and shouted."

"We were highly elated with the thoughts of going home," a Tennessee soldier recalled. Said a comrade in an Indiana regiment, "We were all talking of home and friends and the many good things we would have to eat." "The next day was bright and beautiful and the air was a little chilly," reminisced Charles M. Eldridge of the 3rd Tennessee Cavalry. "I sat all day leaning against the smokestack to keep warm. As the river was on one of its booms it spread all over the lowlands, some places being miles wide."

Alexander C. Brown, an Ohio veteran, fell into a conversation with one of the ship's clerks and asked how many men were aboard. According to Brown, "the clerk replied that if we arrived safe at Cairo[, Illinois,] it would be the greatest trip ever made on the western waters, as there were more people on board than were ever carried on one boat on the Mississippi river." In addition to the crew of about eighty and a paying passenger list of one hundred (including women and children), there were approximately 2,400 soldiers packed onto the *Sultana,* putting the total at more than 2,500. The ship was licensed to carry 376 passengers.

"I know that on the lower deck we were just about as thick as we could possibly lie all over the deck," recollected Chester D. Berry, "and I understand that all the other decks were the same." "The men lay so thick that I could not see any of the deck," insisted a Michigan cavalryman. It soon became evident to everyone that this was not just a typical passage. "I noticed that the boat was top heavy . . . ," wrote a West Virginia trooper. "Under action of one wheel at a time she would keel away over to one side." When the ship made a stop at Helena, Arkansas, word spread among the packed men that a photographer on shore was making a picture of them. As the men rushed as one to that side, "I entreated and exhorted prudence," remembered Captain J. Walter Elliott of the 44th U.S. Colored Troops, "momentarily expecting a capsizing and sinking." The boat's master hurriedly instructed several officers to better control their men so that there would be no repeat of the incident.

At 6:30 P.M. on April 26 the *Sultana* landed at Memphis, where it lay over for a few hours while some of the cargo was taken off and several more paying passengers were brought on. A few soldiers took the opportunity to celebrate ashore, despite strict orders that they were not to leave the vessel. Among the majority who remained on board, several enjoyed an unexpected feast when "one of the hogsheads of sugar was bursted, and a number of the men and boys had quite a picnic." The *Sultana* left Memphis at 11:00 P.M. and paddled across the Mississippi to

Hopefield, Arkansas, where a thousand bushels of coal were loaded in the hold. While this was taking place, a skiff from Memphis pulled up alongside, carrying an Indiana private named George Downing, who had missed the sailing and paid a boatman two dollars to return him to the ship. Downing considered himself lucky: he had got mail while at Vicksburg containing funds requested from his family, and so had been able to afford the ride out. "If I had not sent home for that money I would have been left [behind]," Downing told his friend Henry J. Kline.

The *Sultana* left the coaling station at around one o'clock in the morning on April 27. The acting master's mate of a Federal gunboat anchored nearby found that he could still marvel at the sight of a ship's leaving port: "She was all lit up and presented the usual fine appearance of a large passenger steamer with all her lights aglow . . . as she backed out and started up the river." The soldiers spread out across the boat to find places to sleep. Sergeant Karns located an open spot next to the cabin-deck stairway. "As soon as the boat was under headway again," he remembered, "I fell into a sound slumber and was soon lost in sweet dreams." Another Buckeye soldier, George Hass of the 102nd Regiment, nestled to sleep nearby. Hass had enjoyed prime quarters in a cabin directly over the boilers for part of the trip. "It was warm there and made it a desirable place for sleeping. However, before we reached Memphis we had to vacate in order to make room for some of the sick soldiers," he recalled. Charles M. Eldridge had no such poor luck. His bunk space was directly over the boilers, and the instant the *Sultana* left Memphis he had no trouble falling "sound asleep."

It was a few minutes after 2:00 A.M. The *Sultana* had reached a point approximately eight miles above Memphis and had just worked its way through a group of islands known as Paddy's Hen and Chicks when, with no warning whatsoever, the boat was wracked by a thunderous explosion.

The "first thing that I knew or heard was a terrible crash, everything seemed to be falling," remembered a Michigan soldier. "A piece of iron glanced my head," added a Kentucky comrade, "and in the excitement I thought the rebels had fired a battery on us." "Not more than three feet from where I was lying was a hole clear through the boat," declared an Ohio veteran. "It seemed as if the explosion of the boilers had torn everything out from top to bottom."

Charles Eldridge was blown high into the air. "I was whirling over and over," he later wrote. He came down into the cold Mississippi River, where he had enough presence of mind to grasp a piece of a ladder that was floating by. Ohioan Nicholas Karns sprang to his feet immediately

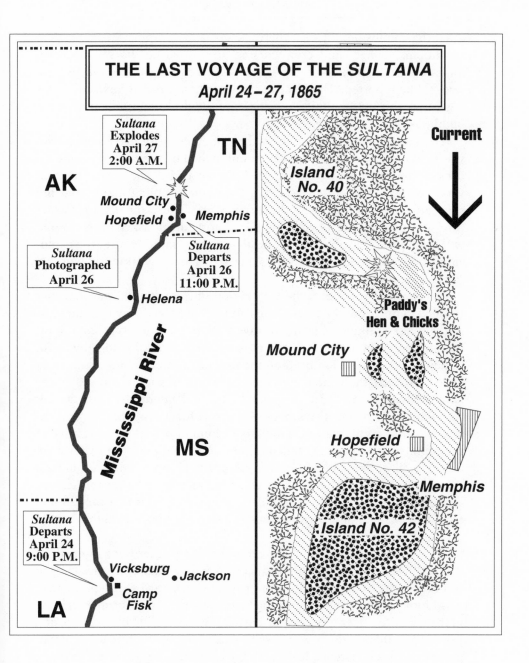

THE LAST VOYAGE OF THE *SULTANA*
April 24–27, 1865

Sultana Explodes April 27 2:00 A.M.

TN

AK

Mound City
Hopefield • • *Memphis*

Sultana Photographed April 26

Sultana Departs April 26 11:00 P.M.

• Helena

Mississippi River

MS

Sultana Departs April 24 9:00 P.M.

Vicksburg • *Jackson*
Camp Fisk

LA

Island No. 40

Current

Paddy's Hen & Chicks

Mound City

Hopefield

Memphis

Island No. 42

after the explosion. "Everywhere steam was escaping, women were screaming, soldiers and crew cursing and swearing, horses neighing, mules braying, splinters flying — the once magnificent *Sultana* [was] a wreck," he reported. The force of the blast had traveled upward, blowing a hole through the middle sections of the decks and obliterating the pilothouse atop the boat.

Thomas Sharp, a soldier from the 2nd West Virginia Cavalry who was sleeping in a section of the boat untouched by the explosion, ran on deck. "Men were lying everywhere," he recalled. "The hurricane deck was crowded. The chimneys fell, killing and crippling many, and fire started from the wreckage in the furnace pit." The *Sultana*'s superstructure was constructed of light wood, almost all of which was covered with highly combustible paint. Less than twenty minutes after the explosion, the ship's midsection was a mass of flames working inexorably toward the stern.*

A Tennessee private, Robert N. Hamilton, ran toward the stern but recoiled in horror at the sight. "Men and women were praying, and most of them not thinking of trying to save their lives. They were leaping off into the water on top of each other — hundreds drowning together." An Indiana soldier who had been on the rear portion of the hurricane deck looked toward the center and found that "this part of the boat was jammed with men. I saw the pilot house and hundreds of them sink through the roof into the flames." "I stood for a few minutes and listened to that awful wail of hundreds of human beings burning alive in the cabin[s] and under the fallen timbers," an Ohio veteran recollected. As the wall of flame closed on the stern, M. H. Sprinkle was among a group who began to throw badly wounded men into the water. According to Sprinkle, he and his comrades thought it "better that they should take their chances of drowning than be left to burn up, which they would do if left on the boat."

As Nicholas Karns saw it, his choice was "to either burn to death or drown." Deciding that a slim chance was better than none, he stripped to his drawers and scanned the river for a spot clear of struggling men. "As I looked out to the right of the boat I saw three or four men fighting in the water for an empty cracker-barrel. It was whirling like a hoop, and I doubt if either of them was saved by it." One of the ship's two gangplanks had been fastened level with the cabin deck; Karns had only just

---

* To the end of his life, Thomas Sharp believed that had it not been for the total panic that ensued, which made any organized firefighting impossible, "three or four men with buckets could have kept the wreck from burning."

clambered onto it when it broke free and crashed to the bow below, crushing those caught under it. Somehow he kept his senses and, with the help of some other men, shoved the plank into the water and jumped after it. "The thought of that ice water makes me shudder yet," he admitted years afterward.

As long as they were standing, the wheelhouses on either side of the *Sultana* acted as jib sails, keeping the stern pointed downwind. But once they collapsed in flames, the steamer, helpless in the current, pivoted around 180 degrees. Now the fire reversed its course and roared toward the bow, where perhaps as many as five hundred people remained. There was no safe place left on board.

George Hass divested himself of everything but his underclothing, grabbed a piece of wood siding, and jumped into the river. "Being a good swimmer I soon got my bearing and swam away from the boat, in order to get out of reach of those who were struggling in the water," he noted. Another who jumped for his life was Joseph T. Elliott, a second lieutenant in the 124th Indiana. "I recollect the sensation I felt on leaping from the steamer into the cold water of that turbulent stream as the flames from the burning vessel cast a weird glow over its surface," he later wrote.

West Virginian Thomas Sharp pushed off alone, clinging to a piece of wreckage. "There were two large cotton stages on board that would have floated 1,000 men," he insisted. "I saw one of them launched with a crowd of men on it and when in the water they all tried to stay on top of it. It got to turning over and over, and I think all got away from it and were drowned."

Aboard the *Sultana* it was hell on earth. "I saw men, while attempting to escape, pitch down through the hatchway that was full of blue curling flames, or rush wildly from the vessel to death and destruction in the turbid waters below," a Tennessee soldier recalled. "The light and screams at this time cannot be described," added an Ohio comrade. "The water was full of struggling and drowning people," said C. J. Lahue of the 13th Indiana Cavalry. "I heard a lady crying for help, asking her husband to rescue her. . . . I also saw the husband, with a little child on his back, struggling in the water for a moment, then sinking. The lady cried out, 'My husband and baby are gone!' "

Those who had survived the blast and escaped the fire now fought for their lives in the rain-swollen river. "I . . . saw that the water was full of men, horses, and mules," remembered one soldier. A Tennessee cavalryman named Andrew Perry watched with fascination and horror as one man, clinging to a part of the wheelhouse, battled a mule for his space:

"The mule would get its front feet on the raft and [the man] . . . would knock it off with a club. It would come again, for several times the mule almost capsized the craft. I don't think I ever saw a more earnest fight. The mule finally gave up or was killed."

Chester D. Berry tried to help one bewildered survivor get into the water. "But I can't swim," the man wailed, "I've got to drown, O dear." Berry showed him the small board he had obtained to help him float, and urged the man to find himself one like it. "But I did get one," the man sobbed, "and someone snatched it away from me." When Berry replied that he should get himself a second board, the man said that he had, but that it too had been stolen. "Well, then," Berry yelled, "get another." "Why," the man whined, "what would be the use, they would take it from me. O dear, I tell you there is no use; I've got to drown, I can't swim." Berry could stand no more. "Drown then you fool," he snarled, giving the man a shove.

"I saw at least twenty drown at once," reflected Stephen M. Gaston. "As fast as one would feel he was drowning he would clutch at the nearest, and I believe many a bold swimmer was drowned that night who could have saved himself if alone."

It was not until nearly two hours later that, alerted by scores of screaming wreck victims floating past with the current, residents of Memphis began their own humanitarian actions. Private citizens all along the river pitched in as well. A flotilla of small boats spread into the river to snatch survivors from the cold waters, while the first rescue craft came on the scene even as the citizens of Memphis were beginning to learn of the tragedy. This was the steamer *Bostonia II,* whose captain spotted the burning wreckage and drew his craft as near as he dared, plucking more than a hundred people from the water. Other vessels soon gathered at the fiery scene to join in the rescue operations, including the steamboats *Silver Spray, Marble City,* and *Rose Hambleton,* as well as the military vessels *Essex, Grossbeak,* and *Pocohontas.*

Sergeant Karns continued to cling to the gangplank, which turned over several times in the current. Each time he and his weary fellows splashed back to it, their number had been diminished by a few more. At last the plank snagged onto a tree, and Karns climbed up into its branches. He was picked up after daylight.

George Hass drifted until he was nearly opposite Memphis, where he was hauled into a small boat. Sailors from the U.S. gunboat *Essex* fished Indiana officer Joseph Elliott out of the river near Memphis as well. Thomas Sharp floated to the Arkansas side of the river, across from Memphis, after being in the water for four hours. Tennessean Charles

M. Eldridge was saved by a farmer who launched his skiff into the dark waters and plucked out about a dozen men. "They carried me out on the bank and built a big fire and worked with me an hour before they could see any signs of life," Eldridge marveled.

Alexander C. Brown, the soldier who had been told by the clerk that the overloaded *Sultana* would set a record, made it to a tree, where he waited four hours for succor. Chester D. Berry also swam to a tree but promptly found himself under assault by "a perfect swarm of buffalo gnats," which tormented him until a small boat picked him up. M. H. Sprinkle, who had helped heave the badly wounded overboard, clung to a raft that was eventually corralled near Memphis. During his drifting voyage, Sprinkle had to fight off a dying man who, even as his head disappeared under the waves, locked an iron grasp on his leg. "The last I can recollect was they were trying to pry the dead man's grip loose from my leg," Sprinkle wrote.

Henry J. Kline survived, but his friend George Downing, who had thought himself lucky to be able to afford a ride out to the *Sultana* from Memphis, did not. Also among the lost was the master of the vessel, J. Cass Mason. Among the surviving members of the crew was the engineer who had approved the boiler patch job, Nathan Wintringer.* No one was ever quite sure how many men had been packed aboard the *Sultana*, so no one knows for certain how many died. The U.S. Customs service at Memphis estimated the number of fatalities at 1,547, but unofficial estimates have put that figure as high as 1,800.†

Several military investigations were conducted in the days and weeks following the disaster. Lacking any firsthand evidence as to conditions at the time of the explosion, however, the investigators could only theorize as to its cause. The principal explanations that emerged pointed to either sabotage, the hasty boiler patch, or a design flaw in the boiler itself. None of these was ever proved or disproved, though the sabotage scenario seems unlikely. Only Captain Frederic Speed was ever called to account. He was found guilty of "neglect of duty" and sentenced to be dismissed from the service, but a review of his case by the judge advocate general reversed that judgment, and Speed was discharged honorably in 1866. Lieutenant Colonel Reuben B. Hatch left the service voluntarily in July 1865 and refused to answer any subpoenas to testify in the matter. Captain George Williams remained in the army, eventually rose to the

* Shortly before his death, in 1886, Wintringer wrote Chester D. Berry a note in which he expressed some remorse over the incident.
† By comparison, the loss on the British-registered *Titanic* was 1,642.

rank of major, and retired in 1870. Major General Napoleon J. T. Dana, in overall command at Vicksburg, resigned from the army little more than a month after the disaster. He enjoyed a successful postwar career in both private and government sectors.

For fully two weeks after the explosion, the Mississippi River continued to release bodies. Some were found as far south as Helena, nearly ninety miles away. Several days afterward, a steersman for a U.S. gunboat spotted what he "supposed to be a large amount of driftwood floating in the river," though the large number of birds circling around the mass made him suspicious. On drawing closer, he saw that the "driftwood" actually consisted of human bodies, and he frantically ran his ship over a sandbar to avoid them.

There was bigger news vying for headline space at this time, but even so, the *Sultana* story got surprisingly little coverage, considering the magnitude of the disaster. Ironically, the number of Union soldiers killed in the early-morning hours of April 27, 1865, exceeded the total Union dead for any single land engagement other than Antietam, Gettysburg, the Wilderness, and Spotsylvania Court House. Although the country soon forgot what had happened eight miles above Memphis,* the survivors of that night of terror could never do so. "Would to God that I could forever blot from memory and sight the events of that terrible disaster," George Hass wrote in 1888. "But they cling to me like a horrible nightmare, even visiting me in my dreams, as well as in my waking moments."

---

* The *Sultana* wreckage today lies buried under a farm field a few miles from Mound City, where it was left by the river waters when the Mississippi shifted its course further east.

Chapter Fourteen

The Lonesome Train

————◀○▶————

THE SPECIAL NINE-CAR train conveying Lincoln's body back to its final resting place in Springfield, Illinois, left Washington a little after 8:00 A.M. on April 21. "A very cold and stormy wet day," noted a sergeant in the honor guard. "Arrived at Baltimore at 8:30 A.M. A large crowd awaited . . . and greeted us with a splendid procession." The train stopped for the night in Harrisburg, where the coffin was put on view in the Pennsylvania State House for thousands to see, despite a series of rain showers that swept through the area.

The decision to bury Lincoln in Springfield had been made by Mary Lincoln only after she considered and then rejected proposals to lay her husband to rest variously in New York, in Washington's Congressional Cemetery, and in the vault under the Capitol rotunda — a place of honor prepared but never used for George Washington. Under powers granted in 1862 that allowed him to control the operation of the nation's railroads, Secretary of War Stanton organized a committee to set the route and timetable for the journey. The committee also saw to other details, establishing guidelines as to who would be permitted to ride in the funeral cars, specifying the size of the train itself, and scheduling several extended stops so that memorials "as may be fitting and appropriate for the occasion" might be conducted.

The route laid out for what became known as the "Lonesome Train" was designed to retrace the journey Lincoln himself had undertaken in 1861 when he traveled from Springfield to Washington to assume the Presidency. Strictly speaking, it was actually the Lonesome Trains, since the engine and several other cars were changed along the way to enable the different railroad companies to take part in the national ceremony. Along with Lincoln's body, the train also carried the disinterred remains of his son Willie, who had died in the White House in 1862.

The funeral train proceeded from Harrisburg to Philadelphia, which it reached at 6:30 P.M. on April 22 and where it would remain until the morning of April 24. Recorded a Pennsylvania soldier in the escort, "The bells throughout the city tolled in muffled strokes as the funeral procession started, keeping up that sad accompaniment till the body was laid in state in the chamber under the very flag pole which Lincoln himself had dedicated." A woman who watched the funeral procession pass by on its way to Independence Hall noted that "everywhere my eyes met some token of mourning, and . . . [I must] say that it . . . made feelings of sorrow rise in the thought."

The body remained on view until early Monday morning, April 24. One of those who paid their respects later wrote, "Our last President certainly was a very homely man, yet there is certainly something more than ordinary in every line of his careworn face."

The train crossed into New Jersey, arrived at the Market Street Station in Newark after 9:00 A.M. on April 24, and was carefully loaded onto the ferry *Jersey City* for the trip into New York. Shortly before 11:00 A.M., as funeral guns boomed, the craft docked at the Desbrosses Street slip.

The solemn cortege wound its way to City Hall Park, where the body would lie in state for twelve hours. At one point along the route a woman leaning out of a tenement window was heard to exclaim, "Well, is that all that's left of Ould Abe?" A voice from the crowd below returned, "It's more than you'll ever be!"

The woman was nonplussed by this riposte. "O, I've nothing against him," she replied. "I never knew him or cared for him, but *he died like a saint.*"

Another woman who viewed the procession left this description of it: "The catafalque was drawn by sixteen white horses, caparisoned in black to their feet, adorned with silver wreaths, crosses, and festoons of natural flowers; General [Winfield] Scott and the foreign consuls, judiciary and city councilmen, etc., in open carriages, three abreast; a fine show of military trailing their arms. Very fine dirge music, and fifty thousand men of different societies, clubs, etc., and a few colored soldiers

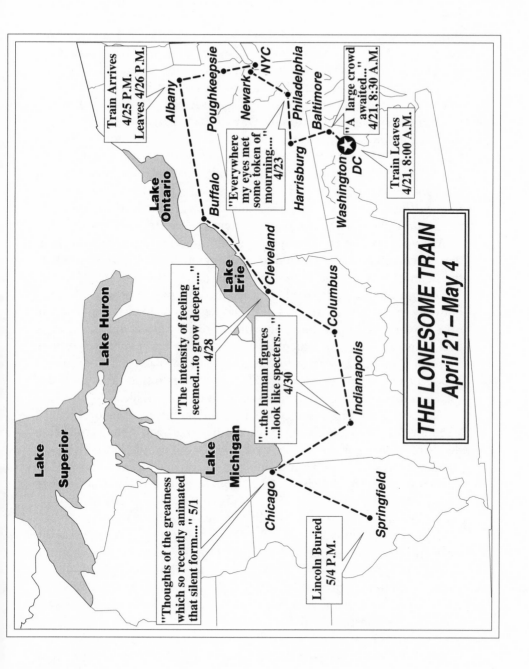

THE LONESOME TRAIN
April 21 – May 4

Train Leaves
4/21, 8:00 A.M.

"A large crowd
awaited..."
4/21, 8:30 A.M.

Washington
DC

Baltimore

Harrisburg

Philadelphia

Newark

NYC

Poughkeepsie

"Everywhere
my eyes met
some token of
mourning...."
4/23

Albany

Train Arrives
4/25 P.M.
Leaves 4/26 P.M.

Buffalo

Lake
Ontario

Cleveland

Lake
Erie

"The intensity of feeling
seemed...to grow deeper...."
4/28

Columbus

Indianapolis

"...the human figures
...look like specters...."
4/30

Lake
Huron

Lake
Michigan

Lake
Superior

"Thoughts of the greatness
which so recently animated
that silent form...." 5/1

Chicago

Springfield

Lincoln Buried
5/4 P.M.

279

with 'Abraham Lincoln, Our Liberator,' etc., on their breasts, guarded by a police force (because the City Council opposed their joining the procession), marched. It was very, very sorrowful."

From New York, which it left at 4:00 P.M. on April 25, the Lonesome Train proceeded along the Hudson River to Albany. At Peekskill, where Lincoln had spoken in 1861 on his way to Washington, the train stopped for three minutes to allow a salute from the crowd present. Night had fallen by the time the train left Poughkeepsie on its way to the state capital. A member of the New York committee on board never forgot the sights along the way: "At every crossroads the glare of innumerable torches illumined the whole population from age to infancy, kneeling on the ground, their clergymen leading them in prayers and hymns."

After pulling out of Albany on the afternoon of April 26 (the same day Sherman and Johnston hammered out the final surrender terms at the Bennett House), the Lonesome Train passed through the Mohawk Valley en route to Buffalo, which it reached the next morning. Here the body lay in view in St. James Hall for eleven hours. "The thought would arise as we gazed upon his quiet smile," one mourner noted, "that he had found the rest for which he must have so often sighed." Among those in the crowd were a former President, Millard Fillmore, and a President-to-be, Grover Cleveland. It was at Buffalo that those on board the train learned of the capture and death of John Wilkes Booth.

The Lonesome Train arrived in Cleveland on the morning of April 28. "The intensity of feeling seemed, if possible to grow deeper as the President's remains went further westward where the people more especially claimed him as their own," a member of the official escort believed. The body was borne to the city's Public Square, where it lay in a pavilion constructed for the occasion. Thousands paid their respects, many waiting in the rain for hours to pass by the casket.

Then the train moved on, to Columbus on April 29 and Indianapolis on April 30. When it pulled out of the Hoosier capital, at midnight, a reporter observed that the "sweet, sad sounds of musical dirges, the occasional muttering of muffled drums, the human figures, passing and repassing, look like specters as the glare of lamps and torchlights send their shadows across the pale faces."

The route to Chicago was filled with moving vignettes. At Battle Ground, Indiana, "Bonfires are blazing, around which some three hundred people are congregated. They slowly wave flags and stand uncovered as the cortege passes." At Francisville, the people crowded near the funeral car, "and stand on tip toe to get a look at the coffin." At Westville, a gathering of over two thousand people was described as a "thoughtful congregation. . . . The men stood with uncovered heads, and women look on in silence. A number of little children were grouped together, holding in their hands white flags with mourning fringes."

It was about eleven o'clock on the morning of May 1 when the Lonesome Train pulled into Chicago on the tracks of the Illinois Central. There were no speeches, prayers, or eulogies given when the solemn cortege arrived; instead, the casket was carried to the courthouse, where the public was admitted beginning at 5:00 P.M. Here a number of tributes took place, including the performance of a new song, "Farewell, Father, Friend, and Guardian," with music by George F. Root, whose tune "Marching Through Georgia" had been a wartime hit.

A soldier in town on furlough wrote in his diary this evening, "Getting into the line, I look upon the still form and calm features of our Lincoln, lying in his narrow bed. There passed through my mind, thoughts of the greatness which so recently animated that silent form; the grand achievements so nearly completed, the lasting results of which will embalm his memory in the hearts of his fellow men."

Lincoln's body lay on view in Chicago until the evening of May 2, when it was moved for the last time, to Springfield, reaching that city the following morning. The sad procession from Washington to the Illinois capital had covered 1,654 miles in twelve days and was only forty minutes off the schedule established before it left.

"The city is so crowded," one newspaperman complained, "that it is impossible to procure lodging in a bar-room or on a pool-table." Travelers arrived from every point on the compass to add to the lines filing past the bier, which had been placed in the Illinois State House. "The soldiers on guard in the Capital and around the grounds kept hurrying the crowd along," one young Illinois infantryman observed. "They had to, you see, for there were always thousands more waiting outside." Every thirty minutes during the daylight hours, a detachment of Battery K, Missouri Light Artillery, fired a salute. The honor guards were drawn from the 146th Illinois, 24th Michigan, 46th Wisconsin, and 14th Iowa, as well as the 23rd Regiment of the Veteran Reserve Corps.

At 1:00 P.M. on May 4, the coffin was carried to Oak Ridge Cemetery for entombment. There were speeches, musical numbers, and poetry. Then the coffins (those of Lincoln and his son) were placed in the stone vault. "People stood on tip-toe, anxiously peering over each other's shoulders, each one determined, if possible, to satisfy himself," wrote a reporter on the scene. "As the guard of honor placed the ashes in the vault, Capt. Robert Lincoln and the intimate family friends were standing close by the door and watching every movement. . . . The ceremonies having terminated, the doors of the vault were closed. . . . Thus we buried him; thus we leave him — the great, the good, the martyr President."

In faraway California, a newspaperman named Bret Harte put into words the meaning of the past fourteen days:

> No other public man seems to me to have impressed his originality so strongly upon the people as did Abraham Lincoln. His person and peculiar characteristics were the familiar and common property of the nation. . . . Even as the martyrdom of this great and good man brought him down to the level of the humblest soldier who died upon the battlefield for his country, so the common sympathy of our loss has drawn us all closer together.

Chapter Fifteen

"God's will be done"

————◦►————

ON THE DAY Lincoln was shot, the refugee Confederate government was in Greensboro, North Carolina, where its members realized they were caught in a three-sided trap — with Sherman approaching from the east, Stoneman threatening from the west, and the Federals who had defeated Lee an ominous presence to the north. To remain still was to invite capture, so plans were made during the early part of April 15 to continue the exodus south. Arrangements for this move were complicated by the fact that the tracks between Greensboro and Charlotte had been cut, meaning that as many personnel and papers as could be managed had to be packed into animal-drawn wagons. The long procession of vehicles and men on horseback, accompanied by a military escort of about 1,300 cavalry, left Greensboro late that same day. A scattered rain had spread over the area, making the journey miserable for everyone. A Greensboro resident watched as Davis and War Secretary Breckinridge rode out of town, noting, "As those great men passed slowly by me on this gloomy April day with their sad faces turned to the South, and as I gazed for the last time in all . . . probability upon the graceful forms and dignified countenances of the two horsemen riding side by side . . . I wept for them and my country."

An English newspaperman was now traveling with the government on wheels. Artist-correspondent Frank Vizetelly of the *Illustrated Lon-*

don News had been with Johnston's men when he learned that the Confederate government was operating out of nearby Greensboro. Vizetelly arrived just in time to scare up a horse and join the lengthy caravan of government officials and clerks. Despite the bad weather and poor roads, which sometimes forced the occupants of the wagons to get out and push, "Mr. Davis was always affable, kind, cheerful, and resolute," a member of the escort recalled.

The procession of people and animals struggled on for fifteen miles before camping the night not far from Jamestown. Davis and his Cabinet found food and lodging at a nearby house, where the host's servant mistook Adjutant General Samuel Cooper for the President and gave him the single bedroom, leaving Davis to make do with a less private space. On April 16 the wagon train reached a point about four miles from Lexington, North Carolina, where an outdoor camp was pitched in a pine grove near the road. There were some messages waiting for Breckinridge in Lexington; one, from Johnston, requested his "immediate presence." After conferring briefly with Davis at around ten o'clock at night, Breckinridge, joined by Postmaster John H. Reagan, rode back to Greensboro.*

The muddy procession of vehicles and riders representing the fugitive Confederate government reached Charlotte on Wednesday, April 19. Although Jefferson Davis's wife, Varina, had come here directly from Richmond before that city's evacuation, she was no longer in town. On learning of Lee's surrender, and being informed that her husband's government was "coming to Charlotte to meet General Johnston and his army," she had realized that she "might embarrass him sadly by remaining there." Her going had been made easier by the fact that Captain William Parker — who, with his cadet detachment, was still responsible for the C.S. Treasury — had decided to move the Confederate funds deeper into the South, and had invited Mrs. Davis and her children to accompany him. Captain Parker's intention was to get through to Macon. His small force moved south by rail to Chester, South Carolina, and then switched to wagons as far as Washington, Georgia, where Parker prudently decided to hold up until the situation ahead of him became less confused. Mrs. Davis and her family left Parker's protection on April 16, at Newberry, where she decided to stay with friends.

The welcome extended to Jefferson Davis at Charlotte combined the outward hospitality he had received at Danville with the cold shoulder he had got at Greensboro. Doors were opened to all members of the

---

* The two arrived in time to take part in Johnston's peace talks with Sherman.

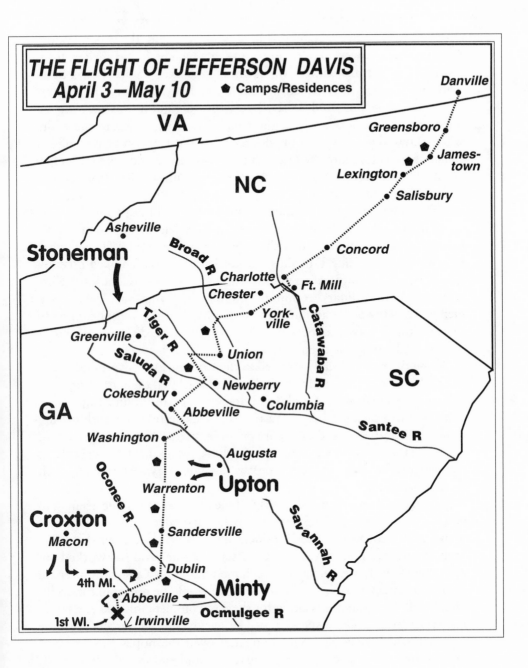

THE FLIGHT OF JEFFERSON DAVIS
April 3–May 10   ⬠ Camps/Residences

VA

Danville

NC

Greensboro
James-
town
Lexington
Salisbury

Asheville

Stoneman

Broad R

Concord

Charlotte
Ft. Mill
Chester
York-
ville

Greenville

Tiger R

Union

Saluda R

Newberry

Cokesbury

Columbia

Catawaba R

SC

GA

Abbeville

Santee R

Washington

Augusta

Oconee R

Warrenton

Upton

Croxton
Macon

Sandersville

Savannah R

4th MI.

Dublin

Minty

Abbeville

1st WI.

Irwinville

Ocmulgee R

285

government save the President — because, it was said, the Federal raider Stoneman had vowed to burn any house in which he found shelter. Ironically, it was a transplanted Massachusetts Yankee named Lewis Bates who finally made his decidedly humble abode available to the fugitive leader. No one bothered to tell Bates that his guest was arriving on horseback, so he was away at the train station expecting to meet him when Davis showed up on his doorstep. While Davis was waiting for someone to let him into the house, a crowd gathered and asked for a few words. He delivered a brief speech, telling the citizens that "the cause is not yet dead, and only show by your determination and fortitude that you are willing to suffer yet longer, and we may still hope for success."

As if cued by some offstage director, a local telegrapher named J. C. Courtney came running up with a short message from War Secretary Breckinridge reporting Lincoln's assassination.* Davis showed no emotion as he read the note, then passed it along with the observation, "Here is a very extraordinary communication." Later this day Davis commented to Navy Secretary Stephen Mallory that if the still-unconfirmed report should prove to be true, "I fear it will be disastrous for our people, and I regret it deeply."

Along the route already covered in the Confederate government's exodus, things were going from bad to worse. After their meeting with Johnston and Sherman, it took John Breckinridge and John Reagan until early on the morning of April 22 to reach Charlotte, what with disruptions to the rail lines and disorder spread by marauding bands of armed military stragglers. Once back in Charlotte, Breckinridge was able to confirm the news of Lincoln's death and give Davis Sherman's draft peace document.

Jefferson Davis sent word to his Cabinet to meet that same evening to consider terms offered by Sherman for the surrender of the Confederate States of America. The C.S. President and his advisers spent Saturday evening and all of Sunday, April 23, discussing the proposal worked out at the Bennett House. Davis told each member of his Cabinet to prepare a written statement of his opinion, so there would be no room for doubt afterward. While he was waiting for them to complete this task, he wrote his wife a letter. "The dispersion of Lee's army and the surrender of the remnant which remained with him, destroyed the hopes I entertained odious options — he could either surrender and endure "the long night

---

* Breckinridge's first report drew upon the grapevine news of the army camps and erroneously placed the assassination on April 11. By the time he met with Davis, Breckinridge had learned the correct date.

of oppression" or continue the struggle and likely "die in vain." He counseled Varina to try to reach an open port and from there sail to a foreign country. For his part, he planned to make his way to Texas and then, if matters seemed beyond salvation, enter Mexico.

The Cabinet delivered its verdict on April 24. To a man, they were in favor of accepting Sherman's terms. Although he remained skeptical that Washington would ratify the agreement, Davis nevertheless sent a telegram to Johnston informing him that his action had been "approved," while also making it clear that any further negotiation would be subject to instructions from the government.

By the time Davis's message reached Johnston, or shortly thereafter, it was rendered null and void by Sherman's renunciation of his proffered terms and termination of the ceasefire. "Have you instructions?" a worried Johnston wired Breckinridge at 6:30 P.M. "We had better disband [i.e., surrender] this small force to prevent devastation to the country."

On April 26, even as Johnston and Sherman were meeting to discuss the terms under which the former might surrender his army, the Confederate government was leaving Charlotte, a little lighter than when it arrived. George Davis, the attorney general, had asked to resign so that he might return home to care for his orphaned children. Jefferson Davis let him go, and also agreed with his sixty-six-year-old adjutant general, Samuel Cooper, that the rigors of the next stage would be too much for him. "I fear the spirit of the people is broken," one of Davis's aides noted sadly, while another declared, "We are falling to pieces."

Shortly after the refugee Confederate government entered South Carolina, on April 27, Jefferson Davis's Cabinet became another member lighter. Treasury Secretary Trenholm, whose health had been poor throughout the journey, tendered his resignation in the morning. Davis hurriedly convened the available Cabinet members, who turned over Trenholm's portfolio to Postmaster General John Reagan, who was not present. When Reagan tried to protest the appointment, Davis managed a bit of graveyard humor, explaining that there was "not much for the Secretary of the Treasury to do, and there is but little money left for him to steal."

On April 28 the procession passed through Yorkville, South Carolina. "Here we found some beautiful houses, and in fact one of the prettiest towns I ever saw," a member of the escort wrote. The column, because of its size and mixed composition, was moving slowly, covering perhaps fifteen miles a day. Some of the veteran cavalry officers in the group worried that the slow pace would allow the fast-moving Federal cavalry to overtake them. Sensing this anxiety, Davis, along with War Secretary

Breckinridge and others, "mingled and talked freely with the men upon this march, and the effect was excellent, largely countering the feeling of uneasiness induced by our lack of activity," an officer noted.

On April 29 the President's party crossed the Broad River, where, during a break for lunch, the members of Davis's inner circle compared their relative wealth. Remembered John Reagan, "After we had joked each other about our fallen fortunes, the President took out his pocket-book and showed a few Confederate bills, stating that that constituted his wealth. He added that it was a gratification to him that no member of his Cabinet had made money out of his position."

On April 30 Davis (who invariably rode at the head of the caravan) met an acquaintance who had ridden up from Abbeville, South Carolina, bearing a note from his wife. As Mrs. Davis later recalled it, it said "that I would not wait his coming, but [would] try to get out of the country as best I might, and meet him in Texas or elsewhere." The column halted for the night a short distance above the Saluda River. Davis and his colleagues were now passing through a region of the Confederacy that had not been directly touched by the war, and that still cherished a sympathy for the Cause. A clerk accompanying the party recollected, "Through the little towns we passed, the ladies ... and the children flocked around us with flowers, eager to see, grasp the hand, and bless their President, God-speeding him on his way."

At Cokesbury, which his column reached on May 1, Davis was joined by a controversial general who had benefited throughout the war from the President's unwavering support — often in the face of badly mishandled campaigns and virtual revolts among subordinate officers. Lieutenant General Braxton Bragg added neither fire nor spirit to the procession when he told Davis of his belief that the end of the Confederacy was near.

Whatever dampening effect Bragg's dour presence may have had on the President's circle was alleviated somewhat by the warm welcome the group received when it arrived at Abbeville, early on the morning of May 2. The whole town was thrown open to the party," a clerk recorded.

Shortly after 4:00 P.M. the same day, Davis summoned the five principal officers of his cavalry escort to what one participant later termed "the last Confederate council of war." It was a military session, with all Cabinet members — save ex-general Breckinridge — excluded, and Braxton Bragg also present. "It is time that we adopt some definite plan upon which the further prosecution of our struggle shall be conducted," Davis said by way of an agenda. He then launched into his usual inspirational speech — well-worn on the ears of his Cabinet but new to these young officers — in which he insisted that the current ill fortunes of the Confederacy were the result of a momentary panic, and that once that panic passed, "the whole people will rally" to the centers of authority that remained.

The young officers were shocked. "I do not remember who spoke first, but we each expressed the same opinion," one of them said afterward. "We told him frankly that the events of the last few days had removed from our minds all idea or hope that a prolongation of the contest was possible." Surprised and taken aback by their reaction, Davis asked why, in that case, they were all still in the field and under arms. When they answered that it was for his protection, and his alone, that they remained together, the C.S. President bristled. "He declared, abruptly, that he would listen to no suggestion which regarded only his own safety." Davis left the meeting very shaken.

Also present in Abbeville were Captain William Parker and his cadets, still in charge of the Confederate gold. They had made it this far on their journey to Washington, Georgia, before Parker decided to hold up. Then, to his great relief, the government itself had appeared on the outskirts of town, and he had been able to return the Treasury to civilian hands. After making his report to the President, Parker repeated the rumors he had been hearing about increasing Union cavalry activity in the region. The officer later remembered Davis's saying "that he would never desert the Southern people; that he had been elected by them to the office he held, and would stand by them. He gave me to understand that he would not take any step which might be construed into an inglorious flight."

Even as Davis was voicing his defiance, the young cavalry commanders, with Breckinridge and Bragg's approval, were telling their men that their mission now was to serve solely as a presidential escort, on a volunteer basis. About half of those in the ranks opted to remain in Abbeville when the President's party again took to the road, shortly after eleven o'clock that night.

The head of the three-mile column crossed the Savannah River at about dawn on May 3. Trouble erupted when a portion of the Treasury train reached the river and a large crowd of cavalrymen gathered around it, declaring that it would be better to distribute the coin among themselves than to allow the Yankees to capture it. War Secretary Breckinridge came on the scene and attempted to convince the men to disperse. He told them that they must not descend into banditry, and that they must preserve their honor. When his arguments failed to sway them, he ordered that the money on hand be distributed among the men. "They were impatient, and helped themselves as soon as they discovered where to get it," a staff officer who was present recalled. "The result was [that] . . . many got nothing."

Unaware that any of this was happening, Davis was saying farewell to one of his closest advisers and confidants, Secretary of State Judah Benjamin. The rotund Cabinet member protested that he could not keep up and would only slow everyone down. "If you should be in a condition to require me again I will answer your call at once," Benjamin assured Davis. Asked where he would now go, Benjamin showed that his sense of humor had survived the journey intact when he responded, "To the farthest place from the United States, if it takes me to the middle of China."

Davis entered the town of Washington, Georgia, early in the afternoon and set up shop in the Bank of Georgia building. Here he accepted the resignation of his Navy secretary, Stephen Mallory. The Confederate government was being reduced to a gaggle of fugitives.

The process of reduction accelerated on May 4. Most of what remained of the Treasury was further divided, with some of the funds going to the loyal members of the cavalry escort, some being given to high officials for their personal use in escaping, and a portion — about $86,000 — being secreted in a false carriage bottom for eventual shipment out of the country. This last sum was later further distributed so that only about $26,000 remained. The stocks of paper money were all burned. Davis also decided that the size of the party itself should be drastically cut back. According to the English correspondent Frank Vizetelly, "It was here that [President Davis] determined to continue his flight almost alone; and, assembling those around him who had sacrificed everything to the defeated cause, he, with tears in his eyes, begged them to seek their own safety and leave him to meet his fate." Jefferson Davis hoped to continue south until he cleared the enemy patrols, whereupon he would link up with Richard Taylor's forces in Alabama. Right after Davis made these announcements, one officer remarked to his assistant, "It is all over; the Confederate government is dissolved."

On May 4, the day Richard Taylor signed the official surrender papers for the troops under his command, Jefferson Davis and his reduced escort left Washington, Georgia. They were followed, a short time later, by John Reagan and what remained of the Treasury train. War Secretary Breckinridge would leave Washington on May 5 to undertake a diversionary move designed to draw attention away from the presidential party. A young soldier who viewed Davis this day noted in his diary, "To see the head and representative of a great and mighty people, fleeing for his life to quit the country is sad indeed. He seems yet hopeful, but I fear our noble cause is gone."

May 5 was a clear, hot day, and the presidential party, which had swelled in size when Reagan and his wagons caught up, managed to cover about thirty-five miles. It was agreed that anyone who asked about the group should be told that it consisted of members of Congress from Texas on their way home.

Having been informed by his wife of her proposed route, Jefferson Davis was privately determined to catch up with and join her if at all possible. This he accomplished on the evening of May 6, when he rode into her camp near the village of Dublin. "Who comes there?" cried out Burton Harrison, who was again accompanying Mrs. Davis on her journey. "Friends," came the reply. Harrison "was astonished to recognize [the voice] as that of President Davis, not suspecting he was anywhere near us." Davis was soon reunited with his family.

On the same evening that Davis joined his wife, Lieutenant Colonel Henry Harnden led a detachment of 150 men belonging to the 1st Wisconsin Cavalry out of their camps near Macon, Georgia. Harnden had been summoned to headquarters a few hours earlier and told that Jefferson Davis had been spotted in South Carolina, and that General Wilson had issued orders for his capture. Harnden's instructions were not quite to take Davis dead or alive, but they came close. "If there is a fight and Jeff. Davis should get hurt, General Wilson would not feel very bad over it," Harnden was told.

Federal attempts to pursue and intercept the Davis party had been virtually nonexistent until after Lincoln's burial. Although Edwin Stanton had from the first suspected that the "President's murder was organized in Canada and approved in Richmond," it was not until a May 2 meeting of Andrew Johnson's Cabinet that Judge Advocate Joseph Holt had presented a formal memorandum charging Davis with complicity in the crime. Johnson at once issued a proclamation that put a price of $100,000 on Davis's head and lesser sums on others implicated in Holt's memo. The hunt was on.

A second, larger expedition was dispatched from Macon on the same mission twenty-four hours after Harnden's departure. Lieutenant Colonel Benjamin D. Pritchard, commanding a force of 419 enlisted men and twenty officers from the 4th Michigan Cavalry, was told to follow the Ocmulgee River "for the purpose of capturing Jefferson Davis and party." Pritchard moved his men out without telling them the purpose of the operation. "Now that was mysterious for a certainty," one of them remarked. "Had we been in the enemy's front, and on the eve of battle, preparation would not have been made with any more caution, but here we were, with the war practically over, asked to observe the utmost secrecy in making a move that apparently had no more significance than moving camp."

Throughout their day of traveling together on May 7, Varina Davis urged her husband to save himself from capture. "Go swiftly and alone," she begged him. Jefferson Davis finally agreed and, after breakfasting with his wife on the morning of May 8, he pushed on alone with his small escort, reaching Abbeville, Georgia,* by evening. Ironically, the horsemen were so delayed in getting across the rain-swollen Ocmulgee River that Varina's party was able to catch up again during the night. Learning from Burton Harrison that Yankee cavalry had been seen in the vicinity, Davis instructed his secretary to keep the wagons moving, promising that his group would overtake them in the morning. This was successfully accomplished before dawn on May 9. The once more combined expedition plodded along the muddy roads until five o'clock in the afternoon, when camp was made for the night less than a mile north of the small village of Irwinville. The plan was for Davis to once again push on ahead, but the horses were so jaded by this time that he decided to let them rest the night.

Lieutenant Colonel Harnden and his Wisconsin detachment had been hard on the trail of Davis's party since May 7, when the Federal officer first learned of the wagon train near Dublin. By May 9 the Yankees had chased down several leads that brought them to Abbeville. There Harnden met outriders from Lieutenant Colonel Pritchard's force of Michigan cavalry and soon was talking with his fellow officer. "After introducing myself, I inquired if he had any news of Jeff. Davis," Harnden remembered. "He said he had not, but that he had been ordered with his regiment to Abbeville to patrol the river and to prevent Davis from crossing." Harnden declined Pritchard's offer of reinforcements and returned to his command to continue the chase.

Hardly had Pritchard reached Abbeville when he received additional intelligence that convinced him that Harnden was on the right scent. "I immediately determined to pursue by another road, believing that if [Davis and his party] were hard pressed at any time they would pass from road to road to baffle the efforts of their pursuers," he later wrote. Pritchard selected a flying squad of 135 men and set off on his own.

By the time darkness had fallen on the night of May 9, Henry Harn-

---

* Not to be confused with Abbeville, South Carolina.

den had reached Irwinville and knew that he was very close to Jefferson Davis. "At that time I felt certain the train was near at hand, but fearing that if we came upon them in the darkness of that night Jeff. Davis and others might escape under cover of the night, I waited until 3 A.M. (May 10), when I again started."

Benjamin Pritchard, coming down from Abbeville with his select force of Michigan cavalrymen, had also learned the location of the wagon camp and moved his troopers in close. "A detail of twenty-five men . . . was sent to make a circuit of the camp and get a position on the road beyond, to send out pickets, and to take precautions for preventing the escape of any of the occupants of the camp in that direction," recalled Pritchard's adjutant, Julian Dickinson.

Dawn was just breaking as Pritchard's main force moved forward. "The charge was uninterrupted by any picket or camp guards, and we speedily took the camp by a surprise so complete that none of the occupants seemed to have been awakened," declared adjutant Dickinson. William P. Stedman, a private in Company B, recollected what happened next. "Then Capt. [Charles T.] Hudson said, 'Go for them!' We gave a yell, and the men went for everything they could find."

As a few sleepy figures began to stumble out of the tents and emerge from underneath the wagons, a crackle of gunfire turned all heads to the south. "I immediately ordered all my forces forward to the scene of the firing," Pritchard reported, "leaving only a force sufficient to guard the camp and prisoners."

Lieutenant Colonel Harnden had sent a scouting party of seven men ahead to locate the camp. The sergeant in command had spotted some shadowy figures ahead, one of whom had called out, "Halt!" "Who are you?" the noncom had asked. "We will show you who we are," came the reply, accompanied by a volley that struck down three of the Wisconsin soldiers. The group retreated to the main body, where Harnden chose ten riders and galloped forward. A second volley ripped into the early-morning air as the Wisconsin soldiers scattered to shoot back. Then there was a third volley, which was met by a charge from Harnden's men that forced their opponents into a swamp. The firefight had been going on for several minutes when a frantic sergeant ran up to Harnden to tell him that his cavalry were shooting at Union men. Yelling, "Stop firing," Harnden rode forward to sort things out. He soon encountered Benjamin Pritchard and learned of the change in plans that had brought the units into collision. The pair rode back into the main camp together while behind them the men counted their losses: three Wisconsin troopers severely wounded and several more slightly injured; two Michigan men killed and one severely wounded.

The sound of the gunfire fully roused the Davis camp. The Davises' coach driver, a black man named James Jones, spread the alarm, but it was too late. "We were taken by surprise, and not one of us exchanged a shot with the enemy," recalled Burton Harrison.

As Jefferson Davis later remembered it, "I stepped out of my wife's tent and saw some horsemen, whom I immediately recognized as cavalry, deploying around the encampment. . . . [My wife] implored me to leave at once. I hesitated from unwillingness to do so, and lost a few precious moments before yielding to her importunity. . . . As it was quite dark in the tent, I picked up what was supposed to be my 'raglan,' a waterproof, light overcoat, without sleeves; it was subsequently found to be my wife's, so very like my own as to be mistaken for it; as I started my wife thoughtfully threw over my head and shoulders a shawl." Davis was accompanied by his wife's maid, who carried a small pail to make it look as if the two were going to the creek for water.

The deception worked for only a few seconds. It was light enough by now for the Yankee troopers to see that one of the two "women" was sporting riding boots with spurs, and they quickly sounded the alarm. According to James F. Bullard, a Michigan private on the scene, "At that Davis threw off the shawl and waterproof that he had been wearing and Mrs. Davis put her arms around his neck and said: 'Please don't shoot him,' and Davis said: 'Let him shoot, I may as well die here as anywhere.' "

By this time Pritchard and Harnden had arrived, and the soldiers were rounding up everyone. A Wisconsin soldier later wrote of Davis's children, "Their young faces expressed more wonder than fear." A few members of the presidential party managed to escape, but most were caught. The Federal troopers helped themselves to the Confederates' personal possessions and valuables; Davis bitterly protested the treatment, but neither Pritchard nor Harnden did much to restrain his men. Davis asked if his family and aides might be left to continue their journey, but Pritchard told him that his orders were to take everyone to Macon.

"God's will be done," Jefferson Davis replied.

Pritchard now assumed overall command. "After allowing the prisoners time to prepare breakfast, I mounted them on their own horses, taking one of the ambulances for my wounded, and one of the wagons for the dead, using the other two ambulances for the conveyance of the women and children, and started on my return by the direct route to

Abbeville, where I arrived at sunset the same day. . . . [After burying my dead] I . . . resumed my march toward Macon at an early hour on the morning of the 11th."*

A Pennsylvania officer under Pritchard, who met the expedition at Abbeville, thought Davis "a very distinguished-looking man . . . who would be noted among a thousand for his striking personality." He saw Mrs. Davis with the other ladies of the party and found all of them "very much distressed, apparently undergoing a severe nervous strain." According to this officer, "No insult was offered Davis, other than the bands of the Division continually played the National airs, such as 'The Star Spangled Banner,' 'Yankee Doodle,' 'Hail Columbia,' etc. which I have no doubt grated harshly on his nerves."

According to Wisconsin trooper John Clark, "The second day on the way to Macon we obtained handbills signed by President Johnson, accusing Davis of complicity, together with his Cabinet, in the assassination of Lincoln, and offering a reward of $100,000 for Davis. . . . When the handbills were distributed among his guard, Davis asked to see one. He ran his eye over the bill, then dropping his head, he groaned: 'This is worse than death itself, to be accused of such a terrible crime.' "

The Yankee column and its captives — Jefferson Davis, his wife and family, and members of his staff and escort — took four days to make the journey from Irwinville to Macon. The Federals troopers were wary. "Some thought Davis would try to escape," a Michigan cavalryman wrote in his diary on the night of May 12. "The guards were doubled & every precaution taken against surprise — but nothing of the kind [occurred]."

The next day the Davis party rested outside Macon in the camp of the Chicago Board of Trade Battery, where gunner James Nourse got a good look at the President's family. "The little girl is very pretty. The boys received some beautiful magnolia blossoms from [the group] and will try to keep them for mementos. . . . My first and last look at Jeff. God's curse rest on all such as he. How easy it would have been for me to have shot him dead with my pistol as he sat on his horse not forty feet from me." An Indiana cavalryman observed that "Jeff seems much troubled, his face wears a sober, anxious look as though he had just recovered from a severe spell of sickness. His wife carries a high head and wears a defiant haughty expression."

---

* On May 10, well before any word regarding the capture of Jefferson Davis had been received, President Andrew Johnson issued a proclamation that threatened trade retaliation against any neutral country providing safe haven to insurgent naval cruisers, such as the C.S.S. *Shenandoah*. In the preamble to his statement, Johnson declared that "armed resistance to the authority of this Government . . . may be regarded as virtually at an end."

With a feeling of disgust undiminished by time, Varina Davis recalled this stop nearly twenty-five years after the fact: "Within a short distance of Macon we were halted and the soldiers drawn up in line on either side of the road. Our children crept close to their father, especially little Maggie, who put her arms about him and held him tightly, while from time to time he comforted her with tender words. . . . It is needless to say that as the men stood at ease, they expressed in words unfit for women's ears, all that malice could suggest."

That night Davis was the guest of James Wilson, who, some hours afterward, set down his impressions in a letter to a friend. "Mr. Davis seemed quite cheerful and talkative, but in his whole demeanor showed no dignity or great fortitude. He remarked with a smile that he thought the U.S. would find graver charges against him than the murder of Mr. Lincoln, and seemed to regret that Mr. L. had been killed. . . . Among other things, Davis said he thought Lee one of the boldest generals of whom he had any knowledge, never needed urging. This was in comparison with Johnston in regard to whom his silence was marked. The thought struck me once or twice that Jefferson Davis was a mad man. The indifference with which he seemed to regard the affairs of our day savored of insanity. He was polite and gracious in his intercourse with me and almost affectionate in taking leave of me."

When Wilson offered the prisoner his choice of transportation north, Davis said that he would prefer going by water since it would be easier on the children. The next evening, for the first stage of the journey, the members of the Davis group were placed on a train that conveyed them first to Atlanta and then on to the rail line leading to Augusta and the Savannah River. In Augusta a crowd gathered when it was learned that the Confederate prisoner would pass through. A New Hampshire soldier assigned to the guard detail never forgot the scene when the party arrived: "It was an anxious moment for that little squad of blue-coats that were nearly surrounded by their bitterest foes, and out-numbered by more than fifty to one. . . . The silence which had thus far prevailed was broken, not by cheers for their chieftain, but by cries from the Confederates on both sides of the street: 'Got any of that gold with you, Jeff?' — 'We want our pay!' . . . And amid such cries of derision from his own troops, the carriages moved on to the landing."

The captives were placed on board a river steamer that took them to Savannah, where they were transferred to a deep-water vessel for the trip to Fortress Monroe, Virginia. Also on the ship were a number of VIP prisoners taken at other points, including Davis's Vice President and political rival Alexander H. Stephens and cavalry officer Major General

Joseph Wheeler. Stephens remembered that when the two met as U.S. prisoners, Davis's "salutation was not unfriendly, but it was far from cordial. We passed but few words; these were commonplace."

The ship anchored off Fortress Monroe on May 19. The group was split up the next day, with General Wheeler and several staff members being sent to Fort Delaware, and Stephens and Postmaster Reagan going to Fort Warren, near Boston. While Mrs. Davis and her children were allowed to return to Savannah, Jefferson Davis was taken into Fortress Monroe and placed in Casemate Number 2, a cell prepared especially for him. Here he would spend the next 720 days while Federal authorities pondered his fate. In a crowning indignity, the commandant of Fortress Monroe, a much-honored Union general named Nelson Miles, on May 23 ordered Davis to be shackled.

The use of restraints having been authorized in this instance by the War Department, Miles decided to place what he described as "light anklets" on the prisoner while the solid wooden door to his cell was being exchanged for a grated one. After the switch had been accomplished, on May 28, Davis's shackles were removed, but the damage had been done. As one powerful politician warned Edwin Stanton, "Until now, our country is honored everywhere. . . . But this wholly unnecessary severity with a *State* Prisoner will loose [i.e., lose] us a great advantage."

Against this backdrop was born one of the most persistent stories regarding the circumstances of Davis's capture at Irwinville. It grew out of his and his wife's actions in the seconds before he stepped out of the tent — his actions in mistaking Varina's waterproof for his own, and hers in attempting to disguise him by throwing her shawl over his head and shoulders. That the two intended that he should try to pass himself off as a woman seems unlikely, but that was how it appeared to one of the Yankees on the scene, who called to a nearby officer, "Adjutant, there goes a man dressed in women's clothes." This comment was related to the Wisconsin officer, Lieutenant Colonel Henry Harnden, who, in turn, mentioned it to James Wilson during a debriefing in Macon. Harnden later stated, "As I saw nothing and heard nothing of any female apparel at the time, I never took any stock in that story."

Wilson's first report to War Secretary Stanton contained no mention of the incident, but in his second, the cavalry officer remarked that Davis had "hastily put on one of his wife's dresses, and started for the woods, closely followed by our men, who at first thought him a woman, but seeing his boots while he was running, they suspected his sex at once." Wilson's statement had the air of authority about it, and the story was picked up and elaborated by the press across the country. "Oh, what a picture for the satirist!" a Philadelphia paper crowed. A Baltimore news-sheet, citing the "extremely ludicrous aspect" of Davis's attempt at disguise, concluded that "the culprit becomes the object of derision much as of excoriation." Most of the major dailies remained skeptical about the tale, though the *New York Herald,* whose war reportage had been among the best, detailed with relish how Davis had "slipped into his wife's petticoats, crinoline and dress, but in his hurry he forgot to put on her stockings and shoes. As our men approached he took to his heels, running for the woods; and, as we are told that his boots betrayed him, he probably neglected to assume the mincing, delicate gait of the sex to which he professed to belong."

Word that the clothing in question had been confiscated by the War Department brought Secretary Stanton a telegram from P. T. Barnum offering to contribute $500 to charity in exchange for permission to display it. A pundit for the *Boston Evening Journal* even set the incident to a bit of verse:

> *Jeff. Davis was a warrior bold,*
> *And vowed the Yanks should fall;*
> *He jumped into his pantaloons*
> *And swore he'd rule them all.*
> *But when he saw the Yankees come*
> *To hang him if they could,*
> *He jumped into a petticoat*
> *And started for the wood.*

The false story would haunt Davis to his grave. Years afterward he was still being asked if it was true, and time and again he was forced to explain that while "there was no impropriety in using a disguise to escape capture, . . . there was no time to have assumed one."

Chapter Sixteen

The Last Battle

———◄o►———

SINCE LATE SEPTEMBER, 1864, the Federal presence near the mouth of the Rio Grande River had consisted of a modest blockading contingent from the Navy and a 950-man garrison occupying a few acres of barren Texas sand dunes on the island of Brazos Santiago. This was all that remained of the grand expedition that in November 1863 had seized large sections of the Texas coastline, briefly extending Union control as far as Brownsville, Corpus Christi, and Ringgold Barracks. The Federal troops assigned to that operation were needed elsewhere and were largely withdrawn by early 1864, leaving behind only a few lonely outposts. Since that time an informal truce had existed between the Yankees offshore and the Rebels inland.

Were it not for its location near the mouth of the Rio Grande, there would have been little to recommend the military post at Brazos Santiago. An officer who served here in early June 1865 reported to his family, "I am finally on land once more, if the low, sandy beach, destitute of trees, shrubs or grass, can be called land." A black soldier assigned to it declared, "We found Brazos a most undesirable place, there were plenty of flies and mosquitos and sand burrs. We had our headquarters at this place which was knee deep in water." Another officer observed, "If you dig down you obtain water, but it is as salt as the sea." Few would dispute that Brazos Santiago was a dead-end assignment.

Union General Lew Wallace (later to achieve fame as the author of *Ben Hur*) had tried to talk Texas out of the war from here in March 1865. Wallace came to this forlorn front for a meeting with the Confederate Western Subdistrict commander, Brigadier General James E. Slaughter, and his subordinate in charge of the Brownsville sector, Colonel John S. "Rip" Ford. Wallace later reported to U. S. Grant that both officers were "anxious to find some ground upon which they could honorably get from under what they admitted to be a failing Confederacy." The Federal envoy prepared a six-point proposal for consideration by the Rebel authorities. Besides demanding that all Confederate soldiers surrender their arms and take an oath of allegiance to the U.S. government, and guaranteeing certain property rights, the draft agreement pointedly left the question of slavery "to the discretion of the Congress of the United States." Slaughter and Ford passed the document up the chain of command, where it was decisively rejected by the District of Texas commander, Major General John G. Walker. "Though nothing was decided of a formal nature," Colonel Ford later reminisced in a curious third-person style, "Ford and Slaughter left General Wallace expecting the peaceful coexistence along the river to continue."

For the first months of 1865, Colonel Robert B. Jones had been in command of the Union outpost at Brazos Santiago. In February he had reported the condition of the Confederate garrison at nearby Brownsville as "in a demoralized state . . . numbers of them are deserting from time to time." Located on the Rio Grande across from the Mexican town of Matamoros, Brownsville (which one visitor described as "a city of strange denizens") was a settlement of some importance. Here Confederate cotton could pass to world markets in return for much-needed hard currency and military supplies. When his superiors asked him if it would be possible to take Brownsville, Colonel Jones answered that he "could occupy the place any day" but added that his thousand-man detachment was far too small to be able to hold the city for very long. Further, Jones feared that any Texas Unionists who revealed themselves during the occupation would suffer once the troops were withdrawn. After digesting this response, Jones's immediate superior replied through an aide that he did "not approve of the temporary occupation of that place, and that there are not forces sufficient that can at this time be spared to make a demonstration in that quarter."

Union

Thursday, May 11, 1865. A storm was coming. Some 250 men belonging to the 62nd U.S. Colored Troops stood waiting to board the steamer that was tied up at the Brazos Santiago landing. Inside the nearby post headquarters, the regimental commander, Lieutenant Colonel David Branson, faced the officer who had replaced Colonel Jones as military commander at Brazos Santiago. Colonel Theodore H. Barrett's orders to Branson were to move across the bay to Point Isobel and to push inland from there on a raid. A member of the steamer's crew had reported that its machinery was broken and that the craft would not be able to transport the soldiers as planned, but Barrett was not going to change his mind. He instructed Branson to shift the crossing to the southern part of the island, where small boats could be used to shuttle the troops to Boca Chica; the raid could begin from there.

Other officers had made reputations for themselves in the war, but not Theodore Barrett. Before his transfer to Brazos Santiago the Federal had commanded occupation troops during the uneventful policing of Louisiana. His reasons for ordering his men into action this day, and thus breaking the "truce" that had existed along the lower Rio Grande, were never fully explained. A correspondent for the *New York Herald* later reported that "Colonel Barrett, who had long stood in need of horses for cavalry and other purposes on the island, sent out a party for the purposes of obtaining them." Indeed, as Lieutenant Colonel Branson began to transfer his command from the island to Boca Chica, he was joined by about fifty men from the Second (U.S.) Texas Cavalry, who, Barrett took pains to note in his official report, were "not yet mounted." Barrett also likely possessed intelligence that an informant had delivered to his superior, which held that the Confederates "don't intend to try to hold Brownsville much longer, and if our forces were ordered to occupy that place, I don't think they would meet with any opposition."

A member of the expedition later openly questioned Barrett's motives, claiming that as he "had no cavalry [to speak of] or artillery, nothing but infantry, . . . what did he want with horses for his men?" The historian for one of the regiments that were soon to be involved concluded that Barrett had acted "either without any definite purpose or for some purpose that has never been made clear." The purpose seemed all too clear to another officer, who afterward wrote that the Brazos "post is commanded by the Colonel of a colored regiment, [who] . . . wishing to establish for himself some notoriety before the war closed, . . . started a colored regiment to Brownsville, on the Rio Grande, in direct violation of orders from headquarters."

With a driving rainstorm causing further delays, it took Lieutenant Colonel Branson until 9:30 P.M. to get his men across the water separating Brazos Santiago from Boca Chica. "At 2 A.M. of the 12th," he later reported, "after making a long circuitous march, we surrounded White's Ranch, where we expected to capture a rebel outpost of sixty-five men, horses, and cattle, but they had been gone a day or two."

Branson rested his troops here for perhaps four hours while he considered his next move. At 6:00 A.M., with Company H of the 62nd U.S.C.T. in the van, Branson marched his men west toward Palmito Ranch, another well-known depot for Confederate matériel. At about 7:00 A.M. his skirmishers came into contact with "rebel cavalry in small force," which gave way slowly before his advance.

The peculiar politics of southern Texas played a part in Branson's march along the U.S. side of the Rio Grande. Mexicans sympathetic to the Confederacy spotted his column from the far bank and, Branson believed, "started to give the alarm to the rebels. At the same time soldiers of the Imperial Mexican Army were marching up that bank of the river."

By midday Branson's soldiers had reached and occupied Palmito Ranch, "capturing 3 prisoners, 2 horses, and 4 beef-cattle." He ordered his men to halt "on the hill at Palmetto Ranch to rest and feed men and animals." At about 3:00 P.M. an organized body of enemy cavalry appeared on the road from Brownsville, and Branson concluded that his position at Palmito Ranch was not a good one. His command retraced its route to White's Ranch, followed closely by the Rebel riders, who were kept at a distance by skirmishers from Company H, 62nd U.S.C.T., and a detail from the 2nd (U.S.) Texas Cavalry.

Couriers were sent back to Colonel Barrett with reports, and late in the evening the Federal commander decided to up the ante. At 10:00 P.M. he ordered the other regiment on Brazos Santiago, the 34th Indiana, to be ready to move. At 1:00 A.M. on May 13, two hundred men from the regiment began the laborious task of boarding skiffs for the trip across the water to Boca Chica. Once ashore on the mainland, the men were assembled and marched seven miles to White's Ranch, reaching it around daybreak. Colonel Theodore Barrett had decided to order "an advance to be again made in the direction of Palmetto Ranch."

Confederate

The troops that had scrapped with Branson's men throughout the day were from Giddings's battalion, under the command of Captain W. N. Robinson. Robinson's men were scattered in picket detachments all along the river line to Brownsville, and after his forward videttes fell back to Palmito Ranch, their captain gathered all of them together for the show of force that convinced Lieutenant Colonel Branson to return to White's Ranch. It was only then that Robinson sent his report of the action back to his superiors in Brownsville, concluding the dispatch, "I think they will return to the island tonight."

The courier carrying this message had arrived late in the evening at Brownsville, where he reported to Colonel Ford that "the Yankees had advanced, and [Robinson] ... was engaged with them just below San Martin Ranch." This seeming violation of the informal truce was something that the combative Texas officer could not take lying down. He sent the courier back to Robinson with a promise that he would "come to his aid as soon as men could be collected." After issuing the orders necessary to marshal his units, Ford stormed into district headquarters and confronted Brigadier General Slaughter.

"General, what do you intend to do?" Ford demanded.

Slaughter was far from confident at this moment. Desertions among his men had become a major problem, and he worried about the large gangs of Mexican bandits that he feared might at any moment make a dash on Brownsville. His only thought was to preserve what few organized troops he had left. Slaughter's answer to Ford was, "Retreat."

"You can retreat and go to hell if you wish!" Ford shouted. "These are my men, and I am going to fight."

The two argued awhile before Slaughter finally agreed to join Ford on the Fort Brown parade grounds the next morning. Together they would march against the enemy.

Union

The black Union troops left White's Ranch at daylight and pushed west toward Palmito Ranch, with Company F skirmishing this time with the omnipresent Rebel horsemen. At first the footsore Indiana veterans were left to secure the area around White's Ranch, but less than thirty minutes after the other troops had departed, orders came for the 34th to follow. As one weary member of the regiment recalled, "We had scarcely got our coffee water warm when we were ordered to fall in, and at once took up our line of march on the Brownsville Road."

Shortly after 9:00 A.M., the lead elements of the 62nd U.S.C.T. reached Palmito Ranch. Colonel Barrett, who was riding with the black soldiers, later reported that "such stores as had escaped destruction the day previous were now destroyed, and the buildings which the enemy had turned into barracks were burned." Barrett's intentions at this point remain somewhat obscure. The 62nd had marched with five days' rations, while the hurried departure of the 34th had not allowed the soldiers time to grab more than one meal before they left. In testimony given after the affair, Barrett stated, "At that point I ordered the 62nd to furnish the 34th Indiana with rations to last until the evening of the next day. I also ordered all the disabled men, and those not able to make a heavy march[,] to be sent back with the wounded men, horses and cattle to Brazos Santiago."

The enemy's cavalry still lingered at long range, maintaining contact but in position to spread the alarm should the blue columns begin to head purposefully toward Brownsville. Soon after he arrived at Palmito Ranch, Colonel Barrett ordered a portion of the 34th Indiana to continue along the river bluff in the general direction of Brownsville. This detachment, under Second Lieutenant Charles A. Jones, moved over Palmito Hill and worked its way for about two miles through the heavy brush that fringed the river. Several parties of mounted Rebels took potshots at his men, but they did not seriously contest the advance. When Lieutenant Jones had gone as far as he thought prudent, he stopped his men and sent for reinforcements. Some time later, Colonel Barrett arrived with them. "Well! Lieutenant, how are you getting along?" he asked.

The young officer explained that he wanted to set up an ambush using fifty men from the main body as bait. He would ease his men further along the thickets on the riverbank, which, he was confident, would conceal them from view. Once in position, he would signal the decoy troops to advance into the open, a move that would draw the Confederate cavalry toward them. His hidden men would wait until the enemy riders passed them and would then open up on their flank and rear. "You may try it," Barrett said.

Before long, the detachment of the 2nd (U.S.) Texas Cavalry ("not yet mounted") appeared, and its commanding officer was briefed on the plan. Jones deployed his men, then scouted ahead to make certain that everything was in place. On his return he spotted a Union line of battle moving out into the open. This proved to be a portion of the 62nd

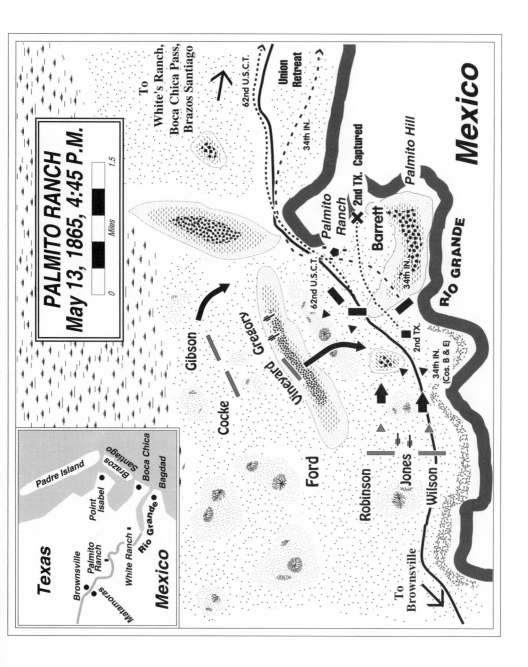

PALMITO RANCH
May 13, 1865, 4:45 P.M.

0   Miles   1.5

To
White's Ranch,
Boca Chica Pass,
Brazos Santiago

62nd U.S.C.T.

Union
Retreat

34th IN.

Mexico

2nd TX. Captured

Palmito
Ranch

Palmito Hill

Barrett

RIO GRANDE

62nd U.S.C.T.

34th IN.

2nd TX.

Gibson

Gregory

34th IN.
(Cos. B & E)

Cocke

Vineyard

Ford

Robinson

Jones

Wilson

To
Brownsville

Texas

Padre Island

Point
Isabel

Brazos
Santiago

Boca Chica

Bagdad

White Ranch

Rio Grande

Palmito
Ranch

Brownsville

Matamoras

Mexico

305

U.S.C.T. under Lieutenant Colonel Branson, who told Jones, "I was ordered by Colonel Barrett to report to you with my command. I do not know what your movements are, or what you are doing." The unexpected presence of extra troops where they were not needed upset Jones's plans. He asked Branson to move his line back under cover to act as a general reserve, then returned to his concealed force, still hoping to put the original scheme into action. However, one of his men fired before the order was given, fully alerting the enemy horsemen to what was happening and prematurely cueing the 62nd, which emerged from its cover to send a few poorly aimed volleys in the general direction of the Rebels. The plan was ruined.

Jones reported his failure to Colonel Barrett. As the lieutenant later recalled, "I asked him if he had any particular point to gain. He said he had not, only to drive them. . . . I told him that I should not advance any further without orders. He says, 'Well, if you think best, we will return to the bluffs and eat supper.' It was now between 4 and 5 o'clock P.M."

Confederate

Colonel "Rip" Ford waited for Brigadier General Slaughter on the Fort Brown parade grounds until 11:00 A.M. Unknown to him, the Confederate commander had received a report of an impending raid on Brownsville from Mexico and had remained at headquarters to coordinate defensive moves. Ford's only thoughts, however, were of those perfidious Yankees, so when Slaughter failed to show up, the Texas colonel "placed himself at the head of the few troops present and marched to a short distance below San Martin Ranch."

He arrived near Palmito Ranch "after 3 o'clock" and at once began to set up an attack. He had under his command some "three hundred cavalry and a light battery," but he estimated the enemy raiding force at eight hundred men. Ford was far from sanguine. "This may be the last fight of the war," he remembered thinking, "and from the number of Union men I see before me, I am going to be whipped."

Nevertheless, he deployed his men for an offensive movement. A two-gun section of Captain O. G. Jones's battery, with Robinson's and Captain D. W. Wilson's battalions alongside, took position in front of the enemy, while two more guns (under Lieutenant William Gregory), accompanied by a detachment led by Lieutenant Jesse Vineyard, were to "move under cover of the hills and chaparral, to flank the enemy's right, and if possible to get an enfilading fire." A third group of men, consisting of units commanded by Captains Cocke and Gibson, was to try to get in the enemy's rear.

Once his riders and gunners were ready, Colonel Ford rode in front of the main body facing the Federals. "Men," he shouted, "we have whipped the enemy in all previous fights. We can do it again." His soldiers cheered and cried "Rip! Rip!" The time was not yet 5:00 P.M.

Union

Colonel Barrett had let most of his men stack their arms and cook their dinners. As he later stated, "Preparations were made to rest there until night, with a view of moving camp at dark, a short distance, and marching in the morning at 3 o'clock in the direction of Point Isobel." While the men relaxed, portions of the 34th Indiana scrounged for souvenirs in the still-smoking ruins of Palmito Ranch. Remembered one soldier, "At the ranche a letter was picked up from a lady to her lover in the Confederate service. Among other matters, she requested him on his return home to bring her a pet Yankee. A number of our boys remarked that the young lady might tame some of our number, but she had given her lover a hard task."

There was an undercurrent of tension running beneath this seemingly placid scene. "Rip" Ford's preparations had not gone unnoticed. A soldier in the 34th later recollected the sight of "the enemy maneuvering — his mounted troopers galloping to and fro." One Hoosier officer loudly remarked, "I don't like the look of things over there." According to Colonel Barrett, "Within fifteen to thirty minutes after the 62nd had gone into camp, the enemy suddenly appeared in large force, in front, on our right flank, and was already attempting to gain our rear, being further down the river than ourselves on the left, having already flanked us." What had begun as a lazy encampment now took on all the appearances of a trap. A medical man with the expedition noted that at about this time, "firing . . . became general along our entire line as well as that of the enemy." To make matters even worse, the Confederates unmasked several cannon, which began to throw shots into and over the Federal camps.

Barrett ordered the officer commanding the 34th Indiana, Lieutenant Colonel Robert G. Morrison, to put out a skirmish line. At the same time, he instructed the 62nd U.S.C.T. to deploy against the enemy force on the right flank. Two companies from the 34th had barely hustled out to take up skirmishing positions when Barrett ordered a general withdrawal.

The retrograde movement quickly became something of a footrace, as few of the veteran Indiana soldiers saw any reason to stand and fight. "It seemed useless slaughter," one later wrote, "and we were at the mercy of the enemy — they having light artillery while we had none." The Union position in the crook of the river bend was an awkward one: the Federals would have to march in a northeastern direction, with their flank toward the enemy, in order to reach the tip of the bend and get astride the Brazos-Brownsville road. In the confused interval during which the Union posture changed abruptly from a defensive stance to a retreat, the Indiana skirmishers and most of the 2nd (U.S.) Texas Cavalry were abandoned as the main lines of battle hastily pulled back. "As I started with the wounded from the field," remembered a medical man, "the skirmishers were falling back, and I could hear them complain of not having been relieved."* The 62nd U.S.C.T. and the 34th Indiana, meanwhile, were marching on a converging course, and for a few moments portions of the two units intermingled under fire. Each side later blamed the other for the mishap, which further disordered the 34th.

Somehow the black and white troops made it to the road without further incident, and from that point on the Union retreat steadied itself, with the men of the 62nd forming the rear guard. "Every attempt of the enemy's cavalry to break this line was repulsed with loss to him," Colonel Barrett later reported, "and the entire regiment fell back with precision and in perfect order, under circumstances that would have tested the discipline of the best troops." A sergeant in the 62nd presented a less rosy view, asserting that the "retreat was saved from being an utter rout by the steadiness of the 62nd USCT and a part of the 34th Indiana."

During this forced withdrawal, the 34th Indiana suffered the indignity of losing both its national and its regimental flag when the footsore color bearers were unable to keep up the rapid pace. The regimental banner was hidden in the brush along the river, where it was found the next day by Confederate troops engaged in mopping up; the U.S. flag was wrapped around the waist of a soldier who then swam across the Rio Grande and turned it over to Mexican officials, who eventually surrendered the standard to Federal authorities.

---

* Colonel Ford later testified that the two Indiana companies had "stood as long as they could, until many of them were run over by my cavalry, and nearly all of them were taken prisoners."

Confederate

"Rip" Ford's pursuit continued for seven miles. "The enemy endeavored to hold various points, but were driven from them," he recollected. Yankee resistance was not the only thing slowing Ford down: his "artillery horses were greatly fatigued (some of them had given out)," he wrote, "[and] the cavalry horses were jaded." The Texan finally called off the chase after the Federals pulled into a defensive position at "a ranch (Cobb's) a mile and a half or two miles from the nearest point on Brazos Island."

Ford worried that Union reinforcements might come out from the island. "It is better to let well enough alone," he told his officers. "We will stop the pursuit." He directed his men to gather in prisoners and any discarded supplies, then watched impassively as the Yankees began to cross some tide-covered mud flats by means of a levee that had been thrown up to bridge them. At that moment Brigadier General Slaughter arrived, accompanied by a small force under Captain W. H. D. Carrington. The rumored border raid had proved to be a bust, and now Slaughter was all for pressing the pursuit. He ordered the riders with Captain Carrington to cut off the enemy's rear guard before it could safely cross the levee. Carrington moved out at once, but the Federals were nearly all over before he got started, and those who were already across were able to lay down a heavy covering fire for their rear guard. As he watched the last of the enemy escape, Slaughter waded into the tidal water and emptied his revolver at the distant foe.

The Battle of Palmito Ranch, later termed by Colonel Barrett "the last actual conflict between hostile forces in the great rebellion," was over.

General Slaughter wrote his report of the action on the evening of May 13 and listed his losses at "four or five severely wounded." From returns supplied to the War Department, the cost to the 62nd U.S.C.T. can be put at two captured and five wounded. The fifty-man 2nd (U.S.) Texas Cavalry just about disappeared after this action, with three wounded and twenty-two captured. Northern newspaper accounts that appeared immediately following the affair claimed that the captured Texans had been shot out of hand, but no reprisals were made. The men of the two skirmishing companies (B and E) of the 34th Indiana, which were captured almost intact, would be speedily paroled and returned to their command within a few days. In his 1865 official report, the Indiana adjutant general calculated the loss to the 34th at "eighty-two in killed, wounded and prisoners." Only one Federal actually died in the fighting, however —Private Jefferson Williams, of the 34th's Company B. Afterward, the survivors of the regiment would present his family with a medallion commemorating him as the last soldier killed in the Civil War.

There were other last actions to be recorded in this affair. As the Confederates pulled back from the shore, a U.S. warship anchored nearby threw a shell at them. According to Captain Carrington, a "seventeen-year-old trooper blazed away in the direction of the exploded shell with his Enfield rifle, using a very profane expletive for so small a boy, causing a hearty laugh from half a score of his comrades. The firing ceased. The last gun had been fired."

In his official after-action report, Colonel Barrett declared that the "last volley of the war, it is believed, was fired by the Sixty-Second U.S. Colored Infantry about sunset of the 13th of May, 1865."

Barrett's performance during this operation drew mixed reviews from the participants. The captain of a company in the black regiment felt that "great confidence was given the men by the intrepid conduct of Colonel Barrett, who remained with the line until the enemy ceased to annoy us seriously." A member of the 34th Indiana, on the other hand, would later maintain that "Col. Barrett, to say the least, showed no ability as a brigade commander." Barrett brought charges against Lieutenant Colonel Morrison for losing control of his regiment and allowing his flags to be captured. A court-martial was convened, testimony given, and a verdict finally delivered absolving the Hoosier officer of any blame.

In an interview conducted long after the war, Lieutenant Colonel Branson of the 62nd U.S.C.T. recalled his thoughts upon hearing that last volley. According to his reminiscence, he turned to one of his company commanders and, "sententiously and with an animation he can never feel again, remarked, 'That winds up the war.'"

Part Three

AFTERSHOCKS

Adieu O soldier,
You of the rude campaigning, (which we shared,)
The rapid march, the life of the camp,
The hot contention of opposing fronts, the long manoeuvre,
Red battles with their slaughter, the stimulus,
    the strong terrific game,
Spell of all brave and manly hearts,
    the trains of time through you and like of you all fill'd,
With war and war's expression.

Adieu dear comrade,
Your mission is fulfill'd — but I, more warlike,
Myself and this contentious soul of mine,
Still on our own campaigning bound,
Through untried roads with ambushes opponents lined,
Through many a sharp defeat and many a crisis, often battled,
Here marching, ever marching on, a war fight out — aye here,
To fiercer, weightier battles give expression.

Walt Whitman, "Adieu to a Soldier"

I am a good old rebel —
    Yes; that's just what I am —
And for this land of freedom
    I do not give a dam'.
I'm glad I fit agin 'em,
    And I only wish we'd won;
And I don't ax no pardon
    For anything I've done.

    Innes Randolph,
        "A Good Old Rebel (Unreconstructed)"

Chapter Seventeen

"They march like the
lords of the world"

———◦———

THE NATION'S TRANSITION from war to peace was nowhere more clearly in evidence than in the shift in focus of its top military commanders. Just a day after Appomattox, U. S. Grant was anxious to return to Washington "with a view to putting a stop to the purchase of supplies, and what I now deemed other useless outlay of money." In the note of April 18 covering his ill-fated peace memorandum, William T. Sherman declared that the "question of finance is now the chief one, and every soldier and officer not needed should be got home at work. I would like to be able to begin the march north by May 1." On April 27, with the ink still wet on Johnston's surrender, Sherman issued orders for four of his six corps to begin the first leg of their homeward journey, a march to Washington, D.C.

The Tenth and Twenty-third corps would remain behind to oversee the paroling of Johnston's army and to garrison the region. The rest of the men began to move north under strict orders to cease all foraging, with trustworthy units sent ahead to secure and protect private property along the chosen routes. All surplus munitions, artillery, and transportation vehicles were left behind.

"On the 30th the march was taken up, the bands playing 'Home again,' and 'We are homeward bound,' and the troops in the most joyous spirits," a Wisconsin soldier in the Twentieth Corps recorded. Added a member of the Fifteenth Corps, "I am glad that old Sherman takes so much interest in his army, he knows that it would not do to crowd us soldiers into ships for we ain't used to being confined and it would kill the half of us."

For the first few days the mood of the march was lighthearted. Soldiers took note of farmers' plowing their fields again, while others, spotting their former foes making their way back home, gladly shared camp rations with them. "We always found these ex-rebels friendly and glad that the war was over, and the parting in the morning would be like leave-taking of old friends," observed an Indiana man.

Three or four days on the road brought the blue columns into Virginia. "When the state line between North Carolina and Virginia was reached, a cracker box was set up with the words 'State line' written on it; and the bands of the Twentieth Corps played, 'Carry Me Back to Old Virginia,' " wrote a Wisconsin man. An Illinois boy noticed that "the citizens seemed glad that the war was over."

But the march soon became something less than a happy jaunt, as officers began to force the pace. "We had marched but two days before we learned that the four corps commanders were marching a race for Richmond," an Illinois soldier remarked. "There has always existed a spirit of rivalry between the 14th and 20th corps, and this feeling has been fostered and encouraged [rather] than otherwise, by the officers. The explanation we find in the fact that one is composed of Eastern and the other of Western troops."

Men paid for this rivalry with their lives. "I saw a number laid out this morning by the roadside looking as if they had been boiled," wrote an Illinois man. "It is said we are racing with 15th A.C. [Army Corps] for the first crossing of the Roanoke," a soldier in the Seventeenth Corps noted in his journal. "It is considered worth an effort to have the advance after crossing the river — perhaps so; but we are flesh and blood, and the sun is hot, and, besides, there is no hurry." "We have never made a much harder march and some of our Generals deserve to have their necks broke for such 'Tom Foolery' after the war," an Ohio soldier declared. Said another, in 1904, "Many were sunstruck, and several deaths occurred on that march, some of whom might still be alive if they had been allowed eight days instead of five to march 140 miles, which is the distance from Raleigh to Richmond."

Tensions only increased when the four columns drew up before the former Rebel capital. Recalled a staff officer in the Seventeenth Corps,

"Our surprise can well be imagined when we received an order prohibiting both officers and men from visiting the city. This order was the occasion of much dissatisfaction and bitter feeling upon the part of the rank and file." "Some of the soldiers got into a row in the town of Manchester [across the James from Richmond] . . . and caused considerable disturbance," an Ohio boy wrote in his diary on May 10. "The difficulty occurred between the Provost Guard & the soldiers in town. Pistols fired & stones thrown freely, goods stolen."

Sherman had planned his tour of the other commands in his sprawling military department in such a way as to allow him to join his men in Richmond for the final stretch to Washington. In the interval, he had received additional newspapers dating from the period between his first peace memorandum and his final settlement with Johnston. Included in the accounts were a number of communiqués undermining his authority, issued by Major General Henry W. Halleck, Lincoln's former chief military adviser and a man who fashioned himself Sherman's friend. If Halleck, who now commanded the Virginia region centered in Richmond, actually thought the fiery Sherman would forgive and forget, he had another think coming. Halleck's dispatches, clearly designed to curry favor with Stanton at Sherman's expense, "simply excited my contempt for a judgment such as he was supposed to possess," Sherman said.

One of those who met Sherman on his arrival in Richmond recalled, "We found him greatly excited and boiling with indignation over an order which had been issued by General Halleck requiring our troops to pass in review before him on the following day. I never before saw him in such a towering passion, or even angry, and never believed that he was capable of using such scathing and denunciatory language as he did in reference to General Halleck. He repudiated the order in toto and directed the column to be moved in ordinary marching form at 3 o'clock A.M. and thus we passed through Richmond just at daylight." Some of Sherman's belligerence managed to trickle down to the rank and file: "Nothing has stopped this Army and if Halleck thinks he can do it, he had better get out of the way," a Wisconsin surgeon exclaimed.

The line of march now took Sherman's men over the bloody battlefields of Grant's Overland Campaign. Quite a number of soldiers were able to visit Spotsylvania, the site of a brutal series of engagements between May 8 and 21, 1864.* A Pennsylvania soldier in the Twentieth Corps noted, "This place looked quite desolate, very few persons remained and what few houses remained standing were pretty well riddled

---

* Covered in detail in my 1989 book, *Bloody Roads South*.

with shot & shell." A New Yorker in the same corps recollected seeing "many evidences of the severity of the contest. One portion of the field which had been covered with pine trees is now cleared of live timber, nearly all the trees having lost their tops."

Sergeant Rice C. Bull made it a point to visit a spot of especial carnage known as the Bloody Angle. "Hardly anything had apparently been changed or disturbed," he remembered. "The doublefaced entrenchments that had been occupied on one side by Union troops and six feet away on the other side by the Confederates still stood as at the time of the battle. I saw the famous tree that had been shot down by bullets fired in the action. . . . Around the foot of the tree were many chips, and I placed several in my knapsack. On the south side of the trench the Confederate dead had been given scant burial, as many as one hundred skeletons were counted in the distance of not more than two hundred feet. On the northern side of the field the dead had not been buried; and as we looked over the ground where the charges had been made by our forces, we saw many places where there were growths of grass in the almost barren field. They marked the remains of Union soldiers, only a skeleton encased in a mouldy uniform of blue with rusty gun and equipment at the side. It was a gruesome sight and made us all the more thankful that the war was at last ended."

Even as Sherman's men were marching north, portions of the Army of the Potomac — the primary force in the Appomattox Campaign — were also converging on Washington. At first the plan had simply been to use the capital as an administrative depot to dispatch the various units to their mustering-out points, but then it began to occur to officials that they could take advantage of the opportunity and stage a grand review. As late as May 16, Grant's chief of staff was advising Sherman, then in Fredericksburg, that a "review has not yet been determined on," but the very next day, Edwin Stanton released a statement promising that a "review of the gallant armies now assembling around Washington will take place here on Tuesday and Wednesday of next week, the twenty-third and twenty-fourth insts." It required two more days for official orders to that effect to reach Sherman, who hastened to assure President Johnson that his men were all "in good order and condition for serenade, reviews, or fighting."

Sherman's men began to gather in encampments spread about Alexandria, Virginia, on May 19. "Nothing but camps as far as we can see which is several miles on three sides and ½ on the other," an Ohio man jotted in his diary. An Illinois soldier was more descriptive: "Grouped around the Capitol City, on every hillside and plain, covering thousands of acres, and extending even beyond our vision, rose the snowy white tents of half a million of veteran soldiers of the Union, who had fought for long years to preserve for themselves and their children, and their successors, all this fair heritage."

The next days were spent in preparation. In Washington routes were laid out, details finalized, and bridges checked to ensure that they could bear the weight of so many men. In the camps, the men also got ready. "All hands have been hard at work polishing guns and brasses, cleaning carriages, and blacking harness," an Army of the Potomac artillery officer noted. A Wisconsin man under Sherman recalled that the "unwonted exercise of blacking shoes, polishing arms and cleaning up was resumed." Railroads worked around the clock to bring more than seventy-five thousand visitors to the city for the event. Saloons were closed, room prices skyrocketed, and many people literally camped out in the parks to await the great event. Reviewing stands were erected in front of the White House, with a special set of seats added across the street (courtesy of a wealthy Bostonian) for the exclusive use of wounded soldiers from area hospitals.

It had been decided that the troops who had been engaged primarily in the Virginia campaigns would march on May 23, while the soldiers who had followed Sherman from Atlanta to the sea would pass in review the following day. Early on the morning of May 23, city fire engines doused Pennsylvania Avenue to settle the dust, and promptly at 9:00 A.M., the troops who had moved before dawn to the staging area near the Capitol began to march.

Major General George Gordon Meade, commander of the Army of the Potomac, led the way with his staff. A national hero after his defensive victory at Gettysburg, Meade had been largely overshadowed by the rise of Grant and his circle in the closing pages of the conflict. Nevertheless, when Meade dismounted at the White House reviewing stand to salute his troops as they passed, he was greeted by Sherman, who said, "I'm afraid my poor tatterdemalion corps will make a poor appearance tomorrow when contrasted with yours."

Behind Meade came the cavalry corps, led by Major General Wesley Merritt in the absence of Phil Sheridan, who had been sent to take command of Union operations aimed at subduing the Trans-Mississippi. "The men were finely mounted and neatly uniformed," a Midwest correspondent reported. "Their bronzed appearance only gave evidence of their veterancy. The horses were in very fine condition, and marched with the utmost regularity, seemingly keeping time to the music that rose from every brigade." "Pennsylvania avenue was packed from one end to the other with a dense mass of humanity," recounted one of those tanned veterans, "and the troops received a perfect ovation at every step." As Brevet Major General George A. Custer drew near the reviewing stands, his horse, spooked by a flowery wreath tossed to its rider by a spectator, bolted down the street. A young bugler who witnessed the affair never forgot "General Custer's superb horsemanship in keeping his saddle on his charging bay stallion, his finally gaining control of him and returning to his place in column with as much grace and ease as if the performance was a part of the original program."

Provost and Engineer troops came next in line, followed by the ranks of the Ninth Corps. Under Ambrose Burnside, at Petersburg, the corps had led the way in the terrible Battle of the Crater; it marched this day under Burnside's successor, John Parke. "Slowly but appreciatively, the audience begin to mark and applaud the tattered banners, some stained and worn, others torn to threads, barely clinging to the staff, and others still carefully gathered around the staff, the threads all too priceless to lose a single one," a reporter wrote. A Pennsylvania soldier remembered this moment as one "the like of which will never be seen again," while a New Hampshire colleague described it as "a sight at once magnificent, soul stirring, and inspiring."

After the Ninth Corps came the Fifth, of Five Forks fame, with Major General Charles Griffin in charge. "I tell you it was a grand sight," a Pennsylvania boy in the ranks wrote to his mother, "one of the grandest things and the grandest mass of people I ever saw in my life." "Little children pressed flowers into the hands of the hardy veterans as they marched in review; kindly smiles and sweet words of welcome greeted the soldiers on every hand," added a comrade. "It is impossible for me to describe that royal scene," a Maine veteran declared. "The buildings were all draped in national colors; . . . the sidewalks were packed with spectators, . . . the bands all played the national airs; the people cheered until they were hoarse; banners waved and handkerchiefs fluttered."

Artillery units marched between the various corps. "The parade of the troops was magnificent," recollected a Rhode Island gunner. "Every tree was crowded with, and every fence covered, with boys," observed a New Jersey artilleryman. "Floral arches spanned the streets, and flags were hanging from every possible point."

The Second Corps, led by Major General Andrew Humphreys, brought this day of the grand review to a close. At Gettysburg this corps had faced and repulsed Pickett's Charge. "The waving sea of bayonets . . . was a magnificent sight as we passed the grand stand," a New Yorker recalled. "The white citizens were not backward in giving to the victorious army a welcome and cheer, whilst the colored people seemed fairly crazed with joy," said a Pennsylvania man.

Not all the participants were wearing rose-colored glasses. "Of all the marches made by the regiment, for rapidity and length, without rest, none would compare with that inhuman tramp for display," a Maine soldier grumbled. "The review was indeed a magnificent spectacle. The vanity of Halleck, that prince of military humbugs, and of President Johnson, must have been fully gratified." One artillery officer turned a cynical eye on the banners that were displayed by the crowd: "Among the last I noticed one: 'The only debt we can never repay; what we owe to our gallant defenders.' I could not help wondering whether, having made up their minds that they can *never* pay the debt, that they will not think it useless to try."

A Cincinnati reporter reflected upon the pageantry and power he had witnessed this day. "You think of the stately poetry of the scriptural words, *'terrible as an army with banners.'* Terrible it is, indeed, in its strength. One wonders that such a power as this in the land could so long have been resisted."

A number of Sherman's men managed to view their "rivals" on parade. "It was a sight of splendor to see the Potomac boys," an Illinois soldier noted. "They were a splendid set of men, and were cheered by us and by the spectators." An Indiana soldier was less impressed. "They had white gloves on, but what does that account to?" he asked.

The next day, May 24, 1865, proved a perfect setting for Sherman's men. "The day was a lovely one, the air was mild and balmy, the sun shone forth resplendently, and scarcely a cloud dimmed the azure vault of heaven," a correspondent wrote. Promptly at 9:00 A.M., the signal guns boomed and Sherman's men moved to march step.

William Tecumseh Sherman proudly led the way. According to a Washington reporter, "On the right of General Sherman rode General [Oliver O.] Howard, distinguished as having but one arm, [having lost the other] at Fair Oaks [in 1862]. . . . He was much observed as any other gentleman in the column. General Sherman's horse was decorated with a large wreath of laurel resting on his shoulders. The noble animal pranced with spirit and seemed to be embued with the fervor of his master." When Sherman reached the Treasury Building, adjacent to the White House, he looked back and was awed by what he saw. "The column was compact, and the glittering muskets looked like a solid mass of steel, moving with the regularity of a pendulum," he remembered.

As Meade had done the day before, Sherman rode past the reviewing stand, dismounted, and joined the notables. He moved along the line, shaking hands first with President Johnson and then with General Grant. Next was the hated Stanton; the war secretary began to hold out his hand but then, realizing that Sherman was going to ignore the gesture, let it fall back to his side. According to one observer, "Stanton's face, never very expressive, remained immobile." Recalled another, "Sherman's face was scarlet and his red hair seemed to stand on end."

All of this happened in a matter of a few moments and went unnoticed by everyone save a few veteran insiders who had been expecting something. The review of Sherman's army proceeded without further incident. His forces were grouped for this occasion as they had been for the final campaign in North Carolina: first came the Army of the Tennessee, consisting of the Fifteenth and Seventeenth corps. "Its record of victories begins with Belmont, notes Donelson, Shiloh, Murfreesboro, Lookout Mountain, Chattanooga, Resaca, Kenesaw, Jonesboro, [and] Atlanta," wrote one reporter. "We were in close column and looking up the long Avenue for a mile you could see as it were a moving wall of bright blue tipped with glittering steel[,] every man keeping step[,] the whole looking like one connected body," remarked an Iowa man. Noted another, "The sidewalks in front of the capital were crowded with ladies, children, citizens & soldiers all looking at us as if they had never seen a crowd of men before & I expect they were disappointed some as the Potomacians told them to wait until Sherman's outlaws marched through if they wanted to see the western savages."

Next came the Twentieth and Fourteenth corps, collectively known as the Army of Georgia. "There is no geographical portion of the country that can exclusively claim this army," a correspondent informed his readers. "It has regiments from the North, the South, the East, and the West." The Twentieth comprised two corps with extensive service in the eastern theater — the Eleventh and Twelfth — while the Fourteenth's service included many western battles. "Long practice in marching, which is in one sense a drill, and the almost entire absence of recruits, conscripts, and substitutes, told greatly in favor of the western troops, and some of the military propriety and exactness was not affected by demonstrations of applause," declared one proud member of the army. A Michigan man long remembered the "perfect sea of bonnets and hats," while a Minnesota soldier was reminded of the "first stages of the war, when the national capital was threatened and the first recruits rushed to its rescue." "Felt kind of queer to get such a welcome," wrote an Ohio infantryman. "Haven't been used to it, makes us feel like the war is over."

A special unit, humorously styled the "Bummer Brigade,"* proved to be a real crowd pleaser. "They were organized under a command by themselves, and seemed to be by brigade and regiment under commanders," explained one observer. "Every man led a pack horse or mule, and various was the make-up of those packs. About the middle of the column was a brigade in which every one had a game cock standing on their pack, and at intervals of a few minutes one would crow, and immediately he could be answered by every one in the brigade. It was amusing, and many were the cheers they got from the sidewalks."

Also a part of this column were squads of black laborers — actually runaway slaves — whose plantation-hardened muscles had helped clear the way for Sherman's men on their march to the sea. Unrepresented either on this day or on the one previous were the thousands of African-American volunteer soldiers who had also paid in blood for the victory signified by the grand review.

By the time it was all over, more than 150,000 men had passed the reviewing stands in a procession that took thirteen hours, spread over two days. The sights and sounds of the event filled the imagination of a ten-year-old onlooker who was already showing great musical promise; in later years John Philip Sousa would claim that the grand review had provided him with a lifetime's inspiration. One participant remembered it as "the grandest pageant that ever took place in modern times"; another felt it must be "one of the most sublime spectacles that human eye ever beheld." In a public career that had spanned more than half a century, former U.S. senator and Sherman family friend Tom Corwin had seen just about every type of official ceremony imaginable, but he could think of nothing to match the proud confidence shown by these victorious veterans. Marveled Corwin, "They march like the lords of the world."

WAR DEPARTMENT, ADJUTANT GENERAL'S OFFICE
Washington, D.C., June 2, 1865

General Orders, No. 108

SOLDIERS OF THE ARMIES OF THE UNITED STATES:

By your patriotic devotion to your country in the hour of danger and alarm — your magnificent fighting, bravery, and endurance —

---

* The "bummers" were bands of foragers who ranged out from the main columns of Sherman's "march to the sea" in search of supplies, loot, and excitement.

you have maintained the supremacy of the Union and the Constitution, over-thrown all armed opposition to the enforcement of the
laws, and of the proclamation forever abolishing slavery — the cause
and pretext of the rebellion — and opened the way to the rightful
authorities to restore order and inaugurated peace on a permanent
and enduring basis on every foot of American soil.

Your marches, sieges, and battles, in distance, duration, resolution,
and brilliancy of result dim the luster of the world's past military
achievements, and will be the patriot's precedent in defense of liberty
and right in all time to come.

In obedience to your country's call you left your homes and families and volunteered in its defense. Victory has crowned your valor
and secured the purpose of your patriot hearts, and with the gratitude
of your countrymen, and the highest honors a great and free nation
can accord, you will soon be permitted to return to your homes and
families conscious of having discharged the highest duty of American
citizens.

To achieve these glorious triumphs, and secure to yourselves, your
fellow-countrymen, and posterity the blessings of free institutions tens
of thousands of your gallant comrades have fallen and sealed the
priceless legacy with their lives. The graves of these a grateful nation
bedews with tears, honors their memories, and will ever cherish and
support their stricken families.

U. S. Grant
Lieutenant-General

Following their part in the grand review, the veterans of Sherman's
armies remained in camp around Washington until early June, awaiting
transfer to Louisville, Kentucky, where they would be mustered out of
the service. The good news was that this time the trip would be by rail;
the bad news was that there simply were not enough cars to carry everyone in the normal fashion. "While we did not expect to be provided with
Pullman coaches, we, nevertheless, did not expect to be given transportation on top of freight and cattle cars," an Iowa soldier complained.

New headquarters were established in Louisville on June 12, and the
soldiers began to flood in. One local newspaper estimated that more
than seventy-three thousand men were camped about the town by mid-
June. "We found the city to be a perfect Sodom," declared a Union
veteran assigned to provost duty. "It was given over to vice, drink and
prostitution. . . . Drunkenness and immorality ran riot; fighting and

322

murders were all but every-day affairs. . . . Some of the saddest experiences of my life were those of the frequent tasks of conducting some of these unfortunates, men and women, the worse for drink or in brawls, to the guard house to be locked up. Such were the kind of service as soldiers of the Republic, we were called upon to render to the country, during the last six weeks of our army life."

It took some while for the four corps to generate the paperwork necessary to send the men home, and in the meantime the residents of Louisville had to endure both the drunken soldiers and the indignities that inevitably occurred with so many men camped on their very doorstep. The worst of it came in late June, when it was widely rumored that Sherman's men were using the city reservoir for bathing and other purposes. Many home owners, reported a correspondent in Louisville, as a result "began to be rather ticklish in the use of hydrant water for drinking and cooking purposes."

Chapter Eighteen

"It was a terrible calamity — beyond description"

---◦---

MOBILE had undergone an amazing transformation in the weeks since its occupation by Union forces. Shortly after the Federal soldiers arrived, on April 12, a reporter set down this word portrait of the Alabama town: "The city is a sad picture to contemplate. The stores look a thousand years old. They wear something of the appearance of the old castles to be seen in some of the countries of Europe. They are empty and forsaken, except [for] here and there an old man seated like some faithful sentinel at his post. . . . The people are distressed. No money except coin and greenbacks will pass. They have little of the former — none of the latter. We have witnessed such sorrow over this order of things as we do not desire again to behold."

Scarcely a month later, following Richard Taylor's surrender, Mobile became an administrative center for the Union army's management of the captured region and a magnet for people uprooted by the war. A paroled Louisiana artilleryman who passed through in mid-May saw "great crowds of Confederate officers and soldiers in the city awaiting transportation to their homes." An Ohio man present at the same time found "the place overrun by officers and soldiers of both Confederate and Union armies." Joining the military men on Mobile's streets were hundreds of now free black laborers, come in from the country to find work with their liberators.

Besides drawing people, Mobile was also becoming a collecting point for cotton (both former Confederate and private) bound for market and munitions confiscated throughout the C.S. Military Department. Circumstances dictated that both materials be stored in the city; the need for their prompt disposal, combined with the lack of adequate facilities to handle them, made the stockpiling of cotton and munitions in an urban area a risk worth taking — or so the Union authorities believed. As a primary storage site for the captured, discarded, and defective ordnance, the Federals selected the two-story Pomeroy and Marshall Warehouse, located on the northeastern side of the city, at the corner of Lipscomb and Commerce streets. The structure was situated on the outer fringes of the commercial district, within three blocks of a large number of cotton presses and sheds as well as other warehouses and offices. Its relatively isolated location and sturdy fireproof construction made it the ideal repository for munitions, at least in the opinion of Brevet Captain William S. Beebe, depot ordnance officer at Mobile. By late May the building's inventory included several thousand artillery shells, hundreds of thousands of rifle and pistol cartridges, hand grenades, bulk powder, and fuses, as well as shot and shell of many different calibers. Security was fairly tight, with sentries outside under orders to enforce a no-smoking zone around the building, and a full-time watchman on patrol inside.

Early on the morning of May 25, noncommissioned officers in the 51st U.S. Colored Troops woke their men and began to form work details to process a large train of captured Rebel ordnance that had been sitting unattended for forty-eight hours. The day promised to be a hot one. Already, recalled an Ohio sergeant, "the shade afforded by the walls was taken advantage of by hundreds of paroled prisoners and colored refugees, who were waiting for transportation, or something to turn up." Labor foreman John Carroll reported to the Pomeroy and Marshall Warehouse at 8:00 A.M. and was told to take a crew of twenty down to the railroad depot to assist in transferring munitions from train cars to wagons, and then to follow these to the warehouse, where they would all be unloaded.

When Carroll arrived at the depot, he found a large detail of black troops also engaged in the task. After a brief conference, Carroll and the white officers in charge of the military party assigned fifty men to move the matériel from the train to the wagons and sent fifty more back to the warehouse to receive it. The first delivery wagons, carrying field and siege ammunition, quickly queued up alongside the Pomeroy and

Marshall loading platform, their drivers impatient to return to the depot.

The black troops who had been assigned to carry the munitions from the wagons into the warehouse seemed not to take their job all that seriously. "The soldiers were handling the boxes of shell very roughly," John Carroll later testified. He watched in shocked surprise as one container of shells was tossed so casually to the platform that it burst open. Soon after this, he saw the soldiers stacking crates right next to the wagon, in such a way that if the pile tipped it would fall onto the munitions that had not yet been taken off. "Boys," Carroll said, "it is fortunate that these are not capped shells; if they were, I would not want to be within three miles of here." His complaints to the officer in charge appeared to have some effect, however, as things seemed under better control by the time he returned to the railroad depot, at 11:00 A.M.

When Dr. N. Walkby, a Mobile resident, stopped by the warehouse on an errand at 1:00 P.M., he was appalled to see some of the black soldiers bowling shells across the platform. "Stop rolling those shells, don't you know better?" he yelled at one of them. The white officer in charge came up to tell the doctor to mind his own business and informed him that there was no danger. Enraged, Walkby stalked out of the warehouse. He tried to report what he had seen to the chief of ordnance, only to be told that that officer was out to lunch and unavailable. Certain that he had witnessed a disaster in the making, the doctor went home and opened all his windows, in order "to save the glass in case an explosion occurred."

Shortly after Dr. Walkby's experience, word of problems at the warehouse reached Julius Becker, a supervisor for the ordnance depot. He hurried to the site in time to see "men . . . dropping the boxes and rolling them end over end, from one side of the warehouse to the other." Becker went looking for the officer in charge but found only a black sergeant, who told him that the men were not taking orders. "At the same time," Becker recalled, "the wagon master stated to me that the teamsters would leave off their work and would not come near the building unless [the soldiers] . . . began to handle the boxes more carefully."

Somebody mentioned that the missing officer could be found aboard a steamer anchored at the shore, not two hundred yards away. Becker located the man, who was resting, and had him return to the warehouse to instruct his men in the proper procedure for handling dangerous explosives. Becker's responsibilities included the other ordnance storage places as well, so shortly before 2:00 P.M. he left the officer and detail working at the Pomeroy and Marshall Warehouse. At about the same time, another officer appeared on the scene with orders for all but twenty-five of the men to report to the railroad depot. These men marched off at about two o'clock.

It was shortly after that when William Johnson, a member of the work detail, left the building on an errand. The officer in charge "was with the men that were unloading the wagons," he later related. "He was a few feet from the wagons, laying against a box inside the building." It was the last time anyone would see either the officer or the work detail alive.

All across Mobile, people went about their business without the least notion of what the next few minutes would bring. Aboard the steamer *Jennie Rogers,* anchored near the city, Arthur H. Burnham, a brevet captain of engineers, was sitting on the boiler deck enjoying a conversation with the vessel's captain, its clerk, and a friend. In the U.S. military headquarters off Government Street, Brigadier General C. C. Andrews was standing next to his seated aide, Alfred Fredberg, and taking care of routine paperwork. On the street just outside headquarters, an Illinois soldier named Bela T. St. John, who had just been relieved from guard duty, set off on a stroll through town. His walk took him to the foot of Government Street, where he turned north as far as Dauphine Street. Shooting the breeze was the exercise of the moment for soldier E. A. Crandall, who sat with friends atop a high woodpile, "telling of the nice things we were going to have when we got home." Captain Fred H. Marsh, of the 46th Illinois, was glad to have escaped the stuffy building that was being used for the court-martial hearing to which he was assigned. The court had adjourned for the day, and Marsh walked quickly along Mobile's streets on his way back to camp. Fatigue, meanwhile, had overcome Brigadier General James Slack, a veteran of the siege operations in April, who gratefully accepted a fellow officer's offer to share his bed in a nearby boardinghouse for a nap.

For most of the soldiers in the camps on the outskirts of the town, there was little to recall in the minutes just after 2:00 P.M. An Iowa soldier named Jasper H. Rice was seated in his tent, bent over his writing desk. Not far away, E. H. Reynolds, of the 46th Illinois, stood outside his tent thinking about the nerve-racking train trip he had just taken as part of a detail accompanying munitions being transferred into Mobile from Gainesville, Alabama. The train had been a smoky, rickety one, and more than once Reynolds had feared for his life.

The time was approximately 2:15 P.M. The city of Mobile, which had survived the entire war virtually unscathed, was about to suffer one of the major tragedies of its history.

* * *

Jasper H. Rice sat bolt upright, startled by what sounded to him like an "18-pound Parrott [cannon] . . . fired at close range." E. H. Reynolds "felt a shock and sudden pressure; at the same instant [I] heard a terrific report." Soldiers in the 33rd Iowa's encampment tumbled out of their tents in a state of perfect astonishment. "We . . . could not imagine the cause of the terrible sound," recollected one of them. To the practiced ear of Brigadier General James Totten, chief of artillery for the Military Division of West Mississippi, there were actually "two distinct explosions, following each other in so quick succession that a person could hardly count one." C.S. veteran and poet Sidney Lanier, sitting at his writing table at Point Clear, across the bay, was shaken by the sound.

Seconds later a blast wave rippled outward from the northeast quadrant of Mobile. Arthur Burnham, who had been chatting on the *Jennie Rogers,* was flung from his chair and sent sprawling on the deck. Staff officer Alfred Fredberg, likewise hurled from his chair by the force of the blast, fell heavily to the floor, while General Andrews, standing next to him, "staggered against the wall." Andrews later recounted, "There was a 'boom' and the glass and frames of the windows came clattering into the room ["like hail," Alfred Fredberg said], and there followed the roar of the falling buildings thrown down by the explosion." The strolling soldier, Bela T. St. John, was aghast "when all of a sudden the sash, glass, shutters &c began to fall around me. . . . The noise was beyond description."

J. E. Lockwood, a sailor aboard the steamer *Col. Cowles,* was resting in a deck chair when the blast wave hit his craft. "It raised me from my chair," he remembered. "I fell down on one knee, picked myself up but seemed propelled by some invisible power and went headlong overboard." He managed to swim safely to shore. Fred H. Marsh, the Illinois officer on court-martial duty, had just reached Mobile's fashionable Battle House when, as he recalled, "all of a sudden the windows and chimneys crashed to the sidewalks." According to an eyewitness account, "In the Battle House was enacted a scene of the wildest panic and confusion. Some hundred or more guests were seated at the dinner table when the explosion occurred. The plastering fell upon them. Shrieking women and pale-faced men all rushed for the doors, midst overturned tables, shivered glass, crockery and mirrors, the very walls seemed about to fall and crush them." A newspaper reported that one of the panicked guests "leaped from the balcony of that building into the street — a height of some thirty-five feet — without the slightest injury." The large woodpile on which E. A. Crandall and his friends had been sitting began to tumble apart, and the men were scattered over the ground. The blast, wrote one

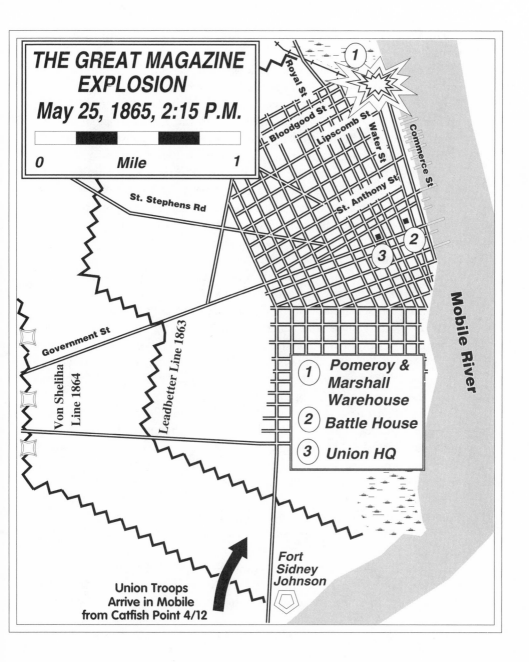

THE GREAT MAGAZINE EXPLOSION
May 25, 1865, 2:15 P.M.

0   Mile   1

Royal St

Bloodgood St

Lipscomb St.

Water St

Commerce St

St. Stephens Rd

St. Anthony St.

3

2

Mobile River

Government St

Von Sheliha Line 1864

Leadbetter Line 1863

1   Pomeroy & Marshall Warehouse

2   Battle House

3   Union HQ

Fort Sidney Johnson

Union Troops Arrive in Mobile from Catfish Point 4/12

dazed Wisconsin soldier, "seemed to lift the whole city from its foundations."

All eyes turned toward the Pomeroy and Marshall Warehouse — or rather, to where it had been mere seconds earlier. The perceptive General Totten saw "an immense mass of shot and shell and fragments flying up vertically as high as five hundred feet in the air, as if a mass of the ammunition had been lifted by the ammunition or powder below it." Wrote a reporter of this blast cloud, "It seemed a writhing giant — gaunt and grim — poised in mid-air, from whose wondrous loins sprang bursting shells, flying timbers, bales of cotton, barrels of rosin, bars and sheets of iron, bricks, stones, wagons, horses, men, women and children, commingled and mangled into one immense mass." An Illinois soldier three miles away saw "rising there that great column of smoke characteristic of an explosion. The smoke mounted up in a dark, thick mass and then spread out like an immense umbrella or mushroom, and through it could be seen broken timbers and *debris* of all kinds flying in every direction."

Related a black soldier in the town, "One old lady thought that Judgment Day had come and cried, 'Thank God, Israel is blowing his trumpet.' " Captain Marsh found himself near a small park, "and just here a lady, all dressed up (a white lady) ran out into the street and clasped hold of me, terribly frightened, saying, 'What is it? What can I do? Where can I go?' Stopping a moment, I pointed to the little park, directing her to hasten there, as there were no buildings there to fall."

General James Slack was jerked awake from his nap when the boardinghouse window shattered and fell across him. Curiously, his sleeping companion was not awakened by the tumult. Said Slack, "I jumped out very quickly and in doing so struck my shin against a window strip that was blown in and bruised it severely. Someone cried out it was a clap of thunder; I thought it pretty odd thunder. Women and children were screaming, men running, glass falling, buildings trembling, everything in the wildest confusion."

Where the Pomeroy and Marshall Warehouse had recently stood, there was now a 254-by-57-foot smoking hole, fully ten feet deep. Of the men on duty in and around the warehouse at the time of the explosion not even fragments remained.

The powerful blast destroyed buildings for blocks and threw flaming timbers into the newly created pyres of wood and cotton kindling. Steamboats and schooners anchored along the city wharf were rocked by the explosion, and their superstructures were shredded by the ordnance and building materials that were hurled at them like canister from the mouth of a cannon. Arthur Burnham, the officer of engineers, remembered "picking up from the deck of the steamer [*Jennie Rogers*] pieces of 12-pounder shrapnel and minie balls, canister balls, pieces of brick and pieces of other ammunition which I cannot characterize." As Bela T. St. John, the Illinois soldier, began to run toward the point of the blast, he observed that "there was cotton burning on the wharf and I noticed a steamer on fire. When I got most there I see 2 wounded men laying on the wharf and a number of persons were gathered around one of them which had a large hole in his head." According to a sailor on a ship located just outside the area of destruction, the "scene on shore was perfectly horrible. The explosion shook the city like an earthquake and all the adjacent buildings were levelled to the ground. The bursting of the shells immediately communicated fire to the ruins and for a long while we thought Mobile was gone up and looked upon her as a doomed city."

Union authorities hurried to the scene. Among the first to arrive was the Thirteenth Corps commander, Brevet Major General Gordon Granger, who, according to a news report, "immediately took steps for the relief of the sufferers and for the safety of the city." Soldier E. H. Reynolds was just one of the many bluecoats who began to congregate downtown. "Throngs were rushing in all directions in search of friends and relatives, while everything possible was being done to extricate the dead and injured from the great masses of timber, brick, etc." Also on hand was Bela T. St. John. "Heavy details of guard were seen on their way to the scene," he recollected, "and driving back all persons that were going down and also driving all soldiers that were not on duty to their quarters."

Fire and the unexploded ordnance now posed a double threat. Remembered General Slack, "About eight squares [blocks] of the city were totally blown into one confused, crushed mass. You can form no conception of the appearance of the buildings, the terrible wreck. The walls of those immense cotton sheds were thrown out and the immense roofs fell in, crushing everything underneath. Immediately following the explosion, the buildings began to burn. A great many persons underneath the rubbish, unable to get out, were roasted alive. Shells were constantly exploding, men crying most piteously for help, the fire approaching them, and no helping hand could save them." "Acres of ground were covered with flames," agreed an eyewitness. According to E. H. Reynolds, "The continued explosions of shells added to the confusion and danger in rescuing the unfortunate ones, and, worst of all, the breaking out of fires in many places, making it impossible to rescue many who must slowly burn to death. Fire companies were called and many streams of water poured in. The bursting shells drove some firemen away, but soldiers with fixed bayonets forced them back to their work and held them there throughout the night."

Reinforcements arrived in the form of a contingent of U.S. sailors led by Fleet Captain Edward Simpson. As the naval officer later reported, "The presence of the sailors in the neighborhood of the exploding shells [was] tending much to restore a partial feeling of confidence to the firemen and others, who were prevented by the bursting shells from working to advantage in extinguishing the fire." A correspondent on the scene wrote of seeing "sailors rush through fire and falling bricks as though they were proof against the accidents common to all men, and come out bearing in their arms some poor fellow buried or crushed almost beyond recognition as a human being. . . . The shrieks of the poor wives, daughters and mothers, as a body would be borne out of the ruins, were heartrending." Two of Captain Simpson's men were killed in the rescue operations.

Soldiers assigned to the Mobile garrison were also pressed into service. "For two hours after the explosion I carried one corner of a stretcher, and on the next morning I assisted in taking from the bay a man who had been shockingly scalded, in the wreck of a vessel, but he was still living," recollected a Wisconsin man. E. H. Reynolds, similarly engaged, never forgot the sight of a "small corral or mule shed where three or four dozen animals were tied. They all laid just as they had fallen away from the explosion, apparently without a struggle." A visitor present that evening noted that the "forked flames rising high in the air — the black eddies of smoke rolling above the flames — the occasional bursting of a shell scattering the burning cinders like a thousand meteors, left an impression on our mind, which time cannot obliterate."

The rescue and cleanup efforts continued for several days. Early on the morning of May 26, Alfred Fredberg reported, "We have just passed a most terrible night, but the danger is, thank God, over." A soldier who visited the site that day remarked that "loaded shells were still exploding in the ruins under the heaps of ashes," while another wrote in his diary that the "fire is still raging in the city." Iowa soldier Jasper H. Rice toured the crushed district that day as well, observing that "they are still finding dead bodies and the stench near the ruins is almost suffocating." "The scene was appalling," a comrade wrote that day. "Whole families were blotted out of existence in that short span of time, bodies torn and mutilated in the blast, and many were burned to death." "For three days the shells kept bursting, thus keeping the men from moving the poor sufferers in the ruins," a sailor recorded. Four days after the blast, a large detail from the 114th Ohio combed the wreckage, finding and removing eight more bodies and 127 dead mules.

A court of inquiry was convened in June. Following several days of investigation, it concluded that although there had been "gross and culpable carelessness on the part of the fatigue party in handling the fixed ammunition," it was now "impossible to render an opinion as to the immediate cause of the explosion, as so far as is known, no person at or in the building survived the explosion." This conclusion missed the point, according to the editorial writers at the *New York Times,* who believed that "some one must be terribly to blame for allowing a quantity of explosive material sufficient to blow up eight squares of buildings to remain stored in the heart of a large city."

Along with its report, the court of inquiry released a list of the military casualties, totaling forty-four wounded and 111 killed or missing. One newspaper took an inventory of Mobile's hospitals immediately following the blast and counted nearly 150 people who had been admitted because of it; no casualty figures were ever given for the black laborers who filled the city's streets. The best guess anyone could come up with was that the warehouse explosion had resulted in between two and three hundred deaths. In addition, two steamers were destroyed, approximately eight to ten thousand bales of cotton burned, and sixty-eight separate structures damaged. An accounting done in the futile hope that the U.S. Congress would help with disaster relief assessed the total damages at $728,892.

The magazine explosion tore the heart out of Mobile's commercial district and crippled its postwar recovery. In October 1865 one of the city's papers took note of the blast's lasting effects when it editorialized, "Observant strangers all remark that for its population and wealth, Mobile is the most ragged, illy-improved and neglected city in the whole country." The full extent of the calamity was made graphically clear in a dispatch filed by a Northern reporter named Whitelaw Reid, who visited Mobile a few days after the disaster:

> Long before we reached the scene of complete destruction, we came upon houses shattered, bottom stories bereft of superstructure, door and window-frames driven in, gable-ends standing up alone, without the roofs they were raised to bear. The streets were filled with the rubbish. Here was a little fragment of a wall, twenty bricks, perhaps, lying sidewise as they fell, still fastened by the unbroken mortar; there the whole outer course of a gable-end dropped flat, and paving the street. Other walls would still be standing; but six or eight feet from the ground the outer course of bricks had been abruptly started outward an inch or more, and thence upward the wall imitated the

direction — but by no means, as we momentarily witnessed, the security — of the leaning tower of Pisa.

All this passed, we came to the scene of the actual explosion. Here, for eight or ten squares, was one waste of broken brick and mortar, still smouldering and smoking, and still — horrible thought! — roasting beneath this parched debris its human victims. Solid warehouses, chimneys, cotton-presses, machinery, all had been flattened as a whirlwind might flatten a house of card-boards.

A Federal officer summed up the entire experience with the comment, "It was a terrible calamity — beyond description."

Chapter Nineteen

The Trans-Mississippi

———◅o▻———

AS DISASTERS for the Cause spread from east to west, all hope for preserving the flickering flame of the Confederacy was centered on that portion of it known as the Trans-Mississippi Department, encompassing Missouri, Arkansas, western Louisiana, Texas, and the Indian Territories (modern Oklahoma). The sprawling department was under the overall command of Lieutenant General Edmund Kirby Smith, a veteran of First Bull Run and Perryville, whose feuds with fellow officers and disagreements with Richmond over policy matters marked a rocky course for his domain. Effectively isolated from the rest of the Confederacy after the capture of Vicksburg and Port Hudson in 1863, Smith had soon afterward begun to extend his authority into many nonmilitary areas. "I feel that I shall now be compelled to assume great responsibilities, and to exercise powers with which I am not legally vested," he informed Richmond.

But Smith lacked sufficient forces to fully impress his will on the Trans-Mississippi. A March 1865 head count showed no more than thirty-six thousand men under arms, and the morale of many of those was poor and getting worse. The "patriotic flash that fired the southern heart in sixty one, meteoric like, has faded away leaving darkness and gloom," one of those thirty-six thousand wrote in mid-April. On April 21, in an effort to counteract the depressing news of Lee's surrender,

Smith issued a proclamation in which he exhorted his men to "stand by your colors — maintain your discipline. The great resources of this department, . . . and the Providence of God [will] be the means of checking the triumph of our enemy and of seeing the final success of our cause."

Surrender was the last thing on the mind of Lieutenant Charles W. Read, a member of the C.S. Navy serving in the Trans-Mississippi. On the night of April 22 he guided his ship, the C.S.S. *William H. Webb*, away from the wharf at Alexandria, Louisiana, on the first leg of a desperate dash down the Red River to the Mississippi, then down that river, past New Orleans, to the Gulf of Mexico.

Once a New York icebreaker, the *Webb* had been converted by the Confederacy into a fast, sturdy ram. Lieutenant Read had supervised its arming and now commanded its last military mission. "As I will have to stake everything upon speed and time," he wrote Navy Secretary Stephen Mallory, "I will not attack any vessel in the passage unless I perceive a possibility of her arresting my progress."

By the following night, April 23, the *Webb*, displaying Federal signal lights, had reached the mouth of the Red River, where it encountered a U.S. naval picket line made up of the ironclads *Tennessee, Manhattan,* and *Lafayette,* as well as a gunboat, the *Gazelle*. In his report of the affair, Lieutenant Robert B. Ely of the *Manhattan* wrote that "at 8:45 [P.M.] a dense cloud of black smoke was discovered by the officer of the deck . . . coming out of the mouth of the Red River. This officer at once beat to quarters. . . . The smoke was now seen to be that of a vessel coming out of the Red River and within 500 yards of this vessel. . . . The turret was immediately revolved, and No. 1 gun was fired. . . . I made . . . General Signal No. 570, 'Strange vessel in sight, positively an enemy.' "

Aboard the *Webb,* Lieutenant Read shouted to the helmsman, "Let her go!" Within a few minutes the swift steamer had cleared the Union squadron and disappeared downstream into the darkness.

Some sixteen hours later the *Webb*, on its run down the Mississippi to open water, drew up to New Orleans. Several times during his passage from the Red River, Lieutenant Read had nudged his craft ashore and sent out parties to cut the telegraph wires running along the bank, so that word of his coming would not reach the Crescent City. As the *Webb* hove within sight of New Orleans, Read added a final touch to the craft's disguise, lowering the U.S. flag he was flying to half-mast in mourning for President Lincoln.

The trick worked at first. The *Webb* passed unremarked under the guns of Fort Parapet, which was manned by a detachment from the 14th

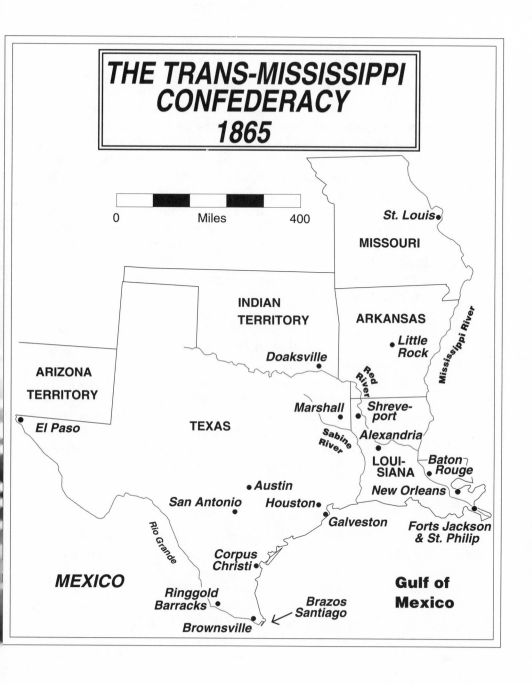

THE TRANS-MISSISSIPPI CONFEDERACY 1865

0 Miles 400

MISSOURI

St. Louis

INDIAN TERRITORY

ARKANSAS

Little Rock

ARIZONA TERRITORY

El Paso

Doaksville

Red River

Mississippi River

Marshall

Shreve-port

TEXAS

Sabine River

Alexandria

LOUI-SIANA

Baton Rouge

Austin

San Antonio

Houston

New Orleans

Rio Grande

Galveston

Forts Jackson & St. Philip

MEXICO

Corpus Christi

Ringgold Barracks

Brazos Santiago

Gulf of Mexico

Brownsville

Rhode Island Heavy Artillery. "To all appearances she was a dispatch boat, and the officers of the battalion, grouped upon the parapet of the river battery, saw her pass the fort without suspecting the nature of the craft," wrote one of those officers. The *Webb* was nearly past the city when a Union sailor who had seen the vessel before its conversion identified it and spread the alarm. Forts along the shore and gunners aboard ships at anchor opened a wild fire that struck the *Webb* only three times (doing no serious damage) while hitting several houses along the bank. Once the ship had been recognized, Lieutenant Read pulled down the U.S. colors and ran a Confederate flag up the staff.

The Rebel vessel got beyond the New Orleans defenses and came close to a storeship, the U.S.S. *Fearnot,* at whose rail could be seen a Union officer and a woman. Lieutenant Read stopped one of his crew from firing a rifle at the two for fear that the woman might be hit.

"That's the first time I was ever ordered not to shoot a Yankee," the crewman grumbled.

A pair of Union steamers now put out from New Orleans in hot pursuit. Read was confident that he could outrace them and was already making plans to run the final gauntlet at Forts Jackson and St. Philip, still sixty miles away, when the lookout spotted a ship ahead.

It was the U.S.S. *Richmond,* a deep-water sloop of twenty-one guns, anchored with engine problems but on full alert. Told by his pilot that shoals would prevent a ramming attack, and unwilling to face the weight of the enemy's broadside, Read opted to run his craft ashore, where the crew set it on fire before scattering into the underbrush. Federal parties landed and took up the chase; by midnight most of the rebel sailors had been captured.

The odyssey of the C.S.S. *Webb* was over.

On the surface, at least, the fighting spirit of the Confederate Trans-Mississippi Department was raised to a fever pitch as the news of Lee's surrender spread throughout the region in late April. Patriotic rallies were held in Shreveport and other towns, newspaper editors closed ranks to trumpet a defiant line, and military leaders issued stirring proclamations. On April 26 Brigadier General Jo Shelby, leader of the famed Rebel "Iron Brigade," declared, "If Johnston follows Lee and Beauregard and Maury and Forrest — all go — and the Cis-Mississippi Department* surrenders their arms and quit the contest, let us never

---

* A reference to the Confederacy east of the Mississippi.

surrender. . . . We will do this: we will hang together, we will keep our organization, our arms, our discipline, our hatred of oppression . . . [preferring] exile to submission, death to dishonor."

Behind this bellicose facade, however, the weary soldiers and civilians of the Trans-Mississippi yearned for their long ordeal to end. One Texas soldier had little patience for those exhorting the masses to fight to the end: "These gentlemen are people [who] I am convinced really would like quite a lot to give themselves up, if only they had the chance," he cynically observed on April 28. The very next day, the officer commanding the Houston garrison asked Trans-Mississippi headquarters in Shreveport to send him some "reliable cavalry," complaining that his "men are deserting by tens and twenties a night."

Even as he maintained a bold front, department commander Edmund Kirby Smith was also trying out some fanciful schemes. On May 2 he wrote to Louisiana businessman Robert Rose, whose dealings often took him south of the border, and asked him to open up an unofficial channel to Maximilian, the French-imposed emperor of Mexico. "There is under my command an army of 60,000 men, [and] of those there are 9,000 Missourians who have been driven from their homes," Kirby Smith asserted, "who . . . would no doubt, upon favorable inducements . . . take service with the power so favoring them." Six days later the lieutenant general met in Shreveport with the representative of his Federal counterpart, who came bearing Grant's Appomattox terms. The Confederate officer rejected the proposals, declaring that they "are not such that my sense of duty and honor will permit me to accept." But Kirby Smith also asked the emissary to stay his return until he could attend a meeting with the Trans-Mississippi governors in nearby Marshall, Texas.

No sooner had Kirby Smith left Shreveport for Marshall than several of his top officers, worried that their commander was planning to capitulate, gathered to figure out how they might best continue the fight. A coup was considered and seriously discussed, but in the end only rhetoric emerged from these meetings, further sharpening the tang of tension in the air. "The clouds thickening around us from every quarter," a Shreveport civilian wrote on May 8, "every countenance is filled with gloom and despondency."

When Kirby Smith returned to Shreveport on May 13, he presented to the Union officer who had come to seek his surrender a list of conditions hammered out by the Trans-Mississippi governors during their meeting in Marshall, Texas. The emissary, in turn, passed these on to his superior, stating that the governors seemed to expect that "more liberal terms should be granted to the Army of the Trans-Mississippi Department than those accepted by General Lee." Federal strength now began to gather along the borders of this last extant department of the Confederacy.

Even as Kirby Smith, the Trans-Mississippi governors, and a few outspoken officers maintained a loud and vocal defiance to keep up public morale, the military strength of the department continued to melt away. In one company, rumors of peace were enough to inspire a drinking spree. The morning report for May 17 noted, "Whole company drunk, raving drunk, except Cpl. Leo Andre." Five days later these soldiers were told to just go home. "And home they went," one remembered.

On May 18 Kirby Smith announced his plans to move his headquarters from Shreveport to Houston, where he believed there were enough loyal troops remaining to form a solid core of resistance. Two days later he began what would turn into a weeklong journey.

On May 21 the troops defending Galveston rioted and seized government property. Two days after that, the loyal Houston garrison went on a rampage, ransacking C.S. supply buildings. "The whole thing is busted up. . . . The soldiers have laid down their arms and want to go home, the war is over," one witness declared. Similar scenes were enacted at Clarksville, Crockett, Gonzales, Henderson, and La Grange.

While Kirby Smith was moving across Texas to Houston, the civil and military authorities of several districts — Arkansas, Texas, and West Louisiana — attempted to capitulate, but the Federals were not interested in a piecemeal surrender. On May 25 the generals who had been left in charge at Shreveport during the transition of authority (including one who had been involved in the coup planning) steamed down to New Orleans and, after a negotiation that lasted into the next day, agreed to surrender all Confederate armed forces on the basis of the Appomattox terms, subject to Kirby Smith's final approval.

When Kirby Smith reached his new Houston headquarters, on May 27, he found that the loyal cadres he was expecting had disappeared into the countryside, and his subordinate commanders had negotiated terms of surrender without consulting him. For three days he stared defeat in the face, acknowledging it only on May 30 in a pair of dispatches. To the Union commander he reported, "The department is now open to occupation by your government." To his men, Kirby Smith issued a bitter farewell address: "Soldiers, I am left a commander without an army — a General without troops. You have made your choice. It was unwise and unpatriotic, but it is final." On June 2 Kirby Smith boarded a Federal steamer standing off Galveston and formally signed the military convention that had been drawn up without his participation.

The last department of the Confederate States of America had ceased to exist.

Interlude

Oldham's Odyssey (Part Two)

———◦———

*W*HEN TEXAS SENATOR *Williamson Oldham left Atlanta on April 13, he was expecting to be able to travel by rail much of the way on his journey back home. But Major General James H. Wilson's capture of West Point on April 16 changed everything. Oldham was in Newnan when the news of the disaster reached him. "Although it was known that the force which captured West Point, and was marching up the country did not exceed twelve or fifteen hundred men, nobody talked of arming and meeting them," he observed with disgust.*

The Yankee action also meant that Oldham's easy route back to Texas was solidly blocked, leaving him no alternative but to strike out westward. After several days of anxious inquiry, he located a C.S. quartermaster wagon train bound from LaGrange to Oxford, Alabama, about sixty-five miles east of Elyton. Using a combination of influence and persuasion, Oldham secured a place for himself on the train, which set out shortly after 1:00 P.M. on Tuesday, April 25. Just as he was about to depart, a young woman who was staying in town ran up with some "glorious news." "France, Great Britain, Austria, and Belgium have recognized the independence of the Confederate States," she said breathlessly, "and have resolved to protect it by armed intervention." Oldham snorted and clambered onto the wagon. "I felt convinced that it was another of the ten thousand hoaxes perpetuated during the war by Yankees who had obtained situations as telegraphic operators, in order to play the part of spies, and a hoax it proved to be," he recalled.

Since beginning his journey in Richmond, little more than a month earlier, Senator Oldham had passed through a Confederacy that was melting around him, like spun glass touched by a blue flame. He had made it through Virginia mere days before Lee's retreat; passed into and out of North Carolina while Stoneman prowled the area to the west and Johnston's position worsened to the east; and been held up in the wake of Wilson's cavalry raid into Georgia. He now moved across northern Alabama, where a Confederate government was more memory than reality, and lawlessness a matter of growing concern. "Confidence was gone," *Oldham realized,* "heart and spirit were gone, resistance had substantially ceased. The country was subjugated and prepared for submission to any conditions [the Union] might impose."

Although the trip from LaGrange to Oxford was not without its tense moments, it was also without serious incident. Oldham arrived in Oxford on April 29 and the next day picked up another wagon train headed for Talledega, which, he had heard, still had rail service. A train did in fact come within a few miles of the town, but it took until May 5 for Oldham to locate the stop and chance upon the train itself, which consisted of "two platform cars, and a very weak locomotive." *Most of the space on the cars had been set aside for building materials designated for track repair further up the line, but more than forty passengers managed to find room aboard before the train pulled out. Remembered Oldham,* "The locomotive barely had the power to draw the train up the steep grades of the road, the dust, smoke and cinders flew back upon us in black columns, and the sun beamed down [on] us with the heat of summer."

The train went as far as Montevallo, where Oldham learned he would have to endure another delay to wait for a small wagon train that would take him to Marion, Alabama. On May 5 the senator heard rumors of Richard Taylor's surrender, which were confirmed the next day. "Thus," *reflected Oldham,* "one by one from the 9th of April . . . the three great armies of the Confederacy had been surrendered, and the whole country east of the Mississippi was conquered."

After a day of riding the wagon, Oldham heard that there were Yankees ahead, at Marion, and that the terms of Taylor's surrender did not apply to nonmilitary personnel. So eight miles short of their destination, Oldham and a traveling companion left the train and turned west. At Demopolis Oldham was surprised to see a large number of military men. "It turned out that they were Confederate soldiers going to Meridan to be paroled under the terms of Gen. Taylor's surrender," *he recalled. While there he caught up on the latest news regarding Jefferson Davis:* "It was understood that President Davis after the surrender of Gen. Lee's army had travelled through North Carolina under the protection of an escort of cavalry, but it was not known where he then was, or whether it was probable he would safely escape or not."

Oldham and his companion had by now decided to abandon their wagon transport, mount a pair of mules, and strike out across country in hopes of finding a place to cross the Mississippi above Vicksburg. They left Demopolis on May 10 and after two days of hard traveling attempted to secure lodging for the night at a well-to-do plantation near DeKalb, Mississippi. The owner refused, and Oldham no longer felt constrained by the bonds of gentlemanly behavior. "I very distinctly informed him that I thought he was a hog and we rode on," he noted. Their next stop offered only a slight improvement. While food and shelter were cheerfully supplied, they were warned that the owner had "a very bad biting dog" in the house. "We had the good fortune to escape his fangs," Williamson Oldham dryly observed.

The next days were marked by steady, if slow, progress. Oldham was convinced that "the South was filled with Yankee spies and detectives" and so had "assumed the character of a Confederate soldier by the name of Bayless."

On May 15 Oldham and his party (which had grown in size to three) made it to the eastern side of the flooded Mississippi River, where they searched for three days for transportation across, listening all the while to rumors about French intervention and Jefferson Davis's successful escape to Texas. Here the senator saw firsthand one of the gangs of surrendered Confederate soldiers that were roving the countryside in search of government property to plunder. In response to Oldham's question, one of the soldiers explained that he was simply taking out in trade what was owed him by the Confederate government for four years' service. "I confess the argument was very strong to my mind, and I could not gainsay it, if they had in all cases limited their spoliations, to Confederate property strictly," Oldham admitted.

Finally, on May 19, the travelers met with a guide who was willing to lead them partway through the maze of bayous, creeks, and swamps toward the western bank of the river. It took six days of effort and several guides to accomplish the task. Each would take them to the next plantation or farm, where they would have to seek fresh hospitality and another guide for the next day's new ordeal. "The timber and undergrowth was so thick, that we had to pursue the roads and bayous, both as a means of making our way and avoiding getting lost in the swamps," Oldham remembered. Hours were lost when a planned route was found to be blocked by solid walls of canebrake; at another point the thorn bushes were so dense that "we were constantly running into them and getting severely scratched." There were bears and snakes to contend *with, as well as sudden currents that threatened to scuttle their fragile boat. The party finally crossed the Mississippi on May 25; eight days after that, on June 2,* Williamson Oldham reached Texas.*

Summing up all that had happened to the Confederacy during his odyssey, Oldham wrote,

> The series of final and crushing disasters to the Confederate cause, commenced on the day I left Richmond, and progressed with me geographically to the Mississippi river. The first occurred on the day I left, which was the defeat of our cavalry and Pickett's Division at Dinwiddie Court House; this was followed by the breaking of Gen. Lee's lines at Petersburg, on the next night, which forced the evacuation of Richmond; then came the surrender of the army of Virginia, followed in quick succession by that of Tennessee, under the command of Gen. Johnston in North Carolina. With these events occurred the fall of Mobile, Selma, and Montgomery, the raid upon West Point, Columbus, and Macon, and the capture of those places; then came the surrender of the Department of Alabama, [and] East Louisiana under the command of Lieut. Gen. Taylor — and finally the surrender of the Trans-Mississippi Department under the command of Gen. E. Kirby Smith, which occurred on the 26th of May, the day that I left the overflow of the Mississippi and reached the highlands of the west. These were the closing disasters to a contest of eight millions of people for their liberty and independence, ending in their subjugation, and the triumph and domination of their enemies.

Of his personal experiences, Oldham added,

> My progress through the country, was necessarily very slow, and by the various modes of travel I was compelled to adopt, I was brought in contact, with all classes of people, with people in the towns and those in the country, with professional men, merchants, planters, and farmers, with citizens and soldiers, secessionists and union men before the war, and patriots and tories while it lasted, and even with deserters and jayhawkers. I carefully watched and marked the effect of those final reverses upon all these classes of the people. The patriot was crushed, the traitor who had taken part in mind or act, against his country wore a satisfied countenance, and some were beginning

---

* This date is conjectural, as Oldham's typescript is confusing on the subject.

openly to speak their sentiments, the brave soldier who had faithfully done his duty was indignant, deserters were coming in from the woods, jayhawkers became bold and active in robbery and plundering — in a word the spirit of the people was broken, and the subjugation was complete.

Chapter Twenty

"All is done — all the Confederacy surrendered"

———◦———

Even as the last military actions were taking place, and as the newspaper columns were filled with the closing incidents of the war, other developments were unfolding that would determine the social agenda for many years to come.

Passions were high at the annual meeting of the Anti-Slavery Society when it convened in New York on May 9. William Lloyd Garrison started things rolling by declaring that the "year of the jubilee is come," that slavery was a thing of the past, and that therefore the society itself should disband. Not so, countered Wendell Phillips, who stated that the "system of slavery stands in the eye of the law untouched." Frederick Douglass, who was also present, agreed with Phillips and insisted, "Slavery is not abolished until the black man has the ballot."

Wendell Phillips felt less commitment to another enfranchisement issue, women's suffrage. He had earlier rejected a proposal from the Woman's Rights Society to merge with the Anti-Slavery Society in order to form an Equal Rights Association. In her speech to the May 10 gathering of the Woman's Rights Convention, Susan B. Anthony asked, "Of what good is negro suffrage as proposed, to negro women? . . . There is, there can be, but one true basis, that taxation and representation must be inseparable; here our demand must now go beyond woman. . . . We therefore wish to broaden our women's rights platform and make it in name what it has ever been in spirit, a human rights platform."

Throughout the South, war-weary civilians took stock of their situation and tried to glean what they could of the future. "We are indeed a conquered people," lamented a South Carolina lady, while a fellow spirit in Arkansas noted in her diary in early June, "All is done — all the Confederacy surrendered."

A North Carolina woman wondered what lay ahead for the newest citizens of America. Writing in late June, she expressed the thoughts of many of her white neighbors when she reflected, "The negro emancipation has been accomplished — the unfortunates have been thrust blindfolded upon the ills of a state of which they know nothing. They enter with confidence and pleasure — expecting that freedom from care which they have hitherto enjoyed together with an entire immunity from all work or all necessity for self-provision. But on the threshold of their new life disappointment awaits them. The Yankees tell them that Freedom does not mean 'freedom from work,' but freedom from the lash and from the degradation of being sold. . . . They occupy themselves ceaselessly trying on their new chains — seeing how little work they can accomplish and yet be fed, and endeavoring to be slave and free at the same moment — a slave on the food, shelter and clothing questions, but free when labor is concerned. Accordingly they are in continual difficulty, and make our lives anything but beds of roses."

The problem posed by the freed blacks was also a vexing one for the Federal officers in charge of the occupation forces:

HEADQUARTERS NORTHERN DIVISION OF LOUISIANA
Shreveport, La., June 11, 1865

General Orders, No. 24

Great and sudden changes in the condition of any class of people are always productive of suffering, and the transition of the blacks from a state of slavery to freedom cannot fail to cause temporary suffering to all classes. Already this is being manifested by the negroes leaving their homes and setting out en masse for the military posts, and with no definite purpose except to leave the scene of their former bondage. The result of this state of things, if allowed, would be —

First. The loss of the crops and the entire ruin of the agricultural interests in this part of the State.

Second. Untold suffering, starvation, and misery among the blacks themselves.

Without attempting, therefore, to regulate all the various interests arising out of this question, . . . the major-general commanding deems it his duty to make such rules as in his opinion will best prevent suffering and restore quiet at the present time. It is therefore ordered: That all persons heretofore held as slaves remain for the present with their former masters and by their labor secure the crops of the present season. The only place where they can obtain a living for themselves and their families is in the field, where they have been accustomed to work. If found wandering about the country or gathering at military posts they will be arrested and punished, and all transports and private steam-boats running on Red River are prohibited from carrying this class of people, except upon a military pass, which will be given only in exceptional cases. . . . But, while it is found necessary during the present unsettled state of the country to make these orders relative to the blacks, the planters are reminded that the matter depends largely on them, and that only by fair treatment of the hands can they hope to mature and harvest their crops and carry on their plantations. Definite contracts must be made with the negroes, which will be binding for the balance of the present season. Planters who endeavor to do this in good faith will be assisted in all proper ways and will do much toward restoring quiet and confidence.

By command of Major-General [Francis J.] Herron.

There were lives linked to the violence and aspirations of the war that would not outlast it.

The end came for that "notorious raskal" William Clarke Quantrill in early June. The enigmatic Ohioan, whose band of bushwhackers had terrorized portions of Kansas, Missouri, and Texas under the banner of the Confederacy, was severely wounded in a May 10 skirmish with Federal troops in Kentucky. When several members of his gang tried to spirit him away from the doctor's house where he was being treated, Quantrill waved them off. "Boys, it is impossible for me to get well, the war is over and I am in reality a dying man, so let me alone," he said.

Quantrill was finally taken to a Federal military hospital in Louisville, where he lingered until 4:00 P.M. on June 6. With his death drawing near, the grim leader whose orders in 1863 to "kill every man big enough to carry a gun" had caused what came to be known as the Lawrence Massacre turned to religion and was baptized a Roman Catholic. Toward the end of his suffering, he thought he recognized one of the doctors attending him as someone he knew from another part of the state. "I am the man," the physician replied. "I have moved here." Replied the dying Quantrill, with a touch of deathbed humor, "So have I."

Eleven days later, in eastern Virginia, the man who symbolized the secessionist fervor of the Confederacy, white-haired, defiant-eyed Edmund Ruffin, ended his own Civil War.

The early years of the conflict had been a heady time for this peppery agriculturalist from Virginia. He was in Charleston during the Fort Sumter crisis and happily joined gun crews engaged in bombarding the enemy bastion. Six days after Major Anderson hauled down the U.S. flag, Ruffin posed for the camera in the uniform of a member of the Palmetto Guard, his fierce expression making it clear for all to see that, for him, at least, there could be no surrender. The decline in the fortunes of the Confederacy after 1863 began to suck the life out of this old man of Southern Independence.

On the morning of Saturday, June 17, Ruffin came downstairs as usual and enjoyed a pleasant breakfast with his family. He spent some time afterward writing in his diary and visiting with friends who called. It was not until shortly after midday that Ruffin was at last alone. Sitting in a chair on the porch of his house, he took up a rifle, rested its butt on a nearby tree trunk, put his mouth over the barrel, and, using a forked stick, pulled the trigger.

The cap flashed with a loud pop, but the gun failed to fire. Inside the house, his daughter heard the noise and ran to get her husband. By the time they reached him, the determined old man had reprimed the weapon, put his mouth again over the barrel, and once more snagged at the trigger. This time it worked.

Next to his body lay his open diary, the ink on its final entry barely dry:

> And now, with my latest writing & utterance, and with what will be near to my last breath, I hereby repeat & would willingly proclaim my unmitigated hatred to Yankee rule — to all political, social & business connections with Yanks, & to the perfidious, malignant, & vile Yankee race.

More and more, as additional regions of what had been the Confederacy came under Union control, combat-trained troops found themselves in the unaccustomed role of occupiers. In towns large and small throughout the South, conquerors and conquered viewed each other with a mix of curiosity, suspicion, and acceptance. An Illinois sergeant on duty in an Alabama town wrote to his wife that the residents "were *not* a *little* surprised to find out that we *didnt* come to eat them up, and before we left them expressed themselves satisfied that Yankees were not such an awful set of ragamuffins as they had been led to believe." A Connecticut soldier with the occupation forces on duty in Virginia recalled their routine: "We had a mail perhaps twice a week, and managed our own affairs as we pleased. As we expected no more military duty, company and regimental drill were abandoned. . . . There was not much affiliation between the soldiers and the society in the village. To the more thrifty of the New England States the whole system of Southern industry seemed fifty years behind the times."

One task common to all occupation troops was the administering of the Oath of Allegiance to ex-soldiers and civilians. A young New Yorker given the assignment in Central Virginia noted in early June that "citizens flock here every day from miles around to take the oath of allegiance, and if they are not able to support themselves take an oath to that effect and receive rations from the government." A soldier similarly assigned in Spotsylvania County, Virginia, found the people who came to him quite candid in their opinions: "They felt that they had submitted the question which had tested the strength of the Union to the highest tribunal, and that their cause had been fully tried and absolutely decided."

The decision as to whether or not to take the oath was a difficult moment of truth for many former Rebel soldiers. For a few, the knowledge that some corner of the Confederacy was still in rebellion was reason enough to refuse: "I would never prove a traitor to the Confederacy as long as she had a soldier in the field," declared a prisoner in Fort Delaware. Yet the writing was on the wall for all to see. "A man of sense ought to yield everything for duty's sake, and 'obey the powers that be,'" a Virginia woman advised her soldier-brother in May. "Come home, . . . for home needs you as well as you need it." "Their hearts cannot change," a Georgia soldier remarked, "but they are compelled to recognize the fact that they are overcome, and to yield, as gracefully as possible."

After G. Moxley Sorrel, an officer in the Army of Northern Virginia, took the oath, the Federal who had administered it smiled at him and asked pleasantly if it had "tasted bad." Following their oath-taking, cannoneer and Fort Delaware POW George M. Neese and his comrades were allowed to walk unmolested through the prison gate. Recalled Neese, "The men were so wild with joy that old veterans playfully tumbled and rolled on the grass like young schoolboys."

Yankee boys from Ohio, Connecticut, and Iowa made up the contingent that garrisoned Selma, Alabama. "I will say it is one of the most pleasant places I ever saw and I don't know that I would do injustice to say that I never saw its equal, in many respects," a Buckeye proclaimed. This despite the havoc wrought by Wilson's men in early April: "The workshops, cars, engines, and depots of both railroads, in fact the entire business part of the city is destroyed beyond repair," a Connecticut gunner observed. "There is not a store opened yet. The people buy their food at our commissary and pay for it in gold of which they have plenty, although Wilson's men took all they could find."

An Iowa artilleryman named John Buttolph managed to get volunteered for a number of provost details that took him out into the countryside. Once, while hunting a white man accused of killing a black, he ordered a search of the suspect's brother's house. The brother's wife wailed her protest as the Union soldiers clumped through her home. "That was what hurt me the most," Buttolph reflected. "A woman's tears would make me forget my duty." On another occasion he was confronted by a widow who wanted to know if she might be able to recover her husband's body from the battlefield at Nashville. "We had to tell her that the Confederate soldiers were buried by our men and we did not think it possible to find him. She took on terribly about it." Still, Buttolph vowed that he would always "remember Selma as the most enjoyable place we saw in the South."

A somewhat different side of the people of that region was seen through the eyes and angled perceptions of a discharged veteran who was now a clerk in the private sector, named Ambrose Bierce. In later years Bierce would establish a unique niche for himself in the annals of American cultural history through his bitterly humorous and often ironically macabre writing, but in 1865 he was charged with the performance of duties that were "exceedingly disagreeable not only to the people of the vicinity, but to myself as well." His job was to locate and seize abandoned Confederate property such as cotton and sell it on behalf of the United States government. It was a situation ready-made for fast operators, and between private dealers who were adept at removing C.S. imprints from the bales and colleagues who were more than happy to accept bribes to issue blanket shipping permits, Bierce saw enough of the shoddy side of human nature to fill several novels.

On one assignment, he and a small military escort accompanied a shipment of six hundred bales on a steamboat headed down the Tombigbee River. His party was ambushed from shore at a narrow part of the passage. "The din of the firing, the rattle and crash of the missiles splintering the woodwork and the jingle of broken glass made a very rude arousing from the tranquil indolence of a warm afternoon on the sluggish Tombigbee," Bierce remembered. The captain and pilot sought deep cover after the first volley, and the escort, it turned out, had been issued rifles but no cartridges. Bierce knew that when the bandits swarmed aboard he, as official government agent, would likely be strung up. "I had never been hanged in all my life and was not enamored of the prospect," he reflected. Fortunately, the ambush site had been poorly chosen, and the vessel drifted away from the shore before the robbers could reach it.

Bierce came to remember the scoundrels he encountered while on occupation duty in Selma with something approaching fondness. "What glorious fellows they were," he wrote, "these my late antagonists of the dark days when, God forgive us, we were trying to cut one another's throat . . . in that criminal insanity that we call battle."

While the civilian populations of the occupied areas seemed for the most part resigned to their fate, the Federal soldiers also had to cope with waves of lawlessness that ranged across the vanquished South. At first it was looting inspired by a distorted sense of justice, with bands of discharged, paroled, or surrendered former soldiers feeling few compunctions about raiding Confederate storehouses and supply depots. One ex-soldier explained his actions to a newspaper editor: "I lived four years on goobers, parched corn and rotten meat, and I saw nothing wrong with taking blankets & such from the commissary as they would have been confiscated anyhow by the Yankees when they arrived."

Once the C.S.A. supplies were gone, however, Southern citizens became the targets. A young Georgia woman named Eliza Andrews watched as a former Rebel soldier stole a neighbor's sole remaining draft animal, despite pleas that the family's survival depended on the creature. The soldier rode past Andrews with a wide grin. "A man that's going to Texas must have a mule to ride, don't you think so lady?" he said.

The response of the U.S. authorities was increasingly harsh. General Order No. 90 of the War Department stated unequivocally that "from and after the first day of June, 1865, any and all persons found in arms against the United States, or who may commit acts of hostility against it east of the Mississippi River, will be regarded as guerrillas and punished with death." Major General E. O. C. Ord, whose words had inspired his men in their grueling march to trap Lee at Appomattox, now counseled his subordinates "to shoot guerrillas, horse-thieves, or marauders." After faithfully chronicling a series of depredations carried out by gangs in the northeastern part of Mississippi, a Presbyterian minister wrote on May 12 that "lawlessness seems to be the order of the day."

Another aspect of the military occupation consisted of stamping out all visible vestiges of the Confederacy:

HDQRS. DEPARTMENT OF VIRGINIA, ARMY OF THE JAMES
Richmond, Va., June 9, 1865

General Orders, No. 70

A sufficient time having elapsed since the surrender of the forces late in rebellion with the United States for all who were of such forces to procure other apparel than their uniform, it is hereby ordered that no person after June 15, 1865, appear in public in this department wearing any insignia of rank, or military or naval service worn by officers or men of the late rebel army.

Where plain buttons cannot be procured those formerly used can be covered with cloth.

Any person violating this order will be liable to arrest.

By command of Major-General [E. O. C.] Ord

In what the newspapers called the "closing pageant of the war," twenty-five thousand veterans belonging to the Army of the Potomac's Sixth Corps marched in review through Washington, D.C., on June 8. Delayed by its expedition to Danville in late April and its subsequent assignment to police the rail lines in the region, the corps had missed the grand parades of May 23 and 24. Even as the proud ranks of the East and West were delighting Washington's crowds, the various divisions of the Sixth Corps were gathering at Richmond. On May 24, the day Sherman's men had the spotlight, Major General Horatio Wright's troops set out from the former Rebel capital on roads north.

As the last corps in the Army of the Potomac to be released from service, these men had little to celebrate, and their mood turned sour when it was rumored that former Rebels traveling south were taking up available train space, forcing the corps to walk instead of ride. "There was some growling as we thought we ought to be used as well as the rebel prisoners who were transported to their homes," a Vermont soldier complained. "It has been called an easy march of about twelve miles a day but I called it anything but easy; I never saw so many stragglers in all my army life; there would hardly be enough men with the officers for a body guard. If we had tried as hard to keep up with the column as we did when following the enemy many would never have reached Washington." Following the route used so recently by both the Eastern and Western armies only compounded the men's misery. "I think I have never met with worse roads," corps commander Wright reported on May 28.

The lead elements of the corps reached the outskirts of Washington on June 2 and went into camp, where the soldiers readied themselves for a display that few thought necessary. "A cattle show of men," was how one participant described it. Newspaper reporters managed to put a more positive spin on the coming affair: "Being the last, there was a very pardonable desire that the troops should appear in the very best possible order, and both commanders and men exerted themselves to improve the personal appearance of the corps," noted the *New York Times*. "Every man . . . wore white gloves, and there were many other indications of special preparations, intended to increase the effect of the several commands."

At precisely 9:30 A.M. on June 8, Wright and his staff, "with the Sixth Corps Headquarters flag floating gaily in the breeze," turned from Fifteenth Street onto Pennsylvania Avenue and headed toward the White House. Behind them came the First Division, Brevet Major General Frank Wheaton commanding. A Connecticut soldier in the ranks never forgot the mood of the men, "in all the misery of full dress, and in a temper that would have carried them against the thousands of acclaiming spectators with savage joy, had it been a host of enemies in arms." The day was brutally hot, and the men were grateful for whatever succor they could find. "Liberal supplies were drawn from the U.S. Sanitary Commission, which were very much needed by our men," a New Jersey veteran wrote. "President Johnson with other dignitaries was seated upon a platform in front of the White House," remembered a Rhode Island officer. "They received us very kindly, but the people with the exception of the ladies who waved their handkerchiefs were very quiet. We expected to meet with a warm reception, as the 6th Corps saved Washington in 1864, but evidently reviews are played out with the Washington people. The city was fearfully hot, and the men suffered much."

Tight behind Wheaton's men came the Second Division, with Brevet Major General George W. Getty in command. The troops "all looked well & the marching was done up in the best of stile," recalled a proud Pennsylvania boy. In this division were the men of the Vermont Brigade, their caps bedecked for the occasion with sprigs of evergreen. One Granite State soldier later remarked that it was a "terrible hot day . . . and many were prostrated by the heat." But he took care to note, "We were the only brigade that saluted the President properly."

Brigadier General James B. Ricketts led the Third Division in review.

355

"They made us wear white gloves and black hats but the dust soon soiled this chicken fixings," a young New Yorker wrote to his parents. A Vermont man in the ranks was pleased to be seen by "a vast concourse of citizens," while a wide-eyed Ohio soldier guessed that "all the women and children in the world were there." The corps's artillery pulled up the end of the long column, which, someone calculated, took an hour and forty minutes all told to pass.

It all seemed frivolous ceremony to surgeon George Stevens, who never forgave authorities for holding this "review of the corps under the scorching rays of the hottest suns ever known in Washington, when hundreds of our men fell down from sunstroke and exhaustion." The review was no picnic, either, for the members of the press corps, who, as in the two previous parades, found themselves with no designated area in the reviewing stands, and their access to prime viewing space blocked by humorless provost guards. One correspondent used his account of the Sixth Corps ceremony as an opportunity to gripe on behalf of his comrades, who "were buffeted and bayoneted about from one point to another, and who, but for their own enterprise and aptitude in accommodating themselves to unfavorable circumstances, must have left unwritten the greatest pageant in history."

Against this backdrop of the ceremony of war, the grim job of cleaning up was getting under way.

WASHINGTON, D.C.
May 31, 1865

Major-General HALLECK:

    I am informed that a great many bodies have been left unburied at Appomattox Court-House. It is possible that some may have been left in the same way at Sailor's Creek. I think a small cavalry force had better be sent to each place to bury any that may still be left above ground.

U. S. GRANT,
Lieutenant-General

——◦——

HEADQUARTERS PROVOST-MARSHAL
Amelia Court-House, June 15, 1865

I have the honor to report that according to instructions I sent a portion of this command to examine into the condition of the dead on the

356

different battle-fields mentioned. The officer in command reports having buried five Federal soldiers on Foster's plantation, two of which had lain on the field since the battle. Found seventeen bodies at Sailor's Creek (ten of which were Confederate) that the recent heavy rains had washed the covering from. These were reburied; also one found near Amelia Springs. Diligent search was made at Appomattox Court-House, but found no bodies uncovered.

I have the honor to be, very respectfully, your obedient servant,

S. R. CLARK,
Brevet Colonel and Provost-Marshal, Amelia Co., Va.

Since his return to Richmond in mid-April, Robert E. Lee had managed to keep a fairly low profile, despite a succession of interview requests from a wide range of people, including many who had fought for him or against him as well as some who were just curious to know his views on the issues now facing the nation. A New York soldier who met him in early June after he attended Mass at Saint Paul's felt that he was "very pleasant, social and accessible. He remained after service a short time in the vestibule, conversed with his friends, and was introduced to all who sought his acquaintance. . . . Though over sixty, he talked with vivacity and moved with agility." To a reporter from the *New York Times* Lee avowed that the question of slavery had been answered. "The best men of the South have long been anxious to do away with this institution, and were quite willing to see it abolished," he said.

Lee's stature as one of the foremost military leaders of the Confederacy placed him in an especially vulnerable position. He belonged to several classifications of citizens exempted from the amnesty proclamation issued by President Andrew Johnson on May 29. That declaration granted full pardon to all who had taken part in the rebellion, save for high-ranking civil, military, and government officials and those whose "taxable property is over $20,000." Individuals excluded from the blanket amnesty (which required the taking of the Oath of Allegiance to become effective) had to apply personally to the President for their pardons. Hardly had Lee decided, as he told his son Custis, that it was "but right for him to set an example by making [a] formal submission [for amnesty] to the Civil Authorities" when he found himself facing indictment for treason by a Federal grand jury in Norfolk.

Robert E. Lee believed in the worth of a man's word, and at Appomattox Court House Grant's terms had promised that all the surrendered soldiers might "return to their homes not to be disturbed by

United States authority as long as they observe their paroles." Through a friendly U.S. senator, Lee was able to learn that Grant not only stood by his promise but was prepared to personally endorse Lee's application for pardon. On June 13 Lee sent his note requesting a pardon to President Johnson through Grant's office. "I am ready to meet any charges that may be preferred against me," he explained to Grant, "but if I am correct as to the protection granted by my parole, I am not to be prosecuted."

Grant was as good as his word. Three days later he forwarded Lee's request to the President, with a covering note that reaffirmed the Appomattox terms and warned that breaching them might "produce a feeling of insecurity in the minds of all paroled officers and men." Grant further urged that the Norfolk judge who had sought the grand-jury action "be ordered to quash all indictments found against paroled prisoners of war, and to desist from further prosecution of them." According to several of his confidants, Grant felt so strongly about this matter that he threatened to resign if Andrew Johnson followed through and actually prosecuted Lee.

The Johnson administration was not prepared to face a public feud with its most honored general, and the treason charge against Lee was quietly filed away, to be formally dismissed only in 1869. Lee's application for a special pardon would not be acted upon in his lifetime, though he was included under the terms of a general amnesty proclamation issued on Christmas Day 1868.

The amnesty proclamation that Andrew Johnson issued on May 29 was one of two important policy directives released that day. The other marked the beginning of Presidential Reconstruction by establishing the steps through which the seceded state of North Carolina might be readmitted to the Union, with the understanding that the Tar Heel example would become the model for other Southern states. Anxious to move quickly on the matter, Johnson acted without waiting for Congressional approval, which would have delayed the decision until the legislative body convened in December.

With the North Carolina proclamation, Johnson was able to appoint a provisional governor, who, in turn, was to arrange for the election of a state convention to draw up a new constitution in conformity with the Federal laws enacted during the war. Only then could the state resume its former relationship to the Union. One provision of this document struck an especially sour note among radicals and reformers: the "loyal citizens" who would elect the convention were to consist only of those who had been eligible to vote in 1861 and had subsequently taken the

Oath of Allegiance. Since slaves had not been enfranchised in 1861, Johnson's plan effectively barred them from the polls.

Those who had hoped to use the ending of the war as an opportunity to clear the slate and correct past injustices were appalled by Johnson's scheme. "Is there no way to arrest the insane course of the President in Washington?" one radical wondered aloud on June 3. In the opinion of Frederick Douglass, Johnson's actions revealed a "bitter contempt and aversion" for African-Americans. On June 8 Johnson continued the reconstruction process with a North Carolina–type proclamation for Mississippi, followed on June 17 by a pair for Texas and Georgia and on June 21 by one for Alabama.

Two days after Johnson issued his Texas declaration, Federal troops began to pour into the Lone Star State. To the accompaniment of a band playing "Yankee Doodle," Brevet Major General Gordon Granger occupied Galveston with a division. Under direct orders from Phil Sheridan, Granger promulgated two decrees, the first freeing all slaves and establishing the relationship between former owner and former human property as that "between employer and hired labor," and the second voiding all acts passed in Confederate Texas and instructing ex-C.S. military and government personnel to take the Oath of Allegiance. On June 20 Houston and Brownsville came under the control of Federal arms.

The Yankee boys did not quite meld into the Texas scene. An Ohio soldier on duty in Houston wrote on June 21, "Before we arrived gold and silver was the only money used. There is any amount of specie here. They do not care about taking our 'greenbacks' but our soldiers in purchasing offer them and if they are not taken (green backs) they, the soldiers, take the goods and walk off. Generally the citizens are courteous but occasionally we meet some rabid rebels. Everybody carries a large bowie knife and a revolver."

Although Union troops would not formally occupy Austin until July — making it the last Confederate capital to haul down its flag — the specter of defeat had already, in the words of one resident, left the city "practically in mourning. . . . The women could hardly believe their men had died, been wounded, [or] mutilated, to be beaten at last."

A short distance south of Washington, the process of remembering the Civil War was beginning.

On the weekend of June 10–11, a pair of pyramid monuments commemorating the two battles of Bull Run, constructed on the battle site during the winter of 1864–65, were dedicated. A reporter for the *New York Times* described them as "plain, simple structures of red sand stone" and noted that the "dedicatory services were of a simple, but impressive character. Rev. Dr. McMurray, of Kentucky, read a portion of the Episcopal service appropriate to the occasion, and two hymns, one for each monument, were sung, having been written expressly for the occasion."

Of all the groups that fought in the Civil War, none was less recognized or more misunderstood than the Native Americans. Most tried to ignore the white conflict or sought to take advantage of the thinning-out of frontier posts by reclaiming authority over regions that had earlier been lost to settlers. But perhaps as many as ten thousand went to war wearing Confederate gray, and many of those took part in several major engagements. Although most operated within the boundaries of the Trans-Mississippi Department, they were not included in the terms of the surrender document signed by Edmund Kirby Smith on June 2.

On June 23 the leader of the last organized body of Confederate troops rode into the village of Doaksville, capital of the Choctaw country in the Indian Territory (modern Oklahoma), to lay down his arms. The tribes that had thrown in their lot with the Confederate Cause had met in a Grand Council of the United Indian Nations on June 10 and there determined that each nation would surrender on its own. The Choctaws had been first, on June 19.

Four days later Brigadier General Stand Watie, principal chief of the Cherokees and commanding general of the Territorial Division, gave up on behalf of the Cherokee forces, as well as the Creek, Seminole, and Osage units serving with them. The nearly sixty-year-old chief had led his men at Wilson's Creek, Pea Ridge, Prairie Grove, and countless smaller actions. He was the last Confederate general to surrender.

On June 29, the military commission charged with determining the innocence or guilt and punishment of the eight individuals arrested for their part in the Lincoln assassination — Samuel Arnold, George Atzerodt, David Herold, Samuel Mudd, Michael O'Laughlin, Lewis Paine, Edman Spangler, and Mary Surratt* — completed its hearing of the evidence and went into a closed session to render its verdicts. The entire process had been controversial, to say the least.

The fact that the trial had taken place under the auspices of a military

---

* Arnold and O'Laughlin had been involved in the abortive kidnap plot, and Spangler was a friend of Booth's employed at Ford's Theater. Surratt ran the boardinghouse where Booth and his coconspirators often met.

court instead of a civil one had divided the country from the outset. War Secretary Stanton was adamant that the defendants face a military tribunal, where the laws of evidence were less confining for the prosecution and the likely punishment was harsher. Andrew Johnson's attorney general agreed, arguing that "if the persons who are charged with the assassination of the President committed the deed as public enemies . . . they not only can, but ought to be tried before a military tribunal."

In New York the diarist George T. Strong noted that there was "much dissatisfaction" over the administration's approach. "There may be reasons for the course adopted of which we know nothing," he wrote, "but it seems impolitic and of doubtful legality." An ex-congressman told Andrew Johnson that the selection of a military commission "will prove disastrous to yourself, your administration and your supporters who may attempt to apologize for it." Several powerful newspapers set themselves in open opposition to the idea, with the writers for the *New York World* titling their editorial against the commission "The Military Star Chamber at Washington."

Adjutant General Edward D. Townsend, the War Department official who had organized the Fort Sumter ceremonies on April 14, was assigned to pick the nine officers who were to serve on the tribunal. Availability was a major factor in the selection process, which resulted in a panel of officers of modest distinction at best, given wide powers and not required to render a unanimous verdict — a two-thirds majority would do. One observer opposed to the whole procedure proclaimed that the commission was made up of "officers too worthless for field service, ordered to try, and organized to convict."

Yet there was deep division among the panel members themselves regarding the part they were expected to play in the unfolding national drama. An officer who was released from the court because he had served on the staff of U. S. Grant, one of the plot's alleged victims,* had wistfully written in his diary just a few days earlier, "I wish I could get off."

For a while it also appeared that the trial would be held in secret, but after a vigorous campaign mounted by the press, the administration decided to open the hearings to the public. Newspaper columns across the country began a regular run of reports to keep their readers abreast of the testimony given by the 169 prosecution witnesses and the 235 called for the defense. Some 34 percent of those appearing for the government

---

* Only the fact that Grant left town on the afternoon of April 14 kept him from becoming a target of the Booth group.

presented statements that had no direct connection to either the assassination plot or the assassination plotters, but instead seemed designed to rouse public wrath against the Confederacy in general. Rules of procedure required the defense attorneys to provide the court with an advance list of witnesses whom they wished to call to the stand, while the prosecutors were free to summon theirs at literally a moment's notice. The harried defenders found themselves having to counter completely unexpected testimony that ranged from the damaging to the utterly unprovable. Further, the defendant's lawyers were not allowed to confer in private with their clients, but had to hold their discussions in the open courtroom, with flanking guards listening in.

One of the defense attorneys himself became an issue in the case. Mary Surratt's chief representative, a former U.S. senator and attorney general named Reverdy Johnson, detested the very idea of a military examination. "Reverdy Johnson," reported one correspondent during the trial, "having made an excellent plea for civil tribunals, and the power of the common law, has become incensed at the cavalier bearing of the court martial officers, whose examinations of witnesses are both informal and arbitrary." Members of the court responded in kind, one of them going so far as to openly question the Maryland barrister's allegiance to the Union. Johnson virtually withdrew from the case, leaving Mrs. Surratt's defense in the hands of two junior members of his law firm. Henry Kyd Douglas, a former Confederate officer who closely followed the trial, later declared, "If justice ever sat with unbandaged, blood-shot eyes, she did on this occasion. . . . Although the Court was organized to convict, the trial need not have been such a shameless farce."

And convict it did. On June 30, after deliberating less than a day, the nine officers sent their guilty verdicts on to President Johnson for his review. Four of the eight defendants received imprisonment, while four were to be hanged. The only real surprise was that Mary Surratt's name was among the doomed quartet, leading five members of the panel to include with their verdicts a petition to the President asking him to commute her death sentence to life imprisonment.

Concluded Henry Kyd Douglas, "The Commission illustrated the very spirit and body of the times; and passion decided everything."

Part Four

VISTAS AGAIN TO PEACE RESTORED

———◄◦►———

To the leaven'd soil they trod calling I sing for the last,
(Forth from my tent emerging for good, loosing, untying the tent-ropes,)
In the freshness the forenoon air,
    in the far-stretching circuits and vistas again to peace restored,
To the fiery fields emanative and the endless vistas beyond,
    to the South and the North,
To the leaven'd soil of the general Western world to attest my songs,
To the Alleghanian hills and the tireless Mississippi,
To the rocks I calling sing, and all the trees in the woods,
To the plains of the poems of heroes, to the prairies spreading wide,
To the far-off sea and the unseen winds, and the sane impalpable air;
And responding they answer all, (but not in words,)
The average earth, the witness of war and peace, acknowledges mutely,
The prairie draws me close, as the father to bosom broad the son,
The Northern ice and rain that began me nourish me to the end,
But the hot sun of the South is to fully ripen my songs.

      Walt Whitman, "To the Leaven'd Soil They Trod"

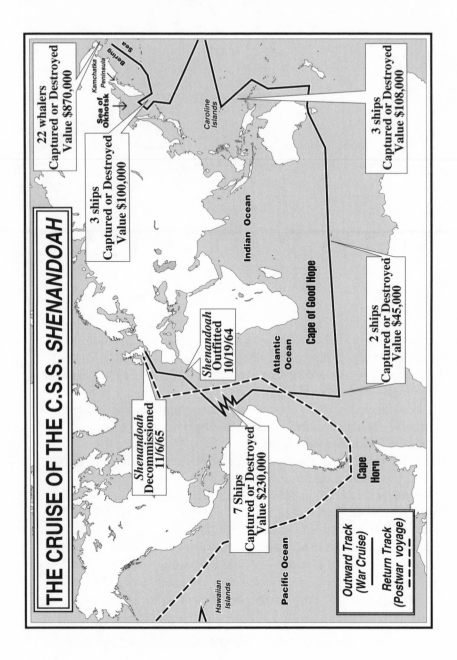

THE CRUISE OF THE C.S.S. SHENANDOAH

22 whalers
Captured or Destroyed
Value $870,000

3 ships
Captured or Destroyed
Value $100,000

3 ships
Captured or Destroyed
Value $108,000

2 ships
Captured or Destroyed
Value $45,000

Shenandoah
Outfitted
10/19/64

Shenandoah
Decommissioned
11/6/65

7 Ships
Captured or Destroyed
Value $230,000

Bering
Sea

Kamchatka
Peninsula

Sea of
Okhotsk

Caroline
Islands

Indian Ocean

Cape of Good Hope

Atlantic
Ocean

Cape
Horn

Pacific Ocean

Hawaiian
Islands

Outward Track
(War Cruise) ——
Return Track
(Postwar voyage) ---

364

Chapter Twenty-one

The Last Raider

———◁○▷———

WHEN THE SOUTH went to war, in 1861, its naval forces existed more in the minds of its leaders than in the actual waters of the Confederacy. But under the inspired leadership of Stephen Mallory, a remarkable force of vessels was assembled, including the C.S.S. *Merrimac,* the first ironclad ship to be used in combat by either side. With its vast merchant fleet spread all over the globe, the United States was especially vulnerable to commerce raiders — fast, powerful warships that prowled the trade lanes seeking to capture or destroy cargo-bearing vessels.

The first in this family of raiders was the C.S.S. *Florida,* built in England and put into commission at sea in April 1862. A second vessel entered the Confederate lists five months later and was christened the C.S.S. *Alabama.* The service of the *Florida* lasted seven months; before the ship was captured by a Federal steam sloop in October 1864, its captain and crew took twenty-three prizes and were responsible for the destruction of four million dollars' worth of U.S. shipping. The *Alabama,* under the command of Raphael Semmes, enjoyed a twenty-two-month life span, over the course of which the Confederacy added to its totals sixty-five Union merchantmen captured and a further fifty-two destroyed, for a value of $4,613,914. The *Alabama*'s career ended in June 1864, in a celebrated sea fight off the port of Cherbourg against the U.S.S. *Kearsarge.*

Following the loss of the *Alabama,* Confederate agents soon put together another deal for a raider that would carry the Confederate flag — and carry on the destruction of war — long after guns had been silenced throughout the South.

The ship in question was purchased from a British shipbuilder and secretly outfitted at an uninhabited island near Madeira. "I do not know why the name *Shenandoah* was chosen," one of its officers wrote afterward, "unless because of the constantly recurring conflicts, retreats and advances through the Shenandoah Valley in Virginia. . . . The burning there of homes over defenseless women and children made the selection of the name not inappropriate for a cruiser, which was to lead a torchlight procession around the world and into every ocean."

The ship's captain, James Waddell, took his first prize on October 30, 1864. By the spring of 1865 that victim had been joined by eight others, on a journey that had taken the raider and its crew from English waters into the South Atlantic, around the Cape of Good Hope, across the Indian Ocean, and into the Pacific.

On April 1, the day that Sheridan crushed Pickett near Five Forks and Wilson bowled over Forrest near Ebenezer Church, the armed cruiser C.S.S. *Shenandoah* crept up to Ascension Island, part of the Carolines chain in the Pacific. The lookout had spotted land at first light, but Lea Harbor was obscured by fog, so the vessel lay to.

Lieutenant Commmanding Waddell had ordered the ship to Ascension Island after learning from a schooner master that four Yankee whalers were anchored in its harbor. Waddell and his crew had seen only one sail in the entire month of March, so their anticipation was intense.

"April 1," Waddell remarked to his executive officer, Lieutenant William C. Whittle. "It would be a good April Fool joke on us if those whalers in Lea Harbor turned out to be neutrals instead of the New Englanders we think they are."

"Yes, no doubt a very fine joke," Whittle agreed, "but I doubt whether I'd enjoy it much."

Waddell's plan was to approach Ascension Island cautiously once the fog lifted; he certainly had not anticipated that the ships there might willingly help him. Nonetheless, a small boat came out from the island and drew up alongside. The Yankee whalers were expecting a U.S. survey ship and wrongly assumed that the C.S.S. *Shenandoah* was it. Waddell was not about to disappoint them; he used the pilot whom the whalers had thoughtfully provided to maneuver his ship into the harbor.

Midshipman John T. Mason described the next events of this day in his journal: "Very soon we made out three American flags & one

Sandwich Islander [which turned out to have United States registry]. The poor Yankees evidently displayed their bunting with the greatest confidence, little dreaming that we were a Confederate man of war." Lieutenant Whittle continued the story: "All four of the captains had gone on a visit to a missionary post near by. As they returned in their boat we intercepted them and brought them on board. It was no April fool for them, poor fellows." "To make matters short," Mason finished his journal entry, "all four of the whalers were made prizes [and destroyed]."

The C.S.S. *Shenandoah* remained in the area for another twelve days in the futile hope of repeating its success. Lieutenant Commanding Waddell then ordered his crew to sail north, into the Pacific trade-wind lanes favored by merchant ships shuttling between the Far East and the western United States. But word that a wolf was on the prowl had made the shippers cautious, and the raider had no luck. Finally, deciding that his best opportunity to wreak havoc on behalf of the Confederacy lay with the whaling fleet then working in far northern waters, Waddell set a course toward the Bering Sea. After fighting their way through a fierce typhoon that more than once threatened to swamp them, the ship and its crew emerged on May 20 in sight of the white-capped mountains of the Kuril Islands, which stretched like a picket line between northern Japan and the Kamchatka Peninsula. Six days later the ship slid past this island chain into the Sea of Okhotsk, where the *Shenandoah* enjoyed a change in its luck, capturing a New Bedford whaler.

But here the Confederate raider faced fresh dangers as well: short, violent gales that struck with little warning, and freezing water that soon covered the vessel with a crust of breathtaking yet deadly beauty. "The braces, blocks, yards, sails, and all other running rigging was thoroughly coated in ice from a half to two inches thick, . . . and when the sunlight burst upon that fairy ship she sparkled from deck to trunk as if a diadem had been thrown about her, awakening exclamations of enthusiastic delight," Waddell noted.

Sailing onto the Bering Sea, the *Shenandoah* scooped up seven more whalers on June 22 and 23, along with some disturbing intelligence. One of the prizes carried a collection of San Francisco newspapers, whose stories suggested that the Cause was not going well. "The papers," Waddell wrote in his journal of the cruise, "contained a number of dispatches and among them was one that stated the Southern Government had removed to Danville and the greater part of the army of [Northern] Virginia had joined General Johnston's army in North Carolina, where an indecisive battle had been fought against General Sherman's army; also that at Danville a proclamation was issued by President Davis, announcing that the war would be carried on with renewed vigor, and exhorting the people of the South to bear up heroically against their adversaries."

The *Shenandoah*'s master apprised his officers of the news and asked if they felt the mission should continue. To a man, they wanted to go on. "So far as we knew," one of the officers recalled, "our armies, though repulsed at many points and sadly depleted in numbers were still making a gallant stand against the Northern hordes . . . ; consequently our hearts were buoyed up with the thought that we were still aiding the great cause to which we had devoted our lives and fortunes."

Lieutenant Commanding Waddell's decision to stick to what he believed to be a good hunting plan began to pay off on June 26, when he hauled in six more whaling vessels in less than twelve hours. Although Waddell and his crew may have taken some professional satisfaction in the destruction of United States shipping of any stripe, these particular targets made for remarkably unappealing victims. "The odor from a whaling ship is horribly offensive," Waddell wrote, though he admitted that "it is not worse than that of the green hide vessels from South America, which can be smelt fifty miles in a favorable wind."

On the morning of June 28, the *Shenandoah* cornered eleven United States whaling ships in East Cape Bay, in the Bering Strait off Alaska. As the warship glided into the bay under sail, with the Stars and Stripes flying from its mast, one of the whalers signaled that it was damaged and asked for assistance. Back from the raider came the quick reply, "We are very busy now, but in a little while we will attend to you."

Twelve hours later the *Shenandoah* stood off from the bay, its work done. Waddell had packed the 327 crewmen he had taken prisoner into two of the captured ships (nine others had decided to enter the Confederate service) and set the rest of the whalers afire. Recalled Waddell, "An occasional explosion on board some of the burning vessels betrayed the presence of gunpowder or other combustible matter. A liquid flame now and then pursued an inflammable substance which had escaped from the sides to the water, and the horizon was illuminated with a fiery glare presenting a picture of indescribable grandeur while the water was covered with black smoke mingled with flakes of fire."

Acting on a report that there were more whalers further north, the C.S.S. *Shenandoah* set sail in that direction. But the cold cruise into the Arctic Ocean proved to be only a frustrating dead end. No ships, just an impenetrable curtain of ice confronted Lieutenant Commanding Waddell and his crew. "To attempt to penetrate such barriers was sheer madness," one of Waddell's officers wrote. "The undertaking would have been attended with the greatest peril, even with the auxiliary of a vessel expressly fortified and strengthened for the rough encounter."

Threading their way back through the floes was no easy task, but by early July the *Shenandoah* and its crew were in warmer waters. Waddell was already formulating a scheme to show the world that the fighting Confederacy was far from extinct. He placed his ship on a course toward the "coast of California, for I had matured plans for entering the harbor of San Francisco and laying that city under contribution [i.e., holding it for ransom]."

On August 2 the *Shenandoah* stopped a British bark thirteen days out of the city. Instead of intercepting valuable information regarding Federal strength there, however, Waddell was presented with irrefutable evidence that the war was at an end. As the *Shenandoah*'s officer of the watch recorded in the ship's log,

> Having received by the bark Barracouta the sad intelligence of the overthrow of the Confederate Government, all attempts to destroy the shipping or property of the United States will cease from this date, in accordance with which the first lieutenant . . . received the order from the commander to strike below the battery and disarm the ship and crew.

Wrote the ship's medical officer, "This is doomed to be one of the blackest of all the black days of my life, for from today I must look forward to beginning life over again, starting from where I cannot tell, how I cannot say — but I have learned for a certainty that I have no country."

Lieutenant Commanding Waddell now made a daring decision. "At the blush of surrender of the *Shenandoah* I saw the propriety of running her for a European port which, though it involved a voyage of seventeen thousand miles, it was the right thing to do." Waddell's determination was not shared by all of the crew, many of whom were still struggling to cope with the painfully abrupt transformation from hunter to hunted. "The hilarity which had so long been observable through the ship was now gone," an officer noted, "and there were only anxious faces to be seen in cabin, wardroom, and forecastle. The lookouts, it was true, still mounted aloft, but it was not to scan the seas for ships that might be captured, but to maintain a faithful watch and word over any suspicious sail that might make its appearance above the horizon." "The very ship seemed to have partaken [of] our feelings and no longer moved with her accustomed swiftness," Waddell observed.

The *Shenandoah* made its way safely and undetected around blustery Cape Horn and entered the lower Atlantic, where a number of destinations presented themselves. Waddell kept his own counsel, but some of his officers resolved to press the issue. On September 28 the senior officers handed him a petition recommending that they sail to Cape Town and not even consider returning the ship to its home port in Great Britain. "What do we gain by proceeding with the ship to England that we would not gain by proceeding there in some neutral vessel from a neutral port?" the petitioners asked. That same day, several steerage officers issued their own statement, likewise counseling a course for Cape Town but also virtually demanding that, should Waddell's decision be otherwise, they be put ashore "at some of the bays to the northward." Cannily recognizing that the majority of his officers would support their captain's authority no matter what their personal feelings were, Waddell summoned his watch officers and put the decision to them: did they wish to follow his plan to make for a European port, or go for Cape Town? The officers backed their commander. As Waddell later noted in his memoirs, "Applications were here made to take the ship to Cape Town, and I declined to do so."

His reminiscence concluded,

On the morning of the 6th of November, 1865, the *Shenandoah* steamed up the River Mersey in a thick fog under the Confederate flag, and the pilot had orders to anchor her near H.M. ship-of-the-line *Donegal*, Captain Paynter, R.N.

Shortly after we anchored a lieutenant from the *Donegal* visited us to ascertain the name of the vessel and gave me official intelligence of the termination of the American war. He was polite. The flag was then hauled down.

After a little diplomatic wrangling, the crew of the *Shenandoah* was allowed to disembark and disperse into the Liverpool masses. The ship was turned over to the American consul on November 11 and eventually found its way into the hands of the Sultan of Zanzibar, who used it in the tea trade. The *Shenandoah* was driven onto a coral reef in 1879 and sunk with a heavy loss of life.

James Waddell remained in England until 1870, when he returned to the United States and settled in Maryland. He was a captain in the Merchant Marine and later was put in charge of the state boats that policed Maryland's oyster beds. When he died, on March 15, 1886, the Maryland Assembly adjourned in his honor.

Litigation over England's part in allowing numerous Confederate commerce raiders to be constructed on its soil went on for years. An international tribunal was convened to investigate the matter and finally ruled in 1872 that Great Britain did bear guilt and was responsible for damages totaling fifteen million dollars in gold. England paid the sum a year later, closing out that chapter of the Civil War.

In his final report of actions, Lieutenant Commanding Waddell proudly declared that the *Shenandoah* "was the only vessel that carried the [Confederate] flag around the world, and she flew it six months after the overthrow of the South. . . . I claim for her officers and men a triumph over their enemies and over every obstacle, and for myself I claim having done my duty."

Chapter Twenty-two

When Johnny Comes Marching Home

———◦›———

QUESTIONS ABOUT CHANGE and the new order of things rumbled throughout the land as the now united states celebrated their first warless Fourth of July in four years.

In South Carolina, Mrs. Mary Chestnut, a personification of Southern aristocracy, described in her diary the distasteful Independence Day celebrations held the previous evening by former slaves of the region. "Thousands of them were in town, eating, drinking, dancing, speechifying," she wrote. "Preaching and prayers were also a popular amusement. They have no greater idea of amusement than wild prayers, unless it be getting married and going to a funeral. But our people were all at home, quiet, orderly, respectful, and at their usual work. There was nothing to show that any of them had ever seen a Yankee or knew that there was one in existence."

In Washington, concern for carrying forward the agenda of social change begun by the war was very much the order of the day at the Colored People's Educational Monument Association in Memory of Abraham Lincoln, whose members today heard words written to them by Frederick Douglass. The black leader stressed that the paramount political goal now was "the immediate, complete, and universal enfranchisement of the colored people of the whole country. . . . The great want of the country is to be rid of the negro question, and it can never be rid of that question until justice, right and sound policy are complied with."

In southern Texas a long column of men, women, and children, now without a country, crossed the Rio Grande into Mexico, seeking to preserve the ideals of the Confederacy. Included in the party were a number of former high officers and officials, including Generals John Magruder, Edmund Kirby Smith, Sterling Price, and Jo Shelby and ex-governors Henry Allen of Louisiana and Pendleton Murrah of Texas. Each had come to a personal decision to go into exile rather than submit to the United States.

Brigadier General Shelby, whose Iron Brigade had served with fierce distinction in Arkansas and Missouri campaigning, paused in midstream. Taking the tattered battle flag of his veteran unit off its staff, Shelby weighted the standard with stones and flung it into the dark waters. There were no speeches to accompany this final act of defiance. There was nothing more to be said.

This refugee column was the forerunner of an exodus of disheartened and displaced Southerners that eventually numbered well into the tens of thousands. The outward movement, which was encouraged by foreign governments anxious to import experienced planters and spurred by a short-lived network of Southern immigration societies, soon established several enclaves, most notably in Mexico, British Honduras, and Brazil. The largest and most enduring settlements were set up in southern Brazil, where the new settlers became known as the Confederados (the modern descendants of whom still cherish their American ancestry). All the others eventually went the way of the Mexican enclave, which centered about a town in the state of Veracruz, named Carlotta by its founders in honor of the French-imposed empress of Mexico. Here, in Carlotta, Shelby, Price, and the others tried to preserve their Southern agricultural society, but it was not long before internal squabbling, coupled with the harsh external realities of Mexican politics, put an end to the experiment. By 1870, the U.S. minister to Mexico could report that of the "large number of citizens of the Southern States of the Union who came to Mexico immediately after the rebellion . . . almost all returned to the United States," and that there was no longer "a single notability remaining out of the many Confederate refugees."

* * *

Brevet Major General John Hartranft had experienced the worst shock a combat commander could receive when, early on the morning of March 25, 1865, he was awakened at his headquarters near Petersburg, Virginia, and told that the Rebels, attacking in overwhelming force, had breached his siege lines. Acting with single-minded purposefulness, Hartranft had not only rallied his defending units but also choreographed a vicious counterattack that completely erased the enemy incursion. Little more than three months later, a few minutes before 1:00 P.M. on July 7, 1865, Hartranft, now serving in Washington, got an even greater shock.

"My God, not the woman too?" he exclaimed loud enough to be heard a few feet away. Major General Winfield Scott Hancock, who had just confirmed the orders to hang Mary Surratt, answered at once, "Yes, the woman too!"

All the legal maneuvers, public outcry, and personal pleadings following the issuance of the guilty verdicts on June 30 had come down to this moment, on a blistering hot day in the courtyard of Washington's Old Arsenal Prison. The four individuals under a death warrant for their part in the Lincoln assassination were only half an hour away from having their sentences carried out.

The quartet were brought into the courtyard at 1:15 P.M. and walked to the high-platformed gallows that had been erected for the occasion. One of the soldiers assigned to spring the trapdoor carefully observed the group. Mrs. Surratt, he noted, was "near fainting after a look at the gallows," and David Herold, too, "trembled and shook and seemed on the verge of fainting." George Atzerodt "shuffled along in carpet slippers, a long, white nightcap on his head. Under different circumstances, he would have been ridiculous." Lewis Paine "was as stolid as if he were a spectator instead of a principal."

The condemned climbed the steps and were placed in seats along the ledge of the trapdoor. (In one of the many sharp ironies of this day, the same chairs had been occupied only a few hours earlier by the officers in charge of the execution as they posed for a group picture made by veteran battlefield photographers Alexander Gardner and Timothy O'Sullivan.) Then their arms and legs were pinioned, the nooses were placed around their necks, and white hoods were adjusted over their heads. While all of this was happening, the two photographers worked rapidly in a small room overlooking the courtyard, keeping their bulky photo boxes supplied with the carefully treated glass plates that would document each step in the terrible proceedings.

General Hancock, a Gettysburg hero and future presidential candidate, had been standing just outside the prison gate, hoping against hope that the line of couriers he had established between the Old Arsenal Prison and the White House might yet bring a reprieve for Mrs. Surratt. Finally he could wait no more.

As he reentered the courtyard, Hancock turned to the officer who would actually signal for the trapdoor to be dropped. "All is ready, Captain. Proceed," Hancock said. The officer could not help himself. "Her too?" he asked. Hancock affirmed the order and clapped his hands in a slow three count, as previously arranged. At "three," the officer signaled to the men underneath the platform to knock out the trapdoor supports. The floor fell away beneath the four at 1:26 P.M.

Mrs. Surratt died at once, and Atzerodt quickly thereafter. For seconds that seemed like hours, David Herold's body writhed in desperate spasms before it, too, was still. It was the taciturn Paine who struggled the longest for life: nearly twenty minutes would pass before his body stopped twitching. The corpses hung for approximately thirty minutes, twisting slowly as weak gusts of dry wind pushed them back and forth. Then they were taken down, pronounced dead, and buried nearby.

Minutes before commanding General Hartranft to proceed, Hancock had confessed his own feelings to a sympathetic member of the defense counsel. Said Hancock, "I have been in many a battle and have seen death, and mixed with it in disaster and in victory. I've been in a living hell of fire, and shell and grapeshot, and, by God, I'd sooner be there ten thousand times over than to give the order this day for the execution of that poor woman. But I am a soldier, sworn to obey, and obey I must."

On November 10 — four days after the *Shenandoah* hauled down its flag in far-off England — Captain Henry Wirz stood on a newly erected gallows in Washington's Old Arsenal Prison and ended one of the more terrible personal journeys in American history. From early 1864 until the general Confederate collapse in 1865, Wirz had served as commander of prisoners at Camp Sumter, better known as Andersonville. Following his arrest by James Wilson in early May, Wirz had been brought to Washington for what would prove to be the only war-crimes trial of the Civil War. Once again the government deemed that the verdict would be rendered by a military tribunal, and an alumnus of the Lincoln assassination trial, Major General Lew Wallace, was named its president.

Any possibility of Wirz's slipping unnoticed through the military justice machinery disappeared abruptly in early June, when stories of the horrible conditions at Andersonville began to circulate in the popular press. After seeing the emaciated forms of the former prisoners of war, even the gentle poet Walt Whitman was moved to anger. "There are deeds, crimes, that may be forgiven," he wrote, "but this is not among them. It steeps its perpetrators in the blackest, escapeless, endless damnation. Over fifty thousand have been compelled to die the death of starvation — reader, did you ever try to realize what *starvation* actually is? — in those prisons — and in a land of plenty!"

The national outrage unleashed by pictures of the camp survivors was further roused by the dramatically embellished reminiscences of soldiers who had escaped from Andersonville. A native antipathy to foreigners served to focus the people's rage on the crippled, Swiss-born Wirz, who maintained that he had only been carrying out orders.

The show trial began on August 21 and nearly closed on its opening day. Secretary of War Edwin Stanton rose and read the charges, which had just been handed to him. To his irritation and embarrassment, he realized that the prosecuting attorney had included in the first charge the names of several prominent Confederate leaders, following the conspiracy line that the government had employed in the trial of the Lincoln assassins. The tactic had nearly backfired in the earlier case when it proved impossible to link those leaders to Booth's accomplices, and Stanton was in no mood to try to make such connections in the case against Wirz. Following a midnight session that lasted into the early hours of August 22, Stanton had all specific references to other high-ranking C.S. military and civil officials removed from the indictment, so that Wirz was now charged only with conspiring "with others unknown."

Wirz's defense attorneys argued that this quick change created an instance of double jeopardy (since he had already submitted a plea in response to the original indictment), and they threatened to withdraw from the case. In fact, three of the four members of the defense team did step down, leaving Wirz's fate in the hands of his friend Louis Schade.

Now began a parade of witnesses and documents that painted a gruesome portrait of the hellish conditions at Andersonville. A stunned North learned how the camp, designed for ten thousand POWs, had eventually been forced to absorb many times that number; and how inadequate water, wood, food, and fuel supplies had led to sanitary and dietary genocide, resulting in the death of more than thirteen thousand inmates.

Wirz's role in the nightmare was central to the government's case, and here the testimony was conflicting. There was little direct evidence linking him to specific acts of murder, and the few eyewitnesses who stepped forward with such claims were unreliable at best. Certain documents introduced at the trial revealed that Wirz had tried but failed through official channels to alleviate some of the camp conditions, while other depositions made it clear that he had ruled the prison with an iron hand, not only establishing a deadline over which the men would be killed for trying to cross without permission, but also inflicting a variety of punishments, including flogging and the use of leg chains.

The verdict was a foregone conclusion. Henry Wirz was found guilty of having conspired to murder prisoners en masse and was personally implicated in the deaths of several prisoners. On November 6, the day Andrew Johnson approved the death sentence, Wirz wrote him, "The pangs of death are short, and therefore I humbly pray that you will pass on your sentence without delay. Give me death or liberty. The one I do not fear; the other I crave."

Now, as he walked the short distance across the open courtyard to the scaffold, the condemned man could hear the soldiers who lined the walls chant, "Wirz, remember Andersonville." After the Federal officer in charge read aloud the execution orders, Wirz looked at him and said, "I know what orders are, Major. And I am being hanged for obeying them."

At 10:32 A.M. Henry Wirz stepped off into eternity. In an open letter written nearly two years afterward, Wirz's defense attorney declared, "We used justly to claim in former times, that ours was 'the land of the free and the home of the brave.' But when one half of the country is shrouded in a despotism which now only finds a parallel in Russian Poland; and when our Generals and soldiers quietly permit that their former adversaries in arms shall be treated worse than the Helots of old, brave soldiers though they may be, who, when the forces and resources of both sections were more equal, have not seldom seen the backs of our best Generals . . . then we may well question whether the 'star-spangled banner still waves over the land of the free and the home of the brave.' "

In what was perhaps the largest military operation of the immediate postwar period, the U.S. government moved quickly to dismantle its massive and expensive war machine.

Before the summer of 1865 was over, great pieces of the machine were sold off. The entire Mississippi squadron — sixty-three boats and tugs — went on the auction block in Mound City, Illinois, and brought $625,000 into Treasury coffers. A short time after that, some twenty-four thousand army mules, advertised as "thoroughly broken . . . gentle and familiar, from being so long surrounded by soldiers," also entered the private sector.

The biggest problem the government faced was how to eliminate the armies themselves. There were 1,034,064 men under arms in Federal service when Robert E. Lee surrendered at Appomattox Court House. An otherwise obscure assistant adjutant general, Brevet Brigadier General Thomas M. Vincent, was told to figure out a way to get these men off the government payrolls as soon as possible. Vincent completed his work on May 1, 1865, and submitted it to U. S. Grant, who returned it with the comment, "Plans and suggestions within approved."

In its simplest sense, Vincent's scheme reversed the mustering-in process. The various army corps were ordered to move to designated points of concentration — George Meade's to Washington, Sherman's to Louisville, George Thomas's to Nashville, E. R. S. Canby's to New Orleans, Vicksburg, or Mobile — where individual service records and unit muster rolls were to be completed. The various regiments were then to proceed to their home states and the camps where they had entered Federal service. There the soldiers would be paid off and sent back to their homes.

Other orders followed, further refining the process. Three-year regiments whose service had begun in July 1862 had first priority; regiments mustered in later that same year would be next to go; and one-year men who had entered the service between May and October 1864 would be retained to the last.

For the most part, the system worked. Between the first of May and the first of August, 1865, some 279,034 soldiers were returned to civilian life. By August 7 the total was 640,806; by September 14, 741,107; and by October 15, 785,205. On November 14, 1866, the secretary of war could report that a grand total of 1,023,021 volunteers had been mustered out.

There were difficulties. It took time to reconcentrate and reorganize the Regular Army, and until it was ready for service, trained volunteer units had to be kept in uniform to patrol the hot spots, such as the Mexican and Canadian borders and the Great Plains, where troubles were looming with the Indian tribes. Few volunteers cared to understand the big picture, and morale problems became serious. Some units mutinied and had to be forcibly disciplined; others were disarmed. Desertions became widespread. Noted one member of a Hoosier cavalry regiment, "There was a growing discontent among the soldiers at being sent further south, when, as they supposed, the war was over. This led to numerous desertions, in fact, the men deserted in squads and platoons. On several occasions nearly the whole command was called out at night, to prevent the threatened desertions of companies and of a regiment." Even the more highly motivated volunteer officers who had been kept in

378

service were champing at the bit; one field commander was moved to complain to U. S. Grant that all his officers were afraid that "everybody at home will have got the start of them in business."

Others worried about the return to civilian life. "I have almost a dread of being a citizen, of trying to be sharp, and trying to make money," one of Sherman's veterans admitted. "I don't think I dread the work. I don't remember shirking any work I ever attempted, but I am sure that civil life will go sorely against the grain for a time." A nearby comrade, who eschewed most capitalization and punctuation, wrote that "the grave question arises what will a person go to work at it is rather a serious question with your humble servant coming as he does under the general Scripture dispensation by the Sweat of thy brow shalt thou eat bread." In a letter to a friend, an Army of the James soldier also faced the question of what to do after army service: "The change from this wild life, where we do not care a fig for a man who does not rank us, and where we march into a man's yard then enter his home and tell the man of [the] house that his family has too much room & that he must move up stairs & we will occupy the balance and do sundry & diverse other impudent things; to the more peaceable association of home is indeed great."

The hardest period came as the men waited for the red tape to finish unrolling. "The work of preparation progresses, but oh, so slowly," a Michigan boy wrote in his diary. "But the work is gigantic. The dismantling of this mighty machine of war, of returning this 'citizen army' to its legitimate and proper field of action, transferring it to an army of citizens, is an herculean task."

The veteran 7th Minnesota was landed at its mustering-in post, Fort Snelling, near St. Paul, in early August. Long days passed as muster rolls were completed and service records filled out. Then there was the final payout. Enlisted men were allowed to take home their knapsacks, haversacks, and canteens but had to purchase their firearms if they wished to keep them. One disgusted infantryman declared this last provision "almost an insult to the veterans who served their country so faithfully," and told the government it could keep its rifle.

On the evening of August 16, those members of the regiment who were returning to Hastings, Red Wing, or Winona boarded the river packet that would carry them home. The regiment's commander, Brevet Brigadier General William R. Marshall, was there to see his boys off. Marshall "bade us good-bye," one of the Minnesota soldiers recalled, "shaking each one by the hand, the tears rolling down his cheeks."

The nature of the largely volunteer Union army was such that companies, and sometimes even whole regiments, were drawn from a single community. When seventy-five members of the 20th Iowa stepped off the riverboat at Davenport on July 27, the local paper reported, they were met by throngs of "anxious relatives and friends, who . . . grasped the returning soldiers as fast as they emerged from the gangway plank. Tears of joy were shed, not only by many of the mothers and wives, and daughters, and sweethearts, but also by a number of the bronzed veterans. . . . The intention was to receive them with an address of welcome, but it was found impossible to keep them together long enough for the purpose. They were snatched away, dragged along, carried off in all directions, and marched up town as soon as they touched *terra firma*."

Finally, however, the Yankee boys came home — *really* home. An Indiana veteran wrote in his diary on the morning after his arrival that it was the "first time i slep in bed since i left home," while an Illinois comrade complained that the bed was "too soft to sleep in. For a long time, I preferred to sleep and to sit on the floor." For a returning Pennsylvania officer, the first night home with his wife was a spiritual and emotional experience. "We so earnestly prayed together," he remembered, "and sought divine help to let the dead past hide its gloomy spots — and looking unto Jesus, rely on Him to work in us and help us to help each other to overcome all evil and to acquire or attain to our ideals as Husband and Wife — as Heads of our Family — as Christians, in the Church and world — Oh! the peace, the joy, the rest that came to and possessed us, and how sweetly we fell asleep in each other's arms —"

A midwestern survivor of the Mobile siege kept a record of his final voyage home: "Before noon left Cairo for St. Louis. As we sailed along the Illinois shore it seems as if we really were almost home. There is a rich green about the foliage you don't often find about Dixie. It looks cool and refreshing, inviting to rest. Sweet home. Illinois is really as good a State as they make. It will do me."

Even as the Union soldiers were returning to their communities in the North, a small band of reporters spread throughout the South, determined, as one of them put it, "to visit some of the scenes of the great conflict through which the country had lately passed." Many made their way to Charleston, South Carolina, where the war's opening shots had been fired. "Dearly has Charleston paid for being the first to attack the national flag, and for leading the van in the path of Secession," wrote John H. Kennaway, an English observer. Sidney Andrews, who reported for the *Boston Daily Advertiser,* described it as a "city of ruins, of desolation, of vacant houses, of widowed women, of rotting wharves, of deserted warehouses, of weed-wild gardens, of miles of grass-grown streets, of acres of pitiful and voiceful barrenness." Yet the city's charm could not be denied — at least not by John T. Trowbridge, a regular correspondent for the *Atlantic Monthly,* who declared that the "ruins of Charleston are the most picturesque of any I saw in the South." Virtually all the other major Southern population centers were likewise visited by these travelers, whose pen portraits captured the often perilous conditions to be found everywhere from Atlanta to Richmond and from Petersburg to Savannah.

These reporters pushed into the former Confederacy to do more than merely observe old battlefields and scenes of destruction. Each, in his own way, tried to understand the mood of the South. "The values and the base of value were nearly all destroyed," explained Andrews. "Many lost everything they had saved. Thousands of men who were honest in purpose have lost everything but honor." A militant ex-Confederate told a reporter from the *New York Times*, "We have no government. We are aliens and foreigners, and will never have our souls so degraded as to have anything whatsoever to do with such a government."

There was tension and violence at almost every point where black aspiration met a fierce white desire to preserve the *status quo ante bellum*. While visiting Selma, Alabama, John Trowbridge came across a black chain gang laboring under the gaze of several whites, who jeered, "That's the beauty of freedom! That's what free niggers come to!" Noted Trowbridgbe, "On inquiring what the chain gang had done to be punished in this ignominious manner, I got the list of misdemeanors, one of the gravest of which was 'using abusive language towards a white man.' " Nothing focused white anger more sharply than the prospect of former slaves' voting. "Everybody admits that the Negro is incapable of intelligently exercising the right of suffrage," John Richard Dennett of the *Nation* was told. Whitelaw Reid, who reported for several different midwestern papers, quickly learned from his conversations with whites that black "suffrage seemed to all the most revolting of possibilities. They were not willing to think their conquerors could mean to inflict such degradation upon a gallant people."

During their wanderings throughout the South, these outsiders often detailed the sad condition of that region's transportation network. "The railroads are worn out," observed Sidney Andrews after passing through the Carolinas, "and there is not a single line in either State that should not be relaid with new iron at the earliest possible day." John Kennaway recalled of his train journey that "many of the seats were broken, and the rails were so worn, and the trains so shaky, that again and again we woke up with a start, thinking that we were off the line."

One message portended failure for President Andrew Johnson's Reconstruction plan, which depended upon the willingness of former Confederate citizens to take an active and positive role in national affairs. John Dennett spoke with several ex-Rebels who stated that it was "only because their country has been subjugated that they now pay obedience to the United States." Relating one conversation he had had, Whitelaw Reid wrote, " 'I was a Rebel,' said a conspicuous Southerner, 'I submit because I was whipped, and have a great respect for the men that whipped me; but I shall have less respect for them if they prove such simpletons as to suppose that the Rebels of yesterday can to-day become fit men to be intrusted with the reorganization of a loyal government, by simply swearing an oath of allegiance."

One sight that became only too familiar to reporters covering the South in mid-1865 was that of paroled and surrendered Confederate soldiers returning to their homesteads. A *New York Tribune* correspondent confided that he was "daily touched to the heart by seeing these poor homesick boys and exhausted men wandering about in threadbare uniforms, with scanty outfit of slender haversack and blanket roll hung over their shoulders, seeking the nearest route home; they have a care-worn and anxious look, a played-out manner."

As the Rebels scattered outward from their former armies, they quickly learned the tricks of passage. "Too many together could not fare so well, so we thought it advisable to travel in less numbers so that people would not dread to feed us as we came along," recalled a Tar Heel soldier. "We would generally stop at nearly every house we passed and beg for something to eat, or for milk or buttermilk; and there being only two of us, we were hardly ever refused, consequently, we never wanted," added a South Carolina comrade.

A young boy in Lincolnton, North Carolina, never forgot the sad procession that passed through his small town: "Some were halt and lame, and some with one arm or one eye. Four years before, these brave men with high hopes went forth to reap the glories and victories of war. They had braved many battles and left many of their comrades slain on bloody fields. They came home discouraged by defeat and found the country impoverished by the long and fruitless struggle." Years afterward, an Alabama woman could reflect, "Often as I sit in the twilight and drift back into the past, it is not easy to restrain tears, as memory views those soldiers in their worn gray, marching home sad and depressed, with the cause they had so warmly espoused, lost."

Although they had been defeated in battle, few of these soldiers were prepared to apologize for their actions. "When I come home if any man reproaches me for being a soldier I will surely hit him," one officer vowed. "I will tell him that we were the ones who suffered and bled and faced the disgrace of having to give up our long arms." Foremost on everyone's mind was concern over the conditions that awaited their return. A North Carolina soldier noted, "Many people say the farm land will not completely recover from the Yankee rape it underwent. Life is bound not to be pleasant for a while."

For the Rebel soldiers, as for their counterparts in blue, the moment finally did arrive when they were home. Mississippian Albert Porter found his "family all in good health and doing well. Some of my children had grown so much I scarcely knew them." When former staff officer Bromfield L. Ridley came home, his "dear old mother threw her arms around me and wept. . . . For a moment I forgot the gloom of surrender." Not all aspects of the homecomings were joyous, however. A member of a Mississippi regiment was part of a group that "reached the neighborhood where some of our company enlisted from. One mother wrung her toil-worn hands in anguish when told that her gallant boy would never come home again. But such is the cruelty of war."

Texan Val C. Giles recalled,

It was late September, 1865, when I reached home in Govalle, outside of Austin, late one Sunday evening, after an absence of four years and five months. Father and mother were not expecting me and were not at home, but my dog, Brave, was on guard. When I left home to join the Army in 1861 he was about three years old.

It was not a "deep-mouthed welcome" that greeted me as I drew near, but a gruff emphatic warning to keep out. Old Brave, now a veteran of more than eight years, took me for a tramp, and was not very far from right about it.

"Brave, old boy," I said, "don't you know me?"

He cocked up one ear and looked at me sideways.

It finally dawned on him who I was, and he came toward me wagging his tail. I opened the gate and he landed on my breast with both paws. I petted him on the head for a moment, then he broke away and circled wildly all around me, expressing in his dumb way his delight at my return.

* * *

The fates of the leaders of the Confederate government were as varied and diverse as the men themselves. **Alexander H. Stephens,** Jefferson Davis's frequent rival and ostensible Vice President, was kept a prisoner in chilly Fort Warren in Boston Harbor until October 1865, when he was released on parole. Turning his thoughts to the question of black suffrage, Stephens foresaw a system of proportional representation for African-Americans, under which he thought it likely that able whites would be chosen to safeguard their interests. Stephens became a Georgia congressman in 1873, served nine years, and was then elected state governor. He died in harness in 1883.

Judah P. Benjamin, the quixotic secretary of state, showed in his successful escape through the Federal dragnet the same kind of resourcefulness that had kept him near the center of power for most of the life of the Confederacy. Soon after leaving the Davis party, Benjamin disguised himself as a non-English-speaking Frenchman, made his way to southwestern central Florida, secured a small boat, managed to survive a harrowing voyage to Bimini, and eventually made passage to England. There he entered the lower rungs of the English bar and within a few years became a leading member of the legal profession. Benjamin retired in 1883 and was dead a year later, a distinguished and much-honored man. He never returned to the United States.

Davis's stalwart secretary of war, **John C. Breckinridge,** also eluded the Yankee patrols, sailing from south Florida to Cuba and weathering a deadly gulf storm in the process. He returned to the United States in 1868 under the terms of an amnesty proclamation and settled in Kentucky, where he practiced law until he passed away, in 1875.

Postmaster **John H. Reagan** returned to Texas, served for ten years in the Federal Congress, entered the Senate in 1887, retired in 1903, and died two years later. Navy Secretary **Stephen Mallory** was kept in Fort Lafayette in New York Harbor until March 1866, despite his willingness to cooperate with the authorities. He even charted the likely course of the C.S.S. *Shenandoah* and suggested ways in which the Union authorities might convince Lieutenant Commanding Waddell to haul down his flag. Mallory lived quietly in Florida until his death, in 1880.

The end of the Confederacy was a deathblow to Texas Senator **Williamson S. Oldham,** whose personal odyssey closely followed the domino-like collapse of that government. He left his adopted state soon after the occupation began and spent time in both Mexico and Canada, where he became a photographer and labored over the manuscript logging his journey across the dying C.S.A. Oldham returned to the United

States in 1867, refused to request a pardon, and was allowed to settle in Houston. He died in that city of typhoid fever on May 8, 1868, unreconstructed to the last.

Following the removal of his leg manacles, **Jefferson Davis** remained under close supervision for two months before steps were taken to improve the conditions of his imprisonment at Fortress Monroe. By September he had been moved from the damp lower level to a dryer and airier cell on an upper floor. In November he wrote Varina, "My health is better than it was three months ago, my food is suited to my health and is abundant as I desire."

While Davis was enduring the indignities and hardships of imprisonment, the U.S. government was sputtering toward an indictment and trial of the former Confederate President. Any idea of prosecuting him for complicity in the Lincoln assassination dissolved for want of hard evidence, so in July 1865 it was determined to charge him with treason instead. Much time was lost while a proper venue for the trial was selected (the final choice was the U.S. Circuit Court in Virginia) and a presiding judge picked (Supreme Court Justice Salmon P. Chase got the nod). During this long period it was also decided to deny Davis any opportunity to post bail.

The search for evidence in the Davis matter was further hampered by interference from congressional inquiries along similar lines, and then nearly sidetracked by the events surrounding Andrew Johnson's impeachment hearings. In the midst of all this, public opinion toward the Rebel leader began to soften, thanks to the publication in June 1866 of a memoir purported to be by Dr. John J. Craven, the Union surgeon at Fortress Monroe. Titled *Prison Life of Jefferson Davis*, it painted a powerfully sympathetic portrait of the suffering of the former Confederate chief executive. Even after it was shown that the book had been largely ghostwritten by a free-lance journalist named Charles Halpine, a number of prominent citizens, including Horace Greeley, editor of the *New York Tribune,* continued to demand that the government either place Davis on trial or allow him bail. This pressure finally resulted in Davis's bond release on May 10, 1867.

When Chief Justice Chase finally convened the court trial, on June 3, 1868, he was told that the defense and the prosecution had agreed to a postponement. Changes in the Johnson Cabinet now removed key figures, causing more delays in the preparation of the government's brief. At last, on February 26, 1869, the U.S. government informed Davis's counsel that it had no case to press against him and that no further investigations would take place.

For a while after his release Davis resided in Canada, but he returned to the United States for good in 1869. He would live for twenty more years, a tireless proponent of Southern ideals and a fierce defender of his wartime decisions. He never applied for a presidential pardon and rejected any suggestions that he seek one. "I have not repented," he declared in 1884. "If it were to do over again I would again do just as I did in 1861." A short time before he died, in 1889, Jefferson Davis told a small group, "I feel no regret that I stand before you a man without a country, for my ambition lies buried in the grave of the Confederacy."

Images of the Civil War were ready materials for the young Winslow Homer. As a combat artist for *Harper's Weekly,* he had seen the reality of fighting firsthand during the Peninsula Campaign of 1862 and been present at the beginning of Grant's Overland Campaign in 1864. Homer's first painting of a war subject was produced in early 1864, a crisp but menacing portrait of a Union sniper at work. Scenes of camp life, soldiers foraging, the boredom of trench warfare, and an almost impressionistic rendering of fighting in the Wilderness followed. None, however, generated quite the amount of interest accorded to his oil-on-canvas work *Prisoners from the Front* when it was first shown, in April 1866, at New York's National Academy of Design. One noted art historian declared that the painting "attracted more attention, and . . . won more praise than any genre picture by a native hand that has appeared of late years." Another proclaimed that it was the "most valuable and comprehensive art work that has been painted to express some of the most vital facts of our war."

A reviewer for the *Evening Post* described the work for his readers: "[The] picture by Homer represents a Union officer . . . receiving a group of rebel prisoners who have evidently just been brought in from the front. The group of prisoners must have been painted from life, for the men are thoroughly characteristic of their class."

A critic who went by the initials E.B. explored the meaning of the figures portrayed for the May 12 edition of the *Round Table:* "[They express] . . . the conditions of character North and South during the war — the South, ardent and audacious at the first, like the young Virginian rebel; bound to the past, and bewildered by the threatened severance of that connection with the past, like the poor old man nervously holding his hat; resting on ignorance and servile habits, as expressed by the 'poor white,' the third prisoner of the group. These are confronted by the dry, unsympathetic, firm face of the Federal officer, who represents the reserved but persistent North."*

A subtle line had been crossed: no longer the object of commercial illustration, the Civil War was now a worthwhile subject of fine art.

The political, social, and economic destiny of the conquered South became a fiercely contested matter in the decade following the end of the armed rebellion. The Reconstruction of the Union, begun in May 1865 by President Andrew Johnson, was undone within a year, due in part to Johnson's unwillingness (or inability) to work with Congress and his complete misreading of Southern attitudes. The state conventions organized under his North Carolina model were not inclined to come meekly back into the Union; some, in fact, refused to repudiate the idea of secession and merely repealed their ordinances to that end, in effect maintaining the principle while revoking its legal expression. Adding insult to injury, most of the states covered by Johnson's various proclamations promptly elected new congressional and Senate slates chock-full of former Confederate leaders. Even more disturbing were the states' so-called Black Codes, which sought to regulate many aspects of African-American life, from legal and property rights to the right to bear arms — this during the period when the same states ratified the Thirteenth Amendment, abolishing slavery.

The fight on the national level between the executive and legislative branches — which climaxed in Johnson's 1868 impeachment trial — resulted in the Congressional Reconstruction Act of 1867, a statute that used force to impose Federal will upon the former states of the Confederacy. Five military districts were created, and each was assigned an army commander to oversee and control all police, judicial, and civil functions. The states were expected to draft new constitutions guaranteeing black suffrage and ratifying certain other reforms. Generals Ord and Sheridan, of Appomattox fame, and General Schofield (from Sherman's campaign) were among the first five chosen to head the occupation districts.

Another military figure from the war, U. S. Grant, became the Republican candidate for President in 1868 and the victor in the general election that year, with an Electoral College margin of 214 to 80. His two terms in the White House were marked by some of the worst scandals and corruption in U.S. history. Grant believed that the type of

---

* In fact, for the Union officer, Homer used as a model his friend Major General Francis Channing Barlow.

organization and management he had employed in the military world would serve him equally well in public life, and he selected his Cabinet and other key officials much as he had picked his staff and command officers during the war. He was attracted to men who had a professed loyalty to him, and to those whom he instinctively trusted. But in contrast to the army, where the hard test of combat had a way of weeding out the opportunists, the more ambiguous arena of national politics (of which Grant knew little) gave free rein to the greedy and corrupt. Grant's appointments, one periodical editorialized, were "probably some of the worst ever made by a civilized Christian government."

Grant was succeeded by Rutherford B. Hayes, who needed a deal to break a tie in the Electoral College and won the votes of Southern Democrats with his promise to pull out the troops. Hayes got his votes, and the Reconstruction era came to an end in 1877.

The process by which the former Confederate states returned to the Union and changed their local laws to conform with new national legislation continued to be contentious. One government agency embodied both the best and the worst aspects of the Northern desire to reshape the South during Reconstruction; this was the Bureau of Refugees, Freedmen and Abandoned Lands, established by Congress on March 3, 1865, to provide humanitarian services for Southern blacks. Although the Freedman's Bureau, as it came to be known, never employed more than nine hundred agents throughout the entire former Confederacy, its broad mandate committed it to a wide range of concerns, from educational and legal reform to labor contracts and social improvement. The bureau's commissioner was Major General Oliver O. Howard, a one-armed veteran of both Eastern and Western theaters of the war, and a man whose concern for human issues led some to dub him the Christian General.

Because it was loosely organized, the Freedman's Bureau attracted not only the most zealously idealistic men and women but also the most baldly unscrupulous. By seeking to quickly enfranchise blacks and fully integrate them into the Southern labor force, the Freedman's Bureau put itself and the people it had been created to protect on a collision course with the rising forces of white reaction. Looking back on this turbulent period during which many blacks were brutalized into quiescence, educational leader Booker T. Washington considered this turn of affairs "unfortunate because during the four years of its existence the freedmen had learned to look to this Bureau and its representatives for leading,

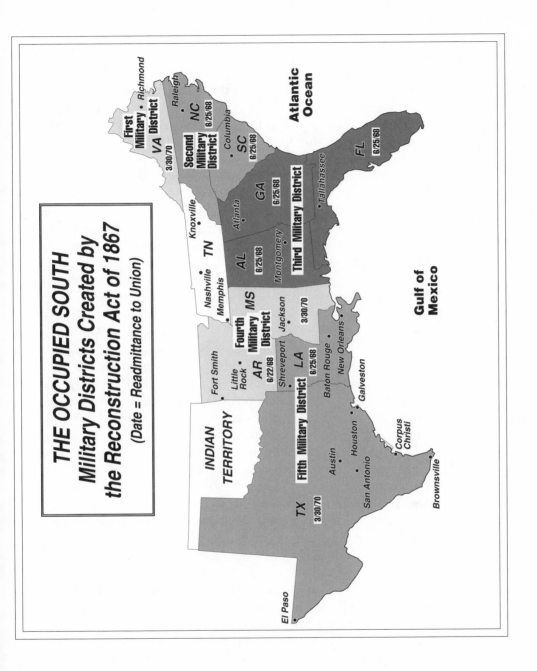

THE OCCUPIED SOUTH
Military Districts Created by
the Reconstruction Act of 1867
(Date = Readmittance to Union)

First Military • Richmond
VA District
3/30/70

Raleigh •
NC
6/25/68

Second
Military
District

Columbia •
SC
6/25/68

Atlantic
Ocean

Knoxville •
TN
Atlanta •
GA
6/25/68

AL
6/25/68
Montgomery •

Third Military District

• Tallahassee

FL
6/25/68

Nashville •
Memphis •
MS
Jackson •
3/30/70

Fourth
Military
District

Fort Smith •
Little
Rock •
AR
6/22/68
Shreveport •
LA
6/25/68

Baton Rouge •
New Orleans •

Gulf of
Mexico

INDIAN
TERRITORY

Fifth Military District

Austin •
San Antonio •
Houston •
Galveston •

Corpus
Christi •

TX
3/30/70

El Paso •

Brownsville •

support, and protection. The whole South has suffered from the fact that the former slaves were first introduced into political life as the opponents, instead of the political supporters, of their former masters. No part of the South has suffered more on this account, however, than the negroes themselves." Accepting the argument that it was no longer needed, Congress in 1869 passed legislation discontinuing most of the bureau's activities, then shut it down completely by 1871.

Southern blacks had entered Reconstruction with amazing amounts of optimism and determination. "The negro of today is not the same as he was six years ago," a reporter for the *New Orleans Tribune* wrote in late 1866. "He has been told of his rights, which have long been robbed." Not only did the newly freed community of Southern blacks now know their rights, but many also had a means to defend them. "As one of the disfranchised race, I would say to every colored soldier, 'Bring your gun home,' " urged a Louisiana activist. The tension between Southern white society, which had seen authority knocked from its grasp by the barrel of a gun, and Southern African-American society, thrust into the power game ill prepared and with only halfhearted support from the North, simmered for only a short time before boiling over into violence. An altercation in Memphis on May 1, 1866, between the city's police (predominantly Irish-American) and a number of recently discharged black soldiers, resulted in a pogrom against the black neighborhoods that left forty-six dead and over a hundred thousand dollars' worth of property destroyed. Less than three months later, the sudden calling of a constitutional convention in New Orleans for the purpose of redrafting the state charter to include black suffrage brought forth opposing demonstrations that quickly escalated into brutal mob violence by whites. Thirty-four African-Americans died, and another 119 were injured. Said a white Union veteran, "I have seen death on the battle field but time will erase the effects of that, the wholesale slaughter and the little regard paid to human life I witnessed here on the 30th of July I shall never forget."

This brutalization of the Southern black population, coupled with the political changes and power realignments occurring on the national level, put an end to any real hope that the Civil War victory might allow African-Americans to enter the mainstream of American society. The question posed by young Lieutenant Edward L. Stevens of Massachusetts, just a few days before his death in one of the last military campaigns of the war, would echo for generations to come: "What is to become of this Race of uneducated, hopeful, anxious people[?]"

* * *

The returning veterans, of course, were quite another story, and the media were almost uniformly hopeful that they would be able to reenter the currents of American society with nary a disturbing ripple to mar the smooth surface. "There is something inexpressly pleasant in the evident satisfaction with which they enter into the delights of domestic life," enthused a writer for the *Philadelphia Public Ledger*. "It is also a fact that they are, as a general rule, more law-abiding than anyone could reasonably expect when the fact of their long experience of camp life is taken into consideration. . . . The American soldier does not lose his personality and become a mere fighting machine when he enters the army. He is still a citizen, with a character to lose and a reputation to master."

The reality was somewhat less rosy. Law-enforcement officials worried that the troublemakers who had been taken off their hands by the military over the past four years were about to come back with a vengeance. Noted one report in the summer of 1865, "On the return of these persons . . . one of two things must happen, — either they will have been reformed in the army, . . . or else they will soon fall again into their old courses. The records of our jails and criminal courts for the last six months will show that the latter has very frequently been the case." Although reliable national figures do not exist, selected statistics reveal that there was a sizable increase in the U.S. prison population in the years 1865–1870, and problems of drug addiction (primarily to morphine and opium), mental illness, and juvenile delinquency spread in the wake of the great demobilization.

Most of the former soldiers, however, returned to the folds of family, friends, and livelihood, anxious to put behind them the memories they could not share with anyone who had not witnessed firsthand the horrors of close-in combat. Walt Whitman expressed something of this attitude when he wrote, "The Four Years War is over, and in the peaceful, strong, exciting, fresh occasions of today, and of the future, that strange sad war is hurrying even now to be forgotten. The camp, the drill, the lines of sentries, the prisons, the hospitals (ah, the hospitals) — all have passed away, all seem now like a dream." Fraternal organizations aimed at veterans could claim few members in this period, while the rare newspapers and periodicals that attempted to cater to that market struggled to survive, and only a handful of wartime reminiscences and unit histories made it into print.

That all began to change dramatically in the 1880s. The mood of the nation had mellowed from the fervent expansionism of the 1870s into a more reflective nationalism, and men who had served in the conflict started to think about what was owed them by a grateful country.

Groups and associations dedicated to caring for the aging population of Civil War veterans began to operate throughout the country. Membership in organizations such as the Grand Army of the Republic and the United Confederate Veterans reached peak levels, and publishers suddenly found there was gold to be had in remembering the conflict. The popular *Century* magazine doubled its circulation the moment it began running a regular series of essays by leading participants in the major military campaigns of the Rebellion. Many of these pieces were later gathered into a four-volume collection that remains in print to this day, *Battles and Leaders of the Civil War.* Billy Yanks refought the war in the pages of periodicals such as the *National Tribune,* or via regular columns in big-city newspapers, such as the *Philadelphia Weekly Times's* "Annals of the War," while Johnny Rebs could turn to the *Confederate Veteran,* the *Southern Historical Society Papers,* or a host of smaller journals. Both regimental histories and military memoirs began to appear on publishers' lists.

The rallying cry for these aging warriors was the effort to win a national pension for those who had served. Many states had already moved to support their veterans with special payments, relief support, and soldiers' homes, but pressure grew on the Federal government to do something as well. Legislation passed in 1890, and enthusiastically signed by President Benjamin Harrison, granted a pension to every honorably discharged soldier who had suffered a disability. With the connivance of administrators who considered old age to be one of those allowable disabilities, the pension roll became a major factor in the national budget, totaling more than a billion dollars in the period 1890–1907.

Remembering the war became a constant theme in the press, thanks in no small measure to the warmhearted spectacles offered by the national organizations in a continuous pageant of encampments, reunions, and battlefield commemorations. In the Northern gatherings the emphasis was always on the priceless contribution the Yankee boys had made in their sacrifices to preserve the United States; as one admiring state governor told those present at an 1879 encampment at Albany, New York, "But for the Union soldiers, there would have been an end to the country." In the Southern conclaves, the precepts of what would become known as the Lost Cause were expounded. The essence of this near-religious faith may have been best expressed by a Georgia soldier writing in September 1865: "Well we Rebs, 'so-called' have been 'overwhelmed,' 'crushed out,' 'subdued,' 'defeated,' or by whatever other name you please to call it except disgraced. In the face of the civilized world the honor of the South stands untarnished and her sons will live in the world's memory as a chivalrous, gallant and brave people."

Perhaps the most poignant occasions were those on which the survivors in blue and gray met on their old fighting grounds to relive past glories and assure an anxious world that once-bitter foes could, in time, clasp hands in friendship. "Once again does this field tremble under the tread of a mighty host," the grizzled veterans of Gettysburg were told at a 1913 commemoration, "not now in fear, but in joy." In one of the more moving scenes played out at the fifty-year Gettysburg observation, the frail and gray-bearded veterans of the Philadelphia Brigade stood on Cemetery Ridge, a hundred feet away from the survivors of George Pickett's doomed division. At the exact hour that the charge had commenced in 1863, the two groups moved together, shook hands, and embraced.

Each year that the former men in arms met to recall the past, they also took stock of those of their former leaders who had passed away.

Ironically, the two principal adversaries in North Carolina in the final weeks of the war were also linked in death. Many honors awaited **William T. Sherman** after the conflict, including service as commander in chief of the U.S. Army under President Grant. After his retirement, in 1884, Sherman was heavily lobbied to make a presidential bid, but he turned down all offers. He died in 1891. Among the honorary pallbearers at his funeral was **Joseph E. Johnston,** whose antagonism toward Jefferson Davis had remained a bitter flame that burned through his military memoir and numerous articles. Johnston had found employment in the transportation, insurance, and communications fields and had even served a term in the House of Representatives. Now, as the old man stood bareheaded in the chilly rain at his post of honor alongside Sherman's coffin, a sympathetic bystander suggested that he at least keep his hat on his head. "If I were in his place and he were standing here in mine," the proud officer replied, "he would not put on his hat." Johnston caught a cold that quickly turned into something worse, and within a month he too was dead.

Dabney Maury, who directed the final Confederate defense of Mobile, helped organize the powerful Southern Historical Society after the war and later served as the U.S. minister to Columbia. He died in 1900. His methodical opponent **E. R. S. Canby** remained in the United States Army and by 1873 was commanding the military forces in the northwest. On April 11, 1873, in the midst of highly charged negotiations with the Modoc tribe in northern California, Canby was brutally murdered by an Indian faction opposed to the talks. **Richard Taylor,** who had traveled to surrender his Department of Alabama, Mississippi, and East Louisiana in a railroad handcar, became an important behind-the-scenes player in the political deal that ended Reconstruction in 1877. Two years later Taylor succumbed to complications from rheumatoid arthritis.

James H. Wilson, whose great cavalry army cut a swath of destruction through Alabama and Georgia, became a prolific writer of histories and biographies notable for their controversial and often unsubstantiated recollections of conversations held at critical points during the war. Wilson saw action in the Spanish-American War and the Boxer Rebellion. He died in 1925, one of the longest-lived of the 583 officers who held full-rank commissions during the Civil War. His fierce adversary **Nathan Bedford Forrest** slowed his pace little in the years after the fighting stopped, though his postconflict career was marred by poor business decisions and further clouded by a brief term of service as Grand Wizard of the Ku Klux Klan. Forrest died in 1877.

Many of the key figures in the Appomattox Campaign remained in the public eye long after the war ended. **Robert E. Lee,** whose surrender of the Army of Northern Virginia marked for many the end of the Civil War, dedicated himself to guiding the South's next generation of leaders by becoming president of a small Virginia college, where he died in 1870. After his death he became *the* enduring Southern symbol of nobility, dignity, and honor. Lee's trusted First Corps commander, **James Longstreet,** threw his fate in with that of the Republican party and staunchly supported U. S. Grant's presidential bid. That stand on the side of Reconstruction, coupled with his blunt outspokenness regarding what he believed had been lapses in command judgment on Lee's part, made him something of a pariah in the former Confederacy. Well into the twentieth century, his image was noticeably absent from the extant memorials throughout the South honoring the military leaders of the Lost Cause. Longstreet died in 1904. **John B. Gordon,** who led the C.S. surrender parade at Appomattox Court House on April 12, enjoyed much success afterward, serving in the U.S. Senate and as Georgia governor. His successful (and much-quoted) memoir, *Reminiscences of the Civil War,* published in 1903, presented a colorful history of the conflict, filled with many incidents that took place only in Gordon's fertile imagination. He too died in 1904.

Of the subsidiary Southern field commanders in the campaign, **George Pickett** lived until 1875, embittered over what he saw as Robert E. Lee's mismanagement of his division at Gettysburg and Five Forks; cavalryman **Fitzhugh Lee** died in 1905, after spending a term in the Virginia governor's house and serving as U.S. consul general in Cuba at the time of the Spanish-American War; **Richard S. Ewell,** the ill-fated commander at Sailor's Creek, became a gentleman farmer and died in 1872.

On the Northern side, the hard-driving **Phil Sheridan** went on to direct many of the military operations against the Plains Indians before ending his public career in the U.S. Army's top post. Sheridan died in 1888. Army of the James commander **E. O. C. Ord** also remained in the service, retiring a major general in 1881. He died in Havana in 1883, a victim of yellow fever. **George G. Meade,** titular head of the Army of the Potomac, continued to perform his duty to the country in the Regular Army. Never a part of Grant's inner circle, Meade was denied the honors he felt he deserved and died brokenhearted in 1872. **Horatio Wright,** the big winner at Sailor's Creek, was another army regular who served his country with distinction in the engineer corps. He died in 1899. **Joshua Chamberlain,** who received the formal surrender of the Army of Northern Virginia on April 12, 1865, left military service soon after the war and went on to enjoy a distinguished public career. He served three terms as Maine's governor, followed by thirteen years as president of Bowdoin College, and was active as a writer and speaker about the war. Chamberlain died in his home state in 1914.

A less sanguine fate awaited the diehard Tennessee Unionist **Daniel Ellis,** whose ambush of a Rebel party had helped usher in the dramatic month of April 1865. Kept busy rounding up Confederate stragglers and Federal deserters in the state until his discharge in September 1865, Ellis was forced to petition Congress for the pay owed him for services rendered in his irregular capacity. As another means of making ends meet for his large family, Ellis memorialized his actions in an 1867 book that he unabashedly titled *Thrilling Adventures of Daniel Ellis.* Too often willing to help others before himself, Ellis lived in virtual poverty until his death, in 1908. Always proud of his service to his country during the war, Ellis named his seventh, and last, child (born in July 1866) U. S. Grant Ellis.

For **U. S. Grant** himself, the postwar years brought the extremes of great success and great failure. Having served as President for two terms (and nearly a third), Grant let his predilection for trusting all the wrong people bankrupt him soon after he left office, and he was forced to surrender many prized war souvenirs as collateral on bad loans. His army pension provided some income, but it was a commitment by publisher Samuel Clemens (who wrote under the name Mark Twain) to issue his personal memoirs that gave the hero, now dying from throat cancer, the purpose to sustain him in the last months of his life. Just days after completing the manuscript, in 1885, Grant died. His book, his final grasp at the golden ring and hope for financial security for his family, was a monumental best-seller.

These thinning ranks presaged the inexorable decline in the once long columns of Civil War veterans. The oldest surviving Confederate general officer, Brigadier General Felix H. Robertson, died in 1928 at age ninety-nine. His opposite number in blue, Major General Adelbert Ames, was ninety-eight when he passed on in 1933. The last surviving common soldiers of the North and South died in 1956 and 1959, respectively.

During its 1869 term, the U.S. Supreme Court took under consideration a property case brought by a "citizen of the United States of color" named Nelson Anderson. Critical to its resolution of the matter was a judicial determination of the legal end of the Civil War.

Anderson was a drayman and cotton sampler in Charleston, South Carolina. In 1863 and 1864 he had invested in forty-eight bales of cotton, which had been seized by Federal authorities in mid-April 1865 and sold at a general auction in New York, with the proceeds going into the U.S. Treasury. Anderson's lawyer contended that the United States owed his client $6,723.36 for property unlawfully taken and sold. Government representatives countered that Anderson's cotton had been legally confiscated, and, besides, he had filed his claim too late, since the Captured and Abandoned Property Act of March 12, 1863, stipulated that all claims had to be submitted within two years after the suppression of the Rebellion. Anderson had entered his case with the U.S. Court of Claims on June 5, 1868.

At that first hearing, depositions had been introduced attesting to Nelson Anderson's loyalty to the United States and to the fact that he had not willingly supported the Confederacy. It soon became clear that the entire matter hinged on fixing the start date for the two-year statute of limitations.

President Andrew Johnson had issued three separate proclamations announcing the end of the Rebellion. The first, on June 15, 1865, dealt with matters in Tennessee; the second, of April 2, 1866, concerned itself with affairs in Georgia, South Carolina, Virginia, North Carolina, Tennessee, Alabama, Louisiana, Arkansas, Mississippi, and Florida. The third, of August 20, 1866, applied to Texas.

The U.S. attorneys argued that the Rebellion had been suppressed following the surrender of the Trans-Mississippi Department, as established in the surrender document negotiated on May 26, 1865. Anderson's lawyer, in turn, argued that the end of the war was a legislative matter, not a military one, and that Congress had previously recognized

President Johnson's August 20 proclamation as the first official declaration that the Civil War had ended everywhere.

The Supreme Court ruled that Nelson Anderson was entitled to recompense by the United States government for his cotton. The court's key determination was that the legal end of the American Civil War had been decided by Congress to be August 20, 1866 — the date of Andrew Johnson's final proclamation on the conclusion of the Rebellion. For legal purposes, at least, the end of the Civil War was a matter of record.

In that document, Andrew Johnson had declared,

> *And I do further proclaim that the said insurrection is at an end, and that peace, order, tranquility and civil authority now exist in and throughout the whole of the United States.*

Chapter Twenty-three

"I die a disgraced soldier"

—◦—

IN AN INTRODUCTION written in 1879 for a collection of articles and memoirs about the Civil War authored by some its leading participants, publisher Alexander K. McClure observed:

> The fierce passions which attend civil war are unequaled in any conflicts between separate peoples, and the advanced intelligence, the community of interest, the common pride of past achievements, and the long maintained brotherhood through generations, all intensified the bitterness of our internecine strife. A war so gigantic, enduring for four long years, so costly in blood and treasure, and reaching almost every household with its sore bereavements, could not but inflame the bitterest passions and resentments, obliterate recollection of virtue in each other's foes, and direct all the agencies of power to color the causes and events of the war to harmonize with the prejudices which ruled North and South.
>
> It was to correct as far as possible the pages of the future history of the war of the late rebellion, that the contributions herein given were solicited, and they have all been written with the view of attaining that purpose. . . . That they are entirely free from prejudice or from the coloring that all must accept in describing momentous events with which they were interwoven by every inspiration of devotion and am-

bition, is not to be pretended; but that they are written in integrity of purpose, and that they give the substance of the truth, can be justly claimed for them.

The search for that "substance of the truth" informed a great deal of the writing that appeared in the decades following the end of the war. While many common soldiers were delighted by the chance to refight the old battles within the pages of a newspaper or journal, for others the argument had far more serious implications. Careers were at stake as prominent military and political leaders on both sides fought to clear their names — and perhaps more important, their reputations — of any imputations regarding their conduct during the conflict.

The Southern side became a literary battlefield as memoirs written by certain individuals to "correct" the historical record were countered by different sets of recollections from other individuals, who felt slighted by statements that had been made by the first group and were equally anxious to see that their "substance of the truth" should see the light of day.

One of the bitterest of these exchanges involved Joseph E. Johnston and Jefferson Davis. Utterly convinced that his war record had been undermined by the C.S. President, Johnston published his memoirs in 1874 to present his side of the matter. "Johnston has [shown] more effectively than another could . . . his selfishness and his malignity," Davis wrote to his wife after reading his former general's book. When Davis completed his own account of the war, which was published in 1881, he took the high road and allowed himself only the most nonspecific and dignified rebuttal of Johnston's charges. Angered by his foe's refusal to either capitulate or engage in literary combat, Johnston permitted his emotions to override his judgment, going so far as to suggest to one reporter that Davis knew more than he was saying about the fate of the Confederate Treasury in the final weeks of the war. It was a sad coda to a military career that, while not without blemish, was more distinguished than many.

To the victors belonged the larger arena of official investigations and public hearings. While the Confederates would be forever limited to trading ink broadsides, Federal officers who believed that their careers had been unjustly scarred during the war had the chance at least to clear their names by officially reopening their cases. Most of these examinations took place within the military family and were quietly settled, but two became headline news.

The first involved Major General Fitz John Porter, who had been dismissed from the army on January 1, 1863, for disobeying orders during the fighting at Second Bull Run. Porter's hearing, which began in 1879 and was widely reported in the press, resulted in his complete exoneration. But for all its spectacle and drama, Porter's court of inquiry was completely eclipsed less than a year later by the official examination of the circumstances surrounding Philip Sheridan's removal of Gouverneur K. Warren from command of the Fifth Corps at the end of the battle of Five Forks, on April 1, 1865.

Warren's life after this incident was a tireless crusade for vindication. He spent the closing months of the war reassigned to rear-echelon districts, then remained in the Regular Army after the conflict, serving as the engineer in charge of several important bridge constructions and navigational improvement projects. All the while, he continued to press for a hearing on his removal. As long as U. S. Grant remained in charge of the army, however, there would be no sympathetic response to Warren's request; and when Grant at last left the army, it was to become President of the United States, so Warren's petition was delayed for eight more years as his former chief enjoyed two terms in office. The only solace for the former Fifth Corps commander lay in the knowledge that the scandals dogging the Grant administration proved that his own case was indeed just.

Grant's immediate successor, Rutherford B. Hayes, was a bonafide Civil War hero and something of a quiet reformer. Warren bided his time until near the end of Hayes's four-year term before meeting with him, on November 21, 1879. Of Warren's three main antagonists, Sherman was still Chief of the Army, and Sheridan had by now won new laurels as an Indian fighter, but Grant was no longer a factor. Hayes agreed to Warren's request.

The Court of Inquiry convened in New York on January 7, 1880. Warren, then acting in his own defense, was described by a reporter who was present as a "dark-complexioned, medium-sized officer, with thin mustache, and eye-glasses, [who] sat at a table a few feet away [from the three judging officers], buried in manuscripts and maps relating to his case." The proceeding opened with the court stenographer's reading into the record Phil Sheridan's official report of the battle of Five Forks. In it the officer gave three principal reasons for his having relieved Warren of his command: first, Warren had failed to move promptly on the night of March 31 from the White Oak Road to Dinwiddie Court House; second, he had been unnecessarily slow in positioning his troops for the April 1 flank assault at Five Forks; and third, he had not exercised effective command control during the attack itself. Included among the report's seemingly matter-of-fact recital of events were several damning asides.

Perhaps the most often quoted recalled Sheridan's anxiety at the slowness of the Fifth Corps in coming into position on April 1. "In this connection," Sheridan had written, "I will say that General Warren did not exert himself to get up his corps as rapidly as he might have done, and his manner gave me the impression that he wished the sun to go down before dispositions for the attack could be completed."

The president of the court was Major General Winfield S. Hancock, who had served alongside Warren at Gettysburg and led a companion corps in the Overland and Petersburg campaigns. The two other general officers, though both war veterans, were decidedly lesser lights than the popular Hancock, who, it was widely rumored, might soon be a presidential candidate. After Sheridan's report was read, Hancock turned to Warren and said, with a touch of dry humor, *"Well, General, have you got anything to say to that? If you have say it."**

Warren, determined to face the man whose action had ruined his life, told the court that he believed Sheridan's real reasons for removing him from command had nothing to do with those set forth in the report. "I therefore wish to have General Sheridan appear, to make out a complete case against me," he demanded.

Hancock was skeptical. *"But General Sheridan is about a three months' sick leave,"* he said, *"and that leave cannot be curtailed. For the matter of that, what certainty have you that he will get back anyhow. Suppose he should die?"*

"I should be very sorry indeed," Warren responded, to general laughter throughout the room.

"Must you have him?" Hancock pressed.

"I do not feel able to make any further statement of the case until he is here," insisted Warren.

After some deliberation, the court agreed to Warren's request. The battle of Five Forks was to be fought over again, and this time the whole world would be watching.

May 4–11, 1880

Sheridan

Phil Sheridan was the sharp tip of the sword. If Grant was the mind that directed the weapon, and Sherman the steadfast blade and handle, then

---

* I have relied on contemporary newspaper reports for much of the dialogue in the trial, a great deal of which was omitted from the "sanitized" official transcript. Quotations taken from newspapers appear in italics in the text.

Sheridan was the point that actually rent the flesh. It was a role for which he was well suited, for there were few actors in the Civil War who could match his ruthless sense of purpose and cold-blooded determination to finish a campaign — not merely with a victory but with the annihilation of the enemy. In the heat of combat he was, one admiring soldier wrote, the "very impersonation of action." Every instinct, every thought, every feeling was totally subordinate to winning. Officers whose performance fell below his expectations would quickly know the taste of disgrace and forever suffer Sheridan's unrelenting wrath. His memory was long, and his contempt for those who had failed him in a moment of crisis was deep and abiding. Phil Sheridan knew how to hate, and he knew how to punish.

Yet for all his dynamism in the field, Sheridan had become a strident voice against change in the postwar years. Asked to support the overhaul of an antiquated system of staff bureaus, Sheridan had refused, with the comment, "It answered well during the war, and we ought to be contented with it in time of peace." He had little interest in facing the serious social issues raised by the conflict. "I never yet have heard a single address by any one in this army society that I thought embodied what the society most wanted to hear," he told a gathering of veterans in 1878. "They all want to talk about the cause which led to the war, and about emancipation, and all such things. We do not care about hearing that. It is all over. The problem is worked out."

Sheridan also felt strongly that army problems were the army's business. He had a sneering distaste for officers who relied on public forums to reclaim reputations that had been lost on the field of battle. He came to Governor's Island without an ounce of pity or remorse, determined that the passage of so many years would not lessen in the slightest the iron strength of purpose that had guided him when he relieved Warren of command on April 1, 1865. To aid him and serve as his surrogate throughout the hearings, Sheridan had engaged the services of a successful and nationally known trial lawyer, Asa Bird Gardner.

Gouverneur Warren had also come to the reconvened hearings with reinforcements. From this point forward his case would be argued by Albert Stickney, a Harvard man who had served as a staff officer during the war and had since enjoyed a successful New York practice. A friend of Warren's who had felt out Stickney beforehand had reported back that the lawyer was "greatly interested and thoroughly in earnest. . . . In short, you will find him the man you need, and in that kind of fight, brains and disciplined profound knowledge tell as much as in your proposition."

Sheridan took his place in the trial room on May 4, 1880, to the fading echoes of a fifteen-gun salute in his honor. His first day of testimony was largely taken up with the reading into the record of an extensive written statement he had prepared, in which he reviewed the actions and his decisions of March 31 and April 1, 1865. According to Sheridan's account, Grant, anxious to press Lee hard lest he slip away from Petersburg and link up with Johnston's army, had ordered him to make a wide flanking swing with his nine-thousand-man cavalry corps. Sheridan's attempt to cut the vital South Side Railroad had been blocked on March 31 by a mixed cavalry-infantry force of the enemy that battled him to a standstill at Dinwiddie Court House. Sheridan had asked for help and been informed by Grant that Warren's Fifth Corps would arrive at midnight. Specific mention was made in Sheridan's statement of Warren's failure to move promptly to his assistance as ordered on the night of March 31, instead delaying while a small bridge was rebuilt to allow the Fifth Corps to pass over Gravelly Run. Declared Sheridan, *"According to the orders of Grant and Meade I felt that there were no circumstances in existence during the night that should have prevented the movement of Warren's two divisions in obedience to orders, and not enough to justify the delay at the bridge by the other division, as the creek could have been forded."*

Sheridan's statement next addressed the attack on the Confederate position at Five Forks. His plans had called for all three infantry divisions to strike the small angle made when the enemy troops refused, or bent back, their left flank; but in the attack as executed by Warren, only one division had actually struck that point, while the other two had marched past the flank and come in well behind the main enemy line stretched along White Oak Road. *"I wish to direct the attention of the court to the fact that the place called Five Forks was not the essential point of this battle; but that the angle made by the enemy refusing his left flank was the essential and objective point,"* Sheridan insisted.

Immediately after the victory was gained at Five Forks, Sheridan maintained, he had faced a whole new set of problems, ranging from a possible enemy counterattack to the need to organize a bold, aggressive pursuit should the enemy retreat. A reporter from the *New York Evening Post* wrote, "In conclusion General Sheridan said: *'General Warren having disappointed me in the movements of his corps and in its management during the battle, in the new emergency that had arisen, and by the new phase that had been given our situation about Richmond by the battle just won, I felt he was not the man to rely on.'* "

Sheridan was now questioned by Warren's attorney, Stickney, who pressed the general hard regarding how much time it should have taken to move fifteen thousand men from the easternmost portion of the White Oak Road to Dinwiddie Court House. In response to one of Stickney's queries, Sheridan allowed that it would have taken a mounted staff officer perhaps fifty minutes to cover the distance. Warren's counsel then slowly pieced together a puzzle of dispatches to demonstrate that the Fifth Corps commander could not have received the instructions to send help to Sheridan until 10:15 P.M. at the earliest. It would have been only after that point that orders could be issued to get the three divisions into marching formation and to move them out along the muddy Boydton Plank Road — and all of this at night.

"Is it your judgment as a soldier that there was any human possibility of General Warren or any of his forces getting down to Dinwiddie Court House before twelve o'clock at night — inside of an hour and three quarters?" Stickney asked. When Sheridan tried to evade a direct answer, Stickney cut him off and drove home the question again. Now Sheridan was angry. He insisted that troops could have been marched that distance (between four and six miles) at a fast enough pace to arrive in time.

"I have marched at the rate of nearly five miles an hour," he said to close off this line of questioning, adding that the same pace had been maintained over a twelve-hour period. "Sixty miles in twelve hours?" Stickney injected incredulously. "Yes," Sheridan answered.

Soon after this, the court adjourned for the day.

The main points of attack and the mood of those involved on the second day of Sheridan's testimony were cogently described by the *New York Herald*'s man on the scene, who wrote, "The counsel endeavored to show by General Sheridan's own admissions that General Warren's orders from Meade were different from what he (Sheridan) supposed they were at the time, and that having these orders, Warren was justified in obeying them rather than realizing the expectation of General Sheridan, who was not in command of him at the time Meade gave him his orders about advancing to Dinwiddie Court House. Mr. Stickney was very polite, self-possessed and persistent; but when General Sheridan began to see the drift of his efforts he grew exceedingly cautious and answered in so non-committal a way that the spectators were forced to smile."

Reported the *New York Herald*'s correspondent of day three, "The proceedings of the Warren-Sheridan inquiry were as lively as a horse radish dinner . . . , and more than once the spectators and counsel found themselves laughing at the way in which General Sheridan converted the

English language into sugar pointed projectiles and hurled them at his adversaries when closely pressed." The representative from the *New York Times* kept a close watch on Warren, who, he noted, "seldom prompts his counsel, or interposes in any way. . . . He sits motionless and silent, without the slightest symptom of interest save an occasional flash of his deep-set, dark eyes."

The events of April 1, 1865, now took center stage. Warren's coolly calculated behavior that day had seemed anything but reassuring to Sheridan, who had "despaired" of having to fight alongside him. Sheridan's military purpose in bringing on the engagement had been a simple determination to *"hit a head wherever I could see one."*

Sheridan's plan to strike the Confederate left flank at Five Forks with Warren's infantry had seemed to go awry from the outset, when two of the three divisions (Crawford's, followed by Griffin's) broke contact with the third (Ayres's). Matters had only gotten worse when that last division fell into a panic upon coming into contact with the enemy, requiring Sheridan to exercise some personal leadership to calm the men. *"I think I sent for Warren several times while the confusion was at its highest,"* Sheridan stated, *"but he had gone to some other quarter of the field. . . ."*

"Have you any actual knowledge what Warren was doing at the time?" Albert Stickney asked.

"No," Sheridan replied, *"but I know where he ought to have been, and it seems to me that if my troops had been in that condition, I should have been on the ground trying to rally them, and to remedy the difficulty."*

On this hard note, the third day of Sheridan's testimony closed.

May 7 proved to be a housecleaning session, with many pages of previous transcript being reviewed and revised for publication. When the court reconvened on May 10, Stickney concentrated on clarifying Sheridan's limited perceptions of what had really taken place during the battle of Five Forks. Right away Sheridan proclaimed that in his opinion, most of the Fifth Corps had had little to do with the victory. "Ayres's division . . . and the cavalry, I think, won the battle," he asserted. "The others didn't get in in time. . . ." Stickney now sought to demonstrate that Sheridan's decision to relieve Warren had been based upon his complete ignorance of the valuable services that the infantry officer had actually performed during the battle.

"So far as I now understand you had no knowledge as to what General Warren did do in this battle after you parted with him in the beginning of the attack?" Stickney inquired.

"No, I had no knowledge," came the reply. Stickney now poured it on.

"You did not learn what General Warren had done with Griffin's, Ayres' or Crawford's divisions?"

"No."

"Did you know at the time that he went himself and sent members of his staff after Crawford's division to bring them back in the rear of the enemy's works?"

"No, I didn't know anything about it."

"Did you learn at any time during the progress of the engagement that it was General Warren who ordered General Griffin to change direction and to make an advance down the Ford Road in the rear of the works?"

"No, sir."

"Did you learn at any time during the engagement that when the last line of defense of the Confederates was taken it was General Warren who led the advance of our troops to the assault, about half a mile west of the Ford road?"

"No, I don't know anything about that."

"If you had known this would it have made any difference in your report . . . ?"

"No, sir, it would not; let me make an explanation. It will be seen that if the enemy was in front of Warren it would have been wrong for him to go on. If he had kept on at the right of Ayres and attacked the enemy that he was fighting all day, in the rear, it would have ended the battle much sooner. If Ayres had been defeated he would have been up a tree, in fact there would not have been trees enough up there for him."

After Stickney sat down, Sheridan's counsel, Asa Bird Gardner, rose and carefully led the general once more through the key points of his case against Warren. The court adjourned at 2:20 P.M. (A friend of Warren's who was following the inquiry closely wrote to the embattled officer that the tables had been turned, and that it was "Sheridan on trial now, instead of Warren. It was his business to know what was going on. . . .")

A final day of testimony remained, but there was little new ground to cover in this session, which began at 11:00 A.M. and ended at 2:55 P.M. The last question came from the president of the court, General Hancock.

"Do you think you would have removed General Warren at the time you did if permission to do so had not been sent to you from General Grant?"

Answered Sheridan, *"I would not have had the authority to do so. I could not have done it."*

◄○►

May 12–27, 1880

Warren's Case Begins

A stream of less exalted witnesses — twenty-four of them in all — passed before the court over the next ten days of hearings, as Warren's counsel crafted his defense. Aides to Sheridan and Warren, along with officers who had commanded troops under them at Five Forks, came forward to describe what they had seen. The weather made it hard going in the hearing room, with temperatures at times well into the nineties.

Sheridan's men presented a generally unflattering portrait of the Fifth Corps commander. Frederick C. Newhall, in 1865 an assistant adjutant general, had thought Warren passive and indifferent at the start of the battle. Cavalry Chief of Staff James W. Forsyth (who spoke in "cold, brief and reluctant sentences") admitted that Sheridan had been impatient but denied that he had acted out of anger in making any of his decisions. The mood changed abruptly when aide-de-camp George A. Forsyth took the witness chair. He had, said a reporter, a "picturesque way of narrating incidents" that "made the spectators laugh in spite of the military surroundings." The aide testified that in carrying messages between Sheridan and Warren after dark on March 31, he had had no difficulty at all in crossing Gravelly Run on horseback. Phil Sheridan's brother and wartime aide, Michael, attested to the panic that had gripped Ayres's troops once the attack began. He recalled how the Fifth Corps skirmishers had "commenced shooting in the air, and all lay down."

In sharp contrast, the infantry officers and staff of the Fifth Corps were nearly of one voice regarding the difficulties of the night march, the severity of the fighting at points other than the angle that Sheridan had declared so critical, and the importance of Warren's leadership on those other portions of the field. The court heard from Major W. H. H. Benyuard, who had investigated the condition of Gravelly Run after dark on March 31 and found it impassible for infantry. Romeyn B. Ayres, whose division had struck and captured the angle, was emphatic about the problems encountered on the march from the White Oak Road line to Dinwiddie Court House. *"It was the most difficult country to move in,"* he declared. *"In fact you could not find anything rougher in the world."* He also denied that there had been any serious panic in his ranks at the start of the attack. "There was no trouble," he maintained.

407

Joshua L. Chamberlain, a brigade commander in Griffin's division at Five Forks, contradicted Sheridan's claim that the battle had been won when the angle was taken. He recounted seeing and hearing Sheridan after Ayres's men had taken that objective, yelling at a follow-up brigade to *"go back and fight the enemy. It's the South Side Railroad we want."*

Walter T. Chester, a captain in a New York regiment during the engagement, testified in great detail about actions late in the fight, in a voice that one reporter likened to that of Mark Twain. Asked by Asa Gardner why his recollections were so vivid, Chester responded, *"The reason of that is very simple. I saw the rebels running away as fast as their legs could carry them, and that was such an unusual thing that it made an impression upon me."* When Warren's aide Frederick Locke repeated the harsh words Sheridan had used in relieving the Fifth Corps general of his command, "the ladies looked at each other as startled as if one of the trees near the window had been struck by lightning," a reporter observed.

Toward the end of this phase of the testimony, Albert Stickney dropped something of a bombshell when he submitted a list of future witnesses to be called, including Fitzhugh Lee, Thomas T. Munford, and others. At this point, noted the *Herald*'s scribe, "Major Gardner wanted to know if those names did not represent men who were in the rebel service at Five Forks. [Court] Recorder Langdon said they sounded familiar, and the spectators smiled. Major Gardner inquired if it would be in good taste to ask ex-Confederates to testify in a little Northern family quarrel." The court disagreed with Sheridan's attorney and issued the necessary summonses.

—◦—

May 28–June 30, 1880

The Rebels

Even though the former C.S. soldiers represented just twelve of the thirty witnesses called during this period, they received the lion's share of the attention from the press. Nearly every one of them was carefully and fully described, as if Northern readers were presumed to be keen to know small personal details about these men from the South. Montgomery D. Corse, one of George Pickett's brigadiers, led off the Confederate parade. The *New York Evening Telegram* took pains to assure its public that Corse was "not a very formidable looking personage, being a kindly looking gentleman of medium size, slightly bald, and wearing spectacles." His statements suggested that the appearance of Federal infantry in the rear of the Confederate position had had a decisive effect on the outcome of the battle. At one point in his testimony, Corse leaned against an unsecured rack of guns and was cautioned by General Hancock to be careful. *"I don't reckon they will hurt me now,"* Corse replied, to general laughter.

Cavalryman Thomas T. Munford (whose "fine, dark features, black mustache and gray hair which stood straight up made him look like a Spanish count") had commanded the men who opposed Ayres's advance. He reported that the Federal line had *"staggered a little"* under his fire, but then *"recovered instantly, and executed the movement to the left in good order."* Fitzhugh Lee ("a sturdy looking man of about medium height and robust form"), though in overall command of the cavalry, admitted that he had seen little of the fighting as he was *"with General Rosser north of Hatcher's Run"* when the battle began. Another of Pickett's brigadiers, Joseph Mayo, downplayed the significance of the cavalry's attack along the front of the Five Forks line as the infantry was flanking the left. *"Oh, no, it was not the cavalry, but the infantry that we were afraid of,"* he stated.

Numerous Federal participants also spoke at this time. Commissary officer D. L. Smith described the last-ditch line that had been formed by the enemy near the Gilliam field, quite some time after the "critical" angle was taken. Especially eagerly anticipated was the testimony of Samuel W. Crawford, whose division was the one that had veered off course, breaking its connection with Ayres's men and leading the reserve division (Griffin's) astray. Crawford was uncomfortable in the public spotlight. "He was somewhat nervous, and his statement and replies were given in so low a tone that they scarcely reached the spectators or the reporters," noted the *Herald*'s account. Crawford took pains to explain that even though his orders had not specifically directed him to maintain a connection with the right of Ayres's division, he had fully understood that to be the spirit of his instructions. In response to a question from the court asking why, then, he had broken that connection, Crawford answered, "Because the enemy were firing, I could not move by the flank to do it. . . ."

There was a minor flap on the last day of June, when Sheridan sent in a request to change the portion of the transcript in which he testified that he had marched an infantry force sixty miles in twelve hours. According to the *New York Evening Sun*'s reporter, "Upon reading his own statement in the proof sheets, General Sheridan concluded to modify it, and asked to be allowed to do so, on the ground that it was made inadvertently. Mr. Stickney said that General Sheridan . . . had most pertinaciously clung to it when pressed. . . . The court ruled that the evidence could not be changed, but said that General Sheridan might insert an explanation he wished to make. On the proof sheets General Sheridan had changed his statement to one that he had marched infantry at a rate of five miles an hour for a short time."

Perhaps the most intriguing news to reach the spectators and reporters had little to do with the testimony being given. The stirrings began on June 8, when the stolid routine of the proceedings was "broken by General Hancock's uniformed messengers bringing in despatches from New York, giving the latest returns from the Chicago Convention." The Republicans had been scrapping over the choice of a presidential nominee, with the largest number of first-round ballots (304) going to U. S. Grant, who fell just 66 votes short of taking up the standard for an unparalleled third term. Grant's support faded fast, however, and after a few days of deadlocked balloting the convention selected James A. Garfield of Ohio. There was a reason for Hancock's interest in these results: just a few days later, he would be selected on the second round of balloting to be the Democratic candidate for U.S. President.

Empty seats in the court became a rare sight as "large numbers of visitors" flocked to Governor's Island to "fix their admiring eyes on the handsome president of the Court." Then, at the conclusion of the June 28 session, Hancock announced, according to a correspondent, that "he had already sent a communication to the War Department asking to be relieved from duty as President of the Warren Court of Inquiry." The next day he turned to the counsels for their opinions on his request. Asa Bird Gardner "was sure that his client would prefer that General Hancock . . . remain," and Albert Stickney said he "hoped that the General would withdraw the application." Hancock himself admitted to being of two minds on the matter. On the one hand, the national attention he was now receiving had created an embarrassing situation, inasmuch "as important personages were continually visiting him," but on the other hand, he recognized that should he withdraw, there could be no replacement "because the person who came could only hear the testimony read, and it is also necessary for members of a court to observe the demeanor of the witnesses on the stand. . . ."

In the end, the national campaign could not be ignored. When the court convened on the last day of June, Hancock was no longer in his usual place. His request to step down had been approved by the War Department. Brigadier General Christopher Columbus Augur, who had commanded the Fifth Corps early in the war, now became president.

———◄○►———

July 1–5, 1880

Warren

As he rose to testify on his own behalf, Gouverneur K. Warren was heartened by the generally positive reaction the press had expressed toward the inquiry. "As one officer after another . . . has related his recollections of that day, . . . it has become more and more plain not only that Warren's command won the battle . . . but that Sheridan really knew very little about the fight . . . ," observed the *Philadelphia Times.* A writer for the *Council Bluffs* (Iowa) *Bugle* declared that "Phil Sheridan is not a little god," and the *Brooklyn Eagle* was confident that the court would vindicate Warren and "place him before the American people in a just and true light."

Warren was under great pressure, and it showed. "He was flurried and nervous, though his wonderful self-control enabled him to maintain an appearance of composure," the reporter for the *New York Times* wrote. Regarding his actions on the night of March 31, Warren pointed out that the contradictory nature of the dispatches he received from both Meade and Sheridan had made it difficult for him to determine the right course of action. *"I was in such great doubt as to the meaning of the despatches, as they came to me in a disjointed form and so separated that I could not tell exactly which one to obey,"* he declared. (When Sheridan's counsel objected to this statement, Warren's man replied, *"I hope my friend will not worry himself needlessly. There will be no applications from our side to amend testimony about moving troops sixty miles a day."*)

Warren also defended his actions in bringing the troops into attack position at Five Forks: *"I know nothing that I could have done to hasten the formation; I cannot imagine what ground General Sheridan could have had for saying that I seemed to want the sun to go down before the troops formed."*

As to the failure of his divisions to move on April 1 in strict accordance with Sheridan's plan, Warren put the blame on the faulty intelligence supplied by the cavalry officer, which had placed the enemy flank fully twelve hundred yards east of where it actually was. When Crawford's troops failed to find the enemy *where they were supposed to be, and having a skirmishing fire in front, it was natural that the troops should push toward that field* [i.e., straight ahead], *thinking that the line of battle would be there. . . ."* He also criticized Sheridan for sending so

411

many aides to redirect the "lost" infantry units. Their appearing with orders, even as Warren's own aides were arriving with different instructions, had only compounded the confusion.

The cross-examination by Sheridan's counsel was "occasionally very severe," remarked one reporter. Said another, "At one point, Mr. Gardner said to General Warren: *'There has never been any doubt that General Warren was as brave and courageous an officer as our service had. General Sheridan never questioned the fact.'* General Warren replied with some warmth of manner: *'General Sheridan seemed to question it after the battle of Five Forks.'* "

Warren's testimony concluded his presentation of evidence. Before Sheridan's counsel began to examine his witnesses, it was decided that the court would adjourn for an extended period to allow Sheridan to travel away from the East Coast on army business, and to give the government printer time to have the transcript prepared. As one newswriter observed about this time, "It takes much longer to fight the battle of Five Forks in New York, than it did down South, but then reputations, not lives, are at stake now. A vast difference indeed."

October 1–22, 1880

Sheridan's Side

A total of thirty-three witnesses appeared before the court of inquiry (now relocated to the Army Building in Manhattan) during the next fifteen days of investigation. The nation had never seen anything like it before. "More distinguished officers are either directly or indirectly interested in it than in any previous military court in the history of the country," stated a writer for the *New York Telegram.*

Sheridan's counsel, Gardner, carefully rebuttressed the key portions of his case. Henry E. Alvord, in 1865 a captain in the 2nd Massachusetts Cavalry, testified that during its attack, Ayres's division had been in "quite a confusion." Other cavalrymen spoke of the severity of the fighting on their fronts. Vanderbilt Allen, then serving on Sheridan's staff, had seen the Fifth Corps commander during the engagement and been struck by his seeming detachment. *"It did not seem to me that General Warren displayed any such energy as he ought to have displayed under the circumstances. He appeared to be entirely indifferent,"* he recalled. Wesley Merritt, who had led one of Sheridan's divisions, offered the opinion that if Crawford and Griffin had been repulsed in their unauthorized flank march, the battle might well have been lost. When witness Francis T. Sherman (the inspector general of the cavalry at the time of the battle) tried to characterize Warren's demeanor as having been "earnestly impassive," he and Albert Stickney engaged in some sharp, if fruitless, exchanges to clarify what he meant.

Some points were hit home time and again, especially the matter of Ayres's division's panicking at the beginning of the attack. The sheer repetitive weight of Gardner's point-making began to wear everyone down somewhat, but an electric current of excitement surged through the room on October 22, when it was revealed that the next day's witness would be none other than U. S. Grant.

---◄○►---

October 23, 1880

Grant

Ulysses Simpson Grant came to the court of inquiry determined to do all he could to preserve Sheridan's reputation. Less than a year earlier, while on a celebrated world tour, Grant had boasted to German Chancellor Bismarck that Sheridan was as great a general as had ever lived.

There were handshakes all around when Grant entered the hearing room shortly after 10:00 A.M. Normally the session got under way at 11:00 A.M.; today's earlier starting time had been specially arranged to accommodate the former President, who had asked to be released by noon if possible.

Much of what Grant said was of no help to either side; as one newspaper reported with a touch of sarcasm, Grant "was invited to take the witness chair, and holding up his right hand, affirmed I DON'T RE-MEMBER." In one key exchange, however, Gardner asked Grant why he had provided Sheridan with discretionary orders to relieve Warren.

"I knew of his previous conduct," Grant answered. *"I was apprehensive that he might fail General Sheridan at the critical moment."*

Here Albert Stickney objected that Grant had exceeded the bounds of the case, since all testimony was to be limited to matters pertinent to actions that had taken place on March 31 and April 1, 1865. There ensued a legal wrangle that ended only when Grant volunteered that he had not acted upon information regarding Warren's behavior on those two days, but had instead based his actions on his previous experience with him.

"And none will be more willing, probably, to own that his opinion may have been erroneous in this instance, than General Grant himself," ventured Stickney.

"Well, no," Grant responded, in a tone that was described as quiet and unhesitating. *"I don't think I will admit that. I have probably made many mistakes in the course of my life; but I don't think I was mistaken in my judgment of General Warren."*

Under further questioning, Grant expanded on this statement: *"I wanted orders promptly obeyed, and generally had them; where officers undertook to think for themselves and consider that the officer who had issued the order did not understand the circumstances and had not considered the work to be done it tended to failure and delay."*

"And that you did not like?" Stickney asked.

"And that I did not like," Grant replied. *"And that kind of conduct led to the removal of one officer."*

Even as Stickney rose to object to the last part of this answer, Grant anticipated him. *"Leave it out,"* he said. The court agreed, and Grant's added comment was removed from the official record.

"Soon after," wrote the correspondent for the *New York Star*, "the General was released from the witness chair, and at once hurried from the room, as if glad to escape from the questioning to which he had been subjected."

———◦———

October 25–November 27, 1880

Winding Up

Although a few new voices would be added, the thirteen days of hearings that followed Grant's testimony were to be devoted largely to concluding statements from the principals and to the recalling of witnesses who had already testified for points of clarification. On October 26 Sheridan's final thoughts were admitted to the record in the form of a long written statement that was read aloud by Asa Gardner. *"The removal of General Warren was done in the midst of circumstances of great urgency and stress,"* the document concluded. *"[There] was no room in my action toward General Warren for anything but a consideration of the perilous situation of my command and of the best interests of the service."*

Warren's last turn came on November 19 and 20. "He wore an anxious look and spent some time in consultation with Mr. Stickney, and then with an air of earnestness that intensified the resolution that usually marks his countenance he seated himself as a witness," wrote a reporter. One final time, Warren talked his way through the events of March 31 and April 1, 1865, which had so changed his life. Toward the end of the

414

period assigned for questioning, Albert Stickney asked Warren if he believed he had made every effort in his power to carry out Sheridan's orders. Asa Gardner promptly objected, saying that it was Warren's actions, not his intentions, that were on trial. Warren huddled for a moment with Stickney and then faced the court.

"I am willing to have that question withdrawn," he said. *"I am willing to stand by my deeds."*

On November 22 the court adjourned to allow the opposing counsels time to prepare their final statements, and to permit the second half of the trial transcript to be printed.

Editors across the nation used the last days of the hearing as an opportunity to wax philosophic about the meaning of it all. "This inquiry will clear up nothing," a writer for the *Washington Post* declared. "It will not even contribute a valuable fact to history. It only makes confusion worse confounded." The editors of the *New York Herald,* after itemizing the staff hours, court time, and witness travel costs of the eighty days of testimony, marveled, "This to vindicate the honor of two soldiers who served the Republic. Who shall again say that republics are ungrateful?" In a less public venue, a Michigan cavalryman named James R. Hutton proved that not all of the old troopers supported their wartime leader. "May you make Sheridan take back tracks as you did the Rebs," Hutton wrote to Warren in a personal letter.

◄◊►

July 21–30, 1881

Final Arguments

Only a handful of the faithful were present when Albert Stickney began his summation. He held the floor for more than two days, drawing freely from the mountain of testimony and evidence to refute each of the specific charges against Warren. His disgust at Sheridan's refusal to take the time to examine all the facts before removing Warren was apparent as he sarcastically paraphrased the cavalryman's position: "Although I was in command of the United States forces ... on that day, I saw only the attack of General Ayres ... ; I know nothing of Griffin's movements; I know nothing of Crawford's movements; ... I do not know anything of what the commander of the Fifth Corps did during the operations of that day; and I cannot give any account of my own personal movements after Ayres's assault. Yet I have had the glory of that day for sixteen years. And I still claim it!" In wrapping up, Stickney said, "For an assassin who takes human life the whole civilized world has the deepest condemnation. For a man who kills reputations, they have the most thorough contempt; and the Constitution of the United States and the Articles of War give to a soldier whose reputation is assailed a proper and sufficient protection. It would be a sad day for the United States Army, if it should ever come, when a soldier's reputation could not have this full and sufficient safeguard. . . ."

Sheridan's counsel, Asa Gardner, began his closing statement by questioning the propriety and validity of hearings held sixteen years after the event, regarding decisions made on a "contested field of battle." He nevertheless went on to consider each point in turn and to marshal all the testimony and evidence on Sheridan's behalf. Although he professed to have no personal animosity toward Warren, Gardner seemed to find Sheridan's scornful attitude infectious. "In those closing days of the great drama around Petersburg and Richmond," Gardner said of Warren, "he seems either to have been bewildered and incapable of sound judgment, or else had an overweening opinion of his own military abilities and a proportionate undervaluation of those senior to himself with whom he was called upon to serve, which made him fail to give efficient support in an emergency." In closing, Gardner expressed the belief that if General Sheridan were to be faced once again with "precisely the same circumstances as presented to him at sunset of the 1st of April, 1865, he would do precisely what he did then."

Endings

Days, then weeks, then months passed without comment from the War Department. In December 1881 Warren confided to Stickney that while he would be pleased if the court vindicated him fully, "I have never been very sanguine that they would do it after Hancock withdrew." A few months later he was putting the best face on things: "I think Grant & Sheridan would have had it published sooner if it would do them any good, for I presume they know what the verdict is already," he wrote.

Sheridan's friends, meanwhile, were rallying to their man's side. Senator John A. Logan, who had commanded a corps under Sherman, promised to do everything in his power to end "this outrageous practice of organizing unauthorized and illegal pretended 'courts' for the purpose of plastering up the reputation of some who could not gain an enviable reputation by their own course of conduct during the war." Sheridan launched his own public-relations campaign by having copies of Asa Gardner's final argument printed and sent to veterans' organizations, libraries, historical societies, and important people (including Bismarck).

For a while Warren toyed with the idea of making a personal appeal to either General of the Army Sherman or President Arthur, but in the end he decided to wait a bit longer. Then, on the last day of July 1882, he fell gravely ill. A physician diagnosed acute liver failure brought on by a diabetic condition, and held out little hope. "I die a disgraced soldier," Warren told his wife shortly before he passed away, at six o'clock in the evening on August 8, 1882.

Eight days later Albert Stickney wrote to President Arthur on behalf of Warren's family, requesting that the court's findings be published. This was finally done on November 21, 1882. The two presiding officers had walked a fine line. Of the three reasons for removing Warren presented by Sheridan in his after-action report, the officers found, in the first instance, that it was not practicable for the Fifth Corps to have marched from the White Oak Road to Dinwiddie Court House in the short time Sheridan allowed (though they did feel that Warren could have moved his men faster than he did); in the second instance, the matter of getting the troops into position on April 1, that there had been no unnecessary delay; and in the third, that Warren's actions during the attack, when he left Ayres's front to direct the movements of Crawford's and Griffin's divisions, had been fully justified.

Almost at once there was a flurry of official actions designed to defuse what was essentially a vindication of Warren's case. In a brief note covering the publication of the findings, William T. Sherman expressed his belief that "General Sheridan was perfectly justified in his actions in this case, and he must be fully and entirely sustained if the United States expects great victories by her armies in the future." In a personal letter to the secretary of war, Sheridan grumbled that the court's opinions "were not in accordance with the evidence." And less than six months after the findings were issued, Sheridan's devoted partisan Frederick C. Newhall wrote a long article for the *Philadelphia Weekly Times* in which he carefully refuted all of the panel's pro-Warren findings.

Yet the testimony and conclusions were there for all to read. An officer who had served under Warren at Five Forks, Joshua L. Chamberlain, reflected, "The traditions of the whole War Department were for sustaining military authority. . . . We can only wonder at the courage of all who gave Warren any favorable endorsement or explanation."

In a letter that he wrote to the U.S. Army Adjutant General in 1868 but never sent, Gouverneur K. Warren tried to explain the larger issue involved in his decision to seek a court of inquiry, saying,

Upon the maintenance of individual rights in all places where the individual has a duty to perform, against the . . . caprice of his superior, depends the prominence eventually of our nation itself. There will be no power to prevent some commander in chief in a future day overthrowing the government when it allows subordinate officers to be disposed on the caprice of the superior, for there would be nothing to protect the subordinates in refusing to obey the order were it to displease the organized government officers or destroy them.

The last battle of the Civil War was over.

Chapter Twenty-four

War without End

———◂◦▸———

I know not whether I shall be understood, but I realize
that it is finally from what I learn'd personally mixing in
such scenes that I am now penning these pages.

Walt Whitman, "Democratic Vistas"

THE STAGE IS DARK, the players have long since gone, but the
play lives on. That great sprawling drama we call the Civil War not only
profoundly touched the generation that lived through it but also left a
deep imprint that is felt to the present time. The Civil War remains with
us, is still a part of us, decades after its centennial (which I experienced as
a boy), and will, I strongly suspect, be no less well remembered at its
bicentennial (which I do not expect to see).

Having traveled those terrible, bloody roads from the Wilderness to
Palmito Ranch, and having lived so long with the words, experiences,
and memories of hundreds of those who fought in those campaigns, I
continue to marvel at how easily, for the most part, the combatants were
able to put away their guns and, once the combat was over, pack away
their personal rancor forever. This was an aspect of the American character of that period that was at once a contradiction and a source of
strength.

On the one hand, these Americans accepted that it was part of the natural order of things to settle with arms those arguments that words could not resolve. The poet Walt Whitman was swept up in this feeling when he wrote,

> War! an arm'd race is advancing! the welcome for battle, no
>   turning away;
> War! be it weeks, months, or years, an arm'd race is advancing
>   to welcome it.

Even when the writing was on the wall in those final months, the wholehearted commitment to battle was no less than it had been in 1862 or 1863. One need only recall the intensity of fighting at Sailor's Creek on April 6, Fort Blakely on April 9, Columbus on April 16, or even Palmito Ranch on May 13 to realize that there was no holding back at the end. But after the guns were stacked, and the standards surrendered, there was remarkably little personal animosity. As one North Carolina officer noted right after Lee's surrender at Appomattox Court House, the "universal sentiment was that the question had been fought to a finish and that was the end of it." A reporter for the *New York Times* caught something of that change in attitude in an article he wrote after traveling through Southside Virginia at almost exactly the same time:

> On the line of the Danville Railroad it was no uncommon sight to see men from both armies walking along together as if they never belonged to hostile forces. . . . White flags were everywhere displayed, and it was no uncommon thing to see women in tears — some overjoyed, others mortified at the result. One lady, smiling through a shower of pearly drops, said to me, "Well, Sir, I hope you are now satisfied, we are at last subjugated." "Did it hurt much?" I inquired, pleasantly; and the person addressed, at once made herself agreeable, and before I left her frankly confessed that subjugation, after all, was more a bugbear than anything else.

The willingness of Americans of both North and South to put aside their weapons and get on with the business of life was strongly reinforced by their leaders. The farewell addresses of Union and Confederate officers were in fact strikingly similar in their basic message. Leave it to that self-made "Wizard of the Saddle," Nathan B. Forrest, to get straight to the point:

The cause for which you have so long and manfully struggled, and for which you have braved dangers, endured privations and sufferings and made so many sacrifices, is to-day hopeless. The government which we sought to establish and perpetuate is at an end. Reason dictates and humanity demands that no more blood be shed. Fully realizing in feeling that such is the case, it is your duty and mine to lay down our arms — submit to the powers "that be" — and to aid in restoring peace and establishing law and order throughout the land.

Forrest's words had an uncanny echo (with allowances for a victor's perspective) in the valediction of the man who had once ordered him hunted down and killed — William T. Sherman. In his farewell, Sherman said,

Our work is done, and armed enemies no longer defy us. . . . As long as that enemy was defiant, not mountains, nor rivers, nor swamps, nor hunger, nor cold, had checked us, but when he who had fought us hard and persistently offered submission your general thought it wrong to pursue him farther. . . . How far the operations of this army have contributed to the final overthrow of the Confederacy, and the peace which now dawns on us, must be judged by others, not by us, but that you have done all that men could do has been admitted by those in authority, and we have a right to join in the universal joy that fills our land because the war is over, and our Government stands vindicated before the world by the joint action of the volunteer armies of the United States. To such as remain in the military service, your general need only remind you that success in the past was due to hard work and discipline and that the same work and discipline are equally important in the future. To such as go home he will only say, that our favored country is so grand, so extensive, so diversified in climate, soil, and production, that every man may find a home and occupation suited to his taste. . . .

It was this willingness on the part of most veterans to divorce action from passion that allowed them in later years to remember those horrific moments with feelings of nostalgia; and that nostalgia, in turn, that laid the seeds for our continued fascination with the Civil War.

Make no mistake: few if any of the profound social and political problems that helped bring on the conflict were resolved by it. The defeat of Southern arms and the collapse of the Confederate government may have eliminated the legal institution of slavery, but the concept survived unaltered in the common white consciousness of the nation. Ahead of black Americans lay a period of history as terror-filled, as soul-destroying, and as racially bigoted as any before the conflict.

On the occasion of the centennial, the great American author Robert Penn Warren concluded in a long essay titled "The Legacy of the Civil War" that

> the word *tragedy* is often used loosely. Here we use it at its deepest significance: the image in action of the deepest questions of man's fate and man's attitude toward his fate. For the Civil War is, massively, that. It is the story of a crime of monstrous inhumanity, into which almost innocently men stumbled; of consequences which could not be trammeled up, and of men who entangled themselves more and more vindictively and desperately until the powers of reason were twisted and their very virtues perverted; of a climax drenched with blood but with nobility gleaming ironically, and redeemingly, through the murk; of a conclusion in which, for the participants at least, there is a reconciliation by human recognition.

Each passing year uncovers more diaries and more letters from soldiers, which add colorful little pieces to the larger pictures of campaigns or battles. Historians writing in the 1990s can draw upon a body of material that simply was not available to the writers of the 1960s, even as those students of the war who have yet to be born will know of people and experiences we cannot. There seems to be a new spirit across the land that recognizes this continuum. In the relatively short period during which I researched and wrote my end-of-the-war trilogy, I witnessed the emergence of several strong grass-roots movements whose whole purpose is to preserve and protect the Civil War battlefields that remain, in the hope that citizens of the future may share in that curious communion of spirit that occurs when one stands upon "hallowed" ground.

For a nation and a people that still cherish the things of youth, the Civil War represents that never-to-be-forgotten moment of transition from adolescence to young adulthood, a mystic time of change from an age when everything is imagined to one when anything is possible. Somehow, in the collective consciousness that makes Americans Americans, that transformation is still shared. Just to say the name Lee, Grant, or Lincoln is instantly to summon up an image that, though perhaps historically inaccurate, is nonetheless complete in our minds. When, even in the midst of a modern orchestral composition, a fleeting reference is made to "Dixie," "Marching Through Georgia," "John Brown's Body," or any one of a dozen other tunes of that era, there is a transmission of values and symbols that takes place on both a conscious and a subconscious level.

The voyage through the fiery trial of war was a coming-of-age for those who experienced it and for the nation that emerged from it. Something of that has been captured in the words of a writer who was born after the war ended but whose imagination was fueled by its raw energy. In *The Red Badge of Courage,* Stephen Crane summed up this personal and national rite of passage when he wrote,

He felt a quiet manhood, nonassertive but of sturdy and strong blood. He knew that he would no more quail before his guides wherever they should point. He had been to touch the great death, and found that, after all, it was but the great death. He was a man.

Notes

———◦———

QUOTATION SOURCES

The abbreviation *OR* is used for *The War of the Rebellion: A Compilation of the Official Records of the Union and Confederate Armies, 1880–1901,* followed by an indication of the volume number and (where applicable) part; the abbreviation *ORN* refers to the *Official Records of the Union and Confederate Navies in the War of the Rebellion, 1894–1922,* followed by an indication of the volume number.

Citations are generally placed in order of their first appearance in the chapter text. Subsequent occurrences within a chapter are not noted, while occurrences of the same citation in subsequent chapters are noted upon their first use.

1. "WE MAY EXPECT WEIGHTY NEWS ANY MINUTE"

The opening incident in Tennessee was related by Daniel Ellis in his *Thrilling Adventures.*

The best overall coverage of the latter stages of the Mobile campaign can be found in two studies, one (Andrews, *History of Campaign . . . Mobile*) by a Union veteran who was there, and the other (Bergeron, *Confederate Mobile*) by a modern historian of the region. Other sources used here were Stevens, *Dear Carrie;* Phelan, *Who Only Stand and Wait;* Maury, "The Defence of Mobile in 1865"; and the Alphonse P. Wolfe letters. Also useful was the *Chicago Tribune* for April 18, 1865.

The insights of the gossipy Mr. Strong will be found in Nevins, *Diary of George Templeton Strong,* while the view from down South comes from Bryan, "A Georgia Woman's Civil War Diary."

Sherman's side of events in North Carolina is laid out in his *Memoirs*. In addition to communications found in *OR* 47/3, other sources used were Bircher, *Drummer-Boy's Diary;* McAdams, *Every-day Soldier Life;* Kirwan, *Memorial History;* and Ridley, *Battles & Sketches.*

Williamson Oldham related his remarkable odyssey in his partially published and partially typescript memoir, *Last Days.*

The only overall study of Wilson's raid in Alabama is Jones, *Yankee Blitzkrieg.* Also used here were Wilson, *Under the Old Flag,* and Mitchell, *Field Notes.*

2. BREAKTHROUGH IN THE EAST

The communications quoted in the opening of this chapter will be found in *OR* 46/3. Other sources were Badeau, *Military History of U. S. Grant;* Wharff, "Chapin's Farm to Appomattox"; Robertson, *Civil War Letters of Robert McAllister;* Freeman, *R. E. Lee;* Dowdey, *Wartime Papers of R. E. Lee;* Crook, "Lincoln's Last Day"; V. Davis, *Jefferson Davis: A Memoir;* and Harrison, "Capture of Jefferson Davis."

The Bearss/Calkins book, *Battle of Five Forks,* is the best extant study of this key engagement. Also invaluable are the one thousand plus pages of testimony in the *Warren Court of Inquiry.* The most up-to-date study of Five Forks from Warren's side is in the unpublished study by Flanagan, *Life of General ... Warren.* Other published quotations came from Starr, "Dinwiddie Court House and Five Forks"; Sheridan, *Personal Memoirs;* Porter, "Five Forks and the Pursuit of Lee"; Agassiz, *Meade's Headquarters;* Johnston, *Story of a Confederate Boy;* Chambers, *Diary;* Peck, *Reminiscences;* Freeman, *Lee's Lieutenants;* Cardwell, "The Battle of Five Forks"; Locke, *Story of the Regiment;* Chamberlain, *Passing of the Armies;* McBride, *In the Ranks;* Denison, *Sabres and Spurs;* Bowen, *Regimental History;* Harris, "With the Reserve Brigade"; Newhall, "With Sheridan"; Day, "Life Among Bullets"; Clark, *Histories* (vol. 3); Smith, *Corn Exchange Regiment;* Swan (in *Papers* 6), "The Five Forks Campaign"; Schilling, "My Three Years"; Day, *A True History;* Elliott, *Southern Soldier Boy;* Hudson, *Sketches and Reminiscences;* Gordon, *Memories & Memorials;* Walker, *Life of Richard Anderson;* Linn, *From Richmond;* Hall, *History of the 97th Regiment;* Roe, *Thirty-ninth Regiment;* Moore, "The Battle of Five Forks"; Robertson, *Reminiscences;* Parker, *Story of the 32nd;* Vautier, *History of the 88th Pennsylvania;* Townsend, *Rustics in Rebellion;* Divine, *35th Battalion Virginia Cavalry;* Cadwallader, *Three Years with Grant;* and Pfanz, *Lincoln at City Point.*

Unpublished and manuscript sources used for quotation were Pickett, Report; Joshua Chamberlain Papers; Warren, Correspondence; Cowart Papers (Munford letters); A. S. Perham Papers (Letter of Thomas B. Roulhac); Rosser, Letter; Munford-Ellis Papers; Harding, Diary; Livermore, Diary; Landis, Diary; Smith, Letters and Diary; and McCabe, Letter. Communications and report excerpts are taken from *OR* 46/1. Also useful were accounts found in the *Richmond Times-Dispatch* for July 5, 1884, August 13, 1897, and October 31, 1909.

The Richmond views on these events are quoted from Simmons, "Flight from Richmond"; Jones, *Rebel War Clerk;* V. Davis, *Jefferson Davis: A Memoir;* Conolly, *Irishman in Dixie;* and Kreutzer, *Notes and Observations.*

3. CAPTURED!!

The Petersburg portions of this chapter for the most part present material researched for, but not used in, my previous book *The Last Citadel.* The quotes come from Hopkins, *Seventh Rhode Island;* Keifer, Letters; Howard, *Recollections;* Davis, *Diary of the War;* Pfanz, *Lincoln at City Point;* Beals, "In a Charge near Fort Hell"; Huyette, *Reminiscences;* Culver, "Entered and Escaped"; McMillan, *Alabama ... Reader;* Clark, *Histories* (vol. 3); Osborne, "Struggle for ... Mahone"; Devereux Family Papers; Stevens (in *Papers* 6), "The Storming of the Lines of Petersburg by the Sixth Corps, April 2, 1865"; Best, *History of the 121st;* Brewer, *History Sixty-first;* Swinfen, *Ruggles' Regiment;* Cummins, *Give God the Glory;* Freeman, *R. E. Lee;* Taylor, *General Lee; Four Years;* Rauscher, *Music on the March;* Smith, *Corn Exchange Regiment;* Gudger, Articles on the 25th Regiment; Pickett, Report; Johnston, *Story of a Confederate Boy;* Newhall, "With Sheridan"; Sheridan, *Personal Memoirs;* Harris, "Nineteenth Mississippi"; Conerly, "How Fort Gregg Was Defended"; Jones, "Defence of Battery Gregg"; Spire, Letters; Clark, *History of the Thirty-ninth;* Dalzell, *Private Dalzell;* Voris, *War Letters;* Gorman, *Lee's Last Campaign;* Howard, "Defence of Fort Gregg"; Gibbon, *Personal Recollections;* Dinkins, "Last Campaign"; Hancock, *Hancock's Diary;* Porter, *Naval History;* Roller, *Last Retreat;* Bartlett, *Soldier's Story;* Bradwell, "On Picket Duty"; Cooke, *War Experiences;* "First and Last Soldiers Killed"; Cooke, *Life of ... Robert E. Lee;* Cadwallader, *Three Years with Grant;* Badeau, *Military History of U. S. Grant;* Haynes, *History of ... Tenth Regiment;* Eden, *Sword and Gun;* Peck, "Recruit"; Cushman, *History of the 58th Regiment;* Grant, *Personal Memoirs;* and Houghton, *Campaigns.* Report and communication quotations are from OR 46/1 and 46/3. Useful newspaper accounts were found in the May 5, 1865, edition of the *New York World,* the August 8, 1897, issue of the *Richmond Dispatch,* the *Philadelphia Weekly Times* for May 5, 1893, and the following editions from the postwar newspaper for Union veterans, the *National Tribune:* July 28, 1887, July 4, 1907, and January 20, 1910.

The Richmond part of the story came from Younger, *Inside ... Government;* Camm, "Naval Officer's Recollections"; Durkin, *Stephen R. Mallory;* Putnam, *In Richmond;* Harrison, *Recollections;* Bruce, "Some Reminiscences"; Howard, *Recollections;* Smith, Diary; Mallory, "Last Days"; Harrison, "From the Diary"; Ballard, *Long Shadow;* Spencer, "French View"; Semmes, *Confederate Raider* Alabama; Parker, *Recollections;* Conolly, *Irishman in Dixie;* Potts, Letter; Handy, "Fall of Richmond"; Pember, *Southern Woman's Story;* Watehall, "Fall of Richmond"; Jones, *Rebel War Clerk;* Barton, *Recollections;* Vandiver, *Civil War Diary of ... Gorgas;* Blackford, *Letters from Lee's Army;* Mixson, *Reminiscences;* Govan, *Haskell Memoirs;* Gache, *Frenchman, Chaplain, Rebel;* Worsham, *One of Jackson's;* Stiles, *Four Years;* Sulivane, "Fall of Richmond"; Sturgis, "About the Burning of Richmond"; Alexander, *Fighting for the Confederacy;* Blackett, *Thomas Morris Chester;* Kreutzer, *Notes and Observations;* Baker (in *Stories of Our Soldiers*), "First Troops in Richmond"; Kautz, *Reminiscences;* Bruce (in *Papers* 14), "The Capture and Occupation of Richmond"; Parsons, *Reminiscences;* Dawson, *First Flag in Richmond;* DeLeon, *Four Years;* Jones, *Ladies of Richmond;* Hunt, Diary; Fontaine, Letters; and Crook, "Lincoln's Last Day." Newspaper accounts of use here were found in the *Richmond Times-Dispatch* for December 19, 1885, and August 11, 1912; the *Philadelphia Weekly Times* for August 27, 1881; the *Richmond News Leader* for April 3, 1935; and the *National Tribune* for September 3, 1887, October 4, 1900, July 20, 1922, and September 24, 1925.

Other points of perspective were provided by Nevins, *Diary of George Templeton Strong;* Gordon, *War Diary;* Wild, *Memoirs and History;* and Jones, *Journal of Catherine Edmondston.*

4. THE DEATH OF AN ARMY

The saga of the Appomattox Campaign has been well told in a number of books, most notably Davis, *To Appomattox*, and Stern, *An End to Valor*. The detailed studies authored by Chris Calkins are of inestimable value toward gaining an understanding of the movements and strategies of these nine days. Quotation sources used here are Bartlett, *Soldier's Story*; Freeman, *R. E. Lee*; Morrill, *My Confederate Girlhood*; Howard, *Recollections*; Longstreet, *From Manassas to Appomattox*; Stonebraker, *Rebel of '61*; Phillips, Journal and Diary; Clark, *Histories* (vol. 2); Dowdey, *Lee*; Cooke, *Life of . . . Robert E. Lee*; Graves, *History of . . . Bedford . . . Artillery*; McCarthy, *Detailed Minutae*; Starr, *Union Cavalry*; Denison, *Sabres and Spurs*; Reece, "Final Push"; Rhodes, *All for the Union*; Craft, *History of the 141st Regiment*; Cheek, *History of the Sauk County Riflemen*; Shaw, *First Maine Heavy Artillery*; Bakeless, "Mystery of Appomattox"; *Under the Maltese Cross*; Camper, *Historical Record*; Livermore, Diary; Wise, *End of an Era*; Dowdey, *Wartime Papers of R. E. Lee*; Alexander, *Fighting for the Confederacy*; Camm, "Naval Officer's Recollections"; Bennett, "Account of the 14th North Carolina"; Dayton, *Diary of a Confederate Soldier*; Bagby, *King and Queen County*; Wiatt, Diary; Boykin, *The Falling Flag*; Lewis, Diary; Mooney, "Union Chaplain's Diary"; Roback, *Veteran Volunteers*; Humphreys, *Virginia Campaign*; Hall, *History of the 6th New York Cavalry*; Preston, *History of the 10th Regiment*; Sheridan, *Personal Memoirs*; Porter, *Campaigning with Grant*; Cadwallader, *Three Years with Grant*; Rich, *Comrades!*; White, *Diary of the War*; Summers, *Borderland Confederate*; Myers, *Comanches*; Cooper, Diary; Anderson, Report; Gordon, *Reminiscences*; Crotty, *Four Years Campaigning*; Trobriand, *Four Years*; Rock, "War Reminiscence"; Best, *History of the 121st*; Johnston, *Story of a Confederate Boy*; Bahnson, *Days of the War*; Barton, *Recollections*; Eckert, *John Brown Gordon*; Marbaker, *History of the Eleventh*; *History of the 57th Regiment*; Snyder, *Recollections of Four Years*; Hall, *History of the 6th New York Cavalry*; Preston, *History of the 10th Regiment*; Haynes, *History of . . . Tenth Regiment*; Woodbury, *Second Rhode Island*; Stevens (in *Papers 6*), "The Battle of Sailor's Creek"; Bowen, *History of the Thirty-seventh*; Keifer, Letters; Walker, *Life of Richard Anderson*; McGlashan, *Our Last Retreat*; Gordon, Report; Thomas, *History of the Doles-Cook Brigade*; Stiles, *Four Years*; Timberlake, "In the Siege of Richmond"; and Aston, *History and Roster*. I also drew on reports and communications found in OR 46/1 and 46/3. Newspaper sources are the *Richmond Times-Dispatch* for April 25, 1897, May 2, 1897, January 1, 1905, and January 26, 1908; and the *National Tribune* for April 28, 1887, August 18, 1887, February 13, 1902, March 13, 1902, and November 25, 1915.

5. "AFTER FOUR YEARS OF ARDUOUS SERVICE"

A thoughtful examination of the events of Lee's capitulation at Appomattox can be found in Cauble, *Surrender Proceedings*. Also useful were the notes and memoranda regarding the fate of the McLean House furniture, compiled in the Monroe Cockrell Papers. Sources for quotation in this chapter are Wise, *End of an Era*; McIntosh, Diary; Gatewood, *Materials*; Jones, "Third Arkansas"; Long, *Memoirs of Robert E. Lee*; Alexander, *Fighting for the Confederacy*; Spaulding, "Nineteenth Maine at High Bridge"; Baker, Diary; Mixson, *Reminiscences*; Humphreys, *Virginia Campaign*; Porter, *Campaigning with Grant*; Gibbon, *Personal Recollections*; Longstreet, *From Manassas to Appomattox*; Freeman, *R. E. Lee*; Grant, *Personal Memoirs*; Calkins, *Battles of Appomattox*

Station; Mohr, *Cormany Diaries;* Moore, *History of North Carolina;* Myers, *Comanches;* Gorman, *Lee's Last Campaign;* Badeau, *Military History of U. S. Grant;* Lang, *Loyal West Virginia;* Denison, *Sabres and Spurs;* Cooke, Letters; Eckert, *John Brown Gordon;* Bradwell, "After the Surrender"; Bennett, "Account of the 14th North Carolina"; Clark, *Histories* (vol. 5); Brady, *Story of One Regiment;* Gordon, *Reminiscences;* Alexander, *Fighting for the Confederacy; Literary and Historical Activities;* Taylor, *Four Years;* Korn, *Pursuit to Appomattox;* (Minnigerode incident) Andrews, *Scraps of Paper,* Cooke, Letters, and Robertson, *Reminiscences;* Talcott, "From Petersburg to Appomattox"; Marshall, *Appomattox;* Agassiz, *Meade's Headquarters;* Chambers, *Diary;* Poague, *Gunner with Stonewall;* Colston, "Last Months"; South Carolina U.D.C., *Recollections;* Silliker, *Rebel Yell & Yankee Hurrah;* Stevens, Letters; Smith, Letters; Dowdey, *Wartime Papers of R. E. Lee;* Calkins, *Final Bivouac;* Chamberlain, "Appomattox"; Gerrish, *Army Life;* Chamberlain, *Passing of the Armies; Under the Maltese Cross;* Scruggs, *Lynchburg, Virginia;* Flood, *Lee: The Last Years;* Southall, "Recollections"; Cooke, *Life of . . . Robert E. Lee;* Ripley, "Personal Reminiscences"; Rogers, Diary; Fatout, *Letters of a Civil War Surgeon;* Cronin, *Evolution;* and Wert, *Mosby's Rangers.* Report and communication quotations are from OR 46/1 and 46/3. Newspaper accounts came from the *Richmond Times-Dispatch* for December 18, 1904, and the *National Tribune* for April 23, 1885, May 11, 1905, September 26, 1912, December 19, 1912, and May 11, 1915.

Reactions to news of Lee's surrender are taken from Wilkinson, "Brandywine Home Front"; Tyler, Letters; Rusk, *Life of Ralph Waldo Emerson;* Nevins, *Diary of George Templeton Strong;* (Melville Poem) Kaplan, Battle-Pieces; ("General Lee's Surrender") Heaps, *Singing Sixties.*

6. "FOR GOD'S SAKE, CEASE FIRING! WE HAVE THE FORT!"

In addition to the core books cited in the notes for the prologue, the following were used as sources for quotation:

MOBILE: St. John, Diary and Letters; Frisbie, Diary; Drish, Letters; Merriam, Letters; Chambers, "Unrecorded Battles"; Sallie L. Tarleton Papers; Eddington, *Civil War Experiences;* Lemke, *Diary of Captain . . . Miller;* Gould, Diary; Potter, Diary; Abernethy, *Private . . . Stockwell;* Hatch, *Dearest Susie;* Elliott, *History of the 33rd Regiment;* Peck, Letter; Lockett, Letter; Stewart, Diary; Stevens, *Dear Carrie;* Wolfe, Letters; Audsley, Letters; Maury, "The Defence of Mobile in 1865"; Sumner, *Diary of Cyrus B. Comstock;* Stephenson, "Defence of Spanish Fort"; Bailey, "The Star Company"; Gibson, "Official Report"; Stockton, War Diary; Gilbert, Letters; Allen, Memoirs and Letters; Holt, *Miss Waring's Journal;* Black, Letters; Clark, *Thirty-fourth Iowa Regiment;* Slack, Letters and Diary; Bentley, *History of the 77th Illinois;* Tarrant, "Siege and Capture"; Smith, *Mobile: 1861–1865;* Mumford, Diary; Morgan, Diary; Ambrose, *Wisconsin Boy in Dixie;* and McMillan, *Alabama . . . Reader.*

WILSON: Wilson, *Under the Old Flag;* Griest, *Three Years in Dixie;* Wyeth, *Life of . . . Forrest;* Mitchell, *Field Notes;* Gilpin, *Last Campaign;* "Rise and Fall of Selma"; Duncan, *Recollections;* McCain, *Memoirs of Henry . . . Ireys;* Lay, Letter on the fall of Selma; Hinrichs, Diary; Montgomery, *Reminiscences;* Stoner, Diary; Pierrepont, *Reuben . . . Kidd;* Wulsin, *Roster;* Riggs, Letters; Larson, *Sergeant Larson;* Harris, *Reminiscences;* Dinkins, "Last Campaign"; Hosea, "Some Side Lights"; Beaumont, "Campaign of Selma"; Nourse, Diary; Rowell, *Yankee Artilleryman;* Latta, Diary; and Peters, Letters.

Also valuable were the following newspapers: *Philadelphia Weekly Press* of June 23, 1886; *Cincinnati Daily Commercial* for April 18, 1865; *Chicago Tribune* for April 18, 1865; *New Orleans Times* for April 6, 8, and 27, 1865; *New York Times* for April 24 and 25, 1865; and *National Tribune* for July 10, 1884; December 31, 1885; August 18, 1887; June 7, 1888; October 1, 1891; May 17, 1900; June 4, 1908; June 2 and December 22, 1910; June 26, July 31, August 28, and November 1, 1913; August 27, 1914; and July 4 and 15, 1923. Useful as well were reports and communications found in ORN 22 and OR 49/1 and 49/2.

7. HEADS OF STATE

The most recent and most thorough biography of the Confederacy's only President is W. C. Davis, *Jefferson Davis: The Man and His Hour.* A shorter but equally valuable study is Ballard, *Long Shadow.* The flight of the Confederate Cabinet is ably described in two books, Hanna, *Flight into Oblivion,* and B. Davis, *The Long Surrender.* Additional quotation sources used in this chapter are as follows:

DAVIS: Durkin, *Stephen R. Mallory;* Davis, *Rise and Fall;* Brubacker, *Last Capital;* Semmes, *Confederate Raider* Alabama; Younger, *Inside . . . Government;* Parker, *Recollections;* Mallory, "Last Days"; Wise, *End of an Era;* Robertson, "Danville under Military Occupation"; Marshall, Diary; Bradwell, "Making Our Way Home"; Noppen, *Stoneman's Last Raid;* Moderwell, "Outline of Stoneman's . . . Raid"; and Brown, *Salisbury Prison.*

LINCOLN: Hunt, Diary; *Story of the 21st Regiment;* Gordon, *War Diary;* Klice, Letters; Blackett, *Thomas Morris Chester;* Graves, "The Occupation of Richmond"; Foote, *Civil War;* Ripley, *Capture and Occupation;* Myer, *Memorandum;* Pember, *Southern Woman's Story;* Collis, *Woman's War Record;* Pfanz, *Lincoln at City Point;* Jaquette, *South after Gettysburg;* Chambrun, *Impressions of Lincoln;* and Crook, "Lincoln's Last Day."

Also useful was the *National Tribune* for May 25, 1911.

INTERLUDES: OLDHAM'S ODYSSEY (PARTS ONE AND TWO)

All material relating to Senator Williamson Oldham came from his partially published and partially typescript *Last Days.*

Additionally helpful were Fontaine, "Hon. Williamson S. Oldham," and King, "Political Career of Williamson Simpson Oldham."

8. SLOW DANCE IN NORTH CAROLINA

Official communications regarding this series of events may be found in OR 47/2 and 47/3, with reports in 47/1. The quotations used here came from *Story of the Fifty-fifth Regiment;* Anderson, *Civil War Diary;* Toombs, *Reminiscences;* Aten, *History of the 85th Regiment;* Ridley, "Last Battles"; Roth, *Well Mary;* Merrill, "16th Kentucky"; Bircher, *Drummer-Boy's Diary;* Adams, "Diary"; Evans, Diary; Woodruff, Diary; Lewis, *Fighting Prophet;* Ridley, *Battles & Sketches;* Thomas, "Their Last Battle"; Clark, *Histories* (vols. 3 and 4); Burt, Diary; Slocum, "Final Operations of Sherman's Army"; Jamison, *Recollections;* Quaife, *From the Cannon's Mouth;* Waring, Diary; Symonds, *Joseph E. Johnston;* (Vance-Graham incidents) Spencer, *Last Ninety Days;* Stratton, Letters and Diary; Sherlock, *Memorabilia;* Dunlap, *Your Affectionate Husband;* Rood, *Story of Service;* Upson, *With Sherman to the Sea;* Bradley, *Star Corps;* Michaels, *Civil War Letters;* Gage, *From Vicksburg to Raleigh;* Hagood, *Mem-*

oirs; Brown, *One of Cleiburne's Command;* Thompson, *History of the 112th Regiment;* Arbuckle, *Civil War Experiences;* Grimes, *Autobiography;* Amis, *Historic Raleigh;* Kinnear, *History of the 86th Illinois;* Puntenney, *History of the 37th Regiment;* Bishop, Letters; and Jackson, *Colonel's Diary.*

Also of use were the *Cincinnati Daily Commercial* for April 11, 1865, and the *Newark Daily Advertiser* for April 29, 1865, as well as accounts from the newspaper for Union veterans, the *National Tribune,* of February 22, 1912, July 15, 1920, and September 1, 1921.

9. "MY GOD — THE PRESIDENT'S SHOT!"

All Townsend quotations regarding the flag raising at Fort Sumter came from his letter housed in the South Caroliniana Library. Other quote sources are OR 47/3; Hill, *Fort Sumter Memorial;* and Rugoff, *Beechers.*

Regarding the assassination of Abraham Lincoln, my account of events is drawn from the following sources: Foote, *Civil War;* Clark, *Assassination;* Welles, *Diary;* Dana, *Recollections;* Reck, *His Last Twenty-four Hours;* Hamlin, "Darkest Hour"; Roe, *Ninth New York Heavy Artillery;* Miers, *Last Campaign;* Rietveld, "Eyewitness Account"; Moss, "Account of the Assassination"; Ward, Diary; Trefousse, *Andrew Johnson;* Hanchett, "Booth's Diary"; Weygant, *History of the One Hundred and Twenty-fourth;* Cronin, *Evolution;* Osborne, *History of the 29th Regiment;* Gregorie, "Diary of Captain Joseph Julius Wescoat"; Turner, *Beware the People Weeping;* Nevins, *Diary of George Templeton Strong;* McCalla, Diary; McAleer, *Days of Encounter;* Stessel, *Soldier and Scholar;* Patterson, Letters; Fleet, "Chapter of Unwritten History"; and Kauffman, "Booth's Escape Route."

10. THE BENNETT FARMHOUSE

In addition to communications found in OR 47/3, the following sources were used for quotation: Green, Diary; Griffith, Diary; Sherman, *Memoirs;* Granger, "A Witness to History"; Merrill, *William Tecumseh Sherman;* Rood, *Story of Service;* Jamison, *Recollections;* Smith, *History of Fuller's Ohio Brigade;* Metz, Diary; *Reminiscences of the Civil War;* Welles, *Diary;* Grant, *Personal Memoirs;* Hughes, *General Johnston;* Aten, *History of the 85th Regiment;* Behrens, *Total War in Carolina;* Hagood, *Memoirs;* Ridley, *Battles & Sketches;* Brown, *One of Cleiburne's Command;* Rowland, *Diary and Letters;* Rennolds, *History of Henry County;* "North Carolina — Held Over from May"; Shingleton, "With Loyalty and Honor"; Watkins, *Co. Aytch;* Arbuckle, *Civil War Experiences;* Ames, Diary; Hurst, *Journal History of the 73rd Ohio;* Barrett, *Sherman's March through the Carolinas;* and Wills, *Army Life of an Illinois Soldier.*

11. POTTER'S RAID

All entries from the journal of Lieutenant Edward L. Stevens came from Moore, "The Last Officer."

In addition to reports found in OR 47/1 and communications in 47/3, other quotation sources are Cooper, Diary; "Potter's Raid"; Gregorie, *History of Sumter County;* Hyde, Notes; and Emilio, *History of the Fifty-fourth.*

12. "THE WHOLE COUNTRY SEEMED TO BE ALIVE WITH DEMONS"

Jones, *Yankee Blitzkrieg,* is the basic source here, supported with reports from OR 49/1 and additional quotations from Brickell, "Reminiscence"; Stanley,

"Story of the Last Battle"; Crouse, Journal; Rowell, *Yankee Artilleryman;* Taylor, "Last Land Battle"; Wilson, *Under the Old Flag;* Hinrichs, Diary; Telfair, *History of Columbus;* Grant, "Recollections"; Scott, *Story of a Cavalry Regiment;* Mitchell, *Field Notes;* and Hatch, *Dearest Susie.*

Also used were accounts found in the following issues of the postwar Union veterans' newspaper, the *National Tribune:* August 11, 1887; May 10, 1888; May 24, 1900; May 15, 1902; August 10, 1905; and May 4, 1910.

The finale for Richard Taylor and his department is drawn from Taylor, Letterbook; Kerby, *Kirby Smith's Confederacy;* Taylor (in *Annals of the War*), "Last Confederate Surrender"; and Taylor, *Destruction and Reconstruction,* with additional material from the *Cincinnati Daily Commercial* of May 31, 1865.

The saga of the *Memphis Appeal* comes from Baker, "Refugee Newspaper," and the "tale is told" article from the *New York Times* for June 25, 1865.

My account of the end of Nathan Forrest's career was based on material in Carter, *When the War Was Over;* Wills, *Battle from the Start;* and Foote, *Civil War.*

The poignant note from Henry Wirz can be found in *OR* (series 2) 8, while Wilson's crowing account of his arrest appears in *OR* 49/2.

The capture of Confederate Florida's capital is detailed in Jones, "Surrender of Tallahassee."

13. "MY HUSBAND AND BABY ARE GONE!"

This chapter is based largely on firsthand accounts found in Berry, *Loss of the Sultana.* Additional survivor reminiscences came from *Ninth Cavalry: One Hundred and Twenty-first Regiment; Records of the Adjutant General's Office: Court Martial of Captain Frederic Speed; Sultana Disaster: Courts of Inquiry;* Dockter, "Andrew T. Perry's Experience on the *Sultana*"; Floyd, "Burning of the *Sultana*"; Hussey, Letter; Walker, "George R. Webb Letter"; Winters, *In the 50th Ohio;* and the following issues of the *National Tribune:* November 15, 1888; October 26, 1893; July 4 and November 21, 1912; July 7, 1921; and June 26, 1924.

Useful secondary sources are Elliott, *Transport to Disaster;* Levstik, "The *Sultana*"; Michael, "Explosion of the *Sultana*"; Potter, *The* Sultana *Tragedy;* and Yager, "*Sultana* Disaster."

A further quotation source not covered above is the *Florida Union* for May 6, 1865.

14. THE LONESOME TRAIN

A core source for materials relating to the Lincoln funeral train is Searcher, *Farewell to Lincoln.* Other sources used for quotation were Longacre, "With Lincoln"; Gibbs, *History of . . . 187th Regiment;* Millice, Letter; Hammond, *Diary of a Union Lady;* Walton, *Private Smith's Journal;* and O'Connor, *Bret Harte.*

Useful as well were the *Chicago Tribune* for May 3 and 5, 1865, and the *National Tribune* for June 26, 1924.

15. "GOD'S WILL BE DONE"

The best modern studies of the end of the flight of Jefferson Davis and his Cabinet are W. C. Davis, *Jefferson Davis;* B. Davis, *Long Surrender;* and Ballard, *Long Shadow.* Other quotations are from Truman, "Incident of the Dying Confederacy"; Tilghman, Diary; Duke, "After the Fall of Richmond"; Reagan, *Memoirs;*

V. Davis, *Jefferson Davis: A Memoir;* Clarke, "Retreat of the Cabinet"; Parker, *Recollections;* Evans, *Judah P. Benjamin;* Hoole, "Vizetelly Covers the Confederacy"; Harrison, "Capture of Jefferson Davis"; Harnden, *Capture of Jefferson Davis";* Thomas/Hyman, *Stanton;* Ripley, "Personal Reminiscences"; Dickinson, "Capture of Jeff. Davis"; J. Davis, *Rise and Fall;* Greeno, "Capture of Jefferson Davis"; Potter, Diary; Nourse, Diary; Griest, *Three Years in Dixie;* Jones, "Your Left Arm"; Buffum, *Memorial of the Great Rebellion;* Dimick, "Capture of Jefferson Davis"; and Barbee, Papers.

Official reports on the affair appear in OR 49/1. Additional material came from the *National Tribune* for February 24, 1910; March 4, 1915; July 16, 1925; and April 14, 1929; the *Philadelphia Inquirer* for July 1, 1886; the *New York Herald* for May 26, 1865; and the *Boston Evening Journal* for May 27, 1865.

Andrew Johnson's proclamation is reprinted in OR (series 3) 5.

16. THE LAST BATTLE

The firsthand accounts that form the basis for this chapter may be found in Branson, *The Last Battle of the War";* Ford, *Rip Ford's Texas;* Wilson, "The Last Battle of The War"; and the following issues of the *National Tribune:* August 27 and October 8, 1885; April 2, 1908; and May 21, 1908.

Also utilized were official reports, communications, and testimony in OR 48/1 and *Proceedings, Findings and Opinions of the Court Martial in the Case of Robert G. Morrison,* as well as accounts published in the *New York Herald* for May 28 and 29, 1865; the *New York Times* for June 18, 1865; and the *San Antonio Express* edition of October 10, 1890.

Useful secondary sources are Brown, *History of Texas;* Fussell, *History of the 34th Regiment;* Horgan, *The Great River;* Hunt, *There Is Nothing Left to Us But to Fight;* Huson, *Refugio;* Oates, *Confederate Cavalry West of the River;* Roberts, *Confederate Military History: Texas;* Schuler, *Last Battle in the War between the States;* and Wooten, *Comprehensive History of Texas.*

Additional quotation sources not covered above are Stevens, *Dear Carrie;* Newton, *Out of the Briars;* and Horrocks, *My Dear Parents.*

17. "THEY MARCH LIKE THE LORDS OF THE WORLD"

The quotation sources used here were Grant, *Personal Memoirs;* Bryant, *History of the 3rd Regiment;* Bush, Letters; Merrill, *Seventieth Indiana;* Stauffer, *Civil War Diary;* Ross, Letters; Wills, *Army Life of an Illinois Soldier;* Jamison, *Recollections;* Porter, Diary; Fryer, *History of the 80th Ohio;* Inskeep, Diary; Sherman, *Memoirs;* Hickenlooper, "Reminiscences"; Schermerhorn, Letters; Foering, Diary; West, Diary; Bauer, *Soldiering;* Elder, Letters; Calkins, *History of the 104th Regiment;* Nevins, *Diary of Battle;* Bryant, *History of the 3rd Regiment;* Cleaves, *Meade of Gettysburg;* Norton, *Red Neck Ties;* Bosbyshell, *48th in the War;* Lord, *History of the Ninth Regiment;* Smith, Letters; *Under the Maltese Cross;* Gerrish, *Army Life;* Rhodes, *History of Battery B;* Hanifen, *History of Battery B;* Roback, *Veteran Volunteers;* Mulholland, *Story of the 116th Regiment;* Small, *Road to Richmond;* Strong, *Yankee Private's Civil War;* Girdner, Letters; Sherman, *Memoirs;* Thomas, *Stanton;* Lewis, *Fighting Prophet;* Mahon, "Civil War Letters"; Tyler, Diary; Aten, *History of the 85th Regiment;* Noble, Letters; Bircher, *Drummer-Boy's Diary;* Porter, Diary; Baker, *History of the Ninth Massachusetts Battery;* Crotty, *Four Years Campaigning;* Stevenson, *Boots and Saddles;* Arbuckle, *Civil War Experiences;* and

Messmer, "The End of an Era." Grant's General Orders No. 108 are published in *OR* 46/1.

Also used were the following newspapers: the *Cincinnati Daily Commercial* for May 24 and 27, 1865; the *New York Times* for May 24, 1865; the *Philadelphia Inquirer* for May 25, 1865; the *Daily Constitutional Union* for May 24, 1865; the *Washington Weekly Chronicle* for May 27, 1865; and the *National Tribune* for February 3, 1916.

18. "IT WAS A TERRIBLE CALAMITY — BEYOND DESCRIPTION"

I have relied in this chapter largely on firsthand accounts found in Andrews, Letters; Black, Letters; Craig, Letters; Glassgow, Letters; Johnson, *Muskets and Medicine;* McLeod, *Brother Warriors;* Nelson, "Recollections"; Patterson, Letters; Reid, *After the War;* Rice, Letters; St. John, Diary and Letters; Sperry, *History of the 33rd Iowa Infantry;* and Stevens, *Dear Carrie.* Useful, too, were the following issues of the *National Tribune:* April 9 and 30, 1903; February 1, 1908; March 1 and April 26, 1923.

I have also utilized official reports, communications, and testimony published in *Record of Proceedings of a Court of Inquiry to Investigate the Fact and Circumstances Connected with the Explosion of the Magazine,* as well as accounts published in the *New York Times* for June 8, 1865, the *New Orleans Daily Picayune* for May 30, 1865, and *New Orleans Times* editions for May 29 and 30, 1865.

Useful secondary sources are Bailey, "Mobile's Tragedy"; Craighead, *Mobile: Fact and Tradition;* Delaney, *Confederate Mobile;* Fonde, *An Account of the Great Explosion;* and Higginbotham, *Mobile: City by the Bay.*

Not covered above but also used here were the *Cincinnati Daily Commercial* for May 10, 1865; Mumford, Diary; and Klein, Letters.

19. THE TRANS-MISSISSIPPI

Besides the reports found in *OR* 48/1 and communications in *OR* 48/2, the following sources provided quotations: Wiley, *Fourteen Hundred and 91 Days;* Kerby, *Kirby Smith's Confederacy;* Winters, *Civil War in Louisiana;* Chenery, *Fourteenth Regiment;* "Confederate Persistency"; Goyne, *Lone Star & Double Eagle;* Kerby, *Kirby Smith's Confederacy;* and White, "Disintegration of an Army."

20. "ALL IS DONE — ALL THE CONFEDERACY SURRENDERED"

Material about black enfranchisement and women's rights came from Garrison, *William Lloyd Garrison;* Foner, *Life & Writings of Frederick Douglass;* and Dorr, *Susan B. Anthony.*

Southern reflections on conditions in the South were quoted from Holmes, *Diary;* Moneyhon, "Diary"; and Jones, *Journal of Catherine Edmondston.* Corresponding Union material is from *OR* 48/2.

Closing scenes with other personalities came from McCorkle, *Three Years with Quantrill;* Connelley, *Quantrill and the Border Wars;* and Mitchell, *Edmund Ruffin: A Biography.*

Other observations were provided by Shannon, *Civil War Letters; Story of the 21st Regiment;* Pierce, "Personal Narrative"; Cronin, *Evolution;* Davis, *Reminiscence;* ["Mary"], "After Appomattox"; Mercer, Diary; Sorrel, *Recollections;* Neese, *Three Years;* Fortney, "Letter"; Buttolph, "Occupation Duty in

Selma"; Bierce, *Collected Works;* Carter, *When the War Was Over;* and accounts in OR 46/3.

The sketch of the Sixth Corps's review was taken from Houghton, "Ordeal of Civil War"; Roe, *Ninth New York Heavy Artillery;* Vaill, *County Regiment;* Haines, *History of the Fifteenth Regiment;* Rhodes, *All for the Union;* Adams, "Civil War Letters"; Cummins, *Give God the Glory;* Haynes, *History of . . . Tenth Regiment;* Stevens, *Three Years;* the *New York Times* for June 9, 1865; and communications in OR 46/3.

The issue of Lee's parole is discussed in Flood, *Lee: The Last Years;* I have drawn additional quotations from Kreutzer, *Notes and Observations.*

Images in other closing scenes were based on material found in Lupold, "Union Medical Officer"; Humphrey, " 'Very Muddy and Conflicting' View"; and the *New York Times* for June 12, 1865.

My account of the trial of the Lincoln assassins utilizes material from Nevins, *Diary of George Templeton Strong;* Turner, *Beware the People Weeping;* Hoehling, *After the Guns Fell Silent;* and Douglas, *I Rode with Stonewall.*

21. THE LAST RAIDER

The sources for this chapter were Horn, *Gallant Rebel;* Whittle, "Cruise of the *Shenandoah*"; Mason, *Private Journal;* Hunt, *The* Shenandoah; Waddell, *C.S.S.* Shenandoah; and Morgan, *Dixie Raider.* Additional material was found in ORN 3.

22. WHEN JOHNNY COMES MARCHING HOME

Opening observations are from Chestnut, *Diary from Dixie;* Foner, *Life & Writings of Frederick Douglass;* and Rippy, "Mexican Projects."

My account of the execution of the Lincoln conspirators was based on material in Katz, *Witness to an Era,* and Tucker, *Hancock the Superb;* information on Henry Wirz's death came from Morsberger, "After Andersonville"; Lowenfels, *Walt Whitman's Civil War;* and a clipping found in the Waring Papers.

Material relating to the soldiers' homecoming was quoted from Cogley, *History of the 7th Indiana; Reminiscences of the Civil War;* Hight, *History of the 58th Regiment;* Dobie, Letters; Lane, *Soldier's Diary;* Trenerry, "When the Boys Came Home"; Barney, *Recollections of Field Service;* Bruce, "Daniel E. Bruce"; Strong, *Yankee Private's Civil War;* Mohr, *Cormany Diaries;* and Stewart, Diary.

Observations by reporters covering the South were taken from Trowbridge, *Desolate South;* Andrews, *South since the War;* Dennett, *South As It Is;* Reid, *After the War;* Kennaway, *On Sherman's Track;* and the June 12, 1865, edition of the *New York Times.*

Other images and comments were quoted from Tarbell, "Disbanding the Confederate Army"; Bush, "Reminiscence"; Mixson, *Reminiscences;* Sherrill, *Annals of Lincoln County;* Hague, *Blockaded Family;* Behrens, *Total War in Carolina;* Porter, Diary; Ridley, *Battles & Sketches;* Lightsey, *Veteran's Story;* and Lasswell, *Rags and Hope.*

For the final years of Jefferson Davis I relied on Dorris, "Pardoning the Leaders," and B. Davis, *Long Surrender.*

The material relating to Winslow Homer's painting *Prisoners from the Front* came from Simpson, *Winslow Homer Paintings.*

Of help on the black experience during Reconstruction were Cornelius, "Freedmen's Bureau of Louisiana"; Foner, *Reconstruction;* and the *New Orleans Tribune* for August 13, 1866. For the Memphis riots I used Rable, *But There Was No Peace;* Ryan, "Memphis Riots of 1866"; Holmes, "Underlying Causes" and "Effects of the Memphis Race Riot"; Richardson, "Memphis Race Riot"; and Lovett, "Memphis Riots." The following sources were used for the New Orleans riots: Rable, *But There Was No Peace;* Taylor, "New Orleans and Reconstruction"; Reynolds, "New Orleans Riot of 1866, Reconsidered"; and Vandal, "Origins of the New Orleans Riot of 1866, Revisited."

For the postwar assimilation of soldiers back into society, I consulted Leventhal, "Disbandment of the Union Army"; Abbott, "Civil War and the Crime Wave"; Nevins, "Major Result of the Civil War"; McConnell, *Glorious Contentment;* Bailey, "Letters"; Murphy, *Nation Reunited;* and Symonds, *Joseph E. Johnston.*

The portion of this chapter dealing with the legal determination of the end of the Civil War draws on Murray, "End of the Rebellion."

23. "I DIE A DISGRACED SOLDIER"

This chapter is based largely on the testimony and evidence given during the Warren Court of Inquiry, later published by the U.S. government under the title *Proceedings, Findings, and Opinions of the Court of Inquiry Convened by Order of the President of the United States in the case of Gouverneur K. Warren,* 1883. Helpful as well were letters, clippings, and memoranda gathered in the Warren Papers held by the New York State Library. Also utilized were contemporary trial accounts contained in the following newspapers: the *New York Herald,* the *New York Evening Post,* the *New York Sun,* the *New York Telegram,* and the *New York Times.*

Useful secondary sources on the subject are Flanagan, *Life of General . . . Warren;* Hutton, *Sheridan and His Army;* O'Connor, *Sheridan the Inevitable;* and Taylor, *Gouverneur Kemble Warren.*

24. WAR WITHOUT END

Alexander K. McClure's observations will be found in the preface he wrote to a collection of articles titled *Annals of the War.* Helpful as well was Symonds, *Joseph E. Johnston.*

The Walt Whitman material came from Geisimar, *Whitman Reader.* Forrest's farewell speech is quoted from Hancock, *Hancock's Diary,* while Sherman's can be found in *OR* 47/3. Also useful was the April 30, 1865, edition of the *New York Times.*

Bibliography

———◁○▷———

MANUSCRIPT SOURCES

ALABAMA DEPARTMENT OF ARCHIVES AND HISTORY
      Harris, Josiah F. *Reminiscence,* 1951.
      Peck, John E. Letter, May 8, 1865.
      Shipman, Stephen V. Diary, 1865.
CITY MUSEUM OF MOBILE, ALABAMA
      Mumford, William T. Diary, 1865.
DUKE UNIVERSITY
      Cockrell, Monroe. Papers.
      Confederate Veteran Papers (Lay, W. B. Letter on the fall of Selma,
         n.d.).
      Cooke, John E. Letters, 1866–1869.
      Cooper, John S. Diary, 1865.
      Cowart, Robert E. Papers (Munford Letters).
      Daniel, John W. Papers.
      Devereux Family Papers.
      Metz, George P. Diary, 1865.
      Munford-Ellis Papers.
      Nourse, James. Diary, 1865.
      Riggs, Philip D. Letters, 1865.
EAST CAROLINA UNIVERSITY
      Tarleton, Sallie L. Papers.
EMORY UNIVERSITY
      Frisbie, Ichabod. Diary, 1865.
      Girdner, Ephrain L. Letters, 1865.
      Pierce, Samuel B. "Personal Narrative," 1865.

FREDERICKSBURG-SPOTSYLVANIA NATIONAL BATTLEFIELD PARK
    Bennett, Risen T. "Account of the 14th North Carolina," n.d.
    Snyder, Thompson A. *Recollections of Four Years,* 1927.
GEORGIA DEPARTMENT OF ARCHIVES AND HISTORY
    Cooke, Giles B. *War Experiences,* n.d.
    Croft, Charlotte. "Personal Experience on the Day of the West Point Battle," n.d.
    Griggs, Carrie. "Reminiscence of Fort Tyler," n.d.
    Marshall, T. J. Diary, 1865.
    Smith, Imogene G. "Battle of Fort Tyler," 1915.
    Stanley, Isham. "Story of the Last Battle at West Point, Ga.," n.d.
GEORGIA HISTORICAL SOCIETY LIBRARY, SAVANNAH
    Burt, Willis P. Diary (in Laura Brantley Papers), 1865.
    Mercer, George A. Diary, 1865.
HISTORICAL SOCIETY OF PENNSYLVANIA
    Foering, John O. Diary, 1865.
    Smith, J. L. Letters, 1865.
ILLINOIS STATE HISTORICAL SOCIETY
    Black, John C. Letters, 1865.
    Drish, James. Letters, 1865.
    Eddington, W. R. *Civil War Experiences,* n.d.
    Gilbert, Edwin. Letters, 1865.
    Hussey, Fenton A. Letter, April 30, 1865.
    Merriam, Jonathan. Letters, 1865.
    Millice, Amos. Letter, April 22, 1865.
    Peters, W. H. Letters, 1865.
    Ross, Levi. Letters, 1865.
INDIANA HISTORICAL SOCIETY
    Crouse, W. O. Journal, 1865.
    Griest, Alvin. *Three Years in Dixie,* n.d.
INDIANA STATE LIBRARY
    Bush, Andrew. Letters, 1865.
    Slack, James R. Letters and Diary, 1865.
    Stratton, George D. Letters and Diary, 1865.
LIBRARY OF CONGRESS
    Allen, Charles J. Memoirs and Letters, 1865.
    Barbee, James D. and David R. Papers.
    Chamberlain, Joshua. Papers.
    Freeman, Douglas S. Papers.
    Gould, William J. Diary, 1865.
    Hotchkiss, Jedediah. Papers.
    Keifer, J. Warren. Letters, 1865.
    Latta, James W. Diary, 1865.
    Lewis, Lathrop L. Diary, 1865.
    McCalla, Helen V. Diary, 1865.
    Mallory, Stephen R. Diary, 1865.
    Mitchell, C. D. *Field Notes of the Civil War,* 1865.
    Perham, A. S. Papers.
    St. John, Bela. Diary and Letters, 1865.
    Smith, Howard M. Letters and Diary, 1865.
    Stevens, Hazard. Letters, 1865.
    Ward, Charles G. Diary, 1865.
    Wilson, James H. Papers.

LOUISIANA STATE UNIVERSITY, BATON ROUGE
    Andrews, George L. Papers (C. C. Andrews letter).
MINNESOTA HISTORICAL SOCIETY
    Bishop, Judson W. Letters, 1865.
MOBILE PUBLIC LIBRARY
    Craig, James. Letters, 1865.
    Rice, Jasper H. Letters, 1865.
MUSEUM OF THE CONFEDERACY
    Fontaine, Mary A. Letters, 1865.
    Harding, Hiram W. Diary, 1865.
    Mason, John T. *Private Journal,* 1865.
    Potts, Frank. Letters, 1865.
    Quarles, Mann S. "Personal Reminiscences," n.d.
    Rogers, Timothy W. Diary, 1865.
    Simmons, Mrs. William A. "The Flight from Richmond," 1865.
    Smith, Caleb M. Diary, 1865.
    Tilghman, T. F. Diary, 1865.
NEW YORK STATE LIBRARY
    Dobie, David F. Letters, 1865.
    Warren, Gouverneur K. Papers.
NORTH CAROLINA DEPARTMENT OF ARCHIVES AND HISTORY
    Bush, J. A. "Reminiscence," 1922.
    Clark, Walter S. Papers.
    Gudger, J. C. L. Articles on the 25th Regiment.
OHIO HISTORICAL SOCIETY
    Ames, Lyman D. Diary, 1865.
    Elder, Robert N. Letters, 1865.
    Griffith, John W. Diary, 1865.
    Inskeep, John D. Diary, 1865.
    Keifer, J. Warren. Papers.
    Porter, Styles. Diary, 1865.
PETERSBURG NATIONAL MILITARY PARK
    Wiatt, William. Diary, 1865.
SOUTHERN HISTORICAL COLLECTION, UNIVERSITY OF NORTH
    CAROLINA
    Barringer, Rufus. Diary, 1865.
    Hyde, Anne B. "Notes about Miss Bee's Father Hung by Gen. Sherman's
        Men in S.C.," n.d.
    Smith, Edmund Kirby. Papers.
    Stewart, William H. Diary, 1865.
    Waring, Joseph F. Diary, 1865, and Papers.
STATE HISTORICAL SOCIETY OF IOWA
    Glassgow, Samuel H. Letters, 1865.
    Green, Levi N. Diary, 1865.
    Morgan, John S. Diary, 1865.
    Patterson, F. J. Letters, 1865.
    Schermerhorn, Winfield S. Letters, 1865.
    Tyler, Loren S. Diary and Letters, 1865.
STATE HISTORICAL SOCIETY OF MISSOURI, WESTERN HISTORICAL
    MANUSCRIPT COLLECTION
    Audsley, Francis F. Letters, 1865.
    Hinrichs, Charles F. Diary, 1865.

TULANE UNIVERSITY
    Army of Tennessee Papers.
    Brickell, William E. "Reminiscence," n.d.
    Rosser, Thomas L. Letter, 1902.
    Taylor, Richard. Letterbook, 1864–1865.
UNITED STATES MILITARY HISTORY INSTITUTE (CARLISLE BARRACKS)
    Baker, Samuel S. Diary, 1865.
    Griest, Alvin. *Three Years in Dixie,* n.d.
    Hickenlooper, Andrew. "Reminiscences," n.d.
    Hunt, Frances C. Diary, 1865.
    Kautz, August V. *Reminiscences,* n.d.
    Klein, Jacob. Letters, 1865.
    Klice, William. Letters, 1865.
    Landis, William J. Diary, 1865.
    Nelson, Joseph K. "Recollections of My Early Life," 1909.
    Parsons, Charles M. *Reminiscences,* n.d.
    Spire, Charles W. Letters, 1865.
    Stockton, Joseph. War Diary, 1910.
    Stoner, Ira C. Diary, 1865.
    West, Samuel. Diary, 1865.
    Wolfe, Alphonse P. Letters, 1865.
UNIVERSITY OF MICHIGAN
    Noble, Henry G. Letters, 1865.
    Patterson, Philo D. Letters, 1865.
    Potter, Henry A. Diary, 1865.
    Ripley, Lauren H. "Personal Reminiscences," 1894.
    Woodruff, Charles. Diary, 1865.
UNIVERSITY OF SOUTH CAROLINA, SOUTH CAROLINIANA LIBRARY
    Stevens, Edward L. "Notes on Potter's Raid," 1865.
    Townsend, Edward D. Letter, May 28, 1865.
UNIVERSITY OF TEXAS AT AUSTIN, BARKER TEXAS HISTORY CENTER
    Davis, Mathew J. *Reminiscence of the War for Secession,* 1934.
    Oldham, Williamson S. *Last Days of the Confederacy,* 1866.
VIRGINIA HISTORICAL SOCIETY
    Gordon, John B. Official Report of the Appomattox Campaign, 1865.
    Livermore, W. T. Diary, 1865.
    Lockett, Samuel H. Letter to D. H. Maury, 1866.
    McCabe, W. Gordon. Letters, 1865.
    McIntosh, David G. Diary, 1865.
    Myer, Gustavus A. *Memorandum,* 1865.
    Phillips, James E. Journal and Diary, 1865.
    Pickett, George. Official Report of the Appomattox Campaign, 1865.
    Robertson, Francis S. *Reminiscences,* n.d.
    Voris, Alvin C. *War Letters,* 1865.
    Warren, Gouverneur K. Correspondence, various dates.
VIRGINIA MILITARY INSTITUTE ARCHIVES
    Gatewood, A. C. L. *Materials Relating to the 11th Virginia Cavalry,* n.d.
VIRGINIA STATE LIBRARY
    Mahone, William. Papers (Longstreet letters).
    Willis, Byrd C. Diary and War Reminiscences, 1865.
WESTERN RESERVE HISTORICAL SOCIETY
    Evans, William D. Diary, 1865.
    Palmer, William P. Collection.

Wild, Fred H. *Memoirs and History of the Baltimore Light Artillery,*
    1912.
WISCONSIN STATE HISTORICAL SOCIETY
    Shipman, Stephen V. Diary, 1865.

PERSONAL ACCOUNTS AND UNIT HISTORIES

Abernethy, Byron R. *Private Elisha Stockwell, Jr., Sees the Civil War.* 1958.
Adams, Bright, ed. "The Civil War Letters of James Rush Holmes." *Western Penn-sylvania Historical Magazine,* 1961.
Adams, Jacob. "Diary." *Ohio Archaeological and Historical Quarterly,* 1929.
Agassiz, George R., ed. *Meade's Headquarters, 1863–1865.* 1922.
Alexander, Edward P. *Fighting for the Confederacy.* 1989.
[An Eyewitness]. "The Capture of President Jefferson Davis." *Register of the Ken-tucky Historical Society,* 1966.
Andersen, Mary Ann, ed. *Civil War Diary of Allen Morgan Geer.* 1977.
Andrews, Christopher C. *History of the Campaign of Mobile.* 1867.
Andrews, Sidney. *The South since the War.* 1866.
Andrus, Michael J. *The Brooke, Fauquier, Loudoun and Alexandria Artillery.* 1990.
Arbuckle, John C. *Civil War Experiences of a Foot Soldier.* 1930.
Aston, Howard. *History and Roster of the Fourth and Fifth Independent Battalions and Thirteenth Regiment Ohio Cavalry Volunteers.* 1902.
Aten, Henry J. *History of the 85th Regiment Illinois Volunteer Infantry.* 1901.
Bahnson, Henry T. *Days of the War, 1863–1865.* 1903.
Bailey, Virginia G., ed. "Letters of Melvin Dwinnell." *Georgia Historical Quarterly,* 1963.
Bailey, W. "The Star Company of Ector's Texas Brigade." *Confederate Veteran* 22 (1914).
Baker, Levi. *History of the Ninth Massachusetts Battery.* 1888.
Barney, C. *Recollections of Field Service.* 1865.
Bartlett, Napier. *A Soldier's Story of the War.* 1874.
Barton, Randolph. *Recollections 1861–1865.* 1913.
Bauer, K. Jack, ed. *Soldiering.* 1977.
Beals, Thomas P. "In a Charge near Fort Hell, Petersburg, April 2, 1865." *Maine MOLLUS* 2 (1902).
Beaumont, E. B. "Campaign of Selma." *The United Service,* 1880.
Bentley, William H. *History of the 77th Illinois Volunteer Infantry.* 1883.
Berry, Chester D. *Loss of the* Sultana *and Reminiscences of the Survivors.* 1892.
Best, Isaac O. *History of the 121st New York State Infantry.* 1921.
Bierce, Ambrose. *Collected Works.* 1966.
Bircher, William. *A Drummer-Boy's Diary.* 1889.
Blackett, R. J. M., ed. *Thomas Morris Chester: Black Civil War Correspondent.* 1989.
Blackford, Susan L., ed. *Letters from Lee's Army.* 1947.
Blakeman, A. N., ed. *Personal Recollections of the War of the Rebellion.* 1907.

441

Bosbyshell, Oliver. *The 48th in the War.* 1895.

Bowen, James L. *History of the Thirty-seventh Regiment Massachusetts Volunteers.* 1884.

Bowen, James R. *Regimental History of the 1st New York Dragoons.* 1900.

Boykin, Edward. *The Falling Flag — The Evacuation of Richmond.* 1874.

Bradley, G. S. *Star Corps.* 1865.

Bradwell, I. G. "After the Surrender at Appomattox." *Confederate Veteran* 17 (1909).

———. "Making Our Way Home from Appomattox." *Confederate Veteran* 29 (1921).

———. "On Picket Duty in Front of Fort Steadman." *Confederate Veteran* 38 (1930).

Brady, Robert. *Story of One Regiment: The 11th Maine Volunteers.* 1896.

Branson, David. "The Last Battle of the War." *The Bivouac,* 1883.

Brewer, Abraham T. *History Sixty-first Regiment Pennsylvania Volunteers.* 1911.

Brown, Norman D., ed. *One of Cleiburne's Command.* 1980.

Bruce, H. W. "Some Reminiscences of the Second of April, 1865." *Southern Historical Society Papers* 9 (1881).

Bryan, T. Conn, ed. "A Georgia Woman's Civil War Diary." *Georgia Historical Quarterly,* 1967.

Bryant, Edwin E. *History of the 3rd Regiment Wisconsin Veteran Volunteer Infantry.* 1891.

Buffum, Francis H., ed. *Memorial of the Great Rebellion.* 1882.

Buttolph, John R. "Occupation Duty in Selma." *Civil War Times Illustrated,* 1966.

Caba, G. Craig, ed. "Incidents of the Grand Review at Washington." *Lincoln Herald,* 1980.

Cadwallader, Sylvanus. *Three Years with Grant.* 1955.

Calkins, William W. *History of the 104th Regiment Illinois Volunteer Infantry.* 1895.

Camm, R. A. "Naval Officer's Recollections of Lee's Retreat." 1884.

Campbell, John A. *Recollections of the Evacuation of Richmond.* 1880.

Camper, Charles. *Historical Record of the 1st Regiment Maryland Infantry.* 1871.

Cardwell, David. "The Battle of Five Forks." *Confederate Veteran* 22 (1914).

Chamberlain, Joshua L. "Appomattox." *New York MOLLUS,* 1903.

———. *The Passing of the Armies.* 1915.

Chambers, Henry A. *Diary of Captain Henry A. Chambers.* 1983.

Chambers, W. P. "One of the Unrecorded Battles." *Confederate Veteran* 22 (1914).

Chambrun, Adolphe de. *Impressions of Lincoln and the Civil War.* N.d.

Cheek, Philip. *History of the Sauk County Riflemen.* 1909.

Chenery, William H. *Fourteenth Regiment Rhode Island Heavy Artillery.* 1898.

Chestnut, Mary. *A Diary from Dixie.* 1949.

Clark, Charles M. *History of the Thirty-ninth Regiment Illinois Volunteer Veteran Infantry.* 1889.

Clark, James S. *The Thirty-fourth Iowa Regiment.* 1892.

Clark, Micajah H. "Retreat of the Cabinet." *Southern Historical Society Papers* 26 (1898).

Clark, Walter. *Histories of the Several Regiments & Battalions from North Carolina.* 5 vols. 1901.

Cogley, Thomas S. *History of the 7th Indiana Cavalry Volunteers.* 1876.

Collis, Septima. *A Woman's War Record.* 1889.

Colston, Frederick M. "Recollections of the Last Months in the Army of Army of Northern Virginia." *Southern Historical Society Papers* 38 (1910).

Conerly, Buxton R. "How Fort Gregg Was Defended." *Confederate Veteran* 15 (1907).

Conolly, Thomas. *An Irishman in Dixie.* 1988.

Craft, David. *History of the 141st Regiment Pennsylvania Volunteers.* 1885.

Cronin, David E. *The Evolution of a Life.* 1884.

Crook, William H. "Lincoln's Last Day." *Century Magazine,* 1907.

Crotty, Daniel G. *Four Years Campaigning in the Army of the Potomac.* 1874.

Culver, F. E. "Entered and Escaped from Fort Mahone." *Confederate Veteran* 18 (1910).

Cummins, Simon. *Give God the Glory.* 1979.

Cushman, Frederick E. *History of the 58th Regiment Massachusetts Volunteers.* 1865.

Dalzell, James M. *Private Dalzell, His Autobiography.* 1888.

Dana, Charles A. *Recollections of the Civil War.* 1898.

Davis, Creed T. *Diary of the War.* 1884.

Davis, Jefferson. *Rise and Fall of the Confederate Government.* 1881.

Davis, Varina. *Jefferson Davis: A Memoir.* 1890.

Davis, William C., ed. "On the Road to Appomattox." *Civil War Times Illustrated,* 1971.

———, ed. *Diary of a Confederate Soldier.* 1989.

Dawson, Henry B. *First Flag in Richmond, April 3, 1865.* 1866.

Day, W. A. *A True History of Company I, 49th Regiment, North Carolina Troops.* 1893.

———. "Life Among Bullets — In the Rifle Pits." *Confederate Veteran* 29 (1921).

Dayton, Ruth W., ed. *Diary of a Confederate Soldier, James E. Hall.* 1961.

DeLeon, Thomas C. *Four Years in Rebel Capitals.* 1890.

Denison, Frederic. *Sabres and Spurs: The First Regiment of Rhode Island Cavalry.* 1876.

Dennett, John R. *South As It Is: 1865–1866.* 1965.

de Trobriand, Regis. *Four Years with the Army of the Potomac.* 1889.

Dickinson, Julian G. "The Capture of Jeff. Davis." *Michigan MOLLUS,* 1888.

Dinkins, James. "The Last Campaign of Forrest's Cavalry." *Confederate Veteran* 35 (1927).

Divine, John E. *35th Battalion Virginia Cavalry.* 1985.

Douglas, Henry K. *I Rode with Stonewall.* 1940.

Dowdey, Clifford, and Manarin, Louis H., eds. *The Wartime Papers of R. E. Lee.* 1959.

Duke, Basil W. "After the Fall of Richmond." *Southern Bivouac,* 1886.

———. "Last Days of the Confederacy." In *Battles and Leaders of the Civil War.* 1889.

Duncan, Thomas D. *Recollections*. 1922.

Dunlap, Leslie W., ed. *Your Affectionate Husband: J. F. Culver*. 1978.

Eden, Robert C. *Sword and Gun: A History of the 37th Wisconsin*. 1865.

Eisenschiml, Otto, ed. *Vermont General*. 1960.

Elliott, Isaac H. *History of the 33rd Regiment Illinois Veteran Volunteer Infantry*. 1902.

Elliott, James C. *The Southern Soldier Boy*. 1907.

Ellis, Daniel. *Thrilling Adventures*. 1867.

Emilio, Luis F. *History of the Fifty-fourth Regiment of Massachusetts Volunteer Infantry*. 1894.

Fatout, Paul, ed. *Letters of a Civil War Surgeon*. 1961.

Fleet, Betsy, ed. "Chapter of Unwritten History." *Virginia Magazine of History and Biography,* 1963.

Floyd, William B. "The Burning of the *Sultana*." *The Wisconsin Magazine of History,* 1927.

Ford, John S. *Rip Ford's Texas*. 1963.

Ford, Worthington, ed. *A Cycle of Adams Letters*. 1920.

Fortney, Peter. "Letter." *Bulletin of the Cincinnati Historical Society,* 1966.

Fryer, David F. *History of the 80th Ohio Veteran Volunteer Infantry*. 1904.

Fussell, I. L. *History of the 34th Regiment Indiana Veteran Volunteer Infantry*. N.d.

Gache, Louis-Hippolyte. *Frenchman, Chaplain, Rebel*. 1981.

Gage, M. D. *From Vicksburg to Raleigh*. 1865.

Gerrish, Theodore. *Army Life: A Private's Reminiscences*. 1882.

Gibbon, John. *Personal Recollections of the Civil War*. 1928.

Gibbs, James M. *History of the First Battalion Pennsylvania Six Months Volunters and 187th Regiment Pennsylvania Volunteer Infantry*. 1905.

Gilpin, E. N. *The Last Campaign.* 1908.

Gordon, Armistead C. *Memories & Memorials of William Gordon McCabe*. 1925.

Gordon, George H. *War Diary of Events*. 1882.

Gordon, John B. *Reminiscences of the Civil War*. 1904.

Gorman, J. C. *Lee's Last Campaign*. 1866.

Govan, Gilbert E., ed. *The Haskell Memoirs*. 1960.

Goyne, Minetta A., ed. *Lone Star & Double Eagle*. 1982.

Granger, Shanton, ed. "A Witness to History." *Civil War Times Illustrated,* 1985.

Grant, Ulysses S. *Personal Memoirs of U. S. Grant*. 1885.

Grant, W. W. "Recollections of the Last Battle." *Confederate Veteran* 23 (1915).

Graves, Joseph A. *History of the Bedford Light Artillery*. 1903.

Graves, Thomas T. "The Fall of Richmond." In *Battles and Leaders of the Civil War*. 1889.

Greeno, Charles L. "The Capture of Jefferson Davis and What I Know of It." *Ohio MOLLUS,* 1911.

Gregorie, Anne K., ed. "Diary of Captain Joseph Julius Wescoat, 1863–1865." *South Carolina Historical Magazine,* 1958.

Grimes, Mrs. Bryan. *Autobiography*. 1908.

Hagood, Johnson. *Memoirs of the War of Secession*. 1910.

Haines, Alanson A. *History of the Fifteenth Regiment New Jersey Volunteers*. 1883.

Hall, Hillman. *History of the 6th New York Cavalry*. 1908.

Hall, Isaac. *History of the 97th Regiment New York Volunteers*. 1890.

Hamlin, Charles. "Darkest Hour." *Maine MOLLUS*, 1898.

Hammond, Harold E., ed. *Diary of a Union Lady*. 1962.

Hancock, R. R. *Hancock's Diary*. 1887.

Handy, Moses P. "The Fall of Richmond in 1865." *The American Magazine*, 1985–86.

Hanifen, Michael. *History of Battery B, First New Jersey Artillery*. 1905.

Harnden, Henry. "The Capture of Jefferson Davis." *Wisconsin MOLLUS*, 1896.

Harris, Moses. "With the Reserve Brigade." *Journal of the United States Cavalry Association*, 1891.

Harris, N. H. "Nineteenth Mississippi Regiment." *Confederate Veteran* 6 (1898).

Harrison, Burton N. "The Capture of Jefferson Davis." *Century Magazine*, 1883.

Harrison, Mrs. Burton N. *Recollections Grave and Gay*. 1911.

Harrison, Francis B. "From the Diary of Wilson Miles Cary." *Tyler's Quarterly Historical and Genealogical Magazine*, 1942.

Harrison, Walter. *Pickett's Men: A Fragment of War History*. 1870.

Hatch, Carl E., ed. *Dearest Susie*. 1971.

Haynes, Edwin M. *History of the Tenth Regiment Vermont Volunteers*. 1870.

Hight, John J. *History of the 58th Regiment of Indiana Volunteer Infantry*. 1895.

History of the 57th Regiment, Pennsylvania Veteran Volunteer Infantry. 1904.

Holmes, Emma. *Diary of Miss Emma Holmes*. 1979.

Holt, Thad, Jr., ed. *Miss Waring's Journal*. 1964.

Hopkins, William. *Seventh Regiment Rhode Island Volunteers*. 1903.

Horrocks, James. *My Dear Parents: The Civil War as Seen by an English Soldier*. 1982.

Hosea, Lewis M. "Some Side Lights on the War for the Union." *Ohio MOLLUS*, 1912.

Houghton, Edwin B. *The Campaigns of the Seventeenth Maine*. 1866.

Houghton, Henry. "The Ordeal of Civil War: A Recollection." *Vermont History*, 1973.

Howard, A. B. "Defence of Fort Gregg." *Confederate Veteran* 3 (1877).

Howard, McHenry. *Recollections of a Maryland Confederate Officer*. 1914.

Hudson, Joshua H. *Sketches and Reminiscences*. 1903.

Hunt, Cornelius E. *The Shenandoah, or the Last Confederate Cruiser*. 1867.

Hurst, Samuel H. *Journal History of the 73rd Ohio*. 1866.

Huyette, Miles C. *Reminiscences of a Soldier in the American Civil War*. 1908.

Jackson, Oscar L. *The Colonel's Diary*. 1922.

Jamison, Matthew H. *Recollections of Pioneer and Army Life*. 1911.

Jaquette, Henrietta, ed. *South After Gettysburg*. 1956.

Johnson, Charles B. *Muskets and Medicine*. 1917.

Johnson, Robert U., and Buel, Clarence C., eds. *Battles and Leaders of the Civil War*. 1889.

Johnston, David E. *Story of a Confederate Boy in the Civil War*. 1914.

Jones, A. K. "Defence of Battery Gregg." *Southern Historical Society Papers* 8 (1880).

———. "Third Arkansas Regiment at Appomattox." *Confederate Veteran* 8 (1915).

Jones, John B. *A Rebel War Clerk's Diary.* 1866.

Jones, Margaret, ed. *Journal of Catherine Edmondston.* N.d.

Kennaway, John S. *On Sherman's Track: The South after the War.* 1868.

King, Spencer B., ed. *War-Time Journal of a Georgia Girl.* 1976.

Kinnear, John R. *History of the 86th Illinois Volunteer Infantry.* 1866.

Kirwan, A. D., ed. *Johnny Green of the Orphan Brigade.* 1956.

Kirwan, Thomas. *Memorial History of the 17th Regiment Massachusetts Volunteer Infantry.* 1911.

Kreutzer, William. *Notes and Observations.* 1879.

Lane, David. *A Soldier's Diary.* 1905.

Larson, James. *Sergeant Larson and the 4th Cavalry.* 1935.

Lasswell, Mary, ed. *Rags and Hope.* 1961.

Lemke, W. J., ed. *Diary of Captain Edward G. Miller.* 1960.

Lightsey, Ada. *The Veteran's Story.* 1899.

Linn, George W. *From Richmond to Appomattox.* 1911.

Literary and Historical Activities in North Carolina. 1907.

Locke, William. *The Story of the Regiment.* 1866.

Long, A. L. *Memoirs of Robert E. Lee.* 1886.

Longacre, Edward G., ed. "With Lincoln on His Last Journey." *Lincoln Herald,* 1982.

Longstreet, James. *From Manassas to Appomattox.* 1896.

Lord, Edward O. *History of the Ninth Regiment New Hampshire Volunteers.* 1895.

Lupold, Harry F., ed. "A Union Medical Officer Views the 'Texians'." *Southwestern Historical Quarterly,* 1974.

McAdams, Francis M. *Every-day Soldier Life.* 1884.

McBride, Robert. *In the Ranks: From the Wilderness to Appomattox.* 1881.

McCain, William D., ed. *Memoirs of Henry Tillinghast Ireys.* 1954.

McCarthy, Carlton. *Detailed Minutae of Soldier Life in the Army of Northern Virginia.* 1882.

McCorkle, John. *Three Years with Quantrill.* 1966.

McGlashan, Peter S. *Our Last Retreat: An Address.* 1893.

McLeod, Martha N. *Brother Warriors.* 1940.

McMillan, Malcolm C., ed. *The Alabama Confederate Reader.* 1963.

Mahon, John K., ed. "The Civil War Letters of Samuel Mahon, Seventh Iowa Infantry." *Iowa Journal of History,* 1953.

Mallory, Stephen. "Last Days of the Confederate Government." *McClure's Magazine,* 1900.

Marbaker, Thomas. *History of the Eleventh New Jersey Volunteers.* 1898.

Marshall, Charles. "General Lee's Farewell Address to His Army." In *Battles and Leaders of the Civil War.* 1889.

———. *Appomattox, An Address.* 1894.

["Mary"]. "After Appomattox." *Confederate Veteran* 31 (1923).

Maury, Dabney H. "The Defence of Mobile in 1865." *Southern Historical Society Papers* 13 (1877).

Merrill, James M., and Marshall, James F., eds. "The 16th Kentucky and the End of the War: The Letters of Henry Clay Weaver." *Filson Club History Quarterly,* 1958.

Merrill, Samuel. *Seventieth Indiana Volunteer Infantry.* 1900.

Merritt, Wesley. "Notes on the Surrender of Lee." *Century Magazine,* 1902.

Michaels, Edward R., ed. *Civil War Letters of Sylvester Rynearson.* N.d.

Mixson, Frank M. *Reminiscences of a Private.* 1910.

Moderwell, E. D. "Outline of Stoneman's Cavalry Raid." 1867.

Mohr, James C., ed. *The Cormany Diaries.* 1982.

Moneyhon, Carl H., ed. "The Diary of Virginia Davis Gray." *Arkansas Historical Quarterly,* 1983.

Montgomery, Frank A. *Reminiscences of a Mississippean in Peace and War.* 1901.

Mooney, Chase C., ed. "A Union Chaplain's Diary." *Proceedings of the New Jersey Historical Society.* 1957.

Moore, J. Staunton. "The Battle of Five Forks." *Confederate Veteran* 16 (1908).

Moore, John H., ed. "The Last Officer — April 1865." *South Carolina Historical Magazine,* 1966.

Morrill, Lily M., ed. *My Confederate Girlhood.* 1982.

Moss, Helen H. "Account of the Assassination of President Lincoln." N.d.

M.R.R. "Potter's Raid." *Our Women in the War* (1885).

Mulholland, St. Clair A. *Story of the 116th Regiment Pennsylvania Infantry.* 1899.

Myers, Frank M. *The Comanches.* 1871.

Neese, George M. *Three Years in the Confederate Horse Artillery.* 1911.

Nevins, Allan, ed. *A Diary of Battle.* 1962.

——, ed. *Diary of George Templeton Strong.* 1962.

Newhall, Frederick. "With Sheridan in Lee's Last Campaign." *Maine Bugle,* 1896.

Newton, Alexander H. *Out of the Briars.* 1910.

Ninth Cavalry: One Hundred and Twenty-first Regiment. 1890.

Norton, Chauncey S. *Red Neck Ties, or History of the 15th New York Volunteer Cavalry.* 1891.

Osborne, Hampden. "The Struggle for Fort Mahone." *Confederate Veteran* 25 (1917).

Osborne, William H. *History of the 29th Regiment of Massachusetts Volunteer Infantry.* 1877.

Parker, Francis J. *Story of the 32nd Regiment Massachusetts Infantry.* 1880.

Parker, William H. *Recollections of a Naval Officer.* 1883.

Peck, George B. "A Recruit before Petersburg." *Personal Narratives of Events in the War of the Rebellion, Being Papers Read before the Rhode Island Soldiers and Sailors Historical Society.* 1880.

Peck, Rufus H. *Reminiscences of a Confederate Soldier.* 1913.

Pember, Phoebe Y. *A Southern Woman's Story.* 1959.

Phelan, Helen C., ed. *Who Only Stand and Wait.* 1990.

Pickett, George E. *Soldier of the South.* 1928.

Pickett, LaSalle C. *What Happened to Me.* 1917.

Poague, William T. *Gunner with Stonewall.* 1957.

Porter, Horace. "Five Forks and the Pursuit of Lee." In *Battles and Leaders of the Civil War.* 1889.

———. "The Surrender at Appomattox Court House." In *Battles and Leaders of the Civil War.* 1889.

———. *Campaigning with Grant.* 1897.

Preston, Noble D. *History of the 10th Regiment of Cavalry, New York State Volunteers.* 1892.

Puntenney, George H. *History of the 37th Regiment Indiana Volunteer Infantry.* 1896.

Putnam, Sallie A. *In Richmond during the Confederacy.* 1867.

Quaife, Milo M., ed. *From the Cannon's Mouth.* 1959.

Rauscher, Frank. *Music on the March.* 1892.

Reagan, John H. "The Flight and Capture of Jefferson Davis." In *The Annals of the War, Written by Leading Participants North and South.* 1878.

———. *Memoirs.* 1906.

Reece, Frances R., ed. "The Final Push to Appomattox." *Michigan History Magazine,* 1944.

Reid, Whitelaw. *After the War: A Southern Tour.* 1866.

Reminiscences of the Civil War (Members of the 103rd Illinois). 1904.

Rhodes, Elisha H. *All for the Union.* 1985.

Rhodes, John H. *History of Battery B First Regiment Rhode Island Light Artillery.* 1894.

Rich, Edward R. *Comrades!* 1898.

Ridley, B. L. "Last Battles of the War." *Confederate Veteran* 3 (1895).

———. *Battles & Sketches of the Army of Tennessee.* 1906.

Rietveld, Ronald D., ed. "An Eyewitness Account of the Assassination of Abraham Lincoln." *Civil War History,* 1976.

Ripley, Edward H. *The Capture and Occupation of Richmond.* 1906.

Roback, Henry. *Veteran Volunteers of Herkimer and Otsego.* 1888.

Robertson, James I., ed. *Civil War Letters of General Robert McAllister.* 1965.

Rock, R. S. "War Reminiscence." *Confederate Veteran* 9 (1901).

Roller, John E. *The Last Retreat: A Memoir.* 1982.

Rood, Hosea W. *Story of Service of Company E, 12th Wisconsin Regiment.* 1893.

Roth, Margaret, ed. *Well Mary.* 1960.

Rowell, John W. *Yankee Artilleryman.* 1975.

Rowland, Charles A. *Diary and Letters.* 1975.

Schilling, Edward. "My Three Years in the Volunteer Army of the United States of America." *Journal of the Alleghenies,* 1984.

Scott, D. M. "Selma and Dallas County, Ala." *Confederate Veteran* 24 (1916).

Scott, William F. *Story of a Cavalry Regiment.* 1893.

Semmes, Raphael. *Confederate Raider Alabama.* 1962.

Shannon, Fred A., ed. *Civil War Letters of Sergeant Onley Andrus.* 1947.

Shaw, Horace H. *The First Maine Heavy Artillery.* 1903.

Sheridan, Philip H. *Personal Memoirs.* 1904.

Sherlock, E. J. *Memorabilia of the Marches and Battles of the 100th Indiana Regiment.* 1896.

Sherman, William T. *Memoirs.* 1875.

Shingleton, Royce, ed. "With Loyalty and Honor as a Patriot: Recollections of a Confederate Soldier." *Alabama Historical Quarterly,* 1971.

Silliker, Ruth, ed. *The Rebel Yell & Yankee Hurrah.* 1985.

Simon, John Y., ed. *The Papers of Ulysses S. Grant.* Volume 15. 1988.

Slocum, Henry. "Final Operations of Sherman's Army." In *Battles and Leaders of the Civil War.* 1889.

Small, Harold A., ed. *The Road to Richmond.* 1939.

Smith, Charles H. *History of Fuller's Ohio Brigade.* 1909.

Smith, John L. *History of the Corn Exchange Regiment.* 1888.

Sorrel, G. Moxley. *Recollections of a Staff Officer.* 1905.

Southall, John R. "Recollections of the Evacuation of Richmond." *Confederate Veteran* 37 (1929).

South Carolina U.D.C. *Recollections and Reminiscences.* 1990.

Sparks, David S., ed. *Inside Lincoln's Army.* 1964.

Spaulding, Joseph W. "Nineteenth Maine at High Bridge." *Maine MOLLUS,* 1915.

Spencer, Warren F., ed. "A French View of the Fall of Richmond." *Virginia Magazine of History and Biography,* 1965.

Sperry, Andrew F. *History of the 33rd Iowa Infantry.* 1866.

Starr, Stephen Z., ed. "Dinwiddie Court House and Five Forks." *Virginia Magazine of History and Biography,* 1979.

Stauffer, Nelson. *Civil War Diary.* 1865.

Stephenson, P. D. "Defence of Spanish Fort." *Southern Historical Society Papers* 39 (1914).

Stevens, George T. *Three Years in the Sixth Corps.* 1866.

Stevens, Thomas N. *Dear Carrie.* 1984.

Stevenson, James H. *Boots and Saddles.* 1879.

Stiles, Kenneth L. *4th Virginia Cavalry.* 1985.

Stiles, Robert. *Four Years Under Marse Robert.* 1903.

Stonebraker, Joseph. *Rebel of '61.* 1899.

Stories of Our Soldiers (Collected from the series written especially for the Boston Journal). 1893.

The Story of the Fifty-fifth Regiment Illinois Volunteer Infantry. 1887.

Story of the 21st Regiment Connecticut Volunteer Infantry. 1900.

Strong, Robert H. *Yankee Private's Civil War.* 1961.

Sturgis, H. H. "About the Burning of Richmond." *Confederate Veteran* 17 (1909).

Sulivane, Clement. "The Fall of Richmond." In *Battles and Leaders of the Civil War.* 1889.

Summers, Festus P., ed. *A Borderland Confederate.* 1962.

Sumner, Merlin E., ed. *The Diary of Cyrus B. Comstock.* 1987.

Swinfen, David B. *Ruggles' Regiment: The 122nd New York Volunteers in the Civil War.* 1982.

Talcott, T. M. R. "From Petersburg to Appomattox." *Southern Historical Society Papers* 32 (1904).

Tarrant, E. W. "Siege and Capture of Fort Blakely." *Confederate Veteran* 23 (1915).

Taylor, Richard H. "The Last Confederate Surrender." In *The Annals of the War, Written by Leading Participants North and South.* 1878.

———. *Destruction and Reconstruction.* 1955.

Taylor, Walter H. *Four Years with General Lee.* 1877.

———. *General Lee: His Campaigns in Virginia.* 1906.

Thomas, Henry W. *History of the Doles-Cook Brigade.* 1903.

Thomas, L. P. "Their Last Battle." *Southern Historical Society Papers* 29 (1901).

Thompson, Bradford F. *History of the 112th Regiment of Illinois Volunteer Infantry.* 1885.

Timberlake, W. L. "In the Siege of Richmond and After." *Confederate Veteran* 29 (1921).

Toombs, Samuel. *Reminiscences of the War.* 1878.

Townsend, George A. *Rustics in Rebellion.* 1950.

Trowbridge, John T. *The Desolate South: 1865–1866.* 1956.

Truman, Benjamin C. "Incident of the Dying Confederacy." *The United Service,* 1896.

Under the Maltese Cross: Antietam to Appomattox. 1910.

Upson, Theodore F. *With Sherman to the Sea.* 1943.

Vaill, Theodore. *County Regiment: A Sketch of the 2nd Regiment Connecticut Heavy Artillery.* 1908.

Vandiver, Frank E., ed. *Civil War Diary of General Josiah Gorgas.* 1947.

Vautier, John D. *History of the 88th Pennsylvania Volunteers.* 1894.

Waddell, James I. *C.S.S. Shenandoah.* 1960.

Walker, Edward R. III. "George W. Webb Letter: A Union Soldier Writes Home." *Smoky Mountain Historical Society Newsletter,* 1983.

Walton, Clyde C., ed. *Private Smith's Journal.* 1963.

Watehall, E. T. "Fall of Richmond, April 3, 1865." *Confederate Veteran* 17 (1909).

Waterman, George S. "Afloat-Afield-Afloat." *Confederate Veteran* 8 (1900).

Watkins, Sam R. *Co. Aytch.* 1882.

Welles, Gideon. *Diary.* 1911.

Weygant, Charles H. *History of the One Hundred and Twenty-fourth.* 1877.

Wharff, William H. "From Chapin's Farm to Appomattox." *Maine Bugle,* 1896.

White, William S. *A Diary of the War, or, What I Saw of It.* 1883.

Whittle, William C. "Cruise of the *Shenandoah.*" *Southern Historical Society Papers* 35 (1907).

Wiley, Bell I., ed. *Fourteen Hundred and 91 Days.* 1954.

Wills, Charles W. *Army Life of an Illinois Soldier.* 1906.

Wilson, D. M. "The Last Battle of the War." *Confederate Veteran* 18 (1910).

Wilson, James H. "How Jefferson Davis Was Overtaken." In *The Annals of the War, Written by Leading Participants North and South.* 1878.

———. *Under the Old Flag.* 1912.

Winters, Erastus. *In the 50th Ohio.* 1905.

Wise, John S. *The End of an Era.* 1902.

Woodbury, Augustus. *The Second Rhode Island Regiment.* 1875.

Worsham, John H. *One of Jackson's Foot Cavalry.* 1912.

Wulsin, Lucien. *Roster of Surviving Members of the 4th Regiment Ohio Volunteer Cavalry.* 1891.

Younger, Edward, ed. *Inside the Confederate Government.* 1957.

SECONDARY SOURCES

Abbott, Edith. "The Civil War and the Crime Wave of 1865–70." *Social Service Review,* 1977.

Amis, Moses N. *Historical Raleigh.* 1913.

Andrews, Marietta M. *Scraps of Paper.* 1929.

Badeau, Adam. *Military History of U. S. Grant.* 1885.

Bagby, Alfred. *King and Queen County, Virginia.* 1908.

Bailey, Mrs. Hugh. "Mobile's Tragedy: The Great Magazine Explosion of 1865." *Alabama Review,* 1968.

Bakeless, John. "The Mystery of Appomattox." *Civil War Times Illustrated,* 1970.

Baker, Thomas H. "Refugee Newspaper: The *Memphis Daily Appeal,* 1862–1865." *Journal of Southern History,* 1963.

Ballard, Michael B. *A Long Shadow.* 1986.

Barrett, John G. *Sherman's March through the Carolinas.* 1956.

Bearss, Ed, and Calkins, Chris. *Battle of Five Forks.* 1985.

Behrens, Roger. *Total War in Carolina.* 1992.

Bergeron, Arthur, Jr. *Confederate Mobile.* 1991.

Bill, Alfred H. *The Beleaguered City: Richmond, 1861–1865.* 1946.

Brown, John H. *History of Texas.* 1888.

Brown, Louis A. *Salisbury Prison: Case Study of Confederate Prisons.* 1980.

Brubaker, John H. *Last Capital: Danville, Virginia, and the Final Days.* 1979.

Bruce, Foster, and Lynch, William O. "Daniel E. Bruce: Civil War Teamster." *Indiana Magazine of History,* 1937.

Bryant, William O. *Cahaba Prison and the* Sultana *Disaster.* 1990.

Calkins, Chris. *Thirty-six Hours before Appomattox.* 1980.

———. "The Final Days: Cumberland County, April 7, 1865." *Cumberland County, Virginia, Historical Bulletin,* 1985.

———. *The Battles of Appomattox Station and Appomattox Court House, April 8–9, 1865.* 1987.

———. *The Final Bivouac.* 1988.

———. *From Petersburg to Appomattox: A Tour Guide to the Routes of Lee's Withdrawal and Grant's Pursuit.* 1990.

———. "The Battle of Five Forks." *Blue and Gray Magazine,* 1992.

Carter, Dan T. *When the War Was Over: Failure of Self-Reconstruction.* 1985.

Carter, Samuel, III. *Riddle of Dr. Mudd.* 1974.

Castel, Albert. *General Sterling Price and the Civil War in the West.* 1968.

———. *The Presidency of Andrew Johnson.* 1979.

Catton, Bruce. *Grant Takes Command.* 1968.

Cauble, Frank P. *Surrender Proceedings at Appomattox Court House.* 1987.

Clark, Champ. *The Assassination.* 1987.

Cleaves, Freeman. *Meade of Gettysburg.* 1960.

"Confederate Persistency." *Confederate Veteran* 5 (1897).

Connelley, William E. *Quantrill and the Border Wars.* 1956.

Connelly, Thomas L. *Autumn of Glory: The Army of Tennessee, 1862–1865.* 1971.

Cooke, John E. *A Life of Gen. Robert E. Lee.* 1873.

Cornelius, John. "The Freedmen's Bureau of Louisiana." *Louisiana Historical Quarterly,* 1949.

Craighead, Erwin. *Mobile: Fact and Tradition.* 1930.

Davis, Burke. *To Appomattox.* 1959.

———. *Sherman's March.* 1980.

———. *The Long Surrender.* 1985.

Davis, William C. *Breckinridge: Statesman, Soldier, Symbol.* 1974.

———. *Jefferson Davis: The Man and His Hour.* 1991.

———, ed. *The Confederate General.* 6 vols. 1991.

Dean, Eric T., Jr. " 'We Will All Be Lost and Destroyed': Post-Traumatic Stress Disorder and the Civil War." *Civil War History,* 1991.

Delaney, Caldwell. *Confederate Mobile: A Pictoral History.* 1971.

Dimick, Howard T. "The Capture of Jefferson Davis." *The Journal of Mississippi History,* 1947.

Dockter, Albert W., Jr. "Andrew T. Perry's Experience on the *Sultana.*" *The Blount Journal,* 1989.

Dorr, Rheta C. *Susan B. Anthony.* 1928.

Dorris, J. T. "Pardoning the Leaders of the Confederacy." *Mississippi Valley Historical Review,* 1928.

Dowdey, Clifford. *Lee.* 1965.

Durkin, Joseph T. *Stephen R. Mallory: Confederate Naval Chief.* 1954.

Eckert, Ralph L. *John Brown Gordon: Soldier, Southerner, American.* 1989.

Elliott, James W. *Transport to Disaster.* 1962.

Evans, Eli N. *Judah P. Benjamin: The Jewish Confederate.* 1988.

Fatout, Paul. *Ambrose Bierce: The Devil's Lexicographer.* 1951.

"First and Last Soldiers Killed in the War." *Confederate Veteran* 3 (1895).

Flanagan, Vincent. *The Life of General Gouverneur Kemble Warren.* Ph.D. diss., City University of New York, 1969.

Flood, Charles B. *Lee: The Last Years.* 1981.

Fonde, Charles H. *An Account of the Great Explosion.* 1869.

Foner, Eric. *Reconstruction: America's Unfinished Revolution.* 1988.

Foner, Philip S. *Life & Writings of Frederick Douglass.* 1950.

Fontaine, E. "Hon. Williamson S. Oldham." *DeBow's Monthly* 7 (1869).

Foote, Shelby. *The Civil War: A Narrative.* 1974.

Fredrickson, George M. *The Inner Civil War.* 1965.

Freeman, Douglas S. *Lee's Lieutenants.* 1944.

———. *R. E. Lee, A Biography.* 1949.

Futch, Ovid L. *History of Andersonville Prison.* 1968.

Garrison, W. P. *William Lloyd Garrison: The Story of His Life.* 1889.

Geismar, Maxwell, ed. *The Whitman Reader.* 1955.

Glatthaar, Joseph T. *The March to the Sea and Beyond.* 1985.

Govan, Gilbert F. *The Chattanooga Country, 1540–1951.* 1952.

Gregorie, Anne K. *History of Sumter County, South Carolina.* 1954.

Hague, Parthenia A. *Blockaded Family.* 1888.

Hamlin, Percy G. *Old Bald Head.* 1940.

Hanchett, William, ed. "Booth's Diary." *Journal of the Illinois State Historical Society,* February 1979.

Hanna, A. J. *Flight into Oblivion.* 1959.

Harter, Eugene C. *The Lost Colony of the Confederacy.* 1985.

Heaps, Willard A. *The Singing Sixties.* 1960.

Hendrick, Burton J. *Statesmen of the Lost Cause.* 1939.

Henry, Robert S. *First with the Most: Forrest.* 1944.

———, ed. *As They Saw Forrest: Some Recollections and Comments of Contemporaries.* 1956.

Higginbotham, Jay. *Mobile: City by the Bay.* 1946.

Hill, Edwin C., ed. *Fort Sumter Memorial.* 1915.

Hill, Lawrence F. "The Confederate Exodus to Latin America." *Southwestern Historical Quarterly,* 1935.

Hoehling, A. A. *After the Guns Fell Silent.* 1990.

Hoehling, A. A., and Hoehling, Mary. *The Last Days of the Confederacy.* 1981.

Holmes, Jack D. L. "The Underlying Causes of the Memphis Race Riot of 1866." *Tennessee Historical Quarterly,* 1958.

———. "The Effects of the Memphis Race Riot of 1865." *Tennessee Historical Quarterly,* 1958.

Hoole, William S. "Vizetelly Covers the Confederacy." 1957.

Hoole, William S., and McArthur, Elizabeth H. "The Yankee Invasion of West Alabama, March–April, 1865." 1985.

Horgan, Paul. *The Great River.* 1954.

Horn, Stanley F. *Gallant Rebel.* 1947.

Huff, Sanford W. "The Eighth Regiment Iowa Infantry and Its Colonel, James L. L. Geddes, at Spanish Fort, Alabama." *Annals of Iowa,* 1867.

Hughes, Robert M. *General Johnston.* 1893.

Humphrey, David C. "A 'Very Muddy and Conflicting' View: The Civil War as Seen from Austin, Texas." *Southwestern Historical Quarterly,* 1991.

Humphreys, Andrew A. *The Virginia Campaign of 1864 and 1865.* 1883.

Hunt, Jeffrey W. *There Is Nothing Left to Us But to Fight.* N.d.

Huson, Hobart. *Refugio.* 1955.

Hutton, Paul A. *Phil Sheridan and His Army.* 1985.

Jones, James P., ed. "Farewell to Arms: Union Muster Out at Louisville." *Filson Club History Quarterly,* 1962.

———, ed. "Your Left Arm: James H. Wilson's Letters to Adam Badeau." *Civil War History,* 1966.

———. *Yankee Blitzkrieg.* 1976.

Jones, James P., and Rogers, William W. "The Surrender of Tallahassee." *Apalachee,* 1967.

Jones, Katharine M., ed. *Ladies of Richmond.* 1962.

Kaplan, Sidney, ed. *Battle-Pieces and Aspects of the War.* 1972.

Katz, D. Mark. *Witness to an Era.* 1991.

Kauffman, Michael W. "Booth's Escape Route: Lincoln's Assassin on the Run." *Blue and Gray Magazine,* 1990.

Kerby, Robert L. *Kirby Smith's Confederacy.* 1972.

King, Alma D. "The Political Career of Williamson Simpson Oldham." *Southwestern Historical Quarterly,* 1929.

Korn, Jerry. *The War for the Union, Volume 4: The Organized War to Victory, 1864–1865.* 1971.

———. *Pursuit to Appomattox.* 1987.

Lang, Theodore F. *Loyal West Virginia.* 1895.

Leech, Margaret. *Reveille in Washington: 1860–1865.* 1941.

Leventhal, Robert M. "Disbandment of the Union Army." *Military Review,* 1961.

Levstik, Frank R. "The *Sultana.*" *Civil War Times Illustrated,* 1974.

Lewis, Lloyd. *Sherman: Fighting Prophet.* 1958.

Lovett, Bobby L. "Memphis Riots: White Reaction to Blacks in Memphis, May 1865–July 1866." *Tennessee Historical Quarterly,* 1979.

Lowenfels, Walter, ed. *Walt Whitman's Civil War.* 1961.

McAleer, John J. *Ralph Waldo Emerson: Days of Encounter.* 1984.

McConnell, Stuart. *Glorious Contentment: The Grand Army of the Republic, 1865–1900.* 1992.

McFeely, William S. *Grant: A Biography.* 1981.

Martin, Samuel J. *The Road to Glory.* 1991.

Merrill, James M. *William Tecumseh Sherman.* 1971.

Messmer, Charles K. "The End of an Era: Louisville in 1865." *Filson Club History Quarterly,* 1980.

Michael, William H. C. "Explosion of the *Sultana.*" *Nebraska MOLLUS,* 1902.

Miers, Earl S., ed. *The Last Campaign.* 1972.

Mitchell, Betty A. *Edmund Ruffin: A Biography.* 1981.

Monaghan, Jay. *Custer: A Life of General George A. Custer.* 1959.

Moore, John W. *History of North Carolina.* 1880.

Morgan, Murray. *Dixie Raider: Saga of the C.S.S. Shenandoah.* 1948.

Morsberger, Robert E., and Katharine M. "After Andersonville: The First War Crimes Trial." *Civil War Times Illustrated,* 1974.

———. *Lew Wallace: Militant Romantic.* 1980.

Murphy, Richard W. *The Nation Reunited.* 1987.

Murray, Robert B. "The End of the Rebellion." *North Carolina Historical Review,* 1967.

Nevins, Allan. "A Major Result of the Civil War." *Civil War History,* 1959.

Nichols, Roy F. "United States *vs.* Jefferson Davis." *American Historical Review,* 1926.

Noll, Arthur H. *General Kirby-Smith.* 1907.

Noppen, Ina W. van. *Stoneman's Last Raid.* 1961.

"North Carolina — Held Over from May." *Confederate Veteran* 6 (1898).

Oates, Stephen B. *Confederate Cavalry West of the River.* 1961.

O'Connor, Richard. *Sheridan the Inevitable.* 1953.

———. *Bret Harte: A Biography.* 1966.

———. *Ambrose Bierce: A Biography.* 1967.

O'Flaherty, Daniel. *General Jo Shelby.* 1954.

Papers of the Military Historical Society of Massachusetts, Volume VI: The Shenandoah Campaigns of 1862 and 1864 and the Appomattox Campaign 1865 (1907) and *Volume XIV: Civil War and Miscellaneous Papers* (1918).

Pfanz, Donald C. *Abraham Lincoln at City Point.* 1989.

Pierrepont, Alice V. D. *Reuben Vaughan Kidd: Soldier of the Confederacy.* 1947.

Porter, David. *The Naval History of the Civil War.* 1886.

Potter, Jerry O. *The Sultana Tragedy.* 1992.

Rable, George C. *But There Was No Peace.* 1985.

Reck, W. Emerson. *A. Lincoln: His Last Twenty-four Hours.* 1987.

Rennolds, Edwin H. *History of the Henry County Commands.* 1904.

Reynolds, Donald E. "The New Orleans Riot of 1866, Reconsidered." *Louisiana History,* 1964.

Richardson, Joe M., ed. "The Memphis Race Riot and Its Aftermath." *Tennessee Historical Quarterly,* 1965.

Richter, William L. " 'It Is Best to Go in Strong-handed' — Army Occupation of Texas, 1865–1866." *Arizona & the West,* 1985.

Rippy, J. Fred. "Mexican Projects of the Confederates." *Southwestern Historical Quarterly,* 1919.

Roberts, Oran. *Confederate Military History: Texas.* N.d.

Robertson, James I. "Danville under Military Occuation." *Virginia Magazine of History and Biography,* 1967.

Roe, Alfred. *Ninth New York Heavy Artillery.* 1899.

———. *Thirty-ninth Regiment Massachusetts Volunteers.* 1914.

Rugoff, Milton. *The Beechers.* 1981.

Rusk, Ralph L. *Life of Ralph Waldo Emerson.* 1949.

Rutman, Darrett B. "The War Crimes and Trial of Henry Wirz." *Civil War History,* 1960.

Ryan, James G. "The Memphis Riots of 1866: Terror in a Black Community During Reconstruction." *Journal of Negro History,* 1977.

Schott, Thomas E. *Alexander H. Stephens of Georgia.* 1988.

Schuler, Louis J. *Last Battle in the War between the States.* 1960.

Scruggs, Philip L. *Lynchburg, Virginia.* 1973.

Searcher, Victor. *The Farewell to Lincoln.* 1965.

Sherrill, William L. *Annals of Lincoln County, North Carolina.* 1967.

Simpson, Marc. *Winslow Homer: Paintings of the Civil War.* 1988.

Smith, Sidney A., ed. *Mobile: 1861–1865.* 1965.

Spencer, Cornelia. *The Last Ninety Days of the War in North Carolina.* 1866.

Starr, Louis M. *Reporting the Civil War.* 1962.

Starr, Stephen Z. *The Union Cavalry in the Civil War.* 1981.

Stern, Philip van Doren. *An End to Valor.* 1958.

Stessel, Edward. *Soldier and Scholar: Emerson's Warring Heroes.* 1985.

Strode, Hudson. *Jefferson Davis: Tragic Hero.* 1964.

Symonds, Craig L. *Joseph E. Johnston: A Civil War Biography.* 1991.

Tarbell, Ida M. "How the Union Army Was Disbanded." *Civil War Times Illustrated,* 1967.

———. "Disbanding the Confederate Army." *Civil War Times Illustrated,* 1968.

Taylor, Betty J. "The Last Land Battle in the War of 1861–1865." *UDC Magazine,* 1985.

Taylor, Emerson G. *Gouverneur Kemble Warren.* 1932.

Taylor, Joe G. "New Orleans and Reconstruction." *Louisiana History,* 1968.

Telfair, Nancy. *History of Columbus, Georgia.* 1928.

Thomas, Benjamin P., and Hyman, Harold M. *Stanton: The Life and Times of Lincoln's Secretary of War.* 1962.

Tidwell, William A. *Come Retribution.* 1988.

———. "Booth Crosses the Potomac: An Exercise in Historical Research." *Civil War History,* 1990.

Trefousse, Hans L. *Andrew Johnson: A Biography.* 1974.

Trenerry, Walter N. "When the Boys Came Home." *Minnesota History,* 1963.

Tucker, Glenn. *Hancock the Superb.* 1960.

Turner, Thomas R. *Beware the People Weeping.* 1982.

Vandal, Gilles. "The Origins of the New Orleans Riot of 1866, Revisited." *Louisiana History,* 1981.

Vandiver, Frank E. *Ploughshares into Swords.* 1952.

Walker, Cornelius I. *Life of Lieutenant General Richard Heron Anderson.* 1917.

Warner, Ezra J. *Generals in Gray.* 1959.

———. *Generals in Blue.* 1964.

Warren, Robert Penn. *The Legacy of the Civil War.* 1961.

Wert, Jeffry D. *Mosby's Rangers.* 1990.

White, William W. "The Disintegration of an Army: Confederate Forces in Texas, April–June, 1865." *East Texas Historical Journal,* 1988.

Wilkinson, Norman B. "The Brandywine Home Front during the Civil War." *Delaware History,* 1964.

Wills, Brian S. *A Battle from the Start.* 1992.

Winters, John D. *The Civil War in Louisiana.* 1963.

Wise, Jennings S. "Boy Gunners of Lee." *Southern Historical Society Papers* 42 (1907).

Wooten, Dudley G. *A Comprehensive History of Texas.* 1986.

Wyeth, John A. *Life of Lieutenant-General Nathan Bedford Forrest.* 1899.

Yager, Wilson M. "The *Sultana* Disaster." *Tennessee Historical Quarterly,* 1976.

NEWSPAPERS

Boston Evening Journal
Brooklyn Eagle
Chicago Tribune
Cincinnati Daily Commercial
Council Bluffs (Iowa) *Bugle*

Daily Constitutional Union
Florida Union
National Tribune
New Orleans Daily Picayune
New Orleans Times
New York Evening Post
New York Freeman's Journal and Catholic Register
New York Herald
New York Sun
New York Telegram
New York Times
New York World
Newark Daily Advertiser
Northern Virginia Pilot
Philadelphia Inquirer
Philadelphia Weekly Press
Philadelphia Weekly Times
Richmond News Leader
Richmond Times-Dispatch
Washington Chronicle

OFFICIAL DOCUMENTS

Gibson, R. L. *Official Report of the Defence and Fall of the Spanish Fort. Southern Historical Society Papers* 4 (1877).

The Official Military Atlas of the Civil War. 1978.

Official Records of the Union and Confederate Navies in the War of the Rebellion. 1894–1922.

Proceedings, Findings and Opinions of the Court Martial in the Case of Robert G. Morrison. N.d.

Proceedings, Findings, and Opinions of the Court of Inquiry Convened by Order of the President of the United States in the Case of Gouverneur K. Warren. 1883.

Record of Proceedings of a Court of Inquiry to Investigate the Fact and Circumstances Connected with the Explosion of the Magazine. N.d.

Records of the Adjutant General's Office: Court Martial of Captain Frederic Speed. N.d.

Report of the Joint Committee on the Conduct of the War at the Second Session Thirty-eighth Congress: Sherman–Johnston. 1865.

Sultana *Disaster: Courts of Inquiry Transcripts.* N.d.

The War of the Rebellion: A Compilation of the Official Records of the Union and Confederate Armies. 1880–1901.

Acknowledgments

---◄o►---

THE RESEARCH FOR THIS narrative of the final months of the
Civil War was, by its very nature, much less concentrated in one region
than that for my two previous books, both of which centered on campaigns in Virginia. My search for fresh voices and hitherto unquoted
sources might well have stretched into many years had it not been for the
talented and dedicated researchers who agreed to serve as my surrogate
eyes at archives all across the country. The debt I owe them seems mis-
erably expressed in the simple words "Thank you," and it is little enough
an accolade to honor each in turn:

Illinois: G. Paul Gerdes; Indiana: Susan H. Truax; Iowa: Jeffrey L.
Dawson; Michigan: Stephen Frank; Minnesota/Wisconsin: James W.
Warren, Paula Stuart Warren; Ohio: Mary Christensen, Alice Coyle
Lunn; Pennsylvania: Steve L. Zerbe; and Texas: Sara Clark.

Once again the historian/researcher Bryce A. Suderow was of inestimable assistance in combing the print and manuscript collections of the
Library of Congress, National Archives, United States Military History
Institute, and Virginia Historical Society. His studies into combat casualty figures for the final months of the war were also extremely helpful.

A number of individuals at manuscript archives and libraries rendered invaluable assistance to this often time-pressed researcher: Jim
Bantin of the Western Historical Manuscripts Collection, University of

Missouri; George H. Schroeter of the Mobile Public Library; Dr. Richard J. Sommers of the U.S. Army Military History Institute at the War College, Carlisle Barracks, Pennsylvania; and Guy Swanson at the Museum of the Confederacy.

Portions of my manuscript benefited in no little measure from a careful review by both professional and amateur historians expert in the specific campaigns: Arthur W. Bergeron, Jr. (Louisiana Office of State Parks), Chris Calkins (Petersburg National Battlefield Park), John H. Friend, Jr.; John C. Goode (North Carolina Department of Cultural Resources); Norman A. Nicolson; Jerry O. Potter; and Ron Wilson and staff (Appomattox Court House National Historical Park). In this context I want to also acknowledge Bruce Aiken, executive director of the Historic Brownsville Museum, who made time available on a Sunday (and on short notice) to accompany me on a tour of the Palmito Ranch battlefield and generously shared with me his profound knowledge of Brownsville's Civil War history. My thanks to all.

In the category of grateful "once agains": once again Robert K. Krick, chief historian at the Fredericksburg-Spotsylvania National Military Park, opened his superb collection of primary and secondary materials to this researcher; once again my friend Christine Malesky patiently read through the typescript and brought grammatical order to the commas, semicolons, and ellipses I had scattered with wild abandon across the pages; and once again I was honored to entrust my manuscript to the tender but firm ministrations of copyeditor extraordinaire Dorothy Straight.

A very special acknowledgment of thanks must go to John E. Stanchak, editor of *Civil War Times Illustrated,* whose commission to write an issue on the last days of the Civil War planted the seed that became this book, and whose permission to quote from that issue (July/August 1990) is deeply appreciated.

And in the "last but not least" category, a tip of the hat to my editor at Little, Brown, Catherine Crawford, for her helpful suggestions in reshaping the first draft of this manuscript.

My thanks for the wise counsel freely offered and humbly received. As always, all judgment calls were made by the home team.

Index